A Limited Edition
of

THE LIFE OF HERBERT HOOVER
Fighting Quaker, 1928–1933

Presented by the Herbert Hoover
Presidential Library Association, Inc.

To:

Copy Number_____

THE LIFE OF HERBERT HOOVER
Fighting Quaker
1928–1933

Elvis Presley, Reluctant Rebel: His Life and Our Times (with David Luhrssen and Dan Sokolovic)

Changing Times: The Life of Barack Obama (with David Luhrssen)

A Time of Paradox: America since 1890

A Time of Paradox: America from Awakening to Superpower 1890–1945

A Time of Paradox: America from the Cold War to the Third Millennium, 1945–Present

Women of the Far Right: The Mothers' Movement and World War II

Transformation and Reaction: America, 1921–1945

Messiah of the Masses: Huey P. Long and the Great Depression

Gerald L. K. Smith: Minister of Hate

Leander Perez: Boss of the Delta

Race, Religion, and Politics: The Louisiana Gubernatorial Elections of 1959–1960

Editor, *Huey at 100: Centennial Essays on Huey P. Long*

Editor, *A Guide to the History of Louisiana*

THE LIFE OF
HERBERT HOOVER

★★★★★

FIGHTING QUAKER

1928–1933

GLEN JEANSONNE

palgrave
macmillan

First published in 2012 by PALGRAVE MACMILLAN® in the United States—a division of St. Martin's Press LLC, 175 Fifth Avenue, New York, NY 10010.

Where this book is distributed in the UK, Europe, and the rest of the world, this is by Palgrave Macmillan, a division of Macmillan Publishers Limited, registered in England, company number 785998, of Houndmills, Basingstoke, Hampshire RG21 6XS.

Palgrave Macmillan is the global academic imprint of the above companies and has companies and representatives throughout the world.

Palgrave® and Macmillan® are registered trademarks in the United States, the United Kingdom, Europe and other countries.

ISBN: 978-0-230-10309-2

Library of Congress Cataloging-in-Publication Data is available from the Library of Congress.

A catalogue record of the book is available from the British Library.

Design by Scribe Inc.

First edition: March 2012

10 9 8 7 6 5 4 3 2 1

Printed in the United States of America.

Transferred to Digital Printing in 2013

To Lauren Priegel Jeansonne
Forevermore

Contents

Acknowledgments   ix

Abbreviations   xiii

Preface   xv

Prologue   The Long Dusty Road from West Branch   1

1   Landslide   15

2   Prepping for the Presidency and Sparring with Congress   43

3   Humanizing Hoover   65

4   A Whirling Dervish   89

5   The Engine of Prosperity Jumps the Track   113

6   The Seventy-First Congress: Fighting the Political Wars   129

7   Hoover and the World: Foreign Policy, 1929–1930   155

8   A Polarized Party   177

9   Combating the Depression: Phase I, 1929–1930   195

10   The Seventy-Second Congress: Frustrating Yet Fruitful   217

11   Combating the Depression: Phase II, 1931–1932   253

12   Frustrated Farmers, Angry Veterans   279

13   Race, Gender, and Labor   303

14   The Grim Reaper Stalks the
World: Foreign Affairs, 1931–1933   329

15   Life in the White House: Personal and Social   347

16   The Peter Pan in Hoover: Children and Fish   367

17   The Fourth Estate   383

18   Running for His Life: The Election of 1932   403

19   The Hard Interregnum   427

20   Fighting Quaker   451

Notes   469

A Note on the Sources   519

Bibliography   521

Index   533

Acknowledgments

I would have written some type of book about Herbert Hoover during my lifetime, but without the support of the Hoover Library Association, it would not have been this book. Dedicated, generous people, they were instrumental in the book's completion. I appreciate the assistance of the director, Rebeckah Allgood, the financial officer, Kathy Frederick, and John Fawcett, the chair of the Biography Committee. The University of Wisconsin–Milwaukee provided a sabbatical in academic year 2006–2007, and the Earhart Foundation provided a crucial grant, complemented by funds from the Helen Bader Foundation of Milwaukee.

Without Timothy Walch, the director of the Hoover Library, this book might have been written by someone, but probably not by me. Tim helped facilitate my authorship and my research at every stage. Thomas Schwarz, who succeeded Walch in 2011, aided the book's promotion and ensures that the Hoover Library remains in good hands. I enjoyed the camaraderie and high morale of the staff. Matt Schaefer, Spencer Howard, Craig Wright, and Lynn Smith belong in the Archivists Hall of Fame. Lynn Smith, the audiovisual archivist; Jim Detlefsen, the audiovisual technician; and Craig Wright selected the photos and duplicated them for me. I owe a special debt to Lynn and Craig, who dropped everything at the last minute to keep the project on schedule. All of the above are more than skilled professionals; they are lifelong friends. In West Branch, and especially at the Hoover Library, it is indeed true that no man is an island. Historians owe a special debt to archivists, whose satisfaction lies in helping other people get the glory.

I recruited local students who photocopied the items I selected virtually nonstop, enabling me to return to Milwaukee with 20 archival boxes of material. The group included graduate student Heather Martens, college student Laurie Fraise, and West Branch ninth graders, Molly Whiteside, Seth Honemann, and Megan O'Neil. I ordered every out-of-print book collected by the Hoover Library. My former student Meredith Vnuk located, purchased, and mailed them to me at West Branch. Most of her work was done gratis. I spent many evenings and weekends reading them, when I did not join the gang swilling to the jukebox at Herb and Lou's below my apartment. They often offered free drinks in return for telling Hoover stories, possibly the only place in America one can find a deal like that.

I might have chosen to live in Iowa City, a lively college town with sophisticated culture, only ten miles down the turnpike from the village of West Branch. Yet for we who appreciate simplicity, West Branch is more like Walden than Gopher Prairie. The winters are cold and blustery, but the people are not. There is a lot of common sense per square foot. Though I arrived there single, without knowing a soul, I never felt lonely. Who would have expected to find in a Quaker hamlet of 1800 a Reiki master, a fine Cajun restaurant (now closed), and a high school football dynasty? Years ago, the team, now known as the "Bears," was known as the "Fighting Quakers." The residents of rural Iowa are no bumpkins—if college standardized entry examinations are any indication—they are among the best in the nation, often *the* best. Corn is brain food.

In the summer of 2008 my fiancée Lauren Priegel accompanied me to the Hoover Institution Archives at Stanford University. I am grateful to the staff of the Hoover Institution Archives, especially Carol A. Leadenham, for her generous assistance. My research assistant at Stanford, Ann Trevor, helped make our journey pleasant and productive. Lauren photocopied materials selected by me at a hectic pace.

I followed a procession of historians who tilled the fertile soil of primary materials, especially George H. Nash, Kendrick Clements, Ellis W. Hawley, and the late Gary Best. Hal Wert, a Hoover scholar, became a close friend and is the major academic referee for my manuscript. Lauren and I spent many pleasant evenings with Hal and I fished his mind for ideas.

The professionals at Palgrave Macmillan helped turn an idea into a book. Chris Chappell, my editor, is patient, professional, and generous. He is the most flexible, considerate editor with whom I have worked. When snags occurred over photographs due to my neglect, he acted quickly and decisively to resolve the issue and put my mind at ease. I value our relationship. I never asked a question that stumped his editorial assistant, Sarah Whalen. My friend and neighbor, Carla Otterson, computerized and organized my data, backing it up electronically, and organizing the bibliography. Carla also rushed over to rescue lost computer data from gremlins in my computer. Laura Godden, my student and fellow Hoover scholar, contributed her formidable talents as a researcher to fleshing out the footnotes and bibliography. Jacque Kelnhofer, a former student with a careful eye and a gift for prose, devoted long hours to scrupulously editing the manuscript. All my students enlivened my life and provided feedback on Hoover.

I am also indebted to my frequent literary collaborator, David Luhrssen and to those who smoothed the rough edges of my life, including Victoria

Leigh, Greg Hoag, Anna Casper, Nancy Retzlaff, Robert Taub, and Joan Hoss. I drew upon the now faint nurture of my 94-year-old mother, and the love of my daughters, Leah and Hannah. I also owe debts to my late father Ryan J. Jeansonne, a person as honest as Herbert Hoover, and to my mentor, the late William Ivy Hair. I am also grateful to the staff of the History Department, Cynthia Barnes, Anita Cathey, and Barisha Letterman. The computer wizards in the Letters and Science Technical support staff made it unnecessary for me to write this tome in longhand. The staff at the Golda Meir Library was efficient and longsuffering. I want to express gratitude for the support of Margaret Hoover, whom I got to know during the final stages of completing my manuscript. All of these, in ways tangible and intangible, are accomplices to the act of creating this manuscript.

Finally, I met my future wife, now Lauren Priegel Jeansonne, through correspondence while in West Branch. She lived in Milwaukee but was willing to wait. I entered the only gift shop in West Branch to purchase a card for Lauren. The owner had no individual cards, only boxes of 50, yet she broke one open to sell me a single card. It read, "And God wrought special miracles" (Acts 19:11–12).

Abbreviations

Accomp.	Accomplishments
Admin.	Administration
B	Box
CF	Clipping File
Coll.	Collection
Corres.	Correspondence
CP	Commerce Papers
C&TP	Campaign and Transition Papers
Dept.	Department
Ed.	Editorial (newspaper)
HHPF	Herbert Hoover Presidential File (Hoover Institution, Stanford University)
HHPL	Herbert Hoover Presidential Library, West Branch, Iowa
LHHP	Lou Henry Hoover Papers
PCP	Precommerce Papers
PP	Presidential Papers
PPP	Postpresidential Papers
Ques.	Question
RF	Reprint File
SF	Subject File

Preface

This is the fifth in a series of volumes about Herbert Hoover sponsored by the Herbert Hoover Presidential Library Association. The three initial volumes, all written by George H. Nash, carry the story of Hoover's life to 1918. The fourth, completed by Kendrick Clements, describes Hoover's life from 1918 through 1928. This volume covers the presidential years, 1929–1933. The concluding study, by the late Gary Dean Best, explains the postpresidential period. These books, written largely from primary sources, are designed to be definitive for the present generation. I feel honored and challenged to be included in the company of such distinguished scholars.

I have divided the opening sections into a preface, which is partly personal in nature, and a prologue, which summarizes Hoover's life before the election of 1928. I have done this in the belief that it is important to understand why and how I wrote the book (here in the preface) and my objectives and point of view, as well as the historical context in which his presidency belongs (through the prologue). The prologue enables this book to stand alone, for those who do not read the entire series. Furthermore, the publication of the individual volumes has been separated by a period of many years, and the prologue provides a refresher.

I decided to write about Herbert Hoover for several reasons. Previously, I wrote biographies of racists and anti-Semites: Leander H. Perez, Gerald L. K. Smith, and profascist women of the 1930s and 1940s such as Elizabeth Dilling, as well as the singular demagogue, Huey P. Long of Louisiana, exhausting my repertoire of finding fault. In Hoover, I found someone I admire: a rare political figure who was pure of heart. Hoover was not perfect; yet he always tried to do the right thing. He never cheated his Maker. In fact, he never cheated anyone.

My previous books have been an apprenticeship for this study. The present book has provided a gratifying sense of purpose. It is rewarding to have a purpose and better yet to consummate it. Moreover, the thirty-first president provided a lode of historical lore with readily available primary sources at a Presidential Library within driving distance of my home in Milwaukee. Hoover represents a challenge and an opportunity to make a difference. Scorned by the public during his tenure and neglected by historians thereafter, his reputation invited resuscitation and a rescue from the dustbin of history. Potentially more original things remain to be said about Hoover than about any but our most recent presidents.

Hoover also represents a major human interest story. He would be less interesting and instructive to study if his career were simply heroic, in which case we could label him a great president and leave it at that, or if he were a complete failure, we could thereby dismiss him with pity. Orphaned at 9, written off in 1933, Hoover lived another 31 years. His adult life bridged the "Gay Nineties" and Populist years, the Progressive Era, the Roaring Twenties, the Great Depression, the First and Second World Wars, the Atomic Age, and the Cold War. When he was born, his father was shoeing horses. When he died, men were planning a voyage of discovery that would set sail upon the Sea of Tranquility. Hoover was one of the first automobile enthusiasts, the first president to have a telephone on his desk, the man responsible for regulating early radio and aviation, and the first American whose face was transmitted via television.

Born in an Iowa village of 300, he knew many of the world's most significant figures in fields that extended far beyond politics and diplomacy. Indeed, if one traces his life, beginning at Stanford during the 1890s, and charts the world-famous figures he encountered, sometimes as a young student or engineer, one cannot help but feel that a synchronous force directed his life. From David Starr Jordan, Jan Paderewski, and Andrew Carnegie, all of whom he met as a Stanford student, to Winston Churchill, Vladimir Lenin (at least by correspondence), Woodrow Wilson, John Maynard Keynes, Adolf Hitler, Douglas MacArthur, Franklin D. Roosevelt, Chang Kai-Shek, and Mahatma Ghandi, the list appears endless. It includes women too: Mary Pickford, Amelia Earhart, and Eleanor Roosevelt. Hoover enjoyed the company of the aviator Charles Lindbergh; the auto magnate Henry Ford; the inventor Thomas Edison; and scores of prominent journalists, statesmen, engineers, and scientists. He knew every president from Theodore Roosevelt to John F. Kennedy. One could almost compile a book simply by making a list of the people he knew. He met them all on equal terms. No one intimidated Hoover, yet no one was too humble for his attention. This is all the more remarkable because his personality was veiled by a shyness that presented a political obstacle in a profession that does not reward modesty. A practical idealist, a man of great fortitude, many of his predictions have borne fruit.

Hoover did not drop names, nor did he indulge in idle gossip. But on occasion, he could be a marvelous raconteur with a fabulous memory for detail. Like all of us, he encountered joy and disappointment. Yet his mountains and valleys were higher and deeper. Seen up close and from afar, or from different angles, Hoover appears a different person, as he does at different times during his life. Yet his core was consistent. I will try to make his story direct. A problem solver and humanitarian, his presidency had tragic undertones. His life, as a whole, however, was fulfilling and marvelously varied. He would be worth writing about even if he had never become president.

An enormously successful engineer who faced political and economic dilemmas with courage, the Great Depression tested his—and every American's—will. Deeply scarred by the death of his parents while a young boy, he loved and understood all children. Never passive or reactive, he epitomized Joan of Arc's adage that in every situation there is always something better to do than nothing. Hoover might not have always been right, but he consistently labored to do the right thing. In more than seven years of research, I found mistakes on his part; the occasional refusal to divulge data that would have sabotaged the economy, but never a deliberate, self-serving lie during his presidential years. This is a remarkable record for a politician. The son of Iowa Quakers, he detested not only political lies but all intellectual dishonesty. He enjoyed helping others covertly, perhaps especially then. This book is written partly to set the record straight but, even more importantly, to add depth to the record and to relate the story of his presidency more thoroughly than it has ever been told. None of us is entirely an innocent bystander, yet sometimes bad things happen to good people. Hoover has been condemned, not purely for his own folly, but for the folly of an era.

After writing about a host of demagogues, it is refreshing to write about someone who was the antithesis of a demagogue: modest, humble, and unselfish—traits common in his fellow Quakers but almost extinct in politicians. As Hoover's life and presidency unfolded during my research, I became increasingly impressed and intrigued. The rest of his life, and that of his individualistic First Lady, will have to wait for other books.

When I was a graduate student at Florida State University, I asked one of my professors if I could write a seminar paper about the administration of Herbert Hoover. He chuckled and said "No, because nothing happened." I wrote the paper anyway, received an "A" for audacity, and my professor and I became lifelong friends. Hoover's presidency, contrary to popular stereotypes, was not a time when nothing happened, nor when only bad things happened. It was not merely a vacuum bookended by frenetic flappers and a government in overdrive.

Even the most sophisticated are sometimes naïve on the subject of Hoover. According to an employee of the Hoover Library, who must remain unnamed to protect his privacy, he once encountered the eminent liberal economist, the late John Kenneth Galbraith, at a dinner on the East Coast. When Galbraith asked him what he did, the man replied that he worked at the Hoover Presidential Library. Galbraith was astounded to learn that such a library existed. "A Library for Herbert Hoover!" he exclaimed. "How sad!"

I see Hoover through the eyes of a small town boy who lived my early years much as he did, in the outdoors; and my later years, much as he did, cloistered and writing books. Young men have the power of energy, and old men have the sagacity of wisdom—the universe's way of making the world work. Like Hoover, I find replenishment from nature, especially from lakes, grass, and trees. Like him, I have always been competitive and continue to believe that my best book will be my next one. Possibly because I enjoyed a similar, if not exact childhood, I do not find him inscrutable. He was, rather, quite straightforward. There paraded through our lives (his on a larger scale) people who seemed unremarkable at the time but who would exert substantial influence. And we share the belief that, as important and enjoyable as book learning is, the least important things we learned are those we learned in books. Neither would either of us deny that luck—some good, some bad—plays a role in life nor that tenacity can often compensate for bad luck. Finally, hard work is its own reward. Writing about his life has been hard work but ennobling.

Hoover was a product of small towns on the American frontier, a Quaker orphan denied some of the love and joy of childhood. However, his childhood was not cheerless, nor was he a morose person. If he had been, he could not have acted so confidently and decisively. As a politician, he wanted to be loved for his accomplishments, but he had no interest in political immortality. He was more profoundly religious than most people, not the kind of religion found between the walls of a church, but the type kindled within. He possessed superior intelligence, especially in certain areas, and human empathy, along with ferocious drive and self-discipline. He cared little for ceremony and was unpretentious. If the meek inherit the earth, he will be among them.

Like Thomas Edison, a genius with common sense, Hoover said little, especially about himself, yet he wrote some 33 volumes. His silence was golden, but his pen was in perpetual motion. A philosophical thinker, he was also a man of action, hardheaded yet not hard-hearted, and privately sentimental. His practical side held that wisdom lay in knowing what to do next and virtue lay in doing it. Some considered him a machine-like workaholic, but even those people respected his ability. There were depths to Hoover's multifaceted personality that led many to misjudge or underestimate him. Sometimes he drew elaborate doodles while his visiting speaker droned on, yet he remembered every word, though he never took notes. He broke the habit of doodling halfway through his presidency. Likewise, early in his career, he developed the habit of avoiding the eyes of his partner in conversation, but this too ended during his presidency. Yet more fascinating, and unknown to the public, was that this sensitive man, who nonetheless possessed a puckish sense of humor, had collected hundreds of cartoon caricatures of himself, some quite vicious, since 1914. He devoted an entire room in the family quarters of the White House to storing them, most pasted in scrapbooks, his favorites framed and hung on the wall. He chuckled when paging through them.

The image of Hoover that permeates the public mind is a paradox. For much of his life, Hoover was considered a visionary, someone ahead of his time. Yet today, the public perception is a dark one. Since the Great Depression, his stereotype fixed indelibly by the presidential campaign of 1932, in which the embattled chief executive was humiliated, is that of a villain. In a word association game, say "Great Depression," and you often will get "Hoover." They might as well be synonyms in *Roget's Thesaurus*. Many believe the Quaker president plotted the stock market crash, orchestrated the Depression that followed, did nothing to stem either, and chortled at the fate of the hungry. A heartless, intolerant plutocrat, he lived secluded with his minions and his millions, oblivious to human misery. In reality, it would be difficult to find anyone who experienced more pain than Hoover himself.

The truth is that Hoover's stereotype, stamped into history, as immovable as the Rock of Gibraltar, is a mirror image. Not only was Hoover not responsible for either the Crash or the Depression, he worked diligently to prevent both and then strove with all his might to mitigate the Depression, with some initial success. A compassionate man, his public service was motivated not by craving for power but by a desire to help others. His personality, of course, made the caricature painted by his opponents plausible. Although neither emotionless nor hard-hearted, he appeared so. His shy introversion played into the hands of his enemies. Protective of his personal and his family's privacy, he was that rare public figure who shunned the limelight. Yet his predecessor, Calvin Coolidge, who was even more shy and more introverted, became an iconic folk hero glamorized by the press. Hoover's personality did not change much from the time he was celebrated as a humanitarian to the time he was vilified as a bland, heartless technocrat. In fact, the man who had suffered early in life and experienced pain and loneliness probably understood the plight of the common man better than any president since Lincoln. He could not make the Great Depression go away any more than Lincoln could make the Civil War go away. Hoover had faults, to be sure, but malice, miserliness, and malign intent were not among them. He was hardly indifferent or lazy nor did he enjoy the trappings of wealth. He gave most of his fortune away, often covertly, and accepted only minimal compensation for public service. His private, stealthy charity helped only a few, but if everyone was able to do what he did, or had actually done so, the Depression would have been washed away by a tsunami of compassion.

This is not a book about the Great Depression, although that is a part of the story. What follows is a biographical account of the man who served as president during the Depression but also had other responsibilities, including some that lay outside the government. This account makes an effort to understand Hoover from the inside out, including his philosophy, his religion, his personality, and his family. The years 1929 to 1933 represented only a slice of his life, and I have attempted to provide some context to understand Hoover in those years in the sense of not only what was occurring in the nation but what was happening in the personal world that Herbert Hoover inhabited. His life includes sadness, like all great lives, but also elements of valor and the redeeming quality of indomitable perseverance. Many books have been written about what Hoover did not do or should have done. This study is primarily about what he did and why. It takes into account what was feasible and realistic in the context of what was known and possible at the time.

Analyzing the presidency of Herbert Hoover, or any presidency, raises the question of how we judge presidents. Often, voters and historians credit them with everything positive that occurs on their watch while blaming them for everything negative, attributing to them a sort of omniscience. We have adopted a more nuanced approach, seeking to determine what role the president actually played in the major events of his administration. This involves attempting to evaluate Hoover according to what he accomplished, what he tried to do, yet failed, and to attribute some events to accident, bad luck, and good luck. Some come out ahead by being lucky rather than wise, and some wise men are unlucky. In this type of analysis, motive, not merely outcome, counts. One may do the wrong thing for the right reason and the right thing for the wrong reason. Playing Russian roulette and winning does not necessarily mean that one has done a smart thing, is an excellent player, and can only improve with practice. We also try to consider how others in the same circumstances might have fared and where paths not taken might have led. The first approach is much easier but is comparable to attributing the law of gravity to the apple that fell on Isaac Newton's head. All presidencies are driven by events and circumscribed by limited options. Many presidents find themselves reacting to things they did not plan. Theodore Roosevelt wanted to be a war president, and Woodrow Wilson desired peace. George W. Bush, a governor with no experience in the federal government or in foreign affairs, planned to be a domestic policy president. Fate determined otherwise. The only occupation more insecure than politics is political prognosticating.

Hoover presided in the White House during dark times. There is a tendency to blame the messenger and, in Hoover's case, to forget his successes before, during, and after the White House years. In another era, Hoover might have been remembered as a reformer, a builder, a principled individualist who worked within limits. If he did not find a total solution to the Great Depression, it might be because there was none. However, what actually happened is grist enough for this writer's mill.

In 1929, the nation stepped to Hoover's beat. By 1932, he was no longer the leader of the band. He accepted massive repudiation with grace. Nonetheless, he was scarred. In later years, when young boys who aspired to the presidency wrote asking for his advice, he replied that public service was a noble profession, but he avoided the word "politics." During his final months in the White House, with no discernable political future in sight, the president worked himself to exhaustion until he stepped into private life, which by no means meant retirement. As if to demonstrate his stubbornness, he lived to be 90 and continued to write an endless stream of books, speeches, and articles. Perhaps, also to prove his stubborn diligence, he wrote them in longhand.

The dominant image of Hoover today reflects the reality that the history of political wars, like the history of military wars, is written by the winners. Yet nothing ever daunted or broke Hoover, from the torrid Australian outback to the Boxer Rebellion, to daring to run for president with no previous political experience. He faced the bitter harvest of the Depression years with unflinching courage and accepted political defeat with dignity.

Of all gifts, drive is the most important. All successful people have it. Hoover had it to an extraordinary degree. How one chooses to channel that drive is a matter of choice. Ambition is one form of drive, but it is not the only form. Saints and martyrs have it; so do tyrants. Hoover answers the question of whether a great man (even if not a great president) can be a good man in the affirmative.

The Long Dusty Road from West Branch

If Jimmy Carter was the twentieth century's most useful former president, Herbert Hoover was the most useful chief executive in the years before he became president. Hoover demonstrated selfless humanitarianism, organizational virtuosity, stamina, and fortitude. In 1928, many Americans believed these achievements and his impeccable character outweighed any lack of political experience as qualifications for the presidency.

Hoover was profoundly shaped by childhood influences: He was orphaned at nine and was raised on the cusp of the frontier, the last president to be born and raised in a frontier environment and the first born west of the Mississippi River. Born in an Iowa farm hamlet of about 400, mostly Quakers, he became perhaps the nation's most cosmopolitan president, circling the globe four times before 1914. The first Quaker chief executive, he was the second engineer president, if one counts George Washington as a surveyor or civil engineer. Hoover's vice president, Charles Curtis of Kansas, was the first vice president born west of the Mississippi and the first to have Indian blood.[1]

From the time of Hoover's birth at West Branch, on the nearly treeless eastern rim of the Great Plains on August 10, 1874, until he left his adopted family in Oregon to enroll at Stanford University, Quakerism dominated his environment. His mother, Huldah, was an itinerant, unpaid Quaker minister. His father Jesse, a witty blacksmith, was also a fervent Quaker. At a psychological level, the thirty-first president never left the frontier villages and austere meetinghouses of his youth.[2]

1

Quakers emphasize the Inner Light, a Divine Spark within that provides moral compass, using their conscience and intuition alone. Persons resemble vessels floating in a sea that is God. There is water within the vessel and greater water without. Early Quakers stripped away the ceremony and superstition that evolved with Christianity, rejecting altars, music, and paid ministers. Services remain silent until someone moved by their Inner Light speaks. Most Quakers enjoy peace of mind.[3]

The sect preaches and practices humility, charity, equality, and treatment of all men as brothers. They are principled, even stubborn, yet tolerant. Opposing slavery and racism, some violated the Quaker belief in pacifism because they were also abolitionists. Still, they are reluctant to fight. Neither as a child nor as an adult did Hoover initiate a physical fight. During his years in adult life, he never lost his temper in public. He was neither verbally nor physically abusive. As a man he fished but did consider hunting cruel. Indians are also brothers, and some of Hoover's playmates were Indians who taught him frontier lore. Quakers paid Indians for their land, and two of Hoover's uncles worked as Indian agents.[4]

Quakers dress plainly and do not flaunt possessions. Serious, purposeful, blunt, and direct, they deny class hierarchies. Self-reliant, they are nonetheless noted for their philanthropy. Hoover's mother embraced Prohibition and women's suffrage. The sect usually moved in groups and kept to themselves. Scripture is paramount, though not all are literalists. Life revolves around the family, home, and community. They take pride in work and are industrious. When Quakers encounter hard times, they are helped by their neighbors. The religion discourages idle gossip or idleness in general. Though they constitute a small sect, Quakers have been unusually successful in fields such as business, education, and science, though few enter politics. In many respects Hoover's was a typical Quaker personality: reticent, modest, and generous—a man who never boasted and refused to attack others verbally. Though common among Quakers, such traits are rare among politicians.[5]

The Quaker boy had a lifelong love of the outdoors, especially fishing and camping, as a child and as an adult. A mediocre student, weak in English, who excelled in math, he enjoyed his time outdoors at recess. Amiably rambunctious, he swam at a muddy swimming hole during the summer and coasted down a sledding hill during the cold, windy winters on the plains. He caught sunfish and dammed small streams to trap trout. Bert demonstrated an early interest in geology by picking fossilized rocks from the gravel along the railroad tracks and labeling them. His free time also involved chores. Holidays were punctuated by picnics and family gatherings. Bert Hoover's boyhood had much in common with Huckleberry Finn's. They fished in the river, roamed the forests, and stretched their imaginations by inventing games. Yet, like Huck Finn's boyhood, Bert Hoover's was darkened by tragedy. The origins were similar: family instability. And each, in his way, left home. However,

Hoover did not flee West Branch of his volition as Huck embarked on a raft down the Mississippi. He was orphaned.[6]

The first blow came when his father, Jesse, died at 34 of a heart attack when the boy was 6. Two years later Huldah succumbed to pneumonia after a frigid walk from a neighboring town where she had preached. Huldah was 35. Bert was nine. A family council decided to disperse the three Hoover children. His older brother Theodore ("Tad") and his younger sister Mary ("May") were sent to live with relatives. Bert boarded with his Uncle John, who owned a farm near West Branch, for two years. Farm work was strenuous but enabled him to be outdoors.[7]

At 11, the family sent Bert to live with his Uncle John Henry Minthorn, who recently had lost his son. The Minthorns could provide a better education than Uncle John in West Branch. Bert made the long train trek to Newberg, Oregon, alone. Minthorn, a Civil War veteran, was learned, versatile, industrious, and tough. He treated the boy like an adult, assigning him chores that exhausted him and a strict regimen of education. His uncle, a country doctor, teacher, and former Indian agent, opened his mind to the boy, whose sponge-like brain soaked it up. When time permitted, Bert escaped into the forests and to the world of reading. His spectrum of literature included major European and American classics, adventure stories, and some of the leading American writers of his time. He struggled with English composition but was proficient at mathematics and developed an aptitude for machinery.[8]

Bert did not attend high school. When his uncle opened a real estate office in Salem, he took Hoover along as an office boy. Self-taught, craving knowledge, and mastering new skills, he kept the books for the company and took night classes in business. Once he talked with a mining engineer who stopped by the office. Hoover was impressed by the opportunities in mining. The geologist told him about a newly opening university, founded by Leland Stanford, a philanthropic California railroad magnate and politician. Hoover decided to attend Stanford although his relatives wanted him to attend a Quaker college. Bert lacked money and preparation. He flunked some sections of the entrance exam but was superb at others, and his gritty determination impressed the professor who gave the test.[9]

On August 29, 1891, Hoover left Salem for Stanford University. He received a few weeks of tutoring that enabled him to enroll. Barely 17, the youngest student, he was the first to arrive. The Pioneer Class included a remarkable number of gifted students and superb athletes, while the faculty boasted academic luminaries. Its benefactor planned to combine the humanities with a practical education. Stanford based admission on ability, not wealth or social standing. The president, David Starr Jordan, was nationally known, as was the head of the Geology Department, John Casper Branner. Hoover flourished in an atmosphere of greater freedom than he had ever known. He was perpetually short on money but never on brains. Bert Hoover became one of the best-known students on campus for his academic ability, his unselfish dedication to student affairs, his intellectual and physical stamina, and his wide range of extracurricular activities. He was elected class treasurer, then student body treasurer; managed the football and baseball teams; helped organize a group of ordinary students who defeated the fraternity clique; and wrote the student body constitution. During the summers he earned money by working on geological surveys.[10]

As a senior, Bert met the love of his life, the only women who ever seriously interested him. Lou Henry was an unusual woman, as individualistic as Hoover himself, with a mind that rivaled his but with more social polish. She could write like one with a natural gift, loved nature as much as he did, and became fluent in five foreign languages. After studying to be a teacher, she was impressed by a speech by Professor Branner and decided to earn a second degree in geology. She was Stanford's first female geology major and the fourth in the country. Lou was a freshman, and Bert a senior when they met in geology lab, though they were about the same age and had been born only a few miles apart in Iowa. It was a rock solid relationship. He possessed superior drive, yet she was better at oral and written communication. She was attractive, vivacious, and athletic. They loved the same things, including each other.[11]

When Bert graduated in 1895, they agreed to marry after Lou graduated and once Bert was financially secure. It was risky: The economy was depressed in the wake of the Panic of 1893. Either might meet someone else. But they knew what they wanted, a marriage made not in heaven but in a geology lab. The pair agreed to correspond, and they did. It must have been intense; Bert burned most of the love letters exchanged between the two. Bert was not comfortable with most women, perhaps completely comfortable with only one. It was not a perfect match, but it was an exceptionally good one.[12]

Degree in hand, Hoover started at the bottom—literally—at the bottom of a mine. The newly minted engineer was not afraid of manual labor; in fact, he enjoyed it. He was sinewy, muscled, and tough, with enormous physical vitality. He later gained weight, but the stamina was lifelong. Bert mastered some of the practical aspects of mining he had not learned at Stanford. He pushed ore carts near Nevada City on the night shift, ten hours a day, seven days a week. When he was laid off he quickly found another job. In December 1895, Hoover gathered his savings and took a chance by quitting his job. He called on Louis Janin, an internationally known West Coast mining consultant and applied for a job. The only position available was secretary. Janin considered the Stanford graduate overqualified, but Hoover accepted. Soon Janin began to pick his brain about the regional mines where he had worked and sent him to inspect mines. His boss was so impressed that when the London consulting firm of Bewick, Moreing, and Co. asked Janin to recommend a mature engineer to oversee their mines in Australia where a gold rush was raging, he selected Hoover.[13]

Hoover quickly won the respect of his men by outworking them and treating them fairly. He worked them hard but paid high wages. Though he was younger than most of the miners, they began calling him "The Chief." For the rest of his life, even as president, his oldest and closest friends called him "The Chief." The Australian desert had more gold than water or women and flies as thick as stew. Living conditions were primitive, and Hoover traveled great distances seeking mother lodes. His first major discovery, the Sons of Gwalia gold mine, made a fortune. The novice did not overlook less valuable metals. He developed profitable lead and zinc mines, weighing the value of the ore against the cost of extraction. Sometimes he made a profit by processing large quantities of low-grade ores. He always looked for numerous minerals, not simply the obvious ones. The young American was intuitive and tireless and willing to take risks—but not foolish ones. By the fall of 1898 Hoover was supervising hundreds of miners, and his salary was $10,000 annually, an enormous sum for that time.[14]

While Hoover was uncovering wealth in Australia, his London-based company was invited to develop mines for the Chinese government. Distrusting Europeans, who had partly parceled up the weak Chinese state, they requested an American. His superiors picked Hoover. He moved to China with a higher salary, a slightly more hospitable climate, and a more prestigious title. Hoover's mind turned to his fiancée in America. He now had the resources to marry and settle in a place suitable for a woman. Meanwhile, Lou had graduated. Patiently, she had kept her word and waited for Bert.[15]

Before traveling to China, Hoover joined Lou in California, where they were married by a Catholic priest, due to the unavailability of a Quaker minister, at her parents' home in Monterrey. They departed quickly for a working honeymoon in China, where they settled at Tientsin, in a rented mansion with servants. The Chinese treated the visitors like royalty, which dismayed the Hoovers. Bert was unimpressed with the efficiency of Chinese labor but doubted American workers would have done as much for such low pay under equally harsh conditions. Hoover was an employee of the Chinese government, which had subcontracted management of its mines to Moreing. Desiring quick wealth, the Chinese encouraged the young engineer to search for gold. He found none but discovered some of the world's richest coal deposits and began developing them.[16]

Hoover's work was curtailed by the rebellion of the Boxers, an ultranationalist Chinese quasimilitary organization that attempted to purge the Celestial Empire of foreign influence. They surrounded Tientsin. Hoover rationed the distribution of food and supervised the construction of barricades. Lou helped operate a hospital. An artillery shell exploded inside their home while she played solitaire. She continued her game. Eventually, foreign troops relieved the settlement, and the Hoovers returned to England. They went back later to revive the company, but it was eventually seized by other foreign interests. During his time there Hoover had made the Chinese mining operations profitable and earned the respect and gratitude of the Chinese. By the time Hoover departed China the *San Francisco Chronicle* featured him in a story describing him as the highest salaried American professional man under the age of 30. He was his young alma mater's greatest success story, and his career was barely beginning.[17]

When he returned to London, Hoover, not quite 28, was made a junior partner in the firm. He specialized in traveling the world resuscitating failing mining ventures. During Hoover's tenure the firm's revenue tripled. However, in 1902 a junior partner and accountant, John S. Rowe, embezzled about $1 million and lost it in speculation. In the absence of the two senior partners, Hoover and another junior partner announced their company would repay the entire debt, although they were not legally liable. The scandal virtually destroyed Hoover's fortune. He began to rebuild. The Hoovers helped support Rowe's wife while the culprit was in prison.[18]

When Hoover's contract expired in 1908, he did not renew it but, at age 34, struck out as an independent consultant. He maintained only a skeleton staff of young engineers who took over and managed failing firms worldwide. The Stanford grad focused on the business and financial end of mining. His base was London, but he established offices in New York, San Francisco, Saint Petersburg, and Paris. He developed a huge copper and iron complex at Kyshtim in the Ural Mountains of Russia on an old estate half as large as Belgium. Yet more impressive was a 200-year-old abandoned Chinese silver mine in northern Burma, surrounded by an impenetrable jungle. Hoover revived the mine, dug deeper, learned to prevent water seepage, and constructed a vast complex employing 25,000 persons of 17 different ethnic groups. Access was obtained by constructing a railroad through the jungle to deliver ore to his smelter. He mined not only silver but lead, copper, and zinc, which made this mine potentially one of the world's most profitable. Hoover had to sell his interests because of World War I. Otherwise, he might have amassed the greatest mining fortune of any engineer in history.[19]

For some time before the war exploded and changed Hoover's and the world's destiny, he had planned to phase out mining and enter some form of public service, perhaps publishing, philanthropy, or politics. He told friends that he had ambitions beyond earning money. He wanted to spend more time with his sons and see them obtain an American education. He was in London in 1914, representing California to persuade Europe countries, especially Britain, to participate in a celebration of the opening of the Panama Canal. His negotiations failed because a bigger crisis erupted. When war was declared, thousands of Americans seeking passage home were trapped on the Continent or in Britain. Hoover and a group of friends arranged private loans for the evacuation, and most repaid them.[20]

A bigger task awaited the engineer. Ambassador Walter Hines Page and a delegation of Belgian and other European leaders asked him to spearhead a mission to save Belgium from starvation. The tiny, densely populated nation was pinned between the British blockade and German occupation. After thinking about it overnight, Hoover created the Commission for the Relief of Belgium (CRB), which ultimately fed Belgium's entire population (7.5 million) plus another 2.5 million trapped in German-occupied northern France. Hoover's initial challenge was to negotiate rights to feed the starving from the suspicious British and French. Neither trusted the other, but both trusted Hoover. He held no public office, represented no nation, and carried no diplomatic credentials. His cardinal weapon was that neither side wanted to alienate Hoover's country, the most powerful neutral, the United States. Hoover proved an adept diplomat. He met with generals, prime ministers, and diplomats and won the grudging respect of the British and the Germans. His integrity was impeccable; he would not betray a trust nor reveal a secret.

Besides diplomacy, Hoover had to compete with troops and munitions for scarce shipping, raise money, purchase supplies, and distribute mountains of food. Virtually all workers for the CRB were volunteers, from friends of Hoover to Belgian housewives. Hoover accepted no money and paid his own expenses. Food was bought or donated in America, tracked by railroad to the coast, and loaded upon a fleet of ships operated by the CRB. The ships carried banners and other insignia to deter sinking by German submarines, but some were sunk anyway. The cargo was unloaded at the port of Rotterdam and from there sent, primarily by canal, to local centers where it was distributed or cooked by Belgian volunteers. Food was sold at a small profit to the solvent, and the profits used to provide free meals to the indigent. Special meals and supplements were prepared for babies, children, and the ill, and the mortality rate in Belgium declined below normal times.[21]

When America entered the war in 1917, Hoover departed to become food administrator for the United States but retained overall direction of Belgian relief, leaving distribution in the hands of neutrals. It was the largest privately organized relief operation in history. Through it, and his later relief operations, Hoover was credited with saving more humans than any individual in history. Combined with his relief in Russia during and after World War II, Hoover is reputed to have saved more humans from starvation than Hitler and Stalin combined killed. The CRB became a forerunner of the United Nations International Children's Fund (UNICEF) and set a precedent for relief by the United States government. Ambassador Walter Hines Page said of Hoover: "He's a simple, modest, energetic little man who began his career in California and will end it in Heaven; and he doesn't want anybody's thanks."[22]

The CRB brought Hoover to the attention of the world, including President Woodrow Wilson, who named him United States food administrator. At Hoover's request, he was unpaid. After protracted debate, Congress enacted the Lever Act, which made the Food Administration official. Hoover now had to feed America, its associated powers, and the neutral countries. Production, shipping, distribution, and public support were vital.

Hoover minimized expenses because many of his friends, including numerous veterans of the CRB, worked without pay. One, his old Stanford classmate Ray Lyman Wilbur, headed the conservation division that promoted voluntary reduction of consumption. While increased production would have to wait until the next harvest, cutting consumption could generate surpluses at once. Every woman over 15 was urged to sign a pledge card to conserve, and 12 million families enrolled. Hoover opposed compulsory rationing because it had worked poorly in Europe. Americans were a people who would rather be led than driven, he explained. Also, a temporary organization with a limited bureaucracy could be dismantled quickly after the war. If sacrifice was mutual and limited in duration, people would accept it. Wilbur coined the slogan "Food Will Win the War," which, in part, it did. His division focused on preventing waste and reducing consumption by working through religious, fraternal, labor, business, women's, and farm groups. He created a press service, a lecture bureau, and an educational section.

Regulations had teeth. Hoover was authorized to cancel licenses of manufacturers, wholesalers, and retailers who violated the rules, but few resisted. Restaurants were asked to reduce portions. Americans ate food that was bulky and difficult to transport in order to save portable food for their Allies. The Food Administration affected virtually every household. Yet, as Hoover had promised, it was completely liquidated within four months of the armistice of November 11, 1918.[23]

Hoover attended the Versailles Peace Conference as Wilson's food adviser. He opposed withholding food from defeated Germans to bludgeon them into signing the treaty, arguing that this would sow resentment that might result in a new war. He took over the relief and rehabilitation of war-devastated Eastern Europe, and during the Russian Civil War he fed that country as well, although he personally opposed Communism. He did not believe children should starve, regardless of the ideology of their parents. In fact, one of his chief motivations for feeding all nations was to protect young children. Though he seldom cried publicly, he did sob at the sight of a parade of children in Poland who had gathered to thank him for feeding them. He declined virtually every decoration offered. Some believed Hoover had done more to deserve the Nobel Peace Prize than Wilson.[24]

Returning to America, now internationally known for his work though he declined most personal interviews, Hoover supported ratification of the Versailles treaty. When the Republicans proved recalcitrant, he backed ratification with reservations. Such a treaty was the only practical course, he believed, and he wrote Wilson to advise him so, but the ailing, angry president refused to reply. Later Hoover wrote a biography of Wilson, largely complimentary, the only biography of a president by a president.[25]

Both parties sought Hoover for their nominee in 1920. The Democrats, including Franklin D. Roosevelt and leading Progressive journalists, courted him ardently. Hoover wanted the presidency but did not want to run for it. He was not ready for the rough-and-tumble of politics and believed the Democrats were destined to lose because Wilson had become unpopular. The Quaker declared himself a Republican and entered the California primary primarily to help deny the nomination to isolationist Hiram Johnson. Johnson won the primary, but Hoover helped block his nomination, making him an unrelenting enemy. Hoover had little chance for the Republican nomination because the conservatives and professional politicians opposed him. They considered him dangerously progressive. He had a mind of his own, in their minds a capital offense. Preferring a pliable candidate, they nominated the affable and malleable Senator Warren G. Harding of Ohio, a man with skeletons in his closet more appropriate for Halloween.[26]

Harding tried to assemble an intelligent cabinet to advise him because he perceived his limitations. He considered Hoover crucial to the cabinet and offered him Commerce or Interior. Interior was more prestigious, but Hoover saw greater potential in Commerce. Harding had to elbow aside several powerful conservatives who distrusted Hoover, arguing he would not place their favorite, Andrew Mellon, in the cabinet unless they accepted Hoover. They did.[27]

Harding was delighted. He knew Hoover was bright, wanted nothing for himself, and would tell the president the unvarnished truth. The Ohioan trusted Hoover's advice on policy and political judgment. In the early days of the Harding administration, Hoover had influence in patronage beyond Commerce. Hoover had a network of contacts among competent individuals, and the president relied on his advice. Hoover helped set priorities for the administration, including the idea of summoning a conference on naval disarmament early during the administration. Harding also asked Hoover to write replies to inquiries about policy questions, which Harding sent out under his own signature. Harding also granted Hoover a voice on all economic questions. Harding delegated much of the work of government to his cabinet because details caused him stress and he was poorly informed about issues. This insecurity made the presidency an excruciating job for Harding. Personally, the president and his commerce secretary got along well. Hoover did not participate in Harding's poker-and-drinking parties because he disapproved of use of alcohol in the White House during Prohibition.[28]

Coolidge relied on Hoover even more than Harding. Unlike the garrulous Harding, Coolidge hoarded words. Nonetheless, the flinty New Englander enjoyed conversing with Hoover. The secretary was respectful and trustworthy. The men unlimbered more in private than in public and enjoyed one another's company. Unlike Harding, Coolidge had succeeded to the presidency unexpectedly. He had not gathered about him a group of cronies who swapped saucy jokes and downed bootleg whisky. Coolidge and Hoover had more in common than Hoover and Harding. Sometimes Hoover's activist adviser stimulated and awed Coolidge to the point of annoyance, even envy. However, Coolidge needed Hoover and tapped his mind. They joined to oppose Agriculture Secretary Henry Wallace's sweeping plans to increase farm prices without limiting production. Both agreed that this would simply encourage more overproduction, which was the basic problem. After Wallace's death, Coolidge offered Hoover the Department of Agriculture. Hoover was not interested but helped select Wallace's successor, William M. Jardine, who became an ally in the cabinet.[29]

Politically, Coolidge leaned on Hoover heavily. He relied on him for patronage recommendations in the entire West, not merely California. Hoover was a major strategist in Coolidge's 1924 campaign, especially in the West. Though Hoover was considered a political novice by outsiders, Coolidge acknowledged his judgment. When Coolidge received policy memos on numerous issues, he often sent them to Hoover before farming them out. Hoover suggested the right department or staffer. Harding was a journalist while Coolidge disliked writing. Hoover ghostwrote even more policy statements sent to Congress and the press under Coolidge's signature than he had written for Harding.[30]

Hoover might have been the nation's greatest secretary of commerce and probably enjoyed the position more than any job he ever held. He cut a broad swath. Although some cabinet members resented his aggressiveness, as secretary, he was not exposed to the microscopic scrutiny of a president. He seized opportunities, and business craved the raw data he was eager to provide. Hoover regulated new industries such as radio and aviation, encouraging their expansion. He enjoyed a variety of relaxed, convivial contacts without the pressure of the presidency. He could focus on economic questions, his chief interest. Moreover, Hoover was a voice of reason in an age of flappers and flivvers.[31]

Hoover's first crisis was the Depression of 1921–22. Some five million workers lost their jobs during the downturn. Hoover asked industrialists to maintain wages in order to preserve consuming power and encouraged public works at every level: private, local, state, and federal, including national highway construction. His brainstorm, The President's Conference on Unemployment, gathered data and planned countercyclical measures. A committee of 14 led by Colonel Arthur Woods coordinated government efforts. Some 209 local committees had been created by the end of 1922. The economy recovered, and by 1923 the famed prosperity of the decade supplanted the stagnation of its first years.[32]

Hoover reorganized and enlarged his department, sometimes swallowing agencies from other departments or creating new ones. He attempted to group agencies according to function. The Bureau of Foreign and Domestic Commerce collected and disseminated statistics, often obtained from trade associations, which collaborated with the government. The Division of Simplified Practice within the Bureau of Standards focused on eliminating waste by diminishing the variety and shape of various products, streamlining production, and facilitating construction by limiting the number of sizes and styles.

A needless assortment of shapes and varieties existed in such products as cans, bottles, automobile tires, paving bricks, electrical fixtures, toilet paper, nuts, bolts, and lumber. Repair, installation, and construction were streamlined.

Hoover used airmail contracts to stimulate the development of commercial aviation and regulated radio informally to protect it from monopoly. He encouraged the home construction industry in the interest of generating jobs and creating a wholesome environment for families, especially children. Hoover considered construction the balance wheel of the economy and believed a reduction in production of durable goods, such as homes and automobiles, was the chief cause of depressions. In both the Great Depression of 1930 and the Great Recession that began in 2007, the sag of housing and automobile sales dragged the economy down. The activist secretary encouraged conservation of human and natural resources, including preservation of game and commercial fishing and prevented the extinction of seals. He helped draft the Agricultural Credits Act, which permitted the War Finance Corporation to grant loans to cooperatives and rural banks and to subsidize exports. Hoover sometimes clashed with the equally strong-willed Secretary of Agriculture Henry Wallace. Partly these were turf battles. Hoover believed crops entered Commerce the instant they left the ground. He believed agriculture should be integrated into the broader economy, while Wallace represented farmers alone. The ambitious commerce secretary also introduced plans for inland waterways and a St. Lawrence Seaway to reduce costs of farmers who shipped primarily by rail. He planned a series of dams that would stimulate reclamation and use of hydroelectric power, including the Hoover Dam.[33]

Hoover preferred to implement reform by cooperation rather than coercion but regulated when necessary. In dealing with water power and conservation of oil resources he wanted to negotiate state compacts, fearing direct federal regulation might be cumbrous and could be unconstitutional. He tried to harmonize the interests of labor and business, which he did not feel were antithetical. Working with Harding, he helped negotiate an end to the exhaustive 12-hour day in the steel industry. Hoover's work was imaginative, sweeping, and expansive. Some who later criticized him for being inactive as president complained he was hyperactive as secretary of commerce.[34]

In the mid- to late-1920s Hoover believed the economy, especially the stock market, was overheating and tried to cool it, although Coolidge and Mellon resisted. Hoover protested against the Federal Reserve's low interest rates, which encouraged speculation; warned against risky foreign loans by private banks that would imminently result in default; and proposed regulation of the New York Stock Exchange by the governor of New York.[35] The breadth of Hoover's plans and the degree to which he consummated them was breathtaking. One of the reasons he aspired to the presidency was to complete the task.

Unexpected events, natural and human, in 1927 helped pave the way to Hoover's election as president. Beginning in the spring, the Mississippi River and its tributaries washed over their banks, drowning people and livestock. The mighty river ripped through its levees in more than 200 places and spread across 25,000 square miles of farms, towns, and rural homes, leaving some 700,000 people homeless. At that time, the federal government had no contingency fund for national disasters, but the dimensions of the catastrophe demanded action. President Coolidge assembled his cabinet and appointed a committee headed by Hoover, which became known as the Hoover Committee, to direct rescue and restoration. Hoover worked through the American Red Cross and six fellow cabinet members. His tasks including plucking stranded individuals, families, and sometimes pets and livestock from treetops, housetops, and high land to safer ground; constructing temporary tent cities; and returning refugees to their homes after the waters had receded, as well as rehabilitation and fundraising.[36]

Operating from his headquarters in Memphis and later in New Orleans, he spent most of his time in the field, traveling in a donated Pullman, in radio contact with his subordinates. Although the waters had taken a toll of more than 300 drowned before Hoover's operation began, only three to six drowned after his work commenced. The commerce secretary commandeered boats from the Coast Guard, the U.S. Navy, the Army Corps of Engineers, and private boats loaned by fishermen, pleasure boaters, and even bootleggers. Naval planes served as spotters for stranded persons. The planes also provided reconnaissance to predict where the next breaches would occur as the waters surged southward.[37]

Hoover's organization followed the model that had served him well in Belgium and in the Food Administration: decisive, instantaneous decision making at the top and delegation to a vast array of volunteers at the local level, involving virtually no bureaucracy and reflecting an appreciation for the human element. The camps were set up by the National Guard and local Red Cross volunteers atop the highest ground available, often on levees. The National Guard maintained order, and the Red Cross served meals and distributed clothing. There were classes, church services, and entertainment in the camps. Most government contributions were in kind rather than in cash. Coolidge did not summon Congress into session to request an appropriation. But money poured in to the Red Cross, about $20.5 million in all, due to radio broadcasts by Hoover, celebrity performances for charity, newspaper appeals, and large donations by private philanthropic foundations. In addition, donations in the form of used clothing and other items amounted to about $1.6 million. Railroads furnished free transportation estimated at $1.5 million.[38]

By midsummer the waters had receded from most of the valley. Railroads provided free transit home, and the enormous cleanup began. Livestock were decimated, crops destroyed, and most of the land was covered with sludge. Total flood damage was estimated at $300 million. Some 10,000 homes lay in ruins; another 150,000 had been damaged. Roads had been washed away, businesses destroyed. After the refugees arrived home, the Red Cross assumed the task of feeding the hungry and distributed clothing, seeds, livestock, and feed and fodder to put the farmers back in business. Morale remained relatively high, thanks in part to Hoover. No president, much less a cabinet member, had ever acted so vigorously in a domestic emergency. According to most accounts, the relatively minor sums spent during the flood of 1927 were considered more effective than the vastly greater sums expended by the federal government in the aftermath of Hurricane Katrina, which struck New Orleans and the Gulf Coast in 2006.[39]

If a rising tide can lift boats, the Great Mississippi River Flood of 1927 certainly lifted Hoover's fame and produced a groundswell of support for the presidency, if it did not exactly sweep him into the White House. It especially gained him the gratitude of the South, a Democratic region where he was not well-known. Prior to the flood, his international reputation as the savior of Belgium had been greater than his reputation in America outside of Washington. Now he had revealed ability that enhanced his reputation as a master of emergencies at home. The commerce secretary was mentioned daily in the newspapers, was watched in newsreels, and was heard via radio. Already recognized as the brightest, most aggressive member of the cabinet, he was seen as a man who married organizational skills with human empathy, undaunted by the most unexpected, most difficult tasks. His imagination, coupled with determined execution, seemed destined to drive the locomotive of 1920s prosperity, with energy in reserve should any circumstance derail it. In that same year, President Coolidge would clear the tracks of any significant political obstacle.

CHAPTER 1

Landslide

Just weeks after Herbert Hoover completed his task of rescuing and revitalizing the Mississippi Valley, on August 2, 1927, President Calvin Coolidge stunned the political and financial world by releasing a cryptic statement at his summer vacation resort in the Black Hills of South Dakota. Nineteen months before his term ended, Coolidge asked the reporters covering him to assemble in a school classroom. When the newsmen filed in, the Vermonter curtly instructed them, "the line forms on the left." As they walked by, he handed each a typed slip of paper with a single sentence: "I do not choose to run for President in nineteen-twenty eight." Asked if he would elaborate, the president replied brusquely, "There will be nothing more from this office today." Coolidge made a fetish of parsing words, but this set a new standard. It jolted the stock market, which had been rising for three years.[1]

Coolidge said little publicly about his reasons for retiring. He almost certainly would have won his party's nomination as well as the 1928 election. However, Coolidge was ill and depressed. Like the stock market, his superficial health was deceiving. His long afternoon naps were due less to lassitude than to chronic indigestion and depression. He lacked stamina, suffered from heart problems (unknown at the time), and was exhausted from stress. Seemingly placid, the president's peace of mind was frayed, and his job preyed on his thoughts. Coolidge's childhood had been unhappy, and the shadow of death haunted him. He lost his mother as a boy and his father while president. The president's personal ordeal and poor health, which contributed to his reticence, were aggravated by the death of Calvin Jr. at 14. The boy died of an infected blister after playing tennis on the White House lawn (a symptom of the poor medical care available even to the family of a president in the 1920s). "When he went, the power and glory of the presidency went with him," Coolidge confessed. Before his next term would have ended, during the interregnum between Hoover and Franklin D. Roosevelt, Coolidge died suddenly in retirement. No one perceived that his announcement would end an era and that his death in 1933 opened a new one.[2]

Despondent, Coolidge was weary of politics. Soon after he withdrew, a friend, James H. MacLafferty, a former California congressman and an assistant in Hoover's Commerce Department, visited the Coolidges. MacLafferty told the president that many of his friends regretted his decision. "Well, it is much better not to want to run and have them want to have you to, than it is to want to run and have them not want you to," Coolidge replied. MacLafferty speculated that since his renunciation of the office, the West Coast would vote for Hoover. The president nodded assent. Grace Coolidge told him that the couple looked forward to relaxing in private life, doing only what they wanted to do.[3]

Hoover was at the Bohemian Grove, an annual camping retreat for California businessmen, politicians, and celebrities beneath the redwoods. More than 100 reporters asked him to comment on the president's surprising, enigmatic announcement, but Hoover sagely declined. He realized the news made him the Republican frontrunner, but he owed respect to Coolidge. He waited to learn whether Coolidge would change his mind. Further, he wished to remain secretary of commerce. He did not want to seem eager for the presidency, and in fact he had mixed feelings. Serving at the highest level would provide the opportunity to accomplish more, yet the Californian knew it would come at a price. He did not intend to actively campaign for the nomination and tried to restrain his friends until Coolidge clarified his intentions. Hoover disliked public speaking and decided he would not make a single political speech before the nominating convention. In fact, he made several speeches, including a few by radio, but none was purely political. He also abstained from fundraising. If there was to be a campaign, it would be conducted by surrogates, and Hoover would direct it from behind the scenes, chiefly by letter writing. In the short run, he would remain loyal to Coolidge. Should Coolidge decide to reenter the contest, Hoover planned to withdraw and turn over his delegates to the president. He believed an intraparty fight would produce fratricide.[4]

Professional politicians did not want Hoover. He was not one of them, had not risen through the ranks, and was too independent and too progressive. A political interloper, the Quaker was not malleable and might not cut deals behind closed doors. The bosses wanted a pliable candidate like Harding or a standpatter like Coolidge. Some of the Old Guard disliked not only Hoover's reputation for progressivism but also his internationalism. After all, Hoover had supported the Versailles treaty, including the League of Nations, and wanted the United States to join the World Court. Elements of the Eastern financial community disliked the commerce secretary because he had opposed lucrative, high-interest foreign bond purchases by Americans on the grounds that the loans were shaky. The commerce secretary also objected to the easy credit policies of the Federal Reserve Board, which had facilitated speculation. Conservative businessmen disliked his proposals for strict regulation. Objections came from some Midwestern farmers who blamed the administration for low prices.[5] Others believed Hoover lacked the speaking skills necessary for politics. Sympathizing, the famous public relations expert and writer Dale Carnegie wrote Hoover, offering to coach him in the art of public speaking. Carnegie's unsolicited letter boasted that he had helped many public figures polish their oratory, including a few engineers. Hoover did not reply.[6]

Still, Hoover possessed an impeccable record, an international reputation, organizational and administration credentials, a fine mind, and grassroots popularity. Journalist Frank Kent, writing for *Plain Talk*, argued that the party should welcome him after a long series of mediocre candidates.[7] Even party hacks realized that his nomination meant an almost certain Republican victory. As secretary of commerce, Hoover had generated a greater degree of *esprit des corps* than any cabinet secretary in memory. He had recently added to his luster by rescuing the Mississippi Valley from the ravages of the river. He had not been tainted by the Harding scandals, and in this respect the fact that he was not a politician was an asset. Despite Hoover's service under the Democrat Wilson, he had subsequently served loyally under two Republican presidents. The Quaker was modest, yet not obsequious. Though some opponents believed Hoover lusted after the presidency, quite the contrary was true. He would take it if it came, but he was not pushy in a political sense. When one of his assistants at Commerce wrote an essay praising his boss and sent it to Hoover for approval, the secretary scribbled, "Please kill this. I want no personal advertising." Craig Lloyd writes, "in light of the evidence, Hoover must be exonerated from the charge that he deliberately used public relations techniques to publicize himself. To Hoover, office seeking was obnoxious." Lloyd explains, "For Hoover himself the kind of exposure that any really ambitious candidate not only accepts, but enjoys, was thoroughly distasteful. Although Hoover was sensitive to criticism, he was also irritated by excessive public acclaim for his achievements."[8]

No candidate appeared sufficiently strong to block Hoover unless a stop-Hoover coalition could be created, resembling 1920s deadlocked convention. Other Republicans coveted the nomination, including Vice President Charles Dawes, former Illinois Governor Frank O. Lowden, Senator Frank B. Willis of Ohio, and Senators Guy Goff of West Virginia and Charles Curtis of Kansas. Yet no other potential nominee had Hoover's strengths, and all had greater weaknesses. Most of his competitors were too old, too obscure, or had only regional appeal. None commanded his grassroots support. Dawes had feuded with Coolidge; Lowden, Curtis, and Goff were regional candidates; and Willis was an Ohio machine politician, similar to Harding. While most were vice presidential timber, none was considered presidential caliber in 1928.[9]

Some believed they could only deter Hoover by reviving interest in Coolidge or persuading the Vermonter to accept a draft. As the campaign progressed, this became increasingly difficult because Coolidge offered no encouragement. The incumbent made it clear that he would neither endorse a successor nor attempt to thwart one. On December 7, 1927, Coolidge informed the Republican National Committee that he did not intend to run.[10] Hoover's confidant, MacLafferty, told Hoover he had never known Coolidge to make a public statement that he later retracted.[11]

Hoover recognized his wide support and was careful not to elbow the incumbent aside. Coolidge was too popular to alienate, and the secretary of commerce treated him deferentially. He respected the New Englander and knew better than to try to pry words out of him. When Hoover's journalist friend, Will Irwin, asked him about his nomination, the secretary responded, "I shall be the nominee, probably. It is nearly inevitable." However, when Irwin followed up by asking what he would do if Coolidge decided to run, Hoover replied, "I won't get in the way, naturally."[12] George Akerson, Hoover's press secretary, stated that only after Coolidge had definitely ruled himself out did Hoover allow his subordinates to unleash a genuine campaign. Lewis Strauss, who had worked for Hoover in the Food Administration, wrote, "Mr. Hoover had told us in no uncertain terms that he was not a candidate and would not consider the subject until Mr. Coolidge had made his own intentions plain."[13] In September 1927, Hoover approached Coolidge gingerly to probe his intentions. Realistically, Hoover knew he could not delay his own campaign indefinitely because rivals were already campaigning. Coolidge remained vague yet refused to permit his friends to enter his name in any primaries. In early 1928, he confidentially told two of his supporters, "I have studied it all over and have finally concluded that I do not want the nomination."[14] The impression was growing that Coolidge could not be coaxed into the race, though diehards persisted. An observer wrote, "Whether Calvin meant it or not, I believe he is fairly out of it. The country has in a large measure accepted the statement at face value, and the active candidates will occupy the field without much elbow room remaining."[15]

In 1928, the stars aligned for Hoover. Along with Coolidge and Andrew Mellon, Hoover was an icon of 1920s prosperity. At 53, he was in the prime of life. His wife, Lou, possessed an impressive academic pedigree and was a talented writer and linguist who had a distinguished record of public service. Their sons, Herbert and Allan, were in college. Hoover counted diverse friends such as John Maynard Keynes, Bernard Baruch, and General Douglas MacArthur. Keynes, who had met him at Versailles, considered the American the only man to have emerged from the contentious peace conclave with an enhanced reputation. Elihu Root and William Howard Taft were among his supporters, and Louis D. Brandeis admired him. Hoover epitomized the selfless public servant who had risen on merit and merged idealism with practicality. His vast European relief programs operated with an overhead of less than one-half of 1 percent. No one found one iota of dishonesty in Hoover in his public or private life, though opponents dredged through political muck. Now his friends strove to win the nomination for the transplanted Californian. These associates were fired with the same work ethic as their leader. They represented no ideological faction or region but a collection of intimates, including numerous writers and journalists.[16]

Because he did not intend to conduct a personal campaign for the nomination, Hoover could treat the Vermonter in the White House with calculated respect. Though opposites in temperament, the respect was genuine. The long-shot candidates had to campaign more aggressively. None percolated with Hoover's energy or commanded his legion of loyal friends. Hoover earned their devotion. He worked his subordinates like dogs, yet wrought miracles. He never sought credit, nor publicly blamed an understudy for failure. One observer claimed that he had enemies but no ex-friends. Many who enlisted in his campaign had a Stanford connection. Stanford had given him an opportunity, and he had become its most illustrious alumnus. He believed California was the center of the universe and Palo Alto its epicenter. During his rescue of flood victims, journalist Will Irwin, who had known Hoover as a Stanford student and as a war correspondent during the Great War, began collecting information for a book that became the first Hoover biography since a 1920 book by Rose Wilder Lane. Published early in 1928, *Herbert Hoover: A Reminiscent Biography* stimulated public interest. It provided more insight into Hoover's private personality than anything in print. The book went through five printings and provided a thoughtful, sympathetic boost to his candidacy.[17]

If Palo Alto was not literally the epicenter of the universe, it might qualify as the epicenter of Hoover's campaign. He had blossomed there, Stanford had shaped his commitment to public service, and he had forged lifelong bonds. Almost immediately he began giving back, and now it was Stanford's turn to help catapult Hoover into the presidency. Many of his friends were eloquent writers and tireless advocates. Their loyalty ran deep. His supporters might have been fervent amateurs, but they were disciplined disciples who collected delegates methodically. Early in 1928, former classmates in California created a Stanford-for-Hoover club, and the movement spread to every state. One of the first to sign up was his old friend and Stanford classmate, Ray Lyman Wilbur, who subsequently attended the Republican convention as an alternate for Hoover. The student newspaper and the Alumni Association endorsed Hoover, the first time the latter had backed a candidate. Much of the campaigning by individuals came at their own initiative, some of them unaffiliated with any group. Some were Stanford classmates or dated to his mining career, the CRB, or the Food Administration. Like Hoover, they were idealistic. Highly motivated, they needed little direction.[18] Hoover's friend and colleague Christian Herter observed that "a small army of men and women dotted all over the United States formed a group of missionaries whose work had been accomplished long before June 12," when the Republican convention assembled at Kansas City.[19]

Hoover's supporters assiduously collected endorsements from individuals and groups and some arrived spontaneously. Among prominent backers were Henry Ford, Thomas Edison, journalist Mark Sullivan, writer Booth Tarkington, and the President of Yale University Dr. James G. Angell. From Hollywood came the support of Cecil B. DeMille, D. W. Griffith, and Louis D. Mayer. "The only opposition to Herbert Hoover is from the politicians," Mayer wrote. "It comes from the same back room clique that acted up in 1920. We will have none of that at Kansas City."[20] Griffith added, "Every line in Herbert Hoover's glowing record as a public servant is a tribute to his unselfishness, integrity, and administrative genius."[21] Ford wrote that Hoover had financial, business, and technical expertise, as well as common sense. "Hoover can bring capital and labor together," the auto magnate explained.[22]

Hoover obtained endorsements from all regions, but his campaign surrogates worked particularly hard to win backing from the Midwest and the South, contested farm sections. James R. Howard, the first president of the American Farm Bureau Federation, wrote, "Hoover has done more for the farmer than any other member of the government during the past eight years." He added, "Actions speak louder than words."[23] Katherine Langley, a Kentucky congresswoman, said Hoover's executive ability foretold a great presidency. She observed that he was loved in Kentucky because of his aid to flood victims.[24] C. D. Street, the Republican National Committeeman of Alabama, said his state was solidly behind Hoover: "Secretary Hoover immensely strengthened himself throughout all the South by his efficient and sympathetic activities in connection with Mississippi flood relief."[25]

The South represented a peculiar problem for Republican candidates during the 1920s. It controlled about one-third of the delegates needed to nominate, yet voted monolithically Democratic in the general election. Republican since Reconstruction, southern blacks remained loyal to the party of Lincoln but were prohibited from voting in general elections by such tactics as the "white primary," property and literacy requirements, local residency stipulations, poll taxes, and flagrant intimidation. Southern Republicans thrived on patronage during Republican administrations. The most certain route to obtaining a large bloc of Southern delegates was to buy them with patronage or bribe them. The party was weak, corrupt, dominated by local bosses, and inefficient at delivering constituent services. Conditions varied from state to state and were complex. In some states, known as lily-white enclaves, the machines were controlled by whites. In other states, where factions called black and tans dominated, a coalition of blacks and whites parceled out jobs and quadrennial delegates.

Hoover hoped his administration could reform the South, but during the nominating process, he accepted the situation as he found it. The Hooverites tended to favor recognition based not on race but on loyalty to Hoover. Though Hoover disliked bossism, at this stage he did not personally intervene in internal struggles, unlike some of his subordinates. A white Tennessean, Horace Mann, was his principal Southern coordinator. In the end, most of Southern delegations, after some initial skirmishing, lined up with Hoover. In the intraparty infighting he had several advantages. No one else who curried favor was likely to win the nomination. If delegates sided with a loser, their demands for patronage were unlikely to be satisfied. The Southern machines might have feared Hoover because of his reputation as a reformer, but they had more to fear from opposing him.[26]

Hoover also had to be concerned about black support in the North, which was more diverse, and he worked diligently to harvest primary delegates and general election votes. Hoover was aided by the fact that he had desegregated the Commerce Department. Harding had given each cabinet member the latitude to desegregate his department, yet Hoover was the only one to do it. Among those aware of the Quaker tradition of tolerance, this was an asset as well. On a personal basis, most Northern blacks could find no compelling reason to vote for one of his opponents.[27]

Hoover benefited from endorsements by groups, too. Most of his fellow engineers backed his candidacy. Women enthusiastically supported him, including reformers such as Jane Addams and thousands of housewives who were grateful for his efforts on behalf of children, recreation, stable homes, temperance, and health care for infants. The Scripps-Howard news chain, which had endorsed LaFollette in 1924, promoted his candidacy, as did a majority of major dailies. Ethnic groups gravitated to Hoover's cause, especially those whose homelands had benefitted from his humanitarianism, such as Poles, Czechs, Yugoslavs, and Russians.[28] Speaking for his fellow Russians, W. W. Bouimistrow, head of a Russian refugee organization in America, praised Hoover. "When famine laid Russia prostrate, there arose a man in America who combined both a great heart and a great brain," he said. "Eleven million people were saved from starvation."[29] A Yugoslav spokesman said, "The name of Hoover is a sacred one to every American of Slavonic origin."[30] A Bohemian writer spoke for many of his Czechoslovakian countrymen when he predicted that Hoover would win the nomination and the election overwhelmingly.[31]

Although Hoover was a candidate of substance and stature, less was known about his views on specific political issues. Prior to his nomination, *The Outlook* asserted, "Not in a generation has there been an outstanding candidate for the presidency of whose partisan commitments so little was generally known." Hoover, it continued, was doubtless a brilliant administrator, but where did he stand within his own party? An interested person could learn much from his published statements. The commerce secretary was an orthodox Republican in that he believed in a protective tariff, immigration restrictions, and resisted radical solutions to farm problems. Hoover had been a bureaucratic central-izer within the cabinet, but he did not favor centralized government in gen-eral. He was dubious of the doctrine of "implied powers" in the Constitution and believed in states' rights. *The Outlook* viewed him as more a Jeffersonian than a Hamiltonian. *Outlook* journalist Silas Bent concluded, "In regard to labor and wages, Mr. Hoover's attitude may be classified as enlightened." He also preferred the two-party system of the United States to the multiparty, parliamentary systems, of Europe. Numerous parties led to fragmentation and often helped elect a leader who represented a minority of the people, he said. Hoover believed it was advantageous for the same party to control Con-gress and the presidency to facilitate implementation of a coherent program. While secretary of commerce, he had been unusually successful in obtaining legislation he wanted from Congress.[32]

The Outlook viewed Hoover as a moderate on Prohibition, certain to be an important issue in the campaign. "There can be no doubt of the economic benefits of Prohibition," he said. "I think increased temperance over the land is responsible for a good share of the enormously increased efficiency of pro-duction." In February 1928, Senator William E. Borah of Idaho mailed the leading Republican candidates a questionnaire asking them to define their position on Prohibition. Borah, an extreme dry, was trying to determine which candidate to support. Hoover responded that he did not favor repeal and would enforce the law more vigorously: "Our country has deliberately undertaken a great social and economic experiment, noble in motive and far-reaching in purpose." Hoover wrote, "It must be worked out constructively."[33] The Quaker never used the phrase "noble experiment" often attributed to him. Many commentators, including *The Outlook* and the Portland *Morning Oregonian*, praised Hoover for his moderate dryness, which in 1928 repre-sented the majority opinion. His response sufficiently satisfied Borah, who campaigned for him during the general election.[34]

As the frontrunner, the commerce secretary became a magnet for slan-derous charges, some resurrected in the general election. His campaign was gaining momentum, alarming adversaries. Lou wrote her sons that "affairs are going with uncanny rapidity toward making your Daddy President." None-theless, Lou was bemused, and sometimes hurt, by rumors circulated about her husband. "I have been asked a great many times if . . . my husband has not invented the Hoover Vacuum Cleaner," she wrote.[35] Some of Hoover's oppo-nents claimed he was ineligible because he was a British citizen. Ohio Con-gressman Charles Brand claimed Hoover had lived in London until age 40, had voted in British elections, and had cheated American farmers by selling American farm products too cheaply to the Allies. He was branded a Demo-crat for having served in the Wilson administration and because he had been entered in the Democratic primary in Michigan by friends in 1920 and had won it.[36]

The frontrunner was also the target of racists. Senator Cole Blease of South Carolina complained on the Senate floor that Hoover had permitted blacks and whites to work side by side in the Commerce Department. Opponents doctored a photograph to show him dancing with a black woman while in the Mississippi Delta. The candidate's enemies claimed that he had defrauded the Chinese and employed slave labor while a mining engineer in the Far East.[37] Groups representing special interests, from farmers to bankers, condemned Hoover. George M. Peek, a prominent farm leader, said in April 1928, "In my opinion, any candidate yet mentioned by either party would be supported by the farm population in preference to Hoover with such a record of duplicity and deliberate exploitation of agriculture."[38] Although farmers were often at odds with Wall Street, both found reasons to criticize the commerce secretary. Financiers feared Hoover, an expert on economics, wanted to regulate them. One journalist wrote that big business and political conservatives "don't like Hoover, don't understand him, and are doubtful about their ability to deal with him."[39] Shortly after his nomination, a Wall Street insider remarked that "some of us who earn our living in Wall Street have sent neither the candidate nor the Republican Convention telegrams of Congratulation."[40]

Hoover's supporters, and some observers who simply believed in fair play, defended him. *The Outlook* pointed out that the Constitution merely specified that a president had to have lived in the United States for 14 years consecutively, which Hoover had done. It did not state that those years must immediately precede his presidency.[41] Irvine L. Lenroot—an attorney, U.S. senator from Wisconsin, and friend of Hoover—issued a legal opinion on December 5, 1927, stating that Hoover was an American citizen and there was nothing that disqualified him from becoming president.[42] The charges of maltreatment of the Chinese were countered by Tang Shao-yi, the only prominent Chinese official still living from those days. He testified that Hoover was actually a hero who had treated the Chinese fairly, protected their interests, and saved many Chinese lives, including his own, during the Boxer Rebellion.[43] His defenders identified Hoover as an advocate for farmers, not their enemy. He had been raised on farms and in farming communities, and he understood the micro- and macroeconomics of farming. During the Great War, prices had been set by a board on which Hoover did not sit, not by the Food Administration. Afterward, when American farmers had been stuck with a surplus, due to the early armistice, he had almost single-handedly pried open the Allied blockade of the defeated Central Powers and disposed of American crops in Central and Eastern Europe, saving farmers from ruin and Europeans from famine.[44] Most of the charges had been made and discredited during the brief Hoover presidential boom of 1920. Only the most gullible could have taken them seriously.

Hoover would have preferred to avoid primary contests, yet significant blocs of delegates were at stake, and he had to demonstrate the ability to win votes. In order to enter the crucial Ohio primary, where Senator Willis was running as a favorite son, Hoover's supporters needed his permission. Once again, Hoover approached Coolidge. If Coolidge had any desire to enter the race at this stage, Hoover promised he would withdraw. Then he asked bluntly if Coolidge thought he should enter the Ohio primary in early February. Succinctly, Coolidge grunted, "Why not?" Coolidge had given his implicit, if not his explicit, blessing. The president did not like Willis, who had often opposed his policies, and preferred Hoover. On February 12, the commerce secretary wrote a letter granting permission to place him on the Ohio ballot.[45]

In fact, without fanfare, Coolidge was slowly clearing the path for Hoover by discouraging those who wanted to promote the president himself. In April, he wrote supporters in Massachusetts urging them not to write his name in on the primary ballot. In other states, where followers were trying to do so, including New York, he asked them to halt efforts. The president complained that the draft campaign was an embarrassment to him.[46] The Senate complemented Coolidge's actions by passing an anti–third term resolution 56–26 on February 10, 1928.[47] In May, Hoover saw Coolidge one last time. By now, he had collected about 400 delegates. Still, he remained willing to step aside. Coolidge responded that, if his commerce secretary actually had 400 delegates, he should keep them. At this point, Coolidge could only have been a spoiler, and he did not desire that role.[48]

Hoover was selective in his choice of primaries. In some cases, he avoided challenging favorite sons because he did not want to alienate them or divide the party. But he was willing to do so where the stakes were sufficiently high, and he had a reasonable chance to win. Hoover believed the crucial contests lay in the farm states of the Midwest because he felt secure about the Northeast, the South, and the West. Farmers, though normally Republican, were on the verge of rebellion because of low prices, especially for wheat. The angst was less directed at Hoover, personally, than at hard times in general. Yet President Coolidge, backed by Hoover, had twice vetoed one of their pet proposals, the McNary-Haugen bill. This measure would have set a guaranteed domestic price for grain. To maintain prices while keeping supply and demand in balance, the government would purchase the surplus and sell it abroad at the lower world price, reimbursing itself with a tax on food processing. The plan, as Hoover and Coolidge pointed out, would only proliferate the problem. It would encourage farmers to produce even more because it lacked production controls, driving prices increasingly downward. Further, most nations, including the United States, had antidumping laws to prevent the underselling of their produce on their own markets. They would retaliate with high tariffs, import quotas, and imperial preferences.

Under Harding, a start had been made to help farmers by enacting the Capper-Volstead Act, which freed cooperatives from the being charged with monopoly; the Grain Futures Act, which curtailed speculation; and the Packers and Stockyards Act, which prevented excessive markups by middlemen. Most farmers wanted more, and there was no question that their income, in a relative sense, had not kept up with that of urban workers. They wanted profits comparable to the period before America entered the Great War, when world demand had driven prices up. Consequently, they had overexpanded in the false belief that the demand would remain permanent. Ironically, American farmers were too good at what they did. They produced more than could be consumed at the prices they desired. The government could not persuade them to cut back, and, in the legal context of the times, it was dubious that any law that compelled them to do so would pass constitutional muster. Moreover, it is unlikely a law limiting production could pass Congress because farmers themselves, and farm-state congressmen, did not support such legislation.

Hoover's chief rivals for the nomination, Illinois Governor Frank Lowden and Vice President Charles Dawes, had farm support because they endorsed the McNary-Haugen bill, but they lacked national backing. At 68, Lowden was old, and he had been complicit in the deadlocked convention of 1920 that resulted in Harding's nomination. Dawes, a distinguished Republican, had been awarded the Nobel Peace Prize in 1925 for his role in negotiating the Dawes Plan to reduce European reparations. However, by supporting the farm plan his own president vetoed twice, he was considered disloyal to Coolidge, alienating friends of the popular incumbent.[49]

Many farmers liked Hoover personally because he had grown up on farms and in farm villages, and he had worked with his hands. They respected his understanding of farm poverty and knew he would treat them fairly, even if he considered some of their pet proposals unworkable. He had a national view and understood the relationship of the farm economy to the total economy. Ironically, farmers wanted the government to do more for them while bankers and business wanted it to leave them alone. Nominating Lowden or Dawes would have divided the party. Either would have been a weaker candidate than Hoover. Further, Coolidge respected Hoover's grasp of agriculture so much that he had asked him to become secretary of agriculture. Hoover, although he remained at Commerce, was a highly influential adviser on farm issues. It was well known that Coolidge preferred Hoover to Lowden or Dawes, and it was inconceivable that the party would nominate one of Coolidge's opponents. This was true of Senator George Norris of Nebraska, as well, who was anathema not only to Coolidge but to regular Republicans. The prudent choice was to nominate the strongest candidate, Hoover.

By mid-February, when Hoover fired up his primary campaign, about one-third of the convention delegates had already been chosen, and Hoover had a substantial lead. Without a candidate sufficiently strong to defeat Hoover directly, his opponents threw their weight behind a multitude of favorite sons, hoping to produce a brokered convention. In the key Midwestern primaries in Ohio and Indiana, Hoover was opposed by Senator Frank R. Willis in Ohio and Senator James E. Watson in Indiana, defending their home turf. Other favorite sons in less important states were Senators Charles Curtis in Kansas and Guy Goff in West Virginia. Willis, a fanatical Prohibitionist and once a paid lecturer of the Anti-Saloon League, waged a largely negative campaign against Hoover. He might have won the primary, yet died shortly before the election. Hoover lost the other primaries, which was not unexpected. He also lost Nebraska and Wisconsin to Norris, who was chiefly a protest candidate. In every state Hoover lost, except Wisconsin, he was defeated by a favorite son.[50]

Hoover's losses were not fatal. He did not travel to any of the primary states to campaign while his opponents ran energetic canvasses and already possessed state political machines. His defeat by Watson in Indiana by the narrow margin of 25,000 votes was a moral victory. Watson had the backing of reactionary elements such as the Ku Klux Klan (Indiana had the nation's largest Klan membership) and the Anti-Saloon League, and Indiana was a largely agricultural state, which favored the McNary-Haugen bill. The vote there did not improve Watson's national prospects.[51]

Overall, Hoover won far more primaries than any other candidate, including major states. He captured California, Oregon, New Jersey, Massachusetts, Michigan, and Maryland, running better in urban than in rural areas. The primaries did not identify any candidate other than Hoover capable of winning the nomination. The primaries singled out Hoover as the man to beat. United, his opponents might pose a nuisance. However, they were no more enamored of one another than they were of Hoover. Most Republicans did not want another deadlocked convention.[52] Hoover looked to the delegate-rich states of Pennsylvania and New York, which could put him over the top. He gained strength in New York after it became clear that Coolidge could not be persuaded to run. Five of his fellow cabinet members had endorsed him by late February, and New York was one of the first states to organize a Hoover-for-President club. Lowden was unacceptable to Eastern farmers who considered the McNary-Haugen measure special interest legislation.[53] Andrew Mellon and the Pennsylvania delegation, which voted under the unit rule, leaned toward Hoover. The treasury secretary initially favored either Coolidge or Charles Evans Hughes, the candidate in 1916. Coolidge's refusal to allow himself to be placed on the ballot in the Eastern states started a move to Hoover. If one of the big Eastern states shifted to Hoover, it would ensure his nomination on the first ballot.[54]

Shortly before the convention, Hoover met with Borah and hammered out the principles of the platform. Both agreed the platform should be dry and should advocate graft-free government, a protective tariff, world peace, relief for farmers, and regulation of utilities. On June 11, the day before the convention opened, Borah released a group of his delegates to Hoover. Borah, a charismatic speaker, helped during the campaign.[55]

Meanwhile, on June 7, Mellon said Hoover would be the best candidate, concurring with William S. Vare, the powerful Philadelphia boss. On June 12, the day the convention opened, Vare made public his commitment, and several New England delegations declared support for Hoover. As an executive committee of corn-belt politicians met to stave off a Hoover nomination, an objective that appeared hopeless, a spokesman for Dawes said his name would not be placed in nomination. The only remaining hope of the diehards was a Coolidge draft.[56]

James W. Good, an influential congressman who, along with Interior Secretary Hubert Work, managed the convention campaign and doused the last embers of the smoldering desire for Coolidge. Good issued a statement from the Hoover headquarters in Kansas City stating that if Coolidge desired the nomination, Hoover remained willing to step aside and lend his support to the incumbent, a tactic designed to force Coolidge's hand. It worked. Coolidge declined the offer and killed the prospect of a draft on the floor. Later, it was learned that Coolidge had written a letter to be read to the convention, only if necessary, renouncing any intention of accepting the nomination. It was not necessary.[57]

Hoover was in constant touch with Good and Work by a direct line from his phone in Washington to campaign headquarters in Kansas City. He canceled personal appointments, permitting only a few close friends to see him. The only family member to attend the convention was Allan, his youngest son, a recent Stanford graduate, who served as a page on the floor. The family and intimate friends gathered nightly at the Hoover home to listen to the major speeches broadcast by radio. Hoover was all business. He kept the press at bay, declining comment.[58]

Professionals were amazed at the single-track effectiveness of the Hoover locomotive. Hoover's name was ubiquitous, as were Stanford alumni. Attractive coeds met delegates with California oranges, dates, figs, and raisins, marching to a brass band. The Hoover machine controlled the Credentials Committee. Contested delegations from the South were mowed down. Race and party standing was ignored; the criterion for seating was fealty to Hoover.[59]

On the afternoon of June 14, the nominations began. Hoover chose an old California friend, Senator John L. McNab, to nominate him. As he began his speech, an enormous demonstration erupted. McNab remained silent and Senator George H. Moses, the permanent chairman, wacked his gavel but did not really intend to quiet the parade. The Californian said that Hoover understood the common people because his roots were in the soil. His nomination was not based on expediency; rather, it was based on a spiritual calling. Hoover had not been chosen by a back-door deal; instead, his support swelled from the grass roots. If the American people had set out a quarter of a century ago to prepare a man for the presidency, they could have devised no better preparation than Hoover's. Next, Arizona yielded to Illinois, which had been expected to nominate Lowden. Instead, Senator Otis Glenn read a letter from Lowden withdrawing because the convention had rejected the McNary-Haugen plan earlier that day. On the first roll-call, Hoover won easily with 837 votes to 74 for Lowden, 64 for Curtis, 45 for Watson, 24 for Norris, and 24 for Coolidge.

Chairman Moses asked the convention to make the nomination unanimous, which it did. Then he cabled Hoover to congratulate him.[60]

On January 15, the delegates nominated Senator Charles Curtis of Kansas for vice president. Hoover did not dictate the nomination but exercised veto power. For the first time, both the presidential and vice presidential nominees of a major party had been born west of the Mississippi River. The Kansas senator was also the first member of a major party ticket to have Indian blood, though only a small amount. Representing a major wheat state, he was expected to help the party in the farm belt. Experienced, a party regular, he would also help Hoover with the conservative faction. Most Republicans believed Curtis strengthened the ticket.[61]

Hoover was gratified but stoic. He listened to the roll-call in the library of his home. His only reaction was to smile and kiss Lou. Overnight, he received thousands of congratulatory telegrams, including messages from Coolidge and Dawes. After staying up late, he arose early, breakfasted with his press secretary, Akerson, and then left for his office to answer mail. Smiling and genial, he remained reticent and declined to comment to the press, only telling them he wanted to meet with congressional leaders first.[62]

Hoover dispatched a telegram to Chairman Moses acknowledging his nomination. It established the tone of the campaign: serious, reflective, and modest. "My country owes me no debt," he explained. "It gave me, as it gives every boy and girl, a chance. It gave me schooling, independence of action, opportunity for service and honor." He concluded, "In no other land could a boy from a country village, without inheritance or influential friends, look forward with unbounded hope." Hoover indicated that the problems of the next four years were not simply economic and material. They involved world peace, and the actions of the president affected every family, a solemn responsibility. The presidency required moral and spiritual leadership.[63]

Hoover orchestrated the details of the campaign. He chose Hubert Work as chairman of the Republican National Committee (RNC). Work, who had led the nominating campaign, along with James W. Good, managed the national effort. Good headed the vote harvesting in the Midwest, Horace Mann in the South, and Tom Gregory in the West. Other lieutenants included Assistant Secretary of Commerce Walter Brown of Ohio, former Senator Irvine Lenroot of Wisconsin, and Edgar Rickard and Ogden Mills of New York. Akerson remained Hoover's press agent and personal assistant.[64]

Work, a psychiatrist, was born in Pennsylvania but lived much of his adult life in Colorado and identified with the West. Appointed postmaster by Harding, he became interior secretary to clean up the Teapot Dome Scandal. Work, Hoover's closest friend in the cabinet, was open, accessible, tactful, efficient, and close to the Old Guard wing of the GOP. He was content to let Hoover make major decisions and focused on implementation. Work helped unite the party. At 68, Work sometimes tired but continued to put in long hours. The staff of the RNC was enlarged to include fundraising and research.

It cultivated relations with blacks, ethnic groups, and labor and created divisions to recruit women, college students, first-time voters, and business and professional people.[65]

A few days after the Kansas City convention, the Hoovers departed by rail for Palo Alto, where the candidate awaited official notification of his nomination. Hoover visited briefly with Vice President Dawes near Chicago and rested for two days with President Coolidge at his summer fishing lodge on Wisconsin's Brule River. The two men said little publicly but fished and chatted. Hoover offered his resignation from the cabinet; however, Coolidge asked him to remain to complete unfinished business.[66]

The trip west was saddened by the news that Lou's father, 84-year-old Charles D. Henry was seriously ill. He died as the Hoovers were en route. The journey provided Hoover's introduction to campaigning. Initially awkward as he shook hands, smiled, and spoke from the rear of the train; he warmed as he headed west. Encouraged by receptive crowds, he began to speak more but confined himself to pleasantries with little political content. Reluctant to make small talk with reporters, at Elko, Nevada, he hugged but refused to kiss a baby.[67] At Palo Alto, the family attended a private memorial service for Lou's father. Hoover spent the remainder of his time visiting friends and politicians, completing Commerce business, and drafting his acceptance speech. He relaxed at the western home Lou had designed for the couple, nestled near their alma mater. Stanford students could not refrain from staging a spontaneous rally at the Hoover home, including cheers, college yells, and fireworks. Speaking from his balcony, the candidate said there was nowhere he would rather be.[68] Getting away for the last time before the campaign, Hoover and a few friends fished one of his favorite spots, near the headwaters of the Klamath River in northern California and nearby Oregon, where he had angled as a boy. He tried to avoid the press and refused to pose for cameras with fish he had not actually caught. Afterward, Coolidge wired acceptance of Hoover's resignation.[69]

The speech accepting his nomination officially opened the campaign. On August 11, Hoover addressed an audience of 60,000 at Stanford Stadium and millions via radio in a peroration he had polished to perfection. Unlike his later campaign speeches, Hoover focused less on specific topics than on a philosophical overview, though he did make some promises. He praised Coolidge and emphasized Republican prosperity but did not mention Harding. Like many of his speeches, it included an element of spiritual uplift. The GOP candidate vowed to continue prosperity, yet overreached in predicting a future without poverty. In reality, poverty is relative, not absolute, and has existed in all civilizations. Still, Hoover vowed to cushion the boom-and-bust cycle. He promised a $1 billion public works program and an interconnected system of transportation with inland waterways complementing railroads. Labor had a place in the American Eden, and he would protect it by reducing the use of injunctions in labor disputes and avoiding labor strife.

Farming was close to Hoover's heart. Farm poverty demanded immediate attention, perhaps a special session. He proposed a multifaceted program
of tariff protection, enhanced marketing through cooperatives, and efficient
transportation. In foreign policy, the candidate vowed to cooperate with the
League of Nations but declined membership. His priority was world peace,
in which naval disarmament would play a vital role. Hoover promised frugal-
ity, elimination of waste, honesty in government, and merit appointments.
Women could help ensure morality in government, as well as the sanctity of
the home and the health and education of children. Hoover knew religious
prejudice might play a role in the campaign, and he called upon his backers to avoid bigotry. The candidate said he came of Quaker stock, a creed in
which prejudice had no place. The bedrock of his philosophy lay in equality
of opportunity. Hoover opposed the repeal of Prohibition and vowed to strive
for stricter enforcement. Reiterating portions of the Republican platform, he
promised to wage a clean campaign, using words to convey, not distort, his
meaning. Hoover was straightforward and transparently sincere. Sprinkled
among specific promises were exhortations to build a united, more spiritual
nation.[70]

The Democrats met at Houston and nominated New York Governor
Alfred E. Smith. Like Hoover, Smith was a self-made man, yet he was as
prototypically urban as the Iowa native was rural. He had grown up, literally,
on the "Sidewalks of New York," which became his campaign song. Unlike
Hoover, Smith was gregarious and a professional politician. Also, unlike his
opponent, he was provincial. He knew little about foreign countries or even
about his own nation west of the Hudson River. He also read little, was poorly
educated, and lacked intellectual interests. A machine politician, he emerged
victorious in two gubernatorial elections but had lost the Democratic presidential nomination in 1924 at a deadlocked convention. Smith was person-
able and enjoyed dealing with people; he was friendly, with charisma and a
sense of humor, but not profound. Uninhibited, he thrived on campaigning.
Politics was his only real profession, and he enjoyed people more than policy.
Smith had managed to work with a Republican legislature to enact significant reform. The candidates had only marginal differences on the issues. The
greater differences lay in style and personality. Both were social reformers
and fiscal conservatives. Of Irish immigrant stock, flaunting a brown derby
worn at a rakish angle, Smith was convivial in his native environment and
somewhat lost outside it. A Catholic, he personally favored repeal of Prohibition, yet the Democratic platform advocated only the state option. Though
Democrats were traditionally a low-tariff party, they did not specifically advocate one in 1928. Although Smith's mercurial temperament contrasted with
Hoover's stoicism, what is surprising is how little they differed in ideological
content. Their personalities led some to misjudge them, believing Smith was
more liberal than he was and Hoover more conservative. Both were essentially
probusiness and favored regulation but not overregulation. Unlike Hoover,

who excelled at administration, Smith was not a good desk man, but the New Yorker mingled better. The men did not know each other well in 1928. However, mutual respect characterized the relationship. Neither man belittled the other, and later they became friends.

Smith was the underdog due to "Republican Prosperity" and because Hoover had higher name recognition nationally. The GOP was better organized at the grass roots, and Smith lacked experience at formulating national strategy. In a normal year, with evenly paired candidates, the GOP was sure to win. Yet 1928 was a better than normal year, and the Republican ship of state sailed upon a sea of prosperity. By necessity and inclination, Smith waged a strenuous, even frenzied, campaign that imitated in macrocosm his individual speeches. He delivered 20 major speeches to Hoover's 7 and fraternized with voters from the back platforms of trains. Neither candidate was an exceptional speaker, though they surpassed Harding's meandering, polysyllabic platitudes and Coolidge's barely audible nasal monotones. Hoover had the advantage on radio, which was used to a greater degree than in previous campaigns. Smith was too fidgety before a microphone, and the stationary sound systems of the era lost some of his words. Further, his East Side accent sounded alien to Americans from the South and Midwest. The Democrats might have been poised to take advantage of agricultural discontent, but Smith lacked knowledge and credibility on agricultural issues. Even the geography of the farm belt confused him. Nonetheless, Smith possessed charisma and kinetic energy, and he was doubtless the most formidable candidate the Democrats could field. Unfortunately for him, he was running in 1928, not in 1924 or 1932.[71]

The preeminent issue of the campaign was prevailing prosperity and Hoover's reputation as a financial expert. In good times, America's are unlikely to reject the incumbent party; in bad times, they are unlikely to reelect them. Most voters recognized both Hoover's financial acumen and Smith's relative lack of economic expertise. Hoover had a long history of managing and mastering large bureaucracies, flexibility in confronting emergencies, and calm confidence in crises. He also possessed a retentive memory that could reel off facts and figures, superb intelligence, practicality, and imagination. Both Smith and Hoover had worked with their hands, and Smith had managed the affairs of a large state, but his experience in finance was not comparable to Hoover's. Hoover had dipped into virtually every sector of the economy, Smith only selectively and in a single state. Hoover's Commerce Department had emphasized the importance of foreign trade as a vehicle for economic growth. Smith knew little about expanding foreign trade, or, for that matter, foreign nations. Hoover was one of the better-traveled, most cosmopolitan candidates in history. Smith was relatively provincial, though no more provincial than Harding or Coolidge, who had won easy victories. Although foreign policy was not a major issue in the campaign, it appeared that Smith lacked interest. Apart from the disparity in world travel, Smith had read little about other nations, their economies, or their peoples. On these issues, he was overmatched. Smith was reasonably bright, but he had a less precise mind, especially on facts, figures, geography, and the complexity of the nation he aspired to govern. In addition to his accent, Catholicism, and public imbibing, some Americans were disillusioned by his connection with the corrupt Tammany Hall machine of New York. Tammany had a bad reputation—muckrakers had immortalized "Boss Tweed"—and it rubbed off on Smith. Many small-town Americans wondered how the New Yorker could understand their problems and proclivities. In 1928 America was still dominated by farms, small towns, and medium-sized cities, and New Yorkers evoked suspicion.[72]

Unlike prosperity, Prohibition was an inflammatory issue, which is deceiving because there were more votes in the former. In 1928 most Americans were willing to give abstention a longer trial, as were both parties. Smith was photographed drinking legally in public, but the differences between the men were greater than the differences between their party platforms. Hoover believed alcohol did more harm than good and undermined the efficiency of workers. More importantly, he believed laws on the books, all laws, should be enforced. If a law was not constructive, it should be repealed. Strict enforcement would expedite repeal. Hoover rarely mentioned Prohibition during the campaign. The GOP nominee never devoted an entire speech to the subject and instructed his subordinates to downplay it, though some could not resist demonizing rum and Smith. Hoover was a moderate Prohibitionist, not a fanatic. He abstained during Prohibition but not before or after, though he never drank much, preferring trout streams to saloons. Some of Hoover's surrogates were overzealous, but the candidate himself was circumspect.[73]

Smears punctuated the campaign, though they did not emanate from the tops of the tickets. Smith was vulnerable on Prohibition, Catholicism, and urban machine politics, especially when combined. Old rumors about Hoover were resurrected: that he was a British citizen, imposed slavery upon Chinese workers, engaged in illicit mining deals, and favored European consumers over American farmers during the Great War. Such canards occur in every campaign, yet anti-Catholic prejudice has been particularly sensitive because of its pervasiveness. Smith was the first Catholic nominated by a major party for president; there was not another until John F. Kennedy. But smears, however vile, were not determining factors. Smith lost his home state of New York, which could hardly be convicted of prejudice after electing him governor twice. In fact, he carried more states in the South—a racist, anti-Catholic region—than in any other section. In most of the Deep South, party loyalties prevailed. Hoover would have defeated a Protestant teetotaler, though perhaps not quite as handily.[74]

Hoover's fears about angry farmers evicting the incumbent party proved unfounded. Smith had little to offer them. Hoover, born on a farm, had dealt with agricultural problems at Commerce. He proposed solutions, though not panaceas. These included tariff protection, a Farm Board to promote cooperative marketing, and cheaper transportation via waterways. The GOP made the farm belt a priority. Farmers were unhappy, but they did not believe Smith understood them. In 1928, the Republican presidential and vice presidential candidates and Hoover's campaign manager were all Westerners. Moreover, the Midwest and trans-Mississippi West were usually Republican.

Although Hoover never considered himself a special interest politician, he reached out to women, blacks, and organized labor. The GOP standard bearer had championed suffrage and the rights of labor. Women were drawn to his humanitarianism, his interest in improving the health and education of children, his emphasis on stable homes, his gentle nature, his strong religious convictions, and his scandal-free public and private life. An internationalist, though a muted one under Harding and Coolidge, witnessing the carnage of World War I had convinced Hoover that disarmament, especially naval reductions, could help avert war. His advocacy of temperance appealed to women, who considered excessive alcohol a rock upon which many marriages foundered.[75]

Hoover's record as commerce secretary brought him substantial union support. Though Smith also had an excellent record on labor, he received few union endorsements. Hoover believed the interests of labor and business, though not identical, overlapped. Most strikes were wasteful. Shop committees representing workers and management could dissipate most problems. In difficult cases, government could arbitrate. Hoover had been a labor troubleshooter for Harding and Coolidge, and workers considered him fair. They remembered his role in abolishing the 12-hour day in the steel industry and his efforts to equitably settle coal strikes during the 1920s. Hoover knew well-paid workers were productive and generated income to drive a strong consumer economy. He considered the American Federation of Labor salutary and was respected by its leaders. Labor, like other sectors of the economy, enjoyed relative prosperity during the 1920s.[76]

Hoover avoided race except to reiterate his Quaker beliefs in equality of opportunity, tolerance, and education. He never appealed to white supremacy. Some Republicans pointed out that Democrats barred blacks from voting in the South and denied black delegates seats at their convention at Houston. Most blacks were grateful for Hoover's rescues and flood relief in 1927. Militant blacks criticized both candidates, and some Southern blacks feared he might deprive them of patronage by basing appointments on merit. The Republican candidate supported a federal antilynching law, a subject on which Smith was silent. Blacks had been Republicans since the Civil War, and the Democrats remained the party of white supremacy. Hoover aggressively sought black votes in the North. He created a Colored Voter's Division that employed 120 persons and contacted about two million black voters. Though there were few black votes to harvest in the South, Hoover's surrogates made some efforts. Hoover faced a challenging situation in the South. He must court white voters without abandoning the party's traditional commitment to blacks. Some of his lieutenants, such as Horace Mann, distributed racist tracts.

Hoover disapproved of and never authorized such material. In fact, he specifically said that he did not want the votes of bigots. Registered Republicans were a minority in the South, and many Southerners who favored Hoover were defecting Democrats. Theirs was more an anti-Smith vote than a pro-Hoover vote; though Southerners, like other Americans, voted their pocketbooks.[77]

After his acceptance speech at Palo Alto, Hoover delivered only six major speeches: on August 21 at his birthplace in West Branch, Iowa; on September 17 in Newark, New Jersey; on October 6 in Elizabethton, Tennessee; on October 15 in Boston; on October 22 in New York City; and on November 2 in St. Louis. This was not a fast-paced campaign, even by the standards of the times, and did not accelerate until early fall. American campaigns, however, usually affect the margin of elections, not their outcomes. Frequently, the underdog wages the more vigorous campaign. William Jennings Bryan, a silver-tongued orator and hyperactive campaigner, lost three presidential elections decisively. Few votes are altered by campaigns because speakers usually preach to their own partisans. Campaigns do help to inspire turnout, energize volunteers, and make marginal differences in close states. But only rarely do campaigns determine elections unless one of the candidates makes a major blunder, which Hoover avoided in 1928. More often, elections are, roughly speaking, a referendum to retain the incumbents or send them packing, and this depends more on circumstances than on oratory. In 1928, cash registers rang louder than political oratory. In more recent times, due to the larger number of primaries, campaigns play a larger role in winning the party nominations than in winning the general election.

Hoover's poor speaking ability was a limited liability, and Smith's provincial outlook hurt him less than prosperous status quo. Hoover's campaign, though, revealed his temperament, his plans for the nation, his organizational skills, and his commitment to social justice. It demonstrated his ability to patiently and diligently organize, to run a disciplined campaign, and to produce speeches more important for content than for pizzazz.

Although Hoover restricted his appearances, Curtis hit the campaign trail hard. At 69, Curtis, much older than his 54-year-old running mate, enjoyed robust health and stamina. Unlike Hoover, he enjoyed speaking, though he was known for his brevity. Representing the greatest wheat-growing state, he understood farming and campaigned chiefly in the wheat and corn belts. Bone dry on Prohibition, unlike Hoover, he considered the matter permanently settled. His energy, if not his glibness, rivaled Bryan's in 1896. Curtis delivered about a thousand speeches and visited nearly every state.[78]

Following his acceptance speech, Hoover traveled east. His first major speech, at West Branch, his birthplace, mingled nostalgia for his Iowa boyhood with empathy for farmers. The village of 745, almost entirely Republican, embraced their hometown hero; they would have applauded him if he had recited from a telephone book. He visited haunts of his youth and explored the woods and fields, seeking the places he had fished, swam, and sledded. He met ex-teachers and classmates. The town was festive, with bands, hot dog stands, balloons, and a huge tent under which he spoke in the evening to a crowd of 15,000.

Hoover told fellow Iowans his homecoming resurrected sentimental memories. Iowa was blessed with the richest soil and the highest scores on intelligence tests in the nation. Hoover expressed his pride in the self-sufficiency of his Iowa ancestors. They grew, raised, and made virtually everything they used, purchasing little. Strong and independent, they were also kind, generous, and God-fearing. Politically, Hoover focused on farm relief and the need for a diversified solution, not a simplistic panacea. The next morning, the native son traveled to Cedar Rapids, a larger city, for two days of meetings: the first day with farmers and farm leaders and the second with farm journalists and editors. He promised to listen, but he ended up doing most of the talking. Specifically, he promised to create a Farm Board with a revolving fund to help sustain prices by purchasing surpluses. Preservation of the family farm was essential because farming was a way of life, not merely an occupation. More than 1,500 leaders attended the conference. Most were impressed by Hoover's grasp of detail and his sincerity. Among those who came doubtful and left endorsing the Republican were Senators Gerald P. Nye of North Dakota and Smith Brookhart of Iowa. Senator James E. Watson, who had defeated Hoover in the Indiana primary, attended as well and was inclined to back him. Just a day earlier, many of the delegates had listened to Smith deliver a radio speech on agriculture and were unimpressed. Smith seemed naïve, unconvincing, and unoriginal.[79]

Returning to the East Coast, Hoover spoke in New Jersey in mid-September, venturing into a Smith stronghold, controlled by powerful Democratic boss Frank Hague. In the farm belt, Hoover had explained his plan for farmers; in the industrial East, he focused on business and labor. The GOP candidate discussed the importance of moderate tariffs and immigration restrictions that protected American workers. Republican administrations, along with technology, had raised the economy to a new apogee. Yet "[h]e would be a rash man who would state that we are finally entering the industrial millennium."[80] Hoover pointed out that the elimination of industrial waste and standardization in manufacturing played a significant role in economic abundance. Reacting promptly to the unemployment crisis of 1921, a Republican administration had helped restore five million jobs. Hoover espoused public works as a tool during economic downturns and suggested contingency plans for such declines. Full employment and job security were essential to a stable economy and helped ensure labor peace. Hoover drove through suburbs around Newark. In Newark, he delivered his principal address to an audience of 10,000 at the state armory. He also visited the inventor, Thomas Edison. Cheering crowds lined the roads to welcome his caravan. Hoover appealed to women and applauded their enthusiasm, yet warned that it would be wasted unless they registered and voted. The results inspired hope, but the GOP still considered New Jersey a tough Democratic enclave.[81]

Next came Hoover's only venture into the South. He gave a major address at the textile city of Elizabethton, Tennessee, on the one-hundred-forty-eighth anniversary of the Battle of Kings Mountain in 1780, a turning point in the American Revolution, whose proximity made it a source of local pride. Unlike most Southern communities, Elizabethton was Republican, surrounded by a Democratic hinterland. A receptive audience of about 60,000 packed the community of 12,000, many from the neighboring states of North Carolina and Kentucky. They sat outdoors on a mountainside, drenched by a downpour, as the speaker stood ankle deep in mud. Hoover appealed to regional pride, noting the contributions of the South to the nation's traditions and observing that his own Quaker ancestors had settled in North Carolina before migrating to Iowa. Hoping to dissipate regional allegiances, he said that he was of the West, which represented a melding of the North and the South. He appealed for religious tolerance and civility in the campaign.

Hoover focused on economic issues of a regional nature, pointing out accomplishments of the preceding GOP administrations that promoted prosperity, including the tariff that aided textile industries such as those located in Elizabethton. He explained that a selective tariff was compatible with promotion of exports. For example, the government could furnish statistical information to aid manufacturers with marketing and restrict immigration to save jobs for American workers. The Iowa native advocated a diverse southern economy that integrated industry and agriculture. America's high standard of living was based on a healthy balance of occupations, labor peace, and improved education, he explained. The government could help construct good roads and develop inland waterways. He reiterated that he would enforce Prohibition, a safeguard of the American home. He also said Southerners should be proud of their rural heritage because cities often bred crime. Hoover's attempt to attract Southern voters proved successful. He carried Tennessee and the Upper South.[82]

Having spoken in the West and the South, Hoover strengthened his support in the Northeast with an overflow audience at Mechanics' Hall in Boston on October 15. As at Elizabethton, he began by praising the hardy pioneers of the colonial era. Then he turned to economic questions that affected New England such as the tariff, foreign trade, and the merchant marine. He observed that nature had not blessed the region with bountiful natural sources but with abundant human resources: an adventurous, inventive people. Massachusetts, like Elizabethton, relied on the textile industry, and he repeated his mantra about protection from cheap foreign labor. The response to the candidate in Coolidge's adopted state increased the GOP hopes of carrying it. No less than one million voters turned out to watch his progress from Springfield to the Boston Common, where 50,000 awaited him. He evoked the magic name of Coolidge in his remarks and promised to continue the incumbent's policies. Earlier, Coolidge had told the Republican state convention he wished to see Hoover elected and had authorized the candidate to use his name.[83]

Hoover ventured into the den of his opponent—New York City—for his last major speech in the East. Warned that the audience might not be appropriate for the topic, his theme was the importance of limited government and the danger of untrammeled federal power. Government should regulate business but abstain from competing with it, he warned. The federal government was too cumbrous to efficiently operate in business, he cautioned, because it operated on patronage rather than merit and based decisions on winning elections. Further, it reacted slowly because inertia was built into the process, which also prevented it from withdrawing promptly when a task was accomplished. He warned against "state socialism" and praised decentralized government, starting with those closest to the people, the localities, and the states. Freedom meant the freedom for entrepreneurs to invent new products and improve production. America should set an example for the world, not tread in its footsteps. He said the American system was not perfect but was practical, evolving through trial and error.

The GOP nominee was more aggressive than he had been in Boston and delivered his speech with greater emotion. He denounced the stultifying effects of big government and a bloated bureaucracy. Not since the days of Theodore Roosevelt had New York cheered a Republican candidate so enthusiastically in the quintessential New York setting—Madison Square Garden. There were requests for 100,000 tickets for the Garden, which seated 20,000. Hoover's 50-minute speech was interrupted by applause 62 times as he attacked the Democrats on such issues as agriculture, control of water power, and Prohibition. Hoover depicted himself as a Jeffersonian, an individualist rather than a collectivist, who would not undermine liberty by economic leveling. Vice President Dawes delivered his first speech of the campaign at New York and was received warmly. He eloquently summarized his party's principles and attacked the Tammany Tiger in its liar.[84]

After his address at New York, Hoover embarked by fast rail for the transcontinental trek to Palo Alto to vote and await the returns. He delivered his last major speech before a cheering throng of 10,000 at the St. Louis Coliseum. En route, the locomotive traversed several doubtful states. Thousands of supporters lined the tracks through West Virginia, Maryland, Ohio, and Kentucky encouraging Hoover. Despite the early hour, huge throngs and two bands greeted him when he halted briefly at Cincinnati. Turning from his jeremiads against big government at New York, Hoover focused on the positive attributes of an active government, singling out public works that benefitted the Mississippi Valley. He reviewed his plans to improve inland waters and flood protection. The Great Engineer's plan would link the heartland with the Gulf through the Mississippi River and the Atlantic via the Great Lakes by constructing a St. Lawrence Seaway. He also believed the federal government should connect major cities through an interstate highway system, an idea ahead of its time. Hoover outlined the government's role in promoting agricultural prosperity and pointed out recent achievements such as the tariff, revival of the War Finance Corporation, establishment of Intermediate Credit Banks, expansion of Farm Banks, legislation encouraging cooperative market- ing, and laws regulating grain exchanges and stockyards. The GOP candidate pledged to convene a special session of Congress to deal with the farm econ- omy. He envisioned a major program of public works, buildings, and dams, staggered in order to ameliorate the business cycle. Hoover concluded, on a note of moral uplift, "I am indebted to my country beyond any human power." He reminded voters than the president was more than an administrator or a legislator. He was the keeper of the flame of liberty, the guardian of world peace, and the protector of the young and the weak.[85]

The commerce secretary enjoyed a wide advantage in newspaper and mag- azine support in 1928. The candidate received the endorsement of 720 news- paper editors, compared to 180 for Smith. A large number of distinguished writers, editors, and publishers backed him. William Allen White, Arch Shaw, Mark Sullivan, William Irwin, and William Hard wrote favorable articles. The *New York Sun*, which had praised Governor Smith previously, now endorsed Hoover. The independent *Milwaukee Journal* considered him better qualified than previous candidates, while the *Detroit Free Press, San Francisco Chronicle, Cincinnati Star Times,* and the *Saturday Evening Post* applauded the nominee. The labor journal, *World's Work*, lent its support, while the liberal *New Repub- lic* praised Hoover as a reliable progressive but questioned whether he could carry his party along with him. The candidate employed former Governor Henry J. Allen as his official public relations director while Alfred J. Kir- chofer, editor of the *Buffalo Evening News*, helped generate and disseminate newspaper publicity. Hoover instructed Kirchofer to keep Prohibition and Smith's Catholicism out of the campaign. Journalists found Hoover one of the most likeable, private personalities they had encountered. Though most politicians craved the limelight, Hoover did nothing to create colorful copy. Even Coolidge, equally reticent, had been a source of quaint stories about his eccentricities. Still reporters were able to find intriguing stories when they dug into Hoover's background as a mining engineer, his feeding of Belgium, his work as food administrator, and his important role at the Versailles Peace Conference. They filled in details about his service as secretary of commerce. Hoover was content to let his record speak; he said little about himself and nothing exotic. He was the most straightforward politician the press had encountered.[86]

Beyond the print media, the influence of radio was substantial in 1928. Politics was beginning to take its place as a staple of radio broadcasting along with music, spectator sports, and news. Hoover was among the first to recognize the potential of the airwaves. Time for a few speeches was pur- chased, but most of the coverage consisted of live broadcasts of the candi- dates' speeches at the networks' expense. Radio stimulated interest, especially among women, and increased registration. Some of the speeches by Hoover and Smith attracted millions of listeners. Politics became truly national rather than regional. Radio was more effective than traditional stumping; a month of radio reached more people than six months of conventional campaigning. Neither Smith nor Hoover was an electrifying radio speaker. Hoover never learned to use voice inflection while Smith's chief problem was his nervousness and regional accent.[87]

Some key Republicans delivered speeches in support of their candidate. Borah made half a dozen addresses in the Midwest, chiefly in August. Hughes spoke several times in October, and Mellon made a few talks on behalf of the nominee. The most important help came from Coolidge. The president felt a speaking tour was beneath presidential dignity, and he was already physically and mentally exhausted, but a few well-spaced comments, both oral and written, assured the business community that his commerce secretary would continue his policies. On August 21, Coolidge praised Hoover's contributions to prosperity through his work in the cabinet. He agreed to be photographed with Hoover at the White House, and after the candidate's speech at St. Louis on November 2, the president dispatched a glowing telegram. Under Hoover, he stated, the government would be in safe hands. He had demonstrated remarkable leadership and possessed outstanding ability. On election eve, the president delivered a short radio address in support of the ticket. Hoover conferred with Coolidge several times during the campaign. Although the meetings were private, they received generous press coverage. In mid-September, the president, the candidate, and Mellon met for an hour and a half at the White House, an unusually long consultation for men of such few words. After his New York speech, Hoover briefed Coolidge about the reception at Madison Square Garden. Both men emerged confident that the GOP would carry the Empire State. The meetings with Coolidge, which complemented the president's endorsements, had the desired effect of establishing a sense of continuity with the popular incumbent.[88]

Lou accompanied her husband on his campaign tours and was more comfortable than him when chatting informally with crowds who greeted their trains. She avoided discussing Prohibition and other divisive issues but did speak briefly over radio, the first wife of a presidential candidate to do so. She utilized her organizational and journalistic talents to recruit friends, write letters, and work through the network of organizations with which she was familiar. The press found her witty, polite, and intelligent. Shortly after her husband's nomination, she received an honorary Doctorate of Literature from Whittier College. In late October, she was the guest of honor at a breakfast for 300 wives of engineers and then spent the afternoon meeting with state leaders at the Women's National Republican Club in Washington. The press, finding Hoover terse, devoted coverage to human interest stories about Lou. Journalists admired her serenity, her independence, her natural dignity, and her sense of humor. Additionally, her world travels and her training in geology made colorful copy.[89]

Hoover ended his campaign with a radio speech from his study in Palo Alto on the eve of the election. It was the first time a candidate had broadcast without a live audience present, and he is believed to have reached the greatest audience to that time. The talk was virtually nonpolitical, calling only for national unity. The candidate praised American democracy and said that the next day more people would vote in a free election than at any time in history. Women and young people had swelled the voting rolls. The Republican asked for an end for voting along regional lines and urged national unity. He said he believed in party government as it was the only effective way to govern a country. He explained that both parties had progressive aims, but differed in how to achieve them. He summoned the American people to solve the problems of their time without abandoning the traditions that had made them strong.[90] Hoover and his family voted at their Stanford precinct then retired to their home to listen to the returns. Their large, Mediterranean-style house was filled with mostly local friends. Special telegraph wires were strung to the home, and for two hours Hoover personally supervised the recording of returns on blackboards. Early returns from the cities showed Smith in the lead, but this was reversed and overwhelmed when town and country votes streamed in. The Republican was delighted to learn he had broken the Democratic monopoly on the South. As guests in the lower rooms consumed sandwiches and coffee, Hoover spent most of his time in his study, quietly puffing his pipe. He occasionally walked into the vaulted living room where his friends and neighbors had gathered, acknowledging their congratulations. He refused to respond to any of the thousands of telegrams that poured in until late in the evening.

Months earlier, when students learned Hoover would be the GOP nominee, they had booked a concert for the Stanford campus by the renowned march composer, John Philip Sousa. The 74-year-old musician vowed to lead his 70-piece band, followed by Stanford students, to the candidate's home if the Stanford alum prevailed. Near midnight, the band appeared at the Hoover home. An airplane flew overhead and dropped exploding fireworks in the midst of a mass celebration, punctuated by college cheers. Hoover and Lou watched and waved from a balcony. When the band burst into the Stanford anthem, Hoover, who rarely showed emotion in public, cried.

Hoover had been confident, but was surprised by the dimensions of his victory. Al Smith, a gracious loser, had not expected to win. He telegraphed his opponent: "I congratulate you heartfelt on your victory and extend to you my sincere good wishes for your health and happiness and the success of your administration."[91]

On November 6, a record number of Americans voted, giving Hoover the largest popular vote and the biggest electoral vote in history. The campaign brought out about eight million more voters than had voted in 1924, about

67.5 percent of those eligible, many of them first-time voters, including the most women ever to vote. The GOP standard bearer won 21,392,190 popular votes to 15,016,443 for Smith and 444 electoral votes to 87 for the New Yorker. Norman Thomas, the Socialist candidate, won 267,420 popular votes and no electoral votes. The Republican won a decisive 58.1 percent of the vote. The dimensions of the margin surprised both Hoover and Smith. It was one of the most lopsided victories in American history up to that time. Hoover won 40 states to only 8 for the Democrat. Smith carried only Mississippi, Alabama, Georgia, South Carolina, Arkansas, Louisiana, Massachusetts, and Rhode Island. The victor cracked the solidly Democratic South, including West Virginia, Kentucky, Tennessee, Virginia, North Carolina, Florida, and Texas. Only the Deep South remained faithfully Democratic, and Hoover won two states even there. Moreover, some of the states in the Southern heartland, where Smith had expected to overwhelm Hoover, were close. Smith did not even carry his home state of New York. The Republican won comfortably among blacks and even more comfortably among women. Blacks in all regions remained convinced that Hoover was not personally racist and that the Republicans were less inimical to their interests than the Democrats. In the old Senate, the division showed 47 Democrats, 46 Republicans, and 1 Farmer-Laborite, who frequently voted with the Democrats. In the Congress-Elect, there would be 54 Republicans, 40 Democrats, and 1 Farmer-Laborite in the Senate. In the House, which was then Republican by a majority of 39, the Hoover administration would have a strong working majority of 95. It was a resounding personal victory for a political novice who ran a flawless campaign. The Republicans' gains in Congress were less decisive than the presidential victory.[92]

The Republicans outspent the Democrats but by less than the usual margin. The report released by the Senate Campaign Expenditures Oversight Committee showed the RNC spending as $4.1 million, the DNC, $3.2 million. The state organizations added $4.8 million for the Republicans and $2.4 million for the Democrats, while other organizations affiliated with the parties spent $700,000 for Republican candidates and $1.7 million supporting Democratic ones. Overall, the RNC raised about $10 million and spent some $9.4 million, while the Democrats raised $7.2 million and spent virtually every penny. Prosperity accounted for relatively high donations on both sides. John J. Raskob, the chairman of the Democratic National Committee, carried a substantial burden for his party. He contributed $150,000 and made three loans, totaling $50,000, to Smith's campaign. Hoover had generous friends but played little personal role in fundraising, and the Republicans did not rely on any single donor to the extent of the Democrats.[93]

Hoover's victory was determined by his personal popularity, his stand on the issues, and the strength of his party during unusually prosperous times. His victory cut across factions and regions. Its geographical breadth was virtually unprecedented since the nation had been polarized by the Civil War. The

Old Guard in his party had fought his nomination, yet most supported him in the election. Still, Lowden never endorsed Hoover and sulked to the end of the campaign. Senator Norris, who deserted his party, made no discernible impact. Hoover carried Wisconsin, the epicenter of Republican insurgency. Dawes was slightly more tactful and delivered one brief speech. Coolidge, though typically subdued, demonstrated clearly that Hoover was his choice. The Republican carried doubtful states in all parts of the nation, demonstrating that no regional issue was dominant. He won wet states, dry states, farm-belt states, and states that sympathized with Smith because of his religion. Given the context of prosperity and a desire for continuity, probably no Democrat could have won in 1928, yet it does not follow that the dimensions of the victory would have been so decisive. After the lackluster campaigns of 1920 and 1924, the 1928 campaign energized voters. Smith's candidacy was path breaking. His real achievement lay in winning the nomination despite his Catholicism. Though his support was not broad, it was intense. By the end of the campaign, he had become "as much a cult as a candidate." Yet there was a consensus in the postmortems that Hoover had won largely because he was the better-qualified candidate. Negative issues might have distorted perceptions of the campaign, but they did not distort the outcome itself. Moreover, they cut both ways. Some believed Hoover's Quaker religion disqualified him as commander-in-chief.[94]

The morning after their victory, the Hoovers were up early, as usual. They celebrated in a typically quiet way, by going for a walk in the foothills and meadows near Stanford, where they had courted as a young couple. They walked leisurely for about an hour and then returned to examine the mail. Awaiting them were more than 13,000 congratulatory telegrams, including messages from Coolidge, Curtis, and Dawes. Hoover read only a few personally and answered selected ones from dignitaries and close friends. Others were read and answered by his assistant, Akerson, and his secretaries. There was no gloating, no uncorking of champagne or other alcohol, merely a sense of quiet satisfaction and gratitude. In his first statement to the press, Hoover accepted the responsibilities "without exultation and in complete dependence on Divine guidance."[95]

CHAPTER 2

Prepping for the Presidency and Sparring with Congress

Herbert Hoover's presidency was not a static experience. He had to do everything he did to get where he ended up. The American people learned along with him, and some of the lessons were difficult and indirect. Sometimes the only way to get from New York to Washington, DC, is via San Diego. When Hoover embarked on his voyage of discovery, like Columbus, he could not know whether he would sail off the edge of the world. He survived, but the world, and his life, were never again the same. The inauguration on a rainy March day culminated in the cauldron of a worldwide depression that resembled Dante's inferno.

During the interregnum between his election on November 9 and his inauguration on March 4, Hoover spent ten weeks on a goodwill tour of Latin America. The incoming president planned to make world peace and hemispheric friendship a major priority. At the outset, he hoped to concentrate on the prevention of another international conflagration, such as the Great War that had dragged the world into an abyss. That nightmare did not occur on his watch, but one almost as insidious did. One wonders if he could have discerned the future whether he would have done anything differently. His first instinct was to extend a hand of comity to the southern neighbors of the United States. Hoover also wanted to allow President Calvin Coolidge to complete his term without distractions from his successor and to escape a horde of patronage-seekers.

The president-elect departed from San Pedro, California, on November 19, 1928, aboard the battleship *Maryland* and steamed south down the western coast of Latin America. From Valparaiso, Chile, he crossed the Andes by rail to Buenos Aires, Argentina, and then proceeded up the East coast to Norfolk, returning to Washington by rail. He visited Honduras, El Salvador, Nicaragua, Costa Rica, Ecuador, Peru, Chile, Argentina, Uruguay, and Brazil, delivering 25 short speeches. Except for the cost of the vessels, Hoover paid his own expenses. Lou, who was fluent in Spanish, accompanied him, along with his son, Allan; press secretary, George Akerson; a few close friends; and about 20 reporters. It was the longest voyage ever made by a president or president-elect, eclipsing even Wilson's trip to Europe. Beginning with an address in Honduras, Hoover emphasized his promise to be a "Good Neighbor," and he repeated the phrase frequently. Franklin D. Roosevelt has been erroneously credited with coining the term and initiating the policy. Roosevelt, who used the words in his inaugural address in 1933, applied the term to the entire world, not specifically to Latin America. The policy was already in place when he took office.[1]

Hoover wanted the trip to emphasize the importance of foreign policy and the special attention Latin America deserved, a relationship based on mutual respect and an appreciation of cultural diversity and without condescension. The incoming president planned to upgrade the diplomatic corps; abstain from intervention; withdraw troops; and promote trade, travel, and cultural exchanges. No force would be used to collect debts and diplomatic recognition would be based on *de facto* control of the government, not ideology. In Central America, due to treaty commitments, the United States would not recognize governments that had seized power through a *coup d'état* that did not represent the will of its own people. Hoover followed through with these promises and improved Latin American relations, which stands as one of the major achievements of his diplomacy.[2]

Hoover usually spent one night in each capital and delivered a single major speech in each nation. Nicaragua, where warring factions clashed and some American troops were stationed, was sensitive. Rather than showing preference for either, Hoover brought the rival leaders together at a joint meeting. Anticipated anti-American demonstrations were defused. In Peru, Hoover was greeted warmly. The reception in Chile, which was involved in a boundary dispute with Bolivia called the Tacna-Arica affair, which had spawned a war that flared sporadically, was much cooler. At Santiago, he emphasized that foreign loans from the United States should be utilized for economic development, not to fuel an arms race.[3]

From Chile, he crossed the Andes by rail to Buenos Aires. Argentine relations were sometimes difficult. Proud of their culture, with a strong economy, Argentines considered themselves rivals of their northern neighbor for leadership in the hemisphere. They also competed with the United States in exporting farm products, especially beef, and resented American tariffs.

Hoover soothed ruffled relations, and the Argentines were unexpectedly pleased by his modesty, his plain manners, and his sincerity. He did not pander, explaining that American farmers needed the tariff but pointing out that the United States purchased many Argentine products. The Quaker said he respected Argentina's achievements and admired the spectacular beauty of the Andes. Several Argentine newspapers, which had vilified him previously, praised Hoover's honest approach, and he won their respect.[4]

Uruguay, the smallest of the South American nations, also harbored resentment, and a parade had to be cancelled. Hoover delivered a forceful speech in which he praised the nation's cultural and material development. Here too, he won converts. When he departed Montevideo, Hoover boarded the battleship *Utah*, which would carry him to Portuguese-speaking Brazil.[5]

Rio de Janeiro, the final leg of his tour, provided the most jubilant celebration. Stepping ashore on December 21, he received an outpouring of affection as thousands of Brazilians, many brandishing small American and Brazilian flags, welcomed the president-elect. With the city in a holiday atmosphere, 100,000 people lined the streets, and his automobile was showered with tons of confetti as he rode with President Washington Luis. Hoover expressed gratitude and observed that it demonstrated the strength of U.S.-Brazilian friendship. The president-elect delivered three speeches: one in response to a greeting by the Brazilian president, a second to the Brazilian Congress, and another to the Supreme Court. The front pages of the daily newspapers were devoted almost exclusively to photos of Hoover. His hosts manifested profound respect at his last port of call. As in other countries, the Hoovers received numerous gifts, such as jewels, laces, rugs, and many kinds of souvenirs, which they donated to museums. The incoming president demonstrated not only sensitivity but substantial knowledge about Latin's America's culture and economy, a solid basis for improving relations. At few times in American history has mutual respect prevailed to the degree it did in 1928. In smaller countries such as Ecuador and major ones like Brazil, from the beginning to the end of his journey, Hoover proclaimed imperialism hypocritical, emphasizing that democracies cannot say one thing at home and do another thing abroad.[6]

Hoover's goodwill tour bore fruit. Beginning with the preinaugural period, attitudes of Latin Americans toward the United States shifted from outright hostility, or at best aloofness, to a sense of common purpose. Probably more than any of his predecessors, Hoover was sensitive to the feelings of Latin American governments. After taking office, he completely reorganized the diplomatic corps in Latin America. Career diplomats, all of them native speakers, replaced patronage appointees in the Latin American capitals. After his tour, letters flooded the president-elect's office, the Pan-American Union, and the Bureau of Foreign and Domestic Commerce of the Department of Commerce, evincing a swelling of goodwill. Peru indicated it would send a special representative to his inauguration. To some degree, the southern republics simply wanted to be left alone. Yet they also wanted, and needed, trade and friendship. Hoover was probably the least confrontational president they had faced, revealing not a trace of arrogance. They appreciated his economic expertise and his good intentions, as well as his frankness and receptiveness to honor differences. There was some suspicion at the beginning of his voyage, but it had almost evaporated by its conclusion. A new tone had been set, and Latin leaders believed Hoover was a man who lacked selfish motives and who could be trusted.[7]

Continuing to cultivate Coolidge, Hoover telegraphed the president and Secretary of State Kellogg from Buenos Aires that his journey had been successful. The president-elect had planned a Florida vacation but decided instead to spend time in Washington organizing his administration before traveling to the Sunshine State. Returning to the capital on January 6, his first appointment was with President Coolidge, whom he briefed on his Latin American mission. Hoover was circumspect; he did his best to avoid overshadowing the incumbent. While in Washington, Hoover kept regular office hours at his home, where he saw a stream of visitors by invitation only. He spent the next two weeks paring down his list of cabinet appointments and conferring with congressional leaders. The president-elect refused to speculate publicly about his cabinet, and communications with the press were filtered through George Akerson, who worked from a suite in the Mayflower Hotel. Starved for copy, journalists had to turn elsewhere because Hoover was all business. Journalists already found it difficult to adjust to a future president who shunned publicity.[8]

On January 20, Hoover left Washington by rail for a respite in Florida, where he resided at the estate of the millionaire J. C. Penney on Belle Island, off the coast of Miami. He adopted a routine that began with church on Sunday. He worked on Mondays and Tuesdays, held appointments on Wednesdays, and devoted the rest of the week to fishing. He wrote his inaugural address, sometimes working on it at sea. While fishing, he landed his biggest sailfish to date, a 45-pounder. The president-elect interviewed a short list of cabinet aspirants and hosted other guests. Horace Mann, who had directed his southern campaign and injected race into it, also visited. Mann, a Tennessee attorney known as a political manipulator, discussed the use of patronage to strengthen the southern wing of the GOP. He believed that if the party was to carry the South, it would have to attract whites, which meant giving patronage to more Southern whites at the expense of blacks. On January 29, Hoover's erstwhile rival, Al Smith, paid a visit, at Hoover's invitation. Smith, who was also vacationing in Florida, enjoyed the company of the Republican, and it marked the beginning of a lasting friendship. The New Yorker said, honestly, that he wished his former opponent good luck and later told reporters that he found Hoover surprisingly amiable. Less than a week later, Hoover entertained James M. Cox, the Democratic candidate in 1920. On February 9, Hoover traveled by houseboat to the lodge of Thomas Edison, where he celebrated the inventor's eighty-second birthday, joined by Henry Ford, Harvey

Firestone, and other guests. Edison, a workaholic, told Hoover that fishing was a waste of time.[9]

Hoover returned to Washington in mid-February, two weeks earlier than he had planned, arriving eager to work. His first major appointment was at the White House, where he spent an hour with the president and Secretary of State Kellogg. Hoover offered to support Coolidge's bills pending in Congress. Circumspect, the president-elect kept a low profile, made no public speeches, and kept the press at a distance. In addition to conferring with Coolidge, Hoover talked with Republican congressional leaders, including John Q. Tilson of Connecticut, Republican leader in the House, and Senator James E. Watson of Indiana, who would become majority leader in the Upper House. They discussed the upcoming special session Hoover planned to call in April to enact a farm bill and revise the tariff. Coolidge's successor continued to screen potential cabinet selections in strict secrecy.[10]

In selecting subordinates, Hoover's chief priority was to select honest, competent, and unselfish public servants. In fact, during the four years of his administration, they spent more than $25 billion without a major scandal. Nor did anyone credibly criticize Hoover with politicizing the federal bureaucracy or the judiciary. Hoover wanted a balanced cabinet. He was less interested in regional or political balance than in having a variety of ideas and viewpoints represented. He did not want "yes men" but strong individuals who could run their departments without micromanagement. Hoover believed in appointing capable assistants and delegating authority, relegating only major policy to his attention.[11] The selection process was meticulous and frustrating. By early January, he had received more than a hundred suggestions for the cabinet. Most came from party leaders, but unsolicited suggestions poured in as well. One volunteer wrote, "I am writing to ask you for a seat in your Cabinet. I had a high school education and am thirty-five years of age. I am strong for Prohibition."[12] An insurance man who had voted for Hoover also had a request: "Please appoint a Post Master who will not economize on mucilage to the point where the stamps will not stick, as has been the case for several years past."[13]

Hoover decided to retain Mellon, even though the treasury secretary initially opposed his nomination. Mellon was considered safe by the business community, and he provided continuity with the popular Coolidge administration. Another member of the Coolidge cabinet Hoover had hoped to retain, Agriculture Secretary William Jardine, announced his retirement. Republican leaders from the East lobbied for a New Englander. The most likely candidate was Charles Francis Adams, the treasurer of Harvard University and a direct descendant of two presidents, a candidate for secretary of the navy. William N. Doak, head of the Brotherhood of Trainmen, was the frontrunner for secretary of labor.

During the first two weeks of February, the selection process bogged down, and Hoover had to go beyond his initial list. Some men he wanted declined for personal reasons, sometimes because they would have to make a financial sacrifice. Hoover's first choice for secretary of state, Charles Evans Hughes, did not wish to return to the cabinet. The most troublesome post was attorney general. William J. Donovan of Buffalo, an assistant attorney general and Hoover supporter, badly wanted the job. The incoming president disliked disappointing Donovan, yet he did not want to appoint a Catholic wet to head the department he intended to use to enforce Prohibition. Hoover considered Justice Harlan Stone, a close friend, but Stone did not want to leave the Supreme Court. He then offered the position to William J. Borah, a leading dry, but Borah wanted to remain in the Senate. The compromise choice was William D. Mitchell, Coolidge's solicitor-general and a Democrat. Hoover would have liked to appoint John L. Lewis, leader of the United Mine Workers, as secretary of labor but did not offer him the position because of a personal indiscretion in his past that might have embarrassed him. (Hoover would not specify the indiscretion, but there was speculation that it was sexual.) The president and Lewis remained personal friends. Other able men selected by Hoover who declined positions included Senator Dwight Morrow of New Jersey, banker Henry Robinson, and philanthropist Julius Rosenwald. In each of his choices, Hoover sought experience, administrative ability, and probity. Special expertise in the department one was to administer was not the chief criterion.[14]

In addition to the cabinet, Hoover recruited a personal staff. The president-elect hired three personal secretaries, although previous presidents had employed only one. Congress approved a request by Coolidge, acting at Hoover's initiative, to fund three secretaries at equal rank and an annual income of $10,000 each. The job of the presidency had grown, and Hoover disliked involvement in minutia. He received more mail, business and personal, than any previous chief executive. Hoover was accustomed to a smoothly functioning office without bureaucratic red tape. He did not utilize speechwriters but did employ a researcher. At the Commerce Department Hoover had also employed three secretaries, whom he paid with his own funds.[15]

At the outset of his administration, journalists also speculated about which of Hoover's close friends might play a major role in the incoming administration comparable to Wilson's alter ego, Colonel Edward House. His closest personal friend outside the government was Edgar Rickard, a mining engineer and businessman who had managed the new president's personal financial affairs since Hoover entered public service. Rickard had assisted Hoover in the CRB, the Food Administration, and the American Relief Administration (ARA). The Hoovers and Rickards often socialized and in earlier years had traveled together in Europe. Rickard was not destined to have much policy input but continued to handle the president's finances, and their private friendship never waned.

Within the cabinet, Hoover's closest friend was Ray Lyman Wilbur, his secretary of the interior. They had become friends as students when both became involved in Stanford politics. Wilbur supervised domestic conservation of food for Hoover during the Food Administration. The Stanford connection was lifelong. Wilbur, a physician, became president of Stanford, and Hoover joined the board of directors and became a major philanthropist to his alma mater. When Hoover asked Wilbur to join the cabinet, he took a leave of absence from Stanford and returned at the end of Hoover's term. Close to Hoover's age, Wilbur shared his interest in child health, conservation, water development, and reform of Native American conditions. He always stayed with the Hoovers when he visited Washington.

The president-elect respected Vernon Kellogg for his brilliant mind and his loyalty. A zoology professor while Hoover was a Stanford student, Kellogg supervised the port of Brussels for the CRB and became a member of the staff of the Food Administration and the ARA. He remained close to the incoming president while Hoover was secretary of commerce. While running the Commerce Department, Hoover also relied heavily on Julius Klein, his most brilliant assistant. Klein, a PhD in economics, had revitalized and expanded the Bureau of Foreign and Domestic Commerce. Another loyal friend, a much younger man, Lewis L. Strauss, had served as Hoover's personal secretary in the Food Administration and accompanied him to the Versailles Peace Conference. He remained until he returned to America to work with Kuhn, Loeb, and Company, a major Wall Street firm. The president-elect also had close ties to another banker, Adolph C. Miller, a member of the Federal Reserve Board at Washington. A Californian, Miller visited with Hoover in Florida during the interregnum and advised him on appointments.

Speculation also focused on Mark L. Requa, a mining engineer who had earned a fortune from oil and other interests. He and Hoover collaborated in several mining enterprises, and subsequently he demonstrated unselfish devotion to "The Chief." Requa's two passions in life were his family and Herbert Hoover. He served in the Food Administration and became general director of the U.S. Fuel Administration during the Great War. In 1927 Requa published a book advocating government regulation of vital natural resources such as coal and oil. Julius Barnes, a wheat exporter from Duluth, also served in the Food Administration. Barnes became president of the United States Grain Corporation, the most important subsidiary of the Food Administration. After the war, he and Hoover failed financially at attempts to publish several newspapers. Barnes combined a keen analytical mind with common sense. Thomas Gregory, a California attorney who had met Hoover as a student at Stanford, managed his legal affairs from his office at San Francisco. Their relationship was both personal and professional. At the end of World War I, Gregory was in Europe as a captain in the American Field Artillery. Hoover placed him in charge of the ARA for Central Europe and Gregory proved innovative in getting food to the fragments of the dismembered Austrian Empire.

Hoover had always enjoyed the company of writers and journalists. Perhaps the closest to him were Will Irwin, George Barr Baker, and Mark Sullivan, whom he also consulted for political advice. Sullivan visited the president-elect in California during the interregnum and also accompanied him to Latin America. The journalist-historian was a regular in Hoover's medicine ball cabinet and a frequent guest at his fishing camp in Virginia.[16]

During the interregnum, Hoover firmed up plans to reorganize the government, drafting a bill for submission at the first regular session of Congress in December. He wanted each executive department to handle tasks suited solely to its jurisdiction. The president's plan would eliminate overlapping and consolidate the activities of agencies scattered throughout the bureaucracy. He also wanted to shift independent bureaus and commissions into appropriate departments. This would save money and serve the public more efficiently. The president-elect also tried to set in motion legislation he had championed throughout the 1920s to provide a contingency fund of $3 billion for use in funding public works during periods of unemployment, a countercyclical measure. The incoming chief executive hoped the idea would complement the work of the Federal Reserve System during downturns. He drafted the proposal for such a contingency fund, known as the "Hoover Plan," introduced at the National Conference of Governors by Governor Ralph Owen Brewster of Maine. About eight governors backed it, as did labor leaders such as William Green, head of the American Federation of Labor (AFL). The majority of governors tabled the proposal, arguing that it would bloat the federal budget. Many also believed prosperity would continue indefinitely. Hoover consulted with agricultural leaders about the farm bill he planned to introduce at the special session. He was told that the farm bill was not complicated and could probably be enacted within weeks. The tariff, however, might prove more troublesome. The incoming president wanted to limit it to agriculture and a few industries suffering from unemployment, without sweeping revisions. Congressional leaders warned the next president that the situation was volatile, especially in the Senate, where labor and industrial groups might logroll. New England manufacturers, for example, wanted protection. The debate could become divisive.[17] The president-elect issued few public statements during the waning days of the Coolidge era, unless he felt strongly. However, shortly after his election, he expressed unequivocal support for the Zionist objective of resettling Palestine. In a telegram to a conference on Palestine, he stated, "I am heartily in accord with the effort to recolonize Palestine and I should like to help the drive for funds."[18]

As one who had never waded into the muddy waters of politics, Hoover was virtually a political virgin. The public accepted him as "pure at heart and noble in spirit," one who had "escaped the Harding muck and mire with scarcely a splatter." Hoover's face had been the first transmitted by the infant image of television in 1927, the same year he had emerged as the savior Mississippi flood victims.[19] Much was expected, too much, in fact. A chorus of voices proclaimed that he was the best-qualified president in memory, the most intelligent, the most diligent, with a focused mind and a generous spirit. He owned a record of unbroken success. "The great majority of Americans signified a strong desire to see the methods of the Department of Commerce transferred to the White House," the *New York Times* explained. The nation was poised for audacious leadership, and "the chance for coincidence between the man and the hour seems almost too good an opportunity to waste," the nation's leading daily proclaimed.[20] Reflecting two years later, *Time* observed, "Rarely, if ever, had a president taken office with public expectation of great achievements whipped to a higher pitch."[21] The son of Iowa expected to usher in a renaissance of reform. "Little had been done by the Federal Government in the fields of reform or progress during the fourteen years before my time," he wrote.[22] Many Americans expected Hoover to become one of the most successful presidents in history, to exercise a Midas touch on the economy. At the time of his election, the *New York Times* stock market average reached an all-time high. It closed at twice the average of 1924, three times greater than in 1918. Every sector of the economy seemed to hum. The nation sensed magic; it did not expect black magic.[23]

Hoover was perceived as the most Progressive Republican since Theodore Roosevelt. Some questioned how one who had never run for political office might fare in the most political job in the land, yet he had managed his campaign superbly. Though more cautious than some who expected instant transformation, Hoover expected to be a reformer. He did not want the presidency for fame, because he already had that, nor for power, because he had a limited view of presidential power. Rather, he wanted the opportunity to give back to the country that had given a poor orphan boy an opportunity. His reforms would begin with children, families, homes, workers, prisoners, and Native Americans.

Nonetheless, there were caveats. The *Outlook and Independent* observed an element of Shakespearean foreboding. "He is regarded as a miracle worker," the *Outlook* wrote. "That is his misfortune. He will be required by his masters, the people, to do the impossible," a task that "seems unreasonable and quite unfair to Mr. Hoover."[24] Similarly, the *San Bernardino Telegram* anticipated that the buildup might set him up for a fall. "The propaganda which seeks to convince the American people that Mr. Hoover is a superman is overreaching itself," the daily warned. "It is teaching the public to expect so much that an ultimate reaction is inevitable."[25] Some later reflected that Hoover was to blame for taking credit for prosperity. In fact, he usually gave his party, not himself personally, credit for it, as an incumbent party usually does; just as the opposition party blames incumbents during hard times. Hoover believed exaggeration could backfire. Economic progress was incremental, not inevitable. "Its miracle is only the constant and everlasting building of brick on brick, stone on stone, by which, in the end, great institutions are created," he told the Gridiron Club shortly after his inauguration.[26] In fact, Hoover was an unusually modest politician, unusually introspective. He disdained flattery as much as he disliked unfair criticism. In 1928 he had waged a campaign that tried to eschew ballyhoo, which would have seemed out of character. In a conversation with Willis J. Abbot, the editor of the *Christian Science Monitor*, during his vacation at the Penney estate in December 1928, he expressed qualms about being oversold. His friends had created the myth that he was "a sort of superman, able to cope successfully with the most difficult and complicated problems," he admitted. The public might "expect the impossible of me and should there arise in the land conditions with which the political machinery is unable to cope, I will be the one to suffer."[27]

Many underestimated the dimensions of Hoover's political problems even before the Depression. Because he succeeded a president of his own party, it would seem insolent to make sweeping changes in the bureaucracy, meaning less patronage was available. He could not expediently criticize his Republican predecessors. A substantial number of members of Congress, including many members of his own party, had wanted someone else for president. The GOP professionals conceded only because the Quaker seemed a certain winner. Some remained openly hostile. Hoover never had a secure working majority in Congress, only a tenuous, unreliable one. He never enjoyed the luxury of the overwhelming majorities that steamrolled the legislative programs of Franklin D. Roosevelt and Lyndon Baines Johnson. For much of his term, factions within the GOP delegation wielded not a shield in front of the president but a dagger at his back.

The president-elect spent the final day before his inauguration at home quietly. He ate a hearty breakfast and read newspapers. The cabinet had been completed two days earlier, and he pondered lesser appointments. He planned to hold his first cabinet meeting the day after his inauguration. The president's family was with him at the house on S Street, which he would soon vacate, including Alan, a Stanford senior, and Hoover's older son, Herbert Jr., with his wife and two babies. On the last evening, the Hoovers dined with the Coolidges at the White House. Hoover appeared relieved that the waiting was ending. On inauguration day, there was little grim but the weather. Enthusiastic crowds celebrated a New Era, a name attached to the new administration that never became popular. Virtually everything the people knew about Hoover was good, but details about his personal life were sparse. He had permitted few glimpses of his private life, though, ironically, he had nothing to hide. The public recognized the incoming president as a superb administrator, but they did not know what was in his heart or on his mind, or what he did for fun. So long as the nation's factories purred, Hoover's surface blandness would not matter much.[28]

The March 4 inauguration, like FDR's first two inaugurations, was held under a steady rain. Hoover was sworn by Chief Justice William Howard Taft on a Bible opened to Proverbs as rain pelted him in the face. The 35-minute address, despite the deluge, was optimistic and uplifting. Hoover brimmed with ideas, but he did not embarrass his predecessor by parading them. The longest section of the speech dealt with world peace. He would build upon the Kellogg Pact, complemented by disarmament. He summoned the nation to practice religious tolerance and strengthen the home, the foundation of liberty and plenty, wedding spiritual and moral imperatives. The president vowed to seek economic justice, to preserve equality of opportunity, and to prevent domination by one interest group or class. He would set an example by honest and frugal leadership, by fairness, and appointments based on merit. He was more specific on the subject closest to his heart: children. The government, he insisted, must strive to improve the health of its people and provide an adequate education for every child. Workers should be insured against unemployment, old age, accident, and death, providing security and social stability. The government must steer a course between the Scylla of centralized bureaucracy and the Charybdis of unrestricted private greed. He hoped the address would help him overcome the stereotype of an engineer who viewed the world mechanistically. While Hoover spoke, newsreel cameras ground. His was the first inaugural captured on audio film. Sound motion pictures had appeared in theaters just two years earlier. Hoover's complete speech was shown in theaters. His low, monotone delivery was unexciting, but the mere fact of listening to a president deliver a speech, with the visual component, stimulated audiences. The content was carefully organized and meticulously thought through. The wet crowd of about 100,000 had not expected Hoover to be dramatic. The Hoovers changed into dry clothes and watched the parade from a balcony at the White House. Lou, who did not serve alcohol during Prohibition, hosted a tea for 1,500 later that afternoon. The president skipped the ball, a small charity affair hosted by Vice President Curtis. The tone of the day had been subdued, as Hoover planned.[29]

Hoover had devoted much time to selecting his cabinet. He considered geography, sound judgment, administrative ability, and personal honesty. The president chose the best administrators, not necessarily those with the most knowledge of their departments. Most pundits found the cabinet above average, though not distinguished. There were no Catholics and no Southerners. The initial cabinet included six attorneys, one banker, an engineer, a college president, and a former steel worker. Eight of the men were older than Hoover; one was his age, 54; and the tenth was three weeks his junior. In his cabinet selections, Hoover tried to unify the party. In key policy positions just below the cabinet level, he placed personal friends and loyalists who sometimes exercised more clout on policy than their superiors. Among the most influential were William R. Castle Jr. in State, Ogden L. Mills in Treasury, Julius Klein in Commerce, Ernest Lee Jahnecke in Navy, and Charles Evans Hughes Jr. in Justice. Hoover departed from precedent by appointing all heads of scientific bureaus by promotion from civil service.[30]

Hoover appointed Mellon, the last holdover of the original Harding cabinet, to assure the business community and appease the GOP's conservative congressional bloc. Mellon was one of the richest men in the nation, considered a financial genius by his admirers, with wide financial interests that included banking, aluminum, and steel. If Coolidge and Hoover were reticent, Mellon was a Sphinx. Sixty-six when he entered Harding's cabinet, he had declined physically and mentally and during the Hoover era became a figurehead. Financially frugal, wanting to rein in government spending during the Depression, his popularity waned as flush times disappeared. Hoover relied more on his young, vigorous, and brilliant assistant, Ogden Mills, a wealthy New Yorker with political and economic experience. Hoover's second press secretary, Theodore Joslin, considered Mellon "a dead weight" who was "a hindrance rather than a help."[31] Mellon was stubborn, and instead of attempting to persuade him, the president often bypassed him. Politically motivated charges were filed against Mellon for owning stock while serving as treasury secretary in 1929 and 1932. The earlier charges were dismissed, but in 1932, after Mellon's credibility had evaporated, Hoover used the charges as an excuse to make him ambassador to England, a convenient refuge from political attacks.[32]

Attorney General Mitchell, a Democrat who had served as Coolidge's Solicitor General, was an effective reformer and administrator who prosecuted Prohibition vigorously after enforcement was transferred from Treasury to Justice. He also helped revitalize and reform Justice, upgrade the quality of special agents, and limit violence in pursuing Prohibition offenders. Mitchell, a firm administrator and hard worker, had been a late addition to the cabinet after others either declined or were eliminated for political reasons. Mitchell, a Democrat, lent a degree of bipartisanship.[33]

Postmaster Warren F. Brown and Secretary of War James W. Good were the most politically oriented of Hoover's appointees. Both had played leading roles in the 1928 campaign, before and after Hoover's nomination. Hoover had known Brown since the early days of the Harding administration and had made him an undersecretary in the Commerce Department. He shared the president's interest in government reorganization and, like Hoover, he was an admirer of Theodore Roosevelt. Brown was the political pivot man in the cabinet. Initially it appeared that Good of Illinois would be the most important political figure in the cabinet. Good had served in the House from 1909 to 1921, retired to practice law, and had managed Coolidge's western campaign in 1924. He played a similar role for Hoover in 1928. Hoover hoped Good would use his personal contacts in Congress to promote the administration's program. He was highly respected in the House, one of the few cabinet members chosen on the basis of his political skills. Sadly, Good survived less than a year, dying at the age of 66 in November 1929 from complications from appendicitis. The death shocked Hoover, who had expected to rely on him. Good's successor was Assistant Secretary of War Patrick J. Hurley, a younger, more aggressive personality: an Oklahoman who had been a soldier, a businessman, and an attorney. A talented public speaker, self-made, and wealthy, he owned eight large buildings in Washington. At the time he entered the cabinet, he was relatively young and not widely known within the GOP inner circle.[34]

Hoover's best friend in the cabinet, Wilbur, was conceivably the most influential, at least in domestic affairs. Both were western outdoorsmen who enjoyed fishing and camping together, and they were ardent conservationists. Hoover planned to work with Wilbur to expand National Parks, Forests, and Monuments and to implement reforms related to children, the infirm, the aged, housing, and American Indians. Like Hoover, Wilbur was adept at raising money from private foundations to facilitate these activities. Providing continuity, James J. Davis, the secretary of labor, was the only holdover from the Coolidge cabinet besides Mellon. The president had planned to select Virginian William N. Doak, vice president of the Brotherhood of Railroad Trainmen, which would have added a Southerner to the cabinet. However, the large labor organizations were unable to agree on Doak or any other candidate, so Hoover asked Davis to remain at his post until he could identify an acceptable successor. In 1930, Davis won a Senate seat representing Pennsylvania, and Doak succeeded him.[35]

During Hoover's tenure, the secretaries of labor and commerce often interacted. Hoover selected a fellow engineer, Robert P. Lamont, as secretary of commerce. Besides a long career as a civil engineer, Lamont had been president of the American Steel Foundries Company and a director on the boards of several large banks and businesses. A surprise selection, virtually unknown in political circles, Lamont became one of the most popular members of the cabinet and was popular in Congress. In August 1932, Lamont resigned from the cabinet, largely for financial reasons, to return to private business. His successor, Roy Dickman Chapin of Detroit, was chairman of the board of the Hudson Motor company. Chapin had also participated in civic and volunteer work. In a tribute to his flexibility, Hoover offered Senator Charles L. McNary of Oregon, author of the McNary-Haugen bill, which Hoover had persuaded Coolidge to veto twice, the opportunity to head the Department of Agriculture. Eventually, the job went to Arthur Hyde, former governor of Missouri and once an auto dealer. Hyde agreed with Hoover and Wilbur about conservation and considered crop limitations the real solution to agricultural problems. The position was stressful, and Hyde nearly suffered a nervous breakdown in April 1932, so Hoover ordered a brief fishing vacation with friends. Navy Secretary Charles Francis Adams, who had never met Hoover, was surprised when the president-elect offered him the navy portfolio. An avid yachtsman and fiscal officer of Harvard, Adams had been a Democrat until 1920. He was recommended to Hoover by Christian Herter, a former secretary to Hoover. Adams was thoroughly loyal to Hoover and defended his program of naval disarmament against the big navy champions in his own department. Hoover found him more flexible than Stimson and later remarked that if he had known him better he would have chosen him for secretary of state. Hoover appointed honest individuals to the cabinet and other noncivil service positions and scrupulously adhered to civil service regulations when applicable. None of his top officials was fired, nor did any resign because of malfeasance or personal or policy differences.[36]

The cabinet was termed the "dark horse" cabinet because many of the appointments had been unexpected and the "highbrow cabinet" because the members had earned more advanced degrees than any previous cabinet. Vice President Curtis sat with the cabinet, which enjoyed an unusual degree of stability. Stimson, Mitchell, Brown, Adams, Hyde, and Wilbur remained for the entire four years. No minutes were kept of meetings, which convened each Tuesday and Friday at 10:30 a.m. There was no fixed order of procedure, and members were free to comment on subjects outside their department. However, Hoover kept the meetings focused, brisk, and brief. Next to Wilbur, Hoover's closest friend was Mitchell. The president found Stimson testy, occasionally insubordinate, and complained about his lackadaisical work ethic, yet Hoover retained him because he was politically influential. Hoover relied on Wilbur to implement many of his domestic reforms. Although the cabinet was efficient at implementing policy, most members were not imaginative at designing it and there was little interaction across departmental lines. Nor was the cabinet involved much in pushing legislation through Congress. Nonetheless, several members campaigned extensively for Hoover's reelection.[37]

Hoover's White House staff worked parallel to the cabinet. All were longtime trusted intimates with specific responsibilities. They labored exhaustively and were thoroughly devoted to the president; their loyalty was personal, not based on policy. Although they advised the president on practical matters, their job was not to generate policy or draft legislation. Hoover personally formulated policy and hammered out details with congressional leaders. The president never criticized his subordinates publicly and took responsibility for their mistakes, which is one reason they remained loyal. In working long hours, they recognized that Hoover worked even longer. They also saw a human side of Hoover nearly invisible to the public. Each had experience in Washington in a different capacity, yet none had significant influence in the higher councils of the GOP.

Lawrence Richey was the closest, personally, to the president, and his tasks were the most diverse, sometimes confidential. A former detective and Secret Service agent, he managed the Secret Service, supervised the office, answered Hoover's personal correspondence, and provided instant information. He was on call for any task. Richey had Hoover's complete confidence, and serving Hoover was his purpose in life. The public face of the administration, George Akerson, the press secretary, was a veteran White House correspondent for the *Minneapolis Tribune*, who also scheduled the president's appointments. Akerson, a Harvard graduate, had been a football star at his alma mater. Although friendly and gregarious, he protected his boss, and under pressure he resorted to alcohol. Like the others, his job wore him down. Walter Newton, a former

U.S. representative, handled relations with Congress, the cabinet, the independent commissions, and the Republican National Committee. He helped Hoover prepare plans for government reorganization and lobbied for administration bills. French Strother, the former associate editor at *World's Work*, was the president's literary assistant and chief researcher. He had input into speeches but did not write them. Hoover also had two clerical secretaries, Ann Shankey and Myra McGrath. Competent and supportive, they handled routine office paperwork, such as typing. Outside the office, Lewis Strauss, a Wall Street financier and an assistant during Belgian relief, continued to offer informal economic advice. James MacLafferty, a former California congressman and businessman who had worked under Hoover at Commerce and campaigned for him in 1928, was placed on the payroll of the Republican National Committee (RNC). He lobbied Congress informally and served as a confidential source of political intelligence. Intensely loyal, he made several fact-finding and campaign tours for Hoover.[38]

The daily grind and constant stress during the Depression punished Hoover's staff. Akerson became unpopular for protecting Hoover from the press and withholding information at Hoover's orders. He resigned and was replaced by Theodore Joslin, another prominent journalist, formerly the Washington correspondent for the *Boston Transcript*. Joslin made sincere efforts to humanize Hoover and generate interesting stories, but Hoover discouraged him. Joslin also clipped important newspapers and provided a news summary for the president. In late August 1932, Joslin took an indefinite leave of absence to recuperate from stress and was replaced by Edward T. Clark, a secretary to former President Coolidge, but after a brief rest returned during the campaign. He kept the most useful diary for political information among Hoover's political insiders. In March 1931, French Strother resigned from the staff to fulfill his ambition to write fiction. He was temporarily replaced by George A. Hastings, an expert in public relations who had engaged in work for charities. Evidently, Strother and Hoover missed each other, and Strother returned to his old position at the White House in February 1932, with Hastings resuming his charitable fundraising. The work at the White House, which often included Sundays and holidays, was unrelenting, yet no one complained or rebelled. The leaves and resignations were due primarily to exhaustion. Akerson, who also missed Hoover's company, returned for the 1932 campaign.[39]

Hoover's first political test came during the special session of the Seventy-First Congress, summoned to provide relief to agriculture and selective tariff increases, principally on farm products, which he had pledged in the 1928 campaign. Hoover has been falsely stereotyped as a "business" president, despite devoting more time to agricultural problems than any previous chief executive. The president empathized not only with farm poverty but with farm traditions and venerated rural values. He agreed with one of his contemporaries, Frederick Jackson Turner, that the farm frontier had helped forge

American democracy. Indeed, both believed that there was more to farming than raising crops. Americans had their roots, both metaphorically and literally, in the soil.

The heart of the farm problem was overproduction and the resistance of farmers themselves to controlling it. Instead, they wanted the government to set prices or pay them some form of direct cash payment, such as an equalization fee or an export bounty, known as a debenture. The problems of farmers had been piling up along with their surplus for a decade and a half after the Great War. They had profited immensely for high European demand and had expanded acreage. When the demand abroad ended with the war, they did not plant less. Farmers suffered other problems. There was a reduction in domestic markets due to changes in diet, a decrease in the rate of population growth, use of synthetic fabrics, and less demand for fodder for farm animals replaced by mechanization. Tractors, reapers, and the gasoline to fuel them were expensive. The prices of what they bought escalated, while the prices for their products fell drastically. Many were mired in chronic debt. Foreclosures on their farms and homes multiplied while land value diminished. The farm depression antedated the Great Depression by more than a decade. Hoover intended to fulfill his pledges to aid farmers, but he believed there was no comprehensive, short-run, simple solution. Paying farmers bounties would only encourage overproduction and further depress prices. Hoover did conceive mitigations that involved a multifaceted approach, implemented incrementally, that would be fair to consumers. He knew that the quick fix many farmers wanted was unrealistic. Moreover, American democracy grinds out legislation slowly and always involves compromise.[40]

The centerpiece to Hoover's legislation program in 1929 was the Agricultural Marketing Act. It would establish a Federal Farm Board of eight members appointed by the president, and the secretary of agriculture, ex officio. The essence of the board's program was to organize individual farmers into cooperatives, which could market products and purchase them cooperatively on more desirable terms and could store surpluses to await better demand, selling them during years of peak demand. The Board would have a revolving fund of $500 million to operate. It could loan money only to cooperatives, created by the type of crop, not individual farmers. The board would also furnish technical advice on matching the right crop to the type of soil and amount of rainfall, instruction on scientific farming, and statistics to aid foreign and domestic markets. The cooperatives could negotiate lower rates for transportation and eliminate cutthroat competition in which farmers underbid one another. They would also encourage crop diversification. The key to the cooperative approach was to eliminate waste and provide efficient distribution, including the reduction of money siphoned from the farmers by speculators, middlemen, and profiteers. In numbers, farmers would possess strength. The entire edifice was designed to operate during ordinary times, not during a devastating depression.[41]

For the president, farming was both an economic and a political problem. Congress and his own party were badly divided. The farm-state progressives, most of them Republican insurgents, were single-minded in promoting the interests of their constituents, obstinate in attempting to block moderate solutions. They wanted more than the congressmen representing industrial districts, or consumers, were willing to give. Some of their proposals were excessively expensive or unworkable. None seriously addressed the problem of overproduction. Most of the western insurgents did not represent populous states, nor did they have a program that was more than regional. Yet because they were fanatically devoted to their constituents, their constituents were fanatically devoted to them. Some were effective orators and crafty parliamentary manipulators, who, combined with Democrats, could obstruct any program. However, few were effective in enacting a program of their own. Some, such as Senator Hiram Johnson of California and Senator George Norris of Nebraska, detested Hoover for personal reasons. The president had helped thwart Johnson's presidential aspirations in 1920 and opposed Norris' fierce determination to implement federal control of water power, though the latter was only a difference in degree. In several cases, the problems went beyond issues to temperament and personality. Senator Robert LaFollette of Wisconsin, for example, who reflexively opposed Hoover's programs, could not claim to do so in the interests of his constituents. Individually, the western insurgents were powerful orators but not powerful legislators. From the beginning, there was nothing Hoover could have done to please them without alienating the larger conservative bloc of Republicans in Congress. The Republican conservatives and insurgents hated each other even more than they hated Hoover.

Most of the insurgents wanted something that would help farmers more directly than Hoover's strategy of cooperative marketing. The wanted the government to fix prices for agriculture or give farmers a cash bonus. After their failure to enact the McNary-Haugen plan in the 1920s, their favorite scheme became a more complicated device called the debenture. Like the earlier panacea, its rationale was to increase exports and thus dispose of surpluses abroad while maintaining high domestic prices. One major difference was that the debenture scheme did not aid farmers directly but worked through middlemen such as brokers or exporters, who themselves would skim off some of the profits. The government would give certificates, or debentures, to farmers exporting grain or other products equal to one-half of the value of the export under tariff protection. In a practical sense, most farmers could not cash in the debentures directly. They had to sell them to a broker or exporter, who could redeem the debentures for payment of import duties. In order to make a profit, the middlemen would not buy the debentures at face value but mark them down when buying them from the farmers. The amount the farmers received would be the value of the debentures minus the profit of the exporters, assuming exporters would purchase them at all. Because exporters redeemed them as exemptions from customs duties, the government would collect less customs revenue, probably resulting in a tax increase. Moreover, the assumption that foreign nations would accept the dumping of cheap American farm products on their markets, undercutting their own farmers, was presumptuous. Most nations, including the United States, already had laws that precluded such dumping. A scheme so complicated would be difficult to implement. It could run aground at any stage, and it failed to address overproduction. Farmers would up the ante, expecting the government to indirectly compensate them infinitely the more they produced. It was simply unrealistic.

In his first encounter with congressional politics, Hoover did not intend to bludgeon Congress because he believed in the constitutional division of powers. Like Harding and Coolidge, he would not lobby individual congressmen. He would assign stewardship of legislation to party leaders, chairman of important committees, and the RNC who would convey his wishes to the rank and file. Occasionally he would send messages to Congress dealing with specific issues. The president expected to wait until Congress had difficulty resolving an issue before intervening. Then he would summon congressional leaders to confer with him at the White House. He believed this approach would preserve harmonious relations with Congress.[42]

The Seventy-First Congress assembled on April 15, and Hoover's message was read to the legislators by the clerks of the House and the Senate the following day. The Republican majority in the House was comfortable and reliable, yet in the Senate, a coalition of Democrats and insurgent Republicans combined to frustrate the president. The House passed the administration farm bill by mid-May. However, the Senate attached the debenture, supported by the western insurgents, who wanted a stronger measure, and the Democrats, whose political aim was to deny the president credit for his first major bill. Deadlocked, the debate dragged on for months and finally went to a conference committee. In conference, the Senate conferees yielded and dropped the debenture. However, when the consensus report was returned to the Senate, it was defeated by the Upper House. Most senators knew that, ultimately, they could not prevail because the president would veto any measure including the debenture and they lacked the votes to pass it over his veto. Moreover, throughout the entire debate, the House solidly backed the president. What the farm insurgents really wanted was the opportunity to prove to their constituents that they had done everything possible to obtain cash payments. However, the insurgents feared that if they blocked farm legislation altogether, the blame would fall on them. Nevertheless, the insurgents, backed by Democrats, fought to the bitter end. William H. Borah and Smith Brookhart, who had campaigned for the president, broke with him and became inveterate enemies, ending Hoover's brief political honeymoon. Henceforth, the insurgents would oppose nearly every administration measure, and their oratory would be hostile. The Agricultural Marketing Act had divided the party, but in the end Hoover got essentially the bill he wanted. The Senate, however, added a provision authorizing the Farm Board to create stabilization corporations to purchase surpluses in order to support prices. Though Hoover initially opposed the amendment, he signed the bill into law on June 15. It had required more than 20 years to enact farm legislation of this magnitude, and Hoover considered it the most important law ever passed dealing with a single industry. The president immediately began the process of selecting his eight appointees to the board. The tariff debate would explode the fracture further. In fact, the Seventy-First Congress dissolved less into two opposing parties able to command discipline than into a variety of factions.[43]

The farm debate was to the tariff debate what a firecracker is to a prolonged nuclear explosion. Making tariffs is a messy business, less akin to surgical precision than to hog butchering, with congressmen hovering like vultures to pick up road kill for their districts. The president believed in moderate tariffs; within his own party he occupied the low end of the tariff spectrum. His version of the tariff was one that would complement the Agricultural Marketing Act as an ingredient of farm relief. Tariff increases on industrial products, he believed, should be limited to manufacturers who were dismissing workers because they could not compete with cheaper foreign labor. The president's guideline was that tariffs should be levied based on the differential between what it cost to manufacture a specific item domestically and overseas. Ironically, farmers, who were vociferous in their demand for higher tariffs on their products, encountered little significant foreign competition on most crops. Only on selected items would farmers benefit from higher tariffs, and it was naïve to assume that tariffs would not also be increased on the things they purchased. Senator Borah played a major role in the tariff debate. He proposed an amendment limiting increases to agricultural products, which pleased the administration, yet failed by a single vote. However, he also attached the much-maligned and much-ballyhooed debenture to the tariff, which created a rerun of the nightmare over the farm bill. The Senate added 1,253 amendments, raising duties on individual items to the already high House bill. With the debenture attached, there was no possibility that the House would pass the cumbrous measure or that the president would sign it.[44]

The role of Democrats in the tariff debate is instructive with respect to their withering criticism of the Smoot-Hawley Tariff during the 1932 campaign. A parade of Democrats appeared before the Ways and Means Committee soliciting higher rates on special items, sometimes produced in a single region, or even a single district, combining with congressmen from other districts to logroll the favored items into the bill. Thus they could take credit from their constituents for protecting home state interests. Then, when the final measure came to a vote, confident that the Republicans had the votes to pass it, they would go on record against the entire bill, claiming to their constituents that they have delivered sustenance to their districts while simultaneous posing as outraged that the Republicans had enacted a law that would wreck the country.[45]

If the farm bill resembled a short-lived, raucous uproar, the tariff represented an even more raucous outrage that filled newspapers columns and left
congressional orators hoarse for months on end while other legislative business lay dormant. If congressmen had been paid for the moments of silence
they observed, it would not have added one cent to the national debt. This was
Hoover's first experience with obstreperous solons. The farm bill had been
only a mild initiative, and Hoover's tactic of exerting pressure only occasionally, and even then through surrogates, had worked reasonably well. He was
not so fortunate in the tariff imbroglio, and it removed some of the luster
from his reputation and some of his own illusions about dealing with Congress. Yet it would have been impractical for the chief executive to haggle over
rates on infinitesimal items. Any rate he tried to personally renegotiate would
have alienated some faction. To have done so would have probably ensured
that no bill at all would have emerged. But after the special session, Hoover
would never be so passive again.

Hoover did take a firm stand on one facet of the tariff. A tariff commission had been created, consisting of experts, which could within limits raise or
lower individual rates without resorting to a new round of logrolling. Congress
could vote only on one rate adjustment at a time. Hoover prodded Congress
to strengthen the commission, to streamline tariff adjustments, and to give
the president, not Congress, the sole authority to approve or veto commission
rate changes. His purpose was to allow rapid adjustments to changing conditions abroad and to take tariff making out of politics. Unfortunately, the last
thing Congress wanted to do was to take tariff making out of politics. When it
came to logrolling, they were professional lumberjacks. Many screamed that
the president was intruding on congressional prerogatives. Hoover countered
that he would not sign the bill without the provision for more flexible tariff
adjustments included.[46]

The deadlock continued throughout the summer and into the fall. The
special session adjourned without completing the Smoot-Hawley Tariff, and
it carried over into the regular session that convened in December and into
the spring of 1930, well after the stock market crash of October 1929. The
final bill was not what Hoover or anyone else wanted. The extended debate
had left business uncertain, weakened morale, and contributed to the general chaos in economic circles during the months before and after the crash.
That, more than the substance of the bill, probably inflicted the most damage.
Hoover had promised a tariff, though not the kind that emerged. Still, he had
succeeded in obtaining the type of tariff commission he wanted, though his
faith in its effectiveness proved unjustified. Many economists believed Hoover
should veto the bill, and the president was troubled by their doubts. But the
greater sin, he believed, was no bill at all. This would plunge Congress into
another round of even more vituperative, endless recrimination and plunge
business into the limbo of protracted uncertainty. In the business community,
hesitation means loss. Besides, the president, and Congress, now had more

important things to attend to than to debate the duties on imported goldfish. So, on June 17, 1930, the Smoot-Hawley Tariff became law and remained law throughout the New Deal.[47]

The Smoot-Hawley Tariff did not cause the crash or the Depression because the crash had occurred before its enactment and the economy was already spiraling downward by the time it was law. More than 40 nations had already increased tariffs before it became law, so it did not initiate trade wars, though it doubtless exacerbated them. Neither did it strangle foreign trade. Americans both imported less and exported less in the coming years, but the chief factor at both shores of the Atlantic was reduced purchasing power. Nonetheless, as Hoover pointed out, many nations still found the lucre to engage in an arms race. Sadly, the bill did more harm than good. It did not produce a bonanza for farmers, who did not need protection anyway. The long period of uncertainty made business, investors, shippers, and exporters nervous; it was difficult to plan for the future. The measure had been proposed under one set of conditions and enacted under different conditions. It had sundered the GOP, which was fractious from the start. But Hoover was the Great Engineer. Hope remained that he could repair the machinery of government.[48]

CHAPTER 3

Humanizing Hoover

Any attempt to understand another human is inherently an oversimplification. Understanding Hoover requires patience and subtlety. Although he said little about himself, he wrote voluminously, and he opened himself to his close friends who, in fact, understood him quite well. Understated, he clearly revealed himself in his actions, which were consistent throughout his life. Even though Hoover grew and evolved, he never departed from seminal values emanating from his Quaker upbringing, his boyhood on the frontier, and being orphaned at nine. Yet environmental determinism does not suffice to understand Hoover. Like all individuals, he was unique. He never outgrew the child inside, a source of joy and insecurity. He forged a joyful childhood and a strong, purposeful manhood out of an environment that seemed unpromising but that in his hands was pregnant with possibilities. Hoover seized the opportunities life offered, and he was blessed with unusual gifts. He never forgot a kindness or ignored the chance to help a friend. He was strong and resilient, mentally and physically, kind and gentle and also tough and smart. To the general public of his time and generations of historians, he seemed a dull skinflint. Nonetheless, he was a fascinating man. It took time to understand him, but it was worth the effort. Those who enlisted in his early causes at Stanford, in Belgium, in the Food Administration, or at the Department of Commerce, bonded with him for life. His superb mind was not his greatest gift; it was his talent for friendship.[1]

If we are to condemn men for shyness, Hoover might merit the death penalty. Shyness, modesty, seriousness, reticence, and restraint are common among Quakers but rare among politicians. Hoover succeeded, to a degree, as a politician because of the decisiveness of his actions, the quality of his mind and imagination, and his ability to bond with people and persuade among small groups. His failures were the reverse side of his success; he could not exhort the masses and could not, or would not, flatter egos, mingle with crowds, slap backs, kiss babies, or tout his achievements. These acts are almost irrelevant to governing, but they are significant in perpetuating oneself in office—the objective of most politicians, but not of Hoover. Some politicians commit larcenies in private; Hoover concealed his good deeds, such as anonymous philanthropies. He always cared more about accomplishing a task than receiving credit. He was curiously an apolitical politician. As president during the Great Depression, he was overmatched, though it is dubious if any president, however clever, could have inspired the crew of a sinking ship. The best any president could have done from 1929 to 1933 was to mitigate the Depression's effects and avoid a popular revolt, which Hoover accomplished. If depressions were due to the personalities of presidents, we would have more frequent downturns. It is well to remember that Calvin Coolidge was equally taciturn and a less effective public speaker, yet he remained popular, though accomplishing little. Neither is it clear that Franklin Roosevelt, if elected in 1928 instead of 1932, would have been more effective than Hoover. He might have gone down with the ship. After all, given two terms to solve the Depression, Roosevelt did not do so.

Being orphaned at nine forever clung to Hoover, however he may have suppressed it. A sense of loneliness haunted him; he disliked being left alone and savored loyal friends. It contributed to his craving for affection and to his inhibition in expressing physical love. It influenced his public persona because he wrapped a security blanket of privacy around his personal life, which became a political liability. Conceivably, lacking physical love from birth parents, being worked incessantly by an uncle who helped raise him, and growing up too soon might have produced an embittered misanthrope, an alcoholic, or a self-destructive personality. That it produced a humanitarian instead—one who had an enduring love for children, enjoyed a happy marriage, made the best of his gifts, and accepted ill fortune with grace—is an argument for the degree of free will humans possess. Reflecting as an adult, Hoover was less bitter about the disappointments of his early life than he was grateful for its opportunities. Adversity made him self-reliant, and when success came, he was generous with credit and in sharing his largesse. Though we have had greater presidents, it is doubtful we ever had a more unselfish one.

The general public obtained the erroneous conclusion that Hoover was a loner who would have enjoyed life as a hermit or a monk. Just the opposite was the case. He craved companionship and good conversation and cultivated friendship. Few people have as many lifetime friends as did Hoover. Hoover conquered fear and loneliness through almost constant companionship. He did not like prying reporters, but he thrived on being surrounded by his intimate friends, whether working, dining, or hiking along mountain brooks. Every evening at the White House, there were dinner guests chosen not for their political significance but for their camaraderie. After dinner, the men retired to the Lincoln Room for several hours of conversation. The president did not dominate; he was both a good listener and a sparkling conversationalist. When he wove tales about his life's adventures, such as the Boxer Rebellion, he did not place himself in the spotlight. He did not boast and rarely complained. He occasionally lost his temper, even using profanity, but never in public, and he never held grudges. He strongly disagreed with some antagonists but did not begrudge their right to disagree. He always felt, however, that it was wrong to oppose vital programs solely for political purposes. Hoover was interested in policy, not politics; progress, not stalemates. He failed to understand self-serving politicians. The problem was not that he was inadequate; the problem was that more did not share his unselfishness.[2]

Although Hoover did not enjoy small talk, he cultivated good conversation. Hoover is one of the few people with whom Coolidge really opened up. They had long, lively conversations, and Coolidge admired Hoover's ability and sound judgment. Hoover, in turn, was deferential to Coolidge and genuinely liked him. Of his three hobbies—fishing, conversation, and reading—Hoover enjoyed the latter two every day. Many presidents summon people to the White House to lecture them. Hoover often invited them in order to listen. He did not want "yes" men in his administration; he wanted lieutenants who would give him the frank truth, even when unpleasant. They were never penalized for disagreeing, which is one reason they bonded.

As a conversationalist, Hoover's interests were as eclectic as his companions. He enjoyed the company of writers, scientists, engineers, businessmen, journalists, and academics. Politicians were among his acquaintances, but they were not there to "talk shop." The president never enjoyed political gossip, and his whimsical sense of humor was far too subtle for most politicians, as was his grasp of literature, economics, and world affairs. From the time he lived in London, the Hoover home had been a Mecca for intellectuals, and Hoover had many friends from the journalistic and literary community, such as William Allen White, Arthur Capper, Will Irwin, Mark Sullivan, David Lawrence, and Ida Tarbell. Conversations with Hoover were never monologues; they were two-way. When inclined, he could be convivial, funny, and informative. But he did not try to dominate. The mix of interesting people with varied life experiences, all connected in some way to Hoover, made White House evenings lively. The atmosphere was spontaneous. Although many of his friends were well educated and brilliant, that was not the basis of their friendship. He disliked snobbish or pretentious people and had been offended by European nobility and class distinctions. Hoover's head was full of stories, jokes, facts, figures, and travels, yet he did not yearn to tell them. However, when enticed, he could sparkle. With friends, he could be the life of the party. In such a setting, the president could relax and be himself. This was the real Hoover.[3]

Those who liked Hoover enough to penetrate his surface reticence were well rewarded. The people who took the trouble to get to know him came to love him. His friendship was genuine; there was no fake feeling. Once someone worked for Hoover, they found they would always be working for him. Among the lifelong, close friends who stood ready to answer his call instantly were Edgar Rickard, Mark L. Requa, Will Irwin, Lewis L. Strauss, and Arch W. Shaw. He not only provided a common purpose, but he was fun to be around, and a sense of accomplishment rewarded them. Although Hoover had one of the finest minds of his generation, his real gift was his capacity for friendship.[4] "Hoover had a multitude of enemies, but no ex-friends," journalist Eugene Lyons writes.[5] Those who once worked for Hoover were enlisted in a reserve army of his helpers for life. They not only bonded with their leader, whom they invariably called "Chief," but they bonded with each other. Many people who knew Hoover considered him the most selfless person they had ever known. The loyalty cut both ways. Hoover never publicly belittled a subordinate. His method was to talk directly to the individual and to shoulder the responsibility himself.[6] A friend in need was never neglected, whether or not they could contribute anything to his undertaking. Loyalty, to him, was a thing of the heart. Hoover always had time for friends, even on his busiest days in the White House. Consequently, they respected their Chief and did not betray him. "Of the top 100 men whom he appointed to office during his term in the White House," Lyons explains, "some died, a few retired for reasons of health, many were promoted—but not one was dismissed." He concludes, "They loved him largely for those very qualities of warmth, kindness, and geniality about which the public knew almost nothing."[7]

Many of Hoover's friends dated to his years at Stanford or had some Stanford connection. Possibly no president, except Wilson, has been so closely identified with a university. An unusual number of the early Stanford alums whom Hoover knew became extremely successful, especially for a small school just getting started. The early years of Stanford produced a galaxy of success stories, some of them highly improbable. In the fall of 1931, the president learned that the football team of 1894, considered unofficially the national champion after having defeated the University of Chicago and their archrival, the University of California, despite being an inexperienced team, planned a reunion in the East. The president invited them to the White House for dinner, followed by reminiscing. As student body treasurer, he had pieced together the money to buy new uniforms. The squad, coached by the legendary Walter Camp, had only 16 members, 2 of whom played every minute of every game. They compensated for their youth and thin ranks with grit and an unusual *esprit des corps*.[8]

On the evening of November 12, the Cardinals assembled on the White House lawn, spiraled a football, executed long-remembered plays, and dropkicked a football over a hedge. Inside, the White House was adorned with Stanford Red, and the former players were entertained by the United States

Marine Band. Hoover invited them back for breakfast the following morning. Finding the president's volleyball cabinet at play, the ex-athletes challenged them to a game and, to their surprise, were soundly defeated. After breakfast, the president arranged for a chauffeur to drive his old friends throughout the Washington area for sightseeing.[9]

Hoover's affection for old friends, which was reciprocated, is only one symptom of the president's sensitive, emotional nature, which the public rarely glimpsed. Hoover understood suffering; he had experienced it and witnessed pain. The reasons he concealed his emotions were not because he lacked feelings but because they were too intense. He did not visit bread lines and soup kitchens, not because he was uncaring, but because he was afraid he would break down in public, as he had done in Belgium. Hoover was very human but was afraid to let it show due to his Quaker upbringing and his own sense that it was inappropriate. Hoover wanted to accomplish great things, but the accomplishments were not ends in themselves; they were ways of expressing love. Business, wealth, and even politics did not make him cynical but provided means to serve humanity. He truly believed that equality of opportunity, which had rewarded him, was the key to potential success for every American. Equality did not guarantee success but made it possible. Hoover believed America should be a meritocracy with a heart, where individuals helped themselves and each other. It is not true that Hoover was incapable of love on a personal level; he was simply incapable of expressing it in words. But he did express it in his actions; in fact, it was the great motivation of his life. Those who understood that his Quaker inhibition blocked physical displays loved him all the more for silent affection.

Hoover did not simply save Belgium, much of Central Europe, and the Soviet Union from famine during the era of the Great War; he performed small acts of kindness virtually every day. He was attentive to incidental people; he respected the humble and was not daunted by the mighty; he was principled yet not dogmatic; he always tried to do the right thing, though he lacked the wisdom to invariably do the right thing. He tried to correct mistakes and not to repeat them. Down-to-earth, thoughtful, and patient, Hoover took people seriously. He was tolerant of interruptions by friends and loved to reminisce with old friends. But perhaps he communicated best with children; he took them seriously, too, well aware of the potential damage inflicted by denial of love at an early age. He loved to be surrounded by children, and his favorites were his grandchildren. He not only understood them, but they seemed to understand him, as if by some curious telepathy. He possessed some of the innocence, simplicity, and naiveté of a child, some of a child's imagination and unconditional love. Yet Hoover found it more difficult to accept love than to offer it. Deprived of love as an orphan, he appreciated his friends and in his own awkward way, reached out to them. He tried to resolve the question of whether a good politician can be a good man, and he resolved the first, at least, in the affirmative.[10]

Hoover not only enjoyed people; he enjoyed his work. He found pleasure in every type of work he ever did, from the hot, dusty outback of Australia, where he searched for gold beneath the desert, to the vastness of China, Siberia, and Burma. He enjoyed his humanitarian work during the Great War, which addicted him to a lifetime devoted to public service. Most of all, he experienced his greatest satisfaction as secretary of commerce during the 1920s. It would have been highly gratifying to remain there, but he always moved up, believing he could do the most good at the top. Hoover was doubtless a workaholic, but it is not necessarily true that workaholics are dull, unhappy people. In fact, Hoover thrived on work, not merely the results, but the process too. This is common among creative people who excel at what they do and lead purposeful lives. Hoover had worked hard through his boyhood, worked his way through Stanford, and won success as an engineer, starting at the bottom. He always won the respect of his peers at every level.

Hoover's work habits were ingrained long before he became president and in fact continued for the rest of his life. That he lived to be 90 in relatively good health and continued to be productive demonstrates not only physical vitality but purposeful living. Compared to other presidents who had served during periods of crisis, including Abraham Lincoln, Woodrow Wilson, Franklin Roosevelt, and Lyndon Johnson, at least in a relative sense, the presidency did not wear Hoover down. He did worry, and he experienced stress, but his work was also cathartic. His physical and his emotional stability compare favorably with even the most resilient of our presidents. Hoover was human, and his presidency was a disappointment to him, as well as to his friends, and to the country. Yet Hoover also savored competition. When he played a game that involved throwing a medicine ball across a net to friends, he wanted to win. When he fished, he wanted to catch fish, and he wanted to eat them. Having a purpose that defines one's life keeps a person strong with vital life force. Hoover's greatest satisfaction was derived from utilizing his gifts of a great mind, a fertile imagination, a remarkable memory, physical vitality, and a hunger for knowledge and synergizing them to produce results. Hoover's working style was consistent, spread throughout the day, over months and years. He did not take a day off during his first six months on the job. During his entire term, he never missed a single day of work due to illness.[11] Ironically, Hoover has been criticized for working *too* hard, for being conscientious to a fault. Yet it is an exaggeration to conclude that the Great Depression would have simply evaporated if he had worked less hard. There is no evidence that his creativity was impaired. In fact, as the Depression lengthened and deepened, Hoover grew more creative. His most successful ideas occurred late in his term. It took him time to learn the office, and like all presidents he made mistakes, but it is difficult to point out specific decisions that indicate that hard work was a hindrance.

Ike Hoover, the White House usher for 41 years, said that despite Hoover's flaws, he had never seen his equal in the White House. Even among political enemies, he earned grudging respect for his fortitude. Hoover's staff lacked his rugged constitution and nearly succumbed to exhaustion, yet their loyalty to the president welded them to their jobs. The president employed technology to keep the wheels of government turning. He was not only the first president to place a telephone on his desk; he used it extensively. Instead of summoning cabinet members or congressmen to the White House, he called them individually, unless he wanted to speak to them as a group. In fact, telephone use multiplied throughout the executive branch. Previous chief executives had taken lengthy vacations to escape Washington's steamy summers. Instead, Hoover became the first president to install air conditioning in the Executive Office Building.[12]

A habitual reader, Hoover carved out time to read for pleasure every day, in addition to stacks of newspapers and news summaries. The writer Christopher Morley, who had a pleasant, relaxed conversation with the president about what he liked to read, found him an intriguing conversationalist, well informed outside of his own fields. The president had read most of the major works of English and classical literature and had sampled popular culture, as well. However, when Morley asked him if this reading gave the busy executive the opportunity to escape thinking about his work, the answer surprised him. "I don't want not to think about it," the president said.[13] Even after his defeat in 1932, journalist Anne O'Hare McCormick found that Hoover's appetite for work had not diminished. "I suspect that Mr. Hoover enjoys the routine, that to wade into a pile of the toughest problems would be what he might do for amusement," she wrote.[14] Hoover smoked thick black cigars all day as he worked, though he sometimes puffed on a pipe. One Quaker lady wrote how he could justify smoking after his strict Quaker upbringing. When his press secretary, Joslin, asked how he was going to answer the letter, the president replied, "I am not going to answer it."[15] While the world seemed imperiled by the whirlwind of a tornado, Hoover worked steadily in the eye of the storm.

The president arose at about 6:45 a.m. and, after a brisk game of medicine ball, enjoyed a brief breakfast, usually with Lou. On most days Lou then walked with him to his office at the Executive Office Building, where he arrived at about 8:30. His first hour was devoted to scanning newspapers and consulting with his three personal secretaries individually. They brought him problems for the day that required his help. The president also cleared up important mail by dictating short replies to his stenographers. He dictated poorly, and his stenographers learned to improvise by filling in words. At about 9:30 the president began the most grinding portion of his day: a series of appointments spaced at eight-minute intervals. He had to absorb information, digest it without taking notes, and render decisions rapidly. Often he had to deny the individual what they wanted, and as the Depression lengthened, this became more difficult. Yet even in the darkest days, this portion of the day was the part he enjoyed most. He was a "people person" to a greater degree than most people realized, and these hours provided the company he craved.

Hoover tried to base his decisions on the logic of the presentation rather than the personality or prestige of the individual. The president looked forward to it as an importunity to be creative. Despite his enjoyment of visitors, he remained on schedule and rarely left a visitor waiting. Each person received his allotted time and no more.[16]

On Tuesday and Friday mornings, the president met with the cabinet from about 10:30 to 12:00. No minutes were taken, and discussions remained confidential. Debate was invited, but once a decision was reached, the cabinet was expected to maintain a united front. Hoover held press conferences on Tuesday mornings and Friday afternoons, timed to meet the needs of the morning and evening dailies. The president had luncheon guests almost daily, usually to discuss policy. Afternoons were reserved for priorities set by the president. Guests came to the White House during these hours by invitation only. Often these were members of Congress, the cabinet, or experts from fields in which Hoover was seeking to resolve problems. He discussed issues such as the tariff, veterans' pensions, and drought relief and drafted speeches, statements, and messages to Congress. The chief executive used the telephone intermittently, sometimes to summon someone to the White House, sometimes for a brief question. The president left his office between 6 and 7 p.m., dined with guests, enjoyed after dinner conversation in the family quarters, and retired to bed around 10:30.[17]

During most of his adult life Hoover had devoted one or two hours to pleasure reading before falling to sleep. As president, his routine slightly changed. Because of his physical workout near dawn and his uninterrupted work, he fell asleep almost immediately. However, his sleep was interrupted. He awoke nightly about 12:30 a.m. and read for an hour or two. Sometimes the reading involved work, but more often it consisted of detective stories or some current interest. Then he slipped back into slumber, awakening promptly at 6:45. The fact that Hoover's sleep was interrupted did not seem to alter its recuperative powers. His tendency to sleep only four to six hours a night characterized his entire adult life and seemed entirely sufficient.[18]

The president cleared his desk twice a day: before meeting visitors in the morning and just before departing for the day. Even many of Hoover's detractors have conceded that he was an exceptionally able administrator, yet few understood his techniques. What worked for Hoover would not necessarily have worked for everyone. They were correct in surmising that he was highly organized, but that was not his real secret, the reason he was able to accomplish a great deal in a short period of time. The secret is that he loved and trusted his subordinates, and they loved and trusted him. Hoover won their respect, gratitude, and confidence by assigning them responsibilities comparable with their skills and permitting them to devise their own solutions with little interference and no criticism, though he assumed ultimate responsibility. He harnessed their creativity and produced the kind of work that only self-motivated lieutenants can provide. Once they adjusted, the freedom was exhilarating. Hoover's method was an extension of his own personality. He respected every person's individuality.[19] He had always worked this way. Once, during his days as leader of the Commission for Relief in Belgium (CRB), he assigned a fellow engineer to operate the CRB's Rotterdam office, the main staging area from which food was imported from overseas, unloaded, reloaded onto barges, and sent through hundreds of canals to destinations in Belgium. When the engineer asked the nature of Hoover's job, he said simply, "Just keep the food moving."[20]

Hoover's work habits were legendary, yet few people in the general public realized that the president was not purely serious—he possessed a puckish sense of humor, one of many sides of his multifaceted personality. Hoover's sense of humor was gentle and never came at the expense of another person. He seldom rehashed old jokes; his humor was as original as his fingerprints. During some talks at the Gridiron Club, he poked fun at the press, who believed the president's job was to provide entertainment on deadline for the morning and evening editions that "shall have the mixed flavor of a human-interest story and a dog fight."[21] More often, his humor was whimsical and self-deprecating and sparkled with originality. Like Hoover's speeches, his humor was the work of his own pen. He rarely told jokes at the expense of others, and he never aimed at the jugular. John Spargo, a friend, observed, "Humorous in a quaint, quiet way, he pours forth, with all the artlessness of a child, a succession of epigrams in which there is something of the whimsicalness and conceit that endeared Charles Lamb to his friends." Hoover's humor was never spiteful: "Even when the mood is satirical, there is a generous and humane quality in the satire."[22]

The originality and subtlety in Hoover's humor are illustrated by a satirical address he delivered on April 27, 1921, at the Gridiron Club. The president facetiously told his audience of journalists that one of the problems that most concerned him was bells. "The whole bell evil has been increasing over a great number of years," he said. "The telephone company alone prides itself on having installed over ten million bells since the Great War. There is no noise in the world that so fills one's heart with alarm and foreboding as the telephone bell." This was especially true of office holders, he lamented: "For its imperious commands you must get out of bed at night." Hoover described the insidious punishment inflicted by bells: "Moreover, our manufacturers have installed mass production in those bells attached to clocks for the evil purpose of an early morning alarm." The president resented having his slumber interrupted. "To interrupt a man's sleep and jerk him from the realm of real bliss into the cold realities of another day is a greater invasion of human liberty than any yet wrought by the Eighteenth Amendment." Bells were ubiquitous. "Wherever one turns there are new and clamorous bells. In the middle of your meals you are summoned to the front door by their strident clang. They even interfere with free burglary." One is reminded of Edgar Allan Poe's poem about bells. "They have been extended to induce the terror in fire engines and ambulances. There are probably 30,000,000 more strident bells clamoring in the nation than before the war." Hoover concluded, "I commend the cure of the abuse to the Gridiron Club."[23]

Some of Hoover's jokes were short quips. Shortly after the Great War, a woman said that he must have undergone terrifying experience supplying Belgium. She asked, "It would interest me to know at what time things looked their blackest?" With no hesitation, Hoover responded, "I should say around three a.m."[24] The president could be self-deprecating. Speaking at the Gridiron Club in December 1932, soon after his humiliating defeat for reelection, Hoover observed: "You will expect me to discuss the late election. Well, as nearly as I can learn," he deadpanned, "we did not have enough votes on our side."[25]

Some of the president's wit reflected his sense of irony. For example, he told the story of a young boy who had asked him for three autographs. "Why three?" he asked. The youth responded that in swapping autographs it took three Hoovers to get one Babe Ruth.[26] During the banking panic, Hoover related the story about a circus in which the animals were starving. The owner had to kill the lion and feed him to the tigers. Soon afterward, the gorilla starved. A jobless banker applied for a job, and the circus owner agreed to dress him as a gorilla and permit him to perform. Shortly, the lion charged out of his cage and the frightened banker-gorilla screamed for help. "Shut up, you fool!" said the lion. "You're not the only banker out of a job!"[27]

Most people who knew Hoover, friend or foe, recognized the superb quality of his mind. Perhaps not more than a half-dozen presidents were his mental equal. A man who was not an admirer commented that Hoover had "a better mental engine than anyone else in Washington."[28] In a city of small minds and big egos, Hoover was the reverse. He was resourceful and imaginative, with a memory so retentive he could reel off facts and figures months after a briefing without ever taking notes. He appeared at cabinet meetings without papers, prepared to spontaneously discuss any matter on the agenda. Engaged in problem solving, he could resolve one issue and shift to a totally unrelated one in the twinkling of an eye.[29] He was both quick and deep, blessed with sound judgment, not easily discouraged. His mind rarely turned off. When he slept, it turned off for a few hours and flicked back on. His assistant, James H. MacLafferty, who had spent a lifetime in politics and business, wrote in his diary, "I have never come in contact with a mind that was the equal of that possessed by Herbert Hoover."[30] Joslin wrote that Hoover had "almost superhuman grasp of detail" yet never lost sight of the big picture.[31] Over the course of his lifetime, Hoover consistently amazed and impressed those he met. John Maynard Keynes, who became well acquainted with Hoover at Versailles, remarked that Hoover, "imported into the Councils of Paris, when he took part in them, precisely that atmosphere of reality, knowledge, magnanimity, and disinterestness which, if they had been found in other quarters also, would have given us the Good Peace."[32] In 1930, the faculty at the Villanova School of Technology in Pennsylvania chose Hoover as one of the 10 greatest engineers of the last 25 years. Others on the list included Thomas A. Edison, George W. Westinghouse, Guglielmo Marconi, and Henry Ford.[33] Yet Hoover was no more simply an engineer than Picasso was merely a painter. He remembered not only facts and figures but people and places. Inscribed in his memory were not only the infinite details of things he had read and heard but the events of his life. These resonated not only in his mind but within his emotions. His learning was derived from books, experience, and people, all available at instant recall.[34]

Despite his active mind, ferocious drive, and encyclopedia of experiences, Hoover was a man of moderate habits, versatile, yet accustomed to a productive routine. He managed his time efficiently, exercised patience, was normally genial, and was collegial rather than dictatorial. Though he became frustrated, he rarely complained or blamed others. Impeccably reliable and punctual, if he accepted a task he would strive to resolve it. He disliked injustice, instinctively trusted people, and never forgot a kindness. He was an exceptionally organized, orderly administrator who rarely took notes or wrote memos. The president, though aware that many of his countrymen hated him, lacked physical fear and never lost his poise. He had reasonable, measured goals, yet considered no task impossible, though possibly not on a rigid timetable. He did not gloat over successes and was undaunted by failures. The label "do-nothing" has never been more inaccurately applied or more maliciously. If there were some who took comfort in Hoover's failures, he never took comfort in anyone's failure. Those who were told he did not care and disdained the needy and accepted it gullibly did not know him well. If there were flaws in Hoover's personality, they were, to some extent, connected to his redeeming qualities. His lack of showmanship was a type of humility. His lack of outward emotion was a reflection of unusual equanimity, which concealed smoldering passions. Though he could be stubborn and self-righteous, among our presidents of substance, he was one of the more flexible. One must accept a man holistically.[35]

Some men are loved, and others are merely respected. By those who knew him intimately, Hoover was both. The president was sincere, and his actions were consonant with his words. He never betrayed a trust and his fidelity to his family and friends was absolute. In research stretching over nearly a decade, this writer has never found a case of Hoover committing a single self-serving lie, though on occasions, he was simply wrong. But he never lied or distorted the truth to further his own ambitious. His fiscal honesty was coupled with intellectual honesty. Hoover never said anything, correctly or mistakenly, that was merely expedient or that he did not believe at the time. That does not mean that he revealed everything he knew. To have done so might have precipitated a financial panic or an international incident. But he came as close to telling the literal truth at all times as any president. His conscience would not permit him to do otherwise. Although politics can be a dirty business, it never soiled Hoover. Though he was an idealist, he was also eminently practical, a man of thought and a man of action. He thought problems through to their ultimate conclusions and then resolved them to the extent possible. Although he wanted to succeed, he was not a perfectionist; he would not dwell indefinitely on one problem to the exclusion of others. Knowledge, he believed, lay in knowing what to do next. Wisdom lay in doing it.

Hoover never developed the hard cynicism of professional politicians. He believed in the American system of government and in the American people, though he had no illusions about the perfectibility of either. He told a young man who inquired about entering public life never to compromise his principles. If he found he was required to do that, he should serve humanity in another line of work. When he departed the presidency, his reputation was tattered, but his integrity remained intact. Hoover had never been patronizing, nor had he ever been subservient. He embraced challenges and never feared anything, including failure. He did not want an easy job. He enjoyed plunging into the unknown, but not recklessly, not without knowing the consequences. He believed imagination had to be harnessed; otherwise it might serve humanity's dark side. It is this poetic, reasoned side of Hoover's temperament that kept him from becoming an advocate of runaway development, a supernationalist like Theodore Roosevelt, or an uncompromising idealist such as Woodrow Wilson, two contemporaries he admired. If he was a technocrat at all, he was a technocrat with a heart, who wanted to heal the nation, to make the system work, to combine mental toughness with human empathy. All setbacks were temporary, he believed. The only thing he wanted for himself was the satisfaction that he had done his best.[36]

Hoover's most significant personality trait was his individualism. He was anticommunist and anti–big government because he believed they stifled individualism. He resisted any ideology that represented regimentation. He derived much of this philosophy from Quakerism, some from personal experience. From boyhood on, there was a streak of individualism, a desire to explore the boundaries of science, humanity, and government that were integral to his being. He believed individuals have a right to fail, as well as to succeed, and that the government should not do things for people that they could do for themselves. He wanted to reconcile individualism with the new industrial state to show that men and machines could coexist in harmony. Although he disliked collectivism, Hoover did not believe the strong should be permitted to crush the weak. He believed in regulation and fair play, and he opposed industrial monopoly and the accumulation of inherited wealth. As a Progressive, he believed strongly in regulation, such as antitrust laws, but within limits, not to the degree that they strangled individual initiative. He disliked class or caste prerogatives and wanted to treat people as individuals, irrespective of race, religion, wealth, occupation, or personal belief. America, he believed, was virtually unique in the fluid nature of its society. He was not a Social Darwinist and explicitly eschewed "rugged individualism." He admired

Lincoln's simplicity and democratic ideals and disliked the attitude that one person was superior to another. He did not, however, believe that everything a person achieved in life was due solely to good luck. Men deserved to keep the rewards of their labors, which were inherently unequal. Pure equality was purely hypothetical.[37]

Some traits that contributed to Hoover's successes in humanitarian undertakings prior to 1929, and that endeared him to his friends, became political liabilities once he ascended to the White House. These were chiefly political failures rather than policy or human failures. Hoover was not a born politician and nothing could make him one. Because he realized this about himself, he did not try to act out of character. He believed that would be a masquerade, intellectually dishonest, and would be placing selfish political motives ahead of the more important work he was meant to do for the country. The presidency was an outlet for his prodigious ability to work, not a vehicle to attract fame or glory or to perpetuate himself in office. He was the opposite of a narcissistic personality. This was a lifelong trait. As he was wrapping up his mission to feed Belgium during World War I, the American Ambassador to Britain Walter Hines Page said of Hoover, "He's a simple, modest, energetic little man who began his career in California and will end it in Heaven; and he doesn't want anybody's thanks."[38]

The president took a no-nonsense approach to his job. He treated it seriously, not as a forum for personal popularity. Instead of publicizing his achievements and giving the public an opportunity to savor them, he moved on rapidly to the next job. He did not believe public relations were an important part of his job; in fact, it distracted him from dealing with important problems. Not only did he conceal his good deeds, performing some of his contributions anonymously, but he did not provide the public or the press, who were naturally curious, with a peek at the private life of the First Family. This led many to conclude, erroneously, that he was drab, uninteresting, and single-minded. It also misled people into believing that he was a passive president, just the opposite of reality.[39]

Hoover complicated his lack of mass charisma by an aversion to the type of activities that many presidents had accepted as routine and that would have reaped him goodwill. For example, he refused to autograph scores of footballs sent to him that were to be sold at charitable auctions. Further, he failed to issue routine endorsements of charitable causes, except for a single annual proclamation praising the Red Cross. This did not extend to local branches of the Red Cross that were conducting drives for the needy. The president could have simply delegated a member of his staff to sign the footballs and write brief charitable blurbs, but he considered this dishonest. Hoover even declined to provide a statement for a tribute to the great Notre Dame football coach Knute Rockne after his death in a plane crash. This was honesty to a fault. Many of the cold receptions Hoover received were due to his own silence. He simply was not savvy in a political sense and probably would not have considered it a compliment of someone had said he was a good politician. He identified that type of politics with Harding's cronyism and glibness. Though no reasonable person would have wanted to exchange Hoover for Harding, the Quaker was overly defensive around the press and unaccustomed to intense scrutiny. None of the things that come naturally to an experienced politician came easily to Hoover. At some conferences, reporters virtually had to drag words out of him. He would not allow his staff to humanize him, to allow photographs of him fishing or having fun. His presidency lacked emotional punch. Too often, he tried to overintellectualize, to convey his messages solely by words without feelings.[40]

Hoover was in fact an intensely passionate and creative man, suppressing smoldering sexual energy, with the drive of a locomotive contained beneath a calm exterior. Perceived as insensitive to human suffering, he was instead too sensitive to reexperience the trauma of the hunger of the Depression, which he had witnessed in Europe during the Great War. He cared so strongly that he feared he might expose himself to ridicule by shedding tears in public. He believed presidents and generals were supposed to be strong, unflappable, iron-willed, leaders, overcoming human emotions lest the nation lose heart. As a Quaker youth, Hoover had learned to accept tragedy and celebration stoically, and it became a lifelong trait but a vice in politics.[41]

Hoover did not demonstrate much emotion in public, nor evoke much. He did not appear amiable, yet he was also too gentlemanly to attack opponents. He believed the synthetic view of the personas some politicians presented to their constituents was hypocritical. A biographer commented that "he overlooks a million chances no politician should overlook."[42] Hoover's lack of superficial charm extended beyond the general public to other politicians. He preferred to work by indirection and let others take the credit. He did not like the role of party leader and never relished political combat, even in self-defense. Following the tradition of most of his predecessors, especially initially, he did not lobby congressmen directly, except for House and Senate leaders and chairs of important committees. He adhered to some positions interminably, which damaged him politically. Hoover would not do things solely for political expediency, such as trading patronage for votes. The president was interested in issues, not political details. He rarely tongue-lashed congressmen, but he was not in the habit of false flattery either. If one received a compliment from the president, it was genuine. He was operating on alien territory. Most politicians, even those who respected him, which included most, had never met anyone like him. Maybe there had never been anyone like him in the White House nor has there been since. A Republican Congressman summed it up when he said, "He didn't know where the votes came from."[43]

This might have been true at the outset of Hoover's administration, but he improved on the job, though it never came naturally. He wrested a great deal of important legislation from a divided Congress. Hoover's overall legislative record was substantial, and it was better in the Seventy-Second Congress, controlled largely by Democrats, than in the Seventy-First Congress, in which his own party held more seats. He even extracted some of his most innovative measures in the volatile election year of 1932, including the Reconstruction Finance Corporation, the Glass-Steagall Credit Act, the Home Loan Bank Act, and the Emergency Relief and Construction Act.[44]

Hoover did not want to be a partisan president and only reluctantly, and rather late, did he accept the role of party leader. He did not enjoy the camaraderie of politics. He preferred to let Postmaster Brown, who had worked as one of his assistants in the Commerce Department, handle patronage. Nonetheless, Hoover was a forceful personality and a strong president, the dominant figure in Washington during his administration. By 1932, he was willing to lobby harder for his program, which included inviting congressmen, whose votes he needed, to the White House. The chief executive learned to work with men he did not like. He had learned from his early mistakes, was less brusque, and chatted more with other politicians. Hoover's kindness was evident when he broke away from work and shared memories with old friends or talked comfortably with children. Whatever the crisis, he never raised his voice. He broke the habit of drawing intricate doodles during conversations, about halfway through his presidency and learned to look visitors directly in the eye, rather than staring at his shoes.[45]

From Daniel Webster and John C. Calhoun to John F. Kennedy and Ronald Reagan, Americans have pulsated to powerful orators. No one would rate Hoover among them, another of his political liabilities. Hoover wrote his own speeches, laboriously, the last president to do so. They were better in content than in style and delivery. They were fact-filled and tightly organized, written more for the eye than the ear.[46] Hoover did not enjoy speaking, and it showed. He stared down at his printed script, rarely looking at his audience, showed little spontaneity, and spoke in monotone, with virtually no inflection or facial expression. If one listened closely, he could find a sparkling epigram here and there, but few listened that closely. Hoover detested bombast and pretention, and he purged his speeches of both. They were informative, but one could be overwhelmed by detail. The logic was convincing, but the delivery bored listeners. Hoover was not equipped to be a cheerleader during the Depression and did not feel that it was his job. Further, speaking to the masses was one of the few tasks that intimidated him. "I have never liked the clamor of crowds," the Quaker president admitted. "I intensely dislike superficial social contacts. I made no pretentions to oratory and I was terrorized at the opening of every speech."[47]

Temperamentally, the president was not equipped to persuade the masses. He lacked dynamism and his style was bland. He did not rehearse his speeches extensively as some presidents do. The message was paramount, the words were secondary. As a radio speaker, he was better. Since his years at Commerce, he had recognized the potential of radio, though he no more enjoyed speaking into a microphone than to a crowd of strangers. As president, Hoover utilized radio more than any of his predecessors, and his cabinet members spoke via the airwaves extensively. Often historians have compared Hoover's effectiveness as a speaker only to his successor, one of the better speakers of the century. Placed in a broader context, Hoover appears better. He was more effective than Harding, who called his own speaking style "bloviating." It was characterized by long, meaningless words virtually devoid of content. Coolidge was a worse speaker than Hoover. On radio, Hoover sounded better than Al Smith, William Howard Taft, Warren G. Harding, Calvin Coolidge, and Alfred Landon and was comparable to Harry Truman and Dwight D. Eisenhower. After FDR, the first president who excelled at public speaking was John F. Kennedy. Reagan was also a virtuoso. But whether via public speaking to the masses; communicating more openly with journalists; or creating a more human, lively image of his personality, no amount of manufactured publicity could have saved Hoover from the dreadful stigma of the Depression. What the nation demanded went beyond oratorical eloquence to the magic of Harry Houdini. Even Houdini produced not magic, but the illusion of magic.

The president refused to deliver a speech unless he had something important to say. Hoover took writing seriously, and he did not believe anyone could convey his convictions as explicitly as he could. He did not enjoy writing, even though he wrote prodigiously. Judged solely on style, Hoover's presidential speeches are mediocre. Judged on content, they are meaty. The president wanted to persuade by the logic of his thought. He did not speak to entertain or dazzle, but to inform and educate. A relentless writer, he labored ceaselessly and in his postpresidential years became witty, erudite, and inspiring. The role of the presidential staff was to research facts, but the president did not permit them to alter his words. Once he started a speech he could not rest until it was complete. Speeches sometimes went through 10 or 15 drafts. Sometimes Hoover would awaken late at night to scribble ideas and revisions.[48]

Yet Hoover was as tenacious a writer as he was at any other task he undertook. His prose was neither florid nor rousing, but his ideas made common sense. Tightly woven, the addresses were direct and tangible, rarely leavened with anecdotes or humor. There was often an underlying moral and spiritual tone. The president was never arrogant and rarely boastful. He strove to make every word count. He was excessively cautious, afraid to be spontaneous. The GOP leader polished infinitely.[49]

Hoover followed the same routine in composing each address. Working alone in the Lincoln Study, often until late at night, he wrote the first draft in pencil, in longhand. He edited it painstakingly, striving to pack in all the relevant information without much regard for order or literary style. He read his first draft repeatedly, set it aside overnight, and examined it again the next morning. Then he submitted the draft to a stenographer, who typed it in triple space, to facilitate further editing. Hoover reduced writing to a mechanical process. One friend complained that he beat the life out of every sentence. He ruthlessly eliminated words and searched for others that expressed his thoughts better. The president was patient. He circulated copies of drafts for critical readings, but rejected ornate language. After several rounds of editing, he had the most recent draft retyped to clean it up. It took a well-trained stenographer to interpret his handwriting. While he worked, a stenographer remained on duty until 10 p.m. each evening. The president himself stayed up much later. Now he began the editing anew, shifting around words and paragraphs. This was the beginning of the organizational stage. He arranged his notes on long sheets of paper and graduated from using a pencil to a fountain pen. Every sentence, every phrase, every paragraph must occupy its exact place. Finally, he took scissors and cut his secretary's typed copy into pieces resembling a jigsaw puzzle. He placed them on the floor and rearranged them until he was satisfied. But many times, he remained unsatisfied. Some speeches continued to be revised until a few minutes before he delivered them.[50]

Hoover's second press secretary, Joslin, believed that if his boss had devoted as much time to polishing his speaking style as he did to honing his prose, the time would have been better spent. Yet there was a medium in which Hoover excelled as a speaker; in which he could be persuasive, witty, and relaxed; in which he could be himself. As a communicator before small groups, especially when content superseded delivery, Hoover could be persuasive, even magnetic, because he was not trying to perform. The strength of his words and the sincerity of his convictions became clear, as did his wit. His capacity for understatement could charm. Anyone who had listened to Hoover as director of the Commission for the Relief of Belgium (CRB) or as Food Administrator during World War I would have found incredulous the idea that he lacked inspirational qualities. He had inspired the world to feed starving nations, and then he inspired Americans to win the war by conserving food. William Allen White described Hoover after hearing him speak for the CRB in 1915: "The whole group . . . was mesmerized by the strange low voltage of his magnetism." Hamilton Holt, who initially met Hoover in Paris in 1919, commented, "Never have I been more enthralled by the charm of the spoken word or by sheer brilliancy of thought, analysis, and exposition. I was in the presence of a master."[51] As director of the CRB, he stood toe-to-toe with such British luminaries as Prime Ministers Herbert Asquith and David Lloyd George. He challenged the German General Moritz von Bissing and even went over his head to Berlin. Hoover's inspired leadership was situational.[52]

Though not inveterately outwardly observant as an adult, Hoover always lived by the internal Quaker creed. Hoover took the doctrine of the Inner Light seriously and lived by it daily. His speeches and his writing are sprinkled with spiritual aphorisms. Quakerism was founded in England by George Fox and brought to American by William Penn. Many immigrated to obtain religious freedom. The name derived from the admonition that they were to "quake" in the presence of the Lord. Hoover's ancestors were Quakers on both sides of his family for many generations, and some had been ministers and influential leaders. They migrated to the upper South and then to the fertile plains of Iowa for better opportunities and to escape slavery. Quakers were among the early abolitionists; by the end of the 1700s no Quaker in good standing was a slaveholder. They also treated Indians justly because they conceived of all men as brothers. Though it conflicted with their equally strong commitment to pacifism, some, including Hoover's uncle John Henry Minthorn, enlisted in the Union Army to abolish slavery and save the Union. Minthorn served in the medical corps, not the infantry, but he believed in self-defense.[53]

Quakers stripped Protestantism of ceremony and ornamentation. Their meetinghouses are plain, without altars or music. Seating is segregated by gender. In traditional services silence prevails until a member is inspired to speak. Later, some Quakers, such as Hoover's mother Huldah, became unpaid "recorded" ministers and the liberal Quakers introduced music into the services. Hoover preferred the traditional, largely silent form of service. Quakers broke with the dominant European denominations at the time they emerged. They oppose Puritan original sin and Calvinist predestination. The sect has no rigid dogma; each individual interprets the Bible according to his or her Inner Light, the Divine Spark within each human. Quakers trust that God will reveal their purpose in life. They respect all types of work, whether mental or manual, which contribute to society, however humble. Quakers are strongly antielitist. They value education, and many are important social and educational reformers, far greater than their percentage of the population. Their purpose is to serve others rather than accumulate idle fortunes; they disdain displays of wealth or ostentations homes or dress; and they have produced philanthropists in disproportionate numbers to their miniscule percentage of the population. Children are expected to obey their parents and master a useful skill, yet Quakers usually rely on affection and cooperation, not compulsion. Helping the downtrodden is part of their obligation, but the downtrodden are also expected to work.[54]

Quakers are goal oriented; while they believe in life hereafter, the denomination focuses on practical deeds wedded to ideals. President Hoover said, "Ideals without illusions are good. Ideals with illusions are no good."[55] A generation later, President John F. Kennedy, who admired Hoover, paraphrased the Quaker president by describing himself as an idealist who had no illusions. Quakers study scripture, yet their formal creed is limited to a few fundamental principles, and church attendance, while encouraged, is a matter of individual conscience. While serious, most Quakers do not obsess over guilt or the prospect of a fiery hell. They reach their conclusions thoughtfully and follow their conscience. Though Quakers are independent, they are unselfish. In the period Hoover grew up, a communitarian tradition prevailed; they often moved in groups, usually to rural areas. They were upwardly mobile. Part of Hoover's love of the outdoors was an outgrowth of his Quaker rearing, as well as his exposure to woods, prairies, lakes, and streams in a relatively pristine environment. Quakers like Hoover see God in nature, indeed, in all things.

One can see, in the adult Hoover, many Quaker traits. He was serious, industrious, inner-directed, generous, thrifty, and an individualist. His earnestness and prudence are Quaker traits, as well as his honesty. Quakers did not need contracts when dealing with each other; the agreements were based on trust. Quakers are strong willed yet restrained in their actions, withholding temper tantrums, letting go of grudges. They are nondemonstrative in the sense of public affection, which is considered a private matter. Hoover's ancestors, like him, believed in order, and that sound decisions were grounded in common sense. Although abandoned by assimilated Quakers, such as Hoover, his ancestors used the biblical language of "thee" and "thou" rather than "you" and "your," another attempt to be plain, simple, and direct. Like his fellow Quakers, Hoover considered excessive materialism tasteless; material things were ephemeral, he believed, as was fame and the acclaim of crowds. Pride could lead to excessive ego. Hoover believed free men had free choices, including the choice to make their own mistakes, and he was generally tolerant of human folly. He did not believe those choices were absolute; some doors were open, others were not. He never took for granted the opportunities offered, nor despaired at setbacks.[56]

Hoover was more inwardly spiritual than outwardly observant. "Fortunately, I belong to a faith that does not depend on outward ceremony," he told a reporter.[57] This, however, did not diminish the profound impact of his faith. "I cannot conceive of a wholesome social order or a sound economic system that does not have its roots in religious faith," he said.[58] When a high school student asked him how he might become a better citizen, Hoover replied that it was essential to have religious convictions. Like other Quakers, Hoover was determined to pursue his own course, regardless of its popularity. Joan Hoff points out that Hoover's Quaker upbringing contributed to his rejection of moral relativism as an adult. During his years abroad, he largely lost touch with his Quaker roots, yet when he returned to the United States permanently, he renewed them. Early in 1929, as he settled into the White House, he planned and helped finance the construction of a small conservative meetinghouse. Lou, though a Presbyterian, always attended services with her husband and agreed with Quaker doctrine. The president invited Stanford classics professor Augustus T. Murray to become minister at the Friends' meetinghouse they attended. When the new, traditional meetinghouse was completed in 1932, Murray returned to Stanford.[59]

Quakers began their religious experience as dissenters, and Hoover respected the right of dissent. Yet some Quaker practices, and their militant allegiance to their beliefs, irritated others, especially atheists, agnostics, or other churches whose doctrines conflicted. Humans tend to be suspicious, even critical, of those who are different, especially those who are deliberately so. We build fences to keep intrusive neighbors out, yet also wall ourselves in.

The distinctive dress and the style of religious observance of Quakers can be obvious. Some consider it threatening, others merely quaint. As nonconformists, they are the objects of curiosity. Quakers can be self-righteous, and even if they are right in principle, this annoys people who consider them too rigid, insular, set in their ways. Their industriousness can make others appear indolent by comparison. They can be tenacious, stubborn, and resistant to change. They prefer to marry within their sect, though many, like Hoover, do not. He accepted minor vices, such as alcohol and tobacco, and sometimes fished or worked on Sundays. Few Quakers are fanatics because tolerance is one of the cornerstones of their creed.

In a larger sense, the fact that Hoover was a Quaker was more important than the fact that John Kennedy was a Catholic. Kennedy's religion was more outward and symbolic. Hoover did not necessarily find God between the walls of a church. As a Quaker, he believed he was a part of God and God was a part of him. They do not honor high position, but rather purity of heart. They seek, above all else in life, peace of mind. Hoover was not a typical Quaker, though he derived many traits from his religion. He had a superb mind and ferocious drive. He remained all his life, a Quaker in the things that mattered. Motive counted, not simply what one did, but why he acted. That is why he believed government should be a last resort rather than a first resort, because it lacked a heart. Government solutions were impermanent and represented the easy way out. They allowed individuals to evade the lessons they learned from becoming self-sufficient and the lessons other people learned from helping those in need. He favored private charity not simply because it aided the needy, but because it ennobled the giver.

The president was steeped in Quaker thought. He read books on Quakerism while secretary of commerce and president. Among the books he checked out from the Library of Congress in 1927 alone were *The Quakers*; *Quakerism and Its Applications to Modern Problems*; *Quakers in War and Peace*; *Quakerism and Politics*; and *Quaker Thought and History*.[60] Hoover also knew the Bible thoroughly. He wrote in 1927 that scriptures had been an extremely significant influence in his life. As a child, he had read the Bible daily, and his prodigious memory stored it indelibly. Ray Lyman Wilbur remembered an occasion in Washington when a delegation of ministers was visiting Hoover. One of the ministers was quoting an Old Testament verse when he stammered, having forgotten the ending. The president completed it for him.[61] Hoover spoke of God and the Bible as beacons that guided his life. On May 6, 1929, he informed a religious convention: "There is no other book so various as the Bible, nor one so full of concentrated wisdom. As a nation we are indebted to this book of books for our national ideals and representative institutions."[62] Elaborating on the central role played by religion in a secure society, the president made it clear that material accomplishments alone could not provide a sound foundation for any nation. "Economic aspiration, though it strongly marks the American system, is not an end in itself," he said, "but is only one of many instruments to accomplish the profound purposes of the American people, which are largely religious in origin." Beyond matter, he felt certain, lies a more permanent realm.[63]

Despite the Depression, Hoover's faith was never shaken. Much of his confidence and self-disciple was also grounded in his faith. But if God provided the inspiration, it remained for him to do the work. He was God's servant, not vice versa. There was nothing wrong with material success, but it did not completely satisfy him. It was ephemeral. It could not be the basis of individual or national greatness. Rather, self-reliance and reliance on God were the creeds by which Hoover lived. Happiness was a gift of God. If one had it, no way could take it away. If a person lacked it, he could not obtain it from someone else, including the government.[64]

Hoover approached the presidency with grand, but not grandiose, expectations. The opportunities and expectations dwarfed his previous experiences. Now no one stood above him to accept ultimate praise or blame. He must range over the entire spectrum of national problems; he could no longer focus solely on those in which he had a special interest; it was not a niche job, like the ones he had held. He knew the president was a magnet for criticism. He rarely complained; after all, he had asked for the job. Hoover knew reform had lagged since the Great War, and he wanted to rebuild the momentum. His ambition was to catch up, to reach into the recesses of neglect, to become an activist president. The new president was no lover of bigness, whether big government, big business, or big fortunes. He wanted to streamline and decentralize government, break up monopoly, regulate monopoly in the few situations that it proved necessary, and disperse big fortunes via high inheritance and estate taxes.   Hoover believed that human leadership should spring from the grass roots, abetted by public education. He considered the family the building block of democracy. The president preferred small towns, especially farming communities, to the cities in which he spent much of his adult life and found peace of mind in the outdoors. He considered strong bodies repositories for strong minds. Hoover believed in individuality, in self-discipline, and that the only type of morality that really counted was when no one was looking. He believed in self-help and in helping neighbors. If government help was essential, it should begin at the local level, ascend to the state level, and should be undertaken at the national level only when the private sector and lower forms of government closer to the people were exhausted. Still, he believed in aggressive government action when the situation demanded it. However, the bureaucracy created to solve temporary problems should be temporary, not the closest thing on earth to eternal life. He detested bureaucracy in all its forms. Bureaucracies were inherently inefficient, inflexible, and self-perpetuating. If there was a need for something, he wanted it taken care of in the simplest, most direct, most humane manner possible. He knew that bureaucracies lacked a human touch and were wasteful, skimming off a great deal of their assets in overhead.[65]

Hoover defined his philosophy, a synthesis, partly borrowed from his personal experience, in his 1922 book, *American Individualism*. It might have warmed the hearts of Jefferson and Franklin. Although not a thorough, theoretical, abstract system, neither was it simply a compilation of platitudes. Hoover was more thoughtful, reflective, and introspective than most modern American presidents and more well read. The central tenet was equality of opportunity protected by the state. This type of individualism, which might be called "Quaker individualism," emanated from the Divine Spark within each human heart. He made it clear that he was not talking about nineteenth-century Social Darwinism, laissez-faire, "rugged individualism" in which "the Devil take the hindmost." No, his type of individualism was a meritocracy with a heart. It was predicated on a fluid society different from other nations. Hoover did not believe that anyone, including the government, could guarantee equality of outcome or that either the rich or the poor were necessarily parasitic. He felt a personal and social obligation to help those who failed—up to a point. But there were boundaries to the degree he would permit the government to intervene in the economy. Hoover's philosophy was premised on the idea that most people were well meaning and could help themselves, but not everyone, in every circumstance. The president did not view the people as masses, or classes, or races but as individual human beings. He believed that life consisted partly of luck but that hard work and native ability were necessary for success too. Humans have choices, but not unlimited ones.[66]

Hoover believed that communism and socialism seductively promised more than they could deliver. The vow to engineer a society of absolute economic equality, premised on equality of ability and character, was utopian. It was based on a degree of altruism that was unrealistic, and the arrogance that industrial managers could assign individuals to jobs more effectively than individuals could choose for themselves. Such views were utopian, based on a romantic view of human nature. Motivation based on individual initiation was the mother of plenty. The Soviet Union, which had resources comparable to the United States, could not even produce enough to feed and clothe its own people. Socialized industry in Europe had reduced productivity and living standards. Hoover disliked the degree of coercion produced by communism and believed it created a creaky bureaucracy. Ultimately, the system would collapse under the weight of its own top-heavy administration. He was right in principle but misjudged the time it would take and the degree of oppression employed to keep it alive. Further, as a society predicated solely on materialism, communism suppressed some basic human needs. Like other inventions of arrogant humans designed to produce a Heaven on Earth, its outcome was just the opposite. Few Americans of his time had seen communism up close or analyzed it so carefully.[67] "The will-o'-the wisp of all breeds of socialism is that they contemplate a motivation of human animals by altruism alone," Hoover wrote. "We in America have had too much experience of life to fool ourselves into pretending that all men are equal in ability, in character, in intelligence, in ambition. That was part of the claptrap of the French Revolution."[68]

Hoover did not believe in fighting ideologies with guns. He was not an absolute pacifist, as were some Quakers, but he came close. Still, he had supported World War I and would support World War II, which he initially opposed, after Pearl Harbor. The Great War, which he had witnessed first-hand, had been the most formative experience of his adult life. It had reinforced his Quaker detestation of carnage and chaos in a way that never left his mind, especially the deaths of civilians, the orphaned waifs, and the famines that followed in wake of war. War was also the enemy of sustained prosperity and caused wanton waste. Hoover believed that war and revolution often arose from economic disparities and political instability. Democratic, middle-class nations rarely waged war of their own volition, he thought. Repression often led to radicalism and war. War was usually unjust, but sometimes it was just. The bitter legacy of the Great War could have been mitigated by a more generous peace. He would have the opportunity to offer similar counsel after the carnage of a yet greater war.[69]

Hoover believed in human progress, yet at a measured, orderly pace. The government should both stimulate and regulate to ensure that the pace of progress neither dashed ahead like the Mad Hatter nor tarried like the Tortoise. Politically and in personality, he was a moderate who served as president during an era when center field was a lonely position. The government must not overreact by proposing solutions that were inappropriate for existing problems, he insisted. It should concentrate on solving immediate problems and not tamper with institutions that had served the nation well; it should refrain from fixing things that were not broken. Americans must realize that many of the problems of the 1930s were due to human mistakes. They should not abandon the system but instead punish the mistaken individuals. They must also understand that not all human problems have solutions, at least not rapid ones, and that humans are not perfectible. Conversely, this meant trying harder, not giving up. It meant never taking the easy way out, or dismissing complexity with glibness. Hoover might have been a more popular president if he had been glib with tongue and pen, but he would not have been true to himself. Though many criticized Hoover and blamed him for the Depression, they were unsure what lessons to take from the economic collapse.[70] Hoover's approach to intricate problems was to preserve; avoid panic; and take practical, incremental steps. "Wisdom consists more in a perception of what to do next than it does in knowledge of the ultimate," he advised.[71]

CHAPTER 4

A Whirling Dervish

Herbert Hoover embarked on his presidency hoping to fulfill the high expectations of his countrymen. Not since the Wilson administration had a president entered office with an agenda so packed with plans for domestic reform. The president realized that little progress had been accomplished during the 14 years prior to his presidency. After 1914 Wilson had been preoccupied with the Great War. The Harding and Coolidge administrations had been absorbed with reconstruction following the war. Coolidge had also been temperamentally reluctant to undertake new initiatives. Hoover also believed that American foreign policy was due for an overhaul.[1]

The new chief executive yearned to learn the job quickly and embark on his journey riding upon the winds of a favorable economy. His early months sizzled with activity, much of it forgotten after the Great Depression stereotype of him as a laissez-faire president was carved in stone by his detractors. Hoover assembled facts and then acted. Conferences were organized on child health, social waste, housing, national land policy, and public education. The government undertook studies on recent social trends and recent economic trends. The chief executive expanded protection of federal workers, including even postmasters beneath the umbrella of civil service. At the end of the Hoover administration, 95 percent of federal employees were covered. The heads of most bureaus, which had been treated as patronage appointments, were now promoted by merit from within. For the first time, federal employees in the District of Columbia were placed under civil service. Hoover left much of the lesser bureaucracy intact. Wholesale removals would have implied criticism of his predecessor.[2]

Hoover intended to regulate railroad and utility rates, reform the banking system, and reorganize the entire federal bureaucracy. The president released radicals who had been imprisoned during the Red Scare. He demonstrated sympathy for women, minorities, and the disadvantaged. Hoover instructed his director of the budget to plan generous increases in appropriations for the bureaus affecting women, children, and Native Americans. He advocated an anti-injunction law to protect labor. Vowing to run an open administration, he abolished the Office of Official Spokesman. Over Treasury Secretary Mellon's objections, the administration published the amounts of major tax refunds. The president vigorously enforced antitrust laws and intervened to prevent a strike on the Texas and Pacific Railroad. Hoover strove to conserve oil, expand national forests, and rein in stock market speculation. Flood control, river and harbor improvement, and construction of hydroelectric dams in central California and the Tennessee Valley punctuated his agenda. The president sought ratification of a treaty with Canada to construct a St. Lawrence Seaway linking the Atlantic Ocean with the Great Lakes, opening an avenue for farm exports. He intended to tap the best minds in the country, place them at the service of social reform, harness technology, and raise the nation's standard of living. The ambitious newcomer wanted to compile a statistical foundation for reform over a sweeping range of activities. This involved systematic attempt to identify problems and draft remedial regulation, dealing with interrelated issues simultaneously. Instead of basking in the glory of his recent victory, he focused like a laser on his job. Hoover appeared the most apolitical president in memory, a refreshing change after Harding's "Ohio Gang" cronies. Most of Hoover's friends were not politicians. A majority were college graduates, including many Phi Beta Kappas.[3]

Most of the press believed the president had roared out of the gates, in contrast to the somnolent Coolidge. Will Rogers wrote that "[Hoover] has no use for politicians, which fact elected him by the largest majority ever recorded. If he will just continue to hate them, we are liable to wake up with another Lincoln or Jefferson on our hands." Senator Arthur Capper of Kansas added, "Hoover is the best President that this country has had in many years."[4] Those who feared change opposed Hoover and Democrats remained skeptical. Yet the press was mostly positive during his first six months. About a month before the stock market crashed, *The Literary Digest* wrote, "Washington is a center of news these days . . . because a quick-witted and aggressive Executive is plainly on the job."[5] Hoover seemed comfortable in the office, upbeat and eager to attack his tasks. He wanted to build upon his achievements as secretary of commerce. The president sensed opportunities on a larger playing field. "Mr. Hoover smiles as often as he ever did, which is more often than his predecessor," the *New York World* observed. "If he ever loses his temper, the fact is admirably concealed."[6] Hoover appeared a rare creature—a sincere politician. He was homespun, with an optimistic view of human nature, sentimental, technically competent, and analytical yet undergirded by a spiritual and humanistic philosophy. He was confident yet modest. Beyond his formal duties as president, Hoover assumed leadership in voluntary organizations promoting outdoor recreations, scientific research, women's interests, peace movements, city and regional planning, conservation, and education.[7]

Hoover's early actions indicated that, although his style was more aggressive than Coolidge's, he might surpass the Vermonter in fiscal economy. Almost immediately he shut down the White House stables and mothballed the presidential yacht as wasteful accoutrements. As a further economy measure, one constituent wrote to suggest that the president abolish the army and the navy. The Quaker dismissed the idea with a chuckle.[8]

At the heart of the president's reform program was reorganization of the executive branch. He assigned his secretary Walter Newton, a former congressman, the task of researching and developing legislation that he could submit to the first regular session of Congress in December 1929. The president believed the federal bureaucracy represented a patchwork of agencies and bureaus that had grown haphazardly and included overlapping and nonessential responsibilities, which needed to be rationalized. Numerous bureaus performed the same function, and some performed no function. The bureaucracy resembled an overgrown plant that had had not been pruned in decades. Hoover wanted to purge the government of waste, group agencies by function, and place them in more appropriate departments. He considered the prison and court systems, the Shipping Board, and the Veterans Bureau ripe for restructuring. Hoover hoped the savings stemming from a more efficient bureaucracy would facilitate tax reductions. He provided Newton with a general outline and instructed his secretary to flesh out the details. The ex-congressman met stiff opposition, because some of his reforms meant eliminating jobs. In every department, vested interests resisted change. Hoover grappled with the problem of reorganization for the remainder of his presidency. His general reorganization plan, repeatedly pigeonholed, was finally defeated on December 3, 1933, after his loss in the 1932 election. It was one of the major disappointments of his administration. Later, under presidents Truman and Eisenhower, he helped implement long-overdue structural reforms.[9]

Nonetheless, significant accomplishments were implemented. In the fall of 1930 Congress enacted a law placing under the new Veterans Administration the existing Veterans Bureau, the Pensions Bureau, and the National Home for Disabled Volunteer Soldiers, which had existed independently. The bill saved about $800 million annually and delivered more humane and efficient services. Hoover was accustomed to a smoothly operating organization and was appalled by some of the malodorous waste he encountered. The government was like a house that creaked and leaked. For example, Coolidge had signed 29,000 official documents in 1928, which consumed about an hour and a half of the president's time daily. Hoover planned to sign only 1,500 in 1929. An opinion from Attorney General Mitchell freed him to sign lists of federal appointments rather than sign for each individual one. The routine tasks of cabinet members were also streamlined.[10]

During his tenure as secretary of commerce, Hoover developed two major plans for old-age and retirement insurance—one based on a privately operated system and the other, a decentralized government system. He made substantial progress and continued the research during his presidency, although the Great Depression and partisan entanglements ultimately made it impossible to implement either during his term. During a second term he might have succeeded. Initially, Hoover preferred a retirement annuity program operated by the major life insurance companies, such as New York Life or Metropolitan Life. Parents could purchase an annuity for a young child by paying a lump sum, or a worker could buy one at a later time. The money would be invested in safe, interest-bearing bonds that would accumulate over time. The cost to the individual would be less if purchased at an early age. Moreover, funds of individuals who died before retirement age would be placed into the pool, reducing the cost for others. The wealthy would be ineligible, as would any retiree who had a private pension plan, to avoid double-dipping. Hoover recommended that the life insurance companies offer the plans on a group basis to employers, who would purchase them for their workers. The advantages of the plan were that it would utilize the existing bureaucracy of the insurance companies, the largest such infrastructure in the country, and would require little investment by the federal government. The government, however, might step in to insure a small number of individuals who could not afford to purchase annuities. As president, Hoover held several conferences at the White House with insurance executives. On September 29, a month before Wall St. crashed, he invited the executive committee of the National Association of Insurance Underwriters to explore the plan at the White House. He planned a publicity campaign, including a series of articles in national magazines such as *Ladies Home Journal* and *Forbes* to promote the idea. The president himself would kick off the plan, which would be voluntary, by purchasing annuities for his two grandchildren for $500 each as presents for Christmas 1929. Unfortunately, after the market crashed interest in the plan virtually evaporated. Insurance companies considered it unwise to expand into a new area during a downturn, and individuals were short of cash and thought short term. Ironically, when Hoover had initially proposed the idea as commerce secretary in the 1920s people had been uninterested, believing the prosperity of the decade would last indefinitely, making such insurance unnecessary.

Hoover also devised a second type of plan, this one financed by the government. It was similar to the plan ultimately adopted, with significant differences. Contributions would be made by workers, employers, and the state and federal governments. All workers pay a flat rate and receive a flat rather than a graduated annuity. Hoover studied state-operated systems in nations such as Germany and Britain and in a few American states such as California. Under this plan, funds would be collected by the federal government and allocated to the states, which would distribute them in block grants. Those lacking an employer, such as private businessmen and farmers, would have their contributions matched by the government. The Hoover Plan, as it was known, was ahead of its time. The program, especially the privately operated version, was quite different from the legislation adopted in 1935 and, in some ways, more efficient. According to the program adopted later, funds contributed from employers and employees are not invested. The Treasury may borrow, at quite low interest, from the fund for general purposes. Because money is not invested and does not compound and because of borrowing from it, the money paid to individuals is not commensurate to that paid in. Social security rates have to be raised periodically. Moreover, government officials subject to political pressure administer the program. In 1935, its very first year of operation, the national government began borrowing social security revenues and diverting them to other purposes in order to avoid tax increases. The plan adopted by the federal government was in deep trouble by the first decade of the twenty-first century. The government had habitually borrowed from surpluses without stockpiling benefits for the maturation of the baby boom generation in the new millennium. Moreover, social security benefits were essentially too meager to provide a comfortable standard of living postretirement. Anyone relying solely on social security, without a retirement plan generated from their former employer, would be virtually a pauper. Hoover's plan would have cost the government less and might have returned higher benefits to the recipients, especially since there would have been less likelihood of a fiscal shell game.[11]

In addition to his plans for old-age pensions, Hoover formulated a plan for unemployment insurance. While secretary of commerce, he initiated research by several commissions to investigate the unemployment cycle. He also approached the Metropolitan Life Insurance Company and proposed that they offer policies that would pay policy holders who became unemployed. Some employers might pool their resources to purchase collective unemployment policies for their employees. Meanwhile, during the mid-1920s, several companies and trade associations conducted experiments in establishing unemployment insurance that included contributions from workers and employers. By 1926 there were about 400 unemployment compensation plans offered by individual companies covering more than four million workers. In 1930 and 1931 the General Electric Company experimented with such a plan. The principle obstacle during Hoover's presidency was the New York State Legislature, which refused to license such a program, and the antipathy of New York Governor Franklin D. Roosevelt to such a plan. Most of the largest life insurance companies were geographically headquartered in New York and required state approval. Nonetheless, research continued. Frederick Ecker, the president of Metropolitan, studied foreign programs and also conferred with Hoover at the White House in 1930 and 1931, spending several nights as the president's guest. However, by 1932, the problem of unemployment had become so overwhelming that Metropolitan conceded that its program would have to be implemented under better conditions. Even the National Association of Manufacturers now opposed the idea. Hoover hoped the states might step into the breach, but like the federal government, they were now swamped by the dimensions of the problem that might have been preempted by earlier intervention. In this, as in other respects, Hoover was ahead of his time.[12]

Hoover adopted a systematic approach to reform. The first step was to gather information, next, to analyze it, and finally, to draft remedial legislation. He believed commissions and committees of experts were useful in assembling and disseminating data. The president appointed groups of experts, often including academicians, businessmen, economists, bankers, and sometimes military men, to contribute. He did not accept their recommendations uncritically, but he did take them seriously. The president strongly believed that the government should act cautiously, not impulsively, because it was possible to enact an overload of legislation. Not every problem was susceptible to a legislative solution. Hoover thought each bill should have a practical purpose. Laws should not be enacted to serve political agendas.[13] "The most dangerous animal in the United States is the man with an emotion and a desire to pass a law," he quipped.[14] There was precedent for Hoover's procedure. His twentieth-century predecessors had appointed commissions, as did governors, such as Robert M. LaFollette of Wisconsin and Franklin D. Roosevelt of New York. Congress also appointed commissions, as did cabinet members. By July 1931, 20 commissions were at work, and several had completed their tasks and disbanded. Hoover did not consider commissions and committees excuses for inaction, but vehicles to prod responsible action. Moreover, they were preferable to enlarging the bureaucracy to undertake such research because they expired when their assignment ended. Many were staffed by volunteers, and most were funded by private philanthropy. Among the problems on which the commissions focused were child health, law enforcement and prison reform, conservation of the public domain, erection of a San Francisco Bay bridge, reorganization of the government of Haiti, reduction of the cost of the military, illiteracy, and unemployment. Some recommendations for dealing with the Depression originated from their work. In pioneering efforts, Hoover appointed committees to study the cost of medical care and to develop plans for security in old age.[15]

In a long-term perspective that had repercussions long after Hoover's term ended, perhaps the most important studies were conducted by the Committee on Recent Economic Changes and the Committee on Recent Social Trends. The former was appointed while Hoover was secretary of commerce and completed its study in 1928. As president, Hoover asked it to expand its work to include the economic downturn of 1929–30. It provided the most thorough investigation then available of the causes and potential resolution of the Depression. Like Hoover's other commissions and committees, it was nonpartisan and provided statistical and other evidence that has proved useful to subsequent economists and social scientists. Part of its value is that the data was gathered while it was fresh. Individuals with knowledge of current events could be interviewed while their memories were fresh and while they were still alive. Even at this early stage, the president recognized that the Depression was a historic event and that fugitive evidence should be preserved.[16]

The Committee on Recent Social Trends, a much larger undertaking, was the most ambitious study of American social problems conducted under the auspices of the federal government up to that time. Hoover had hoped that it would provide a factual, analytical basis for reform during his second term, but his defeat in 1932 prevented that. Nonetheless, the completed research provides not only a panorama of information but fascinating insights into Hoover's plans for a second administration and about his attitude toward social reform in general. On December 19, 1929, the president announced creation of the committee, whose purpose was to examine the entire spectrum of American social problems through the lens of social science, to summarize them, and to recommend remedial action. The president himself and Secretary Wilbur had been active in selecting many of the members, which included the chair, Wesley C. Mitchell, professor of economics at Columbia University, and such eminent academics as Charles E. Merriam and Howard W. Odum. French Strother, the president's research analyst served as the White House liaison. Approximately 300 social scientists participated in the study. Although Hoover was eager to receive and digest the information, some of the scholars lacked his sense of urgency and wanted to incorporate the results of the 1930 census, which delayed completion.[17]

Although the Committee on Recent Social Trends was highly praised both during the 1930s and thereafter, the president's overall strategy of employing committees of experts to delve into complex issues was criticized by some and even ridiculed by his political opponents in subsequent campaigns. Ironically, some of the same partisans who ridiculed Hoover praised FDR for use of his Brain Trust and raised Robert LaFollette to iconic stature for the "Wisconsin Idea" in which he employed academic experts at the University of Wisconsin as a network of advisers to make recommendations for legislation. In his own time, part of the criticism involved a "turf war" with Congress, which argued that the president was trespassing on its prerogative to investigate. Others, including some journalists and historians, dismissed the commissions as excuses for delaying action or ignoring it altogether. Under some administrations ideas might have entered a committee only to never return, but this was not true of most of the Hoover commissions, though some disagreed among their own members and others petered out. Moreover, Hoover's defense is reasonable. He pointed out that he had appointed substantially fewer commissions than Theodore Roosevelt, Woodrow Wilson, or Calvin Coolidge during their first four years of office. If one examined the entire terms of his predecessors, the total appointed by Hoover was lower than that of any twentieth-century president except Harding, who died after three years. Moreover, only seven of Hoover's commissions received public funds, and only four outlived his presidency. In fact, Congress itself was prolific in spawning investigating committees, and all information collected by Hoover's committees was transmitted in its entirety to Congress. Through the years cabinet members had appointed committees and commissions. Most of Hoover's committees addressed specific problems and recommended specific solutions, then expired.[18]

Hoover had helped initiate the regulation of radio and aviation as secretary of commerce, and he was among the first to recognize their potential for commerce and military use and, in the case of radio, for entertainment. As president, his interest in technology provided an incentive to nurture these infant industries and to make the United States a leader in both. The president believed the airwaves should be conduits to consumers and must be strictly regulated to avoid overlapping wavelengths and commercialized exploitation and monopoly. He saw television on the horizon as early as 1927 and understood its commercial potential, although its development was delayed by the Depression and World War II. Hoover even envisioned the potential of atomic energy well before development of the atomic bomb. At the time Hoover became president, the Federal Radio Commission was temporary and exerted only regional authority. On December 3, 1929, the president recommended legislation strengthening the Commission by making it a permanent national regulatory body. Congress approved within two weeks. He combated the development of monopoly in the manufacture of radios. "Whatever other motive may exist for broadcasting, the pleasing of listeners is the primary purpose," he said.[19]

As with radio, Hoover continued the work to improve aviation that he began as secretary of commerce. His older son, Herbert Jr., also became interested in aviation, and his early career involved integrating aviation and radio technology by making it possible for airplanes to navigate by use of radio contact. Hoover employed the U.S. Post Office as a tool to stimulate commercial aviation. The Post Office created incentives for expanding and consolidating routes by offering profitable airmail contracts to lines that carried both mail and passengers. Through the encouragement of the government, four major east-west lines and eight important north-south lines were developed. The McNary-Watres Act of April 1930, inspired by the president, officially inaugurated and codified the operation of the Air Mail Service. The airline industry grew from a disorderly, fragmented arm of transportation to a relatively reliable one. Passenger traffic increased from 165,200 in 1929 to 550,000 in 1933. In addition, air service was initiated to Latin America.[20]

Hoover hoped to use the same tactic, offering mail delivery contracts, to stimulate the construction of a modern, efficient merchant marine, but found the experience frustrating. The U.S. Shipping Board, which operated government-owned lines, many of them using ships that were World War relics, was an independent board beyond the president's control. Hoover believed the fleet was overbuilt and too old. He hoped to transfer the Shipping Board to the control of the Department of Commerce and ultimately abolish it altogether, turning the shipping industry over to private enterprise. However, the system was entrenched and thrived on pork barrel contracts awarded to obsolete ships that embarked largely from southern ports. The keys to their fate were held by powerful southern congressmen. Still, Hoover, operating through Postmaster Brown, encouraged the awarding of new contracts to construct newer, sturdier, and speedy ships. This incentive did result in significant new construction, which had the ancillary advantage of employing an additional 30,000 workers in the shipyards during the Depression.[21]

Hoover also experienced incomplete success in strengthening the Federal Power Commission (FPC) and enhancing its power. When Hoover became president the Commission consisted of three cabinet members who devoted only part of their time to regulating the use of federal water power: the secretaries of agriculture, the interior, and war. The president recommended legislation creating a Commission composed of five full-time, nonpartisan members, who would serve five-year terms with enhanced authority to regulate rates of hydroelectricity sold in interstate commerce. In June 1930, the president signed a weakened measure that deleted the power to regulate rates. Ironically, the regulatory power was stripped because of the opposition of western insurgents, usually supporters of government regulation, on the grounds that they wanted the government to sell electricity directly to consumers.[22]

The insurgents, led by William E. Borah of Idaho, George Norris of Nebraska, and Smith Brookhart of Iowa, clashed again with the president after he appointed the new commissioners, who were promptly confirmed by the Senate, and their certifications signed by the president. They then proceeded to reorganize the FPC and discharged three subordinates who were favorites of the Progressive faction because they had led the fight to regulate aggressively. Based in almost equal portions ideology, personal animosity, and a battle over turf, the Progressives attempted to retroactively revoke the confirmations. There was no precedent for unconfirming a nomination and not much support for such action in the Senate itself. The die-hard senators eventually relented on the confirmations of all but the new chairman, which they carried to the District of Columbia Supreme Court, where they lost. The presiding Justice ruled that the Constitution, parliamentary procedure, and senatorial precedent all lay on the president's side.[23]

Although the small Progressive faction liked to portray Hoover as a lackey of business, that assessment does not withstand scrutiny. After all, it was the Progressives themselves who had gutted the FPC bill of the authority to regulate rates paid by consumers for electricity sold in interstate commerce. As secretary of commerce it had been Hoover's chief task to promote business, and he had done that energetically. Yet his sole interest was never business alone, and he never condoned monopoly. From the early 1920s through the end of his career Hoover opposed price-fixing and monopoly. Later, Hoover opposed the New Deal's National Recovery Administration (NRA) because it encouraged both price-fixing and monopoly. Hoover consistently nurtured competition, and his chief client, he always believed, was the consuming public. Business, labor, and agriculture were all important, yet they constituted only segments of the economy, whereas consumers comprised the entire population. The president believed in stringent regulation of business and prosecuted antitrust suits vigorously, even during the Depression, despite the risk of potentially weakening sectors of the economy. The Justice Department initiated antitrust suits against such leading industries as the Radio Corporation of America (RCA), General Electric, Westinghouse, Appalachian coal producers, California Petroleum Refiners, the Wool Institute, the Sugar Institute, and the Bolt and Nut Association. More antitrust prosecutions were undertaken under Hoover than during any previous administration. As opposed to the insurgents, and later the New Deal, Hoover refused to rhetorically demonize business, because he considered it self-defeating during hard times.[24]

No reform lay closer to Hoover's heart than education, because it pertained to children and young people, the next generation of the nation's leaders. The president's devotion to children was both sentimental and practical. As an orphan, he empathized with them, and he understood their needs. He also realized that democracy could neither survive nor progress without an educated citizenry. The chief executive considered education—especially a high-quality, free, public education—the great leveler, a pathway to upward mobility that would avoid the class and caste distinctions of Europe. It was the key to unlock equality of opportunity, an American birthright to be transmitted from generation to generation. A sound education groomed leaders, and research universities were the fountain of scientific and humanistic breakthroughs. The president understood the complements of scientific and humanistic learning, the former to understand the natural world, the latter to understand human beings. Pure research was necessary to reveal the natural laws that applied research could exploit. The chief executive realized that in the modern world neither lonely inventors nor starving artists thrived in garrets. Education produced not only inventors and poets but citizens who could afford and appreciate their work. Hoover supported education at every level and of all varieties. During the Depression the president focused more on vocational education, especially in the fields of agriculture, commerce, home economics, and trade and industry. Yet he believed education should be well rounded; it should inculcate a love of learning, and athletics could contribute a sense of sportsmanship. Students should immerse themselves in the classics; he even saw virtue in the study of Latin because of the Latin roots of many terms. Education also developed mental discipline and a degree of patience and resilience necessary to succeed in a competitive society. It opened doors to opportunity and provided mental stimulation and enjoyment. He wanted every child to develop a lifelong love of learning. Of our presidents, Hoover was one of the most intimately involved in the educational process. He believed in high pay for college professors to maintain quality, and he argued that education should remain the nation's highest priority even during the dismal days of the Great Depression. He was forcefully antielitist in his approach to education; it should not be limited to a certain class, race, or gender.[25]

Nonetheless, the president remained persuaded that education should be primarily a local responsibility, although he was willing to fill gaps that states were unable to breach, especially by providing aid to poor areas. Educational responsibilities at the federal level were largely the domain of the Interior Department, led by Hoover's friend Wilbur, the president of Stanford University. Wilbur shared Hoover's belief that education should be primarily a local affair; in fact, he felt more strongly about this than the president himself. In 1929 the president created the National Advisory Committee on Education to collect facts and statistics and help define the federal government's role in education. Its 52 members included 3 blacks and 12 Catholics. The committee developed a blueprint for reform, portions of it advanced for its time. In 1930 Hoover considered creating a cabinet-level Department of Education but discarded the idea because of the opposition of Wilbur. The interior secretary preferred to consolidate all federal educational activities within his department and to expand it under the title the Department of Conservation, Education, and Health. Congress did not approve the proposal. Next, Hoover attempted to centralize control of federal educational efforts under an assistant secretary for education within the Department of Interior, yet Congress rejected this as well.[26]

The president was chagrined by the degree of illiteracy that existed in America; many could not write their own names or read a newspaper, an Achilles heel in our democracy. In 1929 the former engineer appointed an Advisory Committee on Illiteracy funded by Julius Rosenwald and John D. Rockefeller. The committee helped organize adult literacy classes in 44 states working through states, local governments, fraternal organizations, and civic groups.[27] The president continued his battle to preserve an oasis of learning amid the barren landscape of the Depression up to the very moment he left office. In January 1933, after his defeat in November 1932, he convened a conference of educational leaders in Washington to focus on how to maintain educational quality during hard times. The chief purpose of the educators was to brainstorm about how to do more with less. Hoover told the leader of the National Education Association that he opposed cuts in education. In one of his last addresses as president, on January 5, 1933, he told Congress: "I ask that throughout your deliberations you bear in mind that the proper care and training of children is more important than any other process that is carried on by our government."[28]

Not all Hoover's educational activities lay within the public sphere. Before, during, and after his presidency he took a special interest in his alma mater, Stanford University. Perhaps his most important accomplishment was the creation of the Hoover Institution on War, Revolution, and Peace, which became one of the world's great research repositories, attracting scholars from throughout the world. Its chief goal was to nurture a peaceful world by learning from the past. Hoover loved the study of history, was widely read in classical and world history, and wanted to furnish the raw materials to inculcate its lessons. Beginning with a crucial mass of primary sources collected by Hoover and his associates documenting the causes and consequences of the Great War, the library expanded through the years, receiving much of its funding from Hoover. Hoover made other contributions, some in the form of personal donations, others by lending his name to fundraising drives and by directly participating in its governance. He was more closely identified with a university than any president except Woodrow Wilson and Princeton and once considered a career as a college president. In 1910 Hoover donated $100,000 to construct a student union and led a campaign to raise the remainder of the funds. Elevated to the board of trustees, he brought to the campus a School of Business Administration and the Stanford Food Institute. As a young engineer he donated much of his collection on Chinese, Asian, and other international books to the Stanford Library. Surreptitiously and publicly, he helped finance the educations of numerous Stanford students.[29]

As a complement to strengthening families and improving education to ensure the fabric of democracy, Hoover tried to improve housing in both rural and urban areas. As secretary of commerce he had made better housing a priority. In 1929 he began planning a major conference to study housing conditions. Twenty-five fact-finding committees were appointed. Some 3,700 experts assembled in Washington in 1931 to discuss their findings, featuring an opening address by the president. They published a multivolume report that suggested remedies such as slum clearance, aid in financing housing, cooperative apartments, and increased attention to zoning. The Home Loan Bank Law enacted by Congress in 1932, which provided low-interest loans, was one of the results. Also, Hoover's Reconstruction Finance Committee in 1932 initiated a slum clearance program. Although the president preferred to work at the local level, he was willing for the federal government to act when local authorities balked or their resources proved inadequate. Like some of the other reforms initiated shortly after Hoover took office, housing reform took some time to materialize.[30]

Hoover probably spent as much time worrying about Prohibition as both a practical and a political problem, with mixed results, than any issue of his administration. A moderate, he found himself trapped between fanatical dries and fanatical wets. Hoover's mother, grandmother, and wife were teetotalers. As a boy in Oregon Hoover had debated another Quaker student on the issue of whether war or alcohol had ruined the lives of more men, with Bert arguing that war had been more destructive. Personally, he considered alcohol more a curse than a blessing to humanity and would say he would be happier if it had never been introduced. Yet he drank wine with meals before and after Prohibition and enjoyed a cocktail before meals. He had owned a wine cellar in California and in London. As president, the Hoovers did not serve alcohol at the White House nor did they attend parties where drinking took place. The president also felt that abstention contributed to the productivity of workers and was partly responsible for the prosperity of the 1920s. Moreover, spending wages on such beverages was a waste of money.[31]

Although humanity would have been better off without alcohol, the genie was, quite literally, out of the bottle. Hoover's chief reason for supporting Prohibition was not moral or religious but pragmatic and principled. He believed in obeying, and enforcing, all laws, whether one liked them or not. He did not believe Americans should choose which laws to obey and which to disobey based on personal preference. That was a prescription for social chaos. The solution to an unpopular law was to repeal it, not to violate it. Strict enforcement would result in more rapid repeal of flawed laws. Still, there was no unanimity during Hoover's term that the Eighteenth Amendment should be repealed, although the country was moving in that direction, especially after the congressional elections of 1930. Not until 1932 had the nation shifted decisively in favor of repeal. As a political tactician, Hoover's strategy was to maintain the unity of the GOP. This was not easy because emotions were tense on both sides. Women, one of Hoover's base constituencies, remained largely opposed to Prohibition. Hoover hoped some compromise, such as a state option that barred the return of the saloon, might suffice. Though dryer than many Democrats, Hoover was not sufficiently dry to satisfy some in his own party, such as Senator Borah. Moreover, there was another aspect of Hoover's philosophy that militated against imposing an unpopular law upon a population that resisted it. He was a tolerant person who believed in voluntarism. It was a cheap morality that relied on the bludgeon. The president stated that laws alone could not reform mankind. He said moral exhortation, childhood training, and self-discipline were equally important. The president prevented Prohibition advocates from circulating pamphlets in the public schools advocating Prohibition, although Congress had appropriated $50,000 to distribute the pamphlets. This type of indoctrination belonged in the home, he thought. In the 1930 congressional elections he did not endorse either dry or wet candidates.[32]

The president believed Prohibition should be given a fair trial. If it could not be enforced, it should be repealed, but the initiative should come from the grass roots, not the president. He did not take the task of repealing a constitutional amendment lightly. It had never been done and might set a bad precedent. Neither did he think tinkering with the definition of what constituted an alcoholic beverage was realistic but considered it a form of evading the issue. Before reforming the Constitution, he would begin by reforming enforcement. He could only deal with federal enforcement, which was only half the problem. Federal jurisdiction extended only to interstate commerce.

Therefore it could interdict only alcohol crossing state lines or entering from outside the United States. Alcohol produced, transported, or sold within states remained the responsibility of state authorities. Under the Eighteenth Amendment, enforcement was defined as concurrent or joint. Enforcement at both levels was atrocious. Speakeasies operated openly, drunks toddled on the streets, mixed drinks were served at fashionable parties, and booze was integral to college life. Neither were public officials spotless. Corruption was rife. Bribery was rampant. Often the best method of locating a speakeasy in a strange city was to ask a policeman. Gangsters dominated entire towns and cities, putting public officials on their payrolls. Gangland killings were frequent, and sometimes innocent bystanders were slain. The mob flaunted their wealth, and expanded into prostitution, "protection," and "numbers." While millions of unemployed stalked the streets in misery, bootleggers paraded their wealth. Yet there would have been no bootleg millionaires if there had been no customers.

Hoover did his best to clean up enforcement at the federal level. Jurisdiction was transferred from Treasury to Justice, and Attorney General Mitchell cracked down. Corrupt officials and judges were weeded out, and their replacements were put under civil service. Prosecutions were streamlined, and convictions increased, while backlogs of cases were cleared up. A new *esprit des corps* infected enforcement officials, abetted by the arrest of high-profile mobsters such as Al Capone, who dominated Chicago and its environs. Moreover, while urging aggressiveness, Hoover also cautioned agents to limit use of firearms to avoid wounding innocent bystanders. Enforcement improved but only at the federal level. The president knew Prohibition could not succeed unless the states were willing to do their part, and they were not. Even some of the states that were most sympathetic to the law in theory were lackadaisical in enforcing it. By late 1931 Hoover was beginning to recognize the futility of the cause, yet practical and political problems obstructed a satisfactory solution. He hoped to find an acceptable compromise, yet like abortion in a later period, the issue was inflammatory. The president felt the nation and the Congress were obsessed with Prohibition at a time when the economy was a more pressing problem. Yet Prohibition was emotionally charged because it was clear-cut; one could be for or against; it was impractical to proselytize for or against the economy.[33]

President Coolidge had signed a bill creating a committee to investigate Prohibition on his last day of office. Congress appropriated $250,000 to fund its work. Hoover fleshed out the concept. In his acceptance speech on August 11, 1928, he promised to appoint a broader, blue-ribbon commission, to explore all aspects of law enforcement and the criminal justice system. He promptly did so, appointing a group that he hoped would either provide a decisive rational for action or banish the controversy quietly into the night. The new president's disappointments began when he sought a chairman of impeccable stature. The chairman, however, was certain to occupy a hot seat, and the heat of the controversy dissuaded some of the better-known men Hoover asked, including World Court Justice Charles Evans Hughes, Supreme Court Justices Harlan F. Stone and Owen J. Roberts, and eminent attorney and future Secretary of State Henry L. Stimson. Hoover settled on George W. Wickersham, a competent legal mind and a prudent man who could soothe fractious debates and craft a reasonable report. Wickersham had served as attorney general under President Taft. The commission included a woman college president and ten lawyers, three of them federal judges. There were eight Republicans and three Democrats representing all regions. Their views on Prohibition were not definitely known at the time, although it was believed the commission had a dry majority of at least one. The commission was to collect and compile statistics on crime from all government agencies. Hoover and Wickersham realized the report, whatever it said, was likely to be controversial and tried to dampen expectations. The president's goal was broad legal reform, not to determine whether Prohibition should be repealed, but this was obscured in the public mind. Hoover intended for the study of crime to be the most comprehensive in history, one that would lay the foundation for changes during and beyond his administration. He wanted to douse the flames of controversy, not fuel them, and to supplant the emotion attached to Prohibition with a logical, well-informed approach. Unfortunately, newspaper reports about the Wickersham report concentrated almost solely on the portion of the report dealing with Prohibition, virtually ignoring the bulk of the report, which encompassed a comprehensive study of crime in America.[34]

The commission split into 11 subcommittees to study specific aspects of criminal activity and law enforcement. Wickersham himself chaired the subcommittee on Prohibition. The preliminary report was released in January of 1930 and the final report one year later. As the president feared, the portion on Prohibition stole the thunder from the majority of the study. The report consisted of a general summary plus opinions by individual members. It satisfied neither the president, nor wets, nor dries because of the equivocal language and lack of consensus. The absence of unity on the commission reflected the divisions throughout the country. In view of later developments, it is worth noting that neither the commission nor the president made any reference to the effect of Prohibition on the economy. The summary concluded that Prohibition was failing; there was a general breakdown in the law. However, it did not propose a definitive solution, and this attempt to straddle the fence was frustrating to partisans on both sides. Sometimes center field is a lonely position. Despite the fact that Prohibition was failing, the main report opposed its repeal, the return of the saloon, or the legalization of wine and beer. Rather, it proposed a further trial with strengthened enforcement. However, it emphasized that more effective enforcement at the federal level would not suffice unless state enforcement improved, and it was not optimistic that it would. The summary portion of the document was acceptable to moderate dries. The specific parts of the document, which represented individual

opinions, were more acceptable to wets. The various opinions were comparable to affirming or dissenting opinions written by Supreme Court Justices,
in which they either support or oppose the general conclusions and provide
elaboration. Within the individual sections, two of the members advocated
repeal, six called for modifications of the law, and four were satisfied with a
further trial of the existing law. One of the members, Monte Lehman, a New
Orleans progressive, refused to sign the summarized report.[35]

Hoover cleared his desk of all other work and devoted 24 hours to reading the entire 90,000-word document. Then he began writing the message
to Congress that would accompany the report when the transmitted it. The
following morning he consulted the cabinet, discussed the contents of his
draft message, and solicited suggestions. He accepted some recommendations and incorporated them into the transmittal message, then retired to his
office to write another draft. Hoover's message was somewhat drier than the
report itself. He stated that he agreed with the thrust of the report that the
law should be given a further trial with stricter enforcement. The president
did not address specific issues such as the legalization of wine and beer, which
he privately opposed. Hoover disagreed with the committee's proposal to
allow Congress to regulate the liquor traffic, objecting that this would politicize enforcement and inject the issue into every congressional election. The
Christian Century, a religious magazine, argued that Hoover had sided with
the dries. His decision to press for more vigorous enforcement seemed to
indicate that he considered Prohibition permanent. From a public relations
aspect, the report was harmful to the president. Rumors circulated that he
had secretly influenced its composition to support the dry position, though
there is no evidence of this. More importantly, the ambivalence of the report
aggravated frustration because it lacked a clear resolution. Some of the public
antipathy over the commission's attempt to straddle the issue was directed at
the president. Congress expressed its unhappiness with the episode by vindictively eliminating the modest appropriation of $100,000 needed to pay the
administrative costs of the commission. Some members of Congress argued
that the legislative branch itself should have conducted the investigation, not
a committee appointed by the president. Both wet and dry congressmen were
critical.[36]

Only minor reforms of federal Prohibition enforcement resulted directly
from the Wickersham Commission's recommendations, although the president did strengthen enforcement through executive reorganization and removing corrupt agents and judges. More significant changes were made in prison
and judicial reform, though some were independent of recommendations of
the commission. Congress seemed reluctant to wade into the swampy morass
of tightening enforcement, which might have been unpopular. Penalties were
reduced for minor offenders, the judicial process was streamlined, and a backlog of court cases cleared. Prosecutions and convictions did increase. Hoover,
the only president to sincerely attempt to enforce the law, made progress,

but Congress and the states demonstrated little enthusiasm. Proposals by the Wickersham Commission to consolidate all border control under the Coast Guard and to codify Prohibition laws died in Congress. Prohibition remained as contentious an issue as ever. The nation insisted that change was needed, but there was no consensus over what type of change. The decibel level of the debate increased.[37]

The results of the 1930 congressional elections showed that more dry than wet Republicans had been defeated and that their numbers were dwindling in Congress. Hoover's personal popularity reached its nadir between June of 1930 and March of 1931. He was partly blamed for the party's losses in the congressional elections and for his stand on the Wickersham report, but no stand he took would have pleased everyone. Clearly, however, public sentiment was drifting more rapidly wet than Hoover was. The Democrats, except for the Southern wing, were wetter. Because of regional loyalties, however, the dry South was likely to vote Democratic anyway. Inaction might prove politically fatal, yet strong action in either direction might also prove fatal. Republicans feared the issue might ruin them in 1932. Tension was so high among Republicans that in December 1932, 64 Republican wets in the House created a bloc to advocate modification of Prohibition laws. Members agreed to cooperate with Democratic wets. The wets were aggressive but failed to unite on any plan. The dries, who were on the defensive, lacked leadership. Hoover attempted to remain aloof and concentrate on economic issues. Prohibition was a symbolic issue, and Hoover was less comfortable with the symbolic, political side of the presidency than he was with its problem-solving side. Within his party, the trend was toward becoming wetter. The dry Republicans, however, were more intense because many of them opposed alcohol on moral and religious grounds. Most adamant wets were Democrats. The president delayed making decisions and refused to show his hand. Hoover's indecisiveness cost him votes in 1932, but it did not cost him the election.[38]

Prohibition might have attracted the most public attention, but President Hoover was more concerned with a general breakdown in obedience to laws and corruption among officials responsible for enforcing them. On April 22, 1929, in a speech to the Associated Press, he declared that law enforcement was the nation's most serious problem. The United States was one of the most dangerous nations in the developed world, he said. Murder, burglary, robbery, forgery, and embezzlement had soared. The United States had 20 times more murders proportionately than Britain and 50 times more robberies. The root of the problem was public apathy. At the first regular session of the Seventy-First Congress in January 1930, the president presented a set of comprehensive reforms to the criminal justice system. He continued the pressure for enactment of his legislation while implementing reforms through reorganization and executive orders. Attorney General Mitchell was assigned the chief responsibility for cleaning up the nation's justice system by weeding out corrupt and inefficient federal officials. Mitchell dismissed corrupt or incompetent federal district attorneys. Lax prosecutors were replaced with aggressive ones. Greater scrutiny was applied to nominations to the federal judiciary. The president initiated the practice of publicizing the sponsors of nominees to diminish political factors involved in appointments. Hoover tried to keep patronage out of the pardoning of prisoners. He granted far fewer pardons than his predecessor.[39]

Under new FBI Director J. Edgar Hoover, appointed by Hoover, the agency became more aggressive and scientific in law enforcement. It established a clearinghouse for fingerprinting and other information, which was shared with state and local authorities. During Hoover's tenure there was a wave of kidnappings, facilitated by the use of automobiles. After the kidnapping and murder of the Lindbergh baby in 1932, Hoover obtained legislation permitting the federal government to pursue kidnappers across state lines. Although the president was a stickler for fair law enforcement, this did not extend to persecuting dissent. At the outset of his administration, he renounced any intention to become involved in witch hunts such as the prosecution of Communists or anarchists for their political beliefs. In late 1929 he ordered the release of Communists who had been arrested for peaceably picketing the White House. Hoover restored civil rights to 35 inmates convicted of political dissent and commuted about one dozen sentences. He fired Assistant Attorney General Mabel Walker Willebrandt for zealotry and intolerance in enforcing Prohibition. Willebrandt had denounced Catholicism while campaigning for Hoover during the 1928 presidential campaign. The president's tolerance was consistent with his Quaker beliefs and his record before reaching the White House. In 1920, during the Red Scare, he had told an unreceptive audience at the Boston Chamber of Commerce that repression only bred radicalism. Hoover tried to set an example of respecting the Constitution in carefully drafting the bills he sent to Congress. He vetoed several measures that his Attorney General had advised him were unconstitutional. Throughout his entire administration, not a single law signed by Hoover was subsequently declared unconstitutional.[40]

Hoover combined aggressive enforcement of laws with expeditious trials and humane treatment of those incarcerated. He had no interest in imprisonment simply for the sake of punishment but rather wanted to rehabilitate inmates and return to society better individuals than those who entered the federal prison system. He was the first president to make prison reform a high priority, even though there were few votes in it. His views on treatment of criminals combined common sense, humanity, and efficiency. The president believed crime was deterred by the certainty of apprehension and conviction, not by the harshness of punishment. The number of criminal cases prosecuted increased substantially from 1928 to 1932, and the percentage of convictions also increased, yet the number of cases pending declined due to Hoover's judicial reforms. In 1931, for example, more than 4,000 more criminal cases were closed than opened. Yet justice was not meted out indiscriminately or vindictively. The president applied humane principles of rehabilitation, job training, reduction of overcrowding, the segregation of hardened criminals from minor ones, and an increase in supervised parole. Hoover took a special interest in the handling of child offenders. He believed that most juveniles were better served by the state and local courts than in federal courts. In June 1932, the president signed a bill moving most juvenile delinquents from the federal criminal justice system to juvenile courts in their own communities, a reform recommended by the Wickersham Commission. Institutions were created specifically to house young offenders, separating them from adult criminals.[41]

The prison system as Hoover found it was a disgrace. Perhaps the most fundamental problem was overcrowding. The urgency of the problem was driven home at the beginning of August 1929 by an outbreak by prisoners at Leavenworth, resulting in the death of one inmate and the injury of three prisoners. Built to accommodate 2,000, the prison was packed with 3,770. It was impossible to find sufficient work to keep them occupied, and the intense heat aggravated tensions. All prisoners but trustees were placed under lockdown. Riots rippled across the country to other federal prisons. The president determined that prisons were operating at 120 percent of capacity. He requested an appropriation of $5 million for a program of construction and remodeling of federal prisons.[42]

In May 1930, a package of administration bills implemented the chief elements of Hoover's program. Congress created a Bureau of Prisons in the Department of Justice, and Hoover appointed Sanford Bates, a prominent reformer who was director of the Massachusetts prison system, as director. The Public Health Service was assigned control of the medical care of prisoners, which improved service, and reformatories for juveniles and women were constructed. Congress also appropriated $500,000 to construct two farms for narcotic addicts, one near Lexington, Kentucky, the other in the Southwest. The addicts received treatment from the Public Health Service and worked outdoors performing agricultural tasks supervised by the Department of Agriculture and designed to be self-supporting. Congress appropriated funds for two new prisons west of the Mississippi and one in the Northeast to relieve overcrowding, a comprehensive program to introduce training schools within prisons to teach trades to inmates, a new hospital for juveniles, and authorized more flexible guidelines for parole. A National Parole Board was established on which women and minorities were represented in proportion to the number of their gender and race incarcerated. Prisoners were permitted to work on government projects, and their sentences were reduced for satisfactory work.[43]

Perhaps no reforms were closer to Hoover's heart than conservation, an interest he shared with Wilbur, a fellow westerner and outdoorsman. The range of his interest in the outdoors was sweeping. It was his source of replenishment, from birth to death. He was so respected in the field that Harding had considered him for secretary of the interior in 1922 and Coolidge had asked him to become secretary of agriculture in 1924. But Hoover added a new aspect to conservation: He wanted to conserve human as well as natural resources and avoid any waste of any kind. For his time, his views were quite advanced. The president favored prudent, planned development that could ensure wholesome recreation and facilitate the restorative powers of nature. He firmly believed that the quality of life could not be measured solely in economic terms. Perhaps the most ardent conservationist president since Theodore Roosevelt, Hoover considered the forests, lakes, and minerals of the country a national trust. Nature's outdoor treasures should be preserved, but humans should not be precluded from using them. The nation must strike a balance between exploitation and pristine isolation, maintaining a high standard of living yet serving the needs of the future. Conservation began with educating individuals about national stewardship. Leaders must persuade people that conservation was in their best interest. Resources vital to the economy were limited, yet prudence could prolong their usefulness. Hoover's vision of conservation was holistic. It stretched from the planting and felling of trees to the sawing of lumber for boards, to nailing boards together for houses. From the hillside to the house, no waste should be tolerated. The president even viewed education of children as a type of conservation. In an aesthetic sense, Americans should learn to respect the wilderness, historic sites, scenic beauty, and the lifestyles of Native Americans. Hoover's views were molded by his frontier rearing and his Quaker beliefs, including his early biblical training.[44]

The Quaker president's partner in the enterprise of conservation, Wilbur, was a lover of the wilderness, and the National Parks represented special reservoirs of beauty for both. As interior secretary, it was the primary responsibility of Wilbur to supervise, protect, and develop the soil, water, forests, and minerals in the national domain. Both Hoover and Wilbur believed in a decentralized approach to conservation in which the states should play a major role.[45]

One of the more egregious examples of wanton waste of a vital national resource lay in oil production. Reckless exploitation, needless waste, and ruthless competition drove prices down because of an orgy of overproduction. Natural gas was flared off heedlessly. Although the United States produced far more oil than it needed and exported most of it, Hoover was sufficiently farsighted to understand that reserves would not last forever. "There is a limit to oil supplies," he wrote. "The time will come when the nation will need this oil much more than it is needed now."[46] Hoover was particularly sensitive to manipulation of oil supplies because of the notorious Teapot Dome and Elk Hill Scandals, which destroyed Harding's reputation. As a result, almost immediately upon taking office, the president cancelled drilling leases on government oil lands. He withdrew drilling permits issued to companies that violated their legal obligations. The new regulations were designed to conserve oil as well as prevent corruption. They generated furor among oil men. Because supply far exceeded demand, Hoover negotiated a deal with the companies to limit 1929 production to 1928 levels. He demonstrated that the two years of greatest overproduction, 1922 and 1927, had been the years of lowest profits.[47]

The one-year agreement and moratorium on drilling on government land was a stopgap. A permanent solution to overproduction required an agreement among the producing states, ratified by their legislatures and approved by Congress, to ration production. The president did not believe the federal government could impose such a compact unilaterally because most oil was produced for intrastate, not interstate commerce. In 1929 Wilbur submitted an agreement drafted by Hoover to the oil states, which rejected it. The oil companies had little interest in limiting production. The president and his interior secretary persisted. Eventually, California, New Mexico, Oklahoma, and Kansas enacted laws curtailing production, yet Texas, the major oil producer, refused. Except for a new oil pool discovered in east Texas, excess oil would have been eliminated. After Hoover's term ended, Texas finally enacted a conservation law. The battle to conserve oil for the future was only partially won in Hoover's time, much to the dismay of later generations of Americans held hostage to soaring prices and embargoes by Middle Eastern cartels.[48]

As if tough negotiations with oil mongers were not sufficient to test the administration's mettle, a month before the 1930 congressional elections, Ralph S. Kelley, an employee of the Interior Department at the Denver Land Office, claimed to have unearthed a scandal dwarfing Teapot Dome. Rather than reporting it to authorities, Kelly accepted $12,000 from the *New York World*, a Democratic daily, to write an exposé. He claimed Secretary Wilbur, had showed favoritism to big oil companies by leasing oil shale lands in the West, potentially worth billions, for a fraction of their value, robbing the government. Corruption was so rife in the Interior Department it made Harding's cronies resemble minnows, he insinuated. Kelly wrote Senator Gerald P. Nye, the chairman of the Senate Lands Committee and asked to testify, and also dispatched a letter of resignation to Wilbur, who declined the resignation and instead fired Kelly. Both Wilbur and Kelly testified. Kelly, a disgruntled employee working exclusively on oil shale projects, had become obsessed with the subject and had lost track of the larger picture. Wilbur patiently explained that the oil shale had little value; the cost of extracting the mineral far exceeded the value of the oil. It could not compete with oil produced by other means. Such land could be purchased for a few dollars per acre from private owners. The Interior Department had more than eight million acres of oil shale land available and had leased only about 43,000 acres. Of this amount, Kelley himself had personally approved the leases on approximately 23,000 acres. The Lands Committee dismissed the accusations, and Wilbur threatened the *World* with a lawsuit, which he withdrew after they promised to print a retraction. The retraction, miniscule and half-hearted, was published well after the 1932 elections. Kelly disappeared into obscurity.[49]

Because of their belief in decentralization and states' rights, Hoover and Wilbur wanted to return the remaining portion of federally owned lands, consisting of nearly 80 million acres, to the states. This consisted of what remained of the original property of the federal government, which was still unsettled, exclusive of national forests, parks, monuments, and Indian reservations. Much was virtually worthless desert land that had been overgrazed and had its topsoil washed away by winds and floods. The president planned to relinquish the property to states, which could lease them to private interests. In 1929 the administration appointed the Commission on Conservation and Administration of the Public Lands, chaired by James R. Garfield, who had served as interior secretary under Theodore Roosevelt. Secretaries Wilbur and Hyde were included as ex officio members. The plan to return the property to the states met obstreperous opposition from many western officials and from conservationists. As a whole, the states had a poor record in conservation. Further, the chief problems were drainage and reclamation to restore watersheds and prevent floods. Many of the rivers in the region crossed state lines and fell under jurisdiction of the federal government, which had superior resources to manage them. Further, the federal government intended to retain mineral rights, which gave the states no incentive to accept the lands. Under the existing system, the states and localities received a share of the fees paid the national government for grazing. The states had nothing to gain but an unwanted responsibility. In September 1931, the Garfield Committee endorsed Hoover's recommendation for state control. In early 1932 the president submitted legislation to Congress authorizing state control, but the legislative branch, preoccupied with the Depression, never acted. Subsequently, the New Deal Congress enacted the Taylor Grazing Act of 1934, which retained federal jurisdiction and gave the national government stronger powers to regulate grazing. The decision was doubtless the best for all concerned. The states lacked both the will and the means to manage the lands and, minus mineral rights, had no incentive to improve the status quo.[50]

National Parks, Forests, and Monuments constituted the core of Hoover's conservation policies because they reflected his love of the outdoors. Being close to nature brought out the highest spiritual values in man he believed, and outdoor recreation was wholesome and therapeutic. The fishing president observed that leisure was not a blessing unless used constructively and complained that Americans had devoted more time to obtaining additional leisure than to thought about how to use it. "Recreation grounds and natural museums are as necessary to our advancing civilization as are wheat fields and factories," he commented.[51] The president believed that a system of expanded national parks would help fill leisure hours. Outdoor exercise released excess energy and helped humans appreciate natural beauty. It also released them from the temptations of destructive leisure. For every man who caught a fish there was one less criminal, he said. Hoover thought the desire to vent anxiety and frustration in the wilderness was crucial during the Great Depression, and his hopes were rewarded. While hard times curtailed other types of recreation, use of national parks increased from 3,370,542 visitors in 1929 to 3,754,596 in 1932. The parks were a bargain in hard times, a place to escape problems amid the serenity of streams, mountains, and forests. The preservation of these treasures contributed to the conservation of human as well as natural resources.[52]

Always practical, Hoover combined refreshment of the soul with conservation and economic benefits. Conservation of the forests meant not only preserving them for campers, hikers, and fisherman but also keeping timber off glutted markets and saving lumber for future needs. He feared that overproduction would exhaust the supply, and thus in 1931 he withdrew some two million acres from logging and set them aside in forest preserves. Later he increased the area of national forests by 40 percent. The president realized that the population was expanding, yet natural resources were finite.[53]

The early Depression years were no period of contraction for national forests, parks, and monuments but a time of expansion. The Forest Service budget rose 46 percent during Hoover's first three years. He appointed a prominent conservationist, Horace Albright, as Commissioner of the National Park Service, and issued executive orders supporting his work. In 1931 Hoover placed superintendents and employees of national parks under civil service protection. Hoover and Wilbur recognized the need for national parks in the more densely populated region east of the Mississippi. In 1929 there was only one national park, Acadian National Park in Maine, east of the Father of Waters. The administration developed projects such as the Great Smokey Mountains National Park in North Carolina and Tennessee, Shenandoah National Park in the Blue Ridge Mountains of Virginia, Mammoth Cave National Park in Kentucky, the Everglades National Park in Florida, and Isle Royale National Park on Lake Superior in Michigan. The federal government developed the Wakefield National Monument, which commemorated George Washington's birthplace, which was within driving distance of millions of Americans. Another development in the East that preserved colonial history was the Colonial National Monument, consisting of about 2,692 acres encompassing James Island, Williamsburg, and the Yorktown Battlefield. Western history sites complemented those in the East. Secretary Wilbur was particularly intrigued by American Indian culture and helped preserve sites such as the cliff dwellings and the archeological remains of Indian villages. Among the projects in the West designed to reflect diverse aspects of scenic beauty were the Petrified Forest in Arizona; the Grande Sand Dunes in Colorado; the Mesa Verde National Park in California; Carlsbad, New Mexico; and Death Valley, California. Perhaps the most impressive accomplishment was the establishment of the Waterton-Glacier International Peace Park overlapping the boundaries of the United States and Canada. It was created by proclamation by president Hoover on June 30, 1932, after approval by Congress and the Canadian Parliament. For administrative purposes, the Waterton Lakes

National Park in Canada and the Glacier National Park in the United States retained their identities, but together they formed a single massive international park. In identifying and developing national parks, the government followed several criteria. They should possess variety, should include diverse types of scenery that were virtually unique, and have scientific and historical importance to the nation as a whole. The president also sought to add to existing parks, particularly by purchasing remaining land within the parks that still belonged to private owners. Hoover obtained a combination of federal, state, and private funds to add to the system. For example, John D. Rockefeller Jr. gave money on a 50–50 matching basis to facilitate the transfer of more than 700,000 acres in North Carolina and Tennessee that were included in the Smokey Mountain National Park. Sixteen of the existing national parks and monuments were increased in size during the Hoover administration.[54]

Complementing the role of parks as sources of scenic beauty and tourist attractions, the administration had a more serious purpose. Hoover, Wilbur, and their conservationist allies took a special interest in preserving wildlife and rare plants. Wilbur strove to protect the habitat of birds, elk, buffalo, and caribou. Like Hoover a lover of trout fishing, he tried to maintain the purity of streams within national control. In addition, the Interior Department set aside certain parcels for scientific research, maintaining their natural conditions virtually unmodified by external influence. Native plants and animals were to remain as undisturbed as possible. In other, less pristine areas, but nonetheless worthy of study, the parks were used for educational purposes. Trained geologists and biologists led camping expeditions of Boy Scouts and Girl Scouts. Wilbur and Hoover believed the national parks served a nurturing purpose as a contact between the people and the government. It was a university of the outdoors, an inviolable trust that must strike a balance between its pristine isolation and access under careful supervision. Inculcating respect for the nation's parks and their plant and animal inhabitants would provide more certain protection than heavy-handed compulsion.[55]

In less than nine months, Hoover launched a movement for social and economic reform and conservation that he hoped would gather momentum, culminating in a second term in which he would anchor in place the ideas suggested by his commissions, especially those still incubating in the Commission on Recent Social Trends. On October 29, 1929, the momentum veered in the opposite direction, and Hoover found that his job consisted of keeping the country afloat. Hoover before the Depression was Noah before deluge.

CHAPTER 5

The Engine of Prosperity Jumps the Track

In the late 1920s, America floated on winds of uplift, which encouraged the myth that human technology had conquered human folly, that a comfortable, secure lifestyle was a reasonable reality for all, that the biblical prescription that the poor would always be with us was mistaken. If pride goeth before a fall, this was a setup for a sucker punch. In his acceptance speech at Palo Alto, Hoover had stated that America was closer to abolishing poverty than any land in history. In a literal sense, this was true. If ever a major civilization in human history prior had come closer to obliterating poverty, in a relative sense, it would be difficult to identify. Yet it did not follow that the highway paved with golden bricks would end with the pot of gold beneath the arching rainbow. An opiate of optimism prevailed. Capitalist economies have always operated on cycles, yet in the 1920s some people believed they were exempt from this law of economics. Many believed reforms enacted during the Progressive Era, such as the Federal Reserve System, which could expand and contract the money supply, made the boom-and-bust cycle obsolete. Generations later, people believed the reforms of the New Deal had made a large economic dip impossible, only to be disproved when the Great Recession of late 2007 exploded in the home mortgage industry and infected the financial infrastructure.

It would be as far from truth to idealize the prosperity of the mid-to-late 1920s, which had numerous weak spots, as to assert that humans are capable of taming their animal passions, achieving permanent world peace, obliterating racism, or, more mundanely, curing the common cold. We are loathe to concede that humans are fallible, yet greed and simple error drives the law of economic cycles. Like physiological mania, economic mania is usually followed by a depression approximately equal in depth to the height of the mania. It is a way of coming back down to earth, of humbling the mighty, of grounding. Nonetheless, the elixir of the 1920s was invigorating and impressive, and there was nothing inexorable in its timing any more than there was inevitable in the way it began. Just because one climbs a mountain does not mean one always falls off. Just as mountain climbers employ ropes, precautions must be taken.

Technology drove the prosperity that preceded the clash. Adrenaline was furnished by inventions such as the automobile, the telephone, radio, motion pictures, and a host of appliances made possible by the magic of electricity, from lighting streets and homes to relieving housework of drudgery. The prosperity, driven by a mass consumer economy, fueled by advertising, employed new tools conceived by inventive minds. Many intellectuals rebelled against materialism, yet most ordinary people wanted to be dealt in. As in 2007, the foreshadowing of a larger collapse occurred in real estate. There was an explosion of land values in Florida, swept away, quite literally, by one of the most destructive hurricanes to that time in the history of the tourist Mecca. But if real estate proved a false god, there remained one sure bet—the stock market, whose epicenter lay in the heart of Manhattan on a short, crooked street, Wall Street. There, fortunes could be made in the twinkling of an eye with a sharp guess, a decisive investment in stocks, and a rapid turnover to someone who would sell them yet higher. Wall Street seemed a money machine, perpetually in motion, gathering momentum. Investors seemed to have the touch of Midas, yet they mimicked the mentality of lemmings; if one went, they all took the plunge.

One of the skeptics of easy money was secretary of commerce, Herbert Hoover, who knew the end would come, the sooner the gentler. It could be cushioned with some reining in of the galloping stock market, but because stocks were selling far beyond what the companies they represented had the potential to earn, an end was imminent. He did not know how near or how calamitous it might be, but he realized that the higher it went, the harder it would ultimately fall, like waxed wings seeking the sun. The mania was propelled by a variety of incentives, the most basic of which was human greed. The ultimate outcome reinforced the adage that a fool and his money are soon parted. The market looked quick and easy, which, for a while it was. It inspired the eternal hope of something for nothing. Playing the market through a broker did not require a great deal of expertise or much initial investment. A few realized it was a game of "hot potato," that the last one caught holding the potato would be burned. The stock market works on supply and demand. Demand bids stocks up and lack of demand bids them down. Ostensibly this depends on the dividends likely to be paid by the company, but that is only true if one is an investor rather than a speculator. Investors buy to make money in the long run based on company stability. Speculators buy solely to resell. As a mining engineer, Hoover had been chiefly an investor. He had managed mines and taken a percentage of the profits. Sometimes he sold properties, but he rarely bought solely to resell quickly. Hoover did not believe that making money was wrong, but he did believe that the speculation had turned reckless. When the house of cards collapsed, it was likely to bring down many buyers with limited resources. It would ripple across the banking and credit industry and wash away the illusion that America had achieved nirvana.

The economy was greased by credit. Most transactions relied on credit, rather than cash. Big ticket consumer goods were bought on credit. But during the waning of the boom, the nation was saturated with consumer goods and the markets for them were running dry. Some companies began investing their funds in the stock market or loaning money to others who in turn would invest. The market had begun to suck capital from productive investment, on which the return was slower and less lucrative. Expansion in many industries seemed to have reached its limits, and capitalists sought other outlets for excess capital. Stock, however, reaped money only for capitalists. It did not employ workers, who in turn, become consumers. Yet in the long run, the only thing that can keep a capitalist economy humming is consumption, and the more widespread, the better. Wage earners had done well but less well than capitalists. Higher wages might have resulted in more consuming power, but it would not have been spread evenly. The workers paid the higher wages would not necessarily buy the products of the company paying them. There had to be a direct connection between high pay and purchase of specific products to provide an incentive for employers to pay more. Moreover, most wage earners were not doing poorly; they simply had bought all they really needed. Farmers were an exception. Their markets had been glutted since Versailles, and they were sinking deeper and deeper into debt. They provided a potential pool of consumers, but the low prices they received were based on the law of supply and demand, which would soon catch up with the industrial sector.

Was there anything the government could do to halt the runaway locomotive before it smashed into a wall? Within the limits of a free society in which people choose how to spend their own money, the government had only a few tools. As secretary of commerce from about 1925 on, Hoover advocated state legislation to regulate the New York Stock Exchange, which he (and probably the Supreme Court) considered an intrastate business. The legislators and governors of New York balked. Franklin Roosevelt, who became governor in 1928 and later blamed Hoover for the crash, not only declined to intervene but dabbled in stocks himself, though he did not need the money. Hoover tried to persuade President Coolidge and Secretary Mellon, who wielded the greatest financial clout within the administration, to issue subtle statements damping the wildfire of market speculation. Both declined. Coolidge realized it would be politically unpopular. Mellon, who had no political ambitions, simply considered it wrong and unnecessary to intervene in the markets.[1]

When the Federal Reserve Act was enacted in 1913 under the Wilson administration, many hoped it could terminate the boom-and-bust cycle by controlling the money supply, either expanding it during deflationary times or contracting it during inflationary times. Making credit harder to get would, presumably, be a disincentive to reckless investment. The Fed's chief tool was control of the rediscount rate, the interest rate it charged for loans to member banks, who then loaned it to the customers. The Fed could also resort to "Open Market" operations, the purchasing of government securities to take them out of circulation, shore up collateral, and dampen inflation. The president had no statutory authority over the Fed, though it sometimes looked to him (in vain under Coolidge) for leadership. Hoover, who next to Mellon wielded the greatest clout in the cabinet on financial matters, attempted to persuade the Fed to raise rediscount rates, beginning in 1925 and continuing during his presidency, by which time it was too late. His most concerted effort occurred in 1925 in collaboration with Senator Irvine R. Lenroot of Wisconsin, who shared the commerce secretary's worries. Lenroot, a Progressive respected for his financial acumen, seemed a more appropriate source of advice than a cabinet member. Hoover had to move cautiously and behind the scenes. A blunt public statement or a leak that he considered speculation risky could send stocks tumbling catastrophically. Hoover wanted to fight a limited war, not Armageddon. Lenroot, using letters ghosted by Hoover or employing statistics provided by him, engaged in a spirited exchange of letters with D. R. Crissinger, governor of the Federal Reserve Board. The senator warned that speculation was reckless and urged the board to raise rediscount rates. Crissinger responded with a series of long letters lecturing the Wisconsin senator and his surrogate, Hoover, about the sound state of the economy. Somewhat sanctimoniously, the chairman bristled at being told how to do his job.[2]

In fairness, the board was in a conundrum from which there was no easy exit. Tightening interest rates might restrain speculation, but it would also hurt legitimate business, including farmers, who were credit starved. To punish the guilty, they would have to punish the innocent. Moreover, Crissinger did not share the anxiety of Hoover and Lenroot about the dimensions of the problem. Neither was the board united on the issue. Eventually, it did raise interest rates, too little, too late, but the Fed could only discourage speculation, not end the spree. Just as the availability of credit did not make speculation inevitable, a lack of credit could not stop the runaway locomotive. Credit stoked the engines but credit did not mandate recklessness. The board's concerns were neither arcane and simplistic nor selfish, though in retrospect its members underestimated the danger.[3]

The Fed was also concerned with the international economy and the problem of foreign loans. Britain, France, and other European nations remained mired in debt and needed money to rebuild wartime destruction. They reminded America that the war had been fought on European soil and that their casualties dwarfed America's. Without credit, they could not repay their own debts, some of which were owed to the United States. The trouble with that argument, Hoover countered, was that they were living beyond their means, with extravagant budgets, elaborate social safety nets, and an accelerating arms race for which they refused to tax their own citizens. Ending the arms race would solve many of their financial problems. These arguments made common sense, yet they were irritating and seemed preachy. Further, Europe needed low interest rates in America to obtain American loans. High interest rates in the United States would lure European capital to America, including gold, when America already had so much excess capital it was pouring much of it into the stock market. A gold drain from Britain might undermine the value of the pound sterling, the basis of international exchange, forcing Britain off the gold standard, which would result in gridlock in international commerce, precipitating an international depression. Whatever the merits of the respective arguments, one cannot examine the behind-the-scenes exchanges without absolving Hoover of blame for the crash. Few on either side of the Atlantic understood the situation with a comparable degree of sophistication or were more audacious in his willingness to bell the wildcat of runaway speculation. The crash did not happen because of Hoover, but in spite of him. No one liked Cassandra, who was labeled insane, or the lamentations of Jeremiah, especially when their arguments are sound. Subsequently, Hoover took no comfort in having led the opposition to the easy-money policies of the Fed, but he did defend himself against accusations that he had fomented the crash.[4]

In the 1920s, Hoover also worried about excessive loans by American private banks to European and Latin American governments. These governments used such loans to finance economic and military expenses without raising taxes on their constituents. In effect, they were foisting risky, high-interest junk bonds upon greedy Americans. Hoover pointed out that these weak governments, including municipalities, could never repay the ridiculously high interest rates they used to lure capital. Further, they were staving off the day of reckoning by pyramiding long-term loans upon short-term loans. The long-term loans were used solely to pay the interest on the short-term loans. Not only was default virtually inevitable, he argued correctly, the high-interest foreign bonds were sucking capital out of legitimate investments in America. Few American investments—except the stock market—offered the payoff of the high-interest foreign bonds. The shaky investments tied up capital and crippled the ability of the American economy to expand in ways that benefitted business and consumers. They provided flimsy security for the banks that held them. When the reckoning arrived, the banks would topple, taking their investors with them. American bankers essentially instructed Hoover to mind his own business. Coolidge inclined to side with the bankers. Secretary of State Hughes opposed Hoover's warnings on grounds of a turf war.

If anyone should issue warnings or invoke some regulation of investments in foreign government bonds, it should be the State Department, not the Commerce Department. Ultimately, European and Latin American governments defaulted en masse, and the financial mess exacerbated the stock market collapse, created chaos in international commerce, and helped destabilize the very governments that had issued the bonds.[5]

By the time Hoover became president, the die was cast, but that did not prevent him from trying. Hoover secretly summoned journalists and newspaper editors, including the publisher William Randolph Hearst, to the White House and described the tidal wave over the horizon gaining momentum. Next, he invited economists and repeated his warning. The president was persuasive, and most cooperated, though a few considered him alarmist. Still, the onslaught of adventurers seeking paper treasures continued undiminished; in fact, it accelerated. The president convinced Mellon, a man of impeccable financial credentials in the orthodox business community, to read a statement to the press indicating that he believed bonds were a safer investment than stocks.[6] Robert Sobel writes that "Hoover's record in the first seven months before the crash is clear. He did more than any of his predecessors to avoid a crash and to mitigate one if it occurred."[7]

Meanwhile, Wall Street rose to a crescendo. Like a Wagner opera, it would culminate in a smashing climax. The market had become increasingly volatile, falling, only to recover, like a cat with nine lives. Yet even cats die. Hoover began to put his own affairs in order. He instructed his financial agent, Edgar Rickard in New York, to move his personal holdings from stocks to secure bonds. A few Wall Street insiders, including Joseph P. Kennedy, surreptitiously tucked away their gains. The bull market peaked on September 3, reaching a level it would not achieve again until 1968. October was the cruelest month. October 24, "Black Thursday," was the worst day on record for losses and volume. That is, until the following Tuesday, October 29, "Black Tuesday," when shares were dumped like Las Vegas brides. Some would not sell at any price, including blue chips. Panic spread. The financial community surveyed the carcass of Coolidge prosperity. But it was only beginning. Many speculators had waited too long to cash in their chips. Greed had a price, on both sides of the Atlantic, even for duped small investors. Few would have predicted it at the time, certainly not Hoover, but it was a catastrophe of biblical proportions. Prosperity had been riding a thin crust, and the stock market signaled a massive cave in, instigated by a loss of morale. A psychology of confidence had helped ensure abundance, but fear and timidity ushered in poverty. Nothing had really changed except people realized the stocks they had been buying on blind faith that did not justify such faith. The businesses, factories, and real assets they represented had not changed one iota. Except for temporary reprieves, some fairly substantial, the decline did not bottom out until the spring of 1933. By then, once mighty corporations had been humbled. By July 1933, about five-sixths of the value of stocks in September 1929 had been lost. By 1932, industrial production had dropped more than 40 percent. Farm prices, already depressed, plummeted by 57 percent between 1929 and 1933.[8]

The crash alone did not cause the Depression, make it inevitable, or dictate its depth and duration. Some believe it was more coincidental than causal. Certainly it was not the only cause, possibly not the chief cause. In all likelihood, it was a catalyst whose major contribution was psychological. People who had spent money wildly now clutched lucre like the Holy Grail. Banks, which had tempted borrowers with low interest rates, now tightened the noose on the money supply, which ensured that money would be scarce for legitimate purposes. Banks, though, did not begin to cascade in an avalanche of failures, at least not right away. Yet by virtually refusing to loan money, some engineered their own demise. Banks cannot earn profits, nor remain in business, if they do not loan money. The crash is important in a symbolic sense to Americans because it marked the end of an era and opened a decade of crushed hopes. The timing of the crash, not the miniscule 2.5 percent of the population who owned stock, constituted a dagger plunged into the heart of the economy. The hemorrhage of assets did not cascade; the wound did not initially appear mortal. The Depression slowly crept up on Americans. The London Naval Conference, not the Depression, was the major news story in the first half of 1930. The course by which the Depression developed was not straight downward, and there were false recoveries. By 1930, the stock market had regained some losses, yet unemployment continued to rise. Breadlines appeared in major cities in mid-1930.[9]

Hoover always pointed to the delayed repercussions of the Great War as having fired the first volley in the Depression. Indeed, some European economies had collapsed in 1927 and 1928, before Wall Street cracked. The United States did not enter the Depression in the vanguard of the Depression but somewhat near the middle. It would be one of the last to recover. The war had ravaged the nations of Europe with unprecedented violence and devastation. The Great War had overthrown the empires of Germany, Austria, and Russia and sown uprisings worldwide: There were revolutions in China, India, Portugal, Spain, Brazil, Argentina, Chile, Peru, and Ecuador.[10] Adolf Hitler, an Austrian soldier recovering from wounds, wrote that when he learned of Germany's surrender while the army remained intact, that was the moment "I resolved to become a politician."[11] The Grim Reaper galloped across Europe and Asia, spewing famine and pestilence, including an infectious influenza epidemic that killed more persons than the war itself. On January 1, 1933, reflecting on the causes of what by then was known as the Great Depression, the *New York Times* attributed it to the dislocations of the Great War. The worldwide downturn was too vast to attribute to a single conspirator or a single cause, although this argument provided political fodder. Though it was later termed the "Hoover Depression" in America, few played a more significant role in striving to prevent the economic holocaust. The heroic humanitarian who had sailed into office upon the seas of prosperity would spend the remainder of his term striving to mitigate the calamity.

The crash inflamed politics almost immediately. On October 31, just two days after Black Tuesday, Democrats hastened to blame the incumbent for the crash. Senator Joseph T. Robinson of Arkansas was among the first. The Democratic National Committee, in an official press release, also identified Hoover as the culprit. In political campaigns continuing into the twenty-first century, Democratic politicians have cited Hoover as an example of a severe economic collapse, which would inevitably follow the election of a Republican administration.[12] Subsequently, a host of denunciations from newspaper editors, labor leaders, bankers, and businessmen sounded the tocsin. As Eugene Lyons has observed, "When the day of reckoning arrived and they needed a 'sacrificial goat,' the man in the White House was 'it.' He would have been 'it' had his name been Smith or Roosevelt."[13] The odds of Hoover escaping blame were about the odds of a mouse escaping from a cat's mouth. Some of the assertions were hair-trigger reactions, and others represented political opportunism or the settling of old scores. However, as Martin L. Fausold points out, "To say that Herbert Hoover as President caused the crash and the depression that would follow, as Roosevelt and the Democrats suggested in 1932, is ludicrous."[14] Other Democrats, who respected Hoover's ability, feared the economic disaster would work to the incumbent's advantage. He would resolve it, as he had competently resolved other emergencies, making him unbeatable in 1932. In all fairness, there was paranoia enough to go around. Some of Hoover's friends believed the Depression was inspired by Democrats to defeat them in the next election. A New Jersey man attributed "the market crash to political forces who want to discredit the administration."[15]

It should be established that the crash did not roll out a red carpet upon which the Depression galloped. The Depression evolved in a series of stages and affected various sectors of the economy differently. The stock plummet was dramatic, but stocks regained substantial ground in the coming months. Unemployment did not exceed that of the downturn of 1920–21 until 1931. The Depression was not a straight country road. It had minirecoveries and backslides. It was affected by events abroad. Not everyone suffered equally. The starkest phase of what became known as the Great Depression did not set in until 1932, and its apogee occurred during the interregnum of 1933, during which Hoover was no longer in effective control.

Hoover realized that if the president panicked, everyone would panic. Thus he issued occasional, mildly reassuring statements, though he refused to encourage people to buy stocks because he did not want to inspire another surge. The president realized stock prices would have to sink to the level of their actual value before they could rebound. Moreover, he understood that the psychological aspect of the crisis was not the sole problem. His priority was to contain the panic to the stock market and to prevent such contagion from spreading to other sectors of the economy. He also knew that rhetoric without results was empty, just as shouting at a drowning man to calm him down would not suffice to save him from drowning. At first, nearly everyone, including the president, believed the downturn would be similar to previous economic setbacks. The model he, and most politicians, as well as the press and the public, had in mind was the most recent recession, the one of 1920–1921, in which he had played a major role in resolving. After saving Belgium and the Mississippi Valley, feeding the Soviet Union, and making America the world's supermarket during the Great War, Hoover seemed better qualified than anyone in public life to manage a crisis. If he had not already occupied high office, he would have been summoned to serve.

The precedent set by previous presidents during panics/depressions was to avoid intervention and ride them out. This policy had been adopted by Van Buren, Grant, Cleveland, and Theodore Roosevelt. Hoover's treasury secretary, Andrew Mellon, publicly respected but overestimated and aged, advised Hoover to follow precedent and let the economic cycle take its course. The downturn, like the earlier ones, would be sharp and painful but brief. From the left, the economist John Maynard Keynes concurred. They concurred that banks and businesses that failed during the purge of the economy were weak and destined to fail anyway. Propping them up only prolonged the agony. Prices would self-adjust. Employment would temporarily fall and then surge. Slowdowns in the economy, which were inevitable aspects of the cycle, were just as inevitably followed by recovery. Wages would revive, as well, and money thrown away in the stock market would be invested in productive enterprises. Chastened, prudent capitalists and consumers would regain economic stability. Capitalism was governed by iron laws. Patience was the essence of virtue under a capitalist system, and recovery would dawn as surely as morning sunshine. It was hubris to believe that nations or individuals completely controlled their destinies, as anyone who had ever stepped in a hole should know.

It has been fashionable since the 1930s to assert that Mellon was an imbecile whose philosophy had been obsolete since Adam Smith. Presumably other explanations are offered for Keynes's similar counsel to wait it out. Orthodox historical accounts claim that Hoover fiddled, and then Dr. Roosevelt stepped in to prescribe medicine that not only saved the patient but guaranteed permanent immunity. Libertarians such as Amity Shlaes, in a popular anecdotal tome, whose argument may nonetheless have some merit, claims that Hoover, and especially FDR, actually prolonged the Depression by economic meddling.[16] The fact remains that the earlier recessions, in which the government remained an innocent bystander, rarely lasted more than two years. None rivaled the longevity of the decade-long Great Depression, which in the end was terminated largely by the historical accident of a victorious world war. Hoover argued that the economy had grown complex, and his humane inclinations and activist intuition mandated intervention, although he later criticized Roosevelt for going too far. Nonetheless, it is possible that the economic and political realities were at odds. Keeping hands off, whether it was an economic option—and no one knows conclusively—was not a realistic political option. A growing consensus had evolved that the government existed to solve problems for its citizens and was capable of doing so. Hoover would become the first to test this thesis on a problem of enormous magnitude. Any president who failed to act was likely to be thrashed politically if not stoned in the streets.

Hoover and Roosevelt were activists by nature, and both were risk takers. Roosevelt was an economic gambler, though he knew little about economics, and Hoover was more willing to gamble politically, though he knew little about politics. Hoover always calculated the odds of success, while Roosevelt sometimes fired into the dark, hoping to hit a moose. Hoover's mind, which fired off neurons like a machine gun, was full of ideas. Roosevelt's mind was largely devoid of original ideas, yet he borrowed them almost randomly, as one plucks books or videos off a library shelf. Hoover embarked into *terra incognito* while FDR had Hoover's example behind him. In addition, many of the ideas the New York aristocrat plucked were generated by Hoover's brain. Both men could not have functioned as fearlessly as they did without enormous self-confidence, for they led an impatient, volatile nation that sizzled like Dante's Inferno.

Hoover could innovate and improvise, and economic problems were his forte. Deeply moved by human suffering, he had dedicated much of his life to alleviating hardship and privation. The president feared that if panic sowed widespread disorder and hunger ravaged the nation without mitigation by government action, the people, in desperation, might turn to ideologies such as Fascism or Communism. Thus his policies were based on political as well as economic considerations.[17] The majority of Hoover's cabinet believed in action, though with varying degrees of assertiveness and inventiveness. His subordinates were loyal and followed the president's lead. Hoover's priority was to avert negativity, bolster public opinion, and stabilize business in order to arrest the decline. The president could not openly express his personal doubts. Once the immediate crisis passed, he could deal with long-range problems. At the time, his actions were more aggressive than many expected—too active, for some. During the first half of Hoover's administration, he received as much criticism for moving too fast as for lassitude. The immediate danger was that the overoptimism of the boom would begat a pendulum swing to pessimism and ossification. He knew the tendency of businessmen to react defensively when they feared inflation. They retrenched, cut back on inventories and orders, and reduced prices. Next, they fired workers and slashed wages. When people retrenched, it forced others to retrench. Employment and consumption spiraled downward. The markets, which had floated on false hope, now cascaded downward in chaos.

Because he considered it his responsibility to help maintain national morale, the president could not reveal all he knew about the economy. Nonetheless, within a month of the crash, he told a small, trusted group at the

White House that they must prepare for the worst. On October 25, while the panic on Wall Street was still in progress, Hoover was already striving to prop up the underlying psychological fears of business. He announced that the fundamental business of the country remained sound, pointing out correctly that the stock market losses represented paper profits. The infrastructure of production remained intact. He worried about unemployment, which was rising. However, no accurate statistics were available, and there would be no conclusive tabulations until the 1930 census. The commander-in-chief resembled a general attempting to inspire his troops not to flee the field of battle. Then the foe, an invisible economic specter, would win. His enemy was more insidious because it was intangible, and the future was uncertain. As the commander, he must remain resolute and appear confident, lest those around him lose hope. The worst thing he could do was to panic and retreat. Hoover's actions in the aftermath of the crash represented a combination of the psychological and the practical. He realized that the underlying enemy was fear and repeatedly said so, long before FDR made the phrase famous in his inaugural address,[18]

Like most successful leaders, Hoover employed tactics that had worked for him in the past. Derived from his experience as head of the Commission for Relief of Belgium (CRB) and the Food Administration during the Great War, his role in managing the postwar recession for Harding, and his rescue of the deluged Mississippi Valley in 1927, the president employed a system that employed centralized policymaking and decentralized implementation. He also relied on men he trusted, many of whom he had met and bonded with during these previous experiences. The federal government in 1929 was a mere skeleton of what it has become in the twenty-first century. The only social benefits it paid were distributed to veterans and through the Children's Bureau. The administration could not control credit because the Federal Reserve System was independent, though at times it could be influenced. Federal expenditures in 1929 comprised only 3 percent of the gross national product (GNP), compared to 20 percent by the end of the twentieth century. In 1929, state and local governments spent five times more than the federal government. Hoover was one of the earliest and most forceful advocates of public spending to energize the economy during economic downturns. Yet the federal government in 1929 was not the powerful force for countercyclical spending it later became. Because there was no precedent for massive spending, it is highly unlikely Congress would have appropriated the money. Both parties, the vast majority of the public, and many academic economists considered a balanced budget sacrosanct. In public construction, capable of creating jobs quickly, the states spent $2 billion, compared to the federal government's $200 million in 1929. The private sector dwarfed both, spending $9 billion. Hoover made his appeal to the private sector only partly because he believed in voluntarism and a decentralized approach. Equally important, given the allocation of existing resources, recovery could only come from private spending. He began by employing the resources at hand.[19]

The chief executive ultimately attacked the developing depression in every facet later identified by economists as a contributing factor to the decline, beginning with fiscal policy. He conferred with Mellon, Mills, members of the Federal Reserve, and Secretaries Lamont and Davis. He also talked with Republican congressional leaders, but he wanted to map out a program before going to Congress. Further, he knew that the national legislature ground out legislation slowly. The Federal Reserve, at Hoover's prodding, reduced the rediscount rate on November 1, from 6 percent to 5 percent, and lowered it again to 4.5 percent on November 15. During the last quarter of 1929, the Fed also made some $500 million in additional credit available through purchase of eligible paper and government bonds. The board's purpose was to pump money previously siphoned into the stock market into business. Credit would be a major weapon. The administration also decided to propose a 1 percent reduction in personal and corporate income taxes, which Congress promptly adopted. The president hoped to stimulate both supply and demand.[20] In a personal gesture, Hoover began donating 20 percent of his annual salary of $75,000 to the government.[21]

The president's most visible attack on the crisis was a series of White House conferences dealing separately with every sector, ranging from a few dozen to several hundred participants. Hoover won the backing of the nation's economic leaders for his program. Nothing like it has ever been attempted— before or since. He outlined a plan and also shook up the status quo, which was riddled by pessimism. The first meeting, on November 19, included railroad executives. The president believed that more jobs lay in repairing and expanding railways than in any industry. The railroad presidents agreed, provided the chief executive seek to achieve rail consolidation to end ruinous competition. Hoover had long backed the idea of consolidating the major trunk lines. Now he had an opportunity to implement mergers. The rail executives agreed to expedite construction and rehabilitation and consider expansion. They scheduled a larger meeting in Chicago to include additional rail men.[22]

On the next day, the president hosted 20 top business and manufacturing leaders, including Henry Ford, Owen D. Young, Julius Rosenwald, Alfred P. Sloan Jr., and Pierre du Pont. The businessmen agreed to continue construction, to avoid layoffs by job sharing, and to resist wage cuts. The president solicited their ideas. Some considered conditions perilous; others believed the shock to be temporary. The chief executive soberly told them that he would not have summoned them if he did not expect the crisis to spread beyond the stock market. He warned that conditions might be bad for an indefinite period and that unemployment would grow. The president warned that they could expect liquidations, deflated prices, and bankruptcies. The collapse was worldwide. Hoover argued that stable employment and reasonable wages were essential to fuel consumption and keep labor peace. Henry Ford raised the ante by announcing that he would give 150,000 Ford workers a pay hike. Ford asserted that the stock market did not determine the health of the economy;

the reverse was true. The problem, Ford said, was that production had out-paced distribution and consumption. Hoover gambled that business would act in its own interest by sacrificing profits before wages. By cooperating, they might encourage consumption. The chief executive used a moral argu-ment, too. Labor was not a commodity to be liquidated, he insisted. Later that day, the president met with labor leaders to consummate a truce. In exchange for employers maintaining existing wage and job levels, prominent labor men promised not to strike or demand wage increases. This included taking exist-ing demands off the table. Management and labor largely kept their promises. During Hoover's administration there were fewer strikes and lockouts than during most periods of comparable length during the twentieth century.[23]

Most large corporations retained existing pay until late 1930 or 1931, when deflation forced cuts. The major steel producers held the line on wages until October 1931. In 1932, the president, by jawboning, forced a reversal of cuts in the income of railroad employees. Most Americans sufficiently fortu-nate to retain their jobs experienced increased wages in real dollars because deflation diminished the cost of living. The industrialists agreed to create a subcommittee to monitor the agreements. A temporary advisory commit-tee was formed, led by Julius Barnes of the Chamber of Commerce. Barnes coordinated activities through trade associations. Barnes's National Business Survey Conference also collected statistics on business and manufacturing. A similar organization was created to monitor the construction industry. Tele-phone companies agreed to expand construction and repair by $600 million, and the steel industry promised to renovate and modernize plants.[24]

Hoover's conferences continued. Leaders of finance, construction, agricul-ture, and utilities paraded into the White House. On November 22, representa-tives of the construction industry visited the Executive Mansion. The president considered construction the "balance wheel" of the economy. It could be accelerated or slowed to mitigate the economic cycle. Hoover implored build-ers to avoid cancellation of jobs and to increase both home and commercial construction. This would generate jobs and would erect useful structures. The contractors were in a strategic position to cushion the blow of unemploy-ment. The president talked with representatives of industries that made brick, cement, and lumber; road builders; the General Contractors' Association; and the National Association of Realtors. Next on the president's agenda were farm leaders. Farming had been troubled even before the market decline. Representatives of farm organizations conferred with the chief executive, Agriculture Secretary Arthur Hyde, the chairman of the Federal Land Banks, created to save mortgaged farms; and Alexander Legge, president of the newly created Farm Board. Among the suggestions offered by farmers were federally financed farm-to-market roads and grain elevator construction. Farmers also pledged to support bond issues for public works. The last meeting was with utility magnates. Like the other leaders who trooped to the White House, most were in agreement with the president's program. The exception was

Samuel Insull of Chicago, who said he saw nothing threatening in the existing situation. However, the industry as a whole promised to expand construction and repairs and to uphold wages. The electric light and power companies vowed to increase their budget by $110 million over their expenditures in 1928. The effect of the conferences was to generate promises of more than $1 billion in new capital outlay. In addition, the meetings helped dispel some of the gloom that had enveloped the nation after the crash. The psychological impact of the meetings, Hoover knew, was as important as the tangible results. With the wolf of want at the door, he hoped to send it scurrying back to its den. He had solidified the support of the financial community and seized the reins of leadership. The public and the press seemed pleased.[25]

The president's backed his words with actions. On November 23 he telegraphed the governors of all 48 states. He asked them to implement planned public works at once. The chief executive also appealed to county and municipal governments. "It would be helpful," he wrote, "if road, street, public building and other construction of this type could be speeded up and adjusted in such fashion as to further employment."[26] Hoover assigned Commerce Secretary Lamont the task of coordinating the efforts of state and local governments to stimulate public works. The states and the private sector possessed far greater resources than the federal government. Hoover promised to complement their efforts with a national public works program, limited only by revenue available. Ultimately, in 1930, more was spent on construction by governments and private individuals than in the boom year of 1929.[27]

Hoover had not parted the Red Sea, but he had demonstrated leadership and held the fear of total collapse at bay. Momentarily, there was a surge of hope. Thousands of congratulatory telegrams and poured in. The press was effusive. "The president's course in this troublous time has been all that could be desired," the New York Times wrote. "No one in his place could have done more; very few of his predecessors could have done as much."[28] "If his efforts prove successful, he will have provided a new technique for dealing with panics," the New York Evening Post added.[29] The Chicago Tribune predicted that success would ensure the incumbent's reelection.[30] In December 1929, the Outlook, which later became critical, predicted, "If he can turn the trick this time there is no reason why prosperity cannot be made perpetual—under proper guidance."[31] Commendations spanned the political spectrum. Even retroactively, the liberal journalist Walter Lippmann, writing in 1936, wrote that "President Franklin D. Roosevelt's position as a radical innovator has been greatly exaggerated. It was Mr. Hoover who abandoned the principle of laissez faire in relation to the business cycle," as well as "established the conviction that the prosperity and depression can be publicly controlled by political action and drove out of the public consciousness that depressions must be overcome by private adjustments."[32] Hoover's policies represented an expansion of his view of government, not a drastic change. He had advocated government activism, including countercyclical spending, since the early 1920s.

Although Hoover was not daunted by what lay ahead, neither was he sure of success. In 1930 he referred to his policies as "a great economic experiment, possibly one of the greatest in our history."[33]

Uncertainty was one of the major enemies of recovery, especially of the stock market. Americans had to be willing to invest and to spend. After a loss of about 30 percent, the market steadied during the first winter of the Depression. By April 1930 Wall Street had recouped about one-fifth of its losses. Some rural banks had failed, but no major banks had stumbled, and total failures were only slightly above normal. There was no nationwide bank panic. Most private employers kept their pledges to Hoover. The statistics of 1929 and the first half of 1930 suggested a slow but nearly normal year, and some considered the crash a fluke. By May 1930, Hoover considered the worst over. Unfortunately, when political rhetoric heated up for the fall 1930 congressional elections, the gains on the market were lost. Other economic barometers fluctuated. The gross national product (GNP) declined 12.6 percent by the spring of 1930, durable goods even more. Still, at the time, the Depression appeared less severe than the one of 1921. In 1921 the GNP had dropped about 24 percent in a single year, almost twice the decline of 1930. Unemployment had been worse in absolute terms in 1921, 4.9 million to 4.3 million. By percentage, unemployment in 1921 had been 11.9 percent compared to 8.9 percent in 1930. There was no reason in 1930 to believe the existing downturn would be more severe or more prolonged than the most recent one. Initially, few faulted Hoover for his analysis of the causes of the downturn or his prescription for dealing with the economy. Most people were willing to give his policies a chance to work. For his first year in office, most people supported the president. Most government officials agreed that Hoover's plan to work from the bottom up rather than the top down was sensible. However, no matter how logical the president's approach, if it did not produce the desired results, patience would wane. Some Democrats and Republican insurgents sharpened their knives. There were doubts about Hoover's ability to whip Congress into line. The criticism arose from opposite camps. Conservatives warned that by not permitting rapid liquidation, he was postponing recovery. Liberals wanted swift government intervention.[34]

Wall Street continued to improve through the spring of 1930, yet this was not reflected in other business indicators. Employment remained shaky, and much of the economy arced downward. In January and February, auto production declined, food prices fell, and railroad car loadings diminished. The rise in stocks that began in January peaked on April 10, when averages were 20 percent higher than at the end of 1929. On May 7, the president predicted that the worst effects of the Depression would be over in 60 days. Compared to previous steep depressions, the economy seemed resilient. Despite Hoover's encouraging statements that business failures were not substantial and despite reductions in the rediscount rate, the market slumped again. In fact, optimistic statements appeared counterproductive. The president's messages were losing credibility. In June, the market collapsed, and the gains made since the beginning of the year were lost. The New York Federal Reserve Bank reduced its rediscount rate from 3 percent to 2.5 percent, the lowest of the year, yet the industrial slide worsened. Credit for construction was available at extremely low rates, yet builders initiated few new projects. Stocks leveled off in August, and during September production improved due to the approach of autumn, but output remained well below 1929 levels. In mid-October the stock market plunged. By November 13, it had dipped below the lowest level of 1929. The remainder of November saw stocks at their lowest level since the middle of 1927. Steel production fell to its nadir since February 1922 except for two months in the middle of 1924. Poison had infected the economy, and there was no doctor with an antidote.[35]

The economy continued to deteriorate during the fall of 1930, running on empty. Hoover's earlier, optimistic predictions were mocked. People, including the president, began to recognize that the Depression might be longer and deeper than the one of 1921. The once-mighty fortress of Wall Street seemed in shambles, with barbarians overrunning the walls. The nascent recovery of the spring, 1930 had devolved into a year of declining trade, prices, and production. There were a record number of bank failures—some 1,345—and larger banks had absorbed some of the smaller ones. At the end of 1930 there were 1,251 fewer banks than at the end of 1929 and 6,733 fewer than at the end of 1921. Prices had dipped as deflation set in. Many important raw materials had declined below the cost of production. This, together with the general decline in commodity prices, decreased the value of exports, and imports declined comparably in value.[36]

Hoover surveyed a bleak economic landscape. The nation faced a bitter winter in 1930–31. The president received advice, solicited and unsolicited, but there was no consensus, no quick, sure solution. The public and the press turned vindictive. Hoover was becoming a sacrificial lamb for the nation's woes. There is no one more vulnerable to morphing into a villain than an ex-hero. But Hoover was neither Hamlet nor Lady Macbeth. He was patient and labored ceaselessly to slice through the Gordian knot of the Depression. He developed new ideas, upping the ante as conditions worsened. He continually invented, yet he faced invective inflicted on him like no president since Lincoln. He had descended, along with the economy, from a superhero to an archvillain. Hoover realized his presidency had become a supreme challenge, and he accepted it as an opportunity. He did not complain, reminding himself that he had asked for the job. The challenge to serve during hard times was an even greater opportunity for public service. As the Depression dragged on, it became clear there was no economic precedent for his dilemma. Hoover did not shirk the responsibility but redoubled his efforts. He would have to crawl out of a deep, dark hole. So he started to climb, one step at a time. The remainder of his term would shape the verdict of history.

CHAPTER 6

![black bar]

The Seventy-First Congress

Fighting the Political Wars

The special session of the Seventy-First Congress adjourned on November 22, 1929, less than two weeks prior to the opening session of the regular long session in early December, still haggling over the Smoot-Hawley Tariff. By this time the stock market fell, importers and exporters continued to withhold orders pending the outcome of the tariff bill, obstructing trade. By now Congress had settled into a pattern of parties and factions. The House, controlled by a comfortable majority of conservative and moderate Republicans, usually supported the president. In the Senate, a coalition of western insurgent Republicans and Democrats joined to wield the balance of power. The president and the House were pitted against the Senate in a battle of wills that endured, to the frustration of both Houses and the president, throughout the session. The Progressives, in particular Senator William E. Borah of Idaho, who had demanded a tariff to protect farmers and had successfully prodded Hoover to summon a special session to enact one, became the bill's most obstinate foe and the president's harshest critic, joined by other western progressives of dubious party loyalty such as George E. Norris of Nebraska, Smith Brookhart of Iowa, Hiram Johnson of California, and Robert M. LaFollette Jr. of Wisconsin. Some detested the president and plotted his defeat in the far-off election of 1932. Most belonged ideologically in the Democratic Party but would have lost their seniority and committee chairmanships because the Republicans theoretically remained the majority party.

Most Progressives represented a thinly populated region and single-interest constituencies. They lacked a comprehensive national program. Most effective at obstructing and orating, few enacted significant laws. Aside from Norris, whose chief interest was Muscle Shoals, a potential dam and hydroelectric complex in the Tennessee Valley, which did not affect his own constituents, their chief concern was farm legislation. On the tariff, they insisted on high tariffs on farm products, which Hoover supported, and low tariffs on products farmers purchased, which was unacceptable to the industrials interests of the East, represented by regular Republicans. The Democrats delighted in the fratricide of the Republicans, realizing the tariff would not satisfy everyone and that they could blame the Republicans.

The clash over the tariff continued unabated even while the stock market slid downward. This further demoralized business, divided Republicans, and delighted Democrats. If the economy toppled into purgatory on the watch of a Republican president and a Republican Congress run amuck, Democrats would reap electoral rewards in 1930 and 1932. In fairness, the Democrats did not then realize they were playing with fire, that the flames licking at the heels of the Republicans would soon scorch the economic infrastructure of the entire nation. Their obstruction was less malicious than expedient. The same could not be said for the Republican insurgents, who could wreck a locomotive but not operate one. Hoover tried to refrain from haggling over specific tariff rates. Presidents had never micromanaged the making of tariffs; they lacked the minute expertise on local issues, and they would only incur enmity by interfering. Yet Hoover provided little leadership at a time when it was badly needed. Early in his presidency, Hoover considered Congress a purely independent branch with which he should not interfere, taking the separation of powers too literally. Thus he permitted the debate to rage. The tariff imbroglio taught the patient Quaker a lesson, however. Never again would he be so patient or so passive when important legislation was pending. His conversion was more evolutionary than St. Paul's on the road to Damascus, but it was nonetheless profound and permanent. For generations, beginning in 1930, politicians, the public, and historians would argue almost as acrimoniously as the Seventy-First Congress over the role the tariff played in the Great Depression. Since it was approved after the Crash, it did not cause the Wall Street fiasco. It did not cripple international trade disastrously, but it certainly did not help it. One thing is clear: It constituted the biggest waste of time in the Hoover presidency. Congress fiddled while Wall Street was reduced to ashes.[1]

The chief protectionists were in the East; the chief low-tariff men were in the West (except that tariffs on farm imports could never be high enough to suit the westerners). Hoover was much closer to the position of the westerners, who ironically were the faction that most bitterly denounced him. Most congressmen wanted a tariff, but they could not agree over its specific provisions. The Republican platform had promised protection to farmers, and

Hoover had pledged to summon a special session to enact one, a promise he intended to keep. Within his own party, Hoover was a moderate, shading to the low-tariff side. Both the East and the West wanted high tariffs on products they produced and low tariffs on those they consumed. Since both were intransigent, the twain could not meet. Hoover considered the emerging bill exorbitant; he wanted selective duties confined solely to producers who really needed it. His criterion was that tariff rates should compensate for the difference between the cost of production abroad (due to cheap foreign wages) and the cost of production at home. Otherwise, Americans workers would be dragged down to international levels, and the standard of living in America would decline. Organized labor backed the chief executive in his intention to base tariff rates largely on wage differentials. The president believed artificially high rates would penalize consumers, who were more important than special interests. But making a tariff was like making and baking mud pies; inevitably it became messy. There were probably more recriminations in tariff debates than in almost any other congressional diatribes. Hoover agreed with Bismarck that the public should be spared the spectacle of making sausages or making laws.

Hoover had three specific objectives: He wanted moderate increases, protection for farmers, and a strong Tariff Commission that could readjust rates ad hoc without returning to Congress. He failed on the first but succeeded on the latter two. The Tariff Commission, created under Wilson, consisted of five members composed of economic experts, appointed by the president. The president wanted a nonpartisan commission that could raise or reduce rates by up to 50 percent subject to his veto. This would facilitate rapid adjustment in response to actions of other nations and take the tariff out of politics. Unfortunately, taking the tariff out of politics was the last thing Congress wanted. They preferred a bill eliminating the commission entirely or giving final approval to Congress, not the president, which would invite interminable logrolling. Though he did not dabble in specific rates, Hoover made clear his preference to limit increases. The president did exert strong leadership on the issue of the commission. He realized the measure likely to emerge would include inequities and wanted the commission to rectify them. The chief executive declared he would veto any bill lacking a strong, presidentially controlled commission. Ironically, the president was later labeled a high protectionist so frequently that the accusation has hardened into a stereotype, when in fact he was a moderating influence. Also ironic, during the tariff debate, as the stock market careened off a cliff, more newspaper inches on the front pages were devoted to the fate of the tariff and negotiations over naval disarmament than to the economic decline, which was expected to be temporary. History read as it happens often reads quite differently than history read backward.[2]

The deadlock between the two Houses and the regional animosities festered from January through June. In early May, when it became evident that a high-tariff measure might emerge, some 1,028 economists signed a petition urging Congress to defeat it. If the legislation passed, the president should veto it. Both the Congress and the president ignored the academic reprimand. The economists might have obtained their wish if the Senate had succeeded in beating down the president's version of the Tariff Commission, in which case Hoover would have vetoed the measure. They also might have been heartened by a presidential veto if the House had not eliminated in conference the pet proposal of the farm belt, a bounty on agricultural exports called the debenture. Farm-state senators had inserted the debenture—a roundabout way of permitting unlimited protection, dumping surplus crops on foreign markets, and reaping infinite profits—after failing to have it included in the Agricultural Marketing Act. Although both the agriculture bill and the tariff had their genesis in extending aid to farmers, agricultural western senators consistently upped the ante until they jeopardized the very type of legislation for which they had clamored so long. Hoover would not agree to a tariff including the debenture, and neither would the House.[3]

Ultimately, the president obtained a bill he felt he could sign, though he pronounced it too high and circulated it around the cabinet for opinions about whether to sign it. After having spent so much time on the issue, vetoing the measure likely would have been viewed as one of the most colossal wastes of time in the history of the Congress, which is quite a statement. So Hoover signed it, with reservations, in the hope that the Tariff Commission might rectify some of the bill's flaws. One of the president's worries during the protracted debate had been that the delay had stalled trade because of the uncertainty during a crucial period. To mitigate the tension, the chief executive announced on June 15, 1930, a day prior to actually signing the bill, his intention to approve it, hoping to allow some of the dust to settle. Instead, the dust became a whirlwind of frantic Wall Street traders dumping stocks like rotting fish, the worst sell-off since the fall of 1929. At the end of the day stocks stood at a new low for 1930, having lost much of the slow ascent since the previous fall. The Democrats promptly blamed Hoover and laid plans to emphasize the Smoot-Hawley Tariff in the 1930 congressional elections. The following day, when the president actually signed the bill into law, stocks rose from the graveyard, though the gain did not entirely compensate for the previous day's sell-off. No one could explain why stocks had declined drastically on the day Hoover announced his intention, nor why they subsequently rose moderately when he followed through. Some simply concluded that the stock market was irrational, as rational an explanation as any. Although the law's economic effects have probably been overestimated, it became a political albatross for the president.[4]

Hoover did not believe that the tariff deepened the Depression much, if at all. First, retaliatory tariffs would have made only a marginal difference in America's economy, which did not operate in the international context of the twenty-first century, a time when many Democrats were protectionists and opposed free-trade agreements. In 1929, imports amounted to only 4.2 percent of the

U.S. gross domestic product (GDP), and exports constituted only 5 percent. Exports declined by only 3.5 percent between 1930 and 1932, and the decreases had begun even before the tariff was enacted. A greater factor, Hoover believed, was declining purchasing power abroad. Statistically, it is difficult to argue that the tariff plunged a dagger into the heart of trade. The decline in imports on which duties had been placed was no greater than the decline in imports on which there were no duties. In some cases, items on the free list fell more.[5] Hoover pointed out that some 63 percent of imports were duty free, including most raw materials. Of the goods taxed, nearly half were agricultural products, which had bipartisan backing. About one-quarter constituted luxury items taxed solely for revenue. The remaining 10 to 11 percent, chiefly on manufactured products, were the only goods disputed. The average duty increase was only 2 percent, which could hardly ruin foreign trade. This was a lower rate of increase than the tariffs of 1894, 1897, and 1909, yet higher than those of 1913 and 1922. Moreover, it is specious to argue that the Smoot-Hawley Tariff ruined world trade, because overall world trade declined during the 1930s, not simply trade among nations that did business with the United States. The argument that the Smoot-Hawley Tariff incited trade wars juxtaposed cause and effect. Nearly 30 nations had already raised their tariffs by the time the American tariff was enacted.[6]

"Both the Fordney-McCumber and Hawley-Smoot tariffs are better regarded as symptoms, not causes of the economic distress in 1921 and 1929, respectively," David Kennedy writes.[7] Probably more important in the stagnation of world trade by 1932 were reduced purchasing power abroad and Britain's introduction of a closed imperial system in 1932. Harris Gaylord Warren writes that the Fordney-McCumber rates were "already . . . high enough to cause a depression if a tariff can have such a result."[8] In the past 40 years there have been 4 tariffs higher than the Smoot-Hawley Tariff that did not adversely affect the economy. Many high-tariff decades experienced prosperity. Historically, at least until 1929, it would be difficult to demonstrate that low-tariff decades had enjoyed superior prosperity to high-tariff decades. In economics, as in historical causation in general, single-cause theories are frequently reductionist. Some analysts assert that domestic producers probably increased their output due to a decline in foreign competition, at least in selected products. The administration claimed that the tariff protected agriculture, as intended, though farmers continued to be their own worst enemies by overproducing. The administration cited figures indicating that during the first year of the Smoot-Hawley Tariff, the number of imported cattle fell from 410,000 to 78,000. Pork imports from Canada dropped from 550,000 pounds to 59,000 pounds. Butter imports declined from 2,851,000 pounds to 1,329,000 pounds, and cattle hides dropped from 294,832,000 pounds to 91,107,000 pounds. Imports of cream, milk, and eggs also decreased. Hoover acknowledged the tariff was imperfect, as were all tariffs, yet he believed it was better because he had worked to prune it of amendments raising some rates and had insisted on a flexible provision to adjust it. He did not consider it important that the public blamed him for a bad bill and that most overlooked the efforts he had made to improve it. The president said that even if a perfect tariff had been passed by Congress, its perfection would be fleeting. Technology and the vicissitudes of world trade soon would make it obsolete. That is why a flexible tariff grounded in a powerful Tariff Commission was so important.[9]

The Democrats equated the tariff with hardship during the congressional campaigns of 1930 and, to a greater extent, during the presidential campaign of 1932. It made effective political fodder because it became a tangible symbol of the Depression and a plausible, if exaggerated accusation, since no one understood the causes of the Depression, nor could historians adequately explain its long duration. Certainly it angered some nations: Canada and England, two of our major trading partners, retaliated by raising their tariffs. England circled the wagons by seeking to monopolize the trade of its empire as did other colonial powers. Many nations dispatched diplomatic protests. Economic nationalism was in vogue during the Great Depression, and virtually every nation turned inward, placing its own interests first. The effect of such policies is mixed. France, a high-tariff nation, probably weathered the Depression most successfully. Britain, a low-tariff nation that attempted to exploit its empire, suffered far more than the United States. The Depression sowed political instability in numerous nations, with apparently little relationship to the tariff policies of those nations.[10]

The tariff imbroglio contributed to political polarization. Hoover, who had progressive inclinations himself, was compelled to rely increasingly on the very conservatives who had opposed his nomination. Borah, an ally during the campaign, became an inveterate foe. Brookhart, Norris, Hiram Johnson, and LaFollette were hostile, but their hostility antedated the tariff. It is also true that if no tariff at all had emerged, Hoover would have been pilloried even more by his own party and blamed by the Democrats as well. Equally true is that, while the press and the Democrats criticized the president for lack of leadership on the tariff issue, the last thing the Republican insurgents wanted was a strong, independent president. They would have preferred a malleable nonentity on the Harding model. Many conservatives would also have preferred a president they could intimidate or at least one who would wheel and deal on patronage and favors. Congress, and the president, learned something about each other from the tariff snafu. Never again would Hoover be so distant from the struggles on Capitol Hill. He would incrementally demonstrate more leadership in congressional affairs, which annoyed a body jealous of its prerogatives but nonetheless virtually clueless as to how to deal with the deepening economic troubles. There was no one on Capitol Hill who could match Hoover in intellect or imagination, and only a few who could match him in stubbornness. The president would often have to pull legislation out of Congress, a process as painful as pulling teeth. Hoover was finding the political process frustrating, but he had learned some lessons. He would never become a polished politician, but he would become increasingly effective at grinding out legislation. It became glaringly obvious during the tariff debate that only the president thought in national rather than parochial terms, and he was gaining the confidence to impose his views. Congress would have to follow Hoover's leadership if it followed any leadership at all.

After the invective levied against the tariff by Hoover's opponents, neither the insurgent Republicans nor the Democrats made significant efforts to repeal it for the remainder of the Great Depression. It was more useful to the Democrats politically if they did not repeal it. Further, subsequent criticisms of Hoover's trade policies include elements of hypocrisy. The New Deal was more highly nationalistic in its approach to world trade than Hoover had been and more isolationist until about 1938, showing no inclination to either arm or disarm until the issue was forced on it. FDR's devaluation of the dollar had much the same effect on international trade as a higher tariff and was more destabilizing. Devaluation made imports (paid for in cheaper dollars) cost relatively more, and exports sold abroad, based on cheaper dollars, earn relatively less. While tariffs (this writer is a free trader) affect only imports and can be targeted to protect specific products, such as agricultural products, devaluation affects prices indiscriminately and triggers trade wars. When one nation devalues its currency, the only options available to other nations are to devalue their own currency, raise tariffs, or impose import quotas to avoid being undersold on their own markets. After the failure of the World Economic Conference of 1933 to achieve currency stabilization, due largely to the nationalistic stance taken by the New Deal, world trade stagnated, delaying recovery not merely in America but throughout the world. Unfortunately, there was no simple, nationalistic road to solving the Depression except possibly the road to war.

In his State of the Union address and his budget message to the long session of the Seventy-First Congress, Hoover submitted legislation to deal with the declining economy and initiate more permanent structural reforms. When the regular session convened, the first major new piece of legislation was the president's request for a 1 percent reduction in income and corporate taxes to stimulate the economy. Cutting taxes is always easier than stiffening regulation or imposing tax increases, and Congress responded in near record time, passing the reduction in just two weeks. There was no bitter factionalism over this measure.[11] When he signed the tax cut into law the president explained that he intended to couple it with rigid economy in order to avoid budget deficits. By February 1930, it appeared that declines in revenue collections would require belt tightening in order to balance the budget. Hoover summoned Republican congressional leaders on the White House to lecture them on the need for economy. On the following day, February 25, he told journalists about the necessity for budgetary restraint. The president urged Congress to resist excessive appropriations. Bills already submitted would, if enacted, exceed revenue by more than $1.5 billion by the end of the fiscal year in July, Hoover warned. This evoked angry rebuttals from some senators. Borah vowed to begin the search for economy by trimming administration bills. Senator Carter Glass, an elderly Democrat representing Virginia, charged the president with blaming Congress for the projected shortfall. Implying that the chief executive was politically naïve, Glass explained that many of the bills were not intended to pass. They had been introduced merely to pacify constituents. The clique of insurgents and a few Democrats critics joined the fray. They pleaded innocent of the charge of excessive spending and insisted the president himself was the culprit. According to them, Hoover had to learn how things worked in Washington, as well as who was boss.[12]

Hoover considered the slack economy an opportunity to reform banking, one of his major priorities. He inherited 24,000 independent banks and a mania for speculation that the Fed was unwilling or unable to temper. Many of the New York banks, which had engaged in speculation, had opposed Hoover's nomination and election. In his first annual message, the president called for congressional authority to create a special commission to investigate banking and suggest legislation. This was denied, and in April 1930, the Senate Banking and Currency Committee decided to investigate banking themselves. Among the reforms Hoover proposed were compulsory membership of all banks in the Federal Reserve System and the separation of savings banks from investment banks. The president was frustrated by the inconsistencies in regulation of banks, which fell solely under state laws. Failing in the Seventy-First Congress, Hoover persisted until the end of his presidency. He believed lax banking regulation had been one of the causes of the stock market crash and yet was unable to prod Congress into acting. Had he succeeded in these early attempts, the banking panic that began in January 1933, during the last months of his presidency, might have been averted.[13]

The president enjoyed more success in perhaps his most significant administrative reform, the consolidation of veterans' services under one agency, improving efficiency and saving about $10 million annually. Services were dispersed among the Veterans Bureau, the Pension Bureau, and the National Home for Disabled Volunteer Soldiers. Veterans' care, which amounted to almost $1 billion in a federal budget of approximately $4 billion, was the largest single item in the budget. The largest portion, which funded the Pensions Bureau, which was located with the Interior Department, consumed 70 percent of Interior's budget. Hoover's plan placed all veterans' services in a new Veterans Administration headed by Brigadier General Frank T. Hines. One of Hoover's innovations was to extend veterans' hospital benefits to those who suffered from peacetime as well as wartime disabilities. Congress, at Hoover's request, provided an allowance for all disabled veterans. No comparable benefits had been extended to veterans since the Civil War era. Some 420,000 additional veterans, the sick and destitute that had become ill after the war, were added to the rolls during Hoover's term, at a cost of $75 million per year. During the Hoover administration 25 new hospitals were constructed or initiated in addition to the 50 existing ones. The number of hospital beds for vets rose from 26,000 to 45,000: an increase of more than 100 percent during the Hoover years.[14]

Despite these significant accomplishments and the administration's generous record on veterans' affairs, the demand for benefits exceeded resources. The issue was politically volatile and became heated as the Depression deepened. Veterans raised their demands, and Congress was reluctant to alienate a large, politically influential voting bloc. Although the president viewed veterans sympathetically, he also considered financial limitations and fairness. Hoover differed with Congress over a bill granting more generous pensions to veterans of the Spanish-American War. The president argued that it would place them in a different category from the veterans of other wars. For example, it would eliminate the provision that a serviceman must have served at least 90 days to become eligible. A man who had served one day would be entitled to full benefits. It would also qualify ex-soldiers and sailors whose disabilities were self-inflicted, such as some who had contracted syphilis, a man who had been court-martialed and discharged because of chronic alcoholism, and another who had deserted his unit and had been dishonorably discharged. In addition, the chief executive felt that wealthy veterans who did not need the money should be excluded. On May 10, 1930, the president vetoed the bill, yet it was overwhelmingly overridden on June 2. The veterans' issue, based as much on politics as policy, remained contentious.[15]

Equally contentious and charged with political venom was the debate over whether and how to develop the nitrate, flood control, and hydroelectric facilities on the Tennessee River in Alabama and Tennessee at a site known as Muscle Shoals. The region had originally been used to produce nitrates for explosives during the Great War and possessed enormous potential. Most aspects of the facility were not overly controversial; it was chiefly the method of distribution of power that was in dispute. The most ardent advocate of government control was Senator George W. Norris of Nebraska, an inveterate foe of Hoover who mixed policy with personal antipathy. The issue had festered throughout the 1920s. The Norris bill for public operation was pocket vetoed by Coolidge. Auto magnate Henry Ford offered to lease and develop the site but withdrew his offer after he was denounced by Norris and his allies for a planning to gouge the public. Norris was intransigent about an issue outside his state, which did not affect his constituents. Another irony is that Hoover was a fervent advocate of dam construction, reclamation, flood control, and generation of hydroelectric power under federal auspices. But he wanted the government to sell electricity directly only when it was impractical for private companies to do so. Otherwise, he wanted the electricity to be leased by the government to companies that would sell it to consumers. The rates they charged in interstate commerce would be regulated by the federal government. Thus the only legitimate issue was a seemingly minor one:

whether the government should sell the electricity to consumers, or lease it to power companies who would deliver it. The president, on principle, believed the government should not compete with private enterprise. But he also had practical reasons. Government operation would inevitably involve layers of bureaucracy and opportunities for patronage. Moreover, government competition would discourage private capital eager to develop hydroelectric sites and result in less, not more, development. His rationale was that no company could compete with the federal government because the government could operate the power plants at a loss, billing taxpayers in other parts of the country a portion of the cost of electricity distributed in the Tennessee Valley. The argument was plausible and indeed made common sense. Yet Norris detested large corporations and was wedded to a conspiracy theory that posited that big corporations cheated their customers by overcharging them. If this were the case, Hoover countered, the solution was to regulate the rates they charged. The president had proposed such legislation, and Norris had repeatedly, and vindictively, killed it. Norris adopted a rule or ruin attitude. Muscle Shoals would be developed his way or no way. Hoover was equally obstinate. Any Norris bill passed by Congress was destined for a presidential veto.[16]

Except for the ideological rigidity on both sides, some compromise might have been reached. Norris wanted the government to produce electricity to test his premise that the government could generate it cheaper and that the utility titans were squeezing consumers. In some cases this was accurate, but Hoover's regulatory measures, which Norris helped defeat, would have protected consumers and investors from such pyramid schemes as Insull Utilities, which collapsed and ruined thousands. Although Hoover's argument was sound on its merits, Norris and his allies, with some success, relied on emotion, which trumped logic. They portrayed Hoover as a pawn and apologist for the interests of big business at a time when big business ranked second only to Satan as an object of public demonization. As on the Spanish war veterans issue, the president took the side of an issue that was sound in principle but made him politically vulnerable. The image of Hoover as an apologist for big business, relentlessly repeated by his political opponents, persists to this day. Hoover followed his conscience; he did not care much about public relations. Neither can the sincerity of Norris be questioned. In fact, his motive was pure; overzealousness and failure to accept the sincerity of others were his flaws. The president thought in national terms; it would be wrong to tax people throughout the nation in order to sell electricity at a loss to a relatively small region. Norris was equally convinced that big business was an ogre, but he was unwilling to accept Hoover's argument that the solution was to regulate it. Unfortunately for Hoover, much of the public and a substantial segment of Congress shared Norris's belief that big business was reprehensible, a perception easy to believe in the aftermath of the stock market crash. Like the tariff, the divisive debate over Muscle Shoals consumed an inordinate amount of time and distracted Congress from dealing with more pressing problems. If the U.S. Senate is the "world's greatest debating society," it seemed at times to debate minutiae endlessly. The president, with a little more flexibility, might have brought the rambling to an end and won plaudits for reconciliation.[17]

As the Seventy-First Congress adjourned for the summer in July, it was remembered as one of the most tempestuous in memory, with clashes between the two Houses. The Lower House usually supported the president, while the Upper House opposed him. The special session that had begun in April 1929 with high expectations had achieved only one major accomplishment, the farm bill. The long session that began in December 1930 proved more productive, yet waged internecine war over intractable issues such as the tariff and Muscle Shoals. With the 1930 congressional elections looming in the fall, the Democrats hoped to gain control of one or both houses, based largely on the economic discontent that followed the stock market crash. Yet a great natural disaster also proved a political albatross for the Republicans—the drought that parched crops in the Mississippi Valley, the Southwest, West, Mountain states, and parts of the South and the Ohio Valley. Seldom have natural and human calamities combined to render a nation so distraught, and its chief executive was pummeled by plagues. Hoover would need to be resilient and resourceful—and perhaps lucky—to prevail.

The Red Cross proclaimed the drought that began in the spring of 1930 the greatest natural disaster in memory, far eclipsing the flood of 1927 during which Hoover had acted as savior of the Mississippi Valley. The drought extended over a broader area, lasted longer, and was more complex to resolve. It affected 30 states to some degree, stretching from Florida and the East Coast to northern Montana. The most distress occurred in the Mississippi and Ohio River Valleys. July was the hottest month in history, and August was almost as hot. In Arkansas the temperature remained above 100 degrees for 42 of 43 days. The intense heat, coupled with lack of rainfall, parched the soil and dried up rivers, and crops and pastures wilted. Fish died and rotted, polluting streams, including Hoover's beloved Rapidan. Forest fires raged out of control. Malnutrition and disease, especially pellagra, haunted rural regions. Human food was less affected than forage and fodder for livestock. Corn and pastures were decimated while wheat and cotton enjoyed about normal years. Yet vegetable gardens on small subsistence farms also suffered losses. The last thing already impoverished farmers needed was a natural disaster that undermined their sustenance. For the president, a great natural affliction would be pyramided upon his plagues of man-made problems.[18]

Preliminary reports revealed that the conditions of pastures on which livestock depended for summer feeding were the worst in history. There was a shortage of water for drinking for livestock and in some places for humans. In the most seriously affected counties it was trucked in or brought in by rail. Some breeding stock—especially cattle, horses, and sheep, which had taken years to develop—died or were slaughtered by owners who could not feed them. In further acts of desperation, some farmers fed seed corn, which had

taken years to develop to dying livestock, jeopardizing not only the next planting but planting for an indefinite future. The livestock that survived were
scraggly, mere skeletons of healthy animals. The corn crop, the smallest in
years, deprived livestock of their basic sustenance, as did the burned out pastures. Farm Board Chairman Alexander Legge suggested that farmers grind
wheat, which was abundant, and feed it to cattle. By early August much of
the corn crop in Ohio, Illinois, and Iowa had been lost. By September the
drought, initially compared to the great drop of 1901, had eclipsed it. Food
shortages for humans were not so widespread but were severe in certain areas.
The northern Great Plains was acutely stricken. The heart of milk-producing
Minnesota was hit hard. Vegetable and fruits were ruined as well. Apples dried
up and fell from trees prematurely. Conditions on the farms affected city families. The price of eggs, milk, and poultry rose as they became scarce and had
to be transported longer distances, meaning cash-short city people ate less and
paid more. States lost tax revenues due to the drought. The president grew
concerned about unemployment of farm hands. Many farmers were finding
it necessary to dismiss all their hired help. During the winter there was likely
to be a pool of unemployed rural people. Hoover, who had planned his first
extended vacation since entering the White House, a camping trip in national
parks in the West, cancelled it to remain in Washington and deal with the
drought. In mid-August rain fell over portions of the area, inducing false hope
that the spell was broken.[19]

On September 2, 1930, Agriculture Secretary Arthur Hyde punctured
the hopes of the optimists by stating that instead of improving, the drought
had worsened. He said that below normal rainfall was now affecting northern Illinois, Michigan, and Wisconsin, which earlier had fared relatively well.
Not only were the length and severity of the drought unprecedented, but so
were the number of people affected, some 17 million.[20] October was the driest month in 1930, the driest year in history since records had been kept. The
Ohio Valley got just a little over half the normal October rainfall, while the
Middle Atlantic states received about one-third. Meanwhile, extension services were working with farm wives to can vegetables and poultry for the coming winter. In schools, home economics classes also participated in canning.
Dr. C. W. Warburton, secretary of the Federal Drought Relief Committee,
emphasized that the types of foods people consumed were important. Reports
from the South and Midwest indicated that tens of thousands of children were
unable to attend school because of lack of suitable clothes. Yet even in the face
of scarcity of some commodities, prices for farm products did not improve
because demand had declined due to decreased purchasing power.[21]

Agriculture Secretary Hyde, at the president's request, made periodic tours
of the stricken areas and provided written assessments, which Hoover used to
formulate policy. Hyde's initial assessment in August had been confirmed by
a yet bleaker report in November, and the drought continued into the winter
through portions of the country, although November rains brought relief to

some drought regions. In November Hyde reported that 236 million bushels of wheat would be fed to livestock compared to 90 million fed in 1929. The wheat crop was satisfactory, and some of the surplus had been depleted by feeding it to cattle, but prices remained low. Cotton, which was largely unaffected, produced the fifth largest crop in history. Because corn seeds had been fed to livestock, leaving none for fall planting, the Department of Agriculture agreed to accept cotton as collateral for seed loans for other crops. The loan would be considered paid when the cotton was sold, though much of the debt was never repaid.[22]

By mid-August 1930, Hoover recognized the crisis was a national emergency whose dimensions posed one of the greatest challenges he faced as president. On August 11, he cleared his desk of all other business to deal with the drought. He modeled his approach on his previous experience with the Commission for the Relief of Belgium (CRB), the American Relief Administration (ARA), the Food Administration (FA), and more recently his experience in rescuing and rehabilitating the Mississippi River Valley during the Great Flood of 1927. In the flood rescue and rebuilding he had collaborated with the American Red Cross, of which he was honorary president. Although the government had contributed substantial resources in kind, few federal dollars had been spent. On that occasion, his actions had been applauded as decisive and effective. In dealing with the drought, decisions would be centralized in Washington, but implementation would be carried out at the state and local levels. There would be a division of authority between the government and the Red Cross, a willing partner, though it had never tackled a tragedy of this scope. The government would deal with structural and economic problems, as well as loans for rehabilitation, taking a national and long-range view. The Red Cross would cope with immediate humanitarian needs such as feeding and clothing the needy. The organization, through its local chapters, possessed an infrastructure of volunteers capable of determining local needs, unlike the federal government. Hoover feared that direct government doles to drought sufferers would result in an avalanche of demands from the urban unemployed for similar aid, which the government simply lacked the resources to meet. He also felt that any such program would be bureaucratic and inefficient, become entangled in favoritism, and inevitably would be manipulated in a fight for spoils and political patronage. Moreover, the Red Cross was better organized to administer such aid. The president also believed that federal direct assistance would discourage donations to the Red Cross and undermine the resources available to private charity because people would consider such donations superfluous. Although the collaboration was mutual, Hoover remained in charge. As in the 1927 flood, the president would devise strategy, and the volunteer organization would employ its workers at the local level in a clear-cut division of labor. Counties that exhausted their resources could appeal to states. States that exhausted their resources could appeal to the federal government. The federal government would also aid in stimulating the fundraising of the Red Cross.

After assessing the situation, in mid-August Hoover summoned the governors of the most seriously affected states to Washington to explain their needs and map out plans. He appointed a National Drought Committee comprised of representatives of the Department of Agriculture, the Federal Farm Board, the Federal Farm Loan Board, the American Red Cross, the American Railway Association, and the Public Health Service to coordinate the national effort, chaired by Hyde.[23] Each governor appointed a state committee, which in turn worked through county committees. At each level, needs would be assessed and provided as far as resources stretched. The president also met with John Barton Payne, the acting Red Cross Director, with leading bankers, because he considered credit for the region essential to recovery; and with railroad presidents, whom he asked to temporarily reduce freight rates by 50 percent for animal and human food transported into the region and livestock transported out for sale or pasturing. They agreed. On August 15, Hoover announced that he was releasing the full year's stipend of federal matching funds for road building in the stricken states to be made available immediately in order to provide employment. States afflicted most seriously were expected to receive between $35 million and $40 million each. Meanwhile, the War Department opened several thousand acres of its lands in Virginia for grazing and watering livestock. About 500,000 cattle and from two to three million sheep were shifted out of the stricken area, the greatest migration of domestic animals in modern times. The U.S. Grain Corporation, a division of the Farm Board, dispatched feed for livestock to needy areas. The Anglo-American Mill Company offered two million gallons of molasses and a great quantity of the company's feeding machines free to farmers whose livestock were suffering from the drought, to be fed under the direction of the Farm Bureau. Credit was provided through the Federal Reserve Banks, the Federal Intermediate Credit Banks, and the Farm Board. Hoover wanted the loans to be based on reasonable collateral in order to limit demand, although he realized that most loans would never be repaid. Like calls for depression aid, he knew the appetite was insatiable and the resources finite.[24]

At the time of the drought, no contingency pool was available to draw upon immediately. All federal money was appropriated for specific purposes. Congressional appropriations would require time, and by statute loans had to be based on sound collateral. The Farm Board could by law loan money only to cooperatives, not to individual farmers. Secretary Hyde found some $800 million left over from an appropriation by the previous Congress for storm and drought assistance. These loans could be made to individual farmers, and they were utilized until exhausted. Likewise, the Federal Intermediate Credit Banks could make loans to institutions such as banks that dealt with farmers, but not to farmers as individuals. The system had been designed primarily to protect taxpayers from default rather than cope with unanticipated emergencies. In most cases, farmers seeking loans went first to local banks. The local banks opposed a federal system of banks that might compete with them by offering lower-interest loans with less secure collateral. This might drive the rural banks out of business. If they failed, their depositors, including some of the farmers in need, would lose their deposits. The government did, however, try to pool funds by creating state or local credit corporations that would increase resources and accept risks. They would serve as intermediaries between the farmers and the local banks, attempting to protect both.[25]

Discharged farm laborers and some farmers who could not earn a profit from farming were offered several types of employment, usually part-time, unskilled labor. States and counties were urged to speed construction and repairs on public buildings rather than spreading them over a longer period. The federal government employed men in the region by stepping up construction of roads in National Forests and National Parks and undertaking other labor-intensive improvements. Logging was increased on public land, employing local labor. Emphasis was placed on expanding work on inland waterways and flood protection within the region, which provided employment. Looking beyond the present crop year, arrangements were made to save the 1931 crop by providing loans for seeds to replace those fed to livestock. These loans could not be used for payment of previous debts, plowing additional untilled land, or erecting new buildings. The campaign to prevent disease, emphasizing proper nutrition and preventive treatment, was undertaken by the Red Cross, the Public Health Service, and the Extension Service of the Agriculture Department. Local schools, including home economics departments, were also enlisted.[26]

The Red Cross played the crucial role in human relief. Some 21 states received some aid from the Red Cross. Hunger was most acute in the Midwestern and Southern states. The Red Cross furnished sustenance to many who had never accepted charity before. Some were foraging for herbs, roots, turnips, and roots found in the forests. The depressed economy limited the ability of their neighbors to help them. Unlike the government assistance, the Red Cross offered food and clothing, not loans. Usually, though not invariably, it provided assistance in kind rather than in cash. During the late fall of 1930 people found their food stocks diminishing. From January 1 to January 15, 1931, the number of persons fed by the Red Cross increased from 225,000 to 507,000. The Red Cross furnished assistance in nearly all Arkansas' 75 counties and in about three-quarters of the counties in Kentucky. In Louisiana about one-third of the parishes received help while more than 40 counties in Oklahoma obtained food. Hundreds of families were fed in southern Missouri, Illinois, Indiana, Ohio, and Mississippi, and many received clothing as well. Suffering was acute where potato crops failed, leaving shortages of calories and starch. Fresh meat was rare, and even forest animals succumbed. In England, Arkansas, the Red Cross temporarily exhausted application forms for aid as people waited in line. Frustration nearly erupted into a mini riot, but the Red Cross dissipated it by simply distributing food on site without applications. The Red Cross was stretched to its limits. In January 1931 Hoover helped promote fundraising appeals for a $10 million relief fund, and the charity ultimately reached its goal, which it claimed was sufficient. On February 10, the president donated one-tenth of his $75,000 salary, or $7,500, to the Red Cross for relief of drought victims. In 1932 he waived virtually his entire federal salary and worked for $1 per year, after Congress legalized such a rebate.[27]

The drought could hardly have come at a worse time for Hoover or the country. The GOP was facing the fall elections of 1930, and, though the drought was less decisive than other issues, it aggravated frustration caused by the prostrate economy. The drought did not really become an inflammatory political issue, however, until after the elections, during the short session of the Seventy-First Congress. Still Hoover's reputation as a "Master of Emergencies," already tarnished, was further damaged. His actions were aggressive for those times. During the congressional elections that year Democrats condemned him for overspending. Still, the suffering from the drought damaged his popularity. In the public mind it was easy to find a human scapegoat for both the Depression and the drought, and Hoover was the most obvious. The drought was almost as resistant as the Depression to a man-made termination. It ended in some states during the winter of 1930–1931, but in others, particularly in North Dakota and South Dakota, where was it was coupled with an infestation of grasshoppers, it seemed to continue interminably. From the fickleness of the weather, the narrative turns to the almost equally unusual congressional elections of the fall of 1930. The drought, the grasshoppers, and the Depression seemed to be allies of the Democrats, and they made the most of it.

As the 1930 congressional elections approached, the president and Republican leaders were apprehensive. Hoover particularly worried about losing the House, which had protected him from the Democrat and Republican insurgent coalition that controlled the Senate and was likely to increase its strength. The House, where every member was running for reelection, was the major battleground. The Republicans expected to lose in wet cities yet compensate in some western states, though senators elected from those states were likely to join the Progressive faction. Support for Prohibition was weakening, and the GOP expected a decline in the number of dries elected in both houses, yet the leadership continued to believe that a majority of Congress and the country, still supported Prohibition. Some feared an adverse reaction to the Smoot-Hawley Tariff comparable to the 1910 elections following passage of the Payne-Aldrich Tariff. However, while many complained that overall rates were too high, they argued that rates on goods they sold, whether agricultural or industrial, were too low. The Republicans had the worst of both worlds. The Depression also resulted in a steep decline in donations to most GOP candidates and to the national party. It appeared the party might be outmanned in dollars, especially since Democratic National Chairman John J. Raskob was willing to finance much of the Democratic campaign single-handedly. The Democrats sensed opportunity, and the Republicans were fragmented and factionalized. They were also demoralized by scandals involving Charles Huston, the chairman of the Republican National Committee, who stubbornly refused to resign. Senator George Moses of New Hampshire, chairman of the Senatorial Campaign Committee, was unwelcome in the West after terming the insurgent senators "Sons of the Wild Jackass" who had betrayed their party.[28]

The Democrats ran against Hoover while the Republicans ran against the Democrats in Congress. The Democratic mantra was to blame the stock market crash and the hard times that followed on Hoover. The president was accused of both being a spendthrift and doing too little to combat the Depression. As in 1928, the economy was the central issue, yet the Republicans were on the wrong side, in a political sense, in 1930. Many prepared to vent their antipathy against the party. Fewer had objections to any specific Hoover policies. If life is unfair, politics multiplies the effect of that adage. The campaign was largely negative. The Republicans defended their record yet produced few new proposals. The congressional Democrats had few accomplishments to boast of, so the administration attacked Democrats for obstructing the president's program without providing alternatives to it. Some claimed the Democrats had a vested political stake in continuation of the Depression. Both parties tried to pin labels of big spenders and "do-nothings" on each other. As an example of Democratic obstruction, Republicans pointed to the protracted struggle over the tariff, which had paralyzed business. Democrats had ostentatiously criticized the tariff even before it passed, the GOP charged, despite inserting high rates to protect their constituents. There was a little truth on each side but a great deal more obfuscation and exaggeration. No one on the Democratic side contributed more scathing invective than journalist Charles S. Michelson, hired by the DNC to skewer Hoover personally for all four years of his administration, a job he relished. Michelson ghosted speeches for senators, representatives, and other public figures, which they lip-synced, and many were inserted in the *Congressional Record*. Michelson was effective less because he employed scurrilous venom, although he possessed a wicked wit, than because he was prolific and unrelenting. The 1930 campaign was for him a warm-up for 1932.[29]

The Democrats made Hoover the central issue. It is simpler and more effective to attack a tangible person than to parade a gumbo of statistics difficult to digest. Emotion ruled the election, and it was difficult to deny that the economy was in bad shape. The theme was whether constituents felt positive or negative about the incumbent party. The DNC unleashed a barrage of speeches, pamphlets, and radio addresses that not only were effective in the short run but began the process of cementing Hoover's place in history as an inept, uncaring president. Similar tactics would be employed in 1932, with greater venom. Low farm prices were attributed to Hoover personally. James M. Cox, the Democratic candidate in 1920, delivered a nationwide radio broadcast on October 13, 1930, in which he blamed the stock market crash on Hoover and his confederates on Wall Street, who then exacerbated their economic carnage with uncaring arrogance. They had sealed the fate of the Republic by enacting the Smoot-Hawley Tariff, which was "forced upon an unwilling people" and "later accentuated the depression." As for the crash, it had been "the direct consequences of Administration propaganda." Cox claimed that if Al Smith had been elected in 1928, the nation would have been spared the Wall Street collapse.[30]

The Democrats rolled out Cox's vice presidential running mate in 1920, Franklin D. Roosevelt, who had offered to run as Hoover's running mate in that election. Roosevelt, now running for reelection as governor of New York, said of his one-time friend and colleague in the Wilson administration: "Not a single step was taken during the years preceding the sharp drop to halt speculation and inflation," a charge that applied more to the New York governor himself than to Hoover. The governor added that, following the crash, "[a]lthough the time called for quick and decisive action by the federal government, nothing happened but words." Roosevelt insisted that the Hoover administration was responsible for an "orgy of inflation" that precipitated the crash and that Hoover had failed to fulfill its campaign promises, bombarding the public with optimistic words that rang hollow. He also branded Hoover a big spender. Roosevelt, who would win reelection by a landslide of 750,000 votes, was already being touted as a challenger to the Republican in 1932 and was priming the political pump. One of his admirers compared the New York governor to one of his predecessors, the tight-fisted fiscal conservative, Grover Cleveland. "We have another Grover Cleveland in Franklin D. Roosevelt," the admirer claimed, "another man of destiny. Our man of destiny, I predict, will travel along the same road." Roosevelt would repeat the same themes in every subsequent campaign for the rest of his life.[31]

An equally inaccurate observation was made by Hoover's vice president, Charles Curtis, shortly after the campaign ended. Though somewhat disappointed in the results, which were nonetheless not on a devastating scale, Curtis predicted the Republicans would bounce back. "They can't beat us in 1932," he vowed. "Good times are just around the corner." That prediction would haunt the Republicans, although many shared it at the time, and it has been erroneously attributed to Hoover. In 1930 some Democrats feared the Depression might end before the next election and that Hoover would be credited with ending it. Much of the general public, to this day, believe Hoover made the statement and use it to label him a false prophet of prosperity.[32]

Although the major issue in the campaign was a protest vote against prevailing conditions, other factors affected the outcome to a lesser degree. Prohibition hurt the Republicans on a regional basis, but a majority of the people nationwide, though rapidly dwindling, still supported it. The East remained wet, parts of the West dry, and the South both solidly dry and solidly Demo-cratic, though the Democratic Party on the whole was wetter than the GOP. Still, both parties had wet and dry factions. The Wickersham Commission had only muddied the situation, though its divisions reflected those of the country. Hoover had accomplished reforms in areas in which there were few votes. In fact his strict adherence to merit appointments denied jobs to the party faithful. The president's attempts to reform the corrupt Southern patronage system cost him support in the short run, though there were pre-cious few Republicans registered there. Finally, the administration's handling of the 1930 drought, or perhaps merely the fact that the drought occurred on Hoover's watch, further poisoned the political well. Some thought the administration could have done more to mitigate the problem, and certainly Hoover failed in his public relations handling of the drought. The politics of the drought would not peak until the short session of the Seventy-First Con-gress, after the election.

The party holding the White House almost inevitably loses seats during midterm elections, and the odds favor the opposition during hard times. Thus it is not surprising that the GOP lost seats. It is somewhat surprising that they did not lose more. Actually, the Republicans polled more total votes that the Democrats, winning 54 percent of the ballots cast. The election produced nearly a dead heat in both houses, in which neither party held a reliable major-ity. The Republicans lost 46 House seats but emerged with an advantage of 2 seats. However, deaths before the seating of the Seventy-Second Congress in December 1932 gave the Democrats a small majority and enabled them to organize the House. The election did not affect the composition of the short session of the Seventy-First Congress, because the new senators and repre-sentatives did not take their seats until December of 1931. The new Senate, prior to adjustments made by the Grim Reaper, would contain 48 Republi-cans, 47 Democrats, and 1 Farmer-Laborite. The Republican vice president could break a tie vote in the Upper House. Although the Democrats would have a working majority in both houses on legislative matters because of the support of the Progressive Republican faction, the Progressives usually voted Republican on procedural matters, such as organization of their chambers, which enabled them to retain their seniority and, in some cases, committee chairmanships. The election was a setback but not a catastrophic one. The major blow was psychological. The Republicans were accustomed to com-manding comfortable majorities during the 1920s, and the election reversed the verdict of 1928. More ominously for Hoover, no president who had lost control of the House in a midterm election had gone on the win the next presidential election.[33]

The Republican campaign had been underfunded, a divided party lacking decisive leadership at the top, in both the White House and the RNC. Hoover disliked the political aspects of his job: distributing patronage designed to win elections, fundraising, and delivering partisan speeches. He did not relish verbal combat and considered emotional rhetoric undignified, and lashing out conflicted with his Quaker principles and inhibited personality. He did not like personal criticism, whether directed at him or even at his political opponents, and this made it difficult for him to defend his policies effectively. The president wanted politics to be based solely on policies logically explained, and he believed that making policies that might end or mitigate the Depression was his chief responsibility. He had a strong sense of duty and found invective unpalatable. Yet politics is largely about personality, even in good times, and voters usually vote based on emotion, even when it only amounts to ratifying the incumbents or expelling them. During early October Hoover was finally persuaded to deliver four speeches, which were billed as nonpolitical and did not solicit votes, but that the GOP understandably hoped he could sway voters. The president began with an address to the American Bankers Association on October 2, followed by speeches to the American Legion at Boston, where he also spoke to a conclave of the American Federation of Labor (AFL). He concluded with an address at Kings Mountain, South Carolina, to celebrants commemorating a famous Revolutionary War battle.[34]

Many observers, both contemporary and historical, underestimated the battle fatigue of the GOP, worn down by internecine strife, especially the bitter animosity spewed at Hoover by the Republican Progressives; the effect of Michelson's churning out reams of propaganda; the party's delay in disgorging itself of its corrupt national chairman; and the demoralization of potential donors, paralyzed by fear and reluctant to contribute to what they considered a lost cause. But it is wishful thinking to postulate that, given the context of the times, the Republicans could have triumphed. They had bigger problems than poor leadership, namely, alienation motivated by the economy. Business blamed them for the crash; workers blamed them for unemployment; and farmers blamed them for low prices and for rejecting their pet panaceas such as the debenture. Even the most savvy, most aggressive, most finely tuned campaign could not have prevented Democratic gains, but better use of resources, planning that started earlier, and a blueprint for a national campaign could have turned a lost cause into a marginal one. All said, 1930 was inauspicious, but it was not Waterloo. The GOP's fate would lie with the course of the Depression. If it ended before 1932 they would probably receive credit, making them victorious. If the economy continued on its downward trajectory, 1932 would be unwinnable.

The country, and the GOP, had been put through the wringer. Yet after a respite, the short session of the Seventy-First Congress produced fireworks of its own. It wrapped up some unfinished business, returned to some remaining controversies, endured partisanship, and achieved its share of accomplishments. Two major controversies involved squabbles debated during the long session: Muscle Shoals and veterans' affairs. Shortly after the congressional elections, with the opening of the congress, which included lame ducks, Norris reintroduced his bill providing for federal operation of Muscle Shoals.

Predictably, it produced another deadlock because neither Hoover nor Norris had moved from their earlier positions. Norris and his allies would accept nothing less than complete federal control, including the direct sale of electricity to consumers. Hoover would have preferred the defeat of the bill by Congress to prevent a confrontation, but both houses approved the bill virtually intact. On March 3, 1931, the president promptly vetoed it, and the Senate fell a few votes short of mustering the two-thirds majority necessary to override. The chief executive complained that an inordinate amount of time, in the doldrums of the Depression, was being devoted to a measure that would serve only 1 percent of the population. He continued to insist that private sale of electricity, with rates scrupulously regulated by the federal government, was simpler and more practical. For his part, Norris attributed the failure to override to the power trust, in connivance with Hoover. In an attempt to settle the issue, a Muscle Shoals Commission, suggested by Hoover and including representatives appointed by the governors of Alabama and Tennessee, devised a plan with progressive features, acceptable to Hoover but not to Norris. There the matter lay, to be revived as an issue during the 1932 presidential campaign in which Norris supported FDR, who endorsed public operation. Development was delayed until the New Deal, but, meanwhile, it left festering sores between Hoover on one side and Norris and his backers on the other. It was the only water power project Hoover did not support during his administration.[35]

Although Hoover won the battle over Muscle Shoals and although he was battered politically, he lost a more important contest during the short session, one that was far more expensive, involved many more people, and opened another political Pandora's Box. By the end of 1930 a strong movement had gained momentum to enact a law permitting veterans to borrow against their bonus certificates, issued during the 1920s but not due to mature until 1945. Veterans would be authorized to borrow up to 50 percent of the value of their certificates at an annual interest rate of 4.5 percent. The movement, politically irresistible, though it would undermine government credit, climaxed during the last two weeks of the short session. Secretary Mellon warned that it could cost between $1 billion and $3 billion at a time when the government was trying to balance the budget, raise money for public works to assist the unemployed, and avoid tax increases that might retard a business revival. Hoover and Mellon argued that such a large expenditure for such a small proportion of the population was unfair. The president was willing to sign a bill granting loans to needy veterans alone, but not to all veterans. Mellon warned that the measure would depreciate the value of all government bonds, including those held by the veterans themselves. It would be more difficult to sell government bonds, which would require higher interest rates to entice buyers, and would drive the government deeper into debt during a period when it was hard-pressed to meet its existing obligations. A large majority of the press considered the legislation unwise. Nonetheless, the veterans' lobby and the potential bloc vote it commanded frightened even House Speaker Nicholas Longworth, who deserted the administration on the issue. Because the bill arose near the end of the session, Hoover could have killed it with a pocket veto. But the president refused to take the politically expedient course, stating he would veto it, go on record in his opposition, and allow both houses the opportunity to override. He cast the gauntlet before Congress. It was a bold but hopeless fight. The House passed the bill by a crushing margin (363–39) and sent it to the Senate, which passed it by an equally crushing vote (72–12). The president, in his veto message, argued that the massive total involved would destabilize the government fiscally and would delay recovery. Nonetheless, the House promptly overrode 328–79 and the Senate followed with an equally lopsided repudiation of 76–17. This was the most serious defeat the president suffered during the Seventy-First Congress and the most costly, fiscally and politically. Moreover, the ease with which the measure passed encouraged veterans to demand payment of the entire bonus during the Seventy-Second Congress, which provoked the most incendiary confrontation of Hoover's entire presidency.[36]

The short session also engaged in fiscal battle, also a matter of principle and politics, over federal appropriations for drought relief for the sunbaked states. Within days after the short session convened in December 1930, the Senate Agriculture Committee approved a bill providing $60 million for drought relief, which allowed purchases of food for drought victims as well as seed and feed for their livestock, far more than the $25 million the president had requested. Hoover also wanted to delete human relief from the bill because he feared urban congressmen would demand the same treatment for the hungry in their districts, which lay beyond the government's resources. The *New York World* editorially supported the president's position. It advised, "If the government feeds one group it should feed all, and once it has embarked on such a policy the politically minded lawmakers will never permit its abandonment."[37] Ultimately a compromise was worked out between the $25 million requested by the president and the $60 million demanded by senators from some affected states. The figure was set at $45 million, and Hoover signed the measure into law on January 15, 1931. Still, some lawmakers clamored from more. One bill proposed appropriating $25 million to the Red Cross, which the organization would distribute to the needy. On January 29, 1931, the Red Cross Central Resolutions Committee went on record as opposing a federal grant. It would jeopardize the independence of the philanthropic group, they argued, making them a quasiofficial arm of the government. The government might insist on attempting to influence how and where the money was spent. Further, government appropriations would handicap the organization's fundraising efforts because the money would appear to make private funds unnecessary. In a fundamental sense, it would undermine the principle of all private charity. John Barton Payne, the director of the Red Cross, said his agency would reject the government money. "If the Senate bill should become law the

Red Cross may as well go out of business, so far as dealing with natural calamities in this country is concerned," the *Washington Post* stated in an editorial.[38]

Hoover promised that no one would starve and argued that all that was at stake was the method of distribution, not whether people would go hungry. Representative Fiorello H. La Guardia, a New York liberal Republican, chimed in that he would indeed demand equivalent treatment for his constituents. Senator Reed Smoot, a Utah Republican, observed that there was some hypocrisy among Democrats who complained that insufficient money was available for drought relief. He said that if every individual in New York City would forego one meal per week and donate the money to the poor, there would be no hungry people anywhere in America. Meanwhile, Farm Board Chairman Alexander Legge said the Farm Board could supply practically unlimited amounts of wheat and cotton to the needy if it were reimbursed. He explained that under law the board had no authority to give away commodities. Congress never acted on the suggestion, which would have helped eliminate the farm surplus. Senator Joseph T. Robinson of Arkansas, who had initiated the initial $60 million appropriation, remained unsatisfied. He attached a $20 million amendment to the Interior Department's appropriation authorization, which had to pass before the session expired. The bill would provide money on top of the $45 million already appropriated, to be used for human food. Robinson, whose own state stood to receive much of the money, was in the process of building a base from which to launch a campaign for president in 1932. None of the actual or proposed appropriation measures included a method for funding them, as was also true of the veterans' bonus. Like, the bonus, the extra benefits had broad political appeal and backed the administration into a corner. Opponents of the measures were labeled enemies of the poor. However, they made responsible government officials of both parties nervous, because the till was nearly empty. Moreover, just weeks before, during the 1930 congressional elections, Democratic spokesmen had taunted the Republicans for excessive spending. Despite the hyperbole, both sides were willing to compromise. Robinson and his allies received their $20 million. It came without an explicit stipulation that it could be used for food, but with the tacit promise that Agriculture Secretary Hyde, who administered the fund, would interpret it generously. Robinson's provision for direct grants to individuals, at Hoover's insistence, was changed to specify that the money would be used for loans, which limited potential demand and also maintained a precedent important to Hoover.[39]

On the legislative front, the battle had been fought to a virtual tie. Money was not imposed on the Red Cross, no doles were provided, and the amount was a compromise. Yet Hoover endured another round of political abuse. One senator complained that Hoover was in league with millionaires, of whom there were not many in 1931, and that they should be taxed to pay for food for the poor. On the extreme left, the newly elected senator from Louisiana, Huey P. Long, was revving up a program that would confiscate millionaires' resources and use their money to provide free homes, guaranteed incomes, free college educations, medical care, and radios. The beauty of the plan was not only that it soaked the handful of millionaires but that no one else would pay any taxes at all.[40]

It might appear superficially that the entire Seventy-First Congress had been a bust for Hoover. Certainly it had been a learning experience. Yet significant reforms in several areas had been initiated, and Hoover's program for combating the Depression was gathering steam. Several bills dealing with public works designed to stimulate employment were enacted. The president had requested $150 million in one measure, which the Senate whittled to $116 million and the House to $110 million. The conference committee settled on $118 million, a modest compromise. A larger struggle ensued over who would control the fund: Congress or the president. Hoover contended that the cabinet and the president could most decisively direct the money to where it was most needed and where projects were most feasible while Congress would use it as a source of political patronage. Al Smith dismayed his fellow Democrats by writing an article, which appeared in the *New York World* on January 5, 1931, siding with his erstwhile opponent in favor of presidential control. Hoover won the conflict.[41] On February 13, 1931, the House passed the Elliot bill, already approved by the Senate, which provided for $415 million in public works outside the District of Columbia, plus an additional $50 million from money to be obtained from the sale of obsolete public buildings, a long-delayed measure for which the president had lobbied arduously. His signature on the bill made it possible to begin work on 200 projects to furnish employment, a major component in his countercyclical program.[42] On February 10, the president, who had already signed a bill sponsored by Senator Robert Wagner, a New York Democrat, to collect more comprehensive statistics on unemployment during the long session, approved a second Wagner measure. This law provided for a contingency planning apparatus to design public works in advance that could be implemented expeditiously during economic downturns. However, Congress stripped the measure of its modest appropriation of $150 million for public works, which would now require a congressional appropriation, slowing the process. Such proposals had been debated in 1921, 1923, and 1928 and had finally come to fruition. Hoover said the measure was not a solution to the present depression but should prove a useful tool during future slumps. On March 9, following the adjournment of the Seventy-First Congress, the president pocket-vetoed the third and final Wagner measure introduced as a package during the long session, a bill to create state unemployment agencies in partnership with the federal government. The chief executive said he had always supported the concept of such agencies, but a similar apparatus already existed in the Labor Department. The creation of new ones would create a lapse during the transition, and the system proposed was no improvement over the existing one. Hoover preferred a direct, centralized system to one operating jointly with the states as more efficient. Hoover pocket-vetoed four bills, of which only the Wagner measure was significant.[43]

The entire Seventy-First Congress had proven a battle of wills, with the president usually winning, sometimes after protracted struggles. Only the bills that involved serious debate have been discussed, which might leave the impression that the Congress was less productive than it actually was. In fact, it dwarfed the achievements of Hoover's immediate predecessors. If Hoover appears restrained in his relations with Congress from the viewpoint of the twenty-first century, it did not appear that way at the time. More often, congressmen accused him of meddling or treading upon their turf. No president in recent years had overcome more determined opposition from his own party. In the end, Hoover emerged as a strong president. He had won the grudging respect of Congress. Initially intending to treat Congress as an entirely distinct branch, he soon discarded that philosophy as impractical. His domestic program in general was the most innovative in scope and significance since the first Wilson administration. Despite resistance, the president had obtained precisely the type of bill he proposed, which became the Agricultural Marketing Act, and a reasonable facsimile of what he wanted in the Smoot-Hawley Tariff, about which he nonetheless had serious reservations. Yet protracted debate to redeem a promise made during the 1928 campaign and reinforced in the Republican platform that ended with no tariff at all would have been a more serious setback. Congress had approved the largest program of inland waterway development in American history; a generous appropriation of federal matching funds for road construction; an initial appropriation to begin work on the Hoover Dam; and reforms in the administration of the Indian Bureau, including increased appropriations, despite the weak economy. Hoover's plans to reorganize veterans' affairs under the rubric of the Veterans' Administration had become reality, and the president's vision of prison and law enforcement reform was under way. The controversial conclusions of the Wickersham Commission should not obscure its contributions to the larger issue of law enforcement in general. Further, Hoover had shamed Congress into appropriating the full $500,000 it had promised to provide in order to complete the commission's work after the national legislature threatened to starve it out of existence. To expedite Prohibition enforcement, Congress had authorized money for new federal judges to hear cases and eliminated trial by jury in minor cases. The president obtained a joint resolution establishing a Bureau of Narcotics in the Treasury Department, separating enforcement of narcotics violations from those of Prohibition, and constructing prisons that focused on the rehabilitation of addicts and of criminals in general. Commissions remained at work producing data and statistics that would serve as blueprints for later administrations. The president had vetoed 11 bills and had been overridden on 2. He had not flinched from confrontations with Congress. Some of his work was unpleasant, yet he relished challenges.

To be sure, the president did not get everything he wanted. He was disappointed in not obtaining banking reform, for he could perceive the seeds of a banking panic. He had only modest success in reorganization of the executive branch and would not obtain the opportunity until the Truman and Eisenhower administrations. He was not entirely opposed to deficit spending in hard times, but he worried that the budget was becoming out of kilter. He wanted to husband funds for ordinary expenditures in order to free additional money for countercyclical recovery measures. No clear-cut resolution to Prohibition had been devised because the nation and its representatives, including the president himself, remained of two minds. The president could not prevent a major raid on the Treasury by proponents of veterans in the waning days of the short session, and it only whet the appetite of the vets for more. Not all the legislation enacted was major, to be sure, but some of it was. The Hoover Dam was under way, the greatest structure to be erected by humans since the Great Wall of China. More than half a billion dollars had been approved for public works, an unimaginable sum in peacetime a few years earlier. Income taxes had been slashed $160 million, another economic stimulus. The effects of the Agricultural Marketing Act and the Smoot-Hawley Tariff might be debatable, but they certainly constituted major legislation. Some of the president's achievements at about midway through his term did not show up in legislation. An unusual degree of labor peace had prevailed. The labor-management agreements negotiated by the president in 1929 were fraying at the edges, yet holding up in many industries. The quality of appointments made by the administration was exceptionally high. There had been no major scandals, and there would be none. The turnover rate in government service was low, and morale was high; no high-ranking official was fired for incompetence or corruption. In foreign policy, the administration had negotiated—and inveigled the Senate to ratify—the London Naval F, the last major international arms limitation agreement prior to World War II. Congressmen who dealt with Hoover might argue with his principles, but no one could credibly claim that he lacked principles, wallowed in glory, wrapped himself in self-serving delusions, or was inert. He was as often criticized for spending too much as for spending too little, for being too tough, rather than too lenient. No one who had seen him in action doubted his capacity for hard work.

When the Seventy-First Congress adjourned it had been in session since April 1929. It had been noisy and reasonably productive but never dull. Hoover had emerged as the dominant figure in Washington. During this time, he had also been catapulted to the epicenter of the world stage.

CHAPTER 7

Hoover and the World

Foreign Policy, 1929–1930

Although John Quincy Adams was well traveled for his time, it is unlikely that any president before the age of jet travel lived and worked abroad as much as Hoover before reaching the White House. By the end of World War I he had visited every nation in Europe, including the new ones carved out of the German, Hapsburg, Turkish, and Russian empires. In his work as an engineer he traversed Australia, China, Siberia, Canada, South Africa, much of Latin America, the Middle East, Burma, Mongolia, and—with the exception of equatorial Africa, traveled widely on every inhabitable continent. Neither did he confine his visits to capital cities or major trade centers. The engineer was at home on camel, horseback, mule, automobile, bicycle, and boat, in the Australian outback, unexplored sections of China and Burma seldom visited by foreigners, remote stretches of Siberia, Japan, the frozen Arctic, and the Mediterranean rim. Before arriving, Hoover read prodigiously about local history, customs, and geography. And beginning with China, he had an accomplished traveling companion in his wife Lou, a woman of insatiable curiosity and tireless endurance who learned to speak five languages. The Hoovers capaciously absorbed what they saw abroad. Fifty years later, Hoover could describe in detail his experience during the Boxer Rebellion of 1900. Although cosmopolitan, Hoover was thoroughly American in his practicality and disdain for pretense. He disliked European aristocracy and elitism, and he found the poverty he observed appalling. However, the Stanford

alum respected foreign cultures and did not believe they should be American-
ized. His appreciations ranged from pottery and poetry to steam shovels. The
president had circled the globe four times by 1914, sometimes with his small
children, reading incessantly on shipboard. He devoured books so hungrily
that some of his friends believed he would have liked wider oceans to provide
more time for his eclectic taste in literature and nonfiction. As an engineer,
Hoover had offices scattered throughout the world with headquarters at London, then the mining capital of the world. World War I brought him into intimate contact with the leading diplomats and businessmen in England. He was
a major figure at the Versailles Peace Conference in 1919. After the war he fed
and helped rebuild the infrastructure of parts of Europe, the Near East, and
Russia. He expressed interest in serving as secretary of state under Coolidge.

Hoover was both a nationalist and an internationalist but never an isolationist. Highly patriotic, never daunted by the stature of foreign leaders,
he nonetheless possessed a sophisticated understanding of the interconnected
nature of world politics, economics, diplomacy, and culture. As a humanitarian, he wished to see the entire world free of poverty, hunger, and disease and
under self-rule. As a dedicated public official and a practical politician, he put
the interests of America first, but knew he must deal within the parameters
set by the Constitution, Congress, and public opinion. During and after the
war, though holding no formal office, Hoover met on equal terms with kings,
generals, and prime ministers. After the war he was better known abroad than
in his own country and was a potential candidate for the 1919 Nobel Prize
awarded to Woodrow Wilson. Hoover's aversion to pageantry caused him to
avoid ceremonies designed to honor him. He was weary of Europe and felt
most at home in America, especially in California. He had no desire to return
to Europe after Versailles.[1]

The war changed Hoover. Always serious, he became more introverted,
fixed with a steely resolve. His Quaker aversion to war was reinforced by the
wanton slaughter he had witnessed and by the hungry, malnourished children
the war left in its wake. Hoover knew that wars killed the innocent, displaced
populations, and often sowed the seeds of future conflicts. One of the tragedies
of Hoover's presidency is that the Depression sidetracked him from fulfilling
his desire to institutionalize peace. As president, he managed foreign crises
cautiously, yet imaginatively, and avoided escalation. Publicly, he strove to
mobilize world opinion against aggressors and to promote friendship on the
basis of respect with Latin America. Though a protectionist, he also desired to
foster commercial relations with the world. He lacked imperialist ambitions
and distrusted those who harbored them. For the most part, Hoover was not
troubled with serious crises until nearly the end of his presidency. Still the
Quaker president was mindful that domestic policy was only one barrel of
a two-barreled shotgun that the chief executive must wield. He must always
train a wary eye on the world, but Hoover was as proactive in foreign policy as
conditions permitted. He proposed more major international initiatives than

any national leader of his time, designed to ensure peace through disarmament and political and economic stability. The president encouraged settlement of disputes through treaties, arbitration, and international organizations. Hoover wanted to venture much further in these directions than most world leaders—and his own countrymen—were willing to follow. The president was not a pacifist, though he might have been as close to one as any modern American president. He had supported World War I and remembered that some of his Quaker ancestors had fought in the Civil War because they hated slavery more than they hated war. Hoover did not believe in unilateral disarmament because he believed that weakness might invite war. Yet he was willing to disarm to the lowest level comparable to other nations.[2]

The zeitgeist in which world diplomats operated during the late 1920s and early 1930s looked backward, from the vantage point of World War I. Many steps Hoover wanted to initiate in diplomacy, including those designed to make war less likely, were handcuffed by the mixed messages Americans attributed to the Great War. This included cooperation with the League of Nations short of membership, joining the World Court, working in concert with other powers to avert a crisis, avoiding military or diplomatic alliances, and diminishing or eliminating war debts. A large portion of public and congressional opinion remained isolationist or at least noninterventionist. By overreacting to perceived mistakes of the past, Americans were destined to commit new, equally fallacious ones. Moreover, after the onset of the Depression, economic desolation shadowed world events, aggravating already volatile conditions. Germany, in the heart of Europe, was plagued by economic and political instability. It was also bent on revenge for defeat in the Great War. It was not merely the punitive Versailles treaty, which was less punitive than a treaty Germany might have imposed on the Allies—and did impose on Russia—that inflamed Germany; it was the humiliation of a military defeat. And the French, frightened by a neighbor more populous, with greater industrial and military potential, reacted defensively, attempting not only to punish Germany for past deeds but relentlessly striving to permanently weaken them, a strategy that outraged Germans. Could powerful nations such as the United States and Great Britain have stepped in, refereed, and separated the prospective combatants? Perhaps, if they had not been democracies. But no American presidential candidate or a potential British prime minister running on a platform of intervening in Central Europe could have been elected. The British, after suffering the grinding ground combat of the Great War, determined to rely almost exclusively on their navy. The United States was also chiefly a naval power, leery of involvement even in a defensive war outside the Western Hemisphere. If there is blame to be shared, it must fall, not solely on the diplomats and politicians of the interwar era, but on the people who elected them to office. This applies to the people who voted for the foreign tyrants as well. Europe and Japan armed to the teeth while the world watched and hoped that common sense would prevail over past enmities, and this was not a safe bet.

Hoover took a long view. He knew dictators thrived on war and swore not to provide one on which they could feed. He did not expect Communism to survive nearly as long as it did, but when the collapse did occur, it came in much the way he expected. The president was justifiably skeptical of economic sanctions as a tool in diplomacy, because he believed they affected only the civilian population, not the dictators or their armies. No really determined aggressor was deterred by sanctions, though some might be goaded into war by them. Most importantly, the Depression preoccupied Hoover. Just as Woodrow Wilson and Lyndon B. Johnson had wanted to be domestic reformers, yet ended up striving to save the world for democracy and from Communism, respectively; Hoover wanted to entrench world peace but was forced to fight an invisible, economic enemy.

At the time he became president, the Great War was the formative experience in Hoover's life, as for many of his generation. He bonded with men who joined him in common crusades during that era and relied upon many of them in government or in voluntary groups for the rest of his life. His life straddled the Great War, which incubated the Great Depression, which incubated a yet greater war, World War II, which contributed to ending the Depression. In retrospect it appears almost a seamless cubicle, inevitable and involuntary, but history is not that dialectical. Hoover's diplomacy was innovative and active yet prudent and measured. He recognized the limits of American power, and he did not intend to risk war for abstract ideals. No American soldier died in battle abroad during his tenure. The United States possessed a tiny army during Hoover's presidency. He did not enlarge it, but he did restructure it and reorganize the command. Although the navy was his chief line of defense, it was also the largest element in the military budget and hence the most amenable to budget cutting, especially if disarmament could be achieved. With savings from the military, the president intended to increase appropriations for the diplomatic corps and for job creation. He realized that resources were finite; he could not spend more in some areas without cutting somewhere else.[3]

Hoover distrusted Europe's class stratification and militarism but got along well with most European leaders. He conducted successful summits in America with Ramsay MacDonald of Britain and Pierre Laval of France. However, he never left America during his presidency. The Quaker entered office with a desire to maintain amicable relations with other nations, especially the Europeans and the Latin Americans, and for the most part he did. The French, in their resolve to defang the Germans, caused the most friction in Europe. In Asia, Japan pursued a relentless imperialist path that produced an ominous crisis in China. Central Europe was in flux. French paranoia aggravated the situation. German economic and political stability was the key to a prosperous and peaceful Europe. Despite Hoover's best efforts, such order could not be cobbled together. The president marginally slowed the arms race and always worked toward that end. The French, however, would not agree to a disarmament treaty without a companion agreement binding the United States to protect them from Germany. This was a political impossibility because the American Congress would never ratify a *de facto* alliance with France.

The president strove to maintain reasonably stable relations with all peaceful nations and to avoid wars that did not affect the vital interests of the United States and achieved these modest ends. The administration placed great faith in the Kellogg-Briand Peace Pact, which outlawed war as an instrument of national policy. Negotiated during the Coolidge administration, it was proclaimed effective by Hoover, who hoped the sanction of public opinion would prove an effective deterrent. However, he did not believe force should be used to enforce such treaties; that would mean going to war to prevent war. The concept was sound legally but shaky in practice. Although used in diplomatic notes, the Kellogg-Briand Pact never prevented a major war, though it served as one basis for the Allied War Crimes Trials after World War II. The chief executive was a pragmatist with a strong idealistic streak. He treated each nation individually, on the basis of its relationship to the best interests of the United States. Quakerism influenced him, but American nationalism influenced him more. As on domestic policy, the president made his own decisions and initiated much of the policy of the administration. Still, he was willing to compromise, both with other nations and with Congress. He seldom broached a matter that he knew Congress would adamantly oppose. For example, his opposition to canceling war debts was based less on principle than on his belief that Congress, backed by the public, would never ratify such an agreement. Hoover was more idealistic than either his immediate predecessors or his successor, indeed, more so than most presidents. For example, he tried to negotiate a treaty immunizing food ships, on the same basis as hospital ships, from attack during times of war. Britain opposed this on the grounds that it would partly nullify the effect of naval blockades.[4] Even more idealistically, in a move he later regretted, the president closed down the State Department's Code-Breaking Office in 1929, stating, "Gentlemen do not read each other's mail."[5] As the nation moved toward war he was heavily criticized for squandering valuable intelligence. Although Hoover considered Theodore Roosevelt his mentor, he had not one iota of Roosevelt's military belligerence. To Roosevelt, war was heroic; to Hoover it was tragic. He had devoted his wartime experience to saving lives, not to killing. He was not a reactive foreign policy president who merely waited for problems to come to him. The president devoted far more time to foreign relations, including trade, during his single term, than did FDR during his first term. Hoover viewed peaceful times as the most auspicious period to erect an enduring edifice of peace. Once war erupted, it was too late. The kind of success he wanted lay in preventing war, not as TR desired, in waging a successful war.[6]

The key figure in the State Department, Henry L. Stimson, was not Hoover's first choice for secretary of state. He offered the position to Senator

William E. Borah and to ex-Supreme Court Justice and New York Governor Charles Evans Hughes, who both declined. Hoover made overtures to New Jersey Senator Dwight L. Morrow and to the incumbent Secretary of State Frank Kellogg, but neither wanted the office. Later, Hoover observed that if he had known Charles Francis Adams better, whom he appointed secretary of the navy, he would have picked Adams to head the State Department. Stimson himself, while honored by the offer, was surprised. He was serving as governor-general of the Philippines and sought about a month to wrap up his activities there. Hoover allowed Stimson time to complete his duties, and Frank Kellogg remained as interim secretary of state.[7] Sixty-one when he became secretary of state, Stimson was serious and aloof. He found cabinet meetings boring, contributed little, and disliked the routine paperwork of his department. "I am afraid I am too much of a loafer and enjoy my recreation too much to be able to stand this thing perpetually," he confessed.[8] The secretary found Washington provincial and the summer heat stifling. One of the more lethargic members of the cabinet, he did not exercise much influence outside of his own department. An impeccable gentleman, Stimson could be opinionated and stubborn. His mind was more ponderous than Hoover's and lacked the president's imagination. The secretary missed the subtlety of the president's wit, and as Stimson aged he tended to overlook, not catch, nuances in conversations.

The chief executive had more disagreements with Stimson than with other cabinet members. Both were strong willed. Yet Stimson respected Hoover and, even when he disagreed, deferred to the president's judgment. He accepted the premise that the president deserved the final say. Reflecting in 1947, Stimson's biographical collaborator, McGeorge Bundy, expressed the opinion of Hoover's ex-secretary of state, "Mr. Hoover was to him one of the great Americans of his time, and one of the most unjustly maligned."[9] Stimson would have liked to dispense with some delicate issues summarily. Hoover was more sensitive to the necessity of dealing with Congress and satisfying public opinion. By nature the secretary was cold, austere, and shy, yet he possessed a hot temper. "There is no blinking the fact," one of his subordinates said, "that Stimson is an unlovable character, a very hard man to work under."[10] Stimson's chief critic in the White House was Hoover's press secretary, Theodore Joslin, who considered the New Yorker abrasive, narcissistic, disloyal, and plodding. "Stimson is a mill stone around the neck of the president," Joslin confided to his diary. "As a negotiator, he is a washout. He does not even carry out instructions given to him painstakingly by the president." Joslin fumed that Stimson thought so slowly that the president had to prompt him during conversations over the trans-Atlantic telephone.[11]

In addition to personality differences, the president and his secretary of state sometimes clashed over policy, especially during the final two years of the administration. Usually, these were differences of degree or opinions about the best strategy to preserve peace. During the Japanese invasion of Manchuria and the subsequent invasion of China in 1932, Stimson wanted to threaten economic sanctions against Japan, which Hoover opposed. However, upon reflection, Stimson admitted that he had underestimated the strength of the isolationist sentiment the president had to cope with. In 1947 he observed that the early 1930s marked the apogee of American isolationism. Stimson also favored outright cancellation of war debts but subsequently agreed that Congress and the public would never have agreed to this. On basic, fundamental principles, the president and his secretary were in agreement. Neither wanted a war in Asia—or elsewhere. They also basically agreed on the efficacy of international public opinion as a deterrent to war. Stimson and Hoover thought the Kellogg Pact might avert another conflagration. Both wanted to cooperate with the League short of membership. Further, to defuse international disagreements and with Hoover's blessing Stimson negotiated 25 bilateral arbitration treaties and 17 treaties of conciliation with foreign nations. Although Stimson's temperament was more militaristic than Hoover's, it would be an exaggeration to conclude that Stimson desired war. Under Hoover, he did everything he was asked to do to avoid war.[12]

Even before he left the Philippines, Stimson had begun putting together his team at the State Department. His first task was to select an undersecretary. Partly upon the recommendation of his friend Felix Frankfurter, he chose Joseph P. Cotton. Cotton became Stimson's chief advisor, and the two were synchronous on policy. His undersecretary also helped soothe egos that Stimson bruised. Stimson came to rely on Cotton heavily, and it came as a staggering personal and professional blow when Cotton died prematurely, at the age of 56, in March 1931. Cotton was succeeded by Assistant Secretary William R. Castle, who had served as chief of the Division of Western Europe. A veteran officer, Castle had entered the State Department in the 1920s. In fact, Stimson inherited an unusually experienced team, though he sometimes chose to ignore their advice. Castle got along better with Hoover than with Stimson. Still, the State Department usually functioned smoothly, and world affairs were in a relatively serene interlude. The Hoover-Stimson team lacked the opportunity to make major diplomatic breakthroughs.[13]

Upon returning from his goodwill voyage to Latin America during the interregnum, Hoover put in motion his plans to make improvement of hemispheric relations a greater priority than any previous president. He wanted to treat all sovereign nations, large and small, with respect and dispel some of the fear of Yankee Imperialism. Hoover's Latin American policies were unusually successful. Alexander DeConde concludes that "he probably traveled farther along the road of Pan-American solidarity than any previous President."[14] Hoover later said that he considered the improvement of relations with Latin American one of the most important accomplishments of his administration. The cornerstone of his commitment was to upgrade the diplomatic corps in the region, which had served as a sinecure. Hoover appointed native speakers who understood the culture and showed respect for the people. The president complemented this empathetic approach by establishing a program to exchange students and professors. He initiated air travel and air mail delivery and began construction of a Pan American highway. His achievements were accomplished despite instability. Some 20 revolutions took place in Latin America during his presidency. His successor adopted Hoover's Good Neighbor policy and built upon it. Their efforts reaped the reward of solidarity during World War II.[15]

In September 1930, Hoover announced a reform in the recognition policy of governments in South America, reversing the precedent set by Woodrow Wilson and continued by his successors. No longer would the United States judge the morality of a new government or how it came to power. Rather, recognition would be determined by certain criteria: physical control of the country; an absence of armed resistance; a commitment to hold elections in due time; and a promise to honor international debts. Hoover's policy was more pragmatic than Wilson's and helped to avoid entanglement in the web of South American factions. It was welcomed by America's neighbors. In Central America, a more stringent criterion was applied based on agreement among the five republics themselves. In 1923, they had signed a treaty disavowing recognition of any regime that had overthrown a constitutionally elected government. Although the United States was not a signatory, it had promised to abide by the treaty and continued to do so. The administration did distinguish between constitutional Latin American governments and insurgents in the sale of arms, adhering to a protocol established at an international conference attended by the regional republics at Havana in 1928. The gathering had agreed to sell arms and munitions to legitimate governments but deny them to rebels. The Hoover administration sold arms to the Mexican government during a revolution. The incumbents prevailed, which helped cement friendly relations. The same policy did not work so well in Brazil. In October 1930, Secretary Stimson authorized the sale of arms to the Brazilian government, which was under the threat of a rebellion. The rebels won and resented the American partiality; nonetheless the policy remained in effect.[16]

The chief executive strove to dispel resentment of the Monroe Doctrine by many Latin neighbors. James Monroe had declared that the Western Hemisphere was no longer open to colonization, a unilateral policy designed to protect Latin America but rendered obsolete by the twentieth century. Theodore Roosevelt's more assertive corollary stated that the United States was the sole enforcer of the doctrine. Hoover considered the policies, especially the Roosevelt Corollary, obsolete. During the Coolidge administration, Reuben J. Clark, a State Department Latin American specialist, researched and wrote a study of the doctrine and its corollary, which he submitted to the outgoing secretary of state, Frank B. Kellogg. Clark argued that the corollary had an adverse effect on Latin American relations and recommended abrogating it. In 1930, Hoover directed Stimson to publish the Clark Memorandum, making it policy. Although Hoover was a "hands-on" president in domestic policy, his sensitivity to Latin American feelings made him increasingly "hands off" with respect to our southern neighbors. He announced that the United States would no longer intervene militarily in South America, not to collect public or private debts or even to save American lives in most cases. The administration would employ all diplomatic means to protect Americans and American interests, but it would abstain from force. Americans who invested abroad did so at their own risk. When Panama experienced a revolution and El Salvador defaulted on bonds, the president refrained from interference. Hoover explained, "I can say at once that it never has been and ought not to be the policy of the United States to intervene by force to secure or maintain contracts between foreign states or their citizens."[17]

The first serious crisis the United States faced in the hemisphere occurred in Haiti, which had been occupied by American Marines since 1915. When Hoover became president, he intended to phase out the 700 Marines stationed there. However, during the first week of December 1929, rioting erupted. The American commissioner, General John H. Russell, declared martial law, and on December 7, the president announced that he was dispatching an additional 500 troops. After two or three days the violence ended, aided by the announcement that the unpopular Haitian president, Louis Borno, would not be a candidate for reelection. Haiti had an indirect method of electing presidents, and the turbulence occurred during a period of political transition. Borno and his opponents compromised on the selection of a moderate, Eugene Roy, a Haitian banker, who would supervise elections for a legislature, which in turn would select the next permanent president. However, Borno initially balked at resigning. Under pressure, he agreed to abide by the original plan. On April 21, Roy was named interim president by the Council of State, which had been appointed by Borno, and the incumbent relinquished his grip on office. On October 14, Haiti voted for its first freely elected legislature in 13 years. The legislature would meet to elect a permanent president in November.[18]

Meanwhile, the president appointed a commission, headed by W. Cameron Forbes, to investigate and suggest a plan for transition. The commission was permitted to go beyond its original instructions when conditions deteriorated, and it improvised a solution. Forbes suggested that the upcoming elections be held under the supervision of local officials rather than Americans, and a candidate neutral toward the United States was elected. Under the direction of the commission, the military administrator on the island was replaced by a civilian. In 1930 the Forbes Commission released its report, which indicated that under American occupation, sanitation, health, and roads were improving. However, the Haitians resented the American presence. Though the commission believed the island was not prepared for independence, it recommended turning over virtually all functions of government to Haitians, with a few American advisers, within six years. Believing an improved educational infrastructure was essential, the president dispatched an all-black commission led by Dr. Robert E. Moton, who had succeeded Booker T. Washington as the principal of the Tuskegee Institute, to gather facts and reach conclusions. The Moton Commission remained in Haiti for 24 days, departing for Washington on July 15, 1930. Moton indicated that the urban population of Haiti was relatively well educated and benefited from good schools. However, education in rural Haiti was poor, and illiteracy was widespread. The island suffered from the deterioration of the world economy, which had depressed the price of coffee, Haiti's chief export. The Moton Commission recommended that education be molded to Haitian needs rather than emulate the education of whites.[19]

The president began removing troops as soon as conditions stabilized. He was eager to withdraw all military forces from Latin America before the termination of his administration. In addition to the Marines in Haiti, there were approximately 1,600 in Nicaragua. Except for these nations, the only American soldiers stationed abroad were 2,605 in China.[20] The Cameron and Moton reports agreed that expeditious withdrawal was desirable. As a result of the reports, the president began a gradual withdrawal of Marines from Haiti. Late in 1931 the Haitian government assumed control of all functions except finances and the military. The Haitian Assembly delayed total withdrawal by refusing to ratify a treaty providing for it. However, in 1934, President Roosevelt completed the pullout via executive agreement without ratification by the Haitians. Except for the Haitian delays, the troops would have departed under Hoover in 1932.[21] Hoover remained patient and flexible in his relations with Latin America, adjusting as conditions changed. His preference would have been to disengage immediately, but almost certainly loss of lives, chiefly among the occupied peoples, would have resulted. He had to tread a line between respecting the sensibilities of the smaller republics and, on the other hand, creating incendiary conditions by precipitous action. In line with his general policy of exerting the least interference practical in Latin America, Hoover reduced the number of Marines in Nicaragua to less than a thousand before the end of 1931 and announced the imminent withdrawal of the remainder.[22] His nuanced approach succeeded reasonably well. Unfortunately, stability was difficult to achieve in the region, particularly during the Great Depression, but due to Hoover's efforts the United States enjoyed unusually warm relations with the republics to the South.

Hoover helped negotiate an end to the Tacna-Arica dispute that had festered for nearly 50 years following the War of the Pacific between Peru and Bolivia on one side and Chile on the other. The Harding and Coolidge administrations had initiated discussions that led to the renewal of diplomatic relations between Chile and Peru. When Hoover toured Latin America in 1928 he was asked to facilitate a settlement. The territory in dispute was chiefly trackless jungle of little value, but national pride obstructed a settlement. Secretary of State Kellogg had made substantial progress during the Coolidge administration, and Stimson and Hoover completed the work. The main point of contention was the port of Arica, the site of the final battle, which had sentimental value for each side. Hoover's compromise awarded Arica to Chile. Peru received a free port there and public works erected by Chile. Peru also received $6 million compensation from Chile. Bolivia remained unhappy because it was still landlocked. The feuding nations erected a monument to symbolize the end of the protracted enmity.[23]

The first year of the administration, 1929, was the high point of idealism for the Hoover-Stimson team, especially for Stimson. The new administration sought to employ the newly minted Kellogg-Briand Pact as a tool to settle international disputes and as a vehicle for disarmament. The first significant opportunity to apply the treaty occurred when Russia and China skirmished in Manchuria over rights to ownership of a strategic railroad. The railway in question connected the Chinese Eastern line and the South Manchurian railway. The former was owned jointly by Russia and China and the latter by Japan. Manchuria was coveted by all three nations because it offered land for colonization, coal and iron deposits, timber, and fertile soil. Nationalism inflamed the three nations, and each was eager to flex its muscles. The Eastern railway, which stretched for about 1,000 miles, held strategic significance for Russia, while China coveted its economic resources. Of the trifecta with interests in the region, China was the weakest militarily but the closest in proximity and was the most aggressive in stirring the pot. The ambitious Chiang Kai-shek believed he could manipulate the local warlord to provoke a fight with the Russians. If he won, the Chinese would have acquired territory. Defeat would mean the elimination of a potential rival to Chiang within the Celestial Empire.

The Eastern had been constructed by the Russians with a French loan, at a cost of about $200,000. During the Great War it passed under the control of the Allies, and it was directly operated by an American colonel. After the war, the Chinese and Russians disputed ownership, but by 1929 the Russians had gained the upper hand. The Chinese provoked hostilities that erupted near the dawn of the Hoover administration. In December 1928, China seized a local telephone line and threatened to take over strategic telegraph communications. In July 1929 the situation escalated when China confiscated the railroad. Russia and China severed diplomatic relations, and war appeared imminent. Stimson planned to use the Kellogg-Briand Pact as a rationale for a ceasefire, claiming that both China and Russia, as signatories, were obligated to observe it. Stimson stirred a hornet's nest. The United States had no relations with Russia and had to convey Stimson's message through France. A direct message went to China. Attempts to obtain collaboration from the leading members of the League, which possessed an enforcement mechanism, were futile. The Russians and the Chinese tartly responded that Stimson should mind his own business. Japan was irritated because it had not been formally consulted. The Japanese correctly pointed out that they had vital interests in the region, where the Americans had none. Hoover, who recognized that

America had no essential interests in the region, was reluctant to intervene, even in the mild form of a diplomatic note.[24]

Neither China nor Russia was prepared for a lengthy war, nor wanted one. The Soviets were still recovering from the Great War, followed by the ravages of a civil war that spewed famine in its wake. China was not a nation in the modern sense. The Chinese army was disorganized, undisciplined, and poorly armed. Much of the damage inflicted on Chinese civilians was caused by the Chinese army in its hasty retreat. Neither side took the Kellogg-Briand Pact seriously. Both replied that the treaty permitted defensive wars, which each claimed to be fighting. Certainly the Russians were stronger in a military sense, but they were not sufficiently strong to impose their rule on a vast expanse of Chinese territory. The fighting seemed to slacken by midsummer and then revived briefly in the fall. The Russians were willing to settle on the basis of the status quo ante before the Chinese began seizing accoutrements of the railroad. Ultimately, the parties settled the issue themselves on the basis of the status quo ante, which meant Russian ownership, in the Sino-Soviet Pact of December 3, 1929. The Russians withdrew by January 2, 1930. Although Stimson liked to claim that he had put teeth into the Kellogg Pact, in reality his diplomacy had no appreciable effect except to irritate all sides. This first foray into the world scene for the new president and his secretary of state was well meaning but not auspicious. It did no serious harm, nor did it affect the dispute, which fortunately was not protracted and did not spread. Militarily and diplomatically, the United States had little leverage in the Far East in the early 1930s, nothing more formidable to contribute than advice.[25]

Defusing wars in faraway places was only secondary to Hoover's primary motivation of unleashing a new era of world peace, and in the early 1930s, the times appeared auspicious. Within a month of his inauguration the president delivered a speech at Arlington National Cemetery in which the suggested that the Kellogg Pact be reinforced by disarmament. Disarmament and peaceful settlement of disputes through mediation and arbitration, as well as expanded international trade, were the pillars of Hoover's foreign relations. He could not rest until the genie of war was restored to its bottle. Hoover took the initiative, yet proceeded cautiously and incrementally, building relationships with other heads of states, and then allowing public opinion to catch up. The key to disarmament was careful preparation and agreements with foreign leaders prior to a conference. The president had been an enthusiastic supporter of the Washington Naval Conference of 1921, which established ratios among the major powers to limit battleship construction. Coolidge had tried to follow up with more general disarmament at the Geneva Conference of 1927 but had failed because of inadequate preparation. The new president planned to build on the foundation of the previous disarmament limits and the Kellogg Pact. Though the Kellogg Pact had been ridiculed by some, Hoover and Stimson believed disarmament might give it tangible meaning.

The logical place for the United States to start was naval disarmament. America, with only 140,000 active soldiers, had the smallest land army of any major power, about the size allotted to the emasculated German military by the Versailles treaty. The navy, however, was second only to Britain's. Hoover believed the American military force should be designed solely for defense, though it would protect the entire Western Hemisphere. The chief executive also believed that a vast military was wasteful during a shaky economy, drained money from productive purposes, and increased taxes. Even with its modest army, the United States had the highest military budget in the world on an annual basis. Before he took office, 25 percent of tax dollars were devoted to defense while 62 percent were used to pay for previous wars by retiring bonds and aiding veterans. This amounted to 87 percent of the federal budget. The cost of constructing a battleship had risen to $50 million. The president also believed an arms race in Europe retarded the continent's economic recovery. In short the arms race, particularly naval competition with Britain, with whom war was inconceivable, violated common sense, and the president believed common sense was the short-term version of ultimate wisdom. The chief executive launched his campaign by asking his friend Hugh Gibson, the ambassador to Belgium and U.S. representative at the World Preparatory Arms Conference in Geneva, to deliver a speech indicating that the president had devised a new yardstick more sophisticated than raw tonnage to measure naval weapons.[26]

Britain was the latchkey to successful naval reductions. There was strong support both in Britain and in America for limitations but also strong resistance. Most Americans remained isolationist, or at least noninterventionist at heart, yet the nation also contained an aggressive big navy faction. Britain's position was realistic yet difficult to reconcile. England needed a large navy to protect its empire, yet could not compete financially with America in a naval race. The Japanese, also stretched to the limit of their resources, were amenable. France and Italy represented more difficult obstacles. Hoover filled the prestigious Ambassadorship to the Court of St. James with a prominent American, the outgoing vice president, Charles G. Dawes. The ambassador opened preliminary discussions with the new Labour Prime Minister Ramsay MacDonald. Both countries wanted to extend the battleship ratios of the Washington Conference to smaller vessels. Most important were cruisers. The British desired a larger quantity of shorter-range, lightly armed cruisers to protect their far-flung Empire. America, lacking Britain's worldwide coaling stations, wanted larger ships that more heavily armed with a longer cruising range. Hoover and MacDonald agreed on basic principles. The decisions were to be made at the top, and the naval experts would iron out details. Then a formula, based on Hoover's ideas, was devised whereby tonnage was not the sole criterion. This facilitated compromise. Hoover was probably the foremost advocate of disarmament of any president up to his time, and in MacDonald he found a kindred spirit. Hoover knew any settlement would have to be ratified by Congress. MacDonald would have to overcome a tradition of centuries during which the British fleet had ruled the seas. The crux of their agreement was naval parity. Neither nation would be realistically threatened by roughly equal fleets. Indeed, Hoover knew that, beyond a certain level, additional ships bought no additional security. His objective was to achieve the minimum number of ships and tonnage feasible in each class.[27]

In late June 1929, the plan was fleshed out. Five-power talks at the ministerial level began in London. This would be followed by a Hoover-MacDonald summit conference at Washington, culminating in a naval conference at London the following autumn. London, rather than Washington, was selected because the United States was not a member of the League of Nations. The early discussions among the diplomats revolved around questions such as whether the conference would focus only on cruisers and battleships or might include additional vessels such as aircraft carriers, destroyers, and submarines. On July 24, 1929, MacDonald announced unilateral reductions as a goodwill measure. He told the House of Commons that he would suspend work on two cruisers, cancel contracts on two submarines, and slow construction on a submarine depot. Hoover and MacDonald synchronized their actions, keeping each other informed during each step of confidence building.[28] The Americans and the British wanted the conference to consider all types of ships, utilizing a flexible yardstick. From the beginning, the major naval powers realized that drawing France and Italy into an agreement would be difficult. France feared the yardsticks developed by the Anglo powers might be inappropriate for them. The French and the Italians, who were competing in the Mediterranean, wanted to omit consideration of smaller vessels, which they considered essential to their Mediterranean fleets. The French wanted superiority over the Italians due to their larger empire, yet the Italians insisted on parity. For each nation, domestic politics was a factor. A French government that accepted parity with Italy might fall while an Italian government that failed to obtain parity would probably collapse. Finally, every achievement possible at the ministerial level had been settled. The remaining issues would have to be determined at the conference itself. Hoover and MacDonald both believed a summit between them would be useful. However, Hoover was cautious about the timing, while MacDonald angled for an invitation. The personal chemistry between the men at a face-to-face meeting would ultimately determine the success of the larger conference.[29]

On September 12, 1929, MacDonald revealed that he had received the desired invitation from Hoover and would sail on September 28, arriving in New York and then traveling by rail to Washington for a six-day sojourn in the United States. The visit began with appropriate pomp, as the prime minister, a widower traveling with his daughter Isabel, arrived on October 4. A ticker-tape parade through America's largest city welcomed him, and Mayor James J. "Jimmie" Walker handed MacDonald the keys to the metropolis. He was honored with a second parade in Washington and spent his first night in the capital at the British Embassy. Then he moved to the White House, where he was honored by being billeted in the Lincoln bedroom. MacDonald also became the guest of honor at the first state dinner of the Hoover administration. The president indicated that he intended to drive his guests to Camp Rapidan for the weekend to experience American informality and to enjoy the fall foliage. The prime minister, who had packed only formal clothes, borrowed pants and a shirt from Hoover for the country outing. Only one State Department official accompanied Hoover. Otherwise, there were no reporters and no advisers for either head of state. The two men spent virtually all their daytime hours together, while Lou, paired with Isabel, took her on long horseback rides and strolls through the forests and gardens. In the bucolic setting of Virginian's Blue Ridge Mountains, the men followed paths beside the gurgling water of Hoover's favorite trout stream. At one point they sat and chatted for nearly an hour at opposite ends of a log overlooking the Rapidan. They discussed only a few serious issues in the picturesque setting, but over the course of MacDonald's visit they covered a variety of topics. The president offered to erase the British war debt in exchange for British withdrawal from Bermuda, Trinidad, and British Honduras, which Hoover wanted for defense. The prime minister demurred, but he did promise to abstain from dispatching British warships to the Western Hemisphere. They agreed that the principal purpose of the coming conference would be to expand to work of the Washington Conference to smaller classes of vessels. MacDonald promised to issue the invitations to the London Conference at the conclusion of his talks in America. Lesser items on the menu included freedom of the seas during wartime, the smuggling of alcoholic beverages into America from British possessions, and Hoover's pet proposal to exclude food ships from submarine attacks during wartime. MacDonald sympathized with the idea but could not persuade the British Admiralty. With the leaders back in Washington, the British government at London issued invitations to the five major naval powers to convene at London early in 1930. The tangible accomplishments of the summit were less important than the symbolism and the bonding of the two men. From that moment, the goodwill that persisted through the Grand Alliance of World War II never faltered. The summit was a diplomatic triumph for both men, whose popularity rose in their native lands. MacDonald's visit was the featured journalistic event of October, overshadowing the crash of the stock market in American newspapers.[30]

The American delegation departed for London on January 7, 1930, to attend what many expected to be the most significant international conclave since Versailles. The president selected a balanced, distinguished delegation, keeping in mind the necessity for ratification by Congress and the importance of the support of American public opinion. Stimson led the delegation, along with Navy Secretary Charles Francis Adams. The American representatives also included Ambassador to Mexico Dwight W. Morrow, known for his tact; Ambassador to Britain Charles G. Dawes; and Ambassador to Belgium Hugh

Gibson, an expert in arms control. Influential senators who might help in the ratification process were part of the team: Joseph T. Robinson of Arkansas, the Democratic minority leader, and David A. Reed of Pennsylvania, a senior Republican. The first plenary session convened on January 21, and most of the early meetings were devoted to speeches and ceremonial activities. Hoover listened to some of the proceedings by radio. Before the nations presented their plans, technical advisory committees had hammered out detailed position papers. The delegates discussed their basic proposals in early February. As with most disarmament conferences, the negotiations proved protracted and frustrating as delegates haggled over minute technical details. Each nation had somewhat different interests, although the United States and Britain remained largely in concert. It proved impractical to simply extend the battleship ratios of the Washington Conference to smaller vessels. The delegates debated the relationship of the caliber of guns, age, armor, speed, maneuverability, cruising range, and the fighting capacity of ships. Some intangibles were impossible to calculate, such as the training and skill of sailors and officers. These could only be determined in battle.[31]

One contentious issue was the American insistence on cruisers armed with 8-inch guns when most cruisers of that time carried 6-inch guns, which Britain preferred. Britain wanted a greater number of ships armed with smaller guns. The United States reduced its demand for the number of ships armed with 8-inch guns from 21 to 18, which broke the deadlock, and the other issues were settled amicably. The conference tried to provide rules clarifying the use of submarines in warfare. This section had no time limit and was ratified by all five nations. However, during World War II, the combatants quickly abandoned the rules. The most obstreperous nation was France, fearful of a revived German military and economy. The French subsequently witnessed such a revival, sown partly as a result of their very policies designed to prevent one, verifying the wisdom of the adage that we attract that which we love, that which we want, and also that which we fear. France insisted on a superior fleet to Italy's, which deadlocked negotiations on the Mediterranean aspect of the naval competition. More problematic was the French insistence on a security pact with the United States or Britain that would protect them from Germany. Hoover, who knew Congress would never ratify such an agreement, scuttled the idea, and the British, reluctant to being drawn into a second land war on the continent, also rejected it. The French additionally wanted provisions that were too sweeping to be realistic, such as land disarmament. Further, they wanted some mechanism to enforce the agreements reached, preferably under the League of Nations. The United States, a nonmember, declined, stating that the French already had sufficient protection under the Kellogg-Briand Pact and the Nine-Power Treaty.[32]

Friction developed between Hoover and Stimson, reaching the point of near-insubordination by the secretary of state. Stimson, in an attempt to prevent a French walkout, tentatively offered the type of guarantee Hoover had forbidden, or at the very least the secretary was inconsistent in what he told to different people. Stimson had somewhat different priorities than Hoover. Ultimately, the French refused to sign the major agreements, though the conference made it possible for them to sign some portions. This eliminated the possibility of the Italians signing because it would have placed them at a disadvantage. All parties, but especially the French and the Italians, were sensitive to the domestic repercussions of concessions. Germany, which was not a participant, in general applauded arms limitations but argued that land armaments also should have been reduced. By mid-April the three major powers had reached agreement in principle, and the remaining tasks were turned over to a drafting committee chaired by Dwight Morrow. Hoover praised the achievement, claiming that it would save the United States approximately $1 billion over the next six years.[33]

The sponsors had to settle for a Three-Power rather than a Five-Power Treaty, but they had considered French agreement unlikely from the outset. The United States achieved most of its objectives, including naval parity with Britain. Fixed limits were set on all categories of ships. The total tonnage of the American fleet remained about the same, but the United States would forego some new construction. The British fleet was reduced by 70,000 tons and the Japanese by 40,000 tons. Submarines were limited to 2,000 tons and aircraft carriers to less than 10,000 tons. Japan was given a slightly higher ratio, in practice, on cruisers, than the 5–5–3 ratio on battleships set at Washington. The United States agreed not to build up to its allotment of cruisers until after 1936, which provided Japan time to close the gap. The Japanese were granted parity in submarines. None of the nations would build new battleships until 1936. However, there was an "escalator clause" stipulating that if one nation exceeded its limits, the others were free to build more. The United States had achieved stability in the fleet strengths of the major naval powers and saved money without sacrificing a significant portion of its navy. In the long run, the absence of France and Italy did not appreciably affect the world balance of power.[34]

It required a vigorous assertion of presidential power to accomplish ratification. Only a handful of senators opposed the treaty, and they came from opposite ends of the spectrum: big navy men and hard-core isolationists. At best, the determined holdouts could delay, but not defeat, ratification. Hoover submitted the London Treaty to the Senate on May 1, but the session expired without a vote. Within 12 hours, Hoover summoned the Senate into special session and said he would keep them in Washington during the sweltering summer until they voted. It took two more weeks, and in that time every conceivable objection was raised. A clique of conspiratorial isolationists claimed nebulous secret agreements might be embedded in the treaty. They demanded that the State Department release thousands of pages of confidential letters and memoranda related to the negotiations. The president and Stimson pointed out the treaties could not be negotiated publicly. If letters written in confidence were publicized, no nation would be willing to negotiate with the United States again. Privately, it was leaked that blunt, derogatory remarks about some foreign leaders existed in the papers, which would jeopardize future relations with those countries. Stimson and Hoover did allow any senators, who wished to review the mountain of material privately, under a vow of confidentially, to tediously read them, and a few did.[35]

Hoover pointed out that not a single military expert claimed that the limitations weakened the United States. In fact, America would actually gain a small advantage of 69 million tons relative to the British fleet. Failure to ratify would compel the United States to spend additional millions without gaining additional security, the president argued. Prosperous nations were less likely to initiate wars, he said. Those who quibbled over details or spread rumors about secret agreements, actually wanted no treaty at all, he insisted. If the United States armed to the teeth, he continued, it would only encourage other nations to do so. There was no comfort in an arms race. "We have only to look at the state of Europe in 1914 to find ample evidence of the futility and danger of competition in arms," the president stated.[36] He further argued, "It is folly to think that because we are the richest nation in the world we can out build other countries. Other nations will make any sacrifice to maintain their instruments of defense against us, and we shall eventually reap in their hostility and ill-will the full measure of the additional burden we may thus impose upon them."[37] Senators Robinson and Reed, who had participated in the negotiations, assured their fellow senators that there were no secret agreements. Robinson lined up Democrats and Reed shored up faltering Republicans. After two weeks of contentious debate, the treaty's supporters overwhelmed the handful of determined opponents, voting to ratify 53–4 on July 21, 1930. The Senate attached a gratuitous reservation providing that the ratification did not apply to any agreements omitted from the text. Twelve other reservations were handily defeated. The following day, the president signed the treaty. Hoover said the treaty was fair to all and dangerous to none, grounded in common sense.[38] The ratification consummated the quarrelsome Seventy-First Congress after 18 months of nearly nonstop turmoil. As with most major issues, the president got his way. The *New York Herald Tribune* editorially observed that it hoped the president could finally get some rest "after a session of Congress which for confusion and cussedness, has had few equals."[39] The other foreign leaders had waited for America to act first before submitting the treaty to their parliaments for approval, which was easily accomplished. Afterward, the United States did not build up to the limits permitted by the treaty, a policy that continued during Roosevelt's first term. The president hoped America could lead by example; the treaty would reassure the world of the nation's peaceful intentions.[40] From a longer perspective, the London treaty remains Hoover's most important diplomatic accomplishment and the best example of his Quaker ideals. There were a few crises and other signal accomplishments, such as the debt moratorium agreement of 1931 and improved relations with Latin American, but for the most part foreign policy under Hoover would be the lull before the storm. During the 1932 campaign, Franklin D. Roosevelt maligned nearly every aspect of Hoover's political policies and his personality, yet he found nothing to criticize in his foreign policy.

Hoover meant what he said about naval disarmament. Even before negotiating the London treaty, the president had developed plans to prune the budget of all branches of the military. Over the weekend of July 26, 1929, he assembled Secretary of War Good and leading military officers at Camp Rapidan to discuss potential cuts. The chief executive opened the discussion by stating that implementation of the Kellogg Pact provided an opportunity to cut defense appropriations. He announced that he was creating a commission within the War Department to identify where reductions could be made without compromising security. Hoover announced that his preliminary agreements with MacDonald would permit him to delay construction of three cruisers authorized by Congress. Once the London treaty was ratified, the president implemented a reorganization of the fleet in the interest of economy and efficiency. Admiral W. V. Pratt, his chief naval officer, cooperated with Hoover in improving efficiency while trimming expenses. They planned to reduce the manpower of the navy by 2,000 to 5,000 enlisted men from its level of 84,500. The Marine Corps of 18,000 would be pared by 500. The decommissioning of three battleships from the scouting fleet, in accordance with the treaty, released 2,100 men for distribution among other units of the fleet and the retirement of some submarines and destroyers made other sailors available. The president announced plans to reduce the civilian staff and curtail recruitment modestly.[41]

Like the navy, but on a smaller scale, the army was assigned the task of deterring aggression and fighting a defensive war in the Western Hemisphere. The president did not intend to dispatch soldiers outside the hemisphere, but he vowed that foreign troops would never set foot on American soil. Defense was relative, not absolute, the president believed. No country could guarantee absolute security, but the United States could maintain a force sufficient for our needs. He wished to demonstrate, by limiting the army to a small, highly trained, professional force, that the United States had no foreign aspirations and posed no threat to any nation. Moreover, manpower was not the sole criterion for an effective defense. A strong economy must complement military preparedness. The nation could spend itself into weakness, he indicated, a view later expressed by President Eisenhower. It was not numbers alone that made an army effective, but quality, disciplined leadership and high morale. The commander-in-chief phased out and retired obsolete equipment. He terminated the policy of basing promotions solely on seniority and promoted General Douglas MacArthur over several senior officers to army chief of staff. Under Hoover, the army command structure was streamlined and the army air force was increased by 40 percent to about 2,800 planes. Living quarters at army posts were improved, and the Coast Guard was strengthened. The drive for economy proved problematical. Although the commission he appointed consented to some economies, it simultaneously recommended substantial pay increases for both officers and enlisted men. In truth, further reductions threatened to cut to the bone, and Hoover did not insist on all his original proposals, lest he jeopardize morale.[42]

One of the international problems Hoover inherited when he became president was the question of Allied war debts owed the United States and, indirectly, German reparations, which some European nations used to pay portions of their debts. Unfortunately, much of Europe was living beyond its means, financing social programs and an arms race, not out of current revenues or increased taxes, but through a shaky house of cards based on American loans and German reparations. Still, the Europeans were suffering, and paying debts to America was no more politically popular there than cancelling them was in America. In Germany, reparation payments aggravated a desire for military revenge. During the 1920s Hoover served on the World War Foreign Debt Commission, on which he was a flexible moderate. In 1922, he suggested canceling the entire debt contracted before the armistice. Told by his colleagues that such an agreement would never be ratified by Congress or approved by the American people, he adopted a strategy of consistently lowering the interest rates and stretching out payment of the principal over a longer number of years. He also sided with colleagues who formulated the idea of reducing debts commensurate with the ability to pay. Although America asked for, and received, no reparations from the Central Powers, two commissions headed by Americans adopted a similar policy of scaling down the reparations in the Dawes Plan of 1924 and the Young Plan of 1929. As president, Hoover negotiated agreements with most of the individual debtor countries based on their capacity to pay. He also wanted to use the debts as leverage to obtain concessions from the Europeans on issues such as arms reductions and opening markets to American agricultural exports. Somewhat inconsistently, he did not believe American tariffs on European products should be reduced. Hoover was a scrupulous bargainer who had no desire to gouge either European debtors or American creditors who would have to foot the bill if the Europeans defaulted. He worked hard to prevent a default by giving a little at a time, within the political context in which he operated. The president did not view the war debts issue in isolation. He considered it part of the jigsaw puzzle of international economics in which goods, currency, and gold flowed from one nation to another. He put American interests first, but he never believed that America could, or should, retreat into a shell, and he recognized the political dimensions of economic problems. Further, he believed maintenance of the gold standard, which was then tied to the British pound, was essential to world economic stability. America and all of Europe remembered the uncontrolled inflation of the early 1920s in Germany, when that country defaulted on reparations and the French and Belgians temporarily occupied Germany's industrial heartland. From this experience, many contemporaries took the lesson that inflation led to economic and political anarchy. Hoover had an appreciation for the dilemma of the Europeans. He worked on the war debts problem up until the last minutes of his presidency, when he saw his fears materialize in defaults.[43]

Another problem Hoover inherited from his predecessors was the issue of whether to diplomatically recognize the Soviet Union. The Quaker's views about Communism were complex. On one hand, he considered it the antithesis of free enterprise and the exercise of individual freedom, including freedom of religion and the right to choose one's own occupation. He considered Communism an unrealistic economic system because it circumscribed incentives and denied rewards for creativity. Indeed, in rescuing the Soviets from famine during the early 1920s, he witnessed firsthand the human suffering in Russia. Nonetheless, he joined neither the First nor the Second Red Scare, believed in free speech for Communists, and never advocated a military war against the Soviets, even at the height of the Cold War. He was fully aware of the repressive systems that had preceded the Soviets and of the poverty of the Soviet peasants. Thus he understood the Russian dilemma, but he did not approve of the solution. On December 6, 1930, Stimson reaffirmed that the existing policy of nonrecognition would remain in effect. To win diplomatic recognition, the Soviets must recognize debts owed to the United States (which the USSR had repudiated), indemnify American citizens for property the regime had confiscated, and, most importantly, terminate propaganda within the United States promoting the overthrow of the American government.[44]

The first two years of Hoover's foreign policy brought significant accomplishments without serious miscues and occurred in a world mostly at peace, though it was not without instability. Unfortunately, as his challenges at home increased with the deepening of the Depression, his plate also became heaped with foreign crises: economic, diplomatic, and military. At home and abroad, Hoover's presidency was becoming a task of crisis management. From the heartland of Central Europe to the unstable Bank of England, revolutions in Latin America, and the roiling Far East, international problems alone would have tested him.

CHAPTER 8

A Polarized Party

When Herbert Hoover became president, the Republican Party was polarized. The fissures almost cracked during the special session to deal with farm relief and the tariff. Ironically, the new president was viewed with suspicion for opposite reasons. The Progressive faction disliked him because he was a moderate and a gradualist, who viewed the country's problems in national rather than regional or parochial terms and who preferred sophisticated, multifaceted solutions to issues such as the farm problem rather than radical, experimental ones, impractical to implement and politically impossible to enact. The party regulars—both conservatives and moderates—comprised a larger faction but created less noise. They disliked Hoover because he was an amateur politician who had not risen through the ranks. He did not trade favors or back special interest legislation targeted to their districts. Hoover was frustrated by the creaky pace of legislating during a worldwide depression. Most previous presidents had worked through congressional leaders, allowing them to shape legislation and guide bills through the labyrinths of Congress. For his first two years, especially during the special session of 1929, Hoover considered the constitutional division of powers sacrosanct. As the Depression worsened, the president grew assertive. After 1930 he was an aggressive president, and although Republican majorities were reduced or eliminated, Congress pounded out most of the major legislation he wanted, though sometimes weakened or delayed. It was not that congressmen were knaves; it was simply that the system had not been designed to act rapidly. During wartime, Congress was willing to cede some of its prerogatives in the face of a common enemy. However, the enemy of the 1930s was invisible, which made it more insidious. Common suffering reaped bickering, not cohesion.

During Hoover's term, the GOP was not a single party, but a party and a faction. The faction, chiefly concentrated in the Midwest and West, called themselves Progressives but were more properly populists or rebellious insurgents. Most represented farm states and were single minded, glued to simple panaceas to raise farm prices and to the persistent farm problems of low prices, high expenses, and indebtedness. They were closer to the provincial single-interest solution of William Jennings Bryan—free coinage of silver—than to the Progressivism of Theodore Roosevelt or Woodrow Wilson. Progressives of the 1900–1920 era developed a comprehensive program for municipal, state, and national reform. The earlier Progressives were an organized, relatively focused, largely urban movement that culminated in the domestic legislation of the first Wilson administration. Hoover had fit in well with this group. He had admired Roosevelt and served under Wilson, and like them he had a national view.

Roosevelt and Wilson had galvanized their parties behind a program, though, ultimately, the harmony collapsed when TR impetuously divided the GOP by challenging Taft in 1912. Then Wilson, by refusing to compromise to ratify an imperfect Versailles treaty, left his party disheartened and rudderless, culminating in the Republican decade of the 1920s. The GOP floated into office on disenchantment with the Democrats and remained in the White House on the uplift of 1920s prosperity. But what prosperity gave, prosperity could take away. Hoover was much more representative of the Progressive model than the insurgents who borrowed the name in the early 1930s, yet the times had changed. The Progressive movement to which he owed his political pedigree was dead, except in name, and most of the old Progressives, including Hoover, later opposed the New Deal, which in degree went beyond anything they conceived. The old Progressives were reformers; the new firebrand insurgents, though some of them might have shared Progressive roots, had no comprehensive program. Historians have quibbled over whether the earlier Progressives were liberals or conservatives; in fact, like Hoover, they were reformers within limits. Hoover was both a highly patriotic nationalist in the sense of Roosevelt and an internationalist similar to Wilson. Most of the insurgent Republicans were intractable isolationists.

These neo-Progressives were more visible in the Republican Party than among Democrats. Their forte was oratory, not enacting legislation. Most of their pet schemes were fiscally impractical and not supported by the mainstream of their own party. They left little tangible mark on the legislation of the Hoover presidency. Most were self-righteous, as was Hoover himself, yet Hoover, who did not try to whip them into line—he would have failed if he did—was more patient and more amenable to compromise. The part of their job the insurgents enjoyed the most was delivering speeches. Hoover considered speechmaking a burden. Temperamentally, they were fire and ice. The volatile insurgents tended to reiterate the same things repeatedly, each time a little louder. They represented the most obstinate faction in Congress and did Hoover more harm than the Democrats. Effective only in opposition, by combining with Democrats, they could defeat or delay legislation, but they lacked the ability, with rare exceptions, to muscle it through. During 1929–30, as part of a coalition with the Democrats, they could marshal a majority in the Upper House. Many had seniority, which they would have lost if they switched parties. Some relied on a cult of personality to generate headlines and perpetuate themselves in politics. Their fate in Congress was martyrdom, though most remained popular in their states, even though they could not deliver legislative manna. In fact, hard times helped them win reelection. This is not to suggest that they were merely cynical exhibitionists. Most were genuine fanatics for a cause to which they were devoted but that they damaged by fracturing their party. By often refusing to accept ameliorative measures that fell short of their demands, they harmed the needs of their constituents. Neither were they unintelligent or lacking in parliamentary or oratorical skills. Their real liability lay in their refusal to compromise in order to attain the best that was possible.[1]

Among the insurgents, several stand out. Senator William E. Borah of Idaho was one of the most difficult men in Congress to get along with, but Hoover knew Borah had influence and tried to remain on his good side. The senator had campaigned effectively for Hoover 1928, yet he broke with the president over the debenture during the special session of 1929 and never returned to the fold.[2] While the differences between Borah and Hoover were political than personal, there was genuine antipathy between Hoover and Senator George H. Norris of Nebraska. Norris was even more of a fair-weather Republican than Borah. Unlike Borah, who worked for Hoover's election, Norris abandoned the Republican presidential nominee in 1924, 1928, and 1932. Norris's fixation on public development of Muscle Shoals frustrated both Hoover and Norris and, along with Hoover's rigidity on the issue, postponed development for years. Unlike most insurgents who focused almost exclusively on measures designed to aid their constituents, Norris's motive was entirely ideological. A dam in Alabama would not help farmers in Nebraska.[3]

More saddening for both men was the defection of fellow Iowan, Senator W. Smith Brookhart. Unlike Norris, Brookhart, had been a good friend, who had campaigned for Hoover in 1928, and the bitter break, which also occurred over the debenture during the special session, caused remorse for Hoover. Brookhart had told Iowans that Hoover was a friend of the farmer who supported the debenture. The former was true, but the latter was not, and Brookhart felt betrayed. Hoover was dismayed as well, because he had never told Brookhart, nor anyone else, that he embraced the debenture. Brookhart not only voted against Hoover's program for the remainder of his term, but like a woman scorned, he poured out a stream of invective against the administration.[4]

With the defection of the Progressive bloc, Hoover was forced to rely on the regular Republicans, the larger conservative faction, to enact his program. Ironically, during the presidential primaries and even during the 1928 campaign, some of the Progressives had been more enthusiastic about Hoover than the conservatives. Hoover had gained the nomination because he was the most electable potential candidate, because he was identified with prosperity, and because he lacked a single, strong opponent. They backed him because they wanted to win.

Major party domination usually does not last more than a decade, especially if conditions decline. Hoover was unfortunate in the timing of his presidency, not simply because it was shipwrecked by the Depression, but because in the normal cycle of politics the Republican well was running dry. This is also true more of the party's control of Congress. A certain amount of volatility, often salutary, is built into the system. Despite lacking a working majority of Congress throughout his presidency, much less a top-heavy majority like his successor, Hoover's relations with Congress were better than might have been expected. Until Hoover's time, presidents had given only the broad outlines of an administration program to congressional leaders, who hammered out the details. With a few notable exceptions (such as Wilson) there had been no consistent theme to presidential domestic policies. There had not even been a national budget until 1921. Although an activist by temperament, Hoover was not inclined to carve legislative notches into his political pistol. The president respected Congress as an independent, equal branch. As he encountered logjams and started to push, Congress pushed back. Hoover had never expected legislative goals to become a battle of wills, nor did he enjoy it. Yet he was determined, even stubborn, as all strong presidents are. As a tactician, Hoover maximized his leadership qualities, which resembled those of Lyndon B. Johnson more than Theodore Roosevelt or Woodrow Wilson. Lacking oratorical finesse, he met with congressmen and national leaders in small groups, where his persuasive powers were at their best, before introducing legislation. The lack of drama in his approach is obvious, but given his personality he had no choice. He scorned propaganda and deliberate exaggeration. The Quaker refused to oversimplify or pander. The president did not enjoy protracted negotiations and believed much time was wasted in futile discussion. He possessed a romantic faith in the good of the people if not always in their judgment or unerring wisdom. He believed most people, including politicians, were basically good. The president did not take expedient shortcuts. He felt members of Congress should vote for measures based on their intrinsic worth rather than their political appeal. Washington insiders did not know what to make of a president so idealistic and so transparently honest. If Coolidge had been scrupulous about using every inch of every government pencil, Hoover believed his office was a sacred trust in a literal sense.[5]

These traits endeared Hoover to his friends, yet made him an anomaly in Washington. He had an excess of Quaker modesty. Hoover ignored political recriminations rather than responding. Nonetheless, his legislative accomplishments, especially during the Seventy-Second Congress are substantial. They represent a coherent program, not a patchwork of bills. Few, if any, of his predecessors, enacted comparable programs under similarly difficult conditions, with less fanfare. Congress during the Hoover years was not a barren wasteland. The president's reaction to a legislative achievement was not to celebrate and wring out the maximum political mileage, but to move on to the next item on his agenda. Over the course of his administration a high percentage of his important measures were adopted. Hoover's methods were unusual but not inept, although they lacked the flair that might have brought him more credit. He was not a complete political innocent. He learned to load down bills he disliked with unpopular amendments that would justify a veto that could not be overridden. The president planned meetings carefully, poring over minute details prior to assembly.[6] His administration, like all administrations, had a patronage side, but he found it too distasteful to handle personally. To the extent possible, he wanted appointments to be made strictly on merit, but he recognized the reality of region and party loyalty. Making a large campaign contribution, however, would not land one an ambassadorship. Postmaster General Brown handled most of the patronage, and the Republican National Committee handled many of the political details, even during election campaigns although strategic decisions were made at the White House. The RNC was also expected to lobby Congress for administration legislation. Cabinet members often shouldered the responsibility of drafting legislation that concerned their departments and ensuring its passage through Congress. This applied only to the smaller legislative items, however. The president firmly held the reins on the big issues, and most of the big ideas originated with him. He did talk them over with his cabinet, his staff, political confidants inside and outside of Congress, and often, the RNC, before submission. Hoover was a good listener yet decisive. He wanted good legislation propelled through Congress by the power of the idea. Although this approach was highly unorthodox, his batting average was pretty good.[7]

Hoover learned some things about the legislative process during his sojourn at 1600 Pennsylvania Avenue, and he departed sadder but wiser. His faith in the system, in himself, and in the people remained unsullied. Some presidents have been equally pilloried, but probably few so literally resembled a punching bag. He explained to his aides, Theodore G. Joslin and James H. MacLafferty, that it is fruitless to punch people whose votes you need to enact legislation. His friend, journalist Edward Eyre Hunt, explained, "His relations with Congress during his presidency might almost be taken as a model of tact and collaboration."[8] The president was tough in the sense of resilience, not aggression. By the same token, he did not necessarily tell even his own followers what they wanted to hear unless he believed it was true. At the end of his term, he was not punch-drunk; he was ready for another round. He did not enjoy either the power or the abuse of the presidency, but he did not shrink from it. The first year of any presidency is a learning process because there is no apprenticeship for the job. Hoover had vast administrative experience, a keen, imaginative, retentive mind, and the drive of a steam shovel. Even before the stock market toppled like Humpty Dumpty, he experienced a baptism of fire in the special session he summoned to deal with farm problems and the tariff. Hoover learned in the tariff battle that tackling tough issues incurs hard feelings. His chief political lesson was that passing controversial legislation would require a greater hands-on approach with Congress. The stock market crash and the economy's downward descent suffused his presidency with urgency. As if propelled by the Furies, the urgency never subsided.[9]

The year 1930 was a transitional one. The economy was running amuck but was a long way from bottoming out, and no one at the time knew how long that would take. Clearly, though, the president's reform agenda was on the shelf. As in Belgium during the Great War and during the Mississippi Flood of 1927, he was summoned to be a "Master of Emergencies" rather than an architect of reform. By the end of 1930 criticism of the president was gaining momentum. The Democrats realized they could make the Depression an effective campaign issue in the November elections by personalizing it and pinning blame on the president. Among the most vociferous critics were Senate Majority Leader Joseph Robinson of Arkansas, Senator Robert Wagner of New York, and Senator Robert LaFollette of Wisconsin. Wagner was scathingly personal: "I want to emphasize that this long and sad procession of weary men in search of work is passing before our eyes even in this land of plenty, in the administration of Herbert Hoover, heralded as the great dispenser of prosperity."[10] LaFollette claimed the administration had invented a Red Scare, comparable to the Palmer Raids of 1919, to divert attention from the Depression.[11] Attorney General Mitchell countered that no Red Scare existed and no arrests had been made, nor were any contemplated. No investigation of Communism was in progress. He said the Justice Department would act only in the event of overt acts. LaFollette did not respond to Mitchell but instead denounced the administration for cutting taxes as an economic stimulus and appointing commissions, which amounted to "passing the buck."[12] Davis also responded to a demand by Senator Brookhart that the administration appropriate $50 million to provide doles to the unemployed. The labor secretary advised that this would not go far. It would mean only $1 weekly for 18 weeks for the three million unemployed. Job creation using larger sums would be more effective, yet the bills to provide for them were idling in neutral in the Senate. Senator John Q. Tilson of Connecticut, the Republican leader in the Senate, pointed to administration achievements, including a farm relief measure, a public buildings bill, and a bill to provide for road construction. The construction and road bills would provide immediate employment.[13]

Senator Robinson complained that the administration was deliberately undercounting unemployment but provided no statistics of his own.[14] Robinson complained that "the shadow of gloom still falls over the United States and envelopes almost every form of enterprise and activity."[15] The Democratic tactic was to blame Hoover for the crash, then to blame him for paralysis in the face of adversity. He was condemned for being too optimistic about recovery and also for being overly negative. Hoover believed such criticism would prove ineffective if recovery occurred and any oratorical retort would be redundant. He believed the politics of the situation as well as common sense mandated that actions would speak louder than words. The GOP pointed out that a large number of recovery-oriented bills were languishing in the Senate, controlled by a Democratic-insurgent coalition. The president could propose, but the Congress must dispose. The congressional Democrats blamed the president, who replied through surrogates that Congress itself was to blame. Meanwhile, legislation was moving through Congress but more slowly than Hoover wanted. Much of the nation remained behind Hoover. He was more popular in the hinterlands than in Washington. Big business, which wanted to be left alone, was suspicious of the president, but small businessmen trusted him. Senators resented the president's independence, yet the public respected it.[16]

The economy was a seesaw. The Republicans rose with it and fell with it. In the blame game the Democrats had an advantage because it was easier to personify an individual than an amorphous collection of individuals like Congress. Moreover, the Republicans had promised prosperity. As the Depression lengthened and deepened, the decibel level of the debate increased. After the 1930 congressional elections, a sense of defeatism set in among some Republicans, who were ready to concede two years before the next elections. The Republicans, accustomed to winning, lacked confidence. Some tried to distant themselves from the president. Shortly after the 1930 elections, a group of Republican congressmen, convinced that if they renominated Hoover the party faced certain defeat, began talking about drafting Coolidge in 1932.[17]

The president, reaching out for support, organized several GOP House members, led by Representative Arthur Free of California, to deliver speeches defending their leader. Free warned the president that he would continue to lose support unless he took more rank-and-file congressmen into his confidence. Hoover agreed. Hoover also relied on Senator Frederick C. Walcott of Connecticut, who by mid-March 1932 had become the most effective administration spokesman in the Senate. An intimate of Hoover who had served in the CRB and the Food Administration and a successful banker, he helped flesh out the administration's recovery program for the Seventy-Second Congress. Walcott could cut deals in the cloak room, at lunch, or on the golf links. Hoover also liked Senator Simeon Fess, the party whip, who became RNC chairman in 1931. His closest friend in the upper house, Ohio Senator Theodore Burton, died early in the administration, depriving the president of a valuable ally. Hoover and Kansas Senator Henry Allen were close, but Allen lost his seat in 1930. One of the brightest stars in the Republican luminary, Senator Dwight Morrow of New Jersey, died in 1931, after serving less than a year of his term. The party infrastructure was weakened not only by dissension and the weak economy but by attrition of some of the president's most reliable allies.[18]

The Republican hierarchy in Congress was weak, ineffective, and sometimes of questionable loyalty. The Senate majority leader, the elderly and lethargic James Watson, had begun his career during the administration of Benjamin Harrison. Hoover believed Watson placed his own interests above those of the president. John Q. Tilson, the House majority leader, seemed lukewarm in his loyalty to the president. He rarely defended the chief executive publicly and disagreed with the president's strategy of organizing representatives to defend him. Tilson did not exert strenuous efforts to expedite administration legislation. The most effective Republican leader in Congress was House Speaker Nicholas Longworth. The speaker was autocratic but genial and popular. An effective speaker, he welded the GOP into a disciplined unit, in sharp contrast to the Senate, where the GOP was factionalized. Longworth's death in 1931, before the Seventy-Second Congress was organized, left a vacuum in the Republican leadership. Tilson, who succeeded him, could not fill his shoes. Under Longworth, the House had been the president's undeviating ally. In the Seventy-Second Congress, support in the House became less reliable. Snell, who moved up the majority leader, was not effective. House Republicans loyal to Hoover complained about Snell's leadership. He failed to communicate how the president wanted them to vote, they said. The party hierarchy lacked an efficient chain of command. Hoover privately complained that some of his political lieutenants were second-rate men.[19]

The crisis in leadership in Congress was aggravated by a prolonged scandal at the Republican National Committee. In August 1929, Hubert Work resigned as chairman of the RNC to return to private life. Hoover's choice as his successor, Claudius H. Huston, had worked for him at the Commerce Department. A native of Tennessee, Huston had been an effective, energetic fundraiser for Hoover in the South during the 1928 campaign. Yet Huston was barely settled into his position before he became embroiled in scandal. Feisty, arrogant, and operating just within the law, he was perhaps the worst appointment of Hoover's administration. Huston had been employed by the Tennessee River Improvement Association, a body representing chambers of commerce, banks, businesses, and other commercial concerns, to lobby Congress to enact a bill authorizing private development of the nitrate and hydroelectric facilities at Muscle Shoals, Alabama. The Union Carbide Company had an interest in the project, especially in power development along the upper Tennessee River. Huston told Union Carbide president Fred H. Haggerston that the association was short of money, and Haggerston wrote him two personal checks totaling $36,000. Huston used the money to speculate on the stock market. He later returned the sum but retained the profits from the speculation. Called before the Senate Lobby Investigating Committee, Huston attempted to bluff and cover up. He claimed he had used the money to purchase maps and charts to use in presentations, yet could not produce the maps and charts. For that matter, there was little evidence of significant lobbying. During the hearings it was revealed that Huston had accepted another $13,000 for which he could not account.[20]

The agony dragged on all summer. Huston, by now a political pariah, continued to protest his innocence and refused to resign. With congressional elections looming in the fall, fundraising was paralyzed. Instead of moving quickly and decisively to replace Huston, Hoover allowed the situation to fester. By late summer, unable to pry a voluntary resignation out of Huston for months, the party was in disarray, straining under the burden of an albatross. In mid-June the Lobby Committee delivered its report, which was less harsh than might have been expected. Republican senators and representatives, especially those standing for reelection, demanded Huston resign instantly. Instead, he traveled, played golf, and said he would only resign at the direct request of the president. The president refused to force his hand. Finally, in late July, James Francis Burke, the general counsel of the RNC, and Joseph R. Nutt, treasurer of the RNC, cornered Huston at New York's Ritz Carlton Hotel and delivered an ultimatum to resign. Otherwise the president and the RNC would fire him. Burke and Nutt hustled Huston back to Washington for a long White House meeting with the president at 9 p.m., the following evening, then conferred with Senate leader James E. Watson and Walter H. Newton, the president's political secretary, at the Willard Hotel. On August 7, Huston finally resigned with very little good grace, claiming he had been framed. The martyr's hair shirt did not fit well, yet the party—and the president—had fiddled too long while the political pot sizzled. At its August 7 meeting, the National Committee elected Senator Simeon D. Fess of Ohio, the president's choice, as Huston's successor. Hoover's selection of a partisan party regular indicated he had decided to cast his lot with the conservatives. A former teacher and professor from Ohio, the Senator had been one of the president's most loyal defenders on the floor, yet he hardly rose above the level of a mediocrity. At that, he appeared a Colossus compared to Huston. The RNC appointed Robert Lucas, a Kentuckian, to a new position, executive director, to handle day-to-day affairs at the Washington office and free Fess to travel. Fess's geographical span was circumscribed, however; the Western Progressives, who detested him, did not want him in their part of the country. Young, energetic, and a brilliant speaker and writer, Lucas was capable of delivering the type of blistering partisan speeches that the more inhibited president could not.[21]

Considering the turmoil, scandal, and closed pocketbooks of donors, coupled with the bone-crushing weight of the Depression, Republicans did not fare as badly in the 1930 elections as might have been expected. Their salvation was that the Democrats were almost as badly disorganized. The only significant money they collected came from a single source, their national chairman, John J. Raskob, who had made a fortune at General Motors and ironically had dabbled in the stock market. The Democrats had never owed so much to a single man as they owed to Raskob. In 1931 the party was said to be in debt to the industrialist for about $800,000. The political atmosphere was combustible in both parties. The Republicans were characterized more by dissonance than harmony, yet they had a coherent program, which the Democrats lacked, and the GOP had no monopoly in intraparty dissension. The Democratic strategy was to criticize Hoover while offering only sparse, individual bills, relying heavily on the caustic speeches ghosted by Charles Michelson, the party's journalistic hatchet man.[22]

After Huston's departure, the Republican national machinery remained unsettled. Senator George H. Moses of New Hampshire remained chair of the Senatorial Campaign Committee. Lucas remained effective, but Fess was worn down by combining the RNC responsibilities with his Senate duties. He wanted to resign, but no adequate replacement could be found to lead what many considered a futile cause. A clique of RNC members were already looking beyond 1932 to 1936 and were priming Dwight Morrow for the nomination. Only Morrow's death in 1931 prevented further splintering. Hoover offered the chairmanship to Postmaster General Brown, who rejected it. Fundraising remained stagnant as the 1932 elections approached, but Hoover delayed picking a chairman. He believed his job was running the government, not running the RNC. Yet it could not run effectively without him. Although he detested delivering speeches, the president remained the biggest attraction and most potent fundraiser in the party. Finally, with the 1932 election looming, he chose another old hand to chair the RNC: Everett Sanders, who had once been personal secretary to Coolidge. Sanders stabilized the party and tied it symbolically to the still popular Coolidge, but he did not infuse the new blood it badly needed.[23]

Political intelligence is valuable to every administration. To a president who prefers not to cultivate congressmen as individuals, it is even more important. Hoover relied on informants he trusted, often those he had known over time, who were loyal and discrete and had no ax to grind. The chief executive consulted with a variety of advisers inside and outside the government. These included elder statesmen such as Charles Evans Hughes and Elihu Root, as well as businessmen, scientists, engineers, and those who had worked under him at the Department of Commerce and in his humanitarian undertakings. The president also had a number of journalistic and literary friends. Hoover's secretaries served as his eyes and ears. Lawrence Richey handled confidential matters, which he never set down on paper and never related to anyone but Hoover. With experience as a Secret Service agent, he possessed investigative skills. Walter Newton, a former congressman, gathered political intelligence. He also lobbied Congress for administrative bills, counted votes, and along with Walter Brown was in charge of patronage, especially in the South.

Akerson and his successor, Joslin, monitored the pulse of the press and of public opinion.[24]

James H. MacLafferty, a former U.S. representative from California who had worked for Hoover in the Commerce Department and during the 1928 campaign, served as the president's chief political adviser, confidential strategist, and liaison with the Republican National Committee. He was a thorough Hoover loyalist, devoted to reelecting the president. MacLafferty met Hoover frequently, at least once a week, and served as an informant on practical politics. He usually saw Hoover early in the morning without an appointment and was admitted immediately by Hoover's press secretary. MacLafferty rarely talked with Hoover for more than 10 or 15 minutes, and their talks were confined to political strategy. MacLafferty was something of a political "errand boy." He took on specific projects: some suggested by Hoover, some selected by himself. He compared his relationship to that of Colonel Edward House with Wilson, but House played a more public role and did not furnish the degree of specific political detail provided by MacLafferty. Few knew of their relationship, and MacLafferty's name rarely appeared in the papers. The ex-congressman made several organizing trips, traveling to every region but the South. He delivered speeches and organized the party's infrastructure at the state level. Politically savvy, he cultivated his contacts in Congress. Hoover's scout was tireless in his efforts to rally Republicans behind Hoover and to provide the president with political intelligence inside and outside of Washington. MacLafferty was more hardened to politics than Hoover and consistently goaded the president to be more aggressive politically. "Can a man who is naturally lovable, gentle, and filled with Hoover's admirable qualities become mean, contentions, and oftentimes seemingly unfair?" MacLafferty asked himself. "It is hard for a man 56 years of age to change habits of a lifetime and the breeding of generations of peace-loving Quakers." After every meeting MacLafferty recorded his conversations, first in longhand, then in typing, for posterity. His diary is the best source of political gossip in the Hoover administration.[25]

The trouble with MacLafferty is that there was only one of him. He possessed the energy, the sound judgment, and the common sense to do Hoover incalculable good. In November 1930, MacLafferty approached Hoover with an idea. He would drive coast to coast, from Washington to California, speaking and organizing along the way, accompanied only by his wife—a one-car campaign caravan. MacLafferty's drive across American had another purpose. It was to gather political intelligence, to relate to the president and to Lucas the mood of the nation in different states, and to use a large sample of the entire nation in what later generations would call a "focus group." MacLafferty delivered relentlessly optimistic pep talks, but he provided the president and party leaders with the unvarnished truth. The journey was arduous, but MacLafferty thrived on it, and his wife endured the travel. He drafted reports of each meeting, which he periodically summarized. He sent one summary to

Lawrence Richey, who funneled it to the president, and another to Lucas. He offered sound advice, which was carefully scrutinized but could not always be implemented on the necessary scale.[26]

Many states were factionalized, and local issues complicated national politics. Democrats sowed rumors designed to debunk the president. In Wyoming MacLafferty heard that Hoover opposed leasing federal oil lands because the president owned large interests in foreign oil. Elsewhere, Hoover's agent heard rumors that the president had introduced the fruit fly into Florida because he was a Californian and wanted to destroy the orange business of Florida. The Democrats also encouraged defeatism among Republicans, telling them there was no reason to vote at all. Among issues, Prohibition was a distant second to the economy, yet it was more emotional, and the solution seemed clear. The electorate leaned increasingly wet and considered the Democrats the wetter party. In general, the Republicans were weakest in the Midwest, the Mountain states, and the Southwest and were almost certain to lose the entire South. When MacLafferty returned, Lucas found his reports enlightening if not encouraging and asked him to undertake a similar tour throughout the Midwest. The ardent Hoover backer found the heartland even angrier than the trans-Mississippi West. Still, he returned satisfied that both expeditions had contributed to strengthening the party infrastructure, providing insights into the issues, and he was gratified by the fact that people had left his meetings more inclined to favor Republican positions. His conclusion was that Hoover's fate lay in the state of the economy in 1932.[27]

It was difficult for Hoover to be a successful politician because he was basically an apolitical president. He had reached office without owing favors, yet neither was he owed any. He was not savvy about politics. He selected his cabinet, his personal staff, and most of his top appointees on the basis of merit and, in some cases, personal loyalty. Few members of his cabinet had clout in the GOP or in Congress. He did not give them *carte blanche* to shore up the administration with patronage appointments. The president's political judgment was not seasoned. Neither Hubert Work, Claudius Huston, Simeon Fess, nor Everett Sanders were equipped to invigorate the RNC, which was especially important because Hoover was not prepared to invigorate it himself. Hoover wanted to be a bipartisan president. He listened to the opposition and made concessions, or he would not have won the substantial amount of significant legislation he extracted from the divided Seventy-Second Congress. The president usually adopted a conciliatory rather than a confrontational approach toward the Democrats. He was more bipartisan than either his successor or most of his predecessors. He did not get along with the Republican insurgents, though some had been personal friends. Much to his dismay, Hoover learned that a president cannot please some people without alienating other people. Of all the lessons he learned in politics, this was perhaps the most bitter. Hoover could not be the type of politician who is sufficiently ruthless to survive in the cauldron of competition for votes.

No one on either side of the aisle doubted Hoover's intelligence. Yet the modern presidency is more a job of dealing with people than about thinking original thoughts. Hoover could in fact deal with people and had done so successfully. What he could not or would not do was to manipulate or bully them. These tactics appeared unsavory to the president. He often felt that Congress lacked direction and a sense of purpose. Part of the problem is inherent in the system. The president can veto, but he cannot legislate. He can devise programs, but he cannot appropriate money. Most agonizingly, in a state of emergency that resembled a war, he could not control the timing with which Congress acted or the degree to which it watered down his bills. The primary interest of most congressmen lay in retaining their jobs, and Hoover did not provide them with much political leverage or largesse to do so. Certainly if Commerce had been the job that made him happiest, the presidency was the position that made him the most frustrated. During ordinary times, he might have been a highly successful, popular president despite his apolitical attitude, which might have won him respect and public acclaim.

It might be unfair to criticize someone for not acting like a professional politician who never wanted to become a professional politician. Hoover wanted to change politics. He did not want it to change him. He would not have considered it a compliment if someone had called him a good politician. To Hoover, politics was no more than a temporary form of public service. Professional politicians constantly have their eyes on the next election and the effect their words and actions might have on voters. These were not Hoover's priorities; in fact, he considered them ignoble. If he had to choose between intellectual honesty and political expediency; he chose intellectual honesty. He did not necessarily tell the voters want they wanted to hear, and sometimes he deliberately took unpopular positions. Hoover rejected politically appealing yet simplistic solutions. Political power was only a means to an end, not a form of self-gratification. He did not shirk power, and he had sought it, but only the things he could accomplish gratified him. He wanted high office because it provided opportunity to serve in a capacity in which he could do the most good. Hoover's mantra was service, along with duty. He found his job trying, but he rarely complained, and he never gave up or doubted himself. It has been said that Hoover failed because he was not a politician. Certainly he was not a typical politician. Yet that is precisely why many people voted for him in 1928, and he did not merely eke into office. In the wake of the Harding scandals, the last thing most people wanted was a conventional retail politician. It has been also been said that he failed because he was too conservative. Yet in the context of his times he was not really conservative at all. During his own time, he received as much criticism from the Old Guard as from the Young Turks, as much for spending too much as for spending too little. In fact, Hoover was a moderate Progressive. Only by reading history backward, by comparing him exclusively with his successors rather than his predecessors, can a case be made that ideology lay at the root of his inability to end the Depression. But history does not happen backward, and the majority of Hoover's ideas were forward-looking, not traditional. Finally, if ending the Great Depression in a single term is the criterion for failure, then we must charge, try, convict, and hang virtually any president who served or might have served in such circumstances, before and since. Fortunately, the American solution is not to hang presidents during hard times but to turn them out of office.

Finally, it is quite possible that Hoover is underrated as a politician. Ellis W. Hawley has argued that much of Hoover's perceived failure was due to circumstances rather than to personal qualities. The image he tried to live up to was not entirely manufactured, nor did he contrive it. Other twentieth-century presidents, such as Woodrow Wilson and Lyndon B. Johnson, have experienced similar reversals in public opinion. No one doubted Johnson's political skills. He was a renowned persuader who produced legislation on an assembly line. In fact, he was one of the master politicians of his generation. Wilson was an eloquent orator, whose speeches sparkled and uplifted the masses and whose delivery was honed to perfection. Yet both toppled from their perch at the apogee of public popularity and are often considered tragic figures. History, and historians, can be unkind.[28]

Hoover hoped to be nonpartisan in his judicial appointments. Throughout the entire judicial system, of the presidents since Grover Cleveland, only Taft nominated fewer judges from his own party than Hoover. A study by the American Bar Association found that Hoover's nominees throughout the entire federal judiciary to be of higher quality than those of Harding, Coolidge, or Franklin Roosevelt. The Quaker appointed fewer from the ranks of big business than his predecessors or his successors. At the beginning of his term he had announced that merit would be the sole criterion for nominations to the federal bench, and his selections reflect this vow.[29]

During his presidency, Hoover had the opportunity to name three justices to the Supreme Court. After Chief Justice William Howard Taft retired on February 9, 1930, because of failing health, the president nominated Charles Evans Hughes. Hughes was superbly qualified. He had served as a Progressive governor of New York as well as a U.S. Supreme Court justice, resigning in 1916 to run for president. Nonetheless, some of the Western Progressives and some Democrats resented Hughes on class grounds and viewed a vote against him as a way to punish Hoover. Among Republicans, Norris, Borah, LaFollette, and Brookhart led the opposition. Borah might have been surprised if he had known that he himself was among the finalists Hoover had considered for the nomination. For four days the insurgents railed that Hughes was a wealthy Eastern elitist whose law practice included large corporations and whose views represented those of the upper classes. The opposition from some quarters fit a pattern. A newspaper that examined the *Congressional Record* found that in 1930 LaFollette had not voted with the GOP a single time and Norris but once. Nonetheless, Hughes' stature was sufficient to overcome the recriminations. The hostility to the nominee was deep but not broad. Hughes was confirmed 56–26.[30]

If the Hughes nomination produced fireworks, Hoover's next attempt to seat a nominee produced a reaction more comparable to a nuclear holocaust. The death of Justice Edward T. Sanford of Tennessee provided the opportunity for the president to name a second justice. There was only one Southerner on the court and none in the cabinet, and the president sought a representative from the Fourth Circuit Court. He believed the circuit courts provided the best proving ground for the Supreme Court, and the Fourth Circuit had not been represented in the past 70 years. After reviewing 125 opinions written by John J. Parker, a Fourth Circuit judge from Charlotte, North Carolina, and upon the recommendation of Attorney General Mitchell, Hoover nominated Parker. Though only 44, he was bright and experienced, having served on the bench for 20 years. Parker was given the highest rating by the American Bar Association.[31]

Initially, it appeared that the only plausible objections to Parker might be that he was too young. However, opposition to Parker was crystallized by two groups: the National Association for the Advancement of Colored People (NAACP), with only 100,000 members in 1930, and the more formidable American Federation of Labor (AFL), with 3.5 million members. The opposition focused solely on one case as well as a single statement of a few lines made during a political campaign. In 1920, while campaigning for governor, Parker had stated that blacks were not yet prepared to enter into participation in North Carolina politics. In reality, Parker was the racial liberal in the race, and his Democratic opponent represented the party of white supremacy in the solid South. Parker had made the remark to keep race out of the campaign, not to inject it. Further, no southern politician who publicly condemned white supremacy in 1920 had the remotest chance of election. As a judge, no decision by Parker had been unfair to blacks as a race, nor would he write any such decisions for the remainder of his judicial career. Indeed, he had stricken a municipal ordinance legalizing restrictive covenants. Walter White, the NAACP secretary, who testified against Parker in 1930, later conceded that he did not consider Parker a racist, nor did his long subsequent career on the bench demonstrate bias.[32]

William Green, who also testified against Parker, considered him inimical to the interests of labor because of a single case, called the Red Jacket Case, in which the jurist had participated in a unanimous decision upholding the right of the Red Jacket mining company to enforce contract provisions requiring potential workers to promise not to join a union as a condition of employment. Parker explained that the U.S. Supreme Court had upheld such contracts and that as a circuit court judge he was bound to follow precedent. To do otherwise would be futile because the higher court would simply overturn it. Indeed, the Supreme Court refused to review the Red Jacket case on appeal, thereby confirming the ruling. Nothing in Parker's subsequent career indicated a prejudice against organized labor.[33]

Hoover initially counted on a comfortable majority for confirmation. Regular Republicans found no objections in Parker's record. Neither did Southern Democrats. Yet Hoover was dismayed to see his supporters melting away as the NAACP and the AFL threatened to punish any senator who voted to confirm by casting a solid bloc of votes against them. Some Republicans standing for reelection asked the president to withdraw the nomination. Hoover refused on the grounds he did not believe in pandering to special interests. Parker himself wanted to remain in contention. The contest resolved into a political tightrope in a handful of states in which organized labor or blacks or both, might determine the outcome. As the controversy heated up, a larger issue emerged that was more ideological than the scrutiny on specific statements or rulings. A significant number of senators considered the makeup of the court too conservative. The replacement of Taft by Hughes had not altered that direction. The addition of Parker might help perpetuate it. Liberal senators wanted a more liberal court. By this criterion, virtually no white Southerner would be acceptable. The situation was not quite that simple, because a majority of both houses, including virtually all the Southern Democrats were conservative, at least in a relative sense. A number of senators who ultimately voted against Parker were more conservative than either Parker or Hoover. Parker's opponents included a variety of both liberals and conservatives, and the swing votes lay in states where senators considered themselves vulnerable. A few, such as Hiram Johnson, cast their votes against Parker based on personal pique against Hoover. In the final tally, Parker was defeated 41–39. If Hoover had been able to persuade one senator to change his vote, the tie would have been broken by Vice President Curtis, and Parker would have been confirmed.[34]

The loss was a severe political setback to the president, largely at the hands of his own party. He had engaged in personal lobbying, even pleading, to a degree unusual for him. His pride had been hurt, and his political reputation had been tarnished. Hoover had been unable to maintain party discipline. He felt chagrined at the role played by special interests, whom he believed would allow no candidate to be confirmed unless they knew in advance how he would vote. Hoover knew his chances of placing a Southerner on the court now were slim. The president felt he had been betrayed by some of his friends and political allies. The ripples of dissent that had begun with the Hughes nomination had swelled into a tide in the fight over Parker. In the long run Hoover made three distinguished nominations to the court that were confirmed. Yet in the minds of many, the single defeat overshadowed them.

Even before the Senate voted on the Parker nomination, a second justice, James C. McReynolds, age 68, declared his intention to retire as soon as a successor could be confirmed. A Democrat appointed by Wilson, he had been on the bench since 1914. Hoover was inclined to appoint a Democrat to replace him. The president did not dawdle in identifying a new nominee to succeed Sanford and accepted the Parker defeat with dignified silence. He promptly nominated Owen J. Roberts of Philadelphia. An attorney rather than a judge, Roberts had earned national acclaim by successfully prosecuting the Teapot Dome Scandal, which sent Interior Secretary Albert B. Fall to prison. A Republican, he was associated with no faction within the GOP. No important interest group opposed him. His ideology has received mixed analyses. Historian David Burner asserts that Roberts had a less progressive record than the rejected Parker, while Donald J. Lisio considers Roberts a liberal, partly because he was a trustee at the all-black Lincoln University. The most curious aspect of the nomination is that it elicited no debate. Senator Borah submitted a favorable committee report. Next, Senator Robinson of Arkansas, the Democratic leader, asked if the report of the Judiciary Committee was unanimous. Senator Norris and Senator McNary replied that it was. Robinson stated that he had no objection to confirmation. Vice President Curtis, in the chair, then announced that Roberts was confirmed without objection and without a roll call. Certainly the haste and the total lack of debate represented a strange contrast the Hughes and Parker nominations.[35]

When Oliver Wendell Holmes retired from the court early in 1932 Hoover chose not to fight the Senate by attempting to nominate a southerner or a conservative. He would have preferred to nominate a judge from the West or the Southwest to bring regional balance to the court, and there were a number of well-qualified conservatives he considered. The president's first choice was his attorney general, William D. Mitchell. He would have replaced him at the Justice Department with Secretary of War Patrick Hurley. Mitchell did not want to make the change, however. He and Hoover talked it over and decided that the insurgents and Democrats in the Senate would join to block anyone close to Hoover. The president observed that there was a good ideological argument to be made for replacing the liberal Holmes with another liberal. Jettisoning the idea of regional balance, the president appointed the best qualified, fairest liberal jurist he knew, Benjamin Cardozo the chief judge of the New York Court of Appeals. As with Roberts, there was no significant opposition to Cardozo. Along with Louis D. Brandeis of Boston, Cardozo was the second Jewish justice. He became the third justice from New York, joining Chief Justice Hughes and Harlan D. Stone. The court was fairly evenly balanced. For the first time since the Wilson administration, it included four Democrats. There were four reliable conservatives on the Supreme Court when Cardozo joined it: Willis Vandevanter, George Sutherland, James Clark MacReynolds, and Pierce Butler. Like Brandeis, Stone had a consistently liberal voting record. The other Hoover appointees, Chief Justice Hughes and Owen D. Roberts, were less predictable.[36]

The political wars of the administration involved all three branches of government: the executive, legislative, and judicial. The opposing parties fought to control all three. The battles over Hughes, and especially over Parker, brought a new dimension to the disputes over the judiciary during the Hoover years. Parker might not have been the best possible nominee, but political pressure, not his qualifications, determined his defeat. The qualifications of Roberts and Cardozo were excellent, but obviously the haste to confirm them without even examining their records casts shadows over the process. In general, all three of Hoover's appointments made distinguished records on the bench. Yet it is clear that political expediency had entered the nominating process to a degree that sullied the reputations of Hoover, the Congress, and special interests, tainting the process. The final result, produced three fine jurists, but the process demonstrated flagrant intellectual dishonesty, not simply in the defeat of Parker, but in the perfunctory examinations of Roberts and Cardozo. It marked a trend that was accentuated later during the twentieth and twenty-first centuries of appointments and confirmation hearings that became increasingly ideologically driven. Hearings seek to determine *how* a potential justice will vote prior to confirming them, and nominees find it prudent to conceal their views.

CHAPTER 9

Combating the Depression
Phase I, 1929–1930

As the country cleared away the rubble from the stock market crash, it slid deeper and deeper into a depression, although no one could predict its severity or duration. The latest panic, of 1921–22, had lasted some two years, about average. Democratic financier Bernard Baruch wrote that he believed Hoover "would be fortunate enough, before the next election, to have a rising tide and then he will be pictured as the great master mind who led the country out of its economic misery."[1]

Hoover knew from the beginning that business recovery and consumer spending relied upon morale. He correctly pointed out that the actual productive and consuming power of the nation were the same after the jolt as before it. Only the psychology changed. "Many thinkers are beginning to recognize the fact that the decrease in business activity during certain periods is largely the result of fear," the *Christian Science Monitor* wrote in early 1931. "President Hoover apparently recognized this when he made the effort to reestablish confidence after the financial crisis of 1929."[2] An economic depression, like a human one, is partly a state of mind. Because causes of depressions are not entirely material, the cure cannot be purely material. The stock operates less on the value of dividends, than on rumor, psychology, and fragments of information. "For the President of the United States to announce we were on the verge of complete collapse would immediately precipitate the collapse," Susan L. DuBrock Wendel writes, "eliminating any chance to reverse the situation."[3]

What would have been the effect on the stock market and the morale of the country if the president had gone on radio in early 1930 and delivered a sermon from his office, stating:

> We are in one hell of a fix! Our entire economy is paralyzed. No one knows what to do. I am getting all kinds of conflicting advice. My personal opinion is that things are going to get much worse before they get better and are going to remain bad for a long time. Unemployment is going to increase. Thousands of banks are going to fail. There will be no end to our misery. God help us! We are at wits' end!

He might have gone on to say that prosperity was as elusive as quicksilver and that for all he knew it might require a decade, even a generation, to recover. People should hunker down, live austerely, buy less, take their money out of banks (most of which were unsafe), ration the dog, and not buy any Christmas presents.

Hoover knew that unless the psychological enemy was defeated, fear and pessimism would feed on themselves. Thus he was at first cautiously optimistic in public. "Ninety percent of our problems are caused by fear," the president said in 1931.[4] "In declaring that there was nothing to fear, but fear," William E. Leuchtenburg writes, "Roosevelt had minted no new platitudes. Hoover had been saying the same thing for three years."[5] Hoover tried to encourage Americans without exaggerating. Although he downplayed the situation publicly, his actions indicate that he considered conditions unstable. His first State of the Union message on December 3, 1929, was packed with legislative proposals. These included a tax cut, increases in public works, and reform of the nation's financial policies. He hoped he could arrest the decline with a combination of persuasion and prompt measures.[6]

Hoover did not believe that positive thinking alone could end the downturn, but it might contain it before it snowballed downhill. The government alone, Hoover continued, could not heal the economy. But it must strive to restore faith that investment would reap profits. Anything the government did to frighten business would prolong hard times. Fear paralyzed. Most people could walk across a board five inches wide laid flat on the floor. But if the same board were placed between two skyscrapers, hundreds of feet high, it would be a difficult task. Louis S. Cates, president of the Phelps Dodge Corporation, explained that the spirit of America must be healed before its economy could be healed. By late 1930, people were wearing their clothes longer, consuming less of everyday necessities, and economizing even if they had no obvious need to do so. Consumption drives a capitalist economy. When it declines at the retail level, this creates slack at the wholesale level, which affects manufacturing. As the economic downturn trickles down, it causes layoffs at every level, which can be restored on a permanent basis only by high levels of consumption. The chief ingredient for recovery is the belief on the part of both producers and consumers that the decline is not of indefinite duration. It would take a series of interrelated acts to rejuvenate the private sector.

Hoover was practical and knew history. He had lived through the financial panics of 1893, 1903, 1907, and 1921–1922. In January 1930, the president requested statistics about previous downturns from the Commerce Department. Hoover used the recession of 1921–22 as a model to chart the duration of the 1929 downturn. The 1921 recession was severe, with unemployment peaking at about six million or 11.9 percent. As secretary of commerce, Hoover was a vigorous advocate of countercyclical measures. Unlike later presidents, however, Hoover did not operate solely from a top-down perspective. He relied on efforts by the federal government in tandem with state and local governments and private business. It was the logical place to start because in 1929 the greatest resources lay outside the federal government. He relied on volunteerism to a greater degree than later downturns but to a lesser degree than previous ones. The 1921–22 recession, not the Depression that followed the 1929 crash, was the first major intervention by the national government during hard times, although modest by later standards. Still, the economy not only recovered but caught a jet stream that propelled it through the prosperity of the Jazz Age.

In 1921 Hoover convened the President's Conference on Unemployment. He focused largely, though not exclusively, on stimulating construction. Construction was the balance wheel of the economy and could be increased rapidly to provide a lift during slack periods. After recovery, Hoover backed several bills that died in Congress between 1921 and 1928. These would have created a federal fund to be used for emergency construction during economic declines. When the 1929 disaster occurred, Hoover again turned to construction, beginning below the federal level, but this time on a much larger scale. Although he was hopeful, he did not believe that an infinite amount of prodding, nor an infinite amount of spending by the government, would produce an infinite number of permanent jobs. Further, he believed federal jobs should be meaningful and provide a useful product. Hoover also tried to improve the statistical basis of tracking employment. The Commerce Department was the mother lode of statistics, yet he wanted more sophisticated data. He was responsible for initiating several major studies on the business cycle. There was a study on Business Cycles and Unemployment and one that dealt with Seasonal Operations in the Construction Industry. More comprehensive was a preliminary study on the U.S. economy in 1928–1929, which evolved into the Committee on Recent Economic Changes and to the 1929–1930 study about Planning and Control of Public Works.[7]

The president was not daunted by the problems of the Depression. Although he detested human suffering, he enjoyed being tested, and he was not averse to taking risks. Yet he wanted to avoid actions that might compromise American institutions. Democratic institutions were permanent; the emergency was temporary. Hoover knew that much of the world was adopting totalitarianism, lubricated by demagoguery. He wanted reasonable assurance that his experiments would succeed and that they would not violate the Constitution or undermine democratic principles. Yet he was not opposed to reorganization of the system. However, he wanted to avoid the creation of a permanent, entrenched bureaucracy to combat an ephemeral emergency. A practical idealist, he would move beyond previous presidents but not sufficiently to undermine private enterprise.[8]

Hoover relied on his experience in feeding Belgium, the work of the American Relief Administration (ARA), the Food Administration (FA), his tenure as secretary of commerce, and rescue and rehabilitation the Mississippi River Valley in 1927. His cardinal principles included centralized decisions, decentralized implementation, and the use of volunteers. Hoover did not micromanage. He picked able subordinates and allowed them to do their jobs. As a Quaker, he believed in self-help and community involvement and in humanizing relief. The president never thought of people as numbers. As president, he felt that his tasks were to deal with the mechanics of the economy and to ameliorate human suffering. The president was not opposed to federal aid but considered it a last resort. He wanted to give private charity, beginning at the local level, the chance to work first. Voluntary giving not only helped the needy; it ennobled the giver. The president also felt that reliance upon a paternalistic government might undermine self-worth and individual initiative, which in fact it has. Yet Hoover was not a hard-hearted man; in fact, he was just the opposite. Hoover was sympathetic to the needy, and he was flexible. He was also venturing, during the Great Depression, into unknown territory in dealing with human problems. His philosophy was not based solely on philosophical principles but on practicality. The government at that time simply lacked the resources to employ, feed, and house all the needy. Moreover, the Depression was still unfolding, and it was impossible to predict where it would lead. His policy was to up the ante when the situation demanded action. He did not have the advantage, as his successor did, of looking back at the years between 1929 and 1933. Effectively fighting the Depression required public and congressional support. Hoover believed the combination of all levels that contributed to the economy was more effective than relying exclusively on the federal government. Yet he was not naïve and was willing to do what had to be done, even some things that he believed were undesirable in the long run but necessary in the short run. "I am willing to pledge myself that if the time should ever come that the voluntary agencies of the country together with the local and state governments are unable to find resources with which to prevent hunger and suffering in my country, I will ask the aid of every resource of the federal government," he explained, "because I would no more see starvation amongst my countrymen than any Senator or Congressman." Hoover also wanted his relief resources to go to the people who needed them, not to be skimmed by a massive bureaucracy, nor traded for votes. The overhead for dispensation of relief during the Hoover administration was about 3 percent. Under the New Deal overhead rose to from 25 to 50 percent.[9]

Hoover not only relied on his own intuition and experience; he consulted a variety of businessmen, economists, journalists, and politicians from both parties. A year after the Crash, most of them did not believe there was much more the government could do. The president did not believe the Depression could be ended solely by legislation. The Congress, as it was then constituted, acted slowly and indecisively. It debated endlessly, packed legislation with pork, and watered down regulatory provisions. Hoover sought remedial legislation, but he believed reliance on Congress alone would yield only partial results. Congressmen thought in parochial terms while the president represented the entire country. Waiting for a consensus often resembled *Waiting for Godot*. Some congressmen even hoped stagnation would benefit their party or their personal ambitions. More basically, Hoover did not believe political solutions to worldwide economic problems were the entire solution. The economy was related to the government, but it did not act at the will of the government. "Economic depressions cannot be cured by legislative action or executive pronouncements," he said. "Economic wounds must be healed by the actions of the cells of the economic body—the producers and consumers themselves." The subsequent failure of the New Deal to end the Depression despite gallant efforts made Hoover a prophet. The government could ease the burden of suffering, but the government could not pull a switch and ignite the engine of prosperity. "We have as a nation a definite duty to see that no deserving person in our country suffers from hunger and cold," he explained. The president believed that taxing then using tax money to create jobs was less efficient than helping private enterprise restore the lost jobs. The government would take money from business, skim some of the funds in overhead, distort the distribution of jobs through political favoritism, and then create a limited number of lower-paying jobs with what was left. Common sense showed that this was a roundabout approach that merely created temporary, relatively low-paying jobs. A better tactic, he believed, was to spread existing work.[10] Hoover realized that the restoration of genuine prosperity would require patience and that democracy was a fickle employer. As an ex-president he ruefully remarked that he had been attacked for not ending the Depression in three years, while Roosevelt was cheered although he had not brought prosperity after six years in office.[11]

The Depression did not, like Athena, emerge fully grown at its birth. It developed and grew incrementally and presented different challenges at different stages. Sometimes it appeared that recovery was approaching, only to be dashed, sometimes by events beyond American borders. The solution, when it ultimately came, almost accidentally, also lay beyond American borders. During the first half of 1930, the Depression and Hoover's attempts to combat it, did not dominate the front pages. Rather, preparations for the London Naval Conference; the nominations of Hughes, Parker, and Roberts to the Supreme Court; and hyperbolic reporting the tariff debate were the major stories. As late as August 1931, a poll of governors revealed that of the 40 who had responded, only 1, Gifford Pinchot of Pennsylvania, representing a relatively rich state, believed he would require federal aid for the coming winter. Most of the nation's mayors told the *New York Times* in September 1931, that they could manage without federal relief. It appeared that the president's appeal to governors and the private sector to expedite plans for construction and repair had been successful. Some 29 governors pledged to increase their 1930 construction by $1.3 billion over the 1929 level. Hoover's appeals to the private sector received an even more encouraging response. Public utilities vowed to spend an additional $14 billion in expansion and maintenance; railroads agreed to implement work totaling $1 billion; and American Telephone and Telegraph planned to spend about $700 million more than the previous year. These pledges were voluntary but were made in good faith and appeared to lift some of the malaise settling over the country, as the president had hoped. The chief executive also planned a smaller package of public works to be constructed by the federal government.[12]

Not all the public jobs created during the Hoover administration resulted in magnificent buildings and bridges or tall dams. Many of them, which do not show up in federal statistics, were undertaken by states and municipalities—with federal encouragement—to employ people at small jobs, sometimes of brief duration, in their own communities. Unlike construction jobs, these did not require special skills and could be implemented quickly. Federal agencies helped in identifying such work. They hunted for jobs that could employ the needy for three or four days a week by improving and beautifying buildings, streets, parks, and schools. Contributions from charity football and basketball games, community chests, local appropriations, and charity drives made such jobs possible. Hundreds of thousands of workers not on the federal payroll were employed in such work, arranged by the federal government, which set priorities for employment, based primarily on numbers of dependents. When individuals applied, they were placed in the most appropriate job for their age and skill. Wages were paid at the level prevailing in the community. Many of the jobs resembled later Works Progress Administration (WPA) work such as cleaning parks; mowing grass; building camp grounds, playgrounds, lakes, and golf courses; landscaping public property; constructing drainage and irrigation facilities; and creating or enlarging picnic areas. Unsafe buildings were razed, swimming pools built, and restrooms sanitized. Water mains, electric lines, and telephone lines were connected. Public buildings were cleaned and painted. Amusement parks were built, and streets paved. Heating was improved in public schools, and parking lots were constructed. These jobs have largely been neglected in histories of the Hoover administration.[13]

The president preferred the creation of jobs to payment of outright doles. He considered doles addictive and demoralizing, though he made exceptions for the handicapped, the infirm, the aged, and especially children. Moreover, he believed that everyone who applied for aid and genuinely needed it should be helped. Hoover believed it was more efficient to work through the infrastructure that already existed within private charities rather than to erect a new federal superstructure. Local officials understood the needs of their own people. In addition, federal stipends might dry up private donations because potential donors might conclude their gifts were superfluous. Hoover never believed in localism at the expense of hungry people, but he did believe in localism. The federal government at that time did not possess more financial resources than the combined state budgets. Raising taxes would take money out of the pockets of consumers and investors, while borrowing would drive up interest rates and require future tax increases. When federal money was used, loans were preferable to grants, because the implication that the money must be repaid would limit demand, and there was only so much money to go around. Public and private sectors should be as meaningful as possible otherwise, skills would atrophy. The workers should feel that they were contributing to a worthwhile accomplishment. Neither should doles be paid when legitimate work was available. Hoover's successor, FDR, and his chief job czars, Harry Hopkins and Harold Ickes, also preferred job relief to outright relief, including the premise that jobs should be as useful as possible under the circumstances. Their philosophy toward work relief differed primarily in scope, the wisdom of massive deficit spending (Hoover accepted modest deficits), and the fact that Roosevelt served slightly more than three terms. On a cost-benefits basis, as well as progress made in ending the Depression, the New Deal programs were only marginally successful. In 1939, the unemployment rate after six years of the New Deal was 17.2 percent as opposed to 15.9 percent in 1931.[14]

Hoover also explored plans to guarantee the employment of workers with the companies that employed them, an idea favored by the AFL. One plan involved guaranteed employment insurance, called work assurance. By the late summer of 1931 the president was attempting to line up commitments from major industries to guarantee their workers a job through the coming winter, perhaps a certain number of days per year, a type of job sharing. Such a plan had been adopted by one major manufacturer. Though backed by the government, such programs would have had to be voluntary because there was no way the government could legally force employers to hire workers.[15]

The president received almost instant action from Congress on a key facet of his program, a $160 million tax cut to stimulate spending and investment, which he signed with little ceremony on December 16, 1929. The president hoped it would inject money into the consumer economy for the Christmas season. The tax cut was targeted. It slashed taxes by 66 percent on small incomes, 4 percent on larger incomes, and 8.33 percent on corporate incomes. It was also a weapon in Hoover's arsenal to provide a psychological boost to consumer and business confidence.[16]

The chief executive fleshed out his plans to combine public and private efforts to aid relief and employment. On October 21, 1930, he asked Colonel Arthur Woods, the former police commissioner of New York City, to chair the President's Emergency Committee on Employment (PECE). Woods, a Harvard graduate who had taught at Groton and worked as a journalist for the *New York Sun,* had helped find jobs for returning veterans after the Great War and had served on President Harding's Conference on Unemployment in 1921. This government committee helped create jobs and served as a clearinghouse to place workers. It helped coordinate the feeding of children in the coal regions by Quaker organizations and the work of the Red Cross in other states. Woods worked within the government to spread work by stretching out the hours among more workers. For example, the War Department, in its work on the Mississippi River near St. Louis and Cairo, implemented a three-day week, which enabled it to employ 1,000 men rather than 500. Woods encouraged similar programs in private companies. He also facilitated direct relief by employers to furloughed workers in the forms of cash, food, clothing, fuel, medical aid, and rent. Fourteen percent of company workers took out loans without interest for employees they expected to rehire when business improved. Woods encouraged Americans to hire carpenters and plumbers to make home repairs and helped persuade voters to approve $450 million in state bonds to provide construction jobs. Thirty prominent Americans served on an advisory committee, and some 3,000 local committees functioned at the community level. Woods consulted governors about their needs for the coming winter and requested an appropriation of $750 million for federal public works. Hoover reduced this to $150 million, and Congress cut it further to $117 million. At the time, unemployment remained at about the 1921–22 level, and there was no surge of support at the grassroots level or in Congress for a program on the scale Woods recommended.[17]

In April 1931, Woods, disappointed that unemployment had continued to swell, announced that he would take two months' leave from the committee to study unemployment insurance programs in England and Germany. The work of the committee continued under its vice chairman, Fred C. Croxton. In August some of the PECE's responsibilities and personnel were transferred to the President's Organization on Unemployment Relief (POUR) under Walter S. Gifford, the president of American Telephone and Telegraph. Three subcommittees under Croxton, Owen D. Young, and James R. Garfield planned the expansion and coordination of relief. The president now realized the Depression would be a lengthy one and began integrating the voluntary efforts into the new Federal Employment Stabilization Board and other permanent government agencies. In August, Croxton, who remained one of the key leaders until March 1933, promised that no one who applied for aid would starve. The shifting of the administration to a more centralized, federally operated program did not mean the end of the voluntary effort. A core of volunteers remained intact until the end of the administration. Hoover saw public and private responsibilities for relief as complementary, not mutually exclusive.[18]

Working in tandem with the Woods and Croxton committees were the Cabinet Committee on Unemployment Relief and a committee of leaders of trade associations, all attacking the problem of unemployment and business stagnation from slightly different angles. The Cabinet Committee, chaired by Secretary of Commerce Robert P. Lamont, was the only one comprising solely federal officials. Lamont's committee was the planning board for devising public works at the federal level. The Cabinet Committee concluded that it would be necessary to erect more public works than during the recession of 1921–22 and predicted that the collapse that began in 1929 would be more severe. It furnished a rationale for the president's request for additional appropriations from Congress. The committee also recommended that money implemented for use over several years be released at once, especially federal matching funds to the states for road construction. Highways constituted the single largest type of state construction, a category in which they far outstripped the federal government. Agriculture Secretary Hyde suggested that farmers be employed on road building near their homes. The federal building program operated on the premise that work should be provided that would avoid the relocation of large numbers of individuals, or separate them from their families, and that would utilize their skills. Earnings must be adequate to provide food and shelter through the winter of 1930–1931, and the work was distributed according to need.[19]

The president and several members of the cabinet also focused on the role credit and banking played in the economy. Some 90 percent of transactions were made on the basis of bank checks. Thus there was a direct relationship between the stability of banks, their credibility with the public, and the willingness of individuals and corporations to deposit funds and borrow. Hoover considered banking the weakest link in the economy. Part of his work was to encourage the free flow of money as in normal times. People, including bankers themselves, resisted taking risks. Bankers, like stock brokers, need confidence to lend money. The credit crisis was based more on fear than on reality. When the panic hit Wall Street it released a great deal of capital that had been tied up in nonproductive speculation. Now that capital was available for investment, but venture capitalists were afraid to use it. Borrowers were afraid to borrow, and lenders were afraid to loan, even though the Federal Reserve, at Hoover's prodding, reduced interest rates well below the level at the height of the boom. Banks feared that reckless loans might lead to failure, but no loans at all meant certain failure for banks and businesses alike. "Fear is death to credit," the president said.[20]

Fear was not the only root of the bank problem. There were genuine, systemic weaknesses evident even during prosperous times that were aggravated by the Depression. There were far too many banks, most were undercapitalized, and they relied on insufficient collateral, including home and farm mortgages, which were rapidly depreciating in value. Foreign junk bonds, usually issued at high rates to attract American capital, were destined for default, and bonds sunk in the deluge of the crash. Much of the problem lay in bad judgment by bankers. But the weakness also lay in the system itself, which was a patchwork of contrasting regulations in different states. Many small banks were organized under state charters because they could operate with fewer restrictions, less capital, and meager collateral. Investment and savings banks were combined, which permitted banks to speculate with their depositor's money and lose it if stocks collapsed. New types of entities were evolving: branch banks and group banks, which by combining resources could dwarf individual unit banks, yet they did not fit neatly into the regulatory systems of many states. Bankers had been lulled into a sense of security by the Federal Reserve Act of 1913, which they believed made a future collapse impossible, just as many were lulled into security years later by New Deal banking reforms, which they believed rendered them invulnerable, only to discover in 2007 that there is always a Grinch lurking to snatch their Christmas presents.

Hoover had been worried about the banking system during his tenure as secretary of commerce. Anyone who looked around should have been worried. The system was honeycombed by small, rural banks that operated on the edge of solvency. From 1921 to 1930, 6,987 banks failed, and only 806 reopened. Most had assets of less than $100,000, some of less than $25,000. Urban banks, which often bought securities issued by smaller, weaker banks, suffered ripple effects. There were almost twice as many state banks as federal banks, with varied regulations. Only one-third of all banks were members of the Federal Reserve System. Hoover included banking reform in every annual message he delivered. The president had definite ideas about reforming banks and the financial system. He wanted commercial banks separated from investment banking to protect depositors. In his first State of the Union message of December 3, 1929, the president called upon Congress to create a commission to recommend specific legislation. Hearings on February 25, 1930, focused particularly on the role branch, group, and chain banking might play. Hoover and some congressmen wanted to loosen restrictions on these larger combinations, which permitted them to pool their resources, making them stronger. No legislation resulted from the committee's inquiry.[21]

After failing to pry banking legislation from Congress, Hoover approached bankers directly in a speech at the American Bankers Association at Cleveland on October 2, 1930. He attempted to persuade them to extend credit to help revive business and stimulate the economy. The bankers were more interested in protecting their liquidity. But near the end of 1930 the foundations of the banking system began to crack. The first shudders began at Louisville's National Bank of Kentucky and spread to neighboring banks in Indiana, Illinois, and Missouri. Next, the fissures spread to Iowa, Arkansas, and North Carolina. Initially, the panic had consumed small, rural banks. But on December 11, 1930, New York City's Bank of the United States shut down, the largest bank failure in history up to that time. Some 400,000 depositors lost nearly $286 million, and it appeared the panic would spread like a prairie fire. In fact, by the end of 1930, some 1,352 banks had failed. Yet the banking system survived, albeit temporarily, and in the first quarter of 1931, not only did bank failures decline, but an economic upturn appeared on the horizon, giving the impression that the worst was over. But the Indian Summer of recovery cooled Unfortunately, steps taken by banks to shore up their reserves in order to stave off collapse, had the effect of further denying credit during a deflationary period. And in 1931, bad news would reach across the Atlantic and chill hopes of rapid recovery.[22]

After the Crash, Hoover wanted the Federal Reserve System, to make credit more readily available. Having been lenient during inflationary times, the lenders should avoid a contraction during deflationary times. The Board was divided during the period after the Crash, both the central Board and the members of the 12 regional banks. In 1929 the death of Benjamin Strong, an influential voice as governor of the New York Federal Reserve Bank, created a leadership vacuum at the nerve center of finance. The Board members squabbled among themselves and with members of the regional banks. In 1930 Hoover appointed Eugene Meyer, a currency expansionist, as governor of the Federal Reserve Board. Although Hoover and Meyer were vigorous expansionists, some members within the system cautioned prudence. Still, caution was not unanimous. In order to arrest the decline, the Fed began to purchase securities in the final months of 1929 to improve the liquidity of member banks. The Board also reduced interest rates, though not sufficiently to satisfy Hoover. Throughout 1930 the Fed continued open market operations and reduction of rediscount rates, which improved the liquidity of member banks. Much of the blame for tepid credit policies must be attributed to the individual banks, whose priority was to husband their resources, and to potential borrowers, who were reluctant to take even modest risks. The potential money supply was sufficient by 1930, yet the actual money supply was restrained by fear. Although credit was available at reasonable rates, the requirements for acceptable collateral had stiffened. No one knew how to bet on an economy that gyrated. This is one reason Hoover considered it essential to preserve the gold standard and to avoid unnecessarily large deficits. The nation began a deflationary spiral in which debtors would have to repay money previously loaned in dollars more valuable than the ones they had borrowed. However, salaried people on fixed incomes would actually be secure because the prices of goods they purchased declined.[23]

As secretary of commerce, Hoover's primary responsibility had been to promote business growth and prosperity, which led some to the deceiving conclusion that he would become a "business" president. Yet as president, Hoover was concerned with the entire economy, including agriculture and labor. His top priority, however, was American consumers. He felt a responsibility to ensure that Americans were offered a variety of affordable products and were provided with jobs that would enable them to purchase these goods. As president he viewed the economy in holistic terms. Hoover wanted business to prosper and realized that without business prosperity, the economy would remain in the doldrums. Yet he considered some capitalists greedy and, like most Progressives, believed fervently in regulation. Left to cutthroat competition, capitalism would devour itself, resulting in one huge monopoly. The tendency of capitalism was to start small and consolidate; the tendency of communism was to start with monopoly and disintegrate. Many American businessmen had initially opposed Hoover because they wanted to be left alone under a lethargic president such as Harding or Coolidge. Hoover believed competition sustained capitalism, and he did not want consolidation to reach the point of monopoly, which is why he rigorously enforced antitrust laws and was somewhat less enthusiastic about large trade associations than he had been at Commerce. Yet Hoover never demonized businessmen or sought to identify businessmen as scapegoats who should be punished to gain political capital. Even when dealing with the opposition party, his preference was not to polarize but to conciliate. He believed laws in the economic sector, as in other areas, should be enforced impartially.[24]

During all previous panics the state and federal governments had retrenched, hoping to squeeze the poison out of the economy. Granted, previous downturns had ended more quickly, and economists have argued ever since whether the course Hoover and FDR pursued actually prolonged the agony. Hoover's secretary of the treasury, the billionaire businessman Andrew Mellon, argued just that. But we will never know for sure. Hoover believed that prudent intervention in the economy could help reverse the economy cycle, though he warned repeatedly that it would be simplistic to assume that we could spend ourselves out of the Depression. Further, it would have been out of character for him to remain inactive. Hoover spent more money on public works than all previous presidents combined, and spending on government construction tripled within three years. Because this did not produce immediate recovery, he was condemned by some for doing too much and by others for doing too little. The measures to implement job-creating public works, which were intended to reverse the economic cycle, began within weeks of the crash, in November 1929. Although the early efforts focused primarily on the state and local sectors, Hoover complemented this with a strong federal program. Congress increased the amount of federal aid to the states for highway construction from $75 to $125 million a year for three years and liberalized the terms for its use. The building program for post offices and other structures in cities and towns throughout the country was increased by $230 million. A $15 million Veterans Bureau hospital construction program was authorized by Congress and implemented immediately. In a number of departments, funds were made available at once instead of at the beginning of the fiscal year on July 1. Every federal agency planning construction advanced the date of its groundbreaking. A Division of Public Construction was established in the Department of Commerce to coordinate and expedite building. Within two years federal spending for construction had grown to $700 million. Hoover said he wanted employment in all parts of the country, providing people with normal jobs in their own homes, in a type of work with which they were familiar. He did not simply fling money at problems, yet acted aggressively and purposefully. On February 10, 1931, Congress created the Federal Employment Stabilization Board, composed of the secretaries of the treasury, commerce, agriculture, and labor. Its task was to provide advance planning and to regulate the pace of public works.[25]

The president wanted public works to be located on the basis of need, not population, so they could serve the jobless, not officeholders. In late 1931 he recommended the creation of a Public Works Administration to rationalize public construction under a single agency. The measure was defeated because it would have removed some of the pork-barrel projects that were used to enhance the reelection of incumbents. The Democrats delighted in submitting pork-barrel bills they knew Hoover would veto. These made them popular among their constituents while it made Hoover appear heartless. Nonetheless, the administration scrupulously avoided favoritism in its dispersal of public works. Despite the hundreds of millions of dollars spent on projects throughout the nation, there was never a single charge of graft or even of inefficiency. The president believed that the targeting and timing of public works was more significant than the amount of money spent. Timed correctly, it could swing the pendulum of employment in a favorable direction. The effectiveness, if timely, was out of all proportion to the size. The president also insisted on paying the prevailing wage in the community to workers employed on government projects. After Congress defeated the Couzens amendment mandating such a prevailing wage, the chief executive implemented the policy by executive order and continued it throughout his administration. Hoover believed high wages for labor stimulated the consumer economy.[26]

The construction programs were an extraordinary accomplishment for their time, especially because Hoover started with virtually no precedents, no procedures in place, and little time to assemble people, plans, and resources. According to David M. Kennedy, not until 1939 did the New Deal increase federal construction to $1.5 billion, its first year above the 1930 spending rate, in 1930 dollars. "Given the constraints under which he labored, in short, Hoover made impressively aggressive countercyclical use of federal policy," Kennedy writes. "Measured against either past or future performance, his accomplishments were remarkable," he explains. "Thanks to his prodding, the net stimulative effect of federal, state, and local fiscal policy was larger in 1931 than in any subsequent year of the decade."[27]

A comprehensive public works program transformed and beautified the national capital. It employed thousands of workers for the duration of Hoover's presidency and beyond. He had planned a construction and beautification program in Washington before the Crash, but the dire need for jobs accelerated and expanded projects that had been part of the president's dream. Both the buildings and the jobs were badly needed. The federal government had neglected to construct buildings to house its employees in Washington for 30 years, from 1900 to 1930. Federal employees were scattered throughout the city in rented buildings, with little unity of purpose. Agriculture was housed in 46 different buildings, Treasury in 27. Many of the buildings were ugly and dilapidated, and the treasury was drained by renting them. Hoover wanted to centralize activities according to function and to make Washington the most beautiful national capital in the world. New buildings, conforming to the ideas of L'Enfant, the original architect, were complemented by parks, highways, bridges, fountains, and landscaped gardens. The president undertook the greatest building program in history in the national capital. Many of the government offices were constructed along the mall, others in a triangle designed to complement one another. They were constructed to last indefinitely, and most are still in use in the twenty-first century. Among buildings started or completed were a new Supreme Court building, additions to the House and Senate Office Buildings, an extension of the Library of Congress, and a new municipal building for the District of Columbia. Nearly completed by the time Hoover left office were buildings for the Commerce Department (the largest building ever constructed by the government to that time), and office buildings for the Post Office, Justice Department, Interstate Commerce Commission, and the National Archives. Other projects included Mount Vernon Boulevard and the Arlington Memorial Bridge. Work was done to enhance the Capitol grounds, including the construction of an underground parking garage with a park above it. An underground irrigation system was built to water the grass and gardens.[28]

When people recall public works, they usually remember large, magnificent public structures. Indeed, there were more such buildings constructed during the Hoover administration than ever before. By the midterm of his presidency, a total of 817 major buildings had been authorized and 131 completed. By the end of Hoover's tenure, 360 such buildings had been completed, and 460 more were under contract. These were being built in more than 400 towns and cities at a cost of about $800 million. If one included all types of projects, such as highways, waterways, and dams, just midway through his term, public works costing $2 billion were under way that provided jobs for about one million workers. Small projects, especially post offices, were scattered throughout hundreds of towns, but the administration also constructed huge post offices in major cities such as Chicago and New York. The administration began the process of phasing out the renting of post offices, which had begun as a cost-saving device during World War I. Although the smaller projects mounted up and spread employment nationally, many of them were not considered sufficiently newsworthy, and Hoover did not receive much credit for them.[29] The president himself established the scope of the public works program. Determination of the relative merits of specific projects was set by him in consultation with the Woods Committee and the Division of Public Construction. Although the president's assertiveness in getting work under way was applauded in many quarters, this was not universally true. Some people advocated government retrenchment, and Congress sometimes reduced administration proposals for appropriations. Yet by the end of 1930, bills were piling up to spend in the range of $3 billion to $5 billion in s single year. Most such bills did not include the means to finance them. Although a few included such activities as the development of roads, rivers, and harbors, the vast majority focused on large public buildings limited to a single city. The president also continued to believe that, wherever possible, public works should be self-liquidating—that is, they should pay for themselves over time. This would minimize the ballooning of the national debt.[30]

One of Hoover's greatest accomplishments in the realm of public works, which produced almost immediate benefits as well as employment for thousands, lay in the development of rivers and waterways. It was appreciated at the time, and probably had more cumulative effect than the construction of large public buildings, but the program has been less noted by historians. Waterway development had always ranked high on Hoover's agenda. His envisioned an integrated plan of navigation, power, irrigation, and flood control on a scale not contemplated by any previous administration. Hoover contemplated the greatest waterway construction program ever attempted, projected to cost three times the amount of the Panama Canal. It would provide employment for thousands and reduce the cost of transportation, providing a cheap alternative for farmers to ship their produce to eastern and foreign markets. The president divided the nation into related water systems for integrated development, with a chief engineer to plan and supervise each. The divisions included the North Atlantic, South Atlantic, Gulf of Mexico, the Upper Mississippi, and the Lower Mississippi. Hoover hoped money saved by the London Naval treaty would help finance the developments. On December 3, 1929, the president outlined his plans in his annual message to Congress. The nation, he said, would systematically develop a system of transportation that included the Mississippi, Ohio, Missouri, Allegheny, Illinois, and Tennessee Rivers, as well as several canals. This would create a north-south trunk line 1,500 miles long and an east-west trunk line of 1,600 miles. The network was to be connected via the Great Lakes by construction of a St. Lawrence Seaway. The cost, exclusive of the St. Lawrence Seaway, would be about $55 million annually for five years, possibly longer. The work on the Ohio had been under way for several years, and Hoover dedicated its completion at Louisville, Kentucky, on October 23, 1929.[31]

The River and Harbor Act of 1930 authorized several important new projects, including the Illinois Waterway connecting the Great Lakes with the Mississippi System at Chicago and the canalization of the Upper Mississippi to a depth of nine feet from the mouth of the Illinois to St. Paul and Minneapolis. This was developed in tandem with a nine-foot depth dredging of the Tennessee River from its mouth to Knoxville, a distance of more than 600 miles. All important harbors were developed to depths justified by their economic potential. Most of the flood control work on the Mississippi, south of Cairo, was complete by the time Hoover left office. The channels connecting the Great Lakes were deepened to 27 feet, and the jetties near the mouth of the Columbia River were repaired. The harbors in the Hawaiian Islands were deepened to accommodate the American military and commercial fleets. In the interest of stimulating employment, the president stipulated that money be spent as rapidly as possible, for as long as it lasted. This applied even though he was attempting to pare the budget in other respects to compensate for declining revenue. The president's plan included the integration of water, rail, and motor transportation in a manner that would provide the best service at the lowest cost. The Inland Waterways Corporation, a government entity, also developed technology for inland waterways, including new types of towboats and tunnels. It created more efficient methods to burn coal and diesel fuel. The number of boats on inland waterways expanded enormously, as did the income generated, and, combined with more efficient methods of diesel and coal propulsion by the Army Corps of Engineers, helped make American products more competitive in international markets.[32]

The most memorable of Hoover's public works, was the Boulder Dam, ultimately known as the Hoover Dam, which provided flood control, irrigation, water storage, and hydroelectric power by constructing the largest dam to that time—some 700 feet high, on the Colorado River. The dam provided cities as distant as Los Angeles and Denver with reliable water supplies. Irrigation produced arable land comparable in size to the admission of a new state. California, much of which would have been a desert wasteland, benefitted most, especially the Imperial Valley, which blossomed with agricultural bounty. The dam generated some one million horsepower, which helped the industrialization of the West. A huge reservoir, Lake Meade, held enough water to cover all of New England with a foot of water. Stocked with fish, operated by the National Park Service, it became a major tourist Mecca, as did the dam itself. Las Vegas, a small town nearby, grew into a resort. The electricity generated ultimately repaid the government for its $165 million investment. During the depths of the Depression, it provided employment for 5,000 workers and their families, including Apache Indians, recruited because they were acclimated to the heat.[33]

Hoover had been a part of the project since the beginning. In 1922 he became chairman of the Colorado River Commission, whose mission was to negotiate a compact among the seven states that would share the water. Arizona, the last holdout, sued to attempt to stop the project. By 1928 agreement had been reached. On June 25, 1929, Hoover proclaimed the compact effective. He then sought an initial appropriation of $10,660,000 to begin the work. Construction began in September 1930 and was about half complete by the end of the administration. The financing was ingenuous. Instead of a public bond issue, bonds issued by the Treasury Department were purchased by the Interior Department, secured by electricity sold by the government to private companies, which distributed electricity to consumers. The guarantee that the bonds would be redeemed enabled the Treasury to offer them at a lower interest rate than bonds sold to the public. No profit and no loss were involved.[34]

On January 9, 1930, Senator Reed Smoot of Utah suggested what had been tentatively known as Boulder Dam be renamed Hoover Dam. Secretary of the Interior Wilbur chose the occasion of dedicating a 22-mile railroad constructed to haul material to the site on September 17, 1930, preliminary to beginning work on the dam itself. The interior secretary, who had been invited to participate in the ceremony by local residents, drove a silver spike that completed the railway. Afterward, he delivered a brief speech. Wilbur noted that important dams built during a president's term were often named for the president who initiated them. There was a Theodore Roosevelt Dam, a Woodrow Wilson Dam, and a Calvin Coolidge Dam. Without giving any advance notice to the press, Wilbur pronounced that the new dam would be named for Herbert Hoover.[35]

Franklin Roosevelt, a great president and the twentieth century's most successful politician, nevertheless, had a cruel, vindictive streak. When the dam on the Colorado River was completed under the New Deal, Hoover was not invited to the dedication ceremonies. In connivance with his vindictive interior secretary, Harold Ickes, the two inflicted a gratuitous insult on ex-president Hoover by changing the name back to Boulder Dam, on Ickes' authority. The renaming had been suggested by Hoover's archenemy, Senator Hiram Johnson of California. Many of Roosevelt's own supporters objected, and some newspapers continued to use the old name. In 1939 the Rand McNally map company resumed using "Hoover Dam." Ickes obstinately insisted on using "Boulder Dam" even after he left office. Hoover and Wilbur maintained a dignified silence. In 1947 Congress unanimously voted to restore Hoover's name to the dam, and the resolution was enthusiastically signed by President Harry S Truman, a friend and admirer of the ex-president. The change "is nothing that will make Herbert Hoover a greater man than he is," journalist George Sokolsky writes. "It will not make the dam more useful. But it is a nice and decent thing to do."[36]

Hoover believed hydroelectric power was the greatest untapped source of energy in America and would be needed by future generations. It was relatively inexpensive, served many functions, and was renewable. Every gallon of water that emptied into the ocean without serving some useful purpose was a waste, Hoover believed. Perhaps no president before or since believed in this form of energy so strongly or advocated it so ardently. Hoover hoped his development of dams and waterways could be expanded during his second term. For employment, as well as multifaceted efficiency, he believed it was perhaps the most useful type of public works the government could undertake.

Next to the Hoover Dam, the most ambitious project he envisioned was the Grand Coulee Dam on the Columbia River in Washington, the second largest dam constructed to that time. The engineering research for the Columbia River dam was begun in 1930, and the final report was delivered in January 1932. The president approved the initiation of construction before leaving office, and work began soon after FDR's inauguration. Plans were also made to begin work on flood control projects in the Central Valley in California. In 1929 Hoover initiated a feasibility study in collaboration with the governor of California. The study was completed in 1932 calling for a series of dams. Even more ambitiously, Hoover had been striving since the 1920s to consummate the St. Lawrence Seaway in collaboration with Canada. The governors of New York, including FDR, opposed the project because it would compete with New York Harbor and the Erie Canal. The two governments reached agreement near the end of Hoover's term. It was submitted for ratification after Hoover's term ended. Lacking FDR's support, ratification was defeated 46–42, far short of the two-thirds majority required. The seaway was finally constructed in the 1950s, about the same time the Interstate Highway system began, another project Hoover had advocated during the 1930s.[37]

During the Depression, many of the major railroads were on the verge of bankruptcy. The issue threatened not only the owners and railroad workers but some of the nation's leading banks and insurance companies that held rapidly depreciating railroad bonds. The railroads were overbuilt and engaged in ruthless competition that threatened to drive them bankrupt. They faced technological obsolescence and ruinous competition from trucks and automobiles. Hoover believed that railroad consolidation might provide a partial solution. The lines could share terminals, coaling stations, and other facilities. Some unions opposed consolidation on the grounds it would cost jobs, which the railroads promised would occur through attrition only. A progressive group, led by Senator Couzens of Michigan and Senator Brookhart of Iowa, hoped to bankrupt the lines because they wanted the government to nationalize them. The president took an active role in catalyzing consolidation in the East, which had been deadlocked for half a decade. He brought the feuding owners together and identified their common interest as well as warned them of ruin if they failed to reach an agreement. The owners negotiated secretly and in December 1930 announced an agreement to unify most of the railroads operating between the Atlantic and Chicago. On Wall St., rail stocks rose. The Interstate Commerce System reviewed and approved a modified plan within a year. It only remained for Congress to pass an enabling act, which was scuttled by an insurgent-Democratic coalition. The timing, coming during the midst of the Depression, was costly in terms of jobs and losses to those who held railroad bonds as investments or collateral. Failure of the effort accelerated the downward trend of the economy. As time made clear, the government could not have operated them at a profit either, or even broken even, because the railroads were eclipsed by highway transportation.[38]

The construction of roads, usually built in partnership with the states, reached into nearly every community and employed hundreds of thousands of workers. The federal financial commitment to road building doubled between fiscal 1930 and fiscal 1931. State road budgets grew at a slower pace yet still amounted to more than the federal government's contribution. In fiscal 1931, federal highway spending was budgeted at $259,897,000, as opposed to $105,648,000 in 1930. The cumulative budget of the states grew only $15 million during the same period, yet nonetheless dwarfed the federal contribution, totaling $1,616,000,000 in 1931. Under Hoover, the miles of highways built with federal aid grew from 78,000 to 115,000, while the numbers of workers employed rose from 110,000 to 280,000. The government's efforts to improve transportation and increase jobs via road work were not confined to urban areas. In 1929 the administration spent $11 million on construction of roads and trails in national parks, rising to $13 million in 1930, falling to just over $11 million in 1931, but growing to $17 million in 1932. The fiscal 1933 budget contained $23 million for roads and trails. Perhaps the most ambitious project designed to encourage tourists to enjoy scenic beauty, which also furnished large numbers of jobs, was construction of the Skyline Drive in Shenandoah National Park in Virginia. The president required employment of local workers using horse-drawn plows and banned heavy machinery for most of the work in National Forests, maximizing employment. In addition, a major reforestation project was undertaken by the Forest Service to create jobs planting seedlings, similar to work later done by the Civilian Conservation Corps.[39] The president was also instrumental in construction of the major bridge project of the era, which spanned San Francisco Bay. The San Francisco Bay Bridge, the greatest engineering achievement of its kind during the 1930s, was built by local authorities who received loans authorized by the federal government. It was the largest bridge in the world.[40]

Many of Hoover's attempts to arrest the Depression went beyond simply providing jobs. The president believed that private home ownership was a cornerstone of the stability of the American family, especially for children. He wanted to make single-family homes more affordable, commodious, and modern, and believed that home construction could provide hundreds of thousands of jobs, using private architects and builders with government assistance. Every new home generated jobs in other basic industries. It was a sustainable industry because the need was universal. As secretary of commerce, Hoover had helped organize a group called "Better Homes in America," which was largely educational. He became chairman of the board in 1921 and was succeeded by Ray Lyman Wilbur in 1929. The organization strove to provide information about how to buy, build, or remodel homes and to furnish them in a practical, economical manner. It was directed largely at the middle and lower-middle class. When the Depression occurred, home construction assumed greater urgency. On March 24, 1930, the president met with Roy A. Young, governor of the Federal Reserve Board. He told Young that the board could help to increase home expansion by making credit easier to obtain and offering lower interest rates. During the months following the stock market crash, the president also exerted efforts to accelerate home modernization and maintenance. Working largely through the Home Modernization Bureau of the National Building Industries organization, the government-private collaboration helped spur home owners to spend $500 million in modernizing existing structures during the first 18 months of the program.[41]

In August 1930 the president appointed a planning committee to organize a national conference on housing. Members were selected from the Departments of Commerce and Agriculture, as well as volunteer and professional organizations and journalists with an interest in housing. The planning committee created 25 committees of experts to study specific aspects of home construction. All the committees were staffed by volunteers and their work was financed by private foundations. The committees worked for months before assembling at a national conference at the Commerce Department in December, 1931. Some 500 members of committees and 3,700 individuals participated. This first national conference was chaired by Interior Secretary Wilbur and Commerce Secretary Lamont. The first tangible effect was passage of the Federal Home Loan Bank Act to provide easier credit. More home construction and modernization occurred because of Hoover's efforts, yet buying or building a home was a risky business, and many were unwilling to take such a risk because of their uncertain future. Further, there were a large number of homes and apartments vacant, which saturated the market.[42]

The president moved decisively on another front. On September 9, 1930, Hoover announced his intention to end all immigration into the United States in order to preserve jobs for Americans. He said those admitted under the per annum quota system amounted to about 150,000, and those from nonquota sources numbered about 100,000. The law permitted the barring of immigrants who were likely to require support from the public welfare systems. Under the existing unemployment circumstances, almost all immigrants were likely to be unemployed. Organized labor strongly supported the Executive Order. A few large businessmen who desired cheap labor opposed it, but, in general, opposition was muted. The number affected was small and because of unemployment, immigration had virtually reversed in the Depression years. Embassies abroad, responsible for issuing visas, were instructed to deny them unless the applicants had families in America who could support them. The order was a suspension of immigration for the duration of the economic crisis, not a permanent change.[43]

Rather than attempting to resolve the problems of the Depression with a single, sweeping approach in the first phase of his attack on the economic Furies, Hoover combined massive public works such as the Hoover Dam and the beautification of Washington, DC, with a host of smaller programs, frequently involving government-private partnerships. Individually some were small, but cumulatively they amounted to a great deal. If there are lessons to his first phase of combating the Great Depression, they might be that a variety of approaches—well timed and targeted, free of political favoritism, and expeditiously implemented—have a chance of mitigating, if not overcoming, declines in the economic cycle. Unselfishly, he did not use the emergency to create patronage jobs or to ensure his own political future.

CHAPTER 10

The Seventy-Second Congress

Frustrating Yet Fruitful

The congressional elections of 1930 resulted in a virtual tie in both houses and during the months before the newly elected Seventy-Second Congress convened in early December of 1931, sufficient deaths occurred, after which the Democrats won more special elections, providing a small Democratic majority in the House. The Republicans held a bare majority of one in the Senate. In both houses there was a clique of Progressives, chiefly western Republicans, who habitually sided with the Democrats, providing them with working majorities in both houses. The Democrats organized the House, electing John Nance Garner of Texas as speaker. The Republican changed their House leadership. John Q. Tilson of Connecticut, who would have been in line to become minority leader, was defeated by Bertrand Snell of New York. Many Republicans felt that Tilson had been ineffective as majority leader and would have been even less effective as minority leader. In the Senate, where the Republicans commanded the votes to organize, the insurgents sabotaged the reelection of George H. Moses of New Hampshire. They refused to vote for the Democratic candidate, Key Pittman of Nevada, and divided their votes among several Republicans, depriving both Moses and Pittman of a majority. The insurgents created a daily deadlock from early December through the two-week Christmas vacation, paralyzing the Senate from conducting business while banks failed, business faltered, and the economy stalled. Finally, on January 6, after 25 ballots, Moses resurrected an old 1890 resolution that permitted the president pro tempore to continue to serve until his successor was elected. Republicans retained their majority leader, Senator James E. Watson of Indiana, a weak leader. At last, in early January, the Senate finally mustered the combustion to conduct business.[1]

The insurgents had no hope of ruling but could, with the Democrats, create an obstacle course through which every piece of administration legislation must navigate. Superficially the Democrats occupied an enviable position. In the Senate, there were 47 Democrats, 12 Progressives, and 1 Farmer-Laborite, constituting a bloc of 60 votes. In the House there were 219 Democrats, supported by 15 Progressives, which created a bloc of 234 against 192 Republicans. On the surface, this was an inauspicious political context for the administration. The insurgents were consistently hostile, but the Democrats realized that with power came responsibility. The Democrats needed to demonstrate that they could lead. Otherwise, they might pay a price at the polls in 1932. Moreover, some Democrats were genuinely wanted to alleviate human suffering. Because they did not have a specific plan to do so, it was either Hoover's program or nothing. As the session opened, a handful of highly influential Democrats, including John Nance Garner; Senator Joseph T. Robinson, the minority leader; 1928 presidential candidate Al Smith; and executive chairman of the Democratic National Committee, Jouett Shouse, promised to cooperate with the president. The Democrats, who lacked a national spokesman, said they would not propose their own solutions to the Depression until they evaluated Hoover's program. This promised hope for an experiment in expedient compromise. The president had a comprehensive program, and the temporary, partial truce helped make the first hundred days of the Seventy-Second Congress the most fruitful period of the Hoover presidency. As conditions had worsened, Hoover had become a more adept politician. The president wrung out of the splintered Seventy-Second Congress more constructive legislation than he had won in the Republican-controlled Seventy-First Congress. Though it nearly shipwrecked on the shoals of the 1932 campaign during the summer, Congress nevertheless ground out important legislation. Throughout the session, even when political maneuvering tried his patience, the president attempted to operate in a bipartisan manner rather than fighting fire with fire.[2]

Hoover planned to ratchet up the machinery of government because the economy had declined further since Congress had last been in session. Most of Hoover's message in the State of the Union address dealt with remedies for specific economic problems. He did not mention foreign affairs or Prohibition. Throughout the long session of the Seventy-Second Congress, Hoover peppered the legislators with frequent messages. Becoming more assertive, he summoned congressional leaders from both parties to the White House to discuss pending bills. Willing to compromise, he rarely rebuked adversaries because he realized he needed Democratic help. The cornerstone of Hoover's agenda was a strong Reconstruction Finance Corporation (RFC) to replace the National Credit Corporation (NCC). The RFC would lend money to troubled banks, businesses, railroads, and agricultural agencies. He also wanted amendments to the Federal Reserve Act, later incorporated in what became known as the Glass-Steagall Act, to liberalize acceptable collateral for gold-backed federal securities, thus shoring up the gold standard and increasing the amount of currency in circulation. The president was both a fiscalist who wanted to expand the money supply and a monetarist who wanted to spend more on job-creating public works. Hoover requested an additional appropriation of $125 million for the system of Federal Land Banks. To complement this, he recommended creation of a system of 12 Federal Home Loan Banks to save homes from foreclosure and provide loans for construction of new family homes. As the president fleshed out his program, it included tax increases and budget cuts to bring the budget more closely into balance. He called for increased public works targeted at areas of high unemployment. Hoover sought bank reform and bankruptcy reform, as well as modification of antitrust legislation. The president suggested a plan to distribute savings denied depositors when their banks failed. The chief executive wanted to help languishing railroads. He asked Congress to reduce the cost and increase the efficiency of government through reorganization, a pet project of his since his days as commerce secretary. He asserted the need for regulation of electrical power, supported the lease of Muscle Shoals, and asked for strengthened laws limiting immigration. The president called for consolidating public works, which were dispersed among a multitude of departments and agencies, under a centralized Public Works Administration. There were some things he asked Congress to avoid: government doles, which destroyed self-respect and were addictive; another general revision of the tariff; greater benefits for veterans, which would overwhelm the budget and deprive the truly needy; and relaxation of antitrust laws, which would encourage monopoly. The package represented a major step in greater involvement in the economy by the federal government, a legislative program that dwarfed the domestic agenda of any previous administration. The plan was meant to provide not only economic sustenance but security and permanent reform.[3]

The president's highest priority was enactment of the RFC bill. It would be stronger than the existing NCC, a voluntary pool contributed by major bankers that Hoover had hastily cobbled together while Congress was out of secession. Unlike the NCC, the RFC would create credit rather than simply redistribute it. The RFC was patterned after the War Finance Corporation (WFC), which had stimulated industry during the Great War and afterward had helped pull the nation out of the recession of 1921–22. The WFC had been phased out in 1929, but many businessmen now clamored for its resuscitation. Hoover's original title of what was, essentially, a bankers' bank, was the Emergency Finance Corporation, so-called to emphasize its temporary nature. In fact, it became an anchor not only of Hoover's recovery program but of the New Deal, lasting until World War II. For such a major bill, Congress moved reasonably rapidly, yet too slowly for Hoover. With banks failing daily, Congress insisted on a two-week Christmas recess, which postponed enactment. There were also doubters, though limited in numbers, on the left and right. Several progressives, who considered anything that might help banks a conspiracy of the mighty against the meek, complained vehemently. Others, including some liberals, claimed it smacked of socialism. From the right, Virginia Senator Carter Glass complained that the RFC might conflict with the work of the Federal Reserve System, in which he took a paternalistic interest. Hoover, forced to compromise with Glass and others, wound up with a weaker bill than he desired. Near the end of the session, he strengthened it. Hoover appeased the Democrats by allowing Garner and Robinson to appoint one director each to the RFC board, making it bipartisan. After accepting amendments from Glass, Garner, and others, Hoover moved the bill swiftly to passage. The House approved it 335–55 and the Senate 63–8. The president signed the bill into law on January 22, 1932. Hoover praised the "patriotism of the men in both houses of Congress who have given proof of their devotion to the welfare of their country, irrespective of political affiliation." The single most important piece of domestic legislation enacted during Hoover's presidency, the law injected the government into the economy to a greater extent than Hoover had earlier considered desirable. Yet his views had evolved, and he considered the new agency a necessity. The RFC was given $500 million in working capital and authorized to issue an additional $1.5 billion in debentures. Hoover appointed longtime Federal Reserve Board member Eugene Meyer as chairman of the board and ex-Vice President Charles G. Dawes as president. The board included seven additional members, apportioned on a bipartisan basis. One representative observed that if it had been passed earlier thousands of banks could have survived. The first piece of Hoover's ambitious recovery plan was in place. It was, up to that time, the largest relief bill ever passed. "Unfortunately, president Hoover has been unjustly maligned by most historians," James S. Olson writes. "In actuality he had long before abandoned laissez-faire strictures for government activism."[4]

The following day, January 23, the president signed the second piece of his legislative package, an appropriation of $125 million in additional capital for the Federal Land Banks. The nation's economy was on life support. The Land Banks helped banks that held mortgages on land and on some farm homes as collateral. As the land values declined, the value of the mortgages fell, jeopardizing the liquidity of banks in farm communities. The Land Banks could discount the mortgage, doing for farm banks what the Federal Reserve did for commercial banks. The banks would be safer than commercial banks, and they would provide additional capital to lend. The money helped provide a psychological lift to farm communities.[5]

Hoover believed the gold standard was essential to the stability of international trade, and he found few dissenters. Gold guaranteed the value of money, set a fixed value on foreign exchange, and provided predictability.

Without such predictability, it was virtually impossible for importers and exporters to plan ahead. Perishable products were the most vulnerable. In the absence of a gold-secured currency, stocks, securities, futures, and prices gyrated wildly. Gold flowing into a country, by increasing the quantity available to back currency, injected additional currency available for commerce. Likewise, gold flowing outward contracted the currency and restricted commerce. The international standard relied on a pool of gold that flowed from weak to strong havens. Ultimately if a nation could not sustain its supply of bullion, it devalued its currency and eventually abandoned the gold standard completely. During the Depression, with the notable exceptions of the United States and France, most nations abandoned the gold standard and devalued their currency. When Great Britain joined the herd of lemmings plunging into the sea, leaving their gold behind, on September 21, 1931, the world was stunned. The world's currency was pegged to the British pound, which had been the international standard for generations. An economic apocalypse seemed imminent.[6]

The fear spread that America might be next, resulting in panic withdrawals by European creditors and redemption of gold certificates by Americans, who hoarded their bullion and currency. The two-pronged assault on American banks also precipitated a rash of failures. Up to this point, American banks had fared better than might be expected. However, in the single month following the collapse of the British pound, 522 U.S. banks failed. By the end of 1931, some 2,294 banks had succumbed. This was double the number of failures in 1930, a new record for a single year. With credit already virtually frozen and business expansion stillborn, the gold crisis added a new dimension to what was now universally known as the Great Depression, and it pyramided Hoover's problems. The president shifted his focus from domestic recovery to stemming the hemorrhage of gold. The last week of September and the first week of October saw America suffer a devastating gold drain. The amount of gold removed from the Treasury from mid-September to mid-October was the greatest amount ever withdrawn from any country. Gold was demanded in sums larger than ships could carry because companies would insure ships for only so much bullion. At the height of the frenzy, gold was leaving the United States at the rate of about $10 million per day. Additionally, by January 1932 domestic hoarding had reached $1.2 billion.[7]

The president believed the United States must protect the integrity of its currency and could not simply abandon the gold standard because it owed gold obligations to creditors based on long-standing contracts. Whether the gold standard is or was necessary to solvency in the long run, it certainly seemed so in the short run, a belief shared by every nation, political leader, and virtually every reputable economist. The collapse of the American gold standard would throw international markets into chaos, and America would suck the worldwide economy into a black hole into which money was drawn in and stayed there. The two-headed monster of foreign withdrawals and domestic hoarding undermined faith in American currency, which was based on the belief that the currency could be redeemed in gold. The Treasury responded by paying out gold on demand, despite the drain. At one point, Hoover later revealed, the U.S. Treasury was less than two weeks away from being emptied of its precious yellow metal. Yet as foreigners looked for safe havens, they found them difficult to locate. When they realized that the U.S. policy of paying on demand must imply a sufficient supply of gold to sustain American obligations, the outward flow slowed. America looked safer than many other places. The United States first weathered a drain of gold, then a drain of cash and currency, and finally a dumping of securities, which drove their values lower. The winter of 1931–32 was colder for the knowledge that the wolf was at the door. When Congress assembled in December, only Hoover and a handful of intimates knew how precarious the situation remained. The policy of paying on demand had temporarily satisfied creditors. Yet the economic wolf remained famished, if at bay. A more permanent solution was needed.[8]

Herein lay the rationale for legislation that became known as the Glass-Steagall Act, another crucial building block in the president's economic program for the Seventy-Second Congress. On February 9, 1932, Governor Meyer of the Federal Reserve Board, Governor Harrison of the Federal Reserve Bank of New York, President Dawes of the RFC, and Treasury Secretary Mills reported to the president of the danger to the gold standard. Foreign gold withdrawals had already climbed to $1 billion. Hoarding was requiring the Federal Reserve to maintain an unusually high supply of gold, while the money removed from circulation was deflating the currency. The free gold available to sustain the gold standard had dipped to $433 million. At that time, foreign governments and individuals held almost $1.4 billion in short-term bills. About $900 million could be withdrawn on demand, and the remainder in less than 90 days. The president had already called upon Congress to liberalize the eligibility requirements for backing Federal Reserve notes. Initially, the Democratic senators on the Banking Committee balked. On February 10, Hoover summoned influential senators to the White House, including members of the subcommittee that would handle the proposal. Glass, a Senate Democrat, enormously influential on financial matters, agreed to sponsor the measure. Representative Henry Steagall, an Alabama Democrat, sponsored the legislation in the Lower Chamber. With Democratic sponsors in both houses, the bill attracted bipartisan support.[9]

It is ironic that the bill is named partly for Glass, because the elderly Virginian was in some respects more of an impediment than an enthusiastic backer of the legislation. Glass was a Senate institution, however, and his imprimatur was important. The Virginian was known as the "Father of the Federal Reserve" for his role in drafting the bill in 1913. Extremely cautious, protective about his handiwork, the Federal Reserve System, Glass was much more fiscally conservative than Hoover. Hoover's differences with Glass prevented the president from accomplishing everything he wanted in the bill.

In particular, Hoover wanted to place the full assets of the system's banks behind the currency and allow greater liberalization of the types of paper eligible for rediscount. Speaker Garner agreed to support Hoover's version, and Glass agreed but vacillated. Second, Glass disliked provisions in the Hoover bill that expanded the money supply, because he erroneously believed there was already too much money in circulation. Finally, Glass considered himself a defender of small bankers, and along with some insurgents, viewed larger bankers as predators. The senator wanted to limit rediscount privileges to small banks capitalized at $2 million or less, which would have denied liquidity to larger banks. A compromise was hammered out, and the final figure was set at $5 million, less than Hoover wanted. The president treated Glass deferentially, consulted with him and Garner periodically, and gave the Democrats a major share of credit. On February 15, the House debated the bill for only a few hours and passed it overwhelmingly, 350–15. The Senate approved a slightly different version on February 19, by a vote of 46–18, and on February 27, both houses approved the conference report without opposition. The president signed the Glass-Steagall Act on February 27, praising Congress for its bipartisanship. Privately, he admitted, "Glass was against the bill and had to be forced to accept some of its provisions."[10]

Treasury officials and most bankers considered the Glass-Steagall Act the most constructive act of the Depression, the most significant banking legislation since the Federal Reserve Act. The law reassured small banks in the Federal Reserve System that there was virtually no bottom to the reservoir of credit available to them. Wall Street applauded the law. Bank stocks rose and lifted other stocks along with them. The new legislation broadened the definition of the type of paper eligible for rediscount and permitted the system to substitute government securities, previously ineligible, as legal backing for Federal Reserve notes. The newly eligible paper allowed the government to get by with less gold and freed gold for other demands, releasing large amounts of the metal, which otherwise would have been tied up as backing for Federal Reserve notes. Now foreign and domestic demand for gold could be met, yet the mere knowledge that they would be met shattered a psychological barrier and reduced the drain. In fact, gold began to flow back into America, expanding the money supply. The measure helped expand the supply of money in circulation without artificial stimulation. It enabled the Federal Reserve system to pursue open market operations more aggressively. By facilitating the purchase of government securities from member banks, it increased their liquidity and their potential for lending. Hoover adhered to a mixed backing of currency, attempting to avoid the Scylla of inflation and the Charybdis of deflation. Passage of the Glass-Steagall Act marked the peak of bipartisan cooperation in the Seventy-Second Congress. Future legislation was extracted more grudgingly, and as the 1932 election loomed, the decibel level of the debates grew acrimonious.[11]

At the end of February, the opposition to Hoover in Congress seemed more rhetorical than real. Every presidential priority had been enacted in near-record time. Much of the press observed that an unusual degree of cooperation prevailed in Congress although the economy remained fragile. The most intemperate language attacking Hoover during the first three months of the session was employed by the insurgent Republicans, joined by a handful of Progressive Democrats. For them, nothing the president could do was enough. Among the insurgents, the most prominent were George Norris of Nebraska, Fiorello La Guardia of New York, William Borah of Idaho, Robert M. LaFollette of Wisconsin, and Bronson Cutting of New Mexico. A small number of Democrats joined the chorus. These included Burton K. Wheeler of Montana, Edward Costigan of Colorado, and Robert Wagner of New York. Hoover had joined other progressives to support Theodore Roosevelt's Bull Moose Progressive Party in 1912. But now, Hoover was too cautious for them, especially pertaining to unemployment relief. Some, such as Norris, held personal grudges against the president. This cast of critics had not changed much since the Seventy-First Congress. Inflammatory orators, they were warriors with words.[12]

Neither party was united. The Democrats had regional and ideological divisions. They were nagged by rural-urban and wet-dry splits, welded together more by tradition and unlikely geographical alliances than by common interests. During Hoover's term they reached no consensus on a program. Hoover seized the reins, and Congress followed, though sometimes it stampeded like a herd of wild horses. By the end of February the mood of cooperation had worn thin. The dilemma facing the Democrats was how to help end the Depression while denying Hoover credit. Hoover, who did not enjoy sleight-of-hand politics, nonetheless correctly perceived that if the Depression ended on his watch, he would win in 1932. If it did not, or if it grew worse, he would lose. Over this, no one had total control, nor could anyone predict the outcome. Few in Congress or among the president's friends at the time prophesied that it would drag on until guns roared once more in Europe, a distant three administrations in the future. The president, though unaccustomed to the rough-and-tumble of holding office, had by 1932 come to accept it. He personally liked Garner and considered him a statesman when he could set aside politics. Though basically a pragmatist, Garner could be a raging partisan. Unlike the Progressives, he had no personal grudge against Hoover. In many respects, he admired and respected him. The two men were quite different, yet each was deft at what he did, though Garner was less inhibited. "I fought president Hoover with everything I had under Marquis of Queensberry, London prize ring and catch as catch-can rules," the speaker explained. He added, in 1948: "If he had become president in 1921 or 1937 he might have ranked with the great presidents. Today I think Herbert Hoover is the wisest statesman on world affairs in America. He may be on domestic affairs, too."[13]

As yet, the Democrats had no single spokesman of national stature. Garner would have liked to be that spokesman, yet he found it impossible to control his own colleagues after February, particularly in dealing with the painful prospect of bringing the budget closer into balance, an objective of both parties, yet a goal on which there was no agreement over method. The only ways to obliterate red ink was to raise taxes or to cut spending—simple solutions but politically difficult ones. If there were a painless way to balance budgets without alienating any important interest group, the budget would always balance. If the Democrats lacked a coherent program to terminate the Depression, the goal of winning the presidency in 1932, after three consecutive lopsided defeats, welded them. With the presidency would come rich rewards of patronage and possibly a more solidly Democratic Congress, though that did not mean that any specific incumbent was safe if the economy continued to tumble.[14]

As the Depression deepened, the Democratic Congress increasingly tried to focus the blame on the president, personalizing the economic tragedy. One Democratic senator argued that his party should avoid "committing our party to a definite program. The issue in the [1932] election is Hoover. Why take any step calculated to divert attention from that issue?"[15] Perhaps the most effective critic of Hoover came not from Congress but from the vinegar pen of the DNC's professional character assassin, journalist Charles Michelson. As conditions worsened, Michelson grew increasingly uninhibited in his language, and many Americans took his words literally.[16] Near the end of the session, Hoover was worn down, but he never demonstrated his frustration with politics publicly. "I am making no complaint," he explained. "I accepted the job of my own free will."[17] While the Democrats were programmatically ineffective, they remained on the offensive rhetorically, claiming credit for legislation that had originated with Hoover. Some Republicans, particularly as the Congress wore on and partisanship erupted more frequently, tried discretely to distance themselves from the president. The congressional Republicans also suffered from weak leadership within the ranks. The chief executive did not get along with Senator Watson, the floor leader in the Upper House. They differed over economic, social, and political issues. He liked Bertrand Snell, the Republican House leader better, but Snell was not an effective communicator. Neither adequately conveyed the president's objectives to the rank and file, and Hoover considered it logistically impossible to talk to all of them personally. Temperamentally, schmoozing was not Hoover's forte; thus he needed persuasive lieutenants. Watson was a major disappointment. "From the time he took office down to the present time," Hoover's press secretary complained on March 30, 1932, "the president has been hampered by Jim Watson being the Republican leader of the Senate." Hoover's secretary Theodore Joslin confided to his diary that Watson was jovial, yet "Sometimes I think he had rather lie than tell the truth. Time and again he has promised faithfully to do a certain thing and has done the opposite."[18]

The president also asked the Seventy-Second Congress to grant him authority to reorganize the executive branch, subject to congressional approval. Reorganization in the interest of economy could avoid more painful cuts and taxes increases. He wanted a streamlined government that would click on all cylinders. The federal government consisted of a hodgepodge of agencies created at different times. Some performed identical functions; some performed no function. It was as if someone had fired a shotgun into the air, and the agencies ended up in whatever department the pellets landed—in a word, randomly. When Hoover investigated the labyrinth of agencies while secretary of commerce, he remarked, "I have found, that the brown bears are under the jurisdiction of the Secretary of Agriculture, the grizzly bears under the care of the Secretary of the Interior, and the polar bears are under my protection as Secretary of Commerce."[19] The merchant marine activities of the government fell under eight agencies. There were 14 agencies within 9 departments engaged in water conservation, 10 agencies doing construction work, and the education work of the government was scattered among 8 departments. Some agencies had outlived their original purpose while others worked at cross-purposes. Each agency possessed its own self-protective pressure group, and congressmen participated in logrolling to protect special interests. In Washington, bureaucracies were immortal. Hoover wanted to reorganize along lines of function and improve accountability. He had demonstrated the potential of providing better service at lower cost by his consolidation of veterans' services, which was already saving $10 million annually. Applying such a model to the entire bureaucracy might save as much as $100 million. There was strong resistance to the president's plan, even among some Republicans. Congress felt the chief executive might lay off some of their constituents and control too many jobs. Garner seized the opportunity to promote not only his party but himself. The speaker, who eyed the presidency, claimed reorganization was a Democratic idea and proceeded to draft legislation. The president responded by releasing a summary of his statements about reorganization dating back 12 years. Ultimately, Hoover's plans failed because Democrats were unwilling to give the authority to consolidate and reduce to a Republican president. Too much patronage was at stake. The debate over reorganization, which began in earnest in February, dragged on until nearly the end of the session. In early July, Congress approved reorganization with the contingency that all changes must be approved by Congress. Since Congress was about to adjourn *sine die* and would not sit again until the following December, this made the possibility of significant reform during the Hoover administration dim. Congress withheld permission until Franklin Roosevelt assumed office, yet Roosevelt did not use the power to make significant changes. Patronage, the manna of politics, expanded during the New Deal and World War II. Control of jobs means control of votes, and this explains, in part, Roosevelt's electoral wizardry. As Hoover predicted, the bureaucracy, once bloated, remained bloated.[20]

Hoover urged banking reform at the opening of the Seventy-First and of the Seventy-Second Congresses. He began before the crash and sent numerous messages to the nation's legislators about the necessity for changes in the nation's banking system. On October 2, 1931, in an address to the American Bankers Association, the president urged bankers to join the movement for reform. The need should have been obvious after the crash, yet bankers themselves were among the most adamant opponents of reform. The president wanted to include all commercial banks within the Federal Reserve System, making them subject to its regulations. Hoover wanted to separate commercial from investment banking and forbid speculation with depositors' money. His plan would have provided for larger pools of capital than many small unit banks possessed, creating a safety net for the smaller, weaker banks. Ironically, the insurgent bloc, who demonized bankers, opposed reining them in, largely because it was a Hoover program. Democrats blocked it for partisan reasons. Senator Glass, considered the dean of Senate financial matters, rejected a change in the status quo. The president continued to seek banking reform during the short session of the Seventy-Second Congress, even as banks shut down in every state, yet Congress remained obdurate. Failure to obtain banking reform was one of Hoover's keenest disappointments. When reform finally did occur under the New Deal, it took the form much like Hoover had proposed years earlier, yet thousands of banks had failed during the interim.[21]

The president had been concerned about the operation of the New York Stock Exchange since the mid-1920s. Prior to the crash he cautioned Governor Roosevelt of New York and Richard Whitney, chair of the exchange, about flaws in the system, yet neither heeded the warning. After the deluge of panic selling helped send the nation's economy into a tailspin, the president consistently prodded Congress to investigate the exchange, yet it took them nearly three years to begin. When the Seventy-Second Congress finally undertook hearings it was during a harried period while it attempted to cut expenses, increase taxes, and enact additional relief legislation. Unfortunately, its purpose was less remedial than aimed at identifying villains. The committee found unethical and dishonest practices that contributed to the catastrophe.[22] Like much that occurred in the Seventy-Second Congress, the hearings were a mixture of substance and showmanship. If ever there was anything more calculated to make the staggering market more nervous than it already was, certainly this attempt to bash the rich, or the ex-rich, was it. Whitney, hauled before the committee, was grilled like a bad piece of meat by the western Progressives yet remained relatively cool. Whitney testified that short selling was not a major contributor to the crash. There had been periods of greater short selling when the market prospered. What really caused the crash was liquidation by frightened investors. By keeping the public frightened about buying stocks, Congress itself contributed to keeping prices low, he explained. Senator Brookhart asserted that the best reform of the market would be to abolish it. That would end speculation permanently. "And then the people of the United States will go to Canada and Europe to do those very things and pay their taxes there," Whitney retorted. Three days later Whitney told the committee that taxes on the sale of stocks and bonds (a provision included in the pending tax bill) would cripple the market and drive prices lower, which was not in the national interest.[23] On June 25, with the long session of the Seventy-Second Congress expiring, the Senate Bank and Currency Committee halted its investigation of the stock market. It had waited so long to begin, and consumed what time it had in hearing witnesses, that no time remained to legislate. Like much unfinished business, it would be carried over into the New Deal.[24]

By early 1932 there was a consensus among the president, the Congress, and most journalist and economists, including the Briton John Maynard Keynes, that the government budget was out of kilter. A large majority of the American public endorsed a balanced budget. The general belief prevailed that large deficits soaked up revenue required to service the debt, drove up interest rates, and starved private business, which needed capital to recover. Big deficits raised questions about the reliability of government-issued bonds and forced the government to pay higher interest rates to attract buyers. Leading Democrats, such as Bernard Baruch, Jouett Shouse, and Franklin D. Roosevelt claimed the president was a profligate spender who wasted money on extravagant projects. During the 1932 campaign, FDR used such words as "shocking," "spendthrift," "appalling," and "bankruptcy" to describe Hoover's fiscal policies. More pragmatically, one economist asked whether an economic catastrophe initiated by excessive borrowing could be rectified by additional borrowing.[25]

Most politicians considered deficit reduction a politically popular issue and wanted credit for accomplishing it, yet balked at specific sacrifices. The Depression placed the government in a whipsaw between increased expenditures on public works and relief and declining revenues because of the stagnant economy. During the 1920s and through the dawn of the 1930s the federal government had run surpluses, one of the reasons for the popularity of Coolidge and Mellon. Yet in fiscal year 1931 ending in July, the surplus became a deficit of more than $900 million, and it threatened to be substantially larger in 1932 if nothing were done. In fact, the government faced the largest peacetime deficit in history. The largest drains on the treasury were service on the federal debt, followed by veterans' pensions, and, a distant third, aid to agriculture. Simultaneous with the greater expenses, revenue declined drastically. The major reductions in government tax collections were attributed to personal income taxes, corporate income taxes, and customs. Revenue fell to the lowest level in any fiscal year since 1917, and expenses were the highest in any years since 1921. To meet the shortfall, the government floated an $800 million bond issue, the largest since the Great War.[26]

One reason that it was extremely difficult to carve out cuts was that about $2.5 billion of the $4.4 billion budget consisted of fixed expenses. Hoover began cuts in areas over which he had direct control: the departments and agencies of the executive branch. He asked each cabinet member to identify cuts, reducing money already appropriated for their department. A pay freeze was placed on employees of the executive branch, and pay cuts were planned, although Hoover and Congress differed vigorously over the type and size of cuts. The president believed he could squeeze $300 million out of the executive offices and intended to ask Congress for an economy bill stipulating about another $250 million in cuts. The optimum would be to obtain $600 million in overall savings and compensate for the remainder with a tax increase. This would not erase the deficit, only reduce it. Some congressmen and economists admonished him to cut deeper, but he believed that was impractical and inhumane.[27]

In mid-April, Hoover proposed an Omnibus Economy Bill to slash federal expenditures by $300 million during the next fiscal year. Hoover and his budget director, Clawson Roop, believed the measure was more likely to pass if the cuts were consolidated in a single bill. On April 4, the president completed an economy message and rushed it to the Capitol. On April 16, Roop spent the entire day explaining the measure to the Ways and Means Committee. One of the major features, expected to save between $80 million and $82 million, was to be obtained by placing federal employees on a five-day week and making all holidays and vacations unpaid. The pay cuts would be limited to only one year, and the military services would be exempted. Congress had proposed a straight 10 percent pay cut, plus layoffs that might affect as many as 15,000 employees, but that would save only about $67 million. Because he was asking other federal employees to accept pay reductions, on April 11, the president offered to waive his constitutional rights barring salary cuts for presidents and work for whatever amount was suggested, as low as $1 per year. In July Hoover cut his own salary by 20 percent, from $75,000 to $60,000. Vice President Curtis took a voluntary cut of 15 percent, reducing his income from $15,000 to $12,500 annually. Members of the cabinet also took reductions. Hoover offered to make the budget reductions himself, shouldering the blame, if Congress would authorize him to do so. Congress, however, believed there was political mileage in balancing the budget, yet could not muster the votes to cut specific items. The House preferred to draft its own bill rather than accept the president's measure. The House eliminated Hoover's five-day week for federal employees and replaced it with a 10 percent across-the-board reduction. The pay cut measure adopted saved only $12 million to $14 million in salaries. The representatives also defeated a proposal to cut their own salaries by $1,000. At the end of April, the House seemed hopelessly muddled. It appeared that only the pressure of meeting the deadline for adjournment would move them to act. Garner lost control over the Democrats on the floor.[28] On April 29, the president talked with 15 members of the House and Senate about the budget. He denounced the idea of draconian salary cuts. "This whole idea of the straight pay cut and the dismissal of thousands of employees because of the flat reduction of appropriations is the most heart-less and medieval action ever proposed by any branch of the government," he complained.[29]

On May 3, 1932, the House finally passed the Omnibus Economy bill with only $30 million of cuts remaining in it, having eviscerated the president's measure. The battle then moved to the Senate, where the debate raged as the national nominating conventions approached and, shortly after that, adjourn-ment. The Senate seemed somewhat more amenable to Hoover's program, though not a great deal more. In a major victory, it accepted his plan to limit the workweek of government employees. The provision received a boost in the form of a letter from AFL President William Green, who supported the five-day week. On June 8, the Senate approved the Omnibus Economy bill, reducing the deficit by about $134 million. Three days later the president conferred with the House and Senate Economy Committees and attempted to persuade them to increase the size of the reductions. The conference com-mittee ironed out differences and on June 28 Congress finally passed the Omnibus Economy bill and sent it to the president, who signed it on June 30, barely in time for the new fiscal year, which began on July 1. Estimates of the amount saved ranged between $130 million and $180 million, well short of the $300 million the president wanted. Most of the reductions came out of the pockets of federal employees. On other proposed reductions, the president believed the Congress had caved in to special interests. Unlike his legislative victories creating the RFC and enacting the Glass-Steagall Act, this one was bittersweet.[30]

Budget cuts represented only half the task of reducing the budget. The second half of the equation, raising taxes, was even more painful. The two bills moved through Congress simultaneously. The tax measures, which were cob-bled together from a variety of ideas, written and rewritten, proved even more contentious than the Omnibus Economy Act. If the American Revolution had tried men's souls, so did the Seventy-Second Congress. The president began with the premise that he could compromise on the method of taxation so long as it raised the requisite sum. Both Hoover and Ogden Mills, who had suc-ceeded the aged Mellon as treasury secretary, with Mellon becoming ambas-sador to Britain, believed taxes should not be so onerous as to retard recovery. They also agreed that the increases, like the budgetary stringency, should last only for the duration of the emergency. Even within the parties, there were substantial differences. One faction, including many Democrats and insur-gents, favored soaking the wealthy through higher income, luxury, and estate taxes. The other favored a broader base including sales taxes. Hoover himself preferred high inheritance taxes but believed higher income and corporate taxes might slow job growth. He did not originate the idea of a sales tax, which was something of a novelty at the time, but found it acceptable. Hoover believed it was necessary both to broaden the tax base and to more steeply graduate taxes at the upper levels. He also felt that the nation was overly reliant on income taxes and customs revenues because these rose and fell disproportionately during hard times. The president believed unearned income should be taxed at a much higher rate than earned income. On February 12, 1932, the leaders of the House Ways and Means Committee, dominated by Democrats, asked Hoover if he could support a general sales tax as a basis for raising revenue. Hoover agreed, provided that necessities, such as food and inexpensive clothing, were exempted, which they were. When the committee finished rewriting the bill, the sales tax was the centerpiece of the legislation.[31]

The sales tax had much to recommend it. Potentially, it could raise more money more quickly than any other type of tax. It was painless to pay, virtually invisible, and fair. The more one bought, the more one paid. This taxed the wealthy on consumption but not on saving or investment, both of which created jobs. Perhaps most importantly, it was the most efficient means of collecting taxes. A huge percentage of income taxes are siphoned off in the cost of collection, which makes tax rates higher for everyone and brings less revenue to the government. It is almost impossible to evade or cheat on sales taxes. They do not require an army of accountants to file them nor to randomly audit them. Because of their straightforward simplicity, without complicated exemptions and deductions, sales taxes rarely result in court battles or penalties for lack of payment. The chief individuals who benefit from income taxes are not the poor, as is erroneously believed, but tax accountants and attorneys. As was noted at the time, people would pay a sales tax virtually without complaining. Every time they paid an income tax they would blame the government. Further, no one intended for the government to rely on the sales tax alone. It was compatible with virtually any other type of tax. Today, most states combine income, sales, property, and other taxes.

The sales tax emerged from the Ways and Means Committee with a 24–1 favorable vote. House Speaker Garner supported it, as did Senator Robinson and most regular Republicans. Democratic leaders Raskob and Shouse supported it. Yet Representative Robert L. Doughton of North Carolina, the only congressman who had voted against the provision in the Ways and Means Committee, launched a rebellion that caught fire. By the second week of March, opposition to the sales tax had gained momentum, and Garner was having trouble holding the Democrats in line. An unlikely coalition formed against the measure. Some, such as Fiorello La Guardia, wanted to defeat it in order to soak the wealthy with higher income taxes. Yet many opponents were Southern Bourbons and congressmen representing Midwestern districts who cared little about soaking the rich. Some of the states in these regions wished to reserve this form of taxation to the states. Since some of the same representatives who opposed a federal sales tax supported such taxes on the state level, it could hardly be argued that their opposition was due to support of the "little man" as La Guardia argued. Thus the battle was not drawn strictly along fiscal or ideological lines. Garner's leadership was publicly attacked by fellow Democrats, and the speaker was close to breaking physically. The Democrats controlled the House and would decide the fate of the measure. On March 24, the sales tax was defeated 223–153 in the House. Only 40 Democrats supported it. Hoover was disappointed because he knew it would be difficult to raise commensurate revenue through any other means. The business community, which placed a premium on balanced budgets, was also disappointed. Perhaps most disappointed was Garner, whose reputation for leadership, and hence his chances for the Democratic presidential nomination, had been tarnished. With the session waning, Congress, with input from Hoover, would have to write an entirely new bill. The Seventy-Second Congress, which had started so auspiciously, with reasonable harmony within and among the parties, had degenerated into a street brawl. Like Hamlet, it could be indecisive. And like Hamlet, it could be self-destructive. And because it comprised many well-meaning individuals, it had redeeming qualities as well.[32]

The rewriting of the bill was painful, because there is no painless way to tax. The tax bill consumed more time than any other legislation of the Seventy-Second Congress. The next version written in the House contained a long list of special excise taxes. Though unpopular, it passed 327–64. The Senate Finance Committee began substitutions and alterations and descended into chaos. In early May Hoover dispatched the sharpest message he had ever delivered and he continued to prod and to conduct personal conferences with small groups of congressional leaders from both parties. A new bill emerged and lingered until May 31, when Hoover made a rare personal appearance and delivered a stinging message to the Senate, the first such appearance by a president since Wilson had pleaded for ratification of the Versailles treaty. In the interim Congress had tacked on tariffs on coal, lumber, copper, and oil and beat back an attempt by Senator Norris, who with single-minded obstinacy made another futile attempt to add the debenture to the bill. The Democrats supported the new tariff levies, although they had campaigned against the tariff in 1930 and Roosevelt would denounce it even more harshly during the 1932 campaign. In late May the Senate had attempted—and failed—to revive the sales tax. In its place, Congress added numerous excise taxes that were in effect sales taxes on selected items. The most pronounced change in the bill was a return to the significantly higher 1922 rates on income taxes, steeply graduated for that era. The new rates were expected to last only two years, by which time the Depression was expected to end. The president did not object to the specific provisions of the bill. However, he was critical because it fell far short of raising enough revenue to reduce the deficit substantially. In this respect, both the revenue bill and the Economy Act, which passed shortly afterward, disappointed the president. Resigned to the fact that he had pushed through the best bill he could get, Hoover signed the Revenue Act of 1932 on June 6. The bill came too late to alter the fiscal 1932 deficit significantly. Importantly, for the short remainder of Hoover's term and throughout the entire New Deal era, no attempt was made to stimulate the economy by cutting taxes. All subsequent revenue measures were directed at raising greater revenues for the government rather than pulling out of the Depression by injection of capital into the private sector, as Keynes and many other economists advocated. Hoover's tax reduction of 1930 was the only major tax stimulus of the entire Depression.[33]

The remaining problem faced by the Seventy-Second Congress was relief. There was general agreement, shared by the president, that the time had come for more vigorous measures because of the continued economic deterioration, widespread unemployment, and the failure of the economy to respond as expected to remedial legislation. There was also a shared feeling that, short of ending the Depression, something must be done to alleviate human suffering. There was no consensus, however, on the form such relief should take, how much money to spend, or the sources from which such money was to come. Some Democrats proposed massive public works programs supported primarily by borrowing. Hoover believed the enormous sums required would undo four months of laborious attempts to bring the budget closer into balance. The president favored utilizing the RFC as the major engine of sustenance and recovery, relying chiefly on loans, not grants, and self-replenishing public works that would, in time, pay for themselves. He still opposed doles, but he no longer believed that private charity alone could suffice for the needy. Politics also figured in the equation. Both parties wanted, not simply relief, but credit for relief. Some individuals, most obviously Garner, who still coveted a place on the 1932 ticket, wanted to appear more generous than his opponents. Most congressmen, when they viewed the problem from a political perspective, wanted to appear responsive to their constituents, even if the till was empty. There was also the practical conundrum that economy in government and expensive relief measures both were politically popular. Hoover was determined to enact some type of relief measure before time expired on the long session, yet he also wanted relief to be consistent with recovery and fiscal responsibility. However, anything that smacked of pork-barrel legislation was anathema to him.

During the Seventy-Second Congress, numerous major public works bills were proposed, mostly in the Senate, as well as bills providing for a direct dole. One by one, they were beaten back. Congress remained cautious about big-spending bills, though the potential political fruits were tempting. The knowledge that most such legislation faced a certain veto that would be impossible to override was also sobering. The hammering out of relief legislation began early during the session and lasted into its waning moments. Two liberal senators, Edward E. Costigan, a Democrat, and Robert LaFollette, an insurgent Republican, introduced a bill to provide $375 million in aid to the states for relief, but the measure was defeated in February. Meanwhile, three Democrats proposed another $375 million bill to assist states for relief and another $375 million for public works in the form of outright grants. This also failed to clear congressional hurdles. Senator Robert Wagner, a liberal Democrat, proposed a bill to allot money to the states for public works, which could be deducted from federal matching funds for roads and repaid later. After this failed, Wagner initiated a more sweeping $1.1 billion public works bill to be financed by a bond issue, which was also defeated. Other variations also fell short. A coalition of Republican insurgents and Democrats could have passed any relief bill in the Senate, and in the House the Democrats commanded a narrow majority. Although there was probably a majority in favor of additional public works, there was no majority in favor of any particular bill. Hoover did not oppose additional public works, but he did oppose public works financed by bond issues, and he opposed a dole, although ultimately he compromised even on that. As the debate over relief evolved, Hoover found himself more in agreement with Wagner than with the other senators. In May, he told the New Yorker that he was willing to compromise with him on a relief measure and hoped such a compromise would prove feasible.[34]

During the spring, the competing ideas mixed and muddled but resolved themselves principally into measures devised by the president, Wagner, Robinson, and Speaker Garner. By this time, presidential politics had intruded by the back door, with the chief rivals being Hoover and Garner. Garner sought to steal Hoover's thunder and up the ante on benefits. The Texan constituted the chief obstacle to smoothing out a compromise. Hoover, Wagner, and Robinson were interested in obtaining some type of useful legislation, although the same Democrats earlier had spoken harshly of the president. In the early stages of the Seventy-Second Congress, Hoover and Garner, if not allies, had agreed upon a *de facto* form of *détente*. As political conditions polarized, they found themselves like intruders in each other's liar. In the end, however, they arranged a satisfactory compromise. By that time, the nation was living not only on borrowed money but on borrowed time. The House, the Senate, and the president wrote legislation expanding federal powers to cope with the emergency. Much of the work was done under intense pressure during late May and June of 1932. The nominating conventions would occur before Congress adjourned, the fiscal year would end on July 1, and the clock was ticking down to the finale of the congressional session. Hoover had planned to submit bills simultaneously in the House and Senate, yet word leaked of his preparations. Robinson trumped him by introducing a bill in the Senate first. Nonetheless, the president went ahead, drafted, and introduced his version of relief legislation. In the Senate, Robinson collaborated with Wagner, a veteran in the struggle over public works and relief. As the session evolved, Wagner and Hoover, once sharply divided, narrowed their differences. Robinson was also willing to compromise in return for a share of credit. All the programs, Garner's, the Robinson-Wagner measure, and the Hoover bill, overlapped. Hoover, for the first time, was ready to loan money to the states for direct relief, which he had previously rejected.

Wagner's original Senate measure was split into two bills. The Wagner-Robinson bill increased the debenture limit of the RFC by $1.5 billion to be lent to states, municipalities, and private companies for self-liquidating public works. A companion bill provided $300 million, which was to be allotted to the states for direct relief. The money would be deducted from road funds escrowed for the states in the future. The legislation also included a $500 million bond issue to be used for public works during the next fiscal year. Senator Wagner and Hoover were not far apart, yet the president disliked the bond issue. The president also opposed a provision in the Senate measure that allocated money on the basis of state population rather than the percentage of unemployed, an attempt to appeal to the highly populated, electoral-rich states.[35]

Hoover considered the Garner bill much worse because the bond issue was larger, although it was supposed to be secured by a small tax on gasoline. The president felt Garner's bill was extravagant and politically motivated. The Garner measure provided that the RFC provide loans directly to private companies and individuals. Under existing rules, the RFC loaned money to banks, which in turn loaned it to people. Hoover believed that bypassing the banking system would in effect nationalize banking and impose an impossible burden of processing tens of thousands of loans on the RFC. Collectively, the private banks had more money to loan than the federal government, and to destroy them would dry up the majority of the credit pool available. Garner's measure, the president argued, smacked of pork-barrel legislation. Jordan A. Schwarz writes of Garner's measure, "Its public works proposals seemed designed more for electing Democrats than providing jobs."[36]

Garner's projects were chiefly buildings, including some 2,300 new post offices scattered among key congressional districts, not necessarily in areas with the highest unemployment. Hoover said the new buildings would require $14 million in annual maintenance whereas $3 million was currently devoted to maintenance. At a cost of $150 million, the bill would employ only 100,000 men for a single year from a pool of eight million unemployed. Hoover called leaders of both parties to the White House for a series of conferences. The Senate leaders were willing to compromise, but Garner was not. The chief sticking point was his insistence that the RFC be authorized to loan money directly to private companies and individuals, including those with shaky collateral who could not secure loans elsewhere. The Democrats, especially Garner, tried to make his legislation a class issue. They claimed that Hoover wanted to loan money to large banks but not to ordinary people. Hoover argued that the banks were only conduits to individuals and private companies and that the RFC could not process so many loans. The RFC directors unanimously agreed, writing a letter stating that they lacked the resources to perform such services. Representative Henry T. Rainey, the Democratic floor leader, was bitter. He complained that the Democrats had cooperated long enough with the president, and now it was the president's time to cooperate. Rainey fumed that "we propose to place the responsibility where it belongs, directly on the President of the United States and his vacillating, incompetent leadership."[37]

In June the House approved Garner's massive spending measure 216–182, followed by Senate approval. Later that month the Democrats assembled in

Chicago to nominate a presidential ticket, and on July 1 chose Franklin D. Roosevelt to head the ticket with Garner as his running mate. The flame of presidential politics now burned white hot in the congressional chambers. The same day the Democrats nominated their ticket, a conference committee that had attempted to cobble together a compromise merging the House and Senate versions, reported their relief bill, which included many of the Garner provisions. On July 5 and 6, the president held conferences at the White House seeking to bridge differences and find a compromise he could sign. He warned that some provisions in the Garner measure would politicize the RFC. Wagner, Robinson, and most Democrats were amenable to Hoover's compromise, but Garner refused. By this time, the sides were relatively close on the amount and nature of spending and on how to finance public works. Yet Garner's intransigence proved a deal-breaker. His bill passed, and the next day, July 9, the president vetoed the measure, which was easily upheld. The marathon negotiations had ended in deadlock, with no victor and no bill.[38]

During the churning of waters by the Garner bill and the Robinson-Wagner legislation, Hoover's own version of a relief bill was making little headway against congressional tides. The president wanted to strengthen and revamp the RFC, increase its funding, and expand its activities. He had written a stronger version of the RFC into his original bill back in January, yet the Democrats had deleted key provisions. If Hoover's more vigorous version of the RFC had been approved in the initial legislation and had operated in the interim, the fiery debate during the final days of the Seventy-Second Congress might have been unnecessary. By the spring of 1932 Hoover had decided plunge ahead and make the RFC the locomotive of credit. He tried to design an agency that would placate liberals yet keep the budget agreements reasonably intact. He considered the Garner bill grandiose and self-serving, and he did not believe it would end the Depression.[39]

On May 31, Hoover presented his ideas to Congress. Over the weekend, he secluded himself at Camp Rapidan to flesh out his theme into a bill. The final version was written by Treasury Secretary Mills and Senator Warren Barbour of New Jersey, whom he selected to manage the legislation on the floor. The Emergency Relief and Construction Bill, the most sweeping such measure to that time, provided many of the powers Hoover had wanted vested in the RFC earlier. The Hoover bill authorized the RFC to issue $3 billion in securities for self-liquidating, reproductive public works. Hoover envisioned projects such as toll roads and bridges, slum clearance and construction of better housing, dams that generated electricity, public utilities, and harbor and dock improvements. These were likely to provide employment of longer duration than public buildings. They would employ a more diverse workforce with different skills. The RFC could also to loan money to modernize private plants that created jobs. Loans could be made to subsidize agricultural exports and domestic marketing, utilizing future crops as collateral. None of the other bills significantly aided agriculture. There would be $300 million in loans for

direct relief (a dole) to help the unemployed, distributed by the states according to their number of needy. He knew most of the loans would never be
repaid, yet the repayment requirement would limit demand during in a time
of limited resources. Senator Barbour introduced the Emergency Relief and
Construction Bill to Congress on June 7. The battle in Congress was heated.
On June 8, by a 9–6 vote, liberals and progressives on the Senate Banking and
Currency Committee killed the Hoover bill. On June 10, the Senate passed
the provision of the Wagner bill providing $300 million relief to the states by
72–8, and on June 23 it approved the Wagner bill bond issue of $500 million
for public works. Neither House gave Hoover what he wanted, and his own
bill failed even to reach the floor.[40]

The Democrats lacked the votes to override Hoover's veto of the Garner
bill. Moreover, even Garner considered a relief bill necessary and feared being
blamed if no bill at all passed. Congress and the White House now hurried to
enact a compromise bill in the few days before adjournment. Garner finally
capitulated on most issues. The redrafted bill deleted most of the provisions
the president opposed. It did not allow the RFC to make loans to individuals or corporations directly, as Garner had proposed. The private banking
system would remain intact, as the president wished. The version rewritten
by the Senate was close to the president's own bill. Unlike earlier drafts, it
did not include public works financed by bond issues. The only corporations
that could borrow funds were in the home construction industry or those
rehabilitating slums. All loans must be based on adequate collateral. The new
bill increased the capital of the RFC by $1.8 billion. It included $300 million
in loans to the states to relieve distress (a dole). The money would be distributed on the basis of need, as Hoover wanted, not proportional to population.
There was a $332 construction fund, but only $136 million in new construction was mandatory. The remainder would be spent when the Treasury certified that resources were adequate. The revised legislation also included the
provisions for agriculture contained in the original Hoover bill. The RFC
was authorized to create a system of 12 regional agricultural corporations to
refinance agricultural debts. The RFC was also empowered to loan money to
banks, agricultural credit corporations, and livestock loan companies.[41]

One provision inserted by Garner at the last moment enraged Hoover.
The speaker added a stipulation permitting Congress to publish a list of banks
that received RFC loans. Hoover and the RFC board warned that this might
panic depositors by inciting a nationwide wave of bank failures and served
no useful purpose. Some banks that needed liquidity might not apply at all
because the revelation could spook depositors and ruin the banks. There
was not even a political advantage to be gained by Hoover's enemies because
the provision would not become effective until after the 1932 elections. The
entire RFC board, including its Democratic members, as well as virtually
every banker, condemned Garner's amendment. Nonetheless, the speaker
vowed that he would not permit the bill to pass without it. Many of Garner's

fellow Democrats saw the danger in the proposal and considered it vindictive. The vote in the House was 169–169, and Garner himself broke the tie. Hoover signed the bill only upon the assurance of Senator Robinson that the dissemination of the information would not actually occur. The records would be retained by the clerk of each House, unless Congress voted to order its release, which seemed unlikely.[42]

Hoover signed the Emergency Relief and Construction Act on July 19, 1932. The legislation, the most comprehensive domestic legislation of Hoover's presidency, injected the federal government into the lives of Americans and lifted Hoover to a new level of presidential activism. Hoover had bowed to necessity, the mother of invention, including provisions he might have rejected a few years earlier. The law set major precedents and demonstrated that Hoover was willing to flex federal muscles when the need arose. He was far less inhibited in doing so than many believed and far less inhibited than some still believe. The bill did not act quickly enough to save Hoover politically. Recovery would take time and, as Hoover had said all along, would require the restoration of old jobs and consumer confidence, not simply government spending. The private sector would have to respond, to make use of the capital available. Ironically, the Emergency Relief and Construction Act was dismissed by Hoover's opponent in the 1932 campaign, yet the strengthened RFC subsequently became a central instrument of the New Deal, lasting until 1945—a sincere form of flattery. The measure helped serve as a model for FDR's Public Works Administration.[43]

Back in December 1931 the president had proposed a system of Home Loan Discount Banks, an important component of his recovery program. Banks that were members of the Federal Reserve System could discount only short-term collateral, not long-term investments such as home mortgages. Hoover's legislation was designed to permit insurance companies, trust companies, deposit banks, and other institutions holding home mortgages to discount them through a new system of banks. Funneling such loans through the RFC would have overwhelmed that agency because of the volume of applications. The bill created 12 Home Loan Discount Banks, one for each Federal Reserve district, controlled by a central board in Washington. The legislation was designed to aid small home owners; homes valued at more than $20,000 were not eligible. Permitting the discount of mortgages would increase the liquidity of institutions holding mortgages and decrease the likelihood of foreclosure. Individuals could not borrow from the system, only member financial institutions. These financial institutions would pool sound mortgages through the regional discount banks, which would use them as collateral to sell government-backed bonds to the public. The plan would provide the same type of security for collateral based on home mortgages as that already permitted for industrial bonds. Replenishing the lending institutions could stave off foreclosures. The greater liquidity acquired by the lending institutions would also thaw credit, making it available for new home construction. The building of new homes would create jobs as well as demand for raw materials. The bill inched forward. It was stuck in committee indefinitely. Senators Glass, Couzens, and Borah opposed it. Even the Republican floor leader, Senator Watson, initially opposed it. Glass feared federal backing of weak mortgages might undermine the stability of the Federal Reserve System. Senator Couzens, who held banking interests in Michigan, considered the banks superfluous and believed they might compete with private lenders. A much larger number of senators and representatives were simply indifferent to the measure. Garner bottled up the bill in the House, hoping to deny Hoover credit for another facet of depression relief. Finally, when he concluded that it was too late to help Hoover much, Garner allowed a vote. Congress belatedly passed the measure on June 16, the last day of the long session, but provided no appropriation. Shortly before Congress adjourned at midnight, Senator Moses slipped the appropriation into an incidental bill to close Virginia Avenue, a deft parliamentary maneuver that no one noticed. Each bank was initially capitalized at from $5 million to $30 million from an appropriation of $125 million in the form of an RFC loan. The bill had taken 220 days to become law. Hoover believed that thousands of foreclosures could have been averted by prompt action. In a final act of political vindictiveness, Senator Borah attempted to repeal the law during the short session of the Seventy-Second Congress after Hoover's defeat but failed. With passage of the Home Loan Bank Bill in the twilight of the long session, the chief elements of Hoover's recovery program were in place.[44]

The president did not receive everything he wanted from the Seventy-Second Congress, although he had a high batting average on important bills. Hoover believed the laws regulating banking had not kept pace with changes in the industry. Antiquated regulations retarded recovery. In some respects regulation was too lenient; in other respects it was unwieldy. First, the president wanted to bring greater uniformity to the patchwork of regulations that governed different states. He wanted to compel all banks to become members of the Federal Reserve System, and he wanted to prohibit speculation with the money of depositors. The president wanted provisions to ensure that depositors received a prorated portion of the assets of failed banks. Further, the government should recognize the large role now played by new types of combinations, such as branch banking, chain banking, and group banking. The banking industry was no longer dominated by the small, unit banks that had characterized earlier eras. The president felt new forms of banking served useful purposes and constituted inevitable outgrowths of expansion, yet required standardized regulations. Hoover also believed that deposits of ordinary bank customers should be insured either by the government or by a pool contributed by banks and organized in cooperation with the government. One possibility was to have banks pay the government to insure deposits. Dozens of bills dealing with deposit guarantees were introduced by both parties, but there was no agreement on a specific plan. Perhaps the biggest obstacle lay in the opposition of bankers themselves, who did not want to pay for insurance. The president attempted to include deposit insurance in the Glass-Steagall Act of January 1932, but the provision was deleted. Most of his bills to reform banking did not even emerge from committee. The Glass Banking bill, submitted on April 18, 1932, was a refinement of earlier efforts by the president and Congress. The measure, which created the Federal Deposit Insurance Corporation (FDIC), was not enacted until the summer of 1933. Like numerous innovations that had their origins under Hoover, it is usually attributed to the New Deal.[45]

During the bank and business failures of the 1920s and the early 1930s, Hoover had labored to win approval of bankruptcy reform. Existing laws gave troubled companies little chance of survival and penalized homeowners, farmers, investors, and bank depositors. Bankruptcy cases in the federal courts had increased steadily from 23,000 in 1921 to 65,000 in 1931 and rose exponentially with the deepening of the Depression. Losses averaged $750 million annually through 1931. On February 29, 1932, the president dispatched to Congress a bill to reduce fraud, conserve assets, and save sound enterprises, but the legislation aroused a cyclone of opposition from special interests. Congress finally enacted bankruptcy reform on March 3, 1933, the day before Hoover left office, but did not include some provisions to facilitate corporate reorganization he had requested. The lateness and the incomplete nature of the legislation were among the president's keenest disappoints. Tens, perhaps hundreds of thousands of businesses and families might have benefitted. When bank failures reached a crescendo during the interregnum, after his defeat, the safety net for which he had pleaded was not there.[46]

No session of any Congress, much less one confronted with the enormous problems of the Great Depression, is perfect. Few presidents get everything they want, and some of the things they want they should not get. Neither can any president upon entering office anticipate the events of their administration. Democracies are inherently more safe than speedy. Institutional inertia and conflicting personalities constitute a drag on the passage of legislation. Often what goes in is not what comes out. Hoover had grown a great deal politically since 1929, even as the economy had caved in beneath him. By 1932, he had a unified, innovative program to present and the grit to push for its passage. He was the same man yet a wiser, tougher person. He was also patient and resilient and more willing to compromise. If the internal personal growth of a person could be measured, Hoover's might be in feet rather than inches. By the time the long session of the Seventy-Second Congress adjourned, part harmony, part dissonance, Hoover believed he had put in place an infrastructure that provided the foundation for recovery. Credit, which he considered the crux of the problem, had been carried about as far as legislation could carry it. Yet no one could compel Americans to use the credit available. The psychological stigma of spending and taking risks to expand business had not been broken, and private investment would not return to normal until the Second World War in the context of the universe of opportunity available in the postwar era—some of it generated by technology, much of it propelled by optimism generated by defeating more human, equally formidable foes, which had unified the nation in a spirit of confident sacrifice.

The Seventy-Second Congress certainly had its moments. Much of the time, it had moved in lockstep with the president, sometimes grudgingly but often willingly. There were men of goodwill on both sides of the aisle. Hoover was not the most articulate man in Washington, but he might have been the smartest and the most determined. Perhaps without the inflammatory rhetoric of the presidential election that followed, the nation might have moved forward, for there were glimmers of an economic liftoff, especially in the stock market, during the summer of 1932. Indeed, much of the world was embarking on a sustained recovery. Hoover desired first stability and then a gradual, measured, march that gathered momentum. But the economy was fragile, and the injection of uncertainty could undo the progress. Though the session had been turbulent at times, both parties were proud of their accomplishments. In some scenarios, a situation in which one party controlled the House and in which the other party controlled the Senate and the presidency but lacked a reliable majority in either house might have been a prescription for interminable gridlock. There was no way either party could simply power legislation through. Lacking a silver tongue, the president was often successful with persistent persuasion. Both parties had focused on immediate problems in place of permanent reform. Yet some of the latter had been accomplished as well, most consequentially the resolution eliminating lame duck sessions and the anti-injunction labor act, both sponsored by Senator Norris. The stars must have been aligned to place Hoover and Norris on the same planet. The program achieved had been the most substantial program of domestic legislation, coherent in purpose, ever enacted in a single session, under harsh circumstances and in turbulent times. The eminent Progressive journalist, William Allen White, summed up the session in an editorial in the *Emporia Gazette*. The president had won every major battle in Congress, he explained, though White did not prophesy the end of the Depression. "That it has prevented further collapse and dire calamity, no one can deny," White writes. The nation might have had more beloved presidents. Yet "America has had no President who has done in eight months such Herculean work for the salvation of the country as Herbert Hoover has done since December 1931."[47]

There were times Hoover must have wished he was still seeking ore in the Gobi Desert, Siberia, or the trackless Australia Outback. Yet in addition to getting most of what he wanted from the Seventy-Second Congress, Hoover was able to block most of what he did not want or had it rewritten in acceptable form. The president vetoed seven measures, all of which were upheld, some dealing with controversial topics such as unemployment relief. After Hoover threatened to veto a veterans' bonus bill, the Senate killed it. Clearly, in the bills he passed and the bills he thwarted, Hoover was in control most of the time.[48]

Herbert Hoover at work in Commerce Department office (1921),
Hoover Presidential Library 1921–31

*Herbert Hoover at work in Commerce Department office (1921), Hoover
Presidential Library 1921–34*

*Mr. Hoover's secretaries: George Akerson, Lawrence Richey, Walter Newton
(December 1928), gift of the George Akerson family,
Hoover Presidential Library 1928–98*

Herbert and Lou Henry Hoover are shown on the steps of the Old Capitol at the University of Iowa with Walter E. Jessup, President of the University and George T. Baker, head of the Iowa State Board of Education (Iowa City, Iowa August 22, 1928), gift of the Kent family, courtesy of Kent Photo 1928–99

Main Street West Branch, Iowa (August 21, 1928), gift of the Kent family, courtesy of Kent Photo 1928-A06A

Portrait of Lou Henry Hoover (1928), Hoover Presidential Library 1928-F03F

Portrait of Herbert Hoover (1928), Hoover Presidential Library 1928-E86E

Herbert Hoover addressing a political gathering in West Branch, Iowa (August 21, 1928), gift of the Kent family, courtesy of Kent Photo 1928-A07A

Herbert Hoover delivers inaugural address (March 4, 1929), U.S. Signal Corp, Hoover Presidential Library 1929-E36E

President Hoover reviewing vessels of the U.S. Fleet from the U.S.S. Salt Lake City—L to R Ernest Lee Jahncke, Charles F. Adams, Herbert Hoover, Admiral Charles F. Hughes (Hampton Roads, Virginia May 20, 1930), U.S. Navy, Hoover Presidential Library 1930-B43B

Commerce Building under construction (July 15, 1930), U.S. Army, Hoover Presidential Library 1930-B87B

*The President and Secretary of War Patrick Hurley on the quarterdeck of
the U.S.S. Arizona (Caribbean tour March 26, 1931), U.S. Navy,
Hoover Presidential Library 1931–21*

*Hoover Dam construction, looking upstream (1935), Bureau of Reclamation,
Hoover Presidential Library 1935–A67A*

Drought—location unknown (ca. 1936), Farm Security Administration,
Hoover Presidential Library 1936–53

CHAPTER 11

Combating the Depression Phase II, 1931–1932

After the stock market crash, the economy did not plummet with the laser-like precision of a smart bomb. Instead, there were small improvements and deeper valleys. Sometimes the nation appeared briefly on the verge of recovery. Yet the trend of production was consistently down while unemployment rose. By early 1931, six million were unemployed, business had declined 28 percent from the year before, and 1,345 banks had failed during the previous 12 months. Conditions steadily, if unevenly, deteriorated. By January 1932, ten million were unemployed. Yet ironically 1932 was Hoover's most active year, the time of his greatest achievements, the best of times during the worst of times. It is plausible to argue that the Depression worsened in spite of Hoover, not because of him. Hoover believed a recovery program was firmly in place by the summer of 1932. The president's immediate objective was to put flesh on the skeleton of his new program, to rev up the engine of recovery in the time left. Yet he was not in the driver's seat. He later reflected that recovery had begun in some European countries at about the time of the 1932 campaign and had continued unabated, while in America it had stalled and imploded during the chaotic interregnum when no one was in control.[1]

At the outset of the Depression, no one predicted that it would continue for a decade. By the end of 1931, however, Hoover realized that it would be longer and deeper than previous downturns. He steeled himself against a more formidable economic foe, and conceded that it would not end during one term. Phase II of his fight against the Depression represented a new approach in depression strategy not only in the Hoover administration but in American history. Yet Hoover's goals were reasonable. He settled on three fundamental priorities: He wanted to maintain the social order, to alleviate distress in the short term, and to prevent panic and unnecessary bankruptcies. His overall objective was to maintain the nation's basic economic system intact so that it could later kick into gear.[2]

Fear represented a mountain between recovery and expansion. The president strove to avert a descent into hopelessness. He knew that the Depression must be conquered mentally before it could be conquered economically. Although America had suffered less than many nations, its standard of living had been higher; thus the decline was steeper. Americans had grown accustomed to comfort and security. They were not a patient people, and voters are notoriously impatient. Yet their worst enemy was not the president; it was themselves. "We have the ability to end it, but we do not," he said. "The banks are full of money in spite of hoarding some months ago, yet because of fear, credit is withheld." The country had been enervated by a state of mind that exaggerated every fragment of bad news and had fallen prey to ominous, self-fulfilling prophecies. "You can be so upset over the loss of part of your business that you let another part slip," Hoover explained.[3] Hoover tried to remain, publicly at least, cautiously optimistic. He labored to hold the country together, avoiding the temptation to blame, especially refusing to demonize business, whose faith in itself was already shaky. The president knew that he could not win the battle alone. "It cannot be won until there is confidence among the people and cooperation one individual with another," he told Theodore Joslin.[4] In an attempt to pry open pocketbooks and gear up industry, the president suggested that individuals place orders for large consumer items, such as automobiles, which would be delivered at a later date. Assurance of a future market would provide an incentive to manufacture major consumer items. People still purchased daily bread, but there was stagnation in the buying of big-ticket, durable goods that provided employment. Everything that could be delayed was postponed.[5]

To drive home the urgency of conditions and inspire unity of purpose, the president employed the analogy of war to his fight against the Depression. He sprinkled his vocabulary with terms such as "tactics," "enemy," "fronts," "attack," and "campaign."[6] Hoover's task was not simple. In a war, everyone fights together. In a depression, everyone fights each other. People sacrifice and accept artificial rationing during a war but complain and refuse to accept natural economic shortages during a depression. Hard times often bring out the worst in people. Blame becomes the national pastime. Economic crises are invisible enemies; it is difficult to discern their causes or their remedies. The nation is fertile for partisanship and demagoguery, and indeed demagogues stalked the land and filled the airwaves with utopian schemes. Economic victories come slowly. Battling a depression is painstaking, repetitive drudgery that requires more patience and endurance than heroism. Medals are not awarded for winning depressions. FDR is fortunate that he ended his tenure on the wings of a victorious war rather than amid the despair of a depression. Had the sequence been reversed, his place in history might also be reversed. The president often becomes a symbol for the mood of the nation, euphoric amid a successful war but cynical, anxious, and frustrated during prolonged economic hardship.[7]

It is a common misconception that Hoover threw overboard the voluntary elements of his depression program when he injected the federal government more aggressively into the economy in 1931 and 1932. In fact, the voluntary and the federal programs coexisted. It is also taken for granted that as government power accrued, the dead weight of the Depression lifted. Whether coincidentally or connected, the reverse is true. The worst years of the Depression are those in which the government was most active. Even while he was pushing his program through the Seventy-Second Congress, Hoover continued to invent, multiply, and employ voluntary organizations. He knew that the credit available under the Reconstruction Finance Corporation would be useless unless businesses and banks were encouraged to borrow, and he enlisted business leaders to calm their colleagues. Following a meeting with business leaders, whom he dispatched as disciples to spread the gospel that low-risk loans were available, the president met with 37 prominent publishers. He asked them to help him push the remainder of his program through Congress, to encourage businesses business, and to break the ice jam of consumer spending. Publishers poured out a steady stream of ink suggesting practical steps individuals could take to lift the economic doldrums. Hoover never considered the government the sole, or even the most effective, emissary to proselytize the public. He wanted to complement political exhortation with articles in daily newspapers and popular and professional magazines. The media had credibility because, unlike politicians, those publications that appealed to general readers had no obvious axe to grind. The president also devoted long hours to listening to business and media leaders, soliciting their ideas, and testing his ideas on them. The administration was a work in progress, and he wanted those he consulted to feel a part of the process.[8]

Hoover became the most effective president in history in stimulating the role of private charity during difficult times. He tapped his organizational and promotional skills to make fighting the Depression a participatory activity that involved ordinary people, infusing the war on the Depression with a common purpose in which the people themselves, not simply the government, played an active role. The people did not simply wait for the government to act; they were encouraged to tap their inner fortitude. No earlier, or later, efforts to deal with a serious economic downturn so fused the public and private tools available to resolve it nor so fully involved the nation's citizens in the effort. The reveille to arouse Americans to act in small and large ways did not reverse the Depression, but it made a significant impact in diminishing it and in lifting morale. There was a higher degree of unselfishness not only in donating to the needy but in a willingness to share jobs and provide gifts in kind to the unemployed than under other presidents. Most public and private projects involved seven-day weeks, which were divided between two sets of workers, each working a three- or four-day week. This employed a larger number of workers; the projects were completed more rapidly and put into use expeditiously. There was less disruption while highway repairs were under way. Workers were paid at the prevailing rate of wages, and unions agreed to work sharing because, of course, the alternative was increased layoffs. There was less labor strife and little domestic violence, during stressful times when both might have been expected to increase. Though not a gifted orator, Hoover was able to inspire many Americans by the example of his own idealism, his relentless work ethic, and his tenaciousness. He believed loss of individual pride and personal responsibility would be more deleterious than physical pain and strove to sustain morale. The test of a nation, he believed, came not during its periods of success, but in its tests from adversity. Individual fortitude was an important weapon against the economic enemy. When Americans were summoned to meet an even greater challenge in 1941, they were sustained, in part by their earlier experience in battling a relentless economic enemy. Some nations in the 1930s did not fare so well.

The administration spawned several major quasigovernment committees headed by prominent Americans and staffed by unpaid volunteers. Sometimes they spun off subcommittees with specialized tasks. Most leaders had experience in business, politics, the military, and government. The purpose of the major committees was similar: to stimulate private giving at the local level, to alleviate unemployment by mobilization of localities and private enterprise, to promote social cohesiveness, to serve as a source of ideas and innovation at the local level, and to serve as a liaison with charities and with the federal government. Arthur Woods, who directed the first committee until April 1931, was succeeded by Fred C. Croxton, who headed the President's Emergency Committee for Employment. The Croxton Committee maintained a staff of 35 in Washington to work with state and local groups. It furnished information to employers, contacted field officers, cooperated with government bureaus, encouraged gardening and self-help, and worked to accelerate construction and sustain wage levels. Croxton persuaded some highly paid executives to take voluntary pay cuts to preserve higher wages for their employees. In cooperation with trade associations, the committee engaged in long-term studies designed to increase industrial output. Never intended to be a total solution, the committee nonetheless considered itself an important line of defense. It gave a human face to the president's efforts: people helping people in their own communities. In the summer of 1931 the president began planning to cope with hunger and cold during the coming winter of 1931–1932. In June, Croxton initiated a survey of cities of more than 25,000 to determine needs for the next winter, relying in part on data collected by the 1930 census. The committee chair believed demand would require twice the resources of the previous winter.[9]

In late August of 1931 the president selected Walter S. Gifford, the president of American Telephone and Telegraph and head of the Charity Organization of New York, to lead a new national relief organization, the President's Organization on Unemployment Relief (POUR) and the old President's Emergency Committee under Croxton was allowed to lapse. Croxton became the assistant director of POUR. The president appointed a blue-ribbon advisory committee of businessmen, industrialists, and academic experts to counsel Gifford. Gifford, his entire staff, and the advisory committee were unpaid volunteers. The new director's assignment included continuation of the work of the Woods and Croxton committees, such as work sharing, stimulation of local employment projects, placement of workers in jobs, and aid in fundraising to local charities such as community chests. There was no national pool of funds available; money was collected and distributed at the community level, where needs could be more accurately identified. The committee helped to identify jobs and provide workers who could fill such positions. POUR compiled lists to match the skills of the jobless with opportunities. The organization attempted to keep workers in their own homes, in their own communities, and with their families. It also discouraged farmers from migrating to the cities, where conditions were worse. Subsistence farming, vegetable gardens, and the raising of livestock and poultry were preferable to bread lines. Under the prodding of the Woods, Croxton, and Giffords committees, cities and individual donors responded. For example, municipal government spending for relief in New York City rose from $9 million in 1930 to $58 million in 1932. Private donations in the metropolis rose from $4.5 million in 1930 to $21 million in 1932.[10]

The Gifford Committee was an umbrella organization led principally by Gifford and Croxton. Beneath it were specialized subcommittees as well as an infrastructure stretching to the local level. The smaller committees and the local groups, like the national structure, were composed of volunteers. The Committee on Cooperation with National Groups and Associations worked with local groups to find employment for individuals in their communities. This subcommittee served as a clearinghouse and kept statistical files. Croxton created another subcommittee that attempted to persuade young people to remain in school in order to avoid competing in an already saturated job market. A separate subcommittee supervised the canning and storing of vegetables donated by farmers for the winter ahead. Perhaps the most prominent of the subcommittees was headed by Owen D. Young, whose members read like a *Who's Who* of American business. The task of the Young Committee was to serve as a catalyst for fundraising for local charities. By mid-September 1931, it was active in 513 cities of more than 25,000. Ten regional executives toured the nation to advise grassroots volunteers. The Young Committee also conducted a national advertising campaign encouraging donations, using space and time provided by national publications and motion picture studios. It helped community chests, welfare organizations, and new organizations created specifically to combat the Depression. It compiled an advisory list of priorities for the allocation of jobs. In the case of comparable applicants, preference was given to married men with dependents. Towns and cities were asked to create part-time jobs, some as menial as mowing, raking, refurbishing schools, and beautification. Even small jobs contributed to morale and helped preserve self-respect. Arrangements were made with farmers to provide food, clothing, and shelter in exchange for farm labor. The job-sharing program included white-collar as well as blue-collar jobs. The committee undertook a thorough study of white-collar unemployment because Hoover realized that most government public works helped chiefly blue-collar workers. To the extent possible, job sharing was applied to transportation, supervisory positions, and the federal civil service. On October 31, the Subcommittee on Employment Plans and Suggestions released a list of practical suggestions to improve the economy. The recommendations applied to private companies, local communities, and individual citizens. The philosophy on which they were based was that production and consumption must resume normal levels to bring the nation out of the Depression. Bankers should not become overly cautious and should continue to make sound loans. Lenders were asked to be more lenient in offering loans, considering the character and past record of the potential borrower, in addition to their collateral. The work of the Young Committee and other subcommittees of the Gifford Committee were designed to ameliorate rather than eradicate unemployment, to provide a bridge to better times, and to boost national morale. None of the subcommittees alone could end the Depression, yet all of them implemented simultaneously increased consumption and fought lethargy and despondency.[11]

In 1930 Governor Franklin D. Roosevelt introduced a relief plan in New York, which while modest by later standards, has been cited as the model that should have been followed on the national level. In fact, Hoover actively encouraged such programs at the state level, because that is where he believed they could do the most good. FDR himself opposed a federal dole. In fact, in 1931 his chief complaint about the Hoover administration was that it was extravagant. Meanwhile, the president drew upon the U.S. Chamber of Commerce to update and amplify unemployment statistics gathered by the U.S. Census and the Labor Department. The president decided to increase public works and to infuse $300 million already appropriated for federal construction into the economy more rapidly. Hoover also donated $2,500 of his personal money to provide relief of the unemployed in the District of Columbia.[12]

Both Gifford and the president had frustrating jobs and agonized over the struggling economy. In February the president summoned Gifford to the White House and asked him to supercharge his committee in order to discourage attempts to legislate direct federal relief. Gifford, however, was discouraged by the grind and the slow pace of progress. Although it is unlikely anyone could have done better, Hoover felt Gifford had given up. The coup de grâce to the Gifford Committee was administered by Congress. In July 1932, the Democrats in Congress defeated an appropriation needed to continue the committee, a politically motivated action. No salaries were involved. The requested appropriation of $120,000 was small and paid only secretarial expenses. The committee thus expired. The Woods, Croxton, and Gifford committees had not eliminated unemployment, but they had reduced it somewhat and had demonstrated that many Americans were willing to make sacrifices for their neighbors. In no other economic downturn has the private sector been tapped so consistently nor organized so effectively. Surely, nothing was lost in the effort, which paralleled federal action rather than diminished it.[13]

On February 5, 1932, Hoover launched another voluntary program to promote job creation but with a slightly different focus and utilizing different resources. The new organization was led by Carl Byoir, a publisher with broad experience in public relations. The group's program was sponsored by the American Legion, the American Legion Auxiliary, the American Federation of Labor (AFL), and the Association of National Advertisers. Henry L. Stevens Jr. of the American Legion and Matthew Woll, vice president of the AFL, played key roles in establishing the organization. Like the other Hoover groups, it relied on volunteers. The field work was done by 7,000 organizations in local communities. The national headquarters in New York knit together field units. The American Legion participated through its 10,800 posts, and the AFL directly informed its 30,000 local unions via its 200 publications. The campaign was subdivided into four divisions: the division of local organizations, the division of advertising, the division of finance, and the division of radio. All of these helped raise funds, food, and clothing for the needy. They encouraged employers to be creative about creating jobs and workers to be creative about seeking them. The Byoir organization was oriented more toward public relations than any of the other voluntary committees. It used large companies as conduits to disseminate advice. The committee lasted only a few months, disbanding in May 1932. It fell short of its goal of finding employment for one million persons, yet during its brief life it placed some 668,607 individuals in jobs. Its component organizations continued to work to achieve its goals.[14]

Fred Croxton remained a key figure in the administration after the expiration of the Gifford Committee, and unlike Gifford he did not fall out of favor with the president. Hoover made Croxton responsible for identifying the most needy cities and states that would draw upon the $300 million congressional appropriation allotted to the RFC Emergency Relief Division. The funds, if necessary, could be used by the states for direct relief—the much-maligned dole—which Hoover now accepted. Croxton and his assistants used the federal funds to complement state and private resources, stretching the money as far as possible. Relief was distributed through local committees modeled on those created by the Woods Committee in 1930 and continued by Croxton and Gifford. In the last stages of his administration, the president folded some of his earlier voluntary efforts into the federal government, where they remained vehicles to disseminate federal appropriations.[15]

The president also utilized quasipublic volunteers to funnel federal credit now available from the RFC to agriculture and industry, streamlining the process. He summoned agricultural and business leaders to the White House to ask for their help in pumping credit into the arteries of the economy, carving out an organization headed by the president's friend, Henry M. Robinson, a Los Angeles banker who supervised six subcommittees. Their purposes included facilitating credit for business, increasing employment through the maintenance of industry, expansion by means of replacing obsolete equipment, stimulation of repair and improvement of homes, and assisting homeowners with mortgages. Hoover urged the economic committees to become active in implementing programs now available. The president tried to pool private, state, and federal resources to make relief funds go as far as possible. Even though most of the money was now federal, Hoover continued to use his decentralized, nonpolitical approach to distribute it.[16]

Hoover forged his last major quasipublic committee in early September of 1932, after the presidential nominating conventions. Newton D. Baker, a recent candidate for the Democratic nomination, led the new umbrella organization. The Baker Committee focused on promoting charitable fundraising and relief of unemployment. In a new wrinkle, the president, Baker, and Croxton delivered national radio addresses calling for support for the committee's efforts. Federal money appropriated for Croxton's RFC fund was supplemented by the money raised by Baker's organization. Hoover never ceased to view relief and recovery as a joint federal, state, and private responsibility. Given that resources were disbursed among this trio and given that federal resources at that time were quite small, it made common sense. To the end of his term he continued to innovate, reinvent, rearrange, and redefine the relationship between the federal government and its constituents. Moreover, Hoover's tactics, his nimble use of resources and personnel, especially the utilization of volunteers and individuals with nothing to gain by employing relief as patronage, help to explain the scrupulous honesty that characterized Hoover's relief program, which had the least costly overhead generated by a large-scale relief operation by any major nation from Hoover's time to the present.[17]

Some voluntary committees were created to deal with specific problems. In the late summer of 1931 the hoarding of dollars and gold by Americans, coupled with foreign withdrawals gold due primarily to financial turmoil in Europe, inspired panic withdrawals of deposits from banks by Americans who feared that their banks were unsafe. Hoover believed that each dollar withdrawn from a bank contracted the available credit by $5 to $10 and that commercial recovery was impossible under such circumstances. Throughout the fall of 1931 and into the winter of 1932, hoarding concerned the administration and the financial community. Hoover addressed the problem through legislation, such as the Glass-Steagall Act, but he combined his program with voluntary efforts to overcome the fear that inspired hoarding, just as he employed dual methods to deal with unemployment. By early February 1932, Hoover inveighed against hoarding publicly, complaining that $1.5 billion had been sucked into a black hole by frightened depositors who would did not trust banks or savings institutions. Credit, already tight, was contracting as was consumer purchasing. On February 8, Hoover announced that Colonel Frank Knox, publisher of the *Chicago Daily News,* had accepted leadership of a committee to combat hoarding called the Citizens' Reconstruction Organization. Like Hoover's other committees, local chapters were created throughout the nation. Dollars returned to circulation would put men back to work.[18]

Hoover recruited the popular ex-president, Calvin Coolidge, to write an article warning about the harmful effects of hoarding, which was published in the *New York Evening Post* on February 29, 1932. Coolidge placed the onus on personal responsibility. There was something virtually every adult American could do. On March 17, President Hoover delivered a national radio address from the White House deploring hoarding, followed by a talk that same evening by Knox, speaking from Chicago. Meanwhile, volunteers fanned out in 2,395 communities for a house-to-house drive to sell "baby bonds," new securities issued by the federal government to lure money out of hoarding. They could be purchased in quantities as small as $50, were redeemable in 60 days, and paid 2 percent interest. Knox called the bonds "an employment agency for idle dollars." Whereas $300 million had been withdrawn in January before the Knox committee was created, during the first three weeks of February, about $100 million was returned to circulation. From February 8, when Hoover created the Knox Committee, until mid-May, about $250 million flowed back into bank vaults. Yet the crisis was not over. The Knox Committee proved only a temporary reprieve. In late June, hoarding resumed, and the situation became increasingly critical as the economy remained ossified. In the second half of May through late June the reversal became pronounced and $125 million was withdrawn from banks. Hoover's tools to reverse hoarding were limited. Beneath the symptom lay a contagion of fear. It would continue to drag the economy down, even if it was unjustified, until the addictive pessimism was punctured.[19]

In late November of 1931 the motion picture industry joined the voluntary effort to raise funds for the needy. At the request of Young, William H. Hays, the motion picture czar, in collaboration with Young's Committee, devised a National Motion Picture Week for Local Unemployment Relief. During the week of November 18–25, some 600 theaters nationally donated the ticket sales from their screenings to charity, estimated at $500,000. Unlike some efforts to raise money in movie houses, there were no speeches, and no collections were taken before or after the showings. The money was derived solely from ticket sales.[20]

On January 25, 1932, the Hoovers entertained the famous Polish pianist and ex-Prime Minister Ignacy Paderewski at the White House. Later in the evening he performed a concert for the benefit of the Unemployment Fund of the American Red Cross. The First Lady, who initiated the contact, sponsored four additional concerts by the eminent musician in American cities, including one in Madison Square Garden, with proceeds going to the Red Cross. Paderewski said his efforts were paid out of the respect of his nation for Hoover and the United States during and after World War I. In addition to her role in arranging the Paderewski benefits, the First Lady mobilized young people, especially the Girl Scouts, to contribute to the effort against the Depression. She asked them to volunteer for chores that would help their parents, neighbors, and the community. They could help the needy with housework, gardening, sewing, yard work, and errands, as well as collect food and clothing. Part of their contribution was psychological uplift; Lou told them they could help to relieve the anxieties as well as the physical needs of older people. In these small ways Lou personalized the Depression and provided the young with motivation to help. On November 7, 1931, she delivered the first nationwide radio address by a First Lady. She suggested practical tasks to her audience of 4-H Club members that could help alleviate the mental and physical effects of the Depression.[21]

Some businesses and merchants made contributions in kind. On April 3, 1932, the American Bakers' Association pledged to give unsold bread at the end of each day to the Red Cross for free distribution to the hungry. Local relief organizations delivered the bread, which amounted to five to ten million pounds weekly. Henry Stude, president of the Bakers' Association, said he realized the serious crisis faced by the nation, and there was no reason for the unsold bread to be wasted. In addition, John Barton Payne, chairman of the Red Cross, arranged for most of the 40 million bushels of wheat allotted to the needy from the Farm Board surplus to be baked at cost by local bakers throughout the nation. In relation to another commodity, New York merchants developed a plan in early August of 1932 to donate unmarketable grades of fruit and vegetable for distribution to the poor. Agriculture Secretary Hyde and the President's Committee on Unemployment approved the idea. Tons of produce, quite edible, was being discarded because it did not meet commercial grading requirements. The plan provided that growers and shippers, when loading, include as many boxes of the noncommercial products as practical. The railroads shipped them without charge. When they reached terminals, the food was unloaded and sent to relief organizations, which distributed them to the poor.[22]

Many voluntary organizations participated in the relief effort, some national but most, local. Most of the breadlines and soup kitchens were privately operated, many of them by churches. The largest national organization that provided relief was the Red Cross. Prior to the Depression, the Red Cross did not ordinarily become involved in efforts that dealt solely with unemployment.

However, the Red Cross spent $3.5 million in relief aid to more than 12 million Americans in the fiscal year that ended on June 30, 1932. The 2,275 local chapters supported activities in which churches and other charities participated. Red Cross chapters provided employment relief to 454,000 families at a cost of $2,215,000. In addition, 90,000 families in 143 counties where coal mining was the chief activity were helped at a cost of $522,000. The greatest disaster relief task of the year was in drought-stricken states, where 58,248 families were carried on relief rolls from August 1931 until June 1932. The organization distributed stock feed in the drought region to 184,188 stock owners, totaling 223,811 tons. Flour was given to almost four million families by the time the first 40 million bushels was exhausted in October. In July, after the end of fiscal year 1932, Congress voted to give an additional 45 million bushels of Farm Board wheat to be milled into flour as well as 500,000 bales of cotton. Distribution began in the fall.[23]

President Hoover received numerous suggestions as to how to eradicate the Depression, some from well-meaning people, some who wanted him to utilize a commodity they produced, others from crackpots. His staff skimmed these and passed along those they considered worthy to the president. When the recommendations originated with prominent individuals, the president usually examined them himself, although few proved helpful. Gerard Swope, the president of General Electric, sent the president several ideas. In October 2, 1930, with unemployment climbing, Swope submitted a plan for a sweeping $1 billion bond issue to be used for direct relief in communities with the highest unemployment rates. Hoover considered the plan impractical. At that point, it was impossible to know whether the Depression would deepen or decline.[24]

In mid-September 1931, Swope proposed a more elaborate program that called for a total restructuring of the American economy. It involved quasigovernment cartels operating through collusion of big businesses under the auspices of trade associations. Swope's plan mandated the suspension of antitrust laws, price setting, and wage controls. His intention was to control production and adjust it to demand. Central planning by the federal government would become the centerpiece of a solution to the Depression. There were to be "general boards of administration" to oversee each major line of work, including representatives of government, business, and labor. Consumers, who had no representatives, would have lacked a voice in the prices established by fiat, without regard for supply and demand. Hoover, who valued individual initiative and opposed monopoly, considered the plan unrealistic. It would create a vast bureaucracy that might outlast the Depression and undermine capitalism. Attorney General Mitchell considered the idea unconstitutional. It interfered with intrastate commerce, a state responsibility; it violated the due process clause; and it also violated the Sherman Act because it constituted a "conspiracy in restraint of trade." Swope's scheme would take years to implement and provide no immediate relief. When FDR adopted a similar program, the

National Recovery Administration (NRA), it was nullified by the Supreme Court.[25]

In addition to Swope, other luminaries weighed in with various schemes. The prominent historian, Charles A. Beard, outlined a complicated program in *Forum* magazine in July 1931. Beard's plan focused on national planning, which he considered vital for a technological society. His idea called for an even more omnivorous federal bureaucracy than Swope's. Beard's octopus centered on a National Economic Council subdivided into syndicates representing the major fields of production. The syndicates would control wages, prices, production, distribution, and marketing. Beard believed domestic markets were the cornerstone of the economy and considered world trade largely irrelevant. Beard's proposal was long on generalizations and vague on details. At its heart was the belief that capitalism was irrational and that only centralization could save the nation. His scheme included an Economic General Staff modeled on the Army General Staff to correlate and rationalize the economy. Hastily conceived, the proposal, which attracted attention because of the prominence of its author, closely resembled the syndicalism of Mussolini's Italy. Like the Swope plan it would have been cumbersome to implement and would have required years to bring relief, if ever. It was more a plan for reform in the sense of economic restructuring than a remedy for the Depression.[26]

Virtually all the schemes proposed by thinkers and writers such as Beard were more complex than anything ever actually attempted by the United States even in wartime. None made the leap from drawing board to reality. The economic planners seemed to operate in a vacuum with no role for the president, the Congress, or the courts or for that matter the voters. Presumably, these plans might destabilize an already shaky economy. It was impossible to predict the state of the economy by the time they became operable. There was no indication of who would appoint the various councils and planning boards or of how they would be financed, even down to such minor details as to who would pay their salaries. It stretches credibility that anything that went from typewriter to publication in a few weeks could have permanently eliminated the Depression. The desperation of the times infected not only the hungry and homeless but the elite and well educated, however well meaning.

In late 1931 William Green, AFL president, visited the White House and offered the president a somewhat more prosaic menu of suggestions. Most had already been suggested by others. Green wanted President Hoover to begin by organizing another conference of industrial, labor, and governmental economists to the White House to brainstorm. Among his specific recommendations were a implementing five-day workweek, holding wages at existing levels, relaxing antitrust laws, canceling of war debts, planning over industry, and guaranteeing job security. Another labor leader, Leo Wolman of the Amalgamated Clothing Workers of America, recommended a $3 billion bond issue to employ 750,000 workers. Wolman urged the government to seize control of the economy and to implement a version of socialism. Hoover was already aware of Green's ideas, and Wolman's had no chance of passing Congress or being signed into law.[27]

The already ailing sectors of the economy, such as agriculture, coal, and railroads, continued to decline. These ill segments dragged down other sectors. Rural banks that relied on virtually worthless farm mortgages for collateral collapsed. Railroad bonds were held by most major banks and insurance companies, and retirement systems were vested in them. In July 1932 the Interstate Commerce Commission approved a modified version of the consolidation plan Hoover had helped shape. Yet implementation required enabling legislation from Congress, which balked. The roads continued to hemorrhage. They asked the ICC for rate increases and the unions for wage concessions. The unions refused without guarantees of job security, and the railways promised to reduce manpower only by attrition. They justified the wage cuts on the grounds that the cost of living had declined. In railroads, agriculture, and coal, the real enemy was the changing nature of competition, technology, and diminished demand. Railroads were overexpanded and could not compete with trucking. Coal faced oversupply, declining demand, and ruthless competition. In agriculture, supply consistently outpaced demand. While hungry people stalked the streets, farmers could not simply give away their produce, lest it bankrupt them. If the government bought the surplus, as it discovered, much to its chagrin, it only encouraged more overproduction. The economic shifts were inexorably painful. The lessons Americans thought they had learned in the 1930s came back to haunt them early in the Great Recession that began in 2007. Some took the superficial lessons of the 1930s literally, rather than metaphorically, as historical lessons actually are.[28]

Hoover continued to ponder the roots of the Depression while he battled its daily problems. In early June 1931 he called upon the Committee on Recent Economic Changes, which had produced a study of changes ending in 1928, to undertake a broader, comprehensive study of the causes of the Depression. Funded by the Rockefeller and the Carnegie Foundations, the new investigation probed the period between 1921 and 1931, utilizing data gathered by the 1930 census. The president hoped its report would be complete by 1932 and that it might serve as a blueprint for reforms during his second administration. Edward Eyre Hunt, a prominent journalist and a close friend of Hoover, served as secretary of the committee. Some 50,000 copies of the earlier report, which was critical of the role of the Federal Reserve System prior to the crash, had already been disseminated. The committee was asked to recommend remedial measures to ameliorate the economic cycle.[29]

In preparing for the winter of 1931–32, the president considered ways to protect workers from unemployment and illness through government or private plans, or a mixture of the two. On August 8, 1931, at Camp Rapidan, he pored over a survey of unemployment and medical insurance programs. At the last session of Congress Senator Robert Wagner of New York had submitted a bill for federal unemployment insurance, and Hoover favored some aspects of the measure. The chief executive was joined at Rapidan by Senator Felix Hebert, a Rhode Island Republican, who had traveled to Europe during the congressional recess to study European programs, focusing on those in Germany and Britain. Unemployment insurance had been a concern of the president since his tenure at Commerce, but there was no political consensus on a specific program, and it was shoved aside by the logjam of legislation during the Seventy-Second Congress. Hoover would have liked to implement such a program during a second term. He did not believe a plan could be enacted and undertaken in time to make an immediate impact. Meanwhile, Secretary of Labor Doak continued his efforts to find employment for jobless workers using his department's employment services. On December 17, 1931, he reported that the Labor Department had placed 800,000 individuals in jobs over the preceding six months. An additional 600,000 had obtained jobs with the assistance of state offices. Doak sought congressional funding for an additional 54 offices at the state and local levels. In contrast to later administrations, the Hoover administration devoted far greater efforts to job creation and placement in the private sector.[30]

In February 1931 the president signed the Wagner-Graham Stabilization Act to plan public works that could be implemented during economic declines. The law created a permanent Federal Stabilization Board. This was a long-range reform designed to nip economic downturns before they became full-fledged depressions. Meanwhile, the pace of countercyclical spending accelerated in fiscal 1931. The federal government spent a record of $780,357, 620 for construction and other types of public projects designed to provide work relief. This was approximately $520,733,000 more than was spent in fiscal year 1928. On January 2, 1932, the president toured the new Commerce Building in Washington, considered the largest office building of its time, covering three city blocks and housing 3,000 workers. In conformity with the classical style Hoover replicated in Washington, it was only seven stories tall. During his tenure as commerce secretary, the department's facilities had been scattered in buildings throughout Washington, many of them rented. Hoover had long envisioned a new structure to centralize the varied activities of the department he had consolidated. Following the adjournment of the Seventy-Second Congress during July of 1932, President Hoover funneled newly available money and credit to job-creating projects rapidly. In addition, he accelerated construction already authorized or under way. The chief executive asked the speaker of the House to ensure that all purchases by the federal government be restricted to goods produced in the United States unless it made them prohibitively expensive.[31]

In fiscal 1932 the federal government spent about $750 million on work relief. It was estimated that from the beginning of the Depression until July 1933 the government provided $2.3 billion to create jobs, twice the normal amount of construction. In addition, state and local governments spent $1.5 billion on public works beyond their normal appropriations over the same span. Among the largest categories of work relief during the final year of the Hoover administration were river and harbor projects, flood control, army housing, naval yards and docks, continuation of the Hoover Dam, and hospitals for veterans. In 1932 large post offices were under way in New York, Boston, Philadelphia, Cleveland, Cincinnati, Chicago, Kansas City, Atlanta, Albany, and in other cities. During the previous 10 months, 105 federal buildings had been completed at a cost of $31 million. Many more were in the pipeline at the end of Hoover's term. Some 130 projects, expected to cost $125 million, were under contract. Plans provided for an additional 150 public buildings costing $75 million, ready for contract. The status of the public building program authorized prior to the Emergency Relief and Construction Act was 98 percent complete, under contract, or up for bids. There were more than 390 buildings then under construction. Under the emergency building program authorized by the Seventy-Second Congress in July 1932, the Treasury had let contracts to construct an additional 400 buildings. Some of these buildings would take three years to complete and are usually attributed to the New Deal.[32]

Hoover had opened the spigots on federal spending. Federal expenditures rose from $3.3 billion in fiscal 1929 to $4.6 billion in fiscal 1932 and 1933, an increase of 40 percent. Meanwhile, federal revenue declined by about one-half, to less than $2 billion. Hoover was so concerned about the Depression, particularly unemployment, that he was willing to incur a budget deficit amounting to about 60 percent of the budget, the largest peacetime deficit in American history. His spending for public works was greater than the sum spent for such projects during the entire previous 30 years. Since 1900, only $250 million had been spent on public buildings. The Iowan built more than 800 major buildings at a cost of over $700 million. Many of the projects began under Hoover were completed under the New Deal, a substantial number financed by loans from the RFC. The 16,000 miles of federally funded highways built in 1932 were more than double the amount built in 1929. During Hoover's four years, 37,000 miles of federal highways were built. More important than the bricks, mortar, and paved highways were the jobs created. At the outset of the Depression in 1929 some 180,000 Americans were employed on federal public works. This rose to 430,000 by August, 1930, to 760,000 by August 1931, and to at least 860,000 by the end of his term. The vast majority of the projects were eminently useful, consummated without waste or corruption, and awarded on the basis of need and merit, and many remain in use, serving Americans in the twenty-first century.[33]

Although Hoover spent billions of dollars on public works, he did not believe that construction alone could lift the nation out of the Depression. Once the spending stopped, the jobs ended, and the gales of unemployment resumed in full fury. The kind of dependency Hoover meant was not simply the dependence of a single individual on a single job. He also meant the dependency of entire industries, cities, and regions on government contracts.

The best example, which proved Hoover prophetic, was the later growth of the military-industrial complex, which made certain manufacturers and regions almost entirely dependent on military orders. Their congressmen fight over the awarding of contracts and the location of bases. Over the long run, a government-driven economy has the insidious effect of discouraging private investment and increasing interest rates, which dries up private credit. It pits regions and companies against one another in a contest decided, not entirely by merit, but by political influence. Government borrowing competes with the raising of private capital while taxation simultaneously drains the private sector. The use of government jobs or contracts as a form of political patronage disturbed Hoover because he considered it a form of buying votes. Another type of dependency was bureaucratic inertia. Once in the budget, it was difficult to extracts items whose original purpose had vanished. The president also believed that unlimited spending dug the government so deeply into debt that it mortgaged future generations who must pay for the spending by severe cutbacks or tax increases, perhaps planting the seeds for later recessions and a reduction in the standard of living when the time came to pay the debts incurred. Even if the government could spend its way out of one depression, limited in duration, Hoover was certain that it could not spend its way out of every downturn or any prolonged one. He believed history substantiated these beliefs. He also believed that the government should not promise more than it could deliver, lest it sow disillusionment against the government itself and promote cynicism among its citizens.

Additionally, government construction helped only a limited number of workers in only certain types of occupations, and was not spread evenly. Projects took time to plan, to let bids and to formalize contracts, to purchase materials, and to initiate work. They did not immediately jump-start the economy as the often-used metaphor implies, because, after all, the economy is only metaphorically, not literally, an engine. Further, many of the bills proposed in Congress would locate large projects in lightly populated areas of low unemployment. The president believed in bringing jobs to people, not in transplanting families or entire communities to work in unfamiliar regions, only to face the prospect of moving elsewhere when the project petered out. By late 1932, Hoover believed that most useful construction projects that were cost efficient and that could provide significant employment had been exhausted. He did not believe the government should become a perpetual motion machine spewing out endless jobs and borrowing endless sums. Moreover, although jobs were essential to recovery, they were not the only essential component. Credit had to be liquid, banks willing to lend, and businesses willing to borrow. Consumers had to be willing to buy. Americans and foreign nations had to have faith in the solvency of the government. Businessmen had to be confident they could earn a profit and not live in fear of losing everything. In 1932 most people with money to invest were seeking ways to preserve it, not to earn additional profits, which stymied a comeback by the economy.

Service on interest on the national debt was already a major item in the budget and consumed money that could be available for more useful purposes. The underlying factor of fear could not be overcome by temporary jobs, because this did not provide the security that made families feel it was safe to spend money and cease hoarding it. Although Hoover was hardly a silver-tongued orator, oratory alone could not persuade Americans that it was safe to resume their normal lifestyles. The turbulence abroad meant that Americans lived in an uncertain nation within a chaotic global economy, which was becoming increasingly unstable politically.

Simplistic solutions might tantalize, but they were will o' wisps that led to oppression. Even if tyranny would have purchased prosperity, Hoover would not have bought it. He agreed that excessive power in an individual, in the government, or in one branch of government did indeed corrupt. Social stability was necessary for recovery. Hoover distinguished between means and ends and rejected any cure worse than the disease. If men ate every day, as Harry Hopkins told a congressman sarcastically, nations as a whole must take a longer view. In his entire life President Hoover had never stood idly by during any emergency. Yet he was, by temperament and in principle, moderate and level headed. Sometimes his predictions of dire consequences were delayed, but seldom entirely wrong. The president realized that if spending money alone could end a depression, it would have already been over by 1932.[34]

Furnishing jobs in the public sector was only one part of the equation, and in the long run, not the most important one. If creation of private jobs was to be rejuvenated, this would require a reliable flow of credit to sustain existing businesses and begin new ones. In early September, 1931, when he learned that Britain planned to abandon the gold standard, the president realized that European conditions would aggravate the credit freeze. The chief executive, as usual, began with a voluntary, private plan to ameliorate the lending crisis, his last major experiment in voluntarism. Hoover hoped a pool of private bankers might resolve the credit problem temporarily, and Congress was not in session. On September 8, 1931, he summoned Eugene Meyer, the governor of the Fed, to the White House for a consultation. The president proposed a pool of $500 million to be set aside by wealthy bankers, especially the big New York banks, to lend money to weaker banks, which held collateral that had declined in value. Meyer agreed to present the president's idea to the bankers. As he expected, they were leery. They did not oppose the expansion of credit but preferred not to risk their own money. The bankers deliberated over the proposition and agreed to meet with Hoover to discuss the idea in Washington on October 4. To avoid detection, they assembled as Secretary Mellon's opulent apartment rather than at the White House. Advising them that his backup strategy was to submit legislation calling for a revived institution modeled on the World War I War Finance Corporation (WFC), he persuaded most. The next step was to approach the politicians. Hoover telephoned or telegraphed congressional leaders of both parties and asked them to assemble secretly at the White House, providing private airplanes to those who needed them. On October 7, the chief executive explained his plan to stabilize banking in the Lincoln Room, with shutters closed. There was general assent to the idea, especially with the caveat that the government assume responsibility if necessary, yet there were some dissenters. The consensus, however, was that it represented a step in the right direction. Even before the plan was publicly announced, rumors of it inspired a surge in stocks and bonds on Wall Street. The fleshed-out proposal was generally praised by the press, including the Democratic *New York Times*. The stock surge slackened within a week, but it had helped put wheels under the new vehicle.[35]

Hoover's attempt to utilize the assets of the larger banks to alleviate the credit crisis made common sense, because they possessed an excess of deposits beyond their needs, in the absence of borrowers. Moreover, Hoover hoped the infusion of liquidity into weak banks would break the logjam of fear that paralyzed commerce. If business picked up, this would aid the stronger banks as well as the weaker ones. It literally did not pay to be selfish. Further, the banks contributing to the pool would be protected. No loans would be made without adequate collateral. To dissuade shaky banks from seeking loans, interest rates were set sufficiently high that only reasonably sound banks could afford them. The system was designed to protect only banks with a realistic chance of survival. The National Credit Corporation (NCC) had a small office in New York with a clerical staff for processing loans. Subdivisions were set up in each of the 12 Federal Reserve districts. Below this, committees at the local level determined the viability of loans. Banks could join the system by subscribing 2 percent of their capital. Loans approved on the local and regional level were taken from the national pool, and loans were repaid to the national office. The NCC lifted spirits temporarily.[36]

On November 9, 1931, the NCC made its first loans, about $2 million, to a group of Illinois banks. Applications from other banks had been approved and were on their way to the national board. Even before loans began flowing in significant numbers, during the first half of November, bank failures plummeted. However, it soon became obvious that bankers were not their brothers' keepers. Perhaps inspired by overconfidence because of the improving economy, the NCC directors tightened the noose on loans and became miserly. Their own liquidity remained their chief priority. The NCC accepted U.S. government securities at only 75 percent of market value and stated that it would make loans at only 40 percent of the market value of other types of collateral. It would not accept real estate or agricultural paper as collateral at all. By November 30, the economy, which had been improving earlier in the month, stood dead in the water. Hoarding resumed, bank failures rose, and industrial stocks fell by 20 percent. The economy lost all the ground that had been regained after the default of the Bank of England. December 1931, opened with a surge in bank failures. Hoover and Congress were frustrated by the pokey distribution of NCC loans. To the bankers who had placed their funds in the pool, a friend in need seemed a pest. It became evident that the bankers' pool provided no permanent solution. President Hoover's made his request for legislation creating a Reconstruction Finance Corporation (RFC) modeled on the WFC the first priority in his initial message to the Seventy-Second Congress, which enacted it with dispatch.[37]

Despite later criticism, the NCC provided a bridge to the RFC while the latter was pending in Congress and, after its creation, while the RFC geared up. In some two months the NCC prevented the failure of several important banks. Hoover of course had hoped for more and felt the big bankers had evinced a selfish streak. Realistically, the weak banks needed new capital not simply loans, yet it would have been politically and practically impossible simply to give them government money. Perhaps a more apt criticism is that the $500 million pool was too small, and its caretakers were minimalists. At best, it was a small solution to a big problem. The NCC also addressed only one segment of the beleaguered financial community. It was empowered to loan money only to commercial banks, yet life insurance companies, credit unions, savings banks, and building and loan associations also were failing. Its successor, the RFC, would become far more than a bankers' bank. By July 1932, with passage of the Emergency Relief and Construction Act, it had become the centerpiece of the recovery effort. That in the long run neither the NCC nor the expansive and more enduring RFC actually ended the Depression does not mean they were bad ideas. The greater problem was not a purely financial one. It was that in the process of losing their livelihoods, many Americans had also become fear mongers. Neither Hoover's innovative ideas nor FDR's rich eloquence could redeem them until they redeemed themselves.[38]

The president was empowered to appoint the board. Eugene Meyer, governor of the Federal Reserve System; Ogden Mills, the treasury secretary; and Paul Bestor, the head of the Federal Farm Board, were ex officio members. Hoover made Meyer chairman of the board and former Vice President Charles G. Dawes president of the corporation. Other directors were chosen partly on a regional basis.[39] The corporation followed Hoover's preference for decentralization. It established 17 regional agencies, each supported by an advisory committee of local representatives, which approved loan applications and forwarded them to the national headquarters in New York. Loans were repaid at the national level. Some of the RFC administrative responsibilities were handled by existing government agencies. The Interstate Commerce Commission reviewed loan applications from railroads while the Federal Reserve banks served as the fiscal agents for the RFC. Thirty local offices were established in the various regions, and a staff of 600 was soon working at the national headquarters. Within two weeks the RFC was extending more than 100 loans daily. Initially most loans were due in six months, and interest was higher than loans obtained from private banks to avoid competing with them. The board insisted on prompt repayment to keep the reservoir fluid for future loans. Managed properly, the RFC could operate indefinitely on its existing capital.[40]

During the first month of its operations, the RFC seemed to be contributing substantially to preventing further decline. Applications were accepted from thousands of banks. In February the RFC helped save the Bank of America in California with a $15 million loan. Two weeks later a $7 million loan rescued the East Tennessee National Bank in Knoxville. Both major loans helped stave off regional crises. Closings declined from 66 in the first week of February to 8 during the final week. In March only 45 banks failed compared to 334 in January and 125 in February. By March 31, the RFC had extended loans to 7,411 institutions totaling $1.78 billion. Banks and trust companies borrowed $1.055 billion while railroads received $331 million. Most loans were to small banks, usually in rural areas, although the size of loans to larger banks was greater.[41]

Only a few weeks after the RFC opened for business, Meyer's wife visited the president to warn him that her husband was on the verge of a nervous breakdown, suffering from exhaustion. Besieged by job seekers, he had sleepless nights. They agreed that the chairman would continue temporarily. Hoover was becoming disenchanted with Meyer, however, and with the timidity of the board in general in extending loans. He wanted a more proactive, bolder board. Meyer refused to loosen the purse strings. There were both personal and policy issues between the men, and neither seemed inclined to bend.[42]

By early June the RFC had loaned money to some 4,000 banks, agricultural credit corporations, and insurance companies. Bank failures, which had averaged nearly 100 a week when the corporation began, had declined to about the rate during normal times. More than 250 building and loan associations had borrowed from the corporation, which enabled them to make routine payments to depositors and also to loan money to additional applicants. In agriculture, the corporation had underwritten $68 million in debentures for the Federal Intermediate Credit Banks, which went directly to farmers for production and marketing. Beyond this, loans had been made directly to farmers for seeds through the Department of Agriculture. These amounted to $75 million to 450,000 farmers. Finally, the $170 million lent to railroads increased employment by continuing construction work. By preventing railroads from falling into receivership, it secured the railroad bonds held as securities by banks and insurance companies. After April, the corporation experienced a steady decline in applications from banks, dropping from 1,269 in that month to 899 in August, indicating that banking conditions were stabilizing. The RFC had achieved its first priority of stopping the hemorrhaging of the banking system. Still, although credit was now available, few businessmen or consumers used it sufficiently to restart the economy. Many bankers used RFC loans not to offer new loans but for the safer purposes of extending old loans or purchasing government securities. Thus the arrest of failures in banking did not lead to a revitalization of business. Although the stock market moved upward during the summer, progress in alleviating unemployment was discouraging. As the calendar crept toward the 1932 election, the public was becoming increasingly critical of Hoover.[43]

The president's relations with Meyer continued to wither. Frustrated by what he considered Meyer's overly conservative policies, and even more frustrated by the failure of the economy to grow, Hoover came to believe that a change in leadership might be necessary. On June 3, Hoover invited the board of directors of the RFC to Camp Rapidan to prod them to act more aggressively. The conference did not go as the president had hoped. He and Meyer quarreled. "Meyer was the malcontent," Joslin recorded. "He came as near to an open break as possible."[44] Meanwhile, Dawes was increasingly alarmed about his personal finances and the condition of his Chicago bank. In May, he had wanted to resign, but Hoover had persuaded him to continue. Early in June Dawes informed the president that he could not delay his resignation much longer. Joslin knew there were strong differences between Dawes and Meyer and that speculation attributing the general's resignation to those differences might cripple the effectiveness of the RFC. On June 6, Dawes submitted his resignation, which the president accepted reluctantly. With the imminent departure of Meyer, Dawes' resignation left a power vacuum at the top of the RFC.[45]

Dawes viewed his task as the reorganization of the Central Republic Bank and Trust Company of Chicago. He had not been an officer of the bank for many years, but Dawes had founded it, and he was its organizational genius. The general was reluctant to apply for an RFC loan because of his past association, but Hoover considered it essential. Another Chicago banker warned the president that if Central Republic failed the entire Chicago banking structure might collapse, and if the Chicago financial markets were disrupted, a national collapse was imminent. "Hoover faced a manifestly simple choice," James Olson writes, "either save the Central Republic Bank or preside over the destruction of the United States banking system." The bank had 122,000 depositors and was closely affiliated with 755 other banks with 6,500,000 depositors in 15 states. The RFC offered a $90 million loan on June 27. As collateral it took every asset of the Central Republic Bank and Trust Company. In the long run, Central Republic failed, but the breathing space provided by the loan avoided the triggering of a series of failures. The crisis in the Midwest subsided, and failures declined in August. Subsequently, Hoover and Dawes were vilified for engineering an "inside job" in which the ex-vice president had applied political pressure to save a bank in which he had a major interest.[46]

The loan to the Chicago Central, coupled with a loan to the struggling Missouri-Pacific railroad, inspired a firestorm of criticism aimed at the administration by Progressives and liberals. Some of the Progressives who were facing reelection campaigns in 1932 wanted to distance themselves from the president. They claimed the RFC and the administration doled out money to rich bankers while neglecting the indigent. Some Progressives considered bankers evil people who should be punished, not helped. The president countered that when a major railroad went bankrupt, thousands of workers lost their jobs, and when a major bank failed, tens of thousands of depositors lost their life savings. Some Progressives seemed to misunderstand how banks and the stock market operated, considering them parasites on society. Democrats, for all the protestations in behalf of the poor, did not want to see the Depression end on Hoover's watch. Even bankers themselves criticized the administration. While liberals and Progressives attacked the RFC for giving handouts to large banks, conservative bankers attacked the corporation for its caution; the RFC, they complained, was stingy to bankers. Interest rates were too high, and collateral requirements were too steep. Hoover and the RFC directors could not satisfy everyone, especially because portions of their constituency demanded diametrically opposite policies. Indeed, the RFC, which in fact worked reasonably well, points out the difficulty of finding a way to run a smoothly operating government bureaucracy, buffeted by political demands, during an emergency. "No other president of the twentieth century has understood and feared the potential of the bureaucracy state as much as Hoover," Olson writes.[47]

By early July the RFC board had been thoroughly reshuffled. The Emergency Relief and Construction Act of July 22 added so much to the board's workloads that the law provided for the replacement of ex officio members with full-time members. Charles A. Miller, a Republican banker, replaced Dawes as president. Finding a successor to Meyer was more difficult. Hoover offered the chairmanship to four men, including Newton D. Baker and Owen D. Young, before ex-Senator Atlee Pomerene, a Democrat from Ohio, accepted. Pomerene served ably in an interim capacity, yet the Democrats in the Senate, in an act of vindictiveness, refused to confirm him. Four Democrats now sat on the board. In August, with the new law in place giving the RFC added responsibilities, the corporation reorganized. A Self-Liquidating Division supervised public works. There was also an Emergency Relief Division and an Agricultural Credits Division.[48]

The Self-Liquidating Division took time to gain momentum because projects had to be approved and planned before contracts were issued. Yet it began construction of important public works. The most important was the Bay Bridge from Oakland to San Francisco, for which the division lent $62 million. The RFC also provided funding for the waterworks system in Pasadena and an aqueduct to carry water from the Colorado River to Los Angeles. Other self-liquidating programs approved included a bridge over the Mississippi River at New Orleans and sewage systems and waterworks systems throughout the South, West, and Midwest. The division set precedents by authorizing slum clearance and the construction of low-income housing financed by federal loans. In efforts to infuse money into the economy more rapidly, the division reduced its interest rate and stretched loan repayments over 25 years. Many of the projects, massive and employing tens of thousands, were not completed during Hoover's administration. In October 1932, the division began to focus on small projects that could put men to work immediately. The Emergency Relief Division had only $300 million to distribute among 48 states that varied in population and need. In order to maximize the money available, the RFC gave preference to states that had exhausted their own resources. The division also attempted to avoid dependence on federal money to an extent that might discourage donations to private charities. It also did not want its loans to be used as a crutch in place of state efforts. One of the first states to receive money was Louisiana, which obtained a $1 million loan to combat floods and droughts. Ohio and Michigan were other early recipients. Gifford Pinchot, the opinionated Progressive Republican governor of Pennsylvania, who had clashed with Hoover previously, demanded $45 million out of the $300 million total for his state alone. The board considered the amount excessive and noted that Pennsylvania, a relatively rich state, had not tapped its own resources sufficiently to receive almost one-sixth of the national total. The board authorized $2.5 million, with more to come later. Pinchot, incensed, wrote Pomerene that "in giving help to the great banks, great railroads, and great corporations you have shown no such niggardly spirit . . . Our people have little patience with giving everything possible to the big fellow and as little as possible to the little fellow." Ultimately, despite Pinchot's outburst, Pennsylvania received the second largest loan in the nation, behind Illinois. The four other largest allotments went to Michigan, New York, Ohio, and Wisconsin.[49]

In the short run, the board was optimistic about the contribution of the RFC. Hoover hoped the appointment of Pomerene and the new Democratic majority would mute congressional criticism. Meanwhile, the economy improved during the summer of 1932, and the RFC became more efficient in processing applications and distributing loans. Bank failures declined from 151 in June to 67 in September. Deposits in Federal Reserve banks increased, and money emerged from hoarding. Applications by banks for RFC loans declined, a sign that they were unnecessary. Securities, railroad stocks, and utility bonds increased in value. In October, for the first time, repayments of RFC loans exceeded new loans. The banking and railroad crisis had stabilized. Still, stronger banks did not lead to industrial recovery because banks were sitting on deposits, even with conditions improving. Industrial prosperity did not return, and employment remained bleak. Hoover's hopes that the tide had been turned against the Depression during the summer of 1932 were crushed in the fall. A crisis in Idaho during the fall was followed by another in Nevada during November, where the governor responded by declaring a bank holiday. Midwestern banking began to tumble into turmoil. From the rural banks the crisis spread to the larger city banks. From October through November, during the peak of the presidential campaign, failures and applications for RFC loans multiplied. Withdrawals from banks resumed. During the last quarter of 1932 the banking system was drained of $300 million in deposits. However, the downturn happened in spite of the RFC, not because of it. The RFC saved many banks that otherwise would have failed. It had been designed as a cushion and a confidence builder and could not literally save every bank. Moreover, its responsibilities now extended well beyond banking to stimulating construction, providing employment, and aiding farmers. It was no longer one-dimensional. Under no circumstances, even after the dawn of the second millennium, can the nation's banks survive a simultaneous nationwide withdrawal of their deposits, whether FDIC-insured or not. The odds against halting a panic by purely economic measures are about as long as exhorting lemmings not to follow their leader over cliffs and plunge to their deaths. Neither lemmings nor human beings are entirely intellectual creatures.[50]

There is another factor in the roiling bank failures that gained momentum beginning in late summer that drives home the point that the absence of reason, not reason, often explains the course of human events. In late August, with Congress adjourned, Garner instructed the clerk of the House of Representatives to publish RFC loans, violating his agreement that the loans would not be publicized and that no action to publish them would be taken without a congressional resolution. Congress was out of session, and a resolution, which probably would not have passed, was impossible until the lame duck session convened in December, after the elections. Garner, now the Democratic vice presidential nominee, ordered the release of the loan recipients in full knowledge that this would start panicked withdrawals from those banks. Depositors would consider the loans a sign of weakness. There was nothing to be gained economically from the release of the figures, which were already available to members of Congress. Yet Garner believed that if a bank panic occurred on Hoover's watch, it would hurt the GOP at the polls in November. Thus Garner deliberately contributed to a nationwide bank panic to enhance his own political ambitions and improve the chances of his party. In a political sense, the strategy worked. In an economic sense, it was catastrophic. The panic swelled and crested with full force during the interregnum after Hoover's defeat.[51]

The Seventy-Second Congress squeezed in one last piece of remedial legislation, passing the Federal Home Loan Bank Bill on July 22. On August 6, 1932, Hoover appointed five members of the Home Loan Bank Board, chaired by Republican Franklin W. Fort, ex-representative from New Jersey. The purpose of the agency was to stimulate new loans for home construction and liquefy mortgages held as collateral by building and loan associations, insurance companies, and savings and loan associations. These institutions could borrow on the basis of their depressed mortgages for more than their current market value, repaying the loan when the mortgage value appreciated. By liquefying the mortgage assets held as collateral, the system freed up credit and made funds available for new loans or for refinancing. The Home

Loan Banks also helped protect the millions of shareholders who owned stock in home-financing institutions. Hoover hoped that stimulating home construction would increase employment. The system was authorized to furnish a maximum of $125 million. The new system filled a gap left by the RFC, which could make only short-term loans, not those of long duration, such as home mortgages. Even before offering their first loans, the Home Loan Banks made a major contribution by declaring a moratorium on mortgage foreclosures held by all closed banks. By the beginning of 1934 approximately 2,000 financial institutions, representing 19 percent of all U.S. building and loan associations with 34 percent of total assets, had joined the system. The Home Loan Banks had authorized more than 2,000 loans valued at more than $107 million, and approximately $94 million had actually been dispersed. The system did not become fully operative until October, late in Hoover's administration, too late to make a major impact either economically or politically during his term, yet it represented a sound idea and established a precedent for government involvement in home financing. The delay in enactment demonstrates that even during the worst economic crisis in the nation's history, evening scores remained the top priority for some.[52]

By the fall of 1932 Hoover's full recovery program was not only in place but operational. His remedies focused on increasing the flow of credit, mitigating unemployment through reproductive public works, increasing construction in the private sector, especially housing, and aiding farmers by a variety of actions that included loans, cooperative marketing, and encouraging exports and crop diversification. There was not sufficient time remaining during his term to determine the ultimate effectiveness of these programs. Hoover demonstrated, however, an enormous fertility of ideas, a sound grasp not simply of theoretical economics but of the way humans behave. He believed he could have made significant progress toward ending the Depression during a second term, but he never believed that he alone, or the government alone, could end it. That would require the return to a mentality of confidence that it was safe to invest, to borrow, and to consume. The president could encourage this, but he could not mandate it. Many of the programs of his successor, borrowed from Hoover and implemented on an enormously larger scale, had only a marginal effect on ending the Depression. Roosevelt, unlike Hoover, believed that the government alone could achieve recovery, but over FDR's three peacetime terms it did not recover, perhaps never could. A few presidents have achieved more complete domestic programs, but few have done so under such trying circumstances and a divided Congress during a single term.

CHAPTER 12

Frustrated Farmers, Angry Veterans

President Hoover devoted more time to farming than to any single issue. He considered family farming more than an occupation; it was a way of life, the crucible of American democracy. The Iowa boy had grown up on farms and in farm communities and had worked with his hands. He understood farm economics and had dealt with the problem of farm debt and low prices as commerce secretary. In fact, he had been Coolidge's closest adviser on agriculture, and Coolidge offered him the position of agriculture secretary. Hoover entered office with a well-defined program for the farm economy, which might have worked under ordinary circumstances. The Depression was a double whammy for farmers already plagued by low prices. They suffered from high fixed costs, especially in transportation; ruthless competition at home and abroad; and ruthless competition among themselves. Most farmers loved what they did but not what they earned. Their hard work was under-rewarded, and they looked to the government to rescue them. Ironically, the better they became at what they did, the worse they fared economically. As the trajectory of production went up, the trajectory of prices went down. Too much success meant failure. They were locked in mortal combat with the law of supply and demand. Hoover devised an imaginative, multifaceted solution. Many farm state politicians blamed the chief executive for depressed prices.

The problem with agriculture was that there were too many farmers who produced too much, victims of bounty. Farming showcased the paradox of the American landscape, the beauty of waving fields of golden wheat and the destitution of the men who grew it. If the problem of overproduction seemed simple, in fact it was not. The nation lacked the political will and perhaps the constitutional authority to impose production controls. Farmers themselves did not want to limit production and neither did farm-state senators and representatives. No bill not supported by the farm states had any chance of clearing Congress. Neither was there any practical means of enforcement short of an army of inspectors or aerial photographs, the present means of enforcement, impractical with the technology of the 1930s. Voluntary controls were unenforceable. If one farmer planted less, other farmers might take advantage and plant more. But there was more to the farm dilemma than simply too much of a good thing. The interest of farmers who mainly grew corn was not identical to that of farmers who fed corn to hogs. It is one thing to control the number of Fords rattling off the assembly line. It is quite another to control the number of piglets a single sow will bear in the spring, much less millions of sows. Farmers differ from industrial workers in another important way. They are not paid wages weekly or monthly. Farmers have to borrow at planting time and are not paid until harvest. If the harvest is meager or the prices low, they become mired in debt. Meanwhile, their fixed costs increased while they paid interest on loans. It must have seemed that all the stars were aligned against them.

Potential excess capacity is not necessarily a vice. It was providential during World War I and World War II. Yet it is difficult to time spring planting with the outbreak of wars. Droughts, floods, insects, and foreign nations do not always cooperate. The idea that hard work reaps economic rewards is no more an iron law than is the inevitability that crops planted in the fall will blossom in the spring. Dumping abroad, on a saturated world market protected by tariffs and antidumping laws, was not realistic. Throughout the Depression, world prices remained well below American prices. Exports could only be traded at prices American farmers would not accept. Hoover's approach was sophisticated but fallible, and it was the only game in town during his administration. If his creation, the Farm Board had flaws, the other ideas had greater flaws. None of them was new, and none of them could pass congressional or constitutional muster. The simplest and most heartless solution would be to permit the extinction of small family farms and encourage their consolidation into agribusiness comparable to Andrew Carnegie's steel empire in order to apply economies of scale. This was not only cruel; it was unrealistic politically. Besides, if farmers left farms, where would they go? Conditions were worse in the cities. Farmers could grow some of what they ate and wore. In fact, a reverse migration from city to farm was under way.

There is another element to farming that is largely psychological but quite real. Not all farmers, farm solely for money. The roots of farming strike emotional chords and are embedded in American history, and many farmers have attachments to the soil. There is the irony in many farm communities that even when times are hard, life is good. For some, including my own grandparents and my father's generation, who grew up in Louisiana, it was all they had ever done and all they wanted to do. Many people yearn to be among grass, trees, ponds, and animals. Farming involves its own type of creativity, the opportunity to be outdoors, and provides the therapy of physical exercise. There have always been more people who want to live on the land than can make a good living farming, an attitude not confined to America. If this is romantic, there is a romantic element in the human condition. There is not much money in writing poetry either, yet there are people who want to do it. Urbanization only increases the desire to escape to a pastoral setting. Farming is grinding work that requires patience, like writing history books, but both have their rewards.

Hoover had the grit and foresight to understand that it was unrealistic to believe that any single panacea, however well intentioned, could solve the farm problem. His approach included protective tariffs; reduced railroad rates for transporting farm products; development of inland waterways as a cheap method of transportation to complement railroads (and compete with them, bringing down prices); cooperative marketing to ration selling when markets were glutted; and production controls probably voluntary out of necessity. He hoped construction of the St. Lawrence Seaway, which he negotiated with Canada, could provide and outlet to the Atlantic for Midwestern agriculture. Hoover's program involved the reorganization of farming into larger units, not by eliminating the family farm, but by integrating thousands of individual farms into cooperatives, which could market and buy in unison. There would be warehouses to store nonperishable crops when the market was glutted and release them gradually to ensure better profits. These cooperatives would receive government loans but would be owned and operated by farmers themselves. The president realized that to prosper farmers would have to adopt the methods of business, but he also believed farming was a different type of business. "The farm is more than a business," he said, "It is a state of living." The Iowa native was Jeffersonian in his view of family farms. Like Frederick Jackson Turner, one of his contemporaries who shared many of his beliefs, the president believed that the American character had been shaped by its agrarian roots. If farmers were to prosper, they would have to change, but the family farm should be retained, not simply for sentimental value, but because of the restorative qualities of the outdoors and the cohesiveness of the rural community. Hoover was a conservationist in more than the sense of preserving natural and human resources; he believed in the preservation of ways of life that had an intrinsic value, from Native Americans to American farmers.[1]

The farm problem was nothing new and neither was a sense of collective identity. Farmers did not believe that urban people, including politicians, understood them or cared about them, and to some degree they were right. They had been coalescing and complaining at least since the 1890s, when their most famous spokesman, William Jennings Bryan, had helped them forge an identity as an interest group. Bryan was popular enough to get nominated for president three times but not sufficiently popular to get elected, in part because his constituency was concentrated in lightly populated states. Yet the farm crisis faced by Hoover dated more specifically to the First World War. As food administrator, Hoover had persuaded consumers that it was patriotic to conserve food and told farmers that it was their duty to produce as much as possible, employing the slogan, "Food will win the War," which in part it did. America fed not only its allies but neutrals, and after the war, it fed its enemies as well as the vast Soviet Union during the famine reaped by the Russian Civil War. Farmers prospered. Many borrowed money, expanded their acreage, and cultivated land that was submarginal under ordinary circumstances, fueled by the temporary euphoria of fat checks and the illusion the demand was insatiable. Yet after the war, Europeans, eventually even the Russians, revived their own agriculture and wanted to become self-supporting. American farmers were stuck with an instant surplus, low prices, and large debts. They did not share the prosperity of the 1920s. A psychology had infected the farm economy that the more they produced, the more they could earn. But unlimited production would yield profits only so long as there was unlimited demand. This was essentially the same problem that had occurred during the 1890s. The law of supply and demand had no statute of limitations. Farmers never recovered from the deflation of 1920, which compounded their indebtedness. They were caught in an iron vise that made them victims of their own success. They also competed in a world market with cheaper foreign labor and sometimes newly broken virgin soils. They were successful as producers but failed at business. No one, most conspicuously farmers themselves, wanted to bell the cat of overproduction. They would have liked government subsidies, and farm-state politicians devised a number of plans, but all of them would only have aggravated overproduction. Hoover's broad approach, while practical, had less political appeal than a simple panacea. There was more aggravation. Use of gasoline-powered machines was expensive and reduced the demand for livestock fodder. Synthetic fabrics competed with cotton and shorter skirts made the South's major staple less fashionable. Diet changes diminished demand for cereals. In addition, new regions such as Argentina, Australia, and New Zealand, provided formidable competition. In a further irony, the U.S. Agricultural Extension Service employed some 5,700 county agents who devoted more than 90 percent of their time to increasing production.[2]

The Depression made a bad situation intolerably worse. Gross farm income fell from $12 billion in 1929 to $5.3 billion in 1932. Farm income nose-dived 20 percent in 1930 and 30 percent the following year. From 1929 to 1932 the prices of crops and livestock declined by almost 75 percent. During the same period farm purchasing power fell by 40 percent and per capita annual income dropped from $602 to $145. All this happened despite the exertions of the Hoover administration to introduce stability and a ray of hope to farm conditions.[3]

The story of agricultural policy during the Hoover administration is largely the story of the Federal Farm Board, created by the Agricultural Marketing Act enacted during the special session of the Seventy-First Congress, which met before the stock market crash. It was a fulfillment of Hoover's 1928 campaign promise to make agriculture his first priority. The premise of the board was that federally sponsored farm cooperatives, each representing a specific commodity, could bring greater efficiency to the business of farming. In 1929 there were approximately two million farmers (about one-third of the total number) who belonged to some 12,500 cooperative associations. The board hoped to induce more farmers to join the cooperative movement in order to increase their leverage in selling and by purchasing supplies in bulk. The cooperatives began at the grass roots. Local associations purchased stocks in regional organizations, which in turn bought stock in the national cooperatives. The national organization made loans to constituent cooperatives; it did not lend money to individual farmers. The cooperatives were a pyramid with their base at the grass roots. The president believed the cooperatives could apply modern techniques of marketing and advertising to rationalize farming. The board had a revolving fund of $500 million that could be used for purposes such as storing crops while awaiting higher prices and selling harvested produce incrementally rather than thrusting them onto the market at peak season. Loans promoted foreign sales, and the government provided technical advice. The Farm Board was authorized to create stabilization corporations, which could purchase produce to sustain prices, but this was not their purpose. Before the Depression, Hoover did not anticipate that this provision would be used at all. In fact, he had not wanted it in the bill.[4]

Hoover selected the men he appointed to the Farm Board on the basis of their ability in marketing, not in farming. Although all eight had experience related to farming, most were executives skilled at selling farm products. Hoover hoped that these men could employ foresight and implement efficiencies such as spreading sales throughout the year in a manner that would raise farm income without increasing prices for consumers. Men sufficiently capable and experienced to serve had to be willing to sacrifice six-figure salaries in the private sector to work at meager salaries as a form of public service. The president appointed Alexander H. Legge of Chicago, the multimillionaire president of International Harvester to direct the Farm Board. The president named James C. Stone of Kentucky, president of the Burley Tobacco Growers' Association, and Vice President C. C. Teague of California, a leader in Citrus Cooperatives, represented the citrus industry. Other members included C. B. Denman, president of the National Live Stock Producers Association; Carl Williams of Oklahoma City, bank director and editor of the *Oklahoma Farmer-Stockman*; and former Nebraska Governor Samuel R. McKelvie, the editor of the *Nebraska Farmer*. Agriculture Secretary Arthur Hyde served as an ex officio member.[5]

Most farmers initially approved of the Farm Board and were willing to give it a chance. However, many wanted it to go further and guarantee that farming would become profitable. This went beyond the power of anyone. Farmers were tough, obstinate, and independent, hardened by a rugged life. Organizing them proved difficult. Some were suspicious of anyone who told them how to conduct their business and resisted change. The board tried to organize regional cooperatives that would not compete with one another, yet farmers were not accustomed to this type of regimentation. To succeed, farmers would have to display a degree of discipline they had never exhibited before. Moreover, Hoover's plan to organize farm cooperatives with government aid was opposed by middlemen such as brokers, because it inhibited their control of the market. The Farm Board was a bold experiment. Never before had the government invested so much energy, effort, and money to address the problems of a single occupation. The onset of the Depression shortly after the experiment began dealt a crushing, unanticipated blow.[6]

After the stock market crash, the prices of wheat and cotton, already abysmally low, plummeted so precipitously that the board felt compelled to intervene by purchasing these commodities to keep them off the market, a tactic called price stabilization. In February 1930, a Wheat Corporation and a Cotton Corporation were created to soak up some of the excess supply. The corporations intended to hold the surpluses until prices resumed normal levels and then sell them. The Wheat Corporation was by far the more important because cotton was chiefly confined to the South. The operations began in February and extended through July. The corporations bought wheat and cotton only from members of cooperatives, not from speculators, who had bet erroneously that prices would rise. The oversupply was so great that the demand for the government to buy was insatiable. In March, Congress appropriated additional money for stabilization, which quickly overshadowed cooperative marketing. The board, and most farmers, did not expect the Depression to last more than a year or two, and stabilization was considered a temporary expedient. By July, the warehouses and silos of the board were nearly full, with no end in sight, and the cost of storing the commodities was consuming a substantial portion of the board's budget. In mid-July, Legge announced the stabilization corporations would cease purchases. It was impractical to fight the law of supply and demand any longer, he explained. Yet in November, in order to prevent a panic, the board resumed buying wheat. The domestic crop in 1930 was estimated to be 840 million bushels, in addition to the 225 million bushels carried over. Meanwhile, the price of wheat continued to plunge, although it remained higher in America than abroad. Legge suggested that farmers feed wheat to livestock to save themselves purchases of fodder and to help eliminate the surplus. Farmers, who were radical in some respects but thoroughly traditional in others, did not take the idea seriously, although it had merit. Legge explained that one grown pig could eat as much ground wheat as a family of five. In Kansas, where farmers accepted his advice, some

27 million bushels of wheat were consumed by the animals. At that ratio, if other states followed, the surplus would disappear into the bellies of hogs.[7]

Some Americans thought they had better ideas. Requests poured in to sell or donate wheat to the "starving Chinese." Americans seemed to believe that everyone in China was starving and that American wheat would save them. A drive was initiated to collect one dollar from every American to buy wheat for the Chinese. Still another drive was launched urging every family to buy a barrel of flour for charity or for use at home. Still others suggested the president give raw wheat to the poor. They could be taught to boil it with water and eat it as mush. One of the strangest manifestations of the attempt to dispose of surplus wheat was the "eat more" movement of 1930. Some advocates urged that all Americans eat one more slice of bread each day to benefit farmers. Others argued that it was unpatriotic to diet. When a proponent of the movement asked Press Secretary George Akerson if the president supported these ideas, Akerson replied, "Frankly and confidentially, Perry, I am wondering if the heat has been too much for your folks out there."[8]

During the summer and fall of 1930, Legge and Hyde toured the wheat states and tried to persuade farmers to reduce planting. Otherwise, in 1931 the board would be overwhelmed by a deluge of new grain that would further depress prices. Legge emphasized that the Farm Board was approaching the limits of its capacity. Legge and Hyde argued that farmers would never achieve the status of other industries unless they cooperatively adjusted supply to demand. Legge said world markets did not offer a price level sufficiently high to remunerate farmers if they relied on exports. The two administration spokesmen proposed reductions of between 10 and 25 percent, phased in over several years. Hoover himself weighed in, coining the slogan, "Grow Less, Get More." The government had neither the legal authority to compel farmers to restrict acreage nor any method of policing it. Nonetheless, a poll by the *Kansas City Star*, a major daily in the leading wheat state, found 77 percent of farmers opposed. The administration spokesmen were shocked, not simply by the dimensions of the opposition, but by its intensity. They were accused of meddling, and farmers questioned their motives. Legge was dismayed by the harshness of the rebuff.[9]

Perhaps the most practical plan was devised by Agriculture Secretary Hyde, who proposed that the government lease marginal land and convert it to pasture or forest. Some could be purchased outright for recreational use. The withdrawal of such lands would align production closer to demand. When market demand increased, the acreage, now replenished by several years of rest, could be planted with crops. The idea was practical, flexible, and not excessively expensive. It was free of bureaucracy, inexpensive, and could be financed by an excise tax of 1 to 2 percent levied on food processors. Hyde also proposed the suspension of all federal programs that encouraged additional planting, such as irrigation and reclamation. The Farm Board implanted Hyde's plan on a trial basis in Kansas, the greatest producer of wheat. However, by the time the program was ready to begin, it was impossible to obtain appropriations from Congress. Once again, the problems of the administration's farm program lay as much in the political domain as in its policy. In government, good ideas do not travel far without money.[10]

In 1931 the winter wheat crop was larger than usual, and the prospects for another dismal year for farm prices appeared imminent. By June, the size of the looming surplus created a dilemma for the Farm Board because the existing surplus was costing $3 million a month to store. The spring wheat crop, however, was smaller than normal due to reduced planting, but the combination of winter and spring wheat was still above market demands. At the end of July wheat dropped to its lowest price ever recorded, 48 cents per bushel. The commodity market was staggered, and buyers of futures were ruined. However, by the fall, prices had increased due to conditions abroad. Argentina, Canada, and Australia harvested less, and much of the Russian crop was ruined because of bad weather. The cumulative effect was to raise world prices.[11]

The year 1931 also brought a bumper crop of cotton. Production in 1931 plus carryover was predicted to be about 24 million bales, out of which the world market could absorb no more than 13 million. This meant that by the end of picking in late October, the United States would have on hand a two-year supply of cotton. Hoover suggested that farmers plow under every second row before harvest, and the Farm Board modified this to recommend destroying every third row. The reaction among Southern governors was mostly negative. Even if desirable, there was no way to get farmers to do it, they said, nor could they guarantee equality of destruction. President Hoover then helped negotiate agreements to sell about one million bales of American cotton out of the current crop to Germany, France, and Poland on credit with adequate collateral. The cotton was not taken from the Farm Board surplus and was sold to overseas brokers, not to foreign governments. The only official federal involvement was that the Federal Reserve Board aided the financing.[12]

Legge announced in February 1931 that he intended to resign, and Hoover accepted his resignation on March 4, praising the Farm Board Chairman for his selfless service. He was succeeded by James Clifton Stone, the vice chairman, who announced that he would continue Legge's policies. The former chairman resumed the presidency of the International Harvester Company. For Legge, chairing the board had been a thankless task. His attempt to prop up farm prices had kept them higher than world prices, but most farmers were bitter and continued to blame the government. The effort to make farming profitable had been undermined by huge surpluses year after year at a time when the world market was depressed. There was no place for the surplus to go except into Farm Board warehouses. Legge had been a consistent, though unsuccessful, evangelist for crop reductions. The board experienced a shakeup, as several other members resigned. In mid-March the board announced that it would cease to support wheat prices beyond May and would begin incrementally to dispose of its huge stores of grain. The board decided that it could not support the 1931 harvest because it lacked the money and the storage capacity. Over a year, the cost of storing the wheat would double the cost to the Farm Board. Plans were to sell the wheat abroad, at a loss. President Hoover estimated that the board had lost about $60 million on its transactions but had added $5 billion to farm income and had saved hundreds of banks holding wheat as collateral from failure.[13]

European commodity exchanges declined with the American announcement that the board would sell its wheat abroad. Inevitably, this would depress world prices, and the American price would decline as well. However, some congressmen were supportive, pointing out that the board's huge surplus automatically depressed prices and created uncertainty in commodity markets. In June the board announced a plan it hoped would minimize disruptions; it would dispose of wheat slowly, at the rate of about five million bushels per month. In August 1931, the board relieved itself of between one-tenth and one-eighth of its surplus by bartering wheat for coffee with Brazil, which normally purchased its wheat from Argentina. The coffee would be withheld from the market for one year and then sold to Americans. Ultimately, the board made a profit on the coffee. In September 1931, the board sold 7.5 million bushels of wheat to Germany on credit over three years at 4.5 percent interest. The board arranged the sale of 15 million bushels of wheat to China, which fell through because of lack of collateral. However, in December 1931, the RFC arranged for the financing of the sale of six million bushels of wheat to China. The sale was from current production by Northwestern farmers. The latter stages of the Farm Board's drawing down of its holdings included giving away the surplus to charity in addition to sales. In 1932 Congress approved the president's recommendation to give $70 million of wheat and cotton to the Red Cross. The board also sent food and fiber abroad to nations suffering from famine or natural disasters. By the fall of 1932 the bins were about empty.[14]

With the stabilization efforts of the Farm Board, Hoover had clearly crossed the Rubicon, elevating government activism in the farm economy to a level never anticipated before the Depression. The real purpose of the Farm Board, the initial motivation for creating it, has been obscured by the attempts at price stabilization necessitated by the Depression. During its existence it organized about 1,000 cooperatives. None failed despite the collapse of thousands of banks. The board's principal objective was to bring to agriculture a degree of organization already existing in many industries, not direct price supports. Because of the fragmentation of the farm economy, characterized by atomization and competing individuals, the law of supply and demand was set by the buyer, not by the seller. Hoover had been disturbed by the degree to which prices increased on their journey from the grower to the consumer. Processors, transporters, packers, and retailers received a far greater share of the profits than farmers, although farmers invested more to produce food than the middlemen did to deliver and sell it. The president believed that more efficient distribution could help rectify this inequity in the same way it had succeeded in manufacturing. The board's chief contribution was not simply to multiply the number of cooperatives but to institutionalize cooperative marketing and to demonstrate its effectiveness. Cooperatives could borrow at lower rates of interest, promote their products, and facilitate exports. Local and regional cooperatives could be merged into national organizations with greater leverage. Some, such as those in the dairy industry, prospered despite the Depression. Almost all cooperatives fared better than unorganized farmers.[15]

The administration complemented the work of the board by helping farmers in many small ways, often overlooked, which helped eased their struggle. The government provided a blueprint for more scientific farming with land utilization studies. These included a survey of the Appalachian region, programs dealing with the public domain, and studies of tenant farming and of soil types. A new program to combat soil erosion was implemented. The farm problem was attacked from the vantage point of agricultural prices and income, supply and demand, the amount of acreage tilled, mortgage debts, taxes, exports and imports, and expansion of credit. Appropriations for the Department of Agriculture were a high priority in the president's budgets and were increased. Additional funds for scientific research in agriculture were appropriated. The administration created a Foreign Agricultural Service to stimulate exports; new field research was undertaken; and conservation was improved in forestry, wildlife, and mineral resources. A treaty was negotiated with Mexico to control animal diseases, and campaigns were launched to eradicate insect pests, plant disease, and predatory animals. The crop pests included the Mediterranean fruit fly, corn borer, and grasshoppers. Plant diseases such as citrus canker and animal diseases such as hoof-and-mouth disease and cattle ticks were included in the eradication programs. Another program battled forest insects and diseases of trees. Construction and maintenance of forests roads and paths provided employment for struggling farmers.[16]

The federal government also improved timber and range management, upgraded the recreational uses of national forests and engaged in fire prevention on public lands. The Agriculture Department made estimates of livestock production in order to make marketing more predictable. It implemented standards for canned foods, fruits and vegetables, livestock, meats, and wool, enabling purchasers to understand what they were buying and helping farmers to market effectively. The Agriculture Department inaugurated tobacco grading and improved cold storage facilities for perishable products. Laws enacted dealing with the agricultural economy included the Animal Quarantine Act, the Cotton Futures and Cotton Standard Act, the Grain Futures Act, the Milk Import Act, the Insecticide Act, the Plant Patents Act, and the Tobacco Standards Act.[17]

Hoover attacked the problem of farm credit. Next to low prices and antiquated marketing methods, inadequate credit was the greatest problem for farm families. Farmers borrowed between harvests, but families also needed long range credit to help stave off foreclosure on their homes and land. During previous administrations, Congress had created the Federal Land Banks under the supervision of the Federal Farm Loan Board. Congress had also set up Intermediate Credit Banks, which provided short-term loans. These credit agencies had been used parsimoniously by Harding, and credit had been tightened further by Coolidge. In 1932 Hoover obtained an additional $125 million appropriation for the Federal Land Banks. Finding the flow of credit still a trickle, he also helped create a system of Agricultural Credit Banks included in the Emergency Relief bill of July 21, 1932. The measure provided for 12 regional banks, capitalized initially at $3 million each. The banks obtained their funds from the RFC. The new banks were permitted to rediscount their loans with the Federal Reserve System and the RFC and ultimately expanded their lending capacity to $1.36 billion, enabling them to offer loans at lower interest rates. The Bankruptcy Reform bill, passed after a year of delay on June 10, 1933, saved the homes of hundreds of thousands of farmers. Hoover also mobilized the private sector. He attempted to persuade local governments to reduce property taxes on homes and land, which burdened farmers. The president had long urged private financial institutions to avoid foreclosures and near the end of January 1933, his efforts bore fruit. Major insurance companies, led by the Prudential Company and New York Life, declared a moratorium on farm foreclosures. The North Central and Western states benefitted the most. New York Life's suspension applied only to Iowa, yet it was an important farm state. As in his fight against the Depression in general, Hoover's attempts to mitigate the effects of the Depression on the farm economy were fought on numerous fronts, some obvious, others subtle.[18]

Farmers did not get what they wanted most from the Hoover administration, consistent prosperity and economy security. Neither did other Americans who lived during the Great Depression, but that was cold comfort to farmers. The failure of stabilization efforts to keep prices from sinking lower and lower was their chief complaint, yet they were accomplices to the crime. "What these farmers apparently expect the government to do is to continue buying up the surplus and storing it while they go on producing an additional surplus," Legge complained.[19] If Hoover had the most frustrating job in government, Legge's ranked near the top. Yet Hoover and Legge went to their deathbeds believing the Farm Board was a sound idea that might have worked well during normal times. If trying counts, and it does, the Hoover administration cannot be faulted for its efforts to help agriculture. The total expenditures of the administration on agriculture amount to about $775 million, far more money than was devoted to any other occupational group. There were types of contributions that cannot be precisely quantified, such as scientific research, conservation, and technical aid. Hoover and Hyde continued to believe that Hyde's plan to retire marginal lands from farming was a sound solution to overproduction, short of the authority to mandate acreage limitations. By the end of the administration, Hoover, Hyde, and farmers themselves were dubious of the government's ability to gratify farmers in the short run. The president concluded by late 1932 that the farm economy would not recover until the entire economy recovered. Most farmers no longer had much faith in panaceas, although some of their spokesmen continued to espouse them, chiefly for political reasons. Hyde had been sobered by the experience. He pointed out that European credit must improve for the export market, on which farmers relied, to increase. In the meantime, agriculture would have to adjust to a limited export trade, which meant adjusting supply to demand. Virtually the entire administration believed the Depression, wherever and however it began and regardless of whose fault it was, had become truly global and that purely nationalistic solutions were futile. Hyde and Hoover also reiterated that American farm prices remained higher than world prices and that, as much as Americans suffered, those in other nations suffered more. This was not popular, not even expedient, for a national leader running for reelection to admit, but it was true. Whatever Hoover's faults, naiveté was not one of them. However, the president was not hopeless about farm poverty. He believed there were solutions to it but no short-term, simplistic governmental ones, unless farmers themselves simply refrained from overproducing.[20]

By the end of his term, the president was content to permit the Farm Board to expire, and after his defeat in November, he knew that was inevitable anyway. The New Deal, as some of its participants later admitted, cribbed much of its farm program from Hoover's administration. Many of Roosevelt's agricultural advisers believed as firmly as Hoover's cadre in voluntarism and decentralization. When the Agricultural Adjustment Act went beyond that, the Supreme Court nullified it, which was predictable. Over passing decades chronic overproduction remained an endemic problem for American agriculture, with mitigations such as war, the opening of markets abroad by wartime devastation, or the mandating of ethanol as a partial solution to overproduction of corn, a solution that dismayed hog breeders and increased the price of gasoline. The history of the Great Depression, and of agriculture as its reflection in microcosm, is not one purely of human folly but of human tragedy.[21]

Hoover's reforms in agriculture, in providing a flow of credit and in furnishing employment for public works, all set precedents not only for the New Deal that followed but for all subsequent administrations. The capstone of his program, the Emergency Relief and Construction Act of 1932, was integral to the fight against the Depression for almost the entire decade that followed, especially its centerpiece, the strengthened RFC. After the initial $300 million appropriation for relief funneled via the states had been exhausted, Congress appropriated an additional $500 for relief under the auspices of the RFC, which were used for the Federal Emergency Relief Administration headed by Roosevelt's most versatile adviser, Harry Hopkins. As under Hoover, states were responsible for implementation. The Commodity Credit Corporation of the New Deal, which furnished money for domestic marketing of agricultural products, also had its roots in the Hoover administration. Hoover's innovations in creating and expanding the RFC, as well as the Federal Land Banks, the Federal Home Loan Discount Banks, and the reforms of the Federal Reserve System were some of the most significant precedents in American history. In addition to ideas and specific programs, much of the personnel in the relief agencies overlapped the Hoover and Roosevelt administrations. The second stage of Hoover's recovery program and the New Deal had more in common than either Hoover or Roosevelt was willing to admit.[22]

March 4, 1932, the third anniversary of Hoover's inauguration, was observed by speeches praising and condemning him in Congress and in the press. Democrats attacked the president from two angles: for doing too little or for doing too much—bankrupting the federal treasury on one hand, while not creating sufficient numbers of new jobs on the other. The press, even the Democratic press, was restrained, generally fair, and evinced an admiration for Hoover's grit and determination, despite his failure to tame the Depression. The *New York Herald Tribune* observed editorially that the real Hoover was better than the myths created by his followers or his opponents, "a general who never loses heart." The *New York Times*, a Democratic paper, wrote that the Democrats were unfair to condemn him as "a wholly incompetent President." Under the circumstances, he had proven resilient and tireless and had performed as well as could be expected. "To lay too much stress upon the personal element in a universal catastrophe is absurd," the *Times* concluded.[23] Representative Bertrand Snell of New York, the Republican leader in the House, said Hoover had earned the respect of his countrymen: "Who could have done better?" Representative John Q. Tilson of Connecticut, the former House Republican leader asked, "What has any one suggested that he should have done that he has not done already? I think when we look back upon these days, when there is not so much partisanship, we will be thankful that we had such a man to guide us."[24]

Farmers represented an occupational group, and the president struggled to ease their burdens. Veterans, however, ranged from the very rich to the very poor, from the unemployed to chairs of corporation boards. Their needs were quite different, yet they often voted as a bloc or threatened to. If there was a common denominator among veterans, it is that they had been underpaid during World War I, when workers on the home front received higher compensation than soldiers and sailors. To rectify the inequity, Congress voted in 1924 to provide veterans of the Great War with certificates due to mature in a lump sum payment of $1,000 in 1924. The bonus was enacted over the veto of Coolidge, who considered it extravagant. Most who voted for the bill believed that the 1920s prosperity would continue indefinitely and that interest earned

by the bonds would permit payment in 1945 without an additional appropriation. After the crash of 1929 and the onset of the Depression, the government
found itself caught in a financial vise. Interest paid on the bonds diminished
during hard times. Hard times also motivated the veterans to demand prompt
payment because their need was urgent. The issue was complex. The veterans
had a legitimate case. They had been underpaid relative to civilians during the
war, and they felt they had been penalized for serving their country.[25]

The administration's record on veterans' interests was generous. Hoover
had consolidated veterans' services in the Veterans' Administration under an
aggressive vets' advocate, Frank T. Hines, and had endorsed many bills that
benefited veterans. When he became president, there were about 367,000
veterans receiving federal benefits. By the end of his administration, this had
grown to 850,000. In addition, the administration had built 25 new hospitals,
raising the number of beds from 26,000 to 45,000. Hospitals that would house
another 7,000 were under construction when he left office. The president
tried to standardize benefits and treat all veterans fairly, regardless of which
war they had served in. He gave special credit for combat service and length
of duty. The chief executive vetoed a few bills that he believed favored some
veterans over others. The World War Disability Act, enacted in 1930 because
of Hoover's prodding, went beyond anything proposed by Congress. David
Burner considers Hoover's disability legislation the most generous of his generation. Some congressmen, in fact, criticized Hoover for spending excessively on veterans during the Depression. The Disability Act cost $73 million.
In addition, the president backed legislation appropriating $12.1 million for
veterans of the Civil War, four acts providing $5.4 million for soldiers' homes,
and appropriation bills requiring $15.9 million for construction. Hoover did
not require disabilities to be service connected. "On the basis of his support
for ex-servicemen, Hoover should have been among the veterans' favorite
Presidents," Donald J. Lisio writes.[26]

Hoover had compassion for needy veterans, yet his compassion extended
to all the needy. He represented all the people not one interest group, however deserving. The demand for relief was infinite, and the supply was finite.
The vets' insistence for full, instant payment of the entire 1945 face value of
the bonus certificates would bankrupt the treasury. It would destroy the credit
of the government and consume a disproportionate amount of the entire federal budget for a small segment of the population, not all of whom were poor
or unemployed. President Hoover was willing to compromise and sign a bill
providing for needy veterans alone. In a practical sense, this would be economically feasible and would not deny other needy Americans. Some nonveterans resented the veterans' militancy. Had they fought for their country, or
were they mercenaries who fought merely for money?[27]

Such arguments made economic sense, but there was a political dimension to the issue. Most representatives and senators realized that the demands
were exorbitant, yet feared being punished at the polls by the veterans. Some,

even Republicans, voted for bills to pay the bonus, hoping that Hoover would veto them. The veterans were asking for a cash payment, not at what the bonds were worth in 1931, but at what they would be worth at maturity in 1945. In February 1931, Congress passed a bill over Hoover's veto providing permitting veterans to borrow half the sum at 4.5 percent interest. The legislation did not provide an appropriation to cover the loans but did mandate the lending. Meanwhile, as the Depression deepened, the pressure built for greater benefits. In the late summer of 1931 a new movement to furnish full cash payments gathered momentum. About 20 bills providing for some form of timely payment were prepared for introduction in the Seventy-Second Congress when it convened in December. The president took the initiative. In September he spoke at the American Legion convention in Detroit, asking the Legion's help in containing spending. The Legionnaires agreed and refused to endorse the bonus bills. In addition, the president vetoed numerous private pension bills, exceeding Grover Cleveland's record for vetoes of similar legislation.[28]

The chief advocate of a cash payment of the bonus was Wright Patman, an ambitious young Democrat and representative from Texas, who had been urging passage of a medley of measures since 1929 that he hoped would culminate in success in the Seventy-Second Congress. In February 1932, Patman introduced legislation providing full, instantaneous payment. The bill would have cost $2.4 billion. At the time, the entire federal budget was only $3.7 billion. Patman proposed to redeem the bonus certificates by printing unbacked currency. The Patman bill became the fulcrum of a congressional melee. Patman, a provocative advocate, tried to turn the matter into a class issue that would provoke national publicity and elicit sympathy for veterans. Taking the offensive, the Texan charged that Hoover's RFC helped bankers whereas his bill would aid the "little fellow." Senator Elmer Thomas, who favored inflation, led the fight for the bill in the upper chamber. The advocates were reinforced by John Rankin of Mississippi, who chaired the House Ways and Means Committee. Father Coughlin, Detroit's demagogic radio priest, testified in favor of the measure and later donated $5,000. Every member of Hoover's cabinet opposed the bill, as did the American Legion. Initially, the House Ways and Means Committee issued an unfavorable report, and the legislation died in committee. However, by June 2, some 104 representatives had signed a discharge petition that assured the bill would reach the floor. Passage in the House was considered certain. Hoover took command more actively than he usually did. He lined up senators to fight the measure. The president hoped that the Senate would either defeat the legislation outright or at least uphold his veto.[29]

Already, thousands of embittered veterans had come to believe that a conspiracy against them existed, with Hoover its provocateur. His past support was forgotten; he became a satanic figure. Some vets spontaneously decided to march on Washington. On May 11, a contingent of about 300 veterans set

out from Portland, Oregon, bound for the capital to lobby for the Patman
bill. They were led by Walter W. Waters, a 34-year-old, indigent, charismatic
veteran of the Great War. The coast-to-coast trip took 18 days. The men
hitched rides on railroad freight cars, drove trucks and cars, and walked. They
attracted little attention until they reached East St. Louis, Illinois on May
20, where officials of the B & O railroad refused to permit them to ride the
rails. A confrontation occurred when the men blocked the tracks. Finally, local
truckers provided transportation to Indiana. There, the governor, eager to rid
his state of troublemakers, trucked them to Ohio. From there, state officials,
meeting them at the borders, hauled them through Pennsylvania and Maryland to the District of Columbia. The protestors were joined by vets from
other states employing the same modes of transportation, often hurried on
their way by state leaders eager to avoid violence. Ultimately, about 20,000
arrived in the national capital. Some of Hoover's advisers wanted him to keep
them out of the District of Columbia, but the president said that had the right
to assemble peacefully[30]

Eventually, the group, known as the Bonus Expeditionary Force (BEF),
included ex-soldiers from virtually every state. Most of them camped in areas
around Washington, one of them in Camp Anacostia, across the Anacostia
River from the capital. A few occupied what they considered more commodious quarters in abandoned buildings along Pennsylvania Avenue. These
dilapidated structures were scheduled to be razed to clear the land for new
federal construction, part of Hoover's plan to provide jobs and new offices
and to beautify Washington. Initially Hoover considered meeting with the
leaders, but he decided that it might only encourage similar groups to travel
to Washington expecting a private audience with the chief executive. Moreover, the president considered the veterans in Washington the responsibility of district authorities. He was preoccupied with the Japanese invasion of
Manchuria, which resulted in the Stimson Doctrine; the disarmament conference at Geneva; pushing the remainder of his recovery program through
Congress; and mapping his fall election campaign. The president treated the
BEF humanely. He made no derogatory comments about them and did not
consider them a menace. Hoover quietly instructed the army and the District
National Guard to provide the men, some of whom had families, with tents,
cooking utensils, food, and clothing. He concealed his generosity, lest other
potential protestors expect it. When disease spread in the camps, the president ordered the government to set up a temporary hospital. Hoover funneled
aid through the District's Superintendent of Police Pelham Glassford. Most
of the veterans believed the support came from Glassford, who actually had
no access to army supplies, and that Hoover snubbed them. A West Point
graduate and Great War officer, Glassford was vain and enjoyed power. Glassford became a hero to the veterans, who considered the man in the White
House heartless.[31]

The veterans in Washington frightened and intimidated some residents, District businesses lost customers, and some vets were arrested for panhandling. The Patman bill passed the House but only by 35 votes, which was not veto proof. On June 16, the day after the House passed the bill, the Senate began debate. By now, even most liberals had soured on the legislation, including George Norris, an inveterate foe of Hoover. Liberals such as Robert Wagner, Robert LaFollette, and Emmanuel Cellar now considered the vets' demands unreasonable. Cellar pointed out that already one-fourth of all federal expenditures were devoted to veterans, who constituted only 13 percent of the unemployed in 1932. Fiorello La Guardia, the New York Progressive Republican, had earlier pointed out that giving $2.4 billion to less than 4 percent of the population would not be a serious contribution toward resolving the Depression. Treasury Secretary Mills had emphasized that issuing unbacked currency would ruin anyone with savings because of the resulting inflation, which would depreciate even the value of the veterans' own bonus certificates. Hoover prepared a veto message, but he need not have worried. The Senate soundly defeated the Patman bill by a vote of 62–18. The veterans under Waters, who had awaited the outcome of the vote on the Capitol steps, surprised many by stoically accepting the verdict. Waters instructed them to sing "America" and then to march back to their camps. Congress adjourned on July 16, 1932. Now, for certain, there was no glimmer of hope for passage of the bonus in the Seventy-Second Congress. Hoover had already signed two appropriation bills amounting to $125,000 to provide transportation home, and about 6,000 vets accepted. After all, their purpose for being there had expired. Yet among an unforgiving core, attitudes hardened. Waters himself vowed to remain in Washington until 1945, if necessary, to obtain his objective. Although in a practical sense, the battle over the Patman bill had ended, a battle of wills remained and moved toward its denouement.[32]

After the adjournment of Congress, conditions in the camps became increasingly filthy and undisciplined. Open, vermin-infested latrines were used during hot weather, and disease spread. Conservative BEF members clashed with Communists who sought to foment the overthrow of capitalism. The Communists sought to exploit the vets as pawns of their revolution. Communists did not control the vets; in fact, no one controlled them. Families and children living in filth on meager rations became ill. Morale declined along with sanitation because their cause was not only hopeless; residents of the District had turned hostile. Neither did they have significant support in the press. By remaining to fight a futile fight they were harming their own cause, which had never had broad support. Waters was losing the allegiance of his men, and his health and stamina were failing. Rival vets competed for leadership. Although discipline was faltering, some thrived on the camaraderie forged in the crucible of common suffering. The veterans baked in the Washington sun and were soaked by downpours. The vets, the city, and the administration, were losing patience. The sit-in could not continue indefinitely.[33]

The time was approaching when the downtown buildings occupied by a few of vets, some with families, would have to be demolished. Federal law prohibited the indefinite occupation of government buildings. But there were also practical reasons. The occupying vets were denying employment to destitute Washington workers who wanted to begin construction on the site once the crumbling buildings were demolished. Caught in the middle of the standoff was George W. Rhine, who owned a salvage company and had paid the Treasury Department $5,251 for the right to demolish the structures and salvage and sell the materials. Rhine was going bankrupt because he could not begin. His debts mounted, and creditors eventually foreclosed on his home in Alexandria, Virginia. His once profitable business was ruined. Hoover took a minimalist approach toward eviction. At first he had no intention of removing anyone but those who were blocking federal public works projects and were on the verge of succumbing to pestilence. He considered them the responsibility of the Washington police force. The squatters could be removed and, if they resisted, arrested. It was a civil matter that did not require federal intervention. As a first step, municipal officials initiated negotiations with Waters for a voluntary withdrawal from the buildings along Pennsylvania Avenue, but nothing could be resolved. Some members of the BEF viewed compromise as a sign of weakness, and Waters wanted to retain his leadership. The Treasury Department issued several deadlines, which were ignored. The deadlines were postponed. Finally, on July 28, after weeks of futile attempts to reach an agreement, the District police decided the time had come to act on a small scale.[34]

The first building was emptied without serious incident. Meanwhile, at Camp Anacostia, Waters and others delivered incendiary speeches. Angry men boarded trucks and sped to the site of the remaining occupied buildings, where they attacked the police with stones, bricks, and clubs. A mass of some 4,000 to 6,000 marchers were joined by angry onlookers, swelling the mob to about 20,000, though not all of them assaulted the 75 police present. The officers called for backups, and about 600 police were rushed to the scene, leaving the rest of Washington virtually unprotected. Glassford was struck by a brick and collapsed. A policeman who tried to rescue him suffered a fractured skull. Shortly after 1 p.m., a more serious scuffle occurred inside one of the buildings. An officer grappled with three assailants, one beating him with his own club, another strangling him, and a third threatening him with a brick. The officer fired his revolver in self-defense, striking two vets. One died immediately, the other later, at a hospital. Glassford apparently asked for federal support, though he later denied it, and his top assistants, who were present, confirmed that troops were necessary. The district commissioners, two of whom inspected the site, telephoned the president for troops. At the time, the riot was still in process. Hoover, who believed Glassford had consented, declined to issue an order without a written request. The commissioners then dispatched a written plea. After receiving it, the commander-in-chief delegated the details of the operation to Secretary of War Hurley, who ordered the army chief of staff, General Douglas MacArthur, to assemble his riot control squad. Hoover instructed Hurley that the troops carry only night sticks, not guns, but Hurley insisted that guns were necessary because there would be only about 600 soldiers opposed by several thousand vets and possibly additional onlookers. The president directed Hurley to instruct MacArthur to move the vets only to the District line. Beyond that, they were to be left undisturbed. Later, they were to be rounded up in an orderly manner and transported home.[35]

MacArthur assembled a show of force intended to intimidate the vets and deter actual force. The army chief of staff decided to take personal command of the operation and assembled a blue-ribbon collection of high-ranking officers to assist him. He delegated field operations to General George Van Horn Mosley. Major Dwight D. Eisenhower served as MacArthur's staff aid, and Major George M. Patton participated. The vets occupying buildings were given more than an hour to evacuate, which they did. The army proceeded slowly and for the most part did not even come in contact with the rapidly retreating BEF. In a few cases, indignant vets lingered to hurl stones, and the army retaliated with tear gas. No shots were fired, and not a single vet or soldier was seriously injured. Hoover monitored the operations by phone. When MacArthur reached the Anacostia River Bridge, the line of demarcation Hoover had set, MacArthur halted and paused for two hours to feed and rest his men. To this point the operation had been disciplined and MacArthur himself remained calm. Hoover reiterated his orders verbally on at least two occasions: that his commander was to leave Camp Anacostia beyond the bridge undisturbed. The general, a World War I hero with an exemplary record, had never defied an order, but he did so now. At the request of a BEF leader, he allowed the vets two hours to evacuate Camp Anacostia and then moved slowly into forbidden territory, which was now empty except for a few stragglers. The few remaining vets set aflame their government-issued tents, a final act of defiance, according to Eisenhower. Later, the army torched the remaining rubbish in a misguided attempt at sanitation. Despite MacArthur's final act of overzealousness, the operation on the whole was a success. The general took the threat of insurrection more seriously than the president, who refused to declare martial law and turned the remaining tasks over to District of Columbia authorities.[36]

Women and children were not removed by the army. They were segregated in the downtown buildings, where they were fed and clothed by the Red Cross, which also provided transportation home. The vets themselves dissipated rapidly. The Veterans Bureau offered them free transportation home by rail or truck. Many of the families took advantage of the offer, but most of the men returned in other ways, possibly because some of them did not want to return home. Some had cars and drove themselves. Others had access to trucks. By a variety of means, they soon left the area, and their long siege of Washington was over.[37]

Hoover was angry at MacArthur and also with Hurley. MacArthur apparently felt he had performed a service by exceeding Hoover's orders, but the president soon disabused him of that idea. After MacArthur boasted of the success of the operation to reporters that evening, with Hurley's backing, the president summoned them to the White House and scolded them severely. After sleeping on it, Hoover gave the general a second tongue-lashing the following morning. The president made it clear that MacArthur worked for him rather than the other way around. Still, he did not leak his critical remarks to the press nor show public anger, which might have been politically expedient. Instead, he shouldered the responsibility himself. Hoover might have had other reasons as well. Publicly chastising MacArthur or firing him might have been unpopular rather than garnering kudos. The general was popular and glamorous, and no one had been hurt. More importantly, the president turned back to his work on what became known as the Stimson Doctrine and other crises abroad. He remained consumed with battling the Depression. Hoover considered the incident over. Nevertheless, much of the public, and many historians, blamed the Quaker president. Some insisted he should have fired MacArthur. The president did not consider the mistake to be one of such magnitude. It was the general's first error in judgment, and the president assumed it would be his last one. Yet there was something more fundamental to Hoover's relationship with those who served him. Throughout his career Hoover never publicly excoriated a subordinate. He dismissed incompetents, but MacArthur was no incompetent. Hoover's policy was to deal with his subordinates face to face and keep their indiscretions within the organization. He never shifted blame, even when deserved. This is one of the facets of his character that created unusually strong bonds of loyalty to those who worked under him, loyalty that cut both ways. MacArthur was retained as chief of staff. When administrations changed, Roosevelt reappointed him chief of staff. After MacArthur's retirement, President Roosevelt called him back into service during World War II, in which he played an important role. Hoover later became more aware of the general's massive ego, which grew over time, and never supported MacArthur's aspirations for the presidency. Although Glassford became a vindictive foe of Hoover, he never uttered a word of criticism of MacArthur. The former District police commissioner and MacArthur remained close friends, and he supported the general's ambition to obtain the Republican presidential nomination in 1952.[38]

Subsequently, questions arose over the role Communists had played in stiffening the veterans' determination. There were Communists in Washington, sent to infiltrate the veterans, subvert their efforts, and provoke violence, inciting an uprising that would inflame other cities, spread, and overthrow and vanquish capitalism in America. This exotic plot had no more chance of succeeding than the cow jumping over the moon, yet some Communist leaders were naively serious about it. At the least, they hoped to use the episode as a vehicle for self-promotion, to glamorize themselves as liberators of the working class. Waters and most of his followers were militantly anti-Communist and were prepared to inflict bodily harm on Communists. The idea of a conspiracy came mostly from public statements issued by Communists themselves, some of whom had been at the scene. To be certain, the Communists were less inhibited at spilling blood than the veterans. Emmanuel Levine, former head of the California Communist Party; John T. Pace, field commander from Detroit; and James W. Ford, who was vice presidential candidate on the Communist Party ticket in the presidential campaign of 1932, were present. Pace later wrote an account of the Communist role in the affair. There were also among the motley stragglers who remained in Washington a cadre of common criminals and nonveterans along for the ride, as well as some veterans who were already receiving pensions. The numbers of the Communists and various hangers on who attached themselves to the movement is impossible to determine precisely, but they probably did not amount to much more than a thousand. The real problem with the veterans' movement after the adjournment of Congress is the relative lack of coherent leadership. The rock-solid support for Waters had fragmented. Lacking a purpose, he did not want to return to obscurity in Oregon and so tried to hold his crew together, organizing groups of thugs he called "Khaki Shirts" to beat and discipline dissenters and Communists. Spread apart into disparate camps and dispersed, the vets did not pose a physical threat. Yet when they gathered as an angry mob as they did on July 28, they became a menace to public safety. Some critics condemned Hoover less for harshness toward the veterans than for giving them the impression that they could remain in Washington indefinitely. The truth is that one would have to delve deep into the annals of American presidents to unearth one who was more reluctant to employ force on any occasion.[39]

The conclusion of some historians who had studied the story of the BEF extensively is that its significance and its effect on the 1932 presidential campaign have been exaggerated. Most national newspapers did not support the BEF cause, either before or after their expulsion from the District. What should have become a footnote to history became in some quarters a cause célèbre. Mayor James Curley of Boston, for example, claimed Hoover had ordered troops to shoot the unarmed vets "like dogs."[40] The rout of the veterans is in no way comparable in scope to use of troops during the urban and campus riots of the 1960s, yet it remains befogged in a historical mystique created in part by the fact that the men involved were veterans. In reality, it has hardly a serious riot, certainly not a brutal assault by soldiers on innocent victims. The Democrats exploited the affair not only in the 1932 campaign but during at least four later elections. Glassford wrote a scathing series of articles designed to defame the president, which appeared in October, just prior to the election. The stories, published in the isolationist Republican daily, the *Chicago Tribune*, were solicited by the *Tribune's* publisher, William Randolph Hearst, who considered Hoover a dangerous Wilsonian internationalist. Much later, in 1952, the former superintendent of police conceded, "Mr. Hoover cannot be accused of prevarication. He knew nothing about the Bonus Army personally."[41] FDR's glib remark to Felix Frankfurter about the expulsion, "Well, Felix, this will elect me," amounted to gloating over a minor tragedy.[42] Any competent pollster or campaign manager could have told Roosevelt that with unemployment near its historical apogee, the New Yorker was already elected unless the stock market soared 800 points on Halloween. "Clearly, Roosevelt's supporters were overly impressed with the impact of the event on the coming election," Donald Lisio writes.[43]

In April 1932, while campaigning for the Democratic nomination, Roosevelt had observed, "I do not see how as a matter of practical sense, a government running behind $2 billion annually can consider the anticipation of bonus payments until it has a balanced budget, not only on paper but with a surplus of cash in the treasury."[44] Soon after becoming president, FDR raced through a Congress with top-heavy Democratic majorities the draconian Economy Act of 1933, which halted benefits for thousands of veterans with disabilities, both service-connected and nonmilitary, thus embittering them. This provoked a second Bonus March. Roosevelt was far harsher on the ex-servicemen than Hoover. He barred them from entering the District of Columbia and confined them within a distant army base. His administration did not supply the vets with food, equipment, and medical care, as Hoover had done. Yet Eleanor Roosevelt's symbolic visit to the vets has attracted more attention from historians than Hoover's painstaking and tangible benefits, including K-rations, army tents, and blankets. FDR also attacked the American Legion as a selfish special interest group. Roosevelt said in 1933, "No one because he wore a uniform must therefore be placed in a special class of beneficiaries over and above all other citizens."[45] In 1935 Congress passed a bonus bill, and Roosevelt vetoed it. In 1936, an election year, the national legislature passed a bonus bill over FDR's veto. The new president did not initiate significant new policies toward veterans of the Great War. He remained a cautious politician, less empathetic toward their needs and less tolerant of their protests than Hoover.[46]

In her 1949 autobiography, *I Remember*, Eleanor Roosevelt wrote that she had been shocked when she learned that Hoover had ordered the Amy to fire on veterans who were peacefully demonstrating in 1932. Patrick J. Hurley, Hoover's secretary of war, wrote a rebuttal, which appeared in *McCall's* later that year. Hurley had continued his public service during the New Deal as a military officer and ambassador to several nations during World War II. He explained that "I cannot ignore Mrs. Roosevelt's erroneous statements, because they do a great injustice to former President Hoover and General MacArthur." Hurley continued, "The truth is, no order was given by anyone to the soldiers to fire on the veterans. The riot was stopped by the army personnel without firing a shot." Hurley added, "Usually when the armed services perform such a duty without firing a shot they are given some credit.

That was not the case with the men who restored law and order in the bonus riots." In response to Hurley's explanation, Eleanor retracted her charges in a paragraph that followed Hurley's story in the same issue of *McCall's*. "I simply stated my impressions of that day, derived from the press which I happened to read," she writes. "I know others had similar impressions, but I am glad to have an authentic account published and I only wonder why it was not done sooner."[47]

Truth is not stranger than fiction, but it is often more complicated. The truth is that the BEF did not loom large among Hoover's priorities until nearly the end of its sojourn in Washington. It exemplifies the distractions the president faced while attempting to salvage the economic wreckage dragging the country to greater depths, amid crises abroad. By overstaying their welcome, the veterans diminished their credibility. Roosevelt's attempt to exploit the incident politically raises doubts about his own intellectual honesty. The great majority of Americans did not pursue elusive panaceas nor turn to authoritarianism. Most did not want to destroy capitalism. They wanted to rev up its motor and be cut in on a larger share—to return, if possible, to the way things were for many Americans in the 1920s before the crash, the time when Hoover was a hero. They suffered yet persevered, pondering questions about their world, their country, and their economy that were both practical and existential. In that sense, their president was much like them.

CHAPTER 13

Race, Gender, and Labor

Hoover's views on race were intellectually honest, the same publicly and privately. As president, he never made racist remarks or indulged in racial humor, which were common in his time. "Neither in his writings, nor in his public utterances later on, would he make statements that could be categorized as 'racist' in the context of the times he lived and the places he worked," Robert Sobel writes.[1] Like his abolitionist Quaker ancestors, the concept of deliberate discrimination was anathema to Hoover. References to racial inferiority, particularly concerning blacks, are absent from his presidential correspondence. After the 1890s, he rarely made racial comparisons at all.[2] Hoover combined compassion with a passionate commitment to philanthropy and social uplift, yet he believed equality of opportunity, the core of his personal philosophy, must be melded with individual and community responsibility. His belief that people must be treated as individuals rather than groups was tempered by his belief that special circumstances required special remedies. He felt that blacks had been set back by the oppression of slavery and there was a sound reason for the government to help them. Yet such assistance should be temporary and coupled with self-help. Hoover's views were free of condescension or paternalism and were more practical than theoretical. Although the president rejected racial prejudice, he considered it impossible for the government to ensure equality of outcome. That would result in an artificial cookie-cutter society. Hoover opposed discrimination, period. His ideal was a color-blind society and a political system blind to special interests. Hoover's tolerance extended to all groups; it was less intellectual than spiritual. Sometimes he took unpopular positions. During 1919–1920, when many public figures remained discretely quiet, Hoover opposed the persecution of Communists, anarchists, and radicals for their political beliefs and opposed their deportation. During and after the First World War he criticized the persecution of Jews and threatened to terminate American food relief to any country that harmed them. As president, Hoover maintained his consistent unflinching record on civil rights. He refused to authorize any prosecution of suspected reds, which he believed violated their freedom of speech, and he permitted peaceful picketing of the White House by Communists. Hoover investigated the incarceration of political prisoners such as the labor leader Thomas J. Mooney. The president forced the resignation of Assistant Attorney General Mabel Walker Willebrandt, who had employed religious invective against Al Smith. The first sentence Hoover commuted was that of a black man convicted of murder on inconclusive evidence. The president instructed his new director of federal prisons to appoint blacks and women to parole boards in proportion to the number of blacks and women incarcerated.[3]

Hoover considered himself a friend of blacks and an advocate of their progress. He wanted to ameliorate poverty and improve education. He believed blacks had made enormous strides in the relatively short time since Emancipation. On the other hand, he believed trading favors for votes was sordid and refused to condone it. Hoover would not bow to the political demands of minorities, particularly on patronage, simply to obtain their bloc of votes. The president believed that if he appointed blacks who were corrupt or political hacks to patronage jobs, it would only confirm stereotypes and entrench white racism. He would not be bullied by militant groups of any stripe, even when he shared empathy for their goals. Nonetheless, when he believed criticism appeared credible, he dealt with it constructively, such as complaints about treatment of blacks in refugee camps during the 1927 Mississippi River flood. His rescue and relief efforts in the flooded area exposed him to Southern black poverty for the first time, and it appalled him. Hoover's experience with the flood began his education on racism. He became more sympathetic to black reformers.[4]

By midsummer 1927 Hoover had a better understanding of racism and the system of peonage that kept blacks chained to plantations as sharecroppers and cheap labor. He believed the salvation of blacks lay in economic independence and developed a program to break up some of the flood-ravaged plantations, many of which were undergoing foreclosure, and transform them into independent small farms of about 20 acres. The plantation owners would be willing to sell because if some land were removed from the market, the value of the remainder would appreciate. Hoover's scheme involved providing the independent farmers with tools, seeds, and animals for the first year, using their crops as collateral. They could purchase the land over a ten-year period, with extensions if necessary. A Land Resettlement Corporation capitalized at about $2 million could implement the program. The commerce secretary believed he could resettle 1,000 families for every $1 million in capital. The new landowners would also become homeowners. The program would be nonprofit, and payments were to be reinvested to resettle additional families. The corporation's board of directors was to include blacks. Northern philanthropists and Red Cross money remaining from the flood recovery should finance the reform. Ultimately the idea failed because Hoover could not obtain the necessary funding. The Red Cross determined that it could not use money raised for flood relief for a different purpose. Julius Rosenwald, an important philanthropist for black causes, declined to participate because he considered the experiment unlikely to succeed, observing that such efforts had failed in the past.[5]

As president, Hoover resumed the effort to persuade wealthy philanthropists to underwrite the program. In 1929 he invited Dr. Robert R. Moton, head of Tuskegee Institute, to meet with Hoover and leading philanthropists to thrash out a solution. Although still struggling, the planters themselves were willing to sell, and the president attempted to persuade the millionaires to open their pocketbooks. Unfortunately, the Depression had dried up philanthropic support, and it seemed an inauspicious time to undertake the reform. Most donors focused on short-term needs and the president himself had to reorder his priorities to deal with the Depression. Nonetheless he never faltered in his belief that the program offered promise to promote a new way of life in the South.[6]

The president developed cordial relations with black leaders who sought assistance for tangible programs. Even before he became president, Hoover befriended prominent black educators and supported black educational institutions. He solicited their advice and took it seriously, without pandering or condescension. As secretary of commerce he desegregated the Census Bureau, the only cabinet member to desegregate a department. Along with Lou, he refused to sign a restrictive covenant prohibiting the sale or rental of his home in Washington to blacks or Jews. Lou, who saw special promise in one of her maids, paid for her college education without announcing it.[7] As commerce secretary, Hoover created a Division of Colored Business, headed by a black official, and in 1925 he supported fundraising drives for black schools at Hampton and Tuskegee. Kicking off the drive he told an audience at Carnegie Hall, "If we are to solve the Negro problem this is the direction of its resolution, and the burden of finding that solution rests upon the American people as a whole." He cooperated with the Negro Business League, the National Urban League, and the Southern Interracial Commission to find jobs for blacks, help migrants to northern cities settle and adjust, and encourage racial harmony.[8]

The racial event that attracted the most notoriety during the early months of Hoover's presidency was the First Lady's invitation to Jessie DePriest, wife of the black Republican Chicago Representative Oscar DePriest, to attend a tea for congressional wives at the White House. The situation was quite different from Theodore Roosevelt's invitation to Booker T. Washington to join him for a working lunch 30 years earlier. Washington was nationally respected by whites, and the affair was a business luncheon. The DePriests, on the other hand, represented a Chicago district known for corruption, and the tea was entirely social. Most Washingtonians could remember no precedent. It was a White House tradition for the First Lady to honor congressional wives with a tea. The Hoovers were not out to prove a point, but neither did Lou intend to snub DePriest. She invited Jessie to the last in a series of five teas. Lou limited the guest list to women she personally knew who were not prejudiced. The final tea was much smaller than the previous four, each of which had included from 180 to 220 women. The list of those invited was not released until shortly before the event. The gathering was brief, informal, and polite. DePriest sipped tea and chatted with the other women. Her husband said afterward that she had made new friends and had been treated kindly. Up until this time, the DePriests had been snubbed by the upper crust of Washington society. The Hoovers never considered excluding Jessie DePriest.[9]

Southern politicians and journalists viewed the tea as the opening wedge of a campaign for social equality for blacks, spearheaded by the Hoovers, who were subjected to venomous attacks. The legislatures of Texas, Florida, Georgia, and Mississippi condemned the invitation. Senator Thaddeus Caraway of Arkansas inserted a racist diatribe in the *Congressional Record*. A 1928 Hoover supporter in Virginia warned that the affair would cost the president 25,000 votes in his state in 1932. Margie Neal, the only woman in the Texas state legislature, was enraged. "The matter of social recognition, as expressed in the White House, is unthinkable," she said. "Mrs. Hoover has violated the most sacred social custom of the White House, and this should be condemned." Crank letters poured in. "Shame on you forever," a Chicago woman wrote the First Lady.[10] Southern newspapers were uninhibited in their criticism. One headline ran, "Mrs. Hoover Defiles the White House." Critical editorials appeared in dailies such as the *Houston Chronicle*, the *Austin Times*, the *Memphis Commercial Appeal*, and the *Daily News* in Jackson, Mississippi.[11] The latter daily, for example, wrote, "The DePriest incident has placed [the] President and Mrs. Hoover beyond the pale of social recognition for the Southern people."[12] Democratic dailies claimed that no Democratic president had ever entertained a black person at the White House, only Republicans: Theodore Roosevelt and Herbert Hoover. An examination of records revealed that Lincoln, Hayes, Grant, Coolidge, and Cleveland all had had black guests at the White House.[13] Both Hoovers reacted stoically, and neither commented publicly. Lou was hurt and lost some respect for reporters. The reaction left her more guarded. To take some of the spotlight off his wife and also to demonstrate that Hoover did not consider the incident a faux pas, the president invited Robert Moton to the White House shortly afterward, demonstrating that blacks were welcome there.

Initially, Representative DePriest was gracious in his comments, yet he soon turned to gloating and inflamed the controversy in order to inflate his status. Ten days after the tea, the Chicago Republican sponsored a "musicale and reception" to help raise $200,000 for the NAACP and to shore up his political base. The congressman exploited his moment in the spotlight by demanding that blacks create their own political party. They could elect 100 representatives in districts where they controlled a majority, he claimed. This aggravated white anxiety about black motives and even alienated some of DePriest's backers. It provoked another round of angry editorials and enabled some Southerners to say "I told you so."[14]

The Hoovers treated the matter routinely, an invitation they would offer to any congressman's wife, and they subsequently made little of it. Nonetheless, the invitation did take political courage, far more than the more highly acclaimed invitation by Eleanor Roosevelt to Marian Anderson to sing at the Lincoln Memorial. In 1932 the Democrats used the affair against Hoover in the South, which returned solidly to the Democratic fold, though chiefly on the basis of the Depression. Walter Newton, the president's secretary, wired a Virginia attorney who complained about the DePriest invitation: "It is unfair to suggest that the first lady of the land can make official discrimination against the wives of colored congressmen, diplomats, or women delegates to civic bodies."[15] The Hoovers also had substantial support, chiefly but not exclusively, in the North. The *Charlotte Observer* in North Carolina insisted that the First Lady was obligated to treat Jessie DePriest courteously. The *Boston Post* wrote that "Here in Massachusetts we should have regarded Mrs. Hoover's failure to receive Mrs. DePriest with the wives of other congressmen as a mistake and insult." The *Philadelphia Record* argued that it would be hypocritical for a nation to profess equality while excluding some on the basis of race.[16] Republican Representative Hamilton Fish of New York argued that it would have been rude to exclude DePriest and criticized Democrats for using the occasion politically.[17] The *Chicago Daily News* praised the White House for standing up for principle, and the Chicago City Council praised them for "true Americanism," while the Women's International League for Peace and Freedom joined the chorus of supporters.[18] The episode was precedent setting and set a good example. Yet in reality the hyperbole was redundant; both sides were preaching to the choir. It did serve to illustrate, however, the passion stirred by race.

The furor incited by the DePriest invitation was not only rude, but the critics seemed to lack a realistic context. About a month earlier, on May 16, 1929, Hoover had invited his closest black adviser, Moton, to the White House. The Tuskegee president met the president there five more times in 1929 and 1930 without comparable press attention. Moton's visits, of course, were related to business and did not raise the issue of social equality for black women. Further, Moton made no attempt to exploit his meetings for personal fame. A few weeks after the DePriest tea garnered headlines, the Hoovers hosted an annual garden party for disabled veterans during which black vets mingled with white veterans. The party attracted little publicity.[19]

The best friend of blacks within the cabinet was Hoover's closest friend, Interior Secretary Ray Lyman Wilbur. Several key black institutions fell under Wilbur's jurisdiction, most importantly Howard University, the all-black university in Washington, DC, funded by the federal government, and the Freedman's Hospital also in Washington, founded in 1871, which provided medical care to blacks, many of them veterans. As of 1931, there were 4,336 inpatients, most, though not all, from the District of Columbia. Only 871 paid for care. In addition, the American territory of the Virgin Islands, largely inhabited by blacks, was transferred to the Interior Department during Hoover's term. Wilbur shared the president's belief that higher education was the crucible of black leadership and a vehicle for upward economic mobility. Their interest went well beyond Howard. Wilbur undertook a national program to improve the health of blacks, especially children. He appointed a specialist in black education to study curricula in secondary schools and recommend improvements. Wilbur established a new Division of Negro Education within the Interior Deptartment. By 1931 it had initiated a survey of the status of black education by a national advisory committee on black education, as well as a 20-year program of development for Howard University. The administration studied education in the Southern states, rural education, and illiteracy. Hoover believed teaching, which he called "practical patriotism," was one of the noblest professions. He delivered an inspiring speech at the Howard commencement and wrote an encouraging letter to the president of Atlanta University emphasizing that education played a vital role in social and economic progress and quality of life.[20]

Hoover and Wilbur made Howard University a showcase of higher education for blacks. When he became president, Hoover doubled the annual appropriation to the black university. Mordecai W. Johnson, president of Howard, termed the increased funding "the most comprehensively helpful appropriation ever received."[21] Established in 1867 for the education of blacks, Howard was partly funded by the federal government. The government was more directly involved in its operation than in any other university because of its mission and its location in the District of Columbia. The student body, however, was drawn nationally, serving about 2,500 students from 40 states, the District of Columbia, and several foreign countries. Its annual budget was about $1,750,000, and its assets were close to $8 million. The administration improved the faculty quality and reduced the faculty-to-student ratio to about 1 to 12. The university included a law school, a graduate school, and a medical school associated with the Freedman's Hospital. Under the Hoover administration the law school became accredited, the library holdings were increased, the college of medicine was enhanced by new faculty appointments, and the college of education initiated publication of the *Journal of Negro Education*.[22]

The administration also promoted economic independence for blacks, a key to self-sufficiency, which was intertwined with education. As secretary of commerce, Hoover had appointed a specialist in black business to his department. As president, he encouraged the work of a private group, the Conference on the Economic Status of the Negro, financed by the Rosenwald Fund. Hoover cooperated with the Urban League and appointed a black employment advisor in the Department of Labor to assist the expanded federal employment service. His task was to analyze black job needs and suggest remedies. The president backed the work of the National Negro Business League, led by Moton. He was especially sympathetic toward Moton's request for federal assistance to black farmers to help enable them to escape the Southern peonage system.[23]

Many of Hoover's committees and commissions emphasized black concerns, including the Committee on Recent Social Trends, the National Conference on Child Health and Protection, and the National Advisory Committee on Education. The problems of black children, especially those related to health, were singled out for attention. Blacks served on the Committee on Child Health and Protection as well as on the Committee on Unemployment. Hoover had been interested in black housing since 1925. In 1930, an all-black subcommittee of the Conference on Home Building and Ownership undertook a study of black housing in urban and rural environments, addressing such problems as home financing, design, and construction. The president also worked closely with private philanthropic organizations to promote black interests, including education and economic development, often tapping the Julius Rosenwald Foundation.[24]

Unfortunately, neither education nor economic independence was a quick fix to the problems of Depression-era unemployment, which exacerbated black status as an underclass. The president, who believed in the value of research, reviewed a study commissioned and published in 1930, *Industrial Background of Study of the Economic Status of the Negro*, which he found grim. By 1930, blacks had lost many of the economic gains they had achieved in the prosperous 1920s. They were largely limited to unskilled jobs, were excluded from unions, and were replaced by white workers at the onset of the Depression. Others had been displaced by technology. Though everyone suffered during the Depression, blacks endured greater suffering. Most did not have a reservoir of savings. In the North, some blacks were employed by municipalities, but jobs in local government were rare in South. Everywhere in the nation, they worked chiefly in open shop plants, and sometimes were used as strikebreakers. Most blacks employed in industry worked at low wages on assembly-line jobs. They were unable to obtain many jobs in construction because of a lack of skills. The report did not come as a surprise, either to Hoover or to blacks themselves. The only way out of the economic morass was to improve skills, which the president hoped could be obtained partly through industrial education. But times were hard and competition for jobs was tough. The report did not examine employment in government or on public works, but these provided merely a limited mitigation. In a general sense, blacks could only hope for better times with the end of the Depression.

Some blacks despaired of the situation so painfully that they desired to be deported. One wrote to the president urging him to deport the entire black population to Liberia, where they would be better off. Another asked for a similar solution, to an unspecified destination.[25]

Although Hoover was scrupulous about appointing highly qualified individuals to federal jobs, he appointed more blacks to government positions than any of his twentieth-century predecessors and provided job security by placing more government officials under civil service. Although he deplored the patronage side of politics, the president had no reservations about appointing qualified blacks; in fact, he was proactive in doing so. Hoover appointed some 54,684 blacks to government positions, which, according to biographer David Burner, is more than Harding and Coolidge combined. The president appointed a black minister to the nation of Liberia, a vice consul to France, an assistant attorney general, and many blacks to significant positions, including a judge in the District of Columbia. Nationally, the Post Office employed 28,400 blacks, the War Department (civilian) 5,914, the Navy Department 5,427, and the Department of Commerce 686, not counting those hired temporarily by the Census Bureau. The Justice Department employed several blacks as assistant U.S. attorneys, while Interior hired 558, including black women as head nurses, clerks, and social workers. Agriculture's employees included two black field agents and 167 county agents as well as more than 123 women, chiefly clerical workers. These were permanent employees of the federal bureaucracy, not those holding temporary jobs created as work relief because of the Depression. While not high by later standards, none of his predecessors in the twentieth century had a comparable record. The numbers do not bear out the stereotype that Hoover was prejudiced against hiring blacks.[26]

Blacks formulated several objectives during the early years of the Depression, and Hoover sought to resolve some of them, with only limited success. First, blacks wanted to obtain employment or some type of economic sustenance and to keep their families intact. They wanted to break the stranglehold on manufacturing jobs held by major unions that excluded them and to penetrate the union movement nationally. Blacks consistently sought the elimination of lynching and segregated public facilities, especially in transportation. Most blacks had an ardent interest in eliminating discrimination in education and gaining greater access to both vocational education and universities. Many blacks believed their interests would be served by the breakup of concentrated wealth, although there was no consensus about how to achieve this. Like other minorities, they desired political advancement, including representation on juries, city councils, and state legislatures as well as in the U.S. Congress. They also had a handful of foreign policy objectives, which were not as pressing and not likely of realization in the short run. These included freedom for the Virgin Islands, the Philippines, and Hawaii and economic aid to Cuba. The president was dubious about the practicality of any of their foreign policy objectives. He opposed segregation and lynching on principle. The president sent a private message to the NAACP convention on June 30, 1931, in which he opposed lynching and considered delivering a message to Congress denouncing it but did not do so. The overriding issue, on which Hoover worked diligently, was finding decent jobs.[27]

Some black concerns were largely symbolic, issues of status and dignity. Hoover received numerous letters and telegrams urging him to commute the sentences of the Scottsboro Boys, condemned to death for rape in Alabama in what had become a cause célèbre. He referred them and those who wanted to see him personally about the case, to Attorney General Mitchell, who explained that the federal government lacked jurisdiction in the cases and that only the governor of Alabama could commute the sentences.[28] The president found it more difficult to deal with black demands related to the military because they involved appropriations and tradition and because black leaders resisted segregation in principle, yet also insisted on preserving the identity of all-black combat units and opposed dispersing blacks to white outposts. The president delegated these decisions to the army itself and never made a public statement about the controversies relating to the army or the army air force. One such issue was the status of the all-black 110th Cavalry unit, which had fought with distinction in the Spanish-American War and First World War. Congressman DePriest complained of rumors that it was to be disbanded and blacks sent to mingle with whites in integrated outposts, where they would be assigned menial tasks. The War Department responded that the 110th would remain intact with its distinctive insignia, yet other black troops would be reassigned as part of overall reductions in manpower that involved both white and black soldiers. The reason was an economy move of the part of the army. The Quaker president, whose record on military preparedness was not good, was determined to reduce expenditures in all government departments. More problematic was the status of blacks in the army air force, a new, elite branch of the military. Blacks were not permitted to enroll in the air force. The army gave as its reason that admission to the air force was limited to college graduates with technical training. There were not sufficient numbers of blacks to create a discrete unit, and blacks themselves desired segregated units. In the early 1930s it was uncertain where the air force would fit into the military paradigm, and later, when limited numbers of blacks were permitted to enlist, they were organized into segregated units.[29]

The administration often received complaints that blacks were not employed in sufficient numbers on public works or suffered discrimination. Every complaint was investigated and, if possible, resolved. The NAACP, for example, complained that inadequate numbers of blacks worked on the construction of the Hoover Dam. The Interior and War Departments, as well as the president, responded. Hoover asked Wilbur to investigate, and the interior secretary found that the reason for low black employment at the Colorado site was that few blacks lived in the area. Further, he negotiated with the six companies constructing the dam, and they agreed to seek additional black labor. The government had no legal power to compel private contractors to hire by quota, he indicated. Further, because blacks were underemployed at government jobs in some regions, the administration attempted to compensate by hiring a higher percentage in areas densely populated by blacks, such as flood control projects on the lower Mississippi. The War Department suggested that the NAACP view employment in terms of numbers on a national basis rather than on specific projects. In 1932, the White House received complaints that blacks employed on Mississippi River flood control projects in the Deep South were paid low wages and compelled to live in unsanitary conditions. Hoover appointed a committee comprising three blacks as well as a representative of the U.S. Army Corps of Engineers to investigate. Finding some of the complaints justified, they took steps to alleviate them. Doubtless, disparities existed, and black leaders monitored the situation closely. The administration made efforts to correct discrimination, but inconsistencies in treatment persisted in work farmed out to private contractors.[30]

Throughout his presidency, peaking with the Parker nomination, Hoover was harshly criticized by Walter White of the NAACP and W. E. B. DuBois, the editor of *The Crisis*, sometimes in highly personal, inflammatory language. DuBois claimed that Hoover perceived blacks as "sub men."[31] The NAACP, especially DuBois, remained relentlessly critical of Hoover's recovery program. *The Crisis* wrote of the RFC, "A breadline of 858 banks, 18 insurance companies, 8 mortgage loan companies, 16 railways and a few other miscellaneous beggars have now been relieved of the immediate necessities to the tune of $200 million and some odd cents." It added, "They are now hoping to totter on until the administration can slip them a few more doles from the taxpayer's money." *The Crisis* dismissed the plight of farmers and the administration's attempt to aid them. "The farmers have been starving for less than twenty years," the journal wrote. "Why should they complain? Let us colored people tell them something about long distance starvation."[32] In May 1932 the *Pittsburgh Courier* claimed that Hoover had treated fish on a fishing trip better than he treated blacks who visited him at the White House. The black press revived old charges that Hoover had mistreated blacks in South Africa and mistreated the Chinese.[33] Ironically, DuBois had suffered less economic deprivation than Hoover during his early life and little overt discrimination during his formative years. His anger was derived more from what he perceived as the historical process rather than personal experience. Hoover, a practical reformer, preferred the approach of the less elitist Moton, whose judgment and common sense he trusted, although the two sometimes disagreed. After the failure of the Parker nomination, Hoover's distaste for the more militant black organizations increased, not because he disagreed with their goals, but because he disliked their confrontational, rule or ruin tactics. The president continued to support black education and moderate reform groups such as the National Urban League. In 1932, he made a $500 contribution to the Urban

League and continued to issue warm messages to black teacher organizations. Given the gulf between their beliefs and the parameters of his party, there is not much the Quaker president could have done to fully accommodate the militants. His successor, FDR, was unable to completely placate them either.[34]

Hoover dealt with racial issues most directly in attempting to reform Republican patronage in the South, a cesspool of cronyism, self-serving bosses, graft, and corruption. The Republican Party in the South was an anomaly, just as the Democratic Party's Southern wing was riven by contradictions. Southern blacks were Republican for historical reasons; the same reasons that made southern whites Democrats. The Southern factions of both parties had little in common with their Northern counterparts. The Republicans were the party of emancipation, and thus Southern blacks became Republicans. Southern whites remembered "Black Reconstruction" imposed on them by the Northern Republicans. Fact, fiction, and myth were intertwined in the historical allegiances of both parties, not to mention a great deal of over-simplification and misunderstanding. To avert black control, never a serious possibility, Southern whites disenfranchised their black neighbors, who were ostracized by the Democratic Party. In the South, blacks could not even vote in Democratic primaries. Because blacks lacked the vote in national elections, they could not contribute electoral support to the Republican cause. Their sole function was to send delegations to Republican National Conventions that helped determine the GOP nominee. The Southern party was a fiction, yet a convenient one for Republicans and Democrats alike.

Black Republicans thrived on the patronage. Hoover's attitude toward South-ern patronage represented in microcosm his philosophy toward all patronage. His priorities for appointments were honesty, ability, and loyalty—in that order. He did not believe in rewarding individuals with patronage solely because of race or party fealty. Moreover, he disliked the funneling of patronage through local or regional bosses who manipulated it to line their pockets, build politi-cal machines, and perpetuate themselves in power. He intended to overturn the corrupt establishment in the South, revitalize the Republican Party there on a biracial basis by providing better government than the Democrats could offer and by waging political campaigns on the basis of economic issues and common interests. He would eschew waving the bloody shirt on one hand or racial demonization on the other. The president believed a government job was a responsibility, not a reward. This was not the way the patronage game was played. There had been previous reformers of the patronage system, such as the Democrat Grover Cleveland, but none had attacked the morass in the South with such audacity or such determination as Hoover. The president was not accustomed to dealing with professional politicians, and they were not accustomed to dealing with a president like him, who seemed apolitical if not antipolitical. Hoover was also as intellectually honest about patronage as about life in general. He ran head-on into a stone wall. Something would have to give.[35]

Such reforms would have been difficult to implement in any region. But Hoover's attempt to impose reform on the South involved the creation of a color-blind party that did not dole out favors or cater to interest groups. People who believe society should be color blind were not yet museum specimens, but organizing a political party on that basis, in the South of all places, was a novel idea. To some it seemed naïve. Yet in reality, it was the only way Republicans could compete in the South. They could not win elections there without white votes, which they could not obtain so long as their patronage was monopolized by corrupt blacks and whites who were equally corrupt and essentially party hacks. Neither could Hoover openly campaign for equal opportunity for blacks without losing white votes in the North and the South. By necessity, his program was one of stealth. Determined he was; invincible he was not. When he turned over the rock of Southern politics, the president unearthed a nest of vipers, which he meticulously set about casting out.

Hoover's tool of reform was the creation of a state advisory committee in each Southern state. A trio of administration advisers, Walter Newton, his political adviser; Postmaster-General Walter F. Brown; and James Burke, counsel of the Republican National Committee, provided liaison with the state committees and, if necessary, tried to reshuffle them. Brown was the leader of the triumvirate. The Justice Department examined each nominee for a patronage office. Those found corrupt or unqualified were rejected at the national level. A series of weak recommendations provided the rationale for reorganizing or dismissing the local advisory committee. Some existing committees were under the control of entrenched bosses accustomed to having their way. The administration indicted Mississippi black political boss Perry Howard twice but failed to convict him. Other strong bosses existed in Tennessee, Florida, Texas, and South Carolina. In some areas, protracted conflicts occurred. Brown was unpopular in the South and somewhat blunt, but black politicians vouched that he was no racist. Some of those purged, white and black alike, had supported Hoover in 1928. The president even retained Democrats whom he felt had served their constituents well.[36]

State bosses were a minor problem compared to regional bosses such as Horace Mann, an attorney who had left Tennessee about ten years earlier to reside in Washington, DC. Mann had been instrumental in Hoover's success in the South in 1928 and wanted to become the postelection power broker and dispenser of patronage. Unlike Hoover, Mann wanted a lily-white Republican party in the South. A power struggle ensued between Mann and Brown, who became archenemies. Initially, a number of state bosses rallied around Mann, and Brown suffered setbacks. Hoover retreated a bit and made more compromises than he intended. Still, by 1930 most of the state organizations were aligned with Hoover, although many blacks were angry at the president. Mann, his power ebbing by late 1931, vowed to work for Hoover's defeat in 1932. Hoover had hoped his choice for chairman of the RNC, Claudius Huston of Tennessee, would help implement his Southern restructuring, but Huston proved a liability: inept, insensitive, and stubborn—ultimately, an embarrassment.[37]

Hoover's attempt to reform patronage in the South was only partly successful. By the spring of 1931 there had been a relapse and many of the old office-holders were back in their positions, though most had pledged their loyalty to Hoover for the 1932 nomination. It was simply too difficult to overcome old political habits in the South. The attempt to outflank white supremacy juxtaposed with the Depression proved an impossible obstacle in Hoover's time. In Virginia, Republicans cobbled together a ticket comprising respectable, reform-minded whites and lost state elections, which demoralized the reform wing of the party. The spoils politician Bascom Slemp remained at the steering wheel of the Virginia machine, and the rest of the South took note. In Tennessee, Hoover protected the black Robert Church as one of two national committeemen and a member of the Republican State Executive Committee as evidence of his commitment to relatively honest blacks. At the local level, partisan politics and the spoils of office proved greater enticements than noble principles. In some places Hoover's strategy backfired. In South Carolina and Mississippi, for example, anti-Hoover black Republicans cooperated with white supremacists to oppose the administration. The attempt to weed out corruption collapsed. Sometimes, convictions could not be obtained. Moreover, leadership was often lacking to replace bosses who were dethroned, leaving the party feeble. Still, it would be an exaggeration to emphasize the role of the patronage wars in the South in Hoover's 1932 defeat. He lost then for the same reason he won in 1928—the economy. In purely political terms, the black vote in the South remained inconsequential. In time, those who advocated basing Southern campaigns on economic issues and common concerns that cut across class lines would come to be known as realists. Good government did matter to Southerners, white and black alike. Events caught up with Hoover's ideas.[38]

Hoover and Moton were discouraged by the failure of Hoover's plan to uplift blacks economically, especially to transplant them to their own farms on defunct plantations. Moton became more distant, but Hoover continued to reach out to the black leader until Moton's death in 1940. If Hoover believed that an educated black elite was necessary to lead Americans out of the trough of racism, he believed this about whites as well. Some found it hard to accept, then and now, that Hoover could be both a friend of blacks and a foe of interest groups and that he believed what developed into the idea of entitlements was demeaning to those who received them. Donald Lisio writes that "it is abundantly clear from the historical record that both the president and his wife were much more sympathetic to blacks than they felt they could reveal publicly."[39] The Hoovers as individuals never discriminated publicly or privately. It went against the grain of the president's Quaker upbringing and his egalitarian ideals. He wanted to believe that a color-blind society could work and would be more stable than a fragmented one. The president underestimated the tenacity of racism because it was removed from his experience. He believed that stable progress most be gradual, not revolutionary or violent; otherwise it would create a backlash that would eviscerate gains or degenerate into dependency. In attempting to reform Southern politics and in the process create a competitive biracial party there, Hoover was, as in other respects concerning his presidency, caught in the whiplash of a man ahead of his times. The kind of economically based Southern politics he envisioned would occur under the New Deal, but under Roosevelt it would be an incidental part of his program, not deliberately designed, as it was with Hoover.

In 1968 General Leslie R. Groves, a friend of Hoover and the man who headed the Manhattan Project for the United States during the Second World War, told Raymond Henle, an oral history interviewer for the Herbert Hoover Presidential Library, about a conversation he had had with the ex-president that seems almost as explosive as the bomb Groves helped develop. The conversation, which occurred in the context of the 1954 *Brown* decision desegregating schools, was placed under a time seal that was not lifted until 2000. According to Groves, Hoover told him there had been a secret agreement between chief justices and presidents from the time of Wilson to the time of Eisenhower to prevent a school desegregation decision from reaching the U.S. Supreme Court. They knew that the court could not deny the moral legitimacy of such a case, yet feared it would create an eruption of public disorder. Every president until Eisenhower had been briefed by the incumbent chief justice, who apparently did not share the pact with other members of the court. If a president appointed a new chief justice, the president briefed the chief justice, and everyone respected a code of silence. Not until the Eisenhower administration was the chain broken because a new president and a new Chief Justice entered office almost simultaneously, both ignorant of the compact that had bound their predecessors. Fred Vinson was chief justice, and he died suddenly in September 1953, one month before the court was to convene and a few months after Eisenhower took office. Not knowing he was going to die, Vinson had not hurried to tell Eisenhower about the accord. Consequently, neither Eisenhower nor Warren knew about it. Previous presidents had simply not permitted their attorney general to handle such a case. That is why the *Brown* case reached the Supreme Court in 1954 and not earlier. Had not both the leader of the Supreme Court and the leader of the executive branch been unable to inform the other about the tacit agreement, it might have continued.[40]

Hoover's interest in Native Americans arose from two sources: his commitment to the brotherhood of all men as a Quaker and his childhood rearing on the frontier. Quakers from William Penn onward usually paid Indians a fair price for their land instead of seizing it. Hoover had Indian playmates as a child in West Branch. He spent several months living on an Osage Indian reservation in Oklahoma, where his Uncle Laban Miles was the Indian Agent. Another uncle, who raised him in Oregon, Dr. Henry Minthorn, was also an Indian agent as well as physician, a teacher, an abolitionist, and a Union veteran of the Civil War. Hoover's lifelong love of the outdoors began in childhood. His Indian playmates taught him how to shoot a bow, trap animals, and build a fire with stones. Young Hoover spent most of his time outdoors, and he thrived on the Great Plains and in the Pacific Northwest. Entering college at Stanford, he undertook the study of geology partly because it permitted him to work outdoors. Hoover considered the Indian lifestyle normal, not exotic, and he respected it.[41]

As president, Hoover's objective was first to improve the health, education, and employment opportunities of Indians and second to provide them with a variety of choices that would enable them gradually to become acclimated to the larger arena of American society, a process he referred to as integration. Many, including Indians themselves, were divided over the wisdom of a melting pot versus separate enclaves. Hoover did not believe Native Americans could ever achieve comparable economic status with whites so long as they remained confined to reservations. Some well-meaning whites wanted Indians to remain on reservations because of romanticized nostalgia for the Indian way of life, while other whites wanted them to remain there for the opposite reason—to exploit them, their land, and their resources. Hoover, as in many aspects of his policies, took a middle path—which invited criticism from both extremes. To some extent, cultural arguments clashed with economic arguments, as they did among other American minorities. However, one thing was certain. The conditions of the American Indians, as he found them, were abysmal, characterized by poverty, poor education, unemployment, alcoholism, and lack of respect. The Depression further aggravated a bad situation. Change might be painful and necessarily would be gradual, but the status quo seemed unacceptable.[42]

The administration preferred to avoid ideological battles over assimilation versus preservation of native cultures. The president's objective was to wean Native Americans from dependency on the government while preserving as much of their traditional lifestyle as was feasible. The objective was to offer Indians free will and increase their opportunities to exercise it. Like all Quakers, his attitude was a mixture of compassion, realism, and common sense. He was also an advocate of gradualism and personal responsibility, with no intention of either tossing Indians into the vicissitudes of the turbulence of Depression-era America or chaining them to permanent status of dependence and impotence. Empowerment and self-esteem were necessary for success. As with blacks, Hoover would have preferred simply to deal with individuals, not groups. Yet he recognized the impossibility of that, even more in the case of Indians than of blacks. Like blacks, they had endured injustices, and like blacks they were among the poorest of Americans. The quickest way to accelerate their economic progress would have been to find them jobs on Ford assembly lines, and some did. But Hoover never based his decisions on purely material grounds. As a spiritual person, he admired the Indian religions and believed they contained profound truths. A conservationist, he applied this philosophy to human resources as well as natural resources and initiated a federal program to record and preserve Indian sign languages before they disappeared. The president attempted to prod Congress into legislation providing for a legal trademark to protect Indian-made crafts from imitations. He never believed it desirable to completely eradicate the Indian culture for reasons of pride, aesthetics, tradition, and history. Interior Secretary Wilbur believed Native American institutions were especially strong among such tribes as the Navajos and Pueblos and were destined to endure indefinitely. They should have industries of their own that would make them self-supporting, he felt. Remnants of Indian culture should be preserved while there was time, including entire villages. In clearing and excavating the National Parks and Forests, the Interior Department strove to preserve Native American artifacts. Hoover and Wilbur felt such evidence of Native American culture was important to whites, especially children, as well as to the tribes themselves. The interior secretary believed that sympathy for the preservation of Indian culture, for Indians and non-Indians alike, could be achieved by exposing it to the entire population. The government could help provide such exposure, which would serve economic, cultural, and educational purposes. Wilbur was also sufficiently flexible to apply different standards to the fiercely independent Florida Seminoles, who had never been subdued by the white man, even though such ruthless generals as Andrew Jackson had tried. The Seminoles remained entrenched on their land in the Everglades after more than 100 years of attempts to conquer them. "Leave them alone and forget about putting them on a reservation," Wilbur said.[43]

The administration of Indian affairs came under the jurisdiction of Wilbur's Interior Deptartment. Wilbur had been an advocate of Indian rights long before he joined the cabinet. He was a longtime member of a Christian organization, the Indian Rights Association, and he also belonged to the more militant American Indian Defense Association. The administration's most tangible contribution to Indian welfare was an immediate increase in appropriations for spending on Indian affairs, rising from $16.7 million in 1929 to $25.6 million 1932, despite the Depression, when other agencies were being cut. The increases came over the objections of Hoover's own director of the budget and were opposed by many members of Congress. The administration did not receive all it requested. The Hoover administration also sponsored legislation to protect the civil rights of Indians, and Hoover introduced, but failed to obtain, measures to provide pensions and old age benefits to Indians. When Wilbur assumed jurisdiction over governmental Indian policies, he found a patchwork of piecemeal legislation enacted sporadically without an overall philosophy. None of the attempts to legislate Indians out of their problems had succeeded; some might have even aggravated the problems. The administration undertook a thorough reform of the existing system. The Indian Bureau was reorganized into five sections: health, education, agriculture, forestry, and irrigation. Each division was headed by a scientist who maintained close communications with reservation superintendents. Special courts were created to speed adjudication of Indian claims. The president did not consider it possible to reopen old land claims during the Depression. The money was not available, and, as with veterans, it would siphon off money available for all needy Americans. Nonetheless, the Interior Department stepped up efforts to provide Indians with remunerative employment. Many were employed in the construction of the Hoover Dam. They lived in the vicinity and were accustomed to the heat. They were also put to work building roads and trails in national parks and forests and on reclamation projects. Indians were given preference for jobs in the Office of Indian Affairs and on reservations, handling most aspects of Indian relations with the government. Whites were not used when Indian workers could be found. By September 1931 there were 1,512 Indians employed by the Office of Indian Affairs. This represented an increase of 465 over 2 years. The range of occupations varied from superintendent of an agency or school to teaching, nursing, and clerical work. "We can hardly expect to place Indians in positions out in the world in general unless we are willing to place them ourselves wherever we are able to do so," Wilbur said.[44]

Wilbur and Hoover assembled a team to lead the Office of Indian Affairs that was both compassionate and competent. James C. Rhoads, appointed commissioner of Indian Affairs and a partner of Brown Brothers bankers of Philadelphia, had a family tradition of concern for Indian welfare. His father was associated with Indian rights for many years, and Rhoads himself had been president of the Indian Rights Association the year before his appointment by Hoover. J. Henry Scattergood, like Rhoads a prominent Quaker and prosperous Philadelphia banker and philanthropist, was named assistant commissioner. Both men relinquished lucrative jobs to enter government service. Hoover had met Rhoads and Scattergood when they worked for the Friends Reconstruction Service after World War I, cooperating with the American Red Cross and the YMCA in feeding Europe. Both shared the philosophy of Hoover and Wilbur of gradually integrating Indians into the larger society. Hoover hoped the Office of Indian Affairs could be dismantled in about 25 years, and Wilbur wanted to begin decentralizing the bureaucracy within 8 years, the amount of time he expected Hoover to remain in office. Health, education, and job preparation were the core of the program with special attention to children. To help keep Indian families intact, boarding schools for children would be phased out. Wilbur believed the idea of educating Indian children separately, on reservations, was flawed because it was premised on the idea that they would all become farmers or work at Indian crafts. Instead, the children, living at home, would be gradually integrated into the state public school systems. Wilbur, who thought Indian children would become overly sheltered if schooled solely on reservations, believed they should be encouraged to continue their education as far as their ability permitted. This would empower them with the skills and self-esteem necessary to succeed in the outside world or in their native environment.[45]

Rhoads also helped to reform and rebuild the bureaucracy dealing with Indians. In the summer of 1930 he summarized accomplishments to date. The commissioner continued to emphasize education as the cornerstone of lifting Indians out of poverty. The courses offered now had a pronounced emphasis on practical and vocational education, directed partly to meeting the hardships of the Depression. The curriculum was designed to train Native Americans for jobs in industry, agriculture, teaching, and clerical work. The Indian school service appointed a former dean at the University of Montana who had worked at the Labor Dept as the assistant director of education. They also hired an experienced educator as supervisor of trade and industrial training. There were plans to hire a director of education for the Indian service who would be placed under civil service. Demonstration teachers had been recruited to tour the schools and instruct teachers. For 1930, an additional $1.1 million was appropriated to provide food, clothing, and discretionary money to students, and higher appropriations were in the pipeline for 1931. Rhoads recognized that education for jobs would be ineffective unless jobs were available and accessible to Indians. A new placement service was created along with guidance counselors to place Indian students and later expanded to include all Indians, not merely students. An employee of the Department of Agriculture was assigned to find work in agricultural occupations. He collaborated with county extension agents and a personnel officer supervised the placement effort. A professor of anthropology at Cornell University received a leave of absence to develop a national educational program for Indians.[46]

Health was another major concern. The administration obtained greater appropriations for health care and had improved hospitals that served Indians, as well as home service. About 140 physicians and 400 nurses were assigned to Indian care. Facilities included 96 hospitals, with 6 more earmarked by Congress. The administration addressed land reform as well. Previously, privately owned Indian land had reverted to the government on the death of the owner. Now such land could be purchased by a relative or by the tribe using government loans. The program facilitated continuity of ownership. Not all educational and occupational efforts involved jobs away from the reservations. Indians were encouraged to perpetuate crafts such as the making of pottery, baskets, rugs, and jewelry, which provided employment especially in the Southwest. The government used modern marketing techniques to promote Indian products and certified their authenticity. Overall, the administration helped Indians become better educated, healthier, better fed, better clothed, and more self-sufficient. They were offered greater choices in vocation. Efforts were made to identify and nurture their talents. The strategy deemphasized paternalism, encouraged pride, and facilitated economic independence. Hoover hoped this would make Native Americans increasingly self-sufficient and less subject to manipulation and the vagaries of changing policies.[47]

Despite the Great Depression, Indian affairs were a priority for Hoover and Wilbur. They had capable, energetic, imaginative advocates in Rhoads and Scattergood. There was never a consensus, even among Indians themselves, about what degree of assimilation or integration was desirable. As lovers of history, yet practical men, Hoover and Wilbur wanted to offer the greatest latitude to Indians themselves, the best of both worlds, yet ultimately, somewhere down the road, the government and Indians themselves would have to make a choice. The administration never wavered from its ultimate goal of economic integration with a degree of cultural autonomy. As with other groups, Hoover foresaw the demeaning aspects of reliance on government support indefinitely. To those who would argue that this was cruel, his counterargument was that permanent dependency was even crueler. The pace was not rigidly set and would relapse and then surge forward, under succeeding administrations and never be determined to the satisfaction of everyone. Like blacks, Native Americans had a history of oppression, and it would take an effort to overcome it. As a practical Quaker, Hoover believed in a combination of compassion and realism. A helping hand would be extended, but it would not provide a permanent solution without an element of personal responsibility. He applied this standard to every group and to every individual, including himself. Indeed, by 1933 Hoover could have very well wallowed in self-pity but choose not to.

Whatever their long-term success, the assertive policies of the Hoover administration relating to Native Americans was intellectually honest, not politically motivated, and they marked an improvement over any previous twentieth-century administration. The fate of the Indian had an important place in the policies of the administration, and its basic impulse was to reform; to move forward at a graduated pace; to improve the tangible areas of Indian life such as health, education, and employment, while preserving Indians skills and their religion; and to provide opportunities for land ownership within and without the tribal system. Some tribes were expected to endure indefinitely, others to shrink and wither. The philosophical question remains as contentious today as it was in Hoover's time, and no one but Indians themselves can determine their destiny. Free will is the greatest weapon for both happiness and misery in the human arsenal. No one who grows up within a certain way of life leaves it without some regret, and gratification and security in the midst of change, much less in the upheaval of the Great Depression, was difficult to come by. But all of us retain some of our heritage within regardless of external circumstances.

Hoover was enthusiastic about the participation of women in public service and had been an early advocate of female suffrage. He knew many of the women reformers of the Progressive movement and had received enthusiastic backing from women in 1928. He had worked in tandem with women's groups to promote causes such as world peace, child health, and the enforcement of Prohibition, and the president was eager to include women in his

administration. Among his personal acquaintances were female writers, journalists, and social workers. Socially, the president had always craved good
conversation. and women outstanding in arts and letters were frequent dinner guests. The chief executive was more socially inhibited with women than
among men, and he bonded most closely with men who had worked for him
over a long period. Fortunately, Lou was a gregarious conversationalist, and
once Hoover opened up, women found him entertaining and knowledgeable.
He also enjoyed a mutual respect with professional women because of their
dedication to humanitarian causes. His own marriage was a true partnership
based on love, loyalty, and common interests, and he did not attempt to dominate. Lou had played an active role in delivering speeches to promote Belgian
relief and food conservation during World War I, but she did not take part
in political campaigns, of her own volition. She shared some of her husband's
modesty and eschewed flaunting her status as First Lady or exploiting it. In
temperament, they were similar though not identical. Lou was independent
and self-sufficient, as demonstrated by her determination to obtain a degree
in geology and engineering after she had already obtained a college degree in
education. She was one of the best educated and most versatile First Ladies.
As First Lady she did not consent to interviews about herself but did speak
and accept interviews about causes she supported, such as the Girl Scouts
and women's athletics. Almost all their social activities and entertaining were
conducted as a couple.[48]

During his first interregnum the president actively recruited women for
positions in government and asked his staff to scout for qualified women he
might appoint. He was eager to place qualified women in positions of responsibility and did so to a greater degree than any of his predecessors. On most
issues, the administration was proactive not neutral. Hoover did not please all
women because they did not have identical aims, yet even some groups with
which he differed, such as the National Woman's Party, whose objective was
a gender-blind Equal Rights Amendment, praised his sincerity. The president
favored legislation limiting the working hours of women and children and
believed they merited special protection. In late 1928 the Columbus, Ohio,
Dispatch wrote that "The Hoover administration has taken a particularly kind
attitude toward the trend of modern feminism that is sweeping women into
positions of responsibility in industry and politics."[49]

Most appointments were in fields related to women's interests or professions. Women were selected by the State Department to represent the United
States at international conferences. The president appointed a woman to the
board that administered trust funds for the Library of Congress. Additional
women were appointed as postmasters and on commissions related to child
health, infant care, juvenile delinquency, the handicapped, Indian welfare,
education, housing, and home ownership. Women were named to the Conservation Commission, and the commission responsible for management of
the currency. For the first time women held high positions in the Offices of

Education and the Bureau of Indian affairs. Women were chosen for assistant commissioner of education and assistant director of Indian education. A woman was appointed to the Board of Income Tax Appeals. When Hoover found women performing well from previous administrations, he kept them on the job. Women were continued as chiefs of the Children's Bureau and of the Women's Bureau, as chairman of the U.S. Employment Compensation Commission, as chief of the Bureau of Home Economics, and as a member of the Civil Service Commission. New appointments included the president of the U.S. Housing Corporation, the Board of Advisers for Federal Institutions for Women (on which two Coolidge appointees were also retained), the Board of Review on Immigration, several state collectors of Internal Revenue, the National Parole Board, and the International Prison Commission. The number of women as customs collectors rose from two to five. Two women represented the United States at the Conference on Codification of International Law at The Hague. In all, about 90,000 women were employed by the federal government, many in clerical positions. Others worked as teachers, as home economics instructors in the Department of Agriculture and as nurses in the Public Health Service. Hoover did not treat these as matters of patronage but sought the most qualified people. The turnover rate was relatively small. The Commerce Department also employed larger numbers of women as census enumerators. Shortly before leaving office, the president signed an executive order granting women equality with men in civil service eligibility. He revoked a civil service rule that required the keeping of separate classification lists for men and women, a change that led to an increase in the number of women employed by the federal government.[50]

Hoover also took an enlightened attitude toward the aspirations of organized labor, dating to his early career as a mining engineer. He treated his men fairly, paid them high wages, and they seldom struck. Hoover was in the vanguard of the Progressive movement on the labor issue. He believed unions were a necessary counterweight to industrialists and helped stabilize society. He also felt that high wages helped drive the consumer economy. In 1909 the young engineer wrote in his first book, *Principles of Mining*, that the days of laissez faire, when business dominated labor, were obsolete and impractical. High morale among workers was a major factor in increasing production. The president believed proper respect could harmonize the interests of management and labor, which were largely mutual, if not identical. He believed strikes and lockouts were wasteful but also that strikes were sometimes necessary as a last resort. Usually neither workers nor employers ever recouped their losses from protracted strikes, however, and the consuming public suffered. Neither did he condone violence, whether by employment of strikebreakers or destruction of property by workers. Hoover opposed the closed shop because he believed it infringed on the rights of individual employees. He also opposed the use of federal injunctions to end strikes. The government should conciliate and mediate but should not terminate strikes by fiat. As secretary of commerce, Hoover promoted the concept of industrial committees representing labor and management at the grassroots level. These would not resemble company unions nor preempt national unions, although national unions often considered them a threat to their authority to negotiate contracts. Rather, the local committees would iron out grievances before they reached the level of causing a strike. Their purpose was to rectify problems before they became aggravated; the shop committees were not designed to browbeat businessmen or to ensure docile workers. Large industries had created mammoth impersonal production lines. The shop committee was a tool to restore a sense of connection at the grass roots. A friend of Samuel Gompers and his successor, William Green, the president believed unions performed a useful function. He considered the American Federation of Labor (AFL) responsible and a bulwark against communism. As president, Hoover became the first president since Wilson to address the annual AFL convention in 1930. Green sometimes clashed with the president, but like Hoover, he opposed a dole. Hoover and John L. Lewis, the militant leader of the United Mine Workers, were mutual admirers. Both were self-educated, brilliant men, committed to the causes they believed in. Lewis was not a Socialist, Hoover said; he wanted a bigger cut from the capitalist system. When he became president, the new chief executive seriously considered appointing Lewis secretary of labor but declined because a scandal in the labor leader's background, which Hoover refused to specify in his *Memoirs*, might embarrass Lewis. Hoover could tolerate Lewis's militancy, given the dire conditions of miners, yet he ordinarily disliked confrontational tactics. On the other hand, he believed repression of labor would only incite radicalism. Prosperity required balance. The economy hummed by integrating waste reduction, worker involvement, just wages, stable employment, and fair prices for consumers.[51]

Hoover largely shaped labor policy under Harding and Coolidge and served as a troubleshooter for both presidents. The secretary of commerce argued against Attorney General Harry Daugherty's sweeping injunction to end the railroad strike of 1922. The commerce secretary devoted a great deal of time to dealing with actual and potential strikes in the railroad and bituminous coal industries in the 1920s and helped engineer the Railway Labor Act of 1926, which supported collective bargaining and established mediation procedures for future strikes. The fundamental problems of these two sick industries remained unsettled, however. At numerous conventions before such unsympathetic audiences as the National Chamber of Commerce, he argued in favor of the rights of labor. Hoover attempted to persuade private insurance companies to provide unemployment insurance and health benefit policies to workers prior to the Depression. Harding relied heavily on the commerce secretary and took seriously his argument that the 12-hour day in the steel industry was inhumane and would only wear down the men in the mills. Profitability required willing workers, and more time off would allow wholesome recreation and additional time with their families. The hard-boiled steel titans were difficult to convince and initially balked in 1922. Hoover audaciously leaked their rejection of administration recommendations to the press, which provoked a firestorm of public criticism directed at the steel moguls. Subsequently, they reconsidered, and Hoover wrote a passage announcing the agreement to reduce hours into a speech delivered by Harding at Tacoma, Washington, shortly before the Ohioan's death. Typically, the precedent-setting reform was accomplished without legislation.[52]

The president devoted a substantial amount of time during his tenure to ensuring that workers were fairly paid, that unions remained intact, and that labor peace prevailed. Despite the Depression, especially through 1931, unusual harmony prevailed. There were fewer strikes or lockouts that during normal times. No federal troops were summoned to quell violence. The major exception occurred in the soft coal industry in eastern Pennsylvania, Ohio, and West Virginia during the summer of 1931. The endemic problems of overproduction and ruthless competition that drove down prices were exacerbated by the Depression. Miners struck out of desperation and even protested that United Mine Worker leader John L. Lewis was a lackey of capitalists. The administration attempted to arrange of conference of mine owners to rationalize the industry, but they declined. They had little in common because they were competing against each other as well as underpaying the miners. The stark law of supply and demand overpowered all attempts at resolution.[53]

Part of the relative peace transpired because of the agreements Hoover negotiated with major industrialists to avoid wage cuts at White House conferences in 1929. The agreements were honored until they began to crack in the summer and fall of 1931, when conditions worsened. By that time most major industries had resorted to every other expedient: cutting salaries and dividends and reducing costs. The principle had been established that labor was not a commodity to be cast aside but a collection of human beings who deserved humane treatment. Still, when the industrialists had agreed to uphold wage levels in 1939, they had expected the downturn to last no longer than six months. By September 1931, after England left the gold standard, their only alternatives to pay cuts was to lay off workers en masse or to go out of business. They justified the reductions in part by arguing that the cost of living had declined comparably and that employed workers had suffered no decline in purchasing power. The announcement of wage cuts by U.S. Steel opened the floodgates, and within weeks nearly every other major type of industry had slashed wages as well, many of them taking effect on October 1. Hoover complained that the reductions would only prolong the Depression by curtailing purchasing power, but this time the industrialists responded that they had no choice. Some complained that artificially propping up wages had prevented the Depression from bottoming out, actually prolonging it. Ironically, the announcement of wage cuts sent the value of stocks and bonds soaring. Wall Street had its best day since the crash, although the momentum was not sustained. Initially, many investors were optimistic that wage reductions would produce increased profits, but that would have happened only if the economy in general had improved.[54]

Hoover's Labor Department helped prevent strikes through its Conciliation Service. The department also expanded the work of the Bureau of Labor Statistics to include statistics on technological unemployment and wholesale price figures, and it monitored wages and hours of labor. It helped job placement by the expansion of the Employment Service, which opened offices in every state. The Women's Bureau investigated the treatment of women in industry and monitored waste. The Child Welfare Bureau coordinated relief for children nationwide. The Seventy-Second Congress extended the Vocational Rehabilitation Act and expanded the five-day workweek to include most permanent federal employees. A bill was enacted prohibiting the counterfeiting of union labels in the District of Columbia, and the five-day week and six-hour day was mandated on public roads financed by the federal government, designed to spread work. In addition, convict labor was prohibited on roads built by the federal government. The Davis-Bacon Prevailing Wage Rate Law provided that when disputes arose over pay for work on public buildings, the secretary of labor would determine the appropriate wages in accordance with prevailing scales. This usually worked to the advantage of labor.[55]

Hoover had been working to free labor from the shackles of federal injunctions used to break strikes since the 1920s. On March 23, 1932, over the objections of conservatives, he signed the Norris-La Guardia Anti-Injunction Act sponsored by GOP Senator George W. Norris of Nebraska and GOP Representative Fiorello La Guardia of New York. It provided full freedom for workers to join the union of their choice, which would serve as their exclusive bargaining agent. The bill drastically limited the use of injunctions in strikes. Injunctions could be granted only in rare instances in which evidence of danger or of injury was proven. The statute also mandated the removal of demonstrably prejudiced judges in labor contempt cases and absolved union officials from prosecution for acts of their individual members. Strikers arrested for perpetrating violence or causing injury were guaranteed a jury trial. Further, the law prohibited "yellow dog" contracts in which employees had to promise not to join a union as a condition of employment. The measure secured many of labor's major objectives, some of which had been under consideration for a decade. Hoover did not originate the bill, but he helped pry it out of a congressional committee when opponents attempted to pigeonhole it. Finally, the president appointed a representative of labor to the Tariff Commission, the first such appointment.[56]

Hoover believed that for the duration of the Depression he should curtail immigration in order to save jobs for Americans. Nonetheless, he had always opposed the provisions in the Immigration Act of 1924 assigning immigration quotas on the basis of national origin. The president considered this discriminatory and had attempted to repeal the quota system during the special session of 1929, yet Congress rejected his recommendation. The Quaker chief executive believed that people of exceptional talent, whatever their origin, should be permitted to immigrate, as should people with families in America. Thus his immigration restrictions of the 1930s were unrelated to race.[57]

The existing law permitted the exclusion of immigrants who would become public charges—that is, they would have to be supported by welfare relief. Under the nagging unemployment existing within the United States, virtually all immigrants without a waiting job or a relative to support them would not be self-supporting. The president, with the vigorous support of organized labor and the general public, issued an executive order instructing American consuls worldwide to withhold visas to immigrants who could not support themselves. This applied to both quota and nonquota countries. At that time, most immigrants were arriving from Canada and Mexico, neither of which was restricted by a quota. In 1929 some 279,678 immigrants came to America, and 69,203 departed. By 1932 this had dramatically reversed. Only 35,576 immigrants entered, and 103,295 departed. In addition to limiting immigration, the administration accelerated the deportation of alien criminals was well as those who had entered the United States legally but had committed crimes while in America. Hoover believed in enforcing all laws and he believed such deportations served the dual purpose of saving jobs for Americans and ridding the country of a criminal element. Virtually all other western nations implemented some type of immigration restrictions during the Depression. William Green, president of the AFL, upon a vote of the union's executive council, commended the president for the policy. Hoover estimated that his immigration policy saved about 400,000 American jobs during his term.[58]

Hoover's policies toward minorities, women, and organized labor emanated from his Quaker conscience, his frontier egalitarianism, his experience in the Progressive movement, and his humanitarian sympathy for those under unusual duress, coupled with a firm belief in personal responsibility, all leavened by common sense. He believed government should lend a helping hand to all in need yet should not play favorites or buy votes with patronage. Neither should such help be extended indefinitely, lest government become a crutch. He always placed the needs of all Americans over the interest of any group, even when it was politically unpopular or when any group commanded a bloc of votes. He was basically a fair man who was deeply compassionate yet not prone to emotional display in public, even with respect to his own family. He lacked the appetite for power and self-preservation that might have made him a more successful politician. He was aware of these qualities and was unashamed of them. When groups received federal money or employment, they would know that they had earned it and that it was rendered with no strings attached. This won him the grudging respect of some who disagreed with him and the affection of those who knew him well. These personal qualities did not make him a great president or even an astute politician, but they did help make him a good and a great man.

CHAPTER 14

The Grim Reaper Stalks the World

Foreign Affairs, 1931–1933

During the first quarter of 1931 the United States economy showed promise that the Depression had bottomed out and was bouncing back. Thus far employment had not dipped below the level of 1921–22. In the first quarter, industrial output grew by 5 percent, payrolls by 10 percent, and stock prices by 10 percent.[1] Then setbacks from Europe occurred that staggered the Unites States and sent the world economy spiraling toward an appointment with the apocalypse. It represented the point at which an ordinary recession became the worldwide Great Depression. Hoover's hopes of ending the collapse in a single term faded. In March, the economy began to decline. A crisis brewed in Germany and Austria, where economic chaos sowed political instability. In Germany, threats came from Communists on the Left and Nazis on the Right. Hoover hoped that he could avert an ultimate Day of Judgment. He injected his administration vigorously into world affairs. Hoover staved off military conflict and economic ruin in the short run, yet his job became infinitely more complicated. For the remainder of his term he dealt with domestic and international crises simultaneously.[2]

Germany and Austria groaned under the burden of debts, some inflicted by reparations and the loss of colonies. Other aspects were self-inflicted. They had been living beyond their means, floating long-term loans at unrealistically high interest rates, certain to default. They resorted to this expediency rather than raising taxes, cutting expenditures, and trimming social benefits. Foreign bankers bought into the shell game, lured by the illusion of stratospheric interest rates offered. Such loans drained American investment capital because no one could earn comparable profits in more prosaic investments. It hurt the former Central Powers too, because the sale of bonds soaked up domestic capital needed for postwar reconstruction, which would have provided jobs. Many impoverished Latin American governments employed the same tactic. When the debts began to fall due, the debtors covered them by issuing short-term securities offering yet higher interest rates. The world economy was linked in a common dependency in which the failure of securities in one nation sucked down creditors abroad. Although some of the offenders were central governments, the most egregious were municipalities and state governments. At the national level, some of the money was being poured, not into productive enterprises, but into armaments. Whether used for arms or social welfare benefits, almost none of the money was spent on self-sustaining projects that generated jobs or consumer products. Hundreds, perhaps thousands, of American banks would drown in the deluge if the debtors defaulted. Now the pied pipers of high-risk investment were beckoning the children of Hamlin.[3] Hoover had been warning against high-yield foreign investments and overpriced domestic stocks since the early 1920s. World investors were riding a merry-go-round that must either stop or spin faster and faster until it spun them off.

In March 1931, Germany and Austria announced formation of a credit union, forbidden by the Versailles treaty, which would have strengthened them economically. The merger was vetoed by the French and the British. The French believed a prostrate Germany would be weakened militarily. Germany was potentially powerful even if temporarily weak, and French memories of the destruction of the Great War were fresh. Yet their militant attitude toward Germany did not cow Germans but inflamed them. Nationalism drove European politics between the wars. Prior to the ascent of Hitler, the most nationalistic nation was France, which had won the last war but feared losing the next one. Hoover considered France intractable, especially on disarmament. The French had the most to gain by disarmament, but they also had the most to lose. Nationalism was a factor in the foreign policies of the United States too but in just the opposite way. Here, it encouraged a militantly anti-interventionist foreign policy rather than an aggressive one. American nationalism was manifested not in an arms buildup but in a build-down, not in a desire for overseas expansion, but in a hands-off policy. In retrospect, lacking a large land army and an ability to transport it, coupled with a reluctance to use it, America's impotence in Europe and in Asia was haunted by inevitability.

By April 1931, the ruinous legacy of the war had led to runs on banks in Austria, including the nation's largest bank, the Kreditanstalt, which contained about one-half of Austrian deposits. The liabilities of the great bank were six times its assets, and it could not withstand a bank run. The French contributed to its demise by withdrawing gold, although France already held the largest reserve of bullion in Europe. In May, the Kreditanstalt collapsed, pulling Europe into a maelstrom of panic that reverberated in America, whose banks held between $1.2 billion and $1.5 billion in European securities. The wave swept across the continent and threatened hundreds, perhaps thousands, of banks in America if not arrested. In early May, the president began contemplating an economic and psychological strategy to dispel the shadow creeping over Europe and threatening to vault over the Atlantic. Over the next six weeks, Hoover devoted most of his time to the crisis in Europe. He consulted economists; members of the cabinet, especially Mellon and Stimson; and his ambassadors to France, England, and Germany. Early in June, he proposed to his advisers a one-year moratorium on all intergovernmental debts (not including private debts). As the largest creditor, the United States would make the biggest sacrifice. The agreement, which he termed a moratorium, would have to be ratified by Congress, which was not in session, and approved by each nation included.[4]

The president sought support from foreign leaders via transatlantic telephone and called members of Congress to the White House. He also employed telephone and telegraph. Most senators and foreign leaders approved. Some equivocated, including the influential Democrats Joseph T. Robinson of Arkansas and John Nance Garner of Texas. The president, remembering the failure of Wilson's Versailles treaty, wanted to ensure domestic support before he announced the moratorium publicly. Later, in a fit of pique, Congress billed the president personally for transatlantic calls. Stimson briefed foreign ambassadors. The British were supportive, the French, dubious. On June 18, Hoover received a cablegram from German President von Hindenburg requesting his intervention. By that time his statement was nearly complete. He planned to release it on June 22, but it was leaked to the press by senators; thus, leading the president to move up the announcement of the moratorium to June 20. A bold stroke, it struck a psychological chord.[5]

Most nations approved promptly. To Germany, Austria, and much of Eastern Europe, it seemed manna from heaven. The French remained recalcitrant. The premature announcement, before they were fully informed, irritated them. More importantly, they did not want to see their archenemy strengthened. They asked, realistically and prophetically, whether the Germans would ante up when the moratorium expired. Privately, Hoover pondered the same question. However, the only options were an immediate default or a potential default later. At least the moratorium would thaw the ice of pessimism. The French public opposed the moratorium, but the French business community supported the delay because otherwise their economy would be dragged down with Germany's. Besides, the French knew that alternatives to President von Hindenburg's government were likely to be militaristically francophobic. Prime Minister Pierre Laval and Foreign Minister Aristide Briand supported the accord, but the decision lay with the Chamber of Deputies, which was divided. Overzealous support by the prime minister might precipitate the collapse of his cabinet. If that occurred, Hoover would lose a friend and partner. After the other nations approved, the French and the Americans haggled over details. Hoover understood France's valid fears. Yet the longer they resisted, the less beneficial impact the announcement would make. After 17 days, the French accepted. It was a historic accomplishment for Hoover. The British hailed it as evidence that America would provide greater leadership in Europe. The lord mayor of Berlin suggested Hoover for the Nobel Peace Prize. The stock market stabilized temporarily. Yet the effect of the French delay was that the hoses were not turned on until the house had nearly burned down.[6]

Congress did not convene until December 7, 1931, and the next installment on war debts fell due on December 15, which left precious little time to ratify. Ratification could be stopped by a determined filibuster led by senators such as Hiram Johnson, an inveterate foe of Hoover and a die-hard isolationist. On December 14, Hoover informed foreign leaders that they would not be held in default if Congress failed to confirm the agreement by the December 15 deadline. Some argued that if the moratorium were approved Germany would never pay. The administration countered that it was certain they would never pay if the agreement were killed. Others claimed Hoover was power hungry or, like Caesar, ambitious. The House approved the moratorium 317–100 on December 19, and the Senate endorsed it soundly with a 69–12 vote, on December 22, giving the president a Christmas present, though with a reservation that stipulated that the U.S. Congress prohibited the cancellation of war debts. The president proposed the revival of the old War Debt Commission to consider adjusting debts based on the ability of the debtor nation to pay, but Congress nailed the coffin shut on that idea.[7]

The moratorium did nothing to deal with private debts owed American and Western European bankers by Germans. In fact, Congress and the president lacked the constitutional authority to intervene in private debts. Most of these loans were short-term securities soon to fall due, which would ensure the collapse of the major Central European banks and some of their creditors. Again, the choice lay between getting nothing and perhaps getting something later. Revolution in Germany was possible if its private banks failed, leaving their depositors penniless and angry. Hoover helped broker a "Standstill Agreement" resembling the moratorium. The Standstill Agreement was among bankers, not governments. It provided that creditors would offer additional time before trying to collect international private debts. Any other solution would have sent stock and bond values plummeting worldwide, including securities held by American banks. The agreement among private creditors was negotiated at the London Economic Conference in July 1931 and finalized at Basel, Switzerland, in late August. However, neither the moratorium nor the Standstill Agreement applied to Latin America, where banking was teetering on an equally precipitous abyss. No one wanted to wade into that thicket.[8]

The moratorium and the Standstill Agreement were only reprieves. Hoover won plaudits as a statesman who had waded into the shark infested waters of European politics and had at least made a valiant effort that gained goodwill for America. Nonetheless, the president's moratorium was followed by a collapse in Germany. In the aftermath of Hoover's initiative and its final acceptance by all nations, two conferences assembled in London. One included economic specialists to plan the tactical implementation of the Hoover plan. More importantly, statesmen from the major powers gathered to determine Europe's economic future. Stimson and Mellon, already in Europe, represented the United States. Mellon, aged and exhausted from his protracted negotiations with the French, played only a minor role. Stimson played a major role but clashed with Hoover for failing to follow the president's instructions and for seeking credit for Hoover's ideas. The conference of statesmen dealt with economic questions. They attempted to salvage the German economy before it disintegrated. Meanwhile, panic spread in Germany as foreign and domestic creditors raced to withdraw deposits in currency and gold. Banks doled out only the minimum to conduct business and pay government obligations. Violence flared as Communists clashed with Nazis. Adolf Hitler claimed his party was the only alternative to Communism. In the days preceding the London conference, which convened on July 20, 1931, diplomats shuttled between London, Paris, and Berlin, in a diplomatic chess game. Stimson and Mellon participated in the international intrigue and were full participants in the London conference. Previously, America had only sent observers to such conferences. Hugh Gibson represented the United States at the meeting of economic experts.[9]

The summer of 1931 witnessed the most feverish diplomatic activity since Versailles. German Chancellor Bruening was at the center of every major discussion, as were the Americans and Laval. The French wanted to cripple Germany's economy and military without destroying its political infrastructure because that might lead to a militaristic government bent on revenge. The Germans and French met face to face, and the Americans parlayed with both. The Germans had hoped the London conclave would produce massive new loans, which Hoover considered impractical. It would be like pouring water into a bucket with holes, he said. Germany received only a $100 million credit for three months, which was spent within nine days. The London Conference made no breakthroughs. For Americans, its significance lay in the major role the United States played in European diplomacy, unprecedented in peacetime. Hoover, an internationalist, was also a realist who knew that he must prod American opinion, yet not move beyond it, as Wilson had done. His task was comparable to prodding a mule train.

As agreed at London, a committee of experts named for its chair, Albert W. Wiggins, chairman of the board of Chase National Bank, convened at Basel to examine Germany's credit needs. The Wiggins Committee locked the Standstill Agreement into place. Experts vowed to convene at the end of six months to consider a further extension. The committee recommended a permanent scaling down of both war debts and reparations, but Hoover declined because Congress was opposed. In fact, Hoover had wanted to make the moratorium for two years but doubted that a longer moratorium could be ratified. The Wiggins group specified that Germany would make up the missed reparations in ten annual installments beginning July 1, 1933, with no option of postponement. In addition, short-term credits were converted into long-term credits. Germany was expected to economize and to consider raising taxes. By now, hope was waning that war debts or reparations would ever be fully paid, yet it was not politically prudent to concede default.[10]

Germany's descent into darkness was only slowed, not avoided, by diplomacy. The Depression did not end in a year, as architects of the Standstill Agreement anticipated. Temporary chaos was averted but not ultimate chaos. The funds saved from reparations were insufficient to stabilize Germany's economy or its politics. President von Hindenburg ruled by decree but could not control Prussia, where fighting between Communists and Nazis, both intent on toppling the government and slaughtering each other, grew pandemic. Parliament was fractured into more than 20 parties. The middle shrunk while both extremes, especially the Right, gained. Bruening despaired of cobbling together a stable coalition. The partnership of Bruening and von Hindenburg, the twin pillars of the old order, was cracking. Gold fled Germany, and the government resorted to draconian fiscal austerity to remain solvent. Britain, attempting to keep Germany afloat, jeopardized its own gold standard. On September 1, 1931, the German stock exchange reopened after being shut for seven weeks, and stocks plummeted from 25 to 40 percent. The only hope was that lack of money to speculate might prevent it from plunging lower. In October 1931, von Hindenburg met with Adolf Hitler, a humiliation to Bruening. On August 1, 1932, groups on the Right, of which the Nazis were the strongest, won 45.5 percent of the vote. Yet economic disarray alone did not drive Germany over the brink. There were other countries that suffered as much or more. Nationalism and a search for scapegoats for the economic malaise and defeat in the Great War were catalysts that toppled a dysfunctional government. What made the hard times hard was more than money alone.[11]

The next nation to tumble off the economic merry-go-round was Britain. The pound sterling, the Rock of Gibraltar of international finance, was stressed enormously by the crisis in Germany. The pound declined in value against other currencies, and investors sought safer havens. The pound had been pegged unrealistically high when Britain returned to gold after the Great War. The government failed to live within its means, and the Depression depleted the Royal Treasury. Generous welfare benefits and high union pay were more than the government could bear, and it resisted raising taxes. On September 14, the Royal Navy mutinied to protest pay cuts. The government compromised by partially restoring pay reductions. Britain sacrificed its own needs by making huge loans to Germany. Now both democracy and the pound sterling were sinking under the weight of hopeless expectations. On September 21, 1931, Britain ceased redeeming domestic credits with bullion. It tried to continue redeeming foreign holders of British securities with gold. This action had the economic impact of the salvo fired at Sarajevo.[12]

The flicker of hope for an early end to the Depression died. The American gold standard and its banking system were undermined. In 1931, gold-backed currency was the common denominator in international commerce. Theoretically, unbacked currency was worthless. A nation could not issue more currency than it could back with gold, lest it risk uncontrolled inflation. Outflowing gold contracted the money in circulation. Gold was pegged at a set value, unlike fluctuating currencies of different nations. It ensured predictability in international exchanges. Now the world's criterion for the worth of items sold from nation to nation resembled Monte Carlo. More than two dozen countries followed Britain off gold. The combination of the British abandoning gold, the moratorium on war debt collection, and the Standstill Agreement meant that much of the world's assets were frozen. Germany turned to autarchy. Britain declared its empire a closed system. The volume of global trade declined from $39 billion in 1929 to about $12 billion in 1932. Foreigners began removing gold from the United States because America might be next. Americans themselves removed money from banks. Depositors staged a run on the banks, demanding gold. By the end of 1931, some 2,294 banks had failed, an all-time record for the United States. The Depression entered a new stage. During the winter of 1931, Hoover had hoped for the best. By the early fall, he feared for the worst. The immediate effect of Britain's departure from the sacrosanct gold standard was a violent fluctuation in the value of world currencies. Second, the stock and bond markets in most countries, including the United States, spiraled downward. The French franc remained the steadiest of all currencies. The Federal Reserve tried to assure depositors by redeeming all demands for bullion, quickly shrinking the American supply. As the gold stock dwindled, Hoover feared to inform the public about how close the nation was to losing control of its currency. He began to preparing a firewall of economic defense. The president organized the National Credit Corporation (NCC) to shore up banks. When Congress convened, he submitted legislation creating the Reconstruction Finance Corporation and, even more significant for the gold standard, the Glass-Steagall Act. Hoover concluded that the roots of the Depression lay not in America's stock market crash, which was only a symptom, but in the economic and political dislocations arising from the Great War and its reverberations in Europe. He realized the saga would not have an early end, and it might not have a happy one.[13]

The French premier, Pierre Laval, redeemed the invitation issued to him by Stimson to parley with the American president in late October 1931. Sailing on October 16, Laval arrived in New York on October 22 and traveled to Washington by train, where he arrived on October 23. The premier had angled for an invitation because a state visit to America might help his stature domestically. Hoover, preoccupied with the Depression and especially the outflow of gold, initially considered the visit a distraction yet soon grew to like the affable Frenchman. There were few dramatic issues at stake, and the summit produced no unexpected results. The talks focused on economics and disarmament. On these issues, the positions of the leaders were immovable due to domestic public opinion. Laval wanted a reduction or elimination of war debts. Hoover responded that Congress prohibited this. The American people did not want to pay higher taxes to relieve the Europeans. The president promised to be as flexible as possible. Hoover wanted French support for disarmament when the Geneva Disarmament Conference convened in February 1932. He pointed out that the French could save more money from arms reductions than from annulment of their war debts. The president wanted to create a linkage between concessions on war debts by America and concessions on disarmament by the Third Republic. The French, however, would not disarm without an implicit alliance with America in the form of a consultative pact. The president countered that no American president could agree to such a pact during an election year and that Congress would defeat any implicit alliance. Hoover emphasized that bigger armies did not guarantee peace, they only added to the degree of carnage that followed if war came. Clearly, the French and American positions on disarmament were irreconcilable. On economic matters, there was basic agreement. The American president asked the French premier to help stem the drain of gold used to back American currency. Laval fully sympathized and said he had already initiated steps to help save the American gold standard. Both men agreed that it was crucial that as many major nations as possible remain on gold.[14] On a personal basis, the talks were straightforward and cordial. Each man understood the political realities faced by the other. Hoover found the Frenchman charming and reasonable, yet a stubborn champion of his country's interests. On some matters they simply agreed to disagree. The conversations occurred in small groups, usually with only interpreters present. Ogden Mills interpreted for the president, who understood French but was not fluent. In person, the president shed inhibitions that marred his appearances before large audiences. Hoover confided that, next to America, France possessed the world's strongest economy and had surpassed Britain's influence in European diplomacy. He promised to consult the French before announcing any major policy. The president and the premier issued a public statement long on generalities but vague on specifics. Laval gained domestic prestige from the summit, and Hoover made a friend.[15]

Hoover hoped to resume work on the Depression, but in early November another visitor arrived, Count Dino Grandi, the young, charismatic Italian foreign minister. Unlike most diplomatic visitors to Washington, Grandi's voyage was purely a gesture of goodwill. He came with nothing to request and with nothing to offer, and there were no significant areas of disagreement.

The suave Italian charmed the American press. Because he was fluent in English, translators were unnecessary. Grandi was best known in Europe as an advocate of world peace who had proposed a one-year moratorium on the manufacture of weapons. He agreed to cooperate with the Americans at Geneva in 1932 and to help persuade the French that security lay in disarmament. Grandi's visit was a social whirlwind, but it included substance. The Italian said that Italy and America were the only well-armed nations willing to disarm. He explained that overpopulation was a major problem for his country, which imported most of its raw materials and food. Grandi stated that Americans might find markets for their agricultural products in Italy, rather than the Italians purchasing them from Rumania or Russia. The visit seemed to have cemented Italian-American friendship. Cumulatively, the visits of MacDonald, Laval, and Grandi, complemented by the travels of Stimson and Mellon to Europe, established the precedent of summitry in peacetime. Now heads of state and their foreign ministers met face-to-face or employed the transatlantic telephone rather than relying exclusively on notes delivered by ambassadors. Beginning with Hoover's tour of Latin America, international diplomacy grew more intimate. Although some visits addressed specific issues, it was more common to seek mutual understanding on general principles.[16]

Grandi might have been too successful for his own good. He cut a high profile in foreign capitals. The young foreign minister was acclaimed at Geneva for bringing style and imagination to diplomacy. His mentor, Benito Mussolini, who seldom traveled abroad, was jealous of subordinates who outshined him. In late July, the axe fell on the foreign minister and four other ministers whom Mussolini fired summarily. The envious premier, too proud and too insecure to tolerate rivals, consolidated his dominance, also dismissing 11 undersecretaries. He seized three additional cabinet portfolios, making himself absolute dictator. Il Duce was moving into a more aggressive stage of his rule. After Grandi's dismissal the tone of Italy's diplomacy hardened, and its direction altered, tilting toward expansionism and eventually gravitating toward Berlin.[17]

Congress continued to reject the president's request to join the World Court, and the war debt controversy continued to simmer. In a conference at Lausanne, Switzerland, from June 15 to July 8, 1932, the powers tried to permanently resolve the issue of reparations. They conceded that Germany was bankrupt. The former European Allies hammered out a treaty providing a virtual end to reparations, contingent on American cancellation of war debts, which was not forthcoming. Hoover argued that he had never considered reparations a good idea and that the United States had never asked for any. The president reiterated his offer to negotiate individually with America's debtors based on capacity to pay. Americans should have realized that their dogged determination to collect was futile. Europeans should have known that an American president could no more cancel debts himself than he could join the League of Nations without congressional consent. Moreover, 1932 was an election year in America, and both party platforms opposed cancellation.[18] More than an expanse of water separated the hemispheres. After Lausanne, only token payments on war debts were made. It is dubious that by the summer of 1932, American acceptance of the Lausanne recipe would have averted the ascendancy of Hitler. Even relieved of reparations, Germany's economy was in shambles. Moreover, money was not Germany's only problem. At the time, Nazism seemed to many Germans the only alternative to Communism. France and Germany had earned each other's enmity. The other nations would be swept into the inferno. The Wisdom of Solomon would not have averted Europe's—and America's—destiny: another bitter war.

Hoover perceived peace as more than the absence of war; he was proactive in making it happen. Those who consider Hoover a passive president should examine closely his record on arms control. On this, he was the most active world leader, unafraid to incur risks. The president considered preserving the peace mankind's greatest challenge. Arms created fear, and fear was the breeding ground for war. Just as it was necessary to break the cycle of fear that nailed the Depression in place, it was essential to break the gridlock of fear that perpetuated wars. In a speech to the International Chamber of Commerce at Washington on May 4, 1931, Hoover emphasized the folly of war and the connection between an arms buildup and a military conflict. The president pointed out that armaments were a relative, not an absolute, concept. Nations armed in response to other nations and raised the stakes when their competitors armed to the teeth. In 1931, the president pointed out, the world was spending $5 billion annually on arms, an increase of 70 percent over the period before the Great War. This created anxiety, imposed a tax burden on all nations, and delayed recovery. He noted that the world had 5.5 million men under arms and another 20 million in reserves, exceeding the prewar years, although the war powers had pledged to demobilize at the war's end. Logically there was less need for arms in peacetime. On December 31, Hoover renewed his appeal for disarmament in an address to the Seventy-Second Congress. The president pointed out that the United States spent 75 percent of its budget, including benefits to veterans, on present and past military expenses, more than any other nation. Yet reductions must be achieved through negotiation; the Quaker did not believe in unilateral disarmament.[19] The president considered the Geneva Disarmament Conference, which convened on February 2, 1932, an auspicious opportunity to save the world from war. Some 40 nations assembled for the most important peace conclave since Versailles. By that time, Hoover was a lame duck. Stimson led the delegation but did not remain for the duration. Hoover's friend Hugh Gibson, the ambassador to Belgium, handled details.[20]

Each power had general and specific goals. The French were the greatest obstacle to disarmament. By 1931, the Depression had disabled the economies of Germany, Austria, and Britain, making France stronger in a relative sense. Domestic politics in each country played a role. One policy was popular in

France while the opposite policy was necessary for political survival in America. France had more to lose from disarmament than the United States because of its proximity to its major foe. On the other hand, America and France had a long history of friendship. They collaborated to maintain the gold standard after England abandoned it. Their leaders were on cordial terms. The philosophical issue was whether states must disarm to obtain security or must have security in order to disarm. In late July, the French practically drove a stake into the heart of the Geneva Conference before it even convened. Putting no faith in treaties without armies to enforce them, they dispatched a note to the League of Nations, arguing that the League must have an army. The army must be equipped with troops and arms, contributed by its members, to preserve the peace. They also resumed their demands on the United States for a consultative pact, a hopeless cause. The French made a valid point: How would any arms reductions be enforced? Hoover had faith in world opinion, but the French considered that naïve.[21]

Initially, Germany was sympathetic to disarmament because it was already disarmed. If other nations disarmed, that would make Germany stronger, in a relative sense. The Germans had other objectives, however. They wanted the war guilt clause deleted from the Versailles treaty, their territory restored, and reparations eliminated. Later, they declared they would abandon the conference unless guaranteed equality in arms. The Geneva Conference was complicated by the fact that the Lausanne Conference met simultaneously. Reparations, war debts, and disarmament were connected because they could be used as bargaining chips. The British, who were floundering financially, welcomed land disarmament because they were not a major land power (neither was the United States). But the British fleet was sacrosanct. America could propose but not dispose. As long as there were no teeth in disarmament, it was no more likely to deter a war than a toy battleship.[22]

The negotiations opened with high-sounding speeches and quickly bogged down. After more than four months of fruitless gridlock, the American president decided to seize control of events. Hoover's formula was to slash offensive weapons drastically and tilt the advantage to defense. The most mobile weapons with the longest range could inflict the most damage. Hoover worked laboriously on his scheme. The president wrote his proposal in two weeks, without assistance, perfecting it through many drafts. On June 22, 1932, Gibson read the plan to the delegates. Simultaneously, Hoover released it to the press. The Hoover Plan banned mobile artillery, armor-breaching guns, bombers, most submarines, and long-range ships. It reduced land armies by about one-third. The president estimated that the reductions would save the world's nations between $10 billion and $15 billion over the next decade with the American share at about $2 billion.[23]

The plan was the boldest, most sweeping initiative presented to any major gathering. It made headlines worldwide. Most small nations approved enthusiastically. But in some quarters it was dead on arrival. The French rejected it, as did the Japanese. The Japanese, fighting the Chinese in Manchuria even while they negotiated in Geneva, wanted to maintain both their imperial navy and their army intact. The British, the most supportive major power, were leery of reductions to the Royal Navy. Grandi of Italy was initially supportive, but Mussolini opposed drastic reductions. In Paris, the press fumed. In America, only a handful of isolationists considered the plan realistic. The Soviet Union hypocritically announced that it was a peaceful nation for which the Hoover plan did not go far enough, proposing that all nations disarm totally. The mixed reviews did not surprise the president. Hoover had not expected the plan to be adopted in its totality. He considered it a basis for negotiation. But it was too sweeping even for that. The British complained that the American leader should have introduced his proposal at the beginning of the conference. Geneva has been the burial ground for numerous peace proposals. At least, Hoover's plan had the advantage of being direct, without complicated formulas, and it applied to all nations equally.[24]

If those who dare greatly, risk failing greatly, Hoover's gamble to disarm was a long shot. The president had too much faith in peace methods that lacked enforcement. The Geneva Conference required unanimous consent for any treaty, which was unrealistic. The patient lingered before expiring. Leadership changed in France, Germany, and America. Positions hardened around the globe while political chaos and economic ruin stalked the world. The Geneva Conference's painful, peaceful death in 1934 was virtually its only peaceful result. Yet until Ronald Reagan met Mikhail Gorbachev at Reykjavik in 1986, no remotely sweeping disarmament proposal was considered.

Hoover began his administration with hopes of improving relations with Latin America. The Good Neighbor Policy was an auspicious beginning, yet implementation meant overcoming decades of instability. The Latin economies were weak. Some lacked industry or relied on a single raw material to export, and frequent revolutions made foreign investment risky.[25] In late March 1931, Hoover toured two American Caribbean possessions, sailing to Puerto Rico for two days and the Virgin Islands for a four-hour stopover. Puerto Rico, obtained from Spain after the Spanish-American War of 1898, had a Hispanic population and culture. Unlike the lightly populated, miniscule Virgin Islands, Puerto Rico was a single, large, overpopulated island. The Virgin Islands, purchased from Denmark in 1917 because of fear that the Germans might construct a submarine base there, included only 22,000 predominantly black inhabitants. Poverty plagued both dependencies. Hoover, therefore, made economic development his priority. Moved by the plight of Puerto Rican children, the president used $600,000 from surplus funds of the American Relief Administration (ARA) and raised $150,000 from private sources to provide milk for children under one year old. Hoover expanded lunch rooms to feed thousands of children who attended schools without meals. The federal government had appropriated $7 million after the territories were struck by a devastating hurricane in 1928, mostly for Puerto Rico.

The Virgin Islands languished in the midst of a three-year drought that devastated their agriculture after the hurricane. Hoover was warmly received during both stops, especially in Puerto Rico. Theodore Roosevelt Jr., whom Hoover appointed governor there, was enormously popular. The Rough Rider's son emphasized economic reform, treated the people respectfully, and had learned to speak Spanish. Shortly before departing, Hoover delivered an address on the Capitol steps to thunderous applause. The Virgin Islands were less effusive because of the dismal state of the economy. Hoover was pessimistic about the short-term prospects there but hoped he could revive the economy once the Depression tapered off.[26]

Cuba was turbulent during Hoover's tenure. In 1925, General Gerardo Machado seized power and imposed a repressive regime. A decline in the price of sugar during the Depression crushed the island's economy. In 1931 a rebellion against Machado erupted, but the army remained loyal, and he subdued the rebels. Following the uprising, the dictator's rule became increasingly harsh, inspiring further uprisings, which drove him from the island in 1933. The administration did not invoke the Platt Amendment, which permitted the United States to police the island, but let events take their course.[27]

Hoover faced volatile conditions in Nicaragua, where American intervention dated to the Taft administration. Implementing his policy of "Dollar Diplomacy," Taft dispatched troops to protect American investments. Coolidge removed them in 1925 but returned them when a civil war inspired by the rebel leader Augustine Sandino erupted in 1927. Stimson arranged an end to the civil war with American troops remaining to preserve order. Sandino fled to Mexico, and Hoover began to phase out the 5,000 Marines. By 1930 only 1,000 remained. However, Sandino returned, and fighting resumed in 1931. Hoover did not send additional troops, but those already there stayed to train the Nicaraguan National Guard. The president demonstrated unusual restraint when American lives were threatened. He sent warships to the Nicaraguan coast to pick up American citizens but refrained from sending armed rescuers inland. The State Department announced that the remainder of the Marines would be withdrawn after the American presidential election of 1932. Meanwhile Americans constructed public works and rebuilt homes and buildings after an earthquake in 1931. Virtually all Marines were withdrawn by the end of 1932 and the last departed on January 2, 1933. The administration also helped settle a boundary dispute between two other Central American nations: Guatemala and Honduras. The dispute dated to the early period of independence from Spain, and the rival nations clashed in 1917 and 1927. In 1929 the parties met in Washington, and in 1930, a Special Boundary Tribunal chaired by Chief Justice Hughes began deliberations. The tribunal divided the territory based on actual occupation, which was accepted by both sides.[28]

By midsummer of 1931, Haitians had become restive because of lack of economic progress and the slow transition to home rule. The economy was stagnant, and the phasing out of American rule was proceeding slowly. The

United States kept 800 Marines on the island, and local factions quarreled over power. Finally, the United States negotiated a new treaty in September 1932, ending the American involvement in 1934. This officially severed most connections. In August 1931, all departments, except sanitation, were handed over to the Haitians. Americans remained only to advise the Haitians. The pullout snagged when the Haitian National Assembly refused to ratify the treaty. By this time, Roosevelt had succeeded Hoover and the new president circumvented the ratification process via an executive agreement, thus finalizing Haitian independence.[29]

Some Latin American problems were not resolved during Hoover's term. The Chaco controversy between Paraguay and Bolivia and the Leticia dispute between Peru and Columbia dragged on. The former involved the remote Chaco Boreal wilderness. The countries had been fighting intermittently since colonial times, yet the matter seemed to have been settled by arbitration in 1930. However, skirmishes continued, and in 1932, while new attempts at arbitration were in progress, another war erupted. The United States applied the Stimson Doctrine denying territory seized by force, created initially for the Far East. Bolivia asserted that the Chaco was already its territory; thus, the Stimson Doctrine was inapplicable. An attempt by the League of Nations also failed to pacify the contending nations. A few months after Hoover left office in 1933, Paraguay declared war on Bolivia.[30]

Like the Chaco wars, the dispute between Peru and Columbia revolved around property that was worthless except for national pride. Leticia was a nearly inaccessible port on the Amazon River. Peru occupied Leticia in 1932, and Columbia dispatched a small flotilla. Planes and ground forces clashed. Young men rushed to volunteer for patriotic combat. Brazil's offer to mediate was rejected by Peru, which appealed to the League of Nations. Columbia countered by appealing to the United States. In February 1933, the League Council, supported by the State Department, proposed a commission to settle the question. The issue still simmered as the Hoover administration expired without U.S. intervention.[31]

The administration's most serious diplomatic problems took place in Manchuria, beginning in 1929 and ending in 1932. In 1929, the Russians and Japanese fought a brief war there. From 1931–1933, the Japanese and Chinese fought a more serious war that expanded onto the Chinese mainland. The Japanese coveted Manchuria as an outlet for expansion of their densely populated home islands. Japan considered Manchuria the cornerstone of its empire. Japan had obtained railroad rights there by the Treaty of Portsmouth in 1905 and subsequent agreements. Nationalism sizzled in the Far East, and the first shots of the Second World War were fired in China. The first mass bombing of civilians also occurred there. China suffered more casualties than any nation save the Soviet Union in the great war that followed.[32]

Japanese militarists sought an excuse to solidify their nation's domination of Manchuria, while the liberal Konoye ministry attempted to restrain them.

On September 18, 1931, a small section of track on the South Manchuria Railway, a few miles north of Mukden, was, according to the Japanese, damaged by a bomb planted by Chinese soldiers. The explosion was probably fabricated. Shortly afterward, a train passed over the alleged gap without difficulty. Meanwhile, the army, without consulting the Konoye ministry, seized Chinese cities along the railroad. The highly disciplined Japanese, although outnumbered, crushed Chinese opposition. The League Council and the United States debated their response and how to contain the spreading conflict. In September, the violence escalated, which alarmed the great powers. The United States dispatched an official protest to the Japanese on September 24, followed by cables from France, Britain, and Italy on October 17, asking them to observe the Kellogg Pact. On November 1, the League Council accepted a suggestion made by the Japanese themselves, and, ironically, opposed by the Chinese, that the League dispatch a commission to the region to investigate. It became known as the Lytton Commission.[33]

Initially, America hoped to encourage Japanese moderates, not isolate them. The administration believed that the militarists had acted without authorization. For the next two months, the State Department pursued a relatively conciliatory policy. The situation was complicated because not all Japanese military men were on one side and all civilians on the other. Second, there was the logistical problem of helping the Chinese. America did not have a land army sufficient enough to dispatch to the Far East. Hoover's priority was to preserve peace or at least localize the war. The president's military advisors told him that a war on the Chinese mainland might last six years with an uncertain outcome. Hoover, who admired the resilience of Chinese culture, believed that China was too large and populous for Japan to digest and assimilate. More importantly, the United States had no vital interests in Manchuria or China that justified war. "These acts do not imperil the freedom of the American people, the economic or moral future of our people," Hoover explained. "I do not propose to sacrifice American life for anything short of this." The president also opposed economic sanctions, which his more truculent secretary of state backed, at least as a tool in a diplomatic bluff. The president did not believe Japan would cower in the face of sanctions. A boycott might provide incentives for the imperialists to seize raw materials elsewhere. Further, he asked Stimson what he would do next if sanctions failed. "I held that the hand that brandishes a pistol must be prepared to shoot," Hoover wrote in his *Memoirs*. When sanctions were imposed on Japan by Hoover's successor, the Japanese reacted more aggressively rather than pulling back, as Hoover had warned.[34]

Conditions escalated. On October 8, Japanese planes bombed Chinchow, killing thousands of civilians. On January 2, they occupied the city, completing the conquest of Manchuria. The occupation of Chinchow became a catalyst for the Stimson Doctrine. On December 9, the president had suggested to Stimson that the United States issue a statement refusing to recognize any conquest gained by aggression. Hoover wanted the doctrine to apply globally. The president viewed Japan's aggression as an opportunity to put teeth into the Kellogg Pact, mobilizing world opinion and ostracizing invaders. On January 3, Stimson drafted such a manifesto, which Hoover softened and then approved. The note, sent to Japan and China, was short but crisp. It stipulated that the United States would not recognize any territorial changes caused by a violation of the Kellogg Pact. The policy, for which both Hoover and Stimson claimed credit and was in fact collaborative, was announced on January 8. Historically, it became known as the Stimson Doctrine, and the secretary of state at the end of his long career considered it his finest accomplishment. Although ineffectual in retrospect, at the time the pronouncement was criticized more for being risky.[35]

Not only did the Japanese continue their advance after Stimson's note of January 7, they expanded operations into the heart of Chinese territory. The most significant move was into Shanghai in late January, where the Japanese attacked the International Settlement and bombed the civilian population, creating 250,000 refugees. Shanghai produced a stronger reaction from the world community and brought the United States and Britain closer. The Western powers were heavily involved in Shanghai. Shanghai raised the stakes because of its foreign presence and also because it was an undisputed violation of Chinese sovereignty. As in Manchuria, however, the Great Depression restrained the response of most major powers. Hoover acted promptly and forcefully. The president dispatched 1,000 soldiers stationed at Manila and an additional 400 Marines to protect Americans, raising the contingent in the International Settlement to about 4,800 men. He also sent a cruiser and six destroyers. The British sent three cruisers and a battalion of troops.[36]

After the Stimson note failed to deter the militarists, the administration determined that stronger medicine was needed, but Hoover still ruled out sanctions or force. At a cabinet meeting, Stimson and Secretary of War Patrick Hurley argued that the United States must back up talk with action. Hurley recommended deploying the fleet. Hoover urged them not to stir the boiling pot. Finally, the administration agreed on a stronger diplomatic message that would reinforce the Stimson note. Stimson wrote a letter to William E. Borah, chairman of the Senate Foreign Relations Committee, dated February 23, 1932, and published the following day. It restated the case for nonrecognition and fortified the diplomatic arsenal by adding that Japan, in addition to violating the Kellogg Pact, had violated the Nine-Power, Four-Power, and Five-Power treaties of 1922, all of which Japan had signed. Again, Hoover tempered Stimson's language. The difference between the president and his secretary was not one of principle but of degree. The letter was intended to caution Japan, encourage China, arouse the American public, and urge the League to act. Hoover decided to water down the message by instructing Undersecretary of State William Castle to deliver an address on May 14, while Stimson was away at the Geneva Conference. Castle stated that the

United States had no intention of employing either force or sanctions. He asserted that America had, in effect, ruled out such actions by refusing to join the League of Nations. Castle pointedly referred to the nonrecognition policy as the Hoover Doctrine rather than the Stimson Doctrine. When Stimson returned, he and Hoover quarreled over the substance of the policy and who deserved credit for it. Hoover also pointed out that a boycott would require an act of Congress, which it would never approve. In addition, economic warfare would cripple American trade at the apex of the Great Depression. The quarrel did not destroy the friendship between the men, and in his *Memoirs* Stimson acknowledges that Hoover had inspired the doctrine that he fleshed out.[37]

The Japanese eventually left Shanghai but remained in Manchuria, where they created the puppet state of Manchukuo. Manchukuo exchanged envoys with the Vatican, Spain, Germany, Italy, and the Soviet Union. The Lytton Commission completed its study in September 1932 but did not publish it until October 1, about two weeks after Japan recognized Manchukuo. The Lytton Report asserted that the Japanese had violated the League Covenant but did not recommend sanctions. The British did place an arms embargo on both Japan and China, but this hurt the poorly armed Chinese more than the well-armed Japanese. The bullets exchanged not only had riddled soldiers and civilians but had punctured the myth of collective security. After its publication in early October, the League debated the Lytton Report for months before finally adopting it on February 24, 1933. It did not faze the Japanese, who quit the League. If the League had been revealed as a paper tiger and the Kellogg Pact as only high-sounding words, that reality should have been self-evident all along. There may or may not have been ways to stop aggression but not simple or painless ones. More ominously, the Stimson Doctrine of nonrecognition did not deter the conquest of Ethiopia and Albania by Italy or the absorption of Austria and Czechoslovakia by Germany. Still, Robert Ferrell writes that the doctrine's critics "overlook the lack of any acceptable substitute."[38]

Hoover, a man of peace, did not have to face the Furies of war on his watch. He juggled diplomacy while struggling with a wretched economy. In the end, the war, when it did come, proved in a sense cathartic for Americans and jolted them temporarily out of the stupor of unemployment until postwar consumerism kicked in and shattered the psychological barrier that presumed that buying goods was risky and that enjoying them was a reason to feel guilty. Hoover played a postwar role in feeding the world and assessing damages that was similar in principle, if not in degree, to his role during the Great War. In his lifetime, he played a major role in the Great War; the Great Depression; and a second, greater war without wavering in his principles, his commitment to peace and justice, and his humanitarian instincts.

CHAPTER 15

Life in the White House

Personal and Social

If Franklin Roosevelt had a second-rate mind but a first-rate temperament and if Herbert Hoover had a first-rate mind but a second rate temperament, Lou Henry Hoover had both a first-rate mind and a first-rate temperament. Yet politics was not her major interest, and she had no ambitions for glory. A modest, secure woman who made friends easily, intellectually honest, she shielded her privacy and her family's. Upon her death, her husband culled their correspondence of its passionate letters and then closed her papers for 40 years. This partly accounts for the fact that she is among the least appreciated and most underestimated twentieth-century First Ladies. Yet she possessed a charming personality and an unusual nimble intelligence and led an exciting life. In fact, comparisons with her more acclaimed successor, Eleanor Roosevelt, are revealing. Lou's father provided the unconditional love that made her a secure, emotionally stable person, capable of self-love—qualities that Eleanor lacked due to her dysfunctional childhood. Lou was better educated than Eleanor, a far superior writer and public speaker, a better mother, and had a happier marriage. Both were caring people. However, Eleanor's drive was directed into politics, and Lou Henry focused on humanitarian actions based on her love of children, especially girls. Lou was less confrontational than her successor and concealed many of her good deeds, including, anonymous personal gifts that she began as a young woman, such as providing food, clothing, and college educations for some of her domestic servants. Even her husband did not know of these private philanthropic deeds. Some measured Lou by later standards that presume that a First Lady should devote herself to political activism. Yet she was active in a variety of arenas, including the League of Women Voters, to which she donated $1,000 annually, and did not accept anybody's model of what she should be, perhaps the best example of all. Strong and independent, Lou was unfazed by flattery or the glamour of politics.

The First Lady's story is important in its own right and also because one cannot understand Herbert Hoover without understanding his family, especially his wife. With Lou Henry as his companion, Hoover was able to fulfill more of his life's ambitions than with any other conceivable spouse. Their interests overlapped and complemented one another's; she not only permitted but encouraged him to pursue his choices in life and provided comfort, nurturing, loyalty, and love. They bonded after knowing each other for only a single year at Stanford, yet the bond endured. It was a marriage made at Stanford, not in heaven, so it included imperfections. But both Hoovers agreed that Stanford was contiguous to heaven.

Although they met at Stanford during Hoover's senior year and Lou's freshman year, each had roots in Iowa. Lou was born in Waterloo, just 70 miles from West Branch, and in the same year, 1874, as Bert. Her parents moved several times because her mother contracted a lung disease, probably tuberculosis, and they settled in Monterrey, California, where Charles Henry became a small town banker. Waterloo, like West Branch, included a strong Quaker influence, and Lou's father had Quaker ancestors. Yet the California towns in which they settled lacked a meetinghouse or association, so the Henrys became Episcopalians. After marrying, Lou attended Quaker services and admired the Quaker lifestyle, yet never formally converted. She was a spiritual person to whom denominational affiliation meant less than internal spirituality. Lou received a degree in education from San Jose State University in 1893 and briefly taught math and science in elementary school but did not feel challenged. After attending two lectures by Hoover's mentor, the eminent geologist John Branner, she was inspired to enroll at Stanford to study geology. Many considered geology an odd choice for a woman, yet Lou liked hard things, including rocks.[1]

Lou's talents went beyond the sciences. She was one of those rare individuals nearly equally balanced in the right- and left-brain hemispheres—creative, intuitive, and imaginative on the one hand and mathematically and scientifically intelligent and analytical on the other. She enjoyed both science and the humanities and could have made a profession of either, yet her innate love was creative writing. She was gifted in composing descriptive prose, journalism, fiction, history, biography, and satire as well as technical writing and translation. At 14, Lou published a paean to the natural beauty of California, which appeared in the *St. Nicholas Magazine* for boys and girls.[2] Her descriptive writing combines a thirst for adventure with the inner calmness of a mind at peace. Lou's depictions of nature are reminiscent of Henry David Thoreau reflecting on Walden Pond and William Wordsworth describing England's Lake country. As a young woman, she described twilight on a camping trip: "We see the dark shapes of the pines, the dim outline of the mountains, and the pale moon just sinking behind the western peaks—but we do not belong to the dark world of which they are a part—we are in a perfect world of light and warmth and happiness of our own."[3]

Lou was entranced by the history of California, and her early works include historical and biographical essays describing the experiences of priests, Indians, and explorers in the seventeenth and eighteenth centuries. Gifted in oral and written communication, as a writer Lou was observant, sensitive, and disciplined, with attention to detail and insight into human nature. She possessed the skill to excel as an academic writer as well. During the mid-1900s, the future First Lady published biographical and cultural profiles as well as several articles of a scientific, technical nature. In 1909 she published "The Late Dowager Empress of China," which appeared in *Contemporary Review*. This was followed by a profile of John Milne, a pioneer in seismology who developed a method for predicting earthquakes, published in the *Bulletin of the Seismological Society*. Unselfish in her writing career, Lou aided her husband and permitted him to receive much of the credit for their collaborations. In 1898 she began translating Chinese mining laws for Hoover as he prepared to codify the Chinese legal system. Her greatest scholarly achievement was the translation from Latin of *De Re Metallica*, a classic sixteenth-century study about mining and metallurgy compiled over 25 years by George Bauer, a Renaissance scholar. The first Latin edition, published in 1556 under the pseudonym of Georgius Agricola, had never been satisfactorily translated into a modern language, chiefly because the author coined Latin words for processes that did not exist when Latin was a living language. The Hoovers worked on the project for five years and published an expensive limited edition at their own expense, including reproductions of the original woodcuts. It was Lou, not her husband, who was primarily responsible for the translation. Hoover, who did not read Latin, added only annotations, yet received the bulk of the credit. Lou was perhaps the most gifted modern First Lady linguistically. In addition to her reading knowledge of Latin, while her husband's mining headquarters was in London, she became fluent in French, Spanish, German, and Italian. She mastered Chinese while Bert managed Chinese mines in the Celestial Empire. Her Chinese teacher said in 1928 that she was the best language student he had ever taught.[4] Bert learned a smattering of Chinese and could speak French haltingly. Sometimes the couple communicated in Chinese, especially before servants, to preserve confidentiality.

At Stanford, Lou tutored her future husband in English while he struggled to satisfy the composition requirement. Later she delivered hundreds of public speeches, which she wrote herself. She was an eloquent speaker, although she did not enjoy it because she preferred to avoid the limelight. Lou made public addresses on behalf of the American Women's War Relief Fund, the Commission for Relief in Belgium, the Girl Scouts of America, the American Red Cross's Canteen Escort Service, the Women's Division of the National Amateur Athletic Federation, and the Salvation Army. In 1928 she delivered a few radio speeches for Hoover, the first candidate's wife to exploit the new medium. In June 1929 she became the first First Lady to deliver a major radio address to solicit relief for the poor. Between 1931 and 1933, she expanded her activities and urged Girl Scouts to help combat the Depression in their communities. Hoover churned out dozens of books through sheer will, but words flowed easily for Lou.

Professor Branner believed he could obtain an academic teaching position for Lou, and she might have flourished in that environment. She had the interpersonal skills to become an academic administrator, perhaps the president of a women's college. Yet an academic life is relatively sedentary, and her life was with Bert and their children. It was not a major sacrifice because she thrived on travel and adventure. Moreover, her real love was writing, and a writer can work anywhere without keeping regular hours. Lou was not only a better writer than her own husband and better than most First Ladies; she was also better than most presidents. None of her husband's successors even wrote their own speeches, and many postpresidential memoirs are ghost written. It was not entirely the pressure of other commitments or lack of opportunity that deterred Lou from professional writing. After all, her husband's prominence opened doors to her that were not open to other aspiring writers. Yet Lou seems to have lacked the drive to push most of her projects through to publication. She would start one, drop it, begin another, and then resume the first. She had offers from publishers that she never followed up on. Lou did not need money from writing and did not desire fame. She simply did not have the kind of self-serving ambition to become a big fish in the literary pond.

The Hoovers' Stanford courtship was a whirlwind affair. They entered three years apart and met in geology class, where Lou was the only female student, and in May 1928 she became the first woman at Stanford to receive a degree in geology. On the day they met, the two lingered to talk after the other students had departed. Afterward, Professor Branner paired his star male student with the vivacious coed at a dinner party. Lou had more experience with men than Bert did with women, but in her company, he shed his inhibitions. Bert told his cousin, Harriette Miles Odell, "[S]he is the only real comrade I could ever have in a woman."[5] Lou was an attractive sorority girl, brilliant, athletic, fun-loving, and popular. She had the ability to rescue her socially inexperienced companion from awkward lapses in conversation. That ability, wrote James M. Harris, is "a sort of a bloom on a woman. If you have it, you don't need anything else; and if you don't have it, it doesn't matter what else you have."[6] Their dates included dances, teas, football games, lectures, and long hikes in the hills surrounding Palo Alto. His senior year was the busiest of Hoover's education. He was running out of money and out of time and trying to graduate, find a job, and woo a mate.[7]

Though thoroughly feminine in her movements and body language, Lou did many things that most women of her time did not do, whether people considered it proper or not. She was proficient at horseback riding, camping, and fishing. Unlike Bert, she also hunted and was a deadeye marksman. Yet she could dance, cook, and entertain and enjoyed music, the arts, and theater. She made better grades than Bert, read voraciously, and had a passion for travel and a desire to make a difference. Her father had given her unconditional love, and her bond with him never broke. In turn, she learned to give unconditional love, and she gave it to Bert in a way he had never experienced. It was the last missing piece to the puzzle of his personality that saw him emerge from his cocoon of a love-deprived childhood at Stanford. Lou did this naturally and unselfishly. Many people were beginning to see sides of Bert that no one realized existed, but Lou saw them all. Lou was interested in both the intellectual and physical sides of life, and she also wanted to find the right man. Marrying well did not necessarily mean marrying rich. Life was an adventure, and adventures are better when shared. Lou admired Bert's intelligence, his ferocious drive, his versatility, his unselfishness, and his determination to accomplish a set task. She found a sense of humor many overlooked. He had quiet strength and undeviating integrity. She liked his independence, which complemented her own. Drawn out, he could be a compelling conversationalist. He was an indefatigable worker, yet he knew how to have fun, especially in Lou's company. Bert's life was purposeful, and he was loyal. So far as is known, neither ever seriously considered marrying another. Other than her father, Bert was the only man Lou ever loved.[8]

When Hoover left Stanford in 1894 with his BS in geology, the nation was deeply bogged down in the financial panic that had begun in 1893. He had to at least obtain a stable job in a suitable place for a woman before he could marry. Initially, he worked in the pits of the Western United States as a common miner, rose to a better job with a prominent San Francisco consultant, and then was hired by the international firm of Bewick, Moering, headquartered in London, which sent him to Western Australia to develop their mining interests there, chiefly gold. Then the parent company, pleased with his work, promoted Hoover to manage Chinese mines in collaboration with the Chinese government. Now he had the money and an appropriate environment for a wife. Upon news of his promotion he cabled Lou, who accepted by return telegram. They were married in a simple ceremony in the Henry home by a Catholic priest because there was no Quaker minister, nor any other Protestant minister available, by special dispensation from the priest's bishop. The following day they traveled by train to Palo Alto then to San Francisco, where they boarded a ship for the Far East, with stops in Hawaii and Japan, laden with books on China, which they read on board. From this point the story of the early years of their marriage reads like *Gulliver's Travels*. As Bert's partner, Lou explored China, Burma, Australia, New Zealand, Tasmania, Russia, Japan, Egypt, and the Middle East. They survived a siege at Tientsen during the Boxer Rebellion of 1900. Lou became the only First Lady to come under fire in wartime. Lou organized a hospital and took the wounded into her home. As Hoover became one of the most sought-after consultants of the prewar era, Lou was a true partner in his work as well as in domestic life. Lou understood the technical side of her husband's work and often traveled with him to inspect mines.[9]

Two sons were born to the Hoovers, Herbert Jr. in 1903 and Allan in 1907. Lou continued to travel with her husband for some time even after the boys were born. Bert said it was easier to travel with children than with grown-ups. Both boys made their first international trips at the age of five weeks. Hoover was never very fond of travel as a tourist—it had to have a practical purpose—though Lou lured him on pleasure trips. The Hoovers often visited historic sites throughout England and Scotland, and Bert read widely about British history. Lou enjoyed travel for its own sake, especially in the company of friends, and they made many friends during the 20 years they lived in London. Like her husband, Lou enjoyed good conversation, and the Hoover home became a salon of social life for Americans traversing Europe during those happy years before the Great War, when Hoover was earning a fortune and building a reputation for his mastery at managing mines. Lou enjoyed collecting antiques, about which Bert was indifferent, and she was fond of the arts and music, in which he was only mildly interested. They both enjoyed reading. Bert, who read voraciously at sea, was the more avid reader. Yet Lou devoured everything from technical journals to the classics, sometimes in the original languages. Bert liked business and finance, and he had a greater interest in newspapers and political magazines.[10]

Lou said that her family priorities were her husband first, herself second, and her children third. In October 1914, she returned to Palo Alto to enroll Herbert and Allan in school because the Hoovers wanted their boys to be educated in American public schools. In November Lou joined Bert in Britain, where he now headed the Commission for Relief in Belgium (CRB). She made several trans-Atlantic commutes, and her role shifted as she undertook more public, charitable roles, many of them related to war relief. When America entered the war in 1917 the Hoovers moved to Washington, where Bert headed the Food Administration. Just as she had made speeches earlier to raise money for Belgian relief, now Lou delivered talks urging housewives to conserve food. She continued her role as parent-in-chief. She camped with her boys, fished with them, and collected rock specimens, trying to compensate for the absence of their father, who was immersed in war work. The Hoovers were lenient parents who wanted their children to explore and think independently. At one point the boys kept a menagerie of pets that included baby chickens, toads, frogs, lizards, salamanders, silkworms, a horned toad, and a small alligator. Still, Bert and Lou wanted their sons to be self-sufficient and tried to avoid spoiling them. The children worked to buy things they wanted. Herbert earned money to buy parts for a car, which he put together himself, demonstrating mechanical ability at an early age. Lou encouraged the boys to work with their hands and did not mind a little dirt. During the 1920s Herbert and Allan grew into young adults. Lou lost both of her parents, her mother in 1921 and her father in 1928. In 1922 Herbert entered Stanford, followed by Allan in 1924. In the latter year, Herbert, a junior, became engaged to Margaret Watson, a fellow junior. The nest was empty. Hoover had a different relationship with his two sons. He had a closer relationship with Allan, whom he found accepting and caring. The two became fishing companions and Hoover confided more in Allan, as did Lou. The correspondence between Allan and his parents is more emotional and spontaneous. Herbert perhaps grew up too much in his father's shadow and found the adjustment difficult. Ironically, he might have been more temperamentally like his father. Herbert was more serious, Allan more fun-loving and attractive to young ladies. Neither of the boys rebelled overtly, and they were relatively normal, more so than many children who grow up in celebrity families burdened by high expectations. Although Lou did most of the parenting when the boys were young, she had her own interests as well. Although she was more outgoing and physically affectionate than her husband, she was also restrained in her affections. Hoover might have privately experienced some guilt at being a less attentive husband and father than he might have been.

The marriage survived strains, although from the beginning Lou realized that she was marrying a man who was also married to his work. Yet their marriage thrived on mutual respect as well as love and the acceptance of differences. At times, the differences produced an element of separation. Hoover always enjoyed the company of male companions. On fishing vacations he spent much of his time with male friends, and the respites he most enjoyed were the Bohemian Grove encampments in California, which emphasized male camaraderie. However, the chief factor in keeping them apart was geographic—his frequent absences because of his work. Even when they lived together and Hoover traveled less, he filled the house with guests on most evenings and weekends rather than spending time alone with his family. Hoover put his work first, believing he should use his gifts in the service of humanity. There was only so much time to go around. Usually it was Lou who moved to be close to Bert rather than vice versa. Their early marriage, before Hoover entered public service, had been a genuine partnership built not only on romantic love but on mutual respect and common interests. They traveled as a family, and they enjoyed leisure time together. By the time the Hoovers reached the White House Hoover had become so involved with his career that the marriage had evolved into a looser relationship in which the couple followed complementary yet essentially parallel paths. He did not share his presidential work with Lou as he had his mining career. They would never again be as close as they had been before 1914. Perhaps the closest they came to sharing genuine enjoyment came during their weekends at Camp Rapidan. They continued to share a love of nature. The couple also shared a lifelong love of Stanford, California, and children. They doted on their grandchildren. Lou worked with young girls and Hoover with boys. After his presidency he devoted much of his time to fundraising for the Boys' Clubs of America.

Hoover found it difficult to show emotion or affection publicly, and this inhibition might have carried over into private moments. Bert was a highly creative person with enormous sexual energy, the basis of creativity, yet sex might have been more a source of emotional relief than of true intimacy. Lou was an attractive, fun-loving woman. Both were healthy personalities with normal, perhaps even greater than normal sexual drives, and had opportunities to stray, but it is doubtful either did. Neither was sexually repressed, yet loyalty meant a great deal to them. Their love never ebbed, and Lou continued to nurture her husband during the most difficult times. She suffered more than he did from the withering criticism the president received, yet she tried to present a face of dignified silence to the world. Lou could reach him more than any person and understood him better, and on important things they agreed. They had minor differences. Lou, a teetotaler, was more opposed to alcohol than Hoover. She did not serve it at the White House nor did she attend parties where liquor was served. Hoover's opposition was based more on his belief in obeying the law. Considering the gloom that settled over the nation during the Depression, the entire family withstood adversity remarkably well. Both Lou and the boys were proud of Hoover's accomplishments and were bound by loyalty. A sense of duty was strong in the family. Hoover's best friends were his family, and his greatest blessing in life was the unconditional love he received from Lou. There is no record of either ever deliberately trying to hurt the other. The boys, although they were independent, were also devoted to their parents. Hoover did not want them to be smaller versions of him. Although public affection was limited, they sometimes strolled together at Rapidan, holding hands. It was a better marriage than the Hardings, the Coolidges, or the Roosevelts, none of whom showed much public affection either. Hoover did not believe politics was the sphere of women, and neither did Lou. However, the president considered her judgment in sizing up people better than his own. It was "uncanny," he wrote in his autobiography. Despite their separations, and the fact that they had different responsibilities, neither was ever seriously lonely. They were too busy for that. Lou breakfasted with her husband alone at 8 a.m. every morning and then walked him to his office. She added spice to his life, and he added gravity to hers. Neither had major regrets, and both had deep feelings for one another; they were both extremely sensitive people. Herbert and Allan grew up to be reasonably successful, happy adults, though they experienced their share of disappointments. Herbert was more serious, like his father, and Allan was more fun-loving, similar to his mother.[11]

Bert was reticent about his private thoughts, and Lou performed most of the religious instruction for Herbert and Allan, neither of whom seems to have been outwardly religious as adults. Before leaving her children to cross the Atlantic in 1914, in order to join Bert in London, Lou wrote an unusually revealing, forthright letter to her sons, in the event she perished in the submarine-infested waters. She wanted to leave them a testament of love, comfort them, and provide guidance. Herbert was to be given the letter immediately, Allan when he was a bit older. She explained "that there is a great power beyond us that controls and guides us and all the affairs about us." However, God did not manage every detail of individual lives. Rather, He gave humans a great deal of latitude by the gift of free will. "Only we have the advantage of having a will with ours, and we can make our forces do almost what we want them to," she wrote. She asked her boys to learn about the soul, "the part that lives inside of us," and to pray for guidance when they needed help. Lou explained that "the soul does not die when our bodies die." It remained to help and comfort others. "I know that if I should die, I can pray my soul to go over to my two dear little boys—and to help and comfort their souls."[12]

From the 1920s onward, Lou was involved in numerous organizations, some professional, but chiefly those dealing with the education, character development, and recreation of girls. Her major activities involved the Girl Scouts of America and the Women's Division of the National American Athletic Association. She also devoted time to the American Association of University Women, the Women's Auxiliary of the American Institute of Mining and Metallurgical Engineers, the Parent-Teachers' Association, the Young Women's Christian Association, and peace organizations. In each of these, she was more than a name on a letterhead. From 1922 until her death in 1944, Lou was the most important leader of the Girl Scouts, serving on the board of directors and as president for two terms. She excelled at fundraising and recruiting and training troop leaders. Lou obtained large grants from the Children's Fund of the American Relief Administration and the Laura Spellman Rockefeller Foundation. On a personal level, she was a troop leader herself, meeting first in the Hoover home on S Street and later at the White House. She upgraded the Girl Scout magazine, *The American Girl*, helped obtain funding for it and helped write the Girl Scout Creed. The Girl Scouts combined two things she loved: children and the outdoors. Like her husband, she feared Americans were becoming overly sedentary and losing contact with nature. Scouting, she believed, should be half education and half recreation. Children needed nurturing and human warmth. The peace of the world of tomorrow lay in the children of today. Scouting could be pure joy, a source of making friends and bonding, and it could also instill responsibility. During the Depression she emphasized the role Scouts could play to help those in need. Lou brought common sense and inspirational qualities to scouting. Scouting never seemed like work to her. In a speech to Girl Scouts at Savannah she said that scouting had helped restore her lost youth. "I am so terribly grateful to you for making joy a duty to me." Lou added, "I have always felt that our play hours have as great an effect upon our lives and our accomplishments as our working hours."[13]

Lou's interest in women's athletics complemented her commitment to outdoor recreation and celebration of natural beauty in her work with the Girl Scouts. She considered physical fitness essential for a happy, healthy life and for self-esteem. Lou was a leader in the creation of the Women's Division of the National Amateur Athletic Federation (NAAF) and was the only woman vice president of the parent group. Her philosophy of athletics differed from that of the NAAF, which emphasized competitive sports designed to train athletes for the Olympics. Lou preferred a more universal model for athletics that included a larger percentage of the population. She felt that overly competitive training placed stress on young people and deprived sports of its joy. Lou wanted a grassroots program based on recreational exercise rather than an elitist one that focused exclusively on winning. She wanted women to learn sports with a carryover value that they could enjoy throughout their lives. However, with the 1932 Olympic Games approaching, the organization adopted the more regimented model, and most of the money and resources were directed toward winning medals. The Women's Division, however, survived as the National Association of Women and Girls in Sport.[14]

Lou's entry into the White House did not change her personality. She was no more intimidated by reporters than she had been by Boxer bullets. She rejected Secret Service protection, shopped alone, drove to New York and North Carolina, managed the White House efficiently, added an atmosphere of western informality, and made guests feel at home. Lou took friends for strolls along the reflecting pool on the National Mall late at night and welcomed guests at the White House that ranged from longtime friends to celebrity entertainers and heads of state. She maintained her interest in the Girl Scouts and when the Depression settled upon the country, made them an arm of her husband's private relief efforts. Lou delivered the first national radio address by a First Lady and by 1932 was speaking periodically. She roused the Girl Scouts and the 4-H clubs to sustain morale, to help the needy, to volunteer to perform chores for shut-ins, and to add a human touch to relieve Depression angst. In addition, she performed "stealth philanthropy," sorting and either answering personally or farming out many of the thousands of letters she received from those in need. She gave her own money anonymously to some, helped place others in jobs, and referred still others to local relief agencies such as the Red Cross. Although it made only a small dent in the Depression, it was a superhuman effort for one person. When her desk was cleaned out after her death, her secretaries found drawers stuffed with uncashed checks from people who had tried to repay loans.[15]

Politically, Lou was equally, if not more, conservative than her husband. She was active in politics yet in a nonpartisan manner. She confined her personal judgments to close friends. Privately, like her husband, she was dubious of Harding's cronies and urged women to vote to keep political hacks from winning office. Winning the vote was only the first step she advised; voting consistently and wisely could help cleanse American politics of corruption. Lou considered moral rectitude a greater qualification for office than intellectual stature. Like her husband, she disdained deal making and intellectually dishonest electioneering. She had always believed that it was better to lose than to win by cheating. An internationalist, Lou backed membership in the World Court. She also chaired a thousand-member nonpartisan Women's National Committee for Law Enforcement, which sought tougher enforcement of Prohibition laws. Lou refused to comment publicly on partisan issues, rarely gave interviews, and usually refused to be quoted for attribution. She would, however, conduct interviews concerning the Girl Scouts or her volunteer efforts to alleviate the Depression. She did not want credit nor did she want to detract attention from her husband's programs.[16]

During her first year in the White House, before the Depression dimmed White House social life, Lou focused on entertaining, which previously had been the sole sphere of First Ladies. She restructured the traditional role by merging social events with her husband's policy agenda using devices such as the selection of guests, seating arrangements, and the timing of events. She helped her husband relax and conserve his resources for important tasks. Lou arranged social events so there would be no wasted time during her the president's day. Although previous First Ladies had entertained with charm, few had been so purposeful in relating social events to a broader agenda. The press observed that next to Martha Washington, Lou was the nation's best-known First Lady prior to living in the White House. She set precedents that later First Ladies adopted. Throughout the nineteenth and early twentieth centuries First Ladies had done little more than entertain and decorate. Lou expanded the role, but she remained an individualist to the core, preserving her privacy and retaining her personal interests. She was a well-organized, hard worker who structured her day yet remained spontaneous. The First Lady excelled at facilitating conversation yet never monopolized conversations. She excelled at drawing other people out, including her husband. Unselfish, she cared about causes, but did not care about receiving credit. Neither did she think much about what historians would say about her, although she had a keen sense of history and made herself the unofficial White House historian, gathering documents and compiling them in order to preserve the story of the executive mansion. Friends remarked that she could have taught metallurgy, geology, or English at the college level. More organized than previous First Ladies, she sometimes worked from early morning until 11 p.m. Thoroughly modern, she used a Dictaphone to answer her voluminous mail. In many respects she was the first modern First Lady. Despite her slim, athletic figure, Lou did not try to be a fashion trendsetter. Her clothes were simple, yet stylish and varied. She presented a soft, feminine presence and never tried to upstage her husband or her guests. The First Lady was firm in her opinions yet did not press them upon others. Like her spouse, she could delegate and did not become lost in minutiae. Lou did not reveal her private thoughts to anyone except her family. She enjoyed company and was a lively companion yet exhibited an element of reserved dignity. During her four years in the White House she received numerous honorary degrees, many of which had nothing to do with the fact that she was First Lady. She enjoyed Washington society but found it somewhat confining and missed California. Lou was the same in public and in private, strong yet sensitive, supportive yet independent. Like Bert, she had been happy and successful throughout her life before coming to the White House.[17]

The Depression cast a pall on the entire family, but Lou considered preservation of morale one of her chief tasks. She encouraged the nation via radio, and newsreels mobilized Girl Scouts and 4-H'ers to do little things to uplift spirits. Lou recognized the psychological challenge posed by the Depression. She remained positive and attempted, in subtle ways, to inspire others to stay hopeful, without raising unrealistic expectations. Lou neither snubbed nor flattered the press. In good times and bad, she was her own person. Her job might have had sad moments, yet its redeeming feature was that she liked people, and her chief task was dealing with people, providing comfort and helping them enjoy the best of life during the worst of times. A Girl Scout leader observed that Lou "was sweet without being sugary; competent and able without being arrogant, dominant, or aggressive." She was also resilient and never seriously depressed. Lou enjoyed a rare degree of peace of mind. Her friend added that "She was that rare combination of simplicity and friendliness and quiet dignity that keeps familiarity away."[18] As late as the twenty-first century, Lou Henry was still largely unknown to the general public, "but her White House activism is too important to be overlooked any longer," writes her most recent biographer.[19]

Life in the White House was not all work, and the Hoover family was an extended one, including their sons, relatives, pets, and old friends who seemed like family. The president remained close to his older brother Theodore, who enjoyed a successful career as an engineer and later as an academic at Stanford, and to his sons, Herbert and Allan, who by graduating from their father's alma mater made the entire family Stanford alumni. The president also loved animals, especially dogs, and was never without one or more at the White House. He had brought from Belgium a German Shepherd named King Tut in 1917. King Tut had virtually free run of the White House, outside and inside. The big dog patrolled the White House grounds and brought the president his morning papers. Yet he was growing old and weak. Hoover sent him to Camp Rapidan where he could romp in the woods, and he died there in peace. The chief executive grieved privately and did not reveal Tut's death to the press for three months. To solace Hoover, European friends shipped him a pup, a Norwegian elkhound, rare in America, the type of dog that had drawn sleds for the Vikings and hunted deer for hundreds of years. The new pup grew into a large dog resembling a Siberian husky. Summers in Washington proved too hot for the Norwegian dog, and he was sent to Alaska, returning in the fall.[20]

The White House was not a "bully pulpit" for the Hoovers. In fact, the Quaker president never used the word "bully." But neither was it a morgue. The president and Lou enjoyed listening to the radio, and Lou's car was equipped with a radio. The First Lady was a skilled photographer and enjoyed snapping the family spontaneously, especially at Rapidan. She also took home movies of the First Family with a portable camera and showed them to close friends. Occasionally she filmed the president and other participants in their prebreakfast game of medicine ball. The Hoovers were also motion picture fans. In May 1929, they installed the first new talkie motion picture equipment in the White House. The Movietone projectors, identical to those used in theaters, were set up in a large reception room and mounted on wheels so they could be moved out when not needed. The White House showed films to groups of 15 to 25 guests beginning at 8:30 p.m. each Monday and Thursday. The program lasted from an hour and a half to two hours. Often senators, representatives, cabinet members, and personal friends were among the guests. The president usually selected the evening's fare. His favorites were newsreels covering domestic and world events. Among feature films, he enjoyed detective stories, just as his favorite light reading consisted of detective novels. Hoover also liked serious drama but nothing racy. Among shorts, he preferred music and singing but did not care much for comedy. Both he and Lou watched travelogues. Among the home movies Lou showed was a lengthy film about their tour of Latin America in 1928.[21]

Although both Hoover sons were grown by the White House years, they remained close to their parents, although frequently separated by distance. Allan graduated from Stanford in June 1929 after joining his parents on their goodwill tour of Latin America. Both Hoover sons had good minds, especially Herbert. Both were mechanically inclined and loved the West. Herbert became an amateur radio operator at 14, developed an interest in air travel, learned to fly, and merged aviation with radio. After earning his BS at Stanford, Herbert taught for two years at Harvard and studied the economics of aviation under the auspices of the Guggenheim Foundation. He accepted a position to adapt radio transmission to commercial aviation and developed a system to guide planes to landings through clouds and bad weather using radio and instruments. In late June of 1929 Herbert was commissioned a first lieutenant in the specialist branch of the Reserve Corps, a designation that permitted the military to use him in any branch in which his expertise was needed. The elder son began working as a radio technician for the Western Air Express and rose to vice president by 1931. He also became a contributing editor to *Aero Digest*, a trade journal, and served on a committee appointed by the Commerce Department, which undertook a study of problems in improving safety in air transportation. Like his father he was inordinately reserved; once he was turned away from the White House by a policeman who demanded that he prove his business there.[22]

Herbert drove himself relentlessly, and his health broke down in September 1930. Initially, Dr. Joel Boone, the White House physician, diagnosed him with an intestinal disorder complicated by overwork and exhaustion and sent him to Camp Rapidan for rest. However, as his condition worsened, Boone concluded that Herbert was infected with tuberculosis. The elder son moved to Asheville, North Carolina, where he was treated at a sanitarium and also by Boone as he recovered in the warmer climate. Herbert obtained a year's leave of absence from Western Air Lines. The president visited him in March 1931, and Lou visited several times, driving herself. Hebert's most frequent visitor was his wife Peggy. For the duration of his recovery, Peggy and the couple's three small children, Herbert III ("Peter"), Peggy Ann, and the infant Joan moved in with their grandparents at the White House. The First Couple thoroughly enjoyed the presence of their grandchildren. The president welcomed Peggy Ann and Peter into his office while working and kept peppermint candy on his desk for treats. He seemed undisturbed by the presence of children while working. A fireproof playroom was built, and Lou collected a cache of toys. During informal meals, the grandchildren dined with their grandparents and their mother, when she was not visiting Herbert. The illness brought the family closer together and gave the president and First Lady an extended opportunity to get to know their grandchildren. By April 1931 Herbert had recovered sufficiently to return to California with his family. In 1932 he began teaching at the California Institute of Technology at Pasadena.[23]

Allan, like all the Hoovers, was independent, publicity shy, and interested in mechanics. He was close to his parents while he attended the Harvard Business School, where he enrolled after graduating from Stanford. Allan avoided crowds when he traveled with his father and spoke little to the press, but he made friends easily with young people. During the summer of 1930 he worked at the Bayonne, New Jersey, plant of the American Radiator Company, where he rotated among different jobs in an effort to gain practical experience to complement the theory he learned at Harvard. He obtained the position on his own, not through his father's influence. On weekends he often traveled to Washington to visit his parents. After returning to Harvard in September and completing the fall semester, the Hoovers sponsored a White House dance for Allan in January 1931. After school at Harvard, Allan returned to California where he accepted a low-paying clerical job at a branch bank in Los Angeles because he did not want to exploit his father's position to obtain a more lucrative position. Like all the Hoovers, he was drawn to California. Both children resisted trading on the family name. Meanwhile, the family fortune shrunk. By late 1932 the president's fortune, which had been estimated at around $4 million in 1914, had shrunk to less than $1 million. This was largely due to stock losses and charitable donations.[24]

The Hoovers were an informal family, but they were by no means inexperienced at formal entertainment. In Europe, Hoover had dined almost routinely with generals, foreign ministers, and prime ministers and had been received by kings. The First Family took entertaining at the White House as a serious responsibility. To a degree, they enjoyed it, and it offered a respite from work. Yet as the Depression dragged on, the president cut back on ceremonial duties because some of them consumed the time he needed to combat the Depression. Further, lavish entertainment seemed in poor taste when people were hungry. Lou strove to make guests at the White House feel at home and to dampen Washington's reputation as the gossip capital of the nation.

The president did not dislike the ceremonial aspects of his job, because he liked people, and Lou felt they were necessary to maintain morale and embellish Hoover's image. However, he hated to waste time, and as the Depression deepened, he came to feel that some traditions that had developed when the presidency was a smaller job distracted him from work. One such tradition was shaking hands with ordinary Americans who dropped by the president's office to grasp his hand briefly and chat. Harding, a gregarious person, and Coolidge, who had time on his hands, had performed this ceremonial task almost daily. Unlike the tight security in place in the White House today, visitors were not screened and lined up at the president's office inside the Executive Office Building. The crowd flowed out of the building and sometimes extended beyond a full city block. In April 1929, the president reduced the number of greeting sessions to twice weekly, and in May he began to limit them to about an hour once a week and then dispensed with them entirely during the hottest months of the summer. In February 1932, Hoover eliminated the tradition of greeting casual visitors and limited visitors to groups recommended by a congressman. They were required to make an appointment with his secretary. By then, the toll of the Depression had expanded the work of the president and made the tradition impractical. In 1934 it was permanently terminated because the new president, Franklin D. Roosevelt, confined to a wheelchair, could not physically perform the task. In addition to consuming time, the tradition drained the president's energy. The chief executive continued to shake thousands of hands at large receptions. On New Year's Day, the gates were thrown open to the public, and the president greeted all comers. On the first day of 1930, people lined up before dawn to see the president, who shook hands with 6,429 visitors for an hour and a half during the morning and two and a half hours in the afternoon. On October 13, 1932, Hoover shook hands with about 3,000 persons at an evening reception of the American Bar Association. His hand began to bleed, he had to step out of the reception line, and he wore a bandage the following day. In 1932, some 160 conventions planned to meet in Washington, and all wanted to send delegations to meet the president. The chief executive was compelled to curtail this tradition as well, limiting visitors to groups with genuine business. His love of children prompted him to make exceptions for them. He met small groups on the White House grounds and allowed himself to be photographed with them. Because the United States lacked a monarch, the president in the past had been expected to perform ceremonial tasks that multiplied as the job grew. Increasingly, ceremonial tasks were delegated to the vice president. Hoover did continue the tradition of shaking hands with ordinary citizens on New Year's Day. By 1932, he was unpopular, and the turnout was diminished by rain. Still, at the end of a long day of grasping hands, the chief usher, who had stood beside him counting the passersby, announced that precisely 1,932 persons had shaken hands with the president. Press Secretary Joslin hoped the coincidence might be an omen for a better year.[25]

The signing of routine papers was another time-consuming burden for the president. No one could read and digest all the documents the chief executive was expected to sign. The attorney general suggested that the president delegate some signing to cabinet members, which lightened the burden. With the Depression, a tidal wave of telephone calls swamped the White House, and the number of letters and telegrams soared. Telephone calls reached about 1,200 per day and letters and telegrams rose to 10,000 per day. Hoover increased the staff to handle the inundation and borrowed help from other departments. Neither Coolidge nor his predecessors had installed a telephone in the Executive Office, fearing the ringing might distract them. Hoover became the first chief executive to place a telephone on his desk, and he created a White House switchboard to screen and direct calls. The president used the telephone to contact cabinet members and other officials, which saved time and trimmed the number of personal visitors.[26]

As hard times increased before Christmas of 1929, Lou distributed gifts to charities and visited the Salvation Army camp, the Walter Reed Hospital, and disabled persons, a practice she continued during later years. No Hoover grandchildren were present at the First Family's initial Christmas at the White House because Herbert and his family decided to remain in California. However, Allan came down from the Harvard Business School to enjoy the holiday with his parents. The Hoovers lit the national Christmas tree, listened to carols, and at noon dined on simple fare featuring turkey. They did not attend church at Christmas because their meetinghouse did not hold services. On Christmas Eve night, Lou sponsored a party for the wives and children of the president's secretaries, with refreshments along with gifts for the children. During the party a fire erupted in the Executive Office Building, which badly damaged the building and destroyed furniture and some papers, though nothing irreplaceable was lost. Allan, his father, and the male parents rushed into the burning building to save essential documents. Some 19 fire companies fought the flames until 11 p.m., and the building was a total loss. The cause was traced to a faulty fireplace, and a new building was constructed while the president temporarily relocated into a commodious office used sporadically by General Pershing. While thousands gathered to watch the firefighters, Lou calmed the children and continued the party inside as the Marine Band entertained them. It might have been a metaphor for the economy, which was going up in smoke.[27]

Lou adjusted to the role of First Lady without undue anxiety. She was well organized, delegated efficiently, liked people, and remembered names and faces. However, she disliked the glare of the spotlight and tried to retain her independence. Her relationship with personal friends changed. They could no longer simply stop by to chat. Callers were required to make an appointment with Lou's social secretary and had to wait in an outer room until the First Lady had completed her visit with the previous caller. This injected a degree of stiffness and distance into friendships. Lou was expected to perform a variety of tasks, many ceremonial, others more substantial. She accompanied the president on public occasions and had to respond to an enormous amount of mail, which swelled as the Depression worsened. She lent her name to charities and tried to aid them. She was expected to attend church regularly, to care about what she wore because it would be described in the press, to host large dinners, and to respond spontaneously to guests her husband brought home. Tourists were allowed on the first floor while the family quarters were on the second floor. She supervised about 30 servants, most of them carryovers from previous administrations. Lou won the affection of her staff because she treated them respectfully. Her official tasks fell chiefly into two categories: managing the White House and hosting social events. In managing the White House, her principal assistant was the housekeeper. Each day began with a conference at which they planned the menus for meals, including formal dinners. Second on the day's agenda was a meeting with her social secretary. She knew a great deal about the traditions and customs of Washington society. The social secretary could provide a buffer between the First Lady and her social demands. She could do some work in the name of the president's wife. Like her husband, Lou employed three secretaries, paying two of them personally. Previous First Ladies had relied on one. Unlike the president's secretaries, the roles of those of the First Lady were less clearly defined. They accepted tasks according to priority rather than specialty. Although the First Lady made the major decisions about important social events, such as the menus and guest lists, the details were implemented by her secretaries.[28]

One reason Lou needed more secretaries is because the Hoovers entertained more than previous First Families. There were dinner guests virtually every night, and it has been estimated that the Hoovers entertained five times as many guests as the Coolidges. While the Coolidges preferred quiet and solitude, the Hoovers were just the opposite. They enjoyed being surrounded by people and had a wide circle of friends, and the president did not like to dine alone. Good conversation was an elixir that lubricated the evenings. Hoover's friends knew that the president enjoyed nothing more than stimulating conversation. He was both a good listener and a gifted raconteur. Lou was a catalyst, steering the conversation into channels and then withdrawing after she had drawn out her guests and her husband. At least before the gloom of the

Depression dimmed the glitter of White House social life, it was the hub of the city, the most exciting place since the time of Theodore Roosevelt. Unlike the garrulous Roosevelt, however, Hoover was not a dominating conversationalist, preferring greater equality among his guests. Lou was also adept in preventing any guest from holding the floor too long. The First Lady introduced an element of western informality into the White House, while venerating its history. During the spring and summer, Lou held outdoor garden parties. At indoor receptions people could sit or mingle rather than simply sit in one place. The First Lady brought in more comfortable furniture for guests who wished to recline. Sometimes the Hoovers varied the routine of the reception line by mixing with the guests and chatting with them in small groups rather than having them file by for a perfunctory handshake. Neither Hoover wore jewelry. Lou dressed simply during the day yet elegantly for evening socials. The First Lady held a larger number of smaller parties to enable guests to talk freely. Instead of the usual tea and cakes of the Coolidge era, guests were served a variety of sandwiches, cakes, coffees, and ice cream. Lou kept events moving and on time. The president ate rapidly and preferred simple fare, yet they set an elaborate table for large, formal dinners. He and Lou practiced a relaxed form of dignity that put guests at ease. Lou was aware that Washington revolved around politics, and even social events reflected that reality. She knew her parties were politically important. Lou planned them to placate critics of the president such as Senator Borah, other congressional opponents, and journalists. Friendly conversation could lubricate the creaky legislative machinery or ingratiate an unfriendly editor. Most people who got to know Hoover in an intimate setting liked him better. Sometimes she surrounded him with an array of friends that included writers, professors, artists, engineers, Stanford alumni, and performers. Many of the White House events included musical entertainment. Lou was the first twentieth-century First Lady to invite black and Native American entertainers to the White House on a periodic basis.[29]

It was difficult not to irritate touchy personalities. Senator Hiram Johnson was inadvertently left off of invitations to a dinner that included other members of the Foreign Relations Committee. Although Hoover apologized, his California rival attributed the oversight to a deliberate snub. It was an unfortunate faux pas but could hardly make Johnson dislike Hoover any more than he already did. The most gossip was churned up over the social status of Dolly Gann, the sister of Vice President Charles Curtis, a widower, because Gann served as Curtis' escort to social events. Gann, a social maverick whose behavior made staid Washingtonians wince, insisted upon the social prerogatives of a vice presidential wife, including seating priorities and invitations to social functions for wives. Some wives ignored the assertive Gann while others deliberately snubbed her. Since politicians were the closest Americans had to royalty, some considered it an affair of state or at least of tradition. Lou refused to comment publicly on the unusual situation. She tried to finesse the problem and appease Gann by sponsoring a special dinner for the vice president, which had never been done, in which Gann occupied a seat of honor. The alternative, inviting the vice president's escort to the dinner for cabinet wives, might have aggravated conflict over the pecking order.[30]

By mid-1930, the malaise of the Depression led the Hoovers to place less emphasis on formal, elegant entertaining, which seemed insensitive at a time when hungry people waited in bread lines, empty handed and unemployed. In June, Lou's social secretary resigned, complaining that the decline in entertaining left her with too little to do. Lou believed that social life played an important role in preserving morale, yet extravagant galas would be tasteless. Some socials were transformed into charity benefits, and Lou "dressed down," wearing cotton gowns made from domestically grown fiber. That winter, the parties were smaller and less ornate. The social season was shortened because of periods set aside to mourn the deaths of Secretary of War James Good and Chief Justice William Howard Taft. Lou's health played a role in curtailing her activities. She suffered several severe colds and, more seriously, fell in her room and sprained her back. For a time, she was confined to a wheelchair. She rested at Rapidan and in her room. In 1931–32 the White House hostess invited fewer and less expensive entertainers to perform. Lou increasingly strove to merge her charitable work with her social obligations and to tailor them to complement her husband's political agenda without appearing too obvious. The First Lady was respected by the Washington social and political community but did not cut a high profile with the general public. Under the radar, she was transforming the role of First Lady.[31]

An administration that had dawned in the sunlit days of unprecedented prosperity had seen the sun set on that prosperity. The Furies that extinguished the flames of prosperity dimmed the affairs of the First Family no less than other families, not simply in their work, but in their private lives. The decline transformed a job of building to one of patching, transforming an atmosphere of heightened expectation to one of deflated hopes. The entire family felt the unyielding pressure of the public spotlight and the acidity of criticism. Although many aspects of life at the White House were daunting, the Hoovers were resilient people who led purposeful lives, still determined to make a difference. Serious people who nonetheless enjoyed life, they persevered. The president and the First Lady demonstrated fortitude and stoic grit, and although enveloped by an atmosphere of gloom, their private lives included many times of joy and quiet satisfaction. Herbert Jr. and Allan had grown up, completed college and graduate study, and embarked on lives of their own. Family bonds remained strong, as did commitment to Quaker ideals. Under stress, they continued to enjoy solitude, the loyalty of their friends, their time together, and interludes away from the office. After Lou Henry's time, there would be different standards by which First Ladies were judged. Just as her husband's tenure marked a transition from lassitude to a more activist presidency, the same can be said of the First Lady. Though there were many in the country who doubted them by 1932, they did not doubt each other.

CHAPTER 16

The Peter Pan in Hoover

Children and Fish

Herbert Hoover loved children. They loved him as well. He treated them with respect, encouraged them to enjoy life, took their problems seriously, and conversed with them as equals. He did not preach to them nor talk down to them. The president's time was never too valuable to turn away children. Hoover had special camaraderie with boys. The saddest part of childhood, he believed, was that it had to end. While it lasted, it existed to be enjoyed. When it did end, children should enter the adult world with healthy minds and bodies and an optimistic outlook. Hoover's love of children never faltered and was one of the most dominant drives in his life. As an adult, the boy in him lived on. He wanted to give children a chance, including some of the chances he had missed. In his own way, Herbert Hoover was one of the great lovers of his time. He realized that what children needed most are love and nurturing. Those are intangibles that no government program can provide, yet without childhoods nourished by love, they grow up with a void inside. He did not believe the problems of children were simple or easy, but he viewed childhood not as a time of surmounting problems, but as a time of joy, to be lived to the fullest, a short precious time. The lost innocence of childhood was never lost on Hoover. His childhood had been one of adversity, and he did not want other children to suffer; otherwise, they might become hardened adults. One of the most important contributions adults can make is to listen. There are complementary things governments and voluntary organizations can do, but they never replace a nurturing family. Though he appeared stoic on the outside, the few times Hoover broke down publicly were when moved by children. His own deprivation forged a bond with the young and he had discovered renewal by helping others. That is why being rich and successful was not enough. Love is the manna on which all humans thrive. Children are the neediest, and the most vulnerable. Childhood is the plastic time of life, not a time to be deliberately molded to conform to adult perceptions, but an opportunity to expand and to dream. The president's heart was open to the young, and he remained young at heart. His chief motivation for his humanitarian work was to save children from starvation, famine, and the ravages of war and the cruelties of life. He was a realist, not a utopian, but he knew that the future lay in children. Humankind was a circle in which children held the hands of their parents, and they in turn held hands with their own children. Breaking the circle meant breaking hearts. He knew. His own heart had been broken. It had healed but never completely. This sense of solitary sadness, which he accepted and came to understand, had made him unusually sensitive and gave his life a purpose beyond fame, money, and political success. All of these could be swept away, but no one who loved, and was loved, would be warped by fear. All humans are motivated to some extent by fear, and Hoover was no different. But he learned, at least intuitively, that fear and security, hate and love, are not opposite emotions, but opposite extremes of the same emotion. In turn, children probably understood Hoover best. They accepted his kindness for what it was, without cynicism, without probing for ulterior motives.

Hoover worked as hard, or harder, for the interests of children, as he ever worked at anything, and unlike the presidency or his mining career, it was lifelong. Even his humanitarian activities were means to an end, not ends in themselves. After all else is forgotten, he would probably prefer to be remembered for his passionate connection with children. The president was sufficiently farsighted to recognize that most of the problems of his time would not be solved by his generation, and he looked to the next generation to carry on the work. Working with children was preventive; it could disperse future storm clouds, including the clouds of war, before they gathered, and it could shine the light of day upon existing problems, some of which were recurrent. Children held the key to scientific advance, the prevention of war, the cure of disease, the elevation of the arts and the humanities, and the improvement in the morality of humankind. It seems impossible to imagine happy adults without happy children. Thus although Hoover's attachment to children was sentimental and nostalgic, it also had a practical side. A little kindness went a long way. More playgrounds today would mean fewer prisons tomorrow. Children are our best investment. Hoover did not desire to "engineer" children, quite the opposite; he delighted in their infinite variety and undiscovered potential. Childhood is and should be a magic time, and it is a mistake to grow up too fast. Childhood is the incubator of the imagination; it is a time to dream; adulthood is a time to make dreams come true. Many of the things

Hoover had dreamed of, beginning at Stanford, had come true, and he wanted to pry open this door of possibilities for other children. Some people who knew Hoover only superficially did not see the boy inside—a Peter Pan who perhaps felt that growing up is a mistake.

Hoover could be moving and eloquent when discussing children. In a speech to a Boy Scout dinner on March 10, 1930, the president emphasized his belief that the nation's children are its most vital resource: "The priceless treasury of boyhood is his endless enthusiasm, his store of high idealism and his fragrant hopes. His is a plastic period when indelible impressions must be made if we are to continue a successful democracy."[1] Hoover believed that it was important for boys to have fun. "There is more joy per inch out of the boy span of life than out of all the fifty years that follow," he said. "I am as strong for the fun side as I am for the serious side—during boyhood—and it's the business of grownups to help on the joy side."[2] Hoover never missed an opportunity to advocate the needs of children, emotionally and eloquently. He was an ambassador for the millions of children who could not speak with a single voice. "They are the most wholesome part of the race, the sweetest, for they are fresher from the hands of God," he told the White House Child Health Conference in 1930. "Whimsical, ingenious, mischievous, we live a life of apprehension as to what their opinion of us might be," adding a touch of irony, "a life of defense against their terrifying energy; we put them to bed with a sense of relief and a lingering of devotion." The president concluded, "We envy them the freshness of adventure and discovery of life; we mourn over the disappointments they will meet."[3] In March of the same year, the chief executive delivered a speech in the same vein when he commemorated the twentieth anniversary of the Boy Scouts of America, a cause to which he was devoted. "Together with his sister, the boy is the most precious possession of the American home," he said. "I sometimes think that one of the sad things of life is that they will grow up." The president explained the role of scouting to scout leaders. "The problem we are considering here is not primarily a system of health or education or morals. It is what to do with him in his leisure time."[4] No less than the future of democracy is at stake, the president told another audience: "Freedom can march only upon the feet of educated, healthy and happy children."[5]

Hoover's eloquence about his love for children expressed the pain of a lost childhood. He carried that pain within him all his life. He remembered much of his childhood as joyous. "I grew up on sand-lot baseball, swimming holes, and fishing with worms," he wrote. Yet later in life one of his regrets was that he had not played enough as a child and spent too much time in the adult world. The world of childhood is wonderful, he told children who wrote him in retirement, and they should play as much as possible. He realized that creative, unstructured play develops the imagination, helps children cope later with unexpected situations, and enhances their ability to make friends. Too much work at an early age produces discipline and direction but also seriousness and lack of spontaneity. In many of his letters to children Hoover was introspective; he was thinking of the facets of life that had been neglected in his own truncated childhood. By communicating with children, he could reflect upon himself in an introspective vein he rarely shared with adults. His hard childhood had not made him mean and bitter. He did not use it an excuse for delinquency, alienation, or hardness, and he never complained. It mellowed him as he aged and helped him understand the suffering of others, and he forged a bond with the young. It resulted in a desire to nurture children, in all countries, in normal times and during war. Hoover reached out to all children, the gifted, the normal, the delinquent, and the handicapped. He believed a normal child was a happy child. He said that it was important to go beyond dwelling on what children lacked and to seek the positive things in them. Adults need to ruminate, not solely on what subnormal children lack, but on the attributes of the best, the brightest, gifted children. Hoover felt positive about the future of the great majority of children if they received love and nurture. Their potential was unlimited, and they would produce the nation's leaders. "Their faces are turned toward the light—theirs is the life of great adventure," he said. "These are the vivid, romping, everyday children, our own and our neighbors, with all their strongly marked differences—and the more the better. The more they charge us with their separate problems the more we know they are vitally and humanly alive." The president was relentlessly optimistic about the nation's children even in the midst of one of the most trying times in its history. "They are not born evil," he wrote. "They are endowed with a cheerfulness and a surplus of dynamic energy," he explained. "They are ambitious, joyous, and anxious to take part in the serious business of the world."[6] Hoover was intrigued by the insatiable curiosity of children, a curiosity he shared. "They are intent on discovering the world for themselves," he wrote, adding that his expertise came from being an ex-boy. One thing the nation could not afford was to give up on its children.[7] When Hoover contemplated running for president in 1928 he told a friend that "the reason above all others why the presidency attracts me is that in that position I would have the greatest of all opportunities to accomplish social betterment, particularly to do something for young people." On his second day in office he discussed the issue of child welfare with senators. Several months later, choked with emotion, he said that child welfare and education "have the widest of social importance that reaches to the roots of democracy itself." Hoover's friend Vernon Kellogg wrote that "I think of him as going down in history as the children's president."[8] Hoover believed harsh discipline could damage a child. They should be given the latitude to develop in their own way. "Standards are wanted, but not standardization of children," he wrote. "We want them different because the greater the variety of good combinations, the richer will be the range of types, and the greater will be the contributions made to our national life."[9]

After he left office, tens of thousands of children wrote the ex-president to tell him that he had inspired them and to solicit his advice. He answered as many in possible, writing in longhand, then had a secretary type and mail them. Hoover usually wrote the letters late at night, often rising after a few hours of sleep. He did not give them pat answers such as "work hard" and "obey your parents" but wrote thoughtful, sincere replies. He responded to one boy who asked if he would be too busy to answer his letter: "I will always be busy, but not too much to answer your letter."[10] Although his letters to adults were often terse and factual, those to children were kind and patient, with a touch of whimsy and humor. In his eighty-fifth year, the former president answered 21,000 letters. In 1962, at the age of 88, he collected a small sample of his correspondence and published it as *On Growing Up*. At 90, the year he died, he was still writing. "Herbert Hoover loved his country, but no more than he loved its children," Richard Norton Smith and Timothy Walch write.[11] Repeatedly, Hoover advised children not to grow up too soon, to enjoy the magic of childhood, to have fun, and to learn good morals through sportsmanship. "The first rule is just to be a boy getting all the constructive joy out of life," he wrote one child. "Play every chance you get—including fishing," he told another. He further advised the boy to "get some indestructible things stored in your head." Education was important, he said, but he did not consider politics a noble profession, he told a correspondent, unless it involved "public service" rather than merely self-gratification.[12] The president believed outdoor recreation helped refresh and balance mind and body. Fishing and camping were his personal favorites, but he was also a fan of organized team and individual sports, especially baseball and football. He played baseball but apparently not much football as a boy. He attended baseball and football games during his presidency. The first portion of the daily newspaper he read was the sports pages. Team sports, Hoover believed, encouraged school spirit, fair play, and learning to collaborate with others toward a common goal. Threaded throughout his advice to young people are the advantages of organized athletics. Hoover never considered his correspondence with young people a chore. He looked forward to it.[13]

Hoover gave money, time, and advice to a variety of organizations that served young people during, before, and after his presidency. Prior to his White House years, his chief children's charitable work was with the American Child Health Association (ACHA), which he helped found, which was devoted to improving the health and well-being of children. Hoover served on the board of directors, as president, as fundraiser-in-chief, and as an apostle of child health, nutrition, and education until the dissolution of the group. Hoover helped finance the organization's operating expenses with money left over from the American Relief Administration. He helped write a "Children's Charter" and a "Children's Bill of Rights" for the ACHA and was the chief impetus behind devoting May Day of each year to the promotion of the welfare of children. Hoover was the most frequent speaker at the semiannual gathering of the association. The chief purpose of the ACHA was educational. It published dozens of books and pamphlets designed to educate the public about the needs of children and to prod the states, the federal government, and private charities to contribute to child health. This group was technical and scientific, more structured than some of Hoover's charities that focused on recreation. It attempted to utilize the work of social scientists and medical researchers to improve the lives of children and to institutionalize the changes.[14]

The president's involvement with the Boys Clubs of America covered his prepresidential and postpresidential careers. Increasingly, he became concerned with the problems of urban youth, who lacked outlets for recreation that came naturally in rural areas. The Boys Clubs accepted members on a nonracial, nonjudgmental basis and offered recreation, classes, athletics, and the opportunity to bond with mentors and with other children. Hoover observed that in cities, "We have increased the number of boys per acre." The city boy had a life "of stairs, light switches, alleys, fire escapes, bells, cobblestones, and a chance to get run over by a truck." Because of his stature, he became a prodigious fundraiser for the organization during his postpresidential years, writing thousands of letters to friends. "I am not a professional beggar," he wrote one, "but this is one cause where I break my rule." During the period from the end of his presidency to his death in 1964, the number of Boys Clubs expanded nationally from 140 to more than 600 locations. He was proud of the fact that whenever a Boys Club opened in a neighborhood, the proportion of youth crime declined.[15] Hoover became chairman of the board in 1936, and he addressed the Boys Clubs directors' dinner at age 86. At 90, he was still engaged with the group. The ex-president remarked that young people needed the freedom to roam and mingle and "if he doesn't contend with nature, he is likely to take on contention with a policeman."[16] Hoover often signed autographs for the boys he met at Boys Clubs ceremonies. One young man got an autograph, scrambled to the back of the line, moved up, and collected another. Hoover asked why he wanted another. He said that "if I get two of your autographs I can trade them to some fellows for one of Gene Autry's."[17] Hoover encouraged the Boy Scouts and the Cub Scouts but was less intensely involved. He contributed a small sum annually to the Boy Scouts and allowed his photograph to be used for fundraising purposes. He wrote one scout that there had been no troop available for him to join as a youth but that one of his sons had been a scout. "I am all for the Scouts," he wrote. "They build up character, health, and sportsmanship."[18]

Hoover worked within the government bureaucracy as well as through private organizations and individual deeds of kindness to advance the cause of children. He kicked off his administration's innovations for child reform with the White House Conference on Child Health and Protection that convened in the fall of 1930 after a year of research by experts. It furnished a blueprint for reform in a variety of realms, yet he was unable to follow through on some because of the Depression and because he was denied a second term. Still, he did make progress. The work of the Children's Bureau was one of the president's special interests, and he steadily increased appropriations for the Bureau despite the reductions in expenditures for other bureaus during the Depression. Hoover said that records of the Public Health Service showed less infant mortality and infant disease than during normal times. The president also supported a congressional initiative to create a National Institute of Health and throughout his public life backed an amendment to ban child labor. Throughout the 1920s Hoover lobbied for a constitutional amendment to regulate child labor. He believed forcing young people to work was detrimental to their health, kept them from attending school, and subjected them to strenuous repetitive motions. Hoover rejected the argument of some manufacturers that use of children in factories was an economic necessity. If waste in production and distribution were eliminated, child labor would be superfluous, he argued. The amendment was passed by Congress after ordinary legislation had been nullified by the Supreme Court. However, it failed to attain ratification by sufficient states.[19]

Some of Hoover's individual kind acts toward children demonstrate the true depth of his commitment to the young, his love of them, and his patience. "When you saw him with the youngsters, you didn't have any doubt that his heart was in the moment," a friend said.[20] In the harsh Depression spring of 1932, the president learned that three desperate children, aged 13, 11, and 10, had come from Detroit to beg the president, their last hope, to help their father return to his family. The man, Charles Feagan, unemployed and broke, had gone West in a futile search for work. Attempting to return, he had been arrested for car theft and jailed. Hoover invited the children to the White House as his first appointment on May 28. He asked the eldest, Bernice, to relate the story. It was a sad tale of an impoverished, close family and a father desperate for employment. The president listened intently, struggling to control his emotions, while the girl begged him to help. As she finished, he told the children that any man who inspired such devotion from his children must be a good man. He promised to do his best to have him released. When the children departed, the chief executive broke down and sobbed. He ordered Theodore Joslin, his press secretary, to obtain the father's release. Then he collected his composure and returned to work. Joslin wanted to use the episode to "humanize" the president, which might help his political prospects in an election year. Hoover rejected the idea, stating that such use of the children's plight would constitute exploitation of them.[21]

In April 1931, Hoover learned about the heroism of Bryan Untied, a 13-year-old student from Colorado whose class had been caught in a snow bank in subzero temperatures when their bus broke down. The driver set out for help, leaving Bryan in charge, but the driver died in the snow. Bryan did his best to save his classmates, including his younger brother. He stripped down to his underwear and gave away his clothes to younger students. He labored to keep the students awake during their 36-hour ordeal. Bryan built a small fire in the bus and tried to keep the students moving; he even incited some to fight. Two days later, a plane spotted the bus with the missing children and soon help arrived. Five of the children had frozen to death, yet due partly to Untied's efforts, 19 survived. The class leader himself suffered frostbite and pneumonia. When the boy recovered, Hoover invited him to the White House to honor him. He set aside time to meet with Bryan at his office and said he was welcome to remain at the White House for as long as he desired, until he had seen all the sights he wanted to see, with meals and transportation provided. Bryan slept in the White House for two days and dined twice with the First Lady, who, driving her own car, took the boy on a tour of Washington, along with her grandchildren. They visited the Washington Monument and other famous sites, but Bryan's most important wish was to see the White House kennels, where the president let him pet the dogs. As in the case of the Feagan children, Hoover allowed only minimal publicity. The sparse information that leaked out came chiefly from the children themselves.[22]

Hoover doted on his granddaughter Peggy Ann and always made time for her when Herbert's children lived in the White House while their father recovered from tuberculosis in Asheville. The president often strolled around the living quarters holding Peggy with one hand and the toddler Peter by the other. Once, Peggy rushed into his office on a Sunday while he was deeply engaged in finishing a speech. The little girl announced that lunch was ready. When the president did not respond, she repeated it, this time as an order. As the president continued to write, Peggy swept all the state papers off his desk, stating emphatically, "I said luncheon is ready; come on, you lazy man." Instead of becoming angry, Hoover put down his work, swept up Peggy into his arms, and carried her to the dining room. On another occasion he dropped everything to take his grandchildren Christmas shopping, realizing that they would be followed by a horde of gawkers and reporters. He patiently taught the small girl the art of trout fishing.[23]

Some of Hoover's kindness was expressed in simple acts, which were meaningful to their young recipients. During the 1928 campaign, Hoover met a 12-year-old Iowa City boy who had never been able to walk. The youth told the candidate that he enjoyed listening to him speak on the radio but that he did not own a set. Hoover remembered the child and later sent him a radio as a gift.[24] The chief executive gave a unique gift to a group of children in May of 1929, when he learned that a small-town high school baseball team in Virginia had lost its "possum" mascot, which had run away. The team captain, who complained that they had lost every game since the departure due to lack of inspiration, wrote Hoover. The president had the White House opossum, which had been presented to him by local children at Camp Rapidan, sent as a replacement. "With the White House 'possum' nothing can stop us from winning now," the team wrote back.[25] During the winter of 1932, Hoover donated $2,500 to the American Friends Service Committee for the feeding of the children of unemployed coal miners. The previous Christmas, the First Family had sponsored a Christmas party at which the children invited were asked to wrap gifts, which were sent to the coal regions.[26]

Such gifts were not merely perfunctory. They made a difference to the people they affected and showed that the president was sincere in his empathy, especially since he refused to exploit them for publicity. Hoover was hurt badly by the outrageous charge—made by his onetime friend, Franklin D. Roosevelt, during the 1932 campaign—that the president had "failed the children." This was perhaps the most ironic charge flung at Hoover. It was sheer fabrication because it was the cause in which he was most deeply involved.[27]

Hoover enjoyed excellent health throughout his life, including remarkable stamina, and incurred no serious illnesses. His early life had been spent largely in the outdoors, yet during his years as secretary of commerce he became sedentary due to his single-minded focus on his work, and his weight ballooned to about 200 pounds. When he became president, his personal physician, Dr. Joel Boone, persuaded him to undertake a regimen of physical exercise for his health. Golf and tennis were too time consuming for the president. A rugged competitor, he enjoyed the challenge of team sports. Hoover and Boone designed a game called "Hoover ball" that provided more exercise in less time than any comparable, practical, activity. No one, before or since, has pursued it with such zest. It involved tossing a medicine ball over a net on a court laid out to resemble a tennis court. There were three men to a side, two near the net and one near the base line. Several games involving Hoover's friends were under way simultaneously, daily, except Sunday. The games began at about 7 a.m. and went on relentlessly, regardless of the weather, even during snow. Sometimes the participants became muddy, yet they played on. The regulars included cabinet members, Supreme Court justices, Dr. Boone, and journalist friends such as Mark Sullivan and William Hard. Those who had to miss a game were required to notify Boone in advance. Politics was off limits, and all participants were equal. The president was one of the strongest and most agile, although some of the taller players, such as Ray Lyman Wilbur, had an advantage. After the game, the players gathered on the White House lawn for juice and coffee, but no one talked "shop." The regimen worked well for the president. By the end of his term he had firmed up and slimmed down to 179 pounds. After the postgame chat, Hoover showered and was ready for his 8 a.m. breakfast. He ate the same meal every morning: one egg and one slice of toast. Sometimes, but only rarely, he had a second cup of coffee. Hoover looked forward to the games and the camaraderie, although he did not like rising quite so early. But the games were energizing and he began each day refreshed and relaxed.[28]

Hoover soaked in nature. He was never happier than in the outdoors. Although other presidents, such as Theodore Roosevelt, were also rugged outdoorsmen, Hoover, who lived much longer, probably spent more time in nature before, during, and after his presidency than any modern president.

He fished, camped, and scaled mountains in some of the most rugged, remote regions of America. Hoover wrote two books and numerous articles about his favorite outdoor avocation, fishing. He had begun pole fishing in Iowa as a child, graduated to fly fishing in Oregon and had perfected the art by the time he became president. He occasionally engaged in deep sea fishing off the Florida Keys and later off the California coast, but until it became physically onerous, he preferred pursuing the elusive trout. In trout fishing he was a purist who even as president rejected advice or assistance. Part of his joy of fishing was the solitude and communion with nature it provided. The only two times the president could be alone, he remarked, were fishing and praying, and he could not pray all the time. But solitude among the trees and streams was only part of his purpose. He also enjoyed catching fish, cooking them over an open fire, and eating them. In fishing as in life, he was competitive and practical. Fishing nourished the soul, and fresh trout nourished the body.[29]

Though many people might have found it strange coming from Hoover, he frequently said that life was more than work. Hoover's writing and speeches about fishing show his poetic and whimsical side and demonstrate his power of expression, which would have surprised the general public during his presidency, partly because it was subtle and he never flaunted it. In *Fishing for Fun and to Wash Your Soul*, published in 1963, the year before his death, he demonstrated, as friends already knew, that he not only could write inspirationally but possessed the linguistic artistry of a poet. He explained what made life meaningful. "It is the break of the waves in the sun, the contemplation of the eternal flow of the stream," he wrote, "the stretch of forest and mountain in their manifestation of the Maker—it is all these that soothe our troubles, shame our wickedness, and inspire us to esteem our fellow men—especially other fishermen."[30] Fishing contributed to humility, the fishing president said. It was the most democratic form of recreation because "all men are equal before fishes."[31] Fishing also kept people out of trouble during their idle moments, the president quipped whimsically. "There were lots of people who committed crimes last year who would not have done so if they had been fishing." He added, "Unless we can promise at least 50 fish per annum, including the occasional big one for recounting and memory purposes, we may despair of keep the population from further moral turpitude."[32] Americans did battle against their finny opponents armed to the teeth, the cracker-barrel philosopher observed. "We have arrived at a high state of tackle, assembled from the steel of Damascus, the bamboos of Siam, the silk of Japan, the lacquer of China, the tin of Bangkok, the nickel of Canada, the feathers of Brazil, and the silver of Colorado," the president said, "all compounded by mass production at Chicago, Illinois, and Akron, Ohio."[33] Fishing was a positive addiction, he explained. "Two months after you return from a fishing expedition you will begin again to think of the snowcap or the distant mountain peak, the glint of sunshine on the water, the excitement of the dark blue seas, and the glories of the forest," Hoover wrote. "And then you buy more tackle and more clothes for next year. There is no cure for these infections. And that big fish never shrinks."[34] Summing up the virtues of fishing, Hoover wrote that they include "discipline in the equality of men, meekness and inspiration before the works of nature, charity and patience toward tackle-makers and the fish, a mockery of profits and conceits, a quieting of hate and a hushing to ambition, a rejoicing that you do not have to decide a blanked thing until next week."[35]

Part of Hoover's reputation as a conservationist stemmed from his love of fishing. Fishing could lure people into the outdoors and involve them in therapeutic, wholesome recreation, he believed, but a sufficient supply of fish must be ensured to attract fishermen. During the Harding and Coolidge administrations, he was the chief advocate of conservation, playing a greater role than the secretaries of the interior or agriculture. His own interior secretary, Wilbur, was an ardent conservationist and one of the president's favorite fishing companions. In the 1920s Hoover served as president of the National Parks Association and honorary president of the Izaak Walton League. As secretary of commerce he helped control coastal oil pollution, developed fish stocking programs on inland waters, and helped conserve fish stocks for both recreational and commercial fishermen. He devised and implemented a plan to grow fingerlings to greater maturity before releasing them into internal waters, giving them a greater chance to survive the carnivorous appetites of larger fish. He believed that the government and fishing organizations could provide more nurseries to grow the young fish before their release, increasing the fish available to anglers. Hoover also realized that environmental pollution poisoned fish and encouraged sound environmental policies.[36]

Hoover might have been more popular with the general public if he had permitted his staff to humanize him by publicizing his interest in fishing, yet that would have defeated one of his purposes for fishing—he wanted to be left alone. Unrelated to his fishing, yet equally indicative of his sense of humor and his humility is another side of Hoover that neither the public nor historians ever recognized. The president maintained a special room at the White House with one of the largest private cartoon collections in the world. All were caricatures and depictions of him from many countries, dating from 1914. By the time he entered the White House the collection had grown to 20,000, most of them placed in bound portfolios, some of his favorites framed. Many, and most from the Depression era, were critical, even cruel, yet the president, who was less sensitive to criticism than most people believed, could laugh at himself. When he wanted a few moments of relaxation and private reflection, the president would retire to what he termed his "art gallery" and peruse the caricatures. The collection included 1932 caricatures denouncing him for his role in the Bonus March and caricatures drawn by angry Japanese nationalists. He was depicted as Uncle Shylock and the patron Saint of the New York Stock Exchange. Among the drawings were quite savage ones from *Punch*. After 1928 the president began adding depictions of himself from the Soviet

Union and Latin America. New cartoons arrived at the White House every day, and many cartoonists who knew of his hobby mailed him originals.[37]

During their first summer in Washington, which in those days lacked air conditioning, the Hoovers concluded that they needed a respite from the heat as well as a secluded spot where the president could relax in the outdoors and fish in relative solitude. The chief executive appointed an informal committee that included his staff, led by Lawrence Richey, to find such a site at a high elevation, wooded, with good trout fishing, within a hundred-mile radius of Washington. Lou, who loved the outdoors as much as her husband, wanted a spot where she could appreciate the spring flowers and the fall foliage and enjoy horseback riding. The president, who traveled less than most chief executives, wanted a location where he could get away for weekends, yet return to Washington quickly in the case of an emergency. His friends identified several locations in Virginia and Maryland, and Hoover selected the exact spot, near the headwaters of the Rapidan River in the Blue Ridge Mountains of Virginia, at an elevation of 2,500 feet, a 3-hour drive from Washington, which required traversing rugged terrain and which discouraged the press.[38]

The president bought 164 acres at $5 per acre, the prevailing price, and personally spent about $15,000 on building supplies and material. Hoover rejected a $48,000 congressional appropriation to construct a more elaborate camp and turned down between $75,000 and $100,000 offered by the Virginia Conservation and Development Commission to improve access and amenities. A detachment of about 50 Marines from a nearby camp constructed the cabins and made some of the furniture. They also provided protection for the First Family, although Lou insisted on driving her own car to and from the camp, sometimes at breakneck speeds. Nestled in the mountains and adjoining the Rapidan, the site included some virgin forests, but much of it had been logged and consisted of second-generation growth. There were rattlesnakes among the scrub growth, some of which were eaten by wild boars, but there was never a snake bite at the camp. Initially, ten tents were pitched on wooden platforms to house the family and visitors before the buildings were erected because the president was eager to fish. His son, Herbert, spent several months in the tent camp recuperating from tuberculosis before the weather cooled and he moved to a warmer climate, still at a high elevation, in Asheville, North Carolina. Although previous presidents had favorite vacation spots, Rapidan was the first permanent retreat erected for a president. Lou, who possessed architectural skills and had designed the family's home at Palo Alto, designed the layout of the camp as well as the interior and exterior of the cabins and the landscaping. She occasionally used the camp to convene meetings of the Girl Scouts and delivered a national radio address from Rapidan in 1929.[39]

The focal point of the cluster of cabins, connected by paths, was a "Town Hall," a gathering place during the evenings and in cool weather for conversation, games, crossword puzzles, and ping-pong. The president never played the games but did read prodigiously from the generously stocked bookshelves, including an entire shelf of detective novels. Upon arising, he and the First Lady started the day by sipping coffee, often outdoors, and devouring newspapers, magazines, and mail, which were dropped by an airplane twice daily in a nearby meadow. The president also took work to read and sometimes retired to his cabin to work on speeches, interspersing work and recreation. He was connected to the White House by telephone and a radio broadcasting set and monitored crises from there, including the progress of the debt moratorium in 1931 and the economic downturn in 1932. In the latter year, as the economy deteriorated, he made fewer trips to the camp. The main building was also used for small conferences. When he had a problem to hash out, the president sometimes took staff, congressmen, researchers, businessmen, economic experts, and cabinet members to the camp, which could accommodate about 30. There, they met in relative seclusion and discussed delicate policy decisions and potential appointments, as well as foreign policy, away from Washington gossip and the prying press. Journalists, who were not allowed at the camp, stayed in small towns nearby. The president never held press conferences there and invited journalists only once, in 1932.[40]

The other central building was the mess hall. These were the two largest buildings, constructed to be all-weather gathering places. Both contained stone fireplaces, as did the individual cabins. The president's cabin, the most commodious, had two large fireplaces, two bedrooms, two bathrooms, a work area, and a porch. The Town Hall also had two large fireplaces where guests gathered for conversation, Hoover's favorite indoor activity, before a crackling fire. Smaller guest cabins also included fireplaces, porches, and different numbers of bedrooms. The visitors and the First Family dined together at appointed times, in an informal setting, often outside. Meals were prepared by Filipino chefs, detached from the presidential yacht, which Hoover had decommissioned as an economy move. Sometimes Hoover himself cooked fresh trout or scrambled eggs and ham. Lou enjoyed horseback riding and hiking, but the president never rode and hiked only to find a choice fishing spot. Hoover dressed informally, yet sometimes upon arrival, he was so eager to hook the hungry trout that he pulled on his boots and splashed into the stream without removing his coat and tie, which created the fable that he always dressed formally, even when fishing. Lou fished with companions, but the president fished in solitude. Pathways interwove the surrounding woods, and sometimes the president and First Lady enjoyed old-fashioned picnics. The harsh economy and serious nature of his job caused presidential stress, which lifted the instant he crossed the Potomac en route to Rapidan. As in all things, Hoover thrived on simplicity. The camp helped Hoover return to his frontier roots. There, he could be a boy again. Rapidan was more than a fishing camp. In reality, the fishing season in the spring was brief, and the camp closed during the winter. Rather, it was an excuse to draw nourishment from nature, to thrive in a pristine environment. Guests at the camp varied from the famous, such as Charles and Ann Lindbergh and Ramsay MacDonald, to friends the Hoovers had known for decades. Even when important decisions had to be made, when the caravan of cars from Washington arrived at the rippling stream, life slowed down. His vacations there were not expensive. The Hoovers paid for the food consumed. Each weekend cost the government an average of $200.[41]

The mountain people from the surrounding countryside and villages loved the Hoovers and basked in the attention Camp Rapidan brought to their remote region. Very few of them were voters; most were illiterate and too poor to pay taxes. The chief occupation was subsistence farming. The state of Virginia, which boasted Mount Vernon and Monticello, both en route to Rapidan, considered the president an adopted son. On August 17, 1929, the Chamber of Commerce of Madison County sponsored a "Hoover Day" celebration to welcome the Hoovers as their neighbors. Governor Harry F. Byrd arrived at the county seat in a blimp, the Marine Band played, and a newsreel crew filmed the gala. The weekly paper announced that the all-day picnic was the most important event in the history of the county. The sponsors asked each county resident to bring a picnic basket sufficient to feed only their family and others. In addition, cattle, pigs, and 500 chickens were roasted, and 5,000 cups of squirrel stew were served. Upon his arrival, the chief executive received a 21-gun salute while the band struck up "Hail to the Chief." The Hoovers dined on local fare: fried chicken, ham, barbecued beef, pie, and cake but abstained from squirrel stew. After feeding about 10,000 people, the leftovers were sent to feed Marines at the nearby camp. Hoover delivered a brief address in which he thanked the people for their hospitality and praised Virginia as the cradle of presidents. "We hope to be good neighbors," he concluded, "and we know from experience already that you will be."[42]

The warm relationship between the mountain people and the Hoover was cemented by the chance encounter of Dr. Boone with a local boy, 11-year-old Ray Burraker, while the physician was horseback riding in the late summer of 1929. Boone invited Burraker to meet the president, but the shy youngster declined. When Boone told Hoover of the encounter, the president told his physician to tell the boy the head of state would pay him $5 for an opossum. It took Ray two weeks to work up the courage, but he arrived with a 15-pound opossum on August 10, Hoover's fifty-fifth birthday. The president closed the possum deal, giving the animal to his son Allan as a pet. Hoover learned that Burraker had never gone to school—indeed, there was no school in the region because the residents did not make sufficient money to pay taxes—and could not read and write. Burraker had eight siblings, all illiterate like him. Hoover introduced the lad to Charles Lindbergh, a weekend guest. Ray commented that he had never heard of Lindbergh, which delighted the famous aviator, who felt oppressed by fame. The president invited Burraker to join the First Family for his birthday dinner. Still shy, Ray declined, but he ate with the servants. Subsequently, the youth returned and tried to sell the chief executive two raccoons, but Hoover decided the opossum was enough. Coming out of his shell, Burraker later visited the White House, where he had his tonsils out, gratis, at the Navy Hospital.[43]

The Hoovers were moved by the plight of the mountain people who lived in the region known as "Dark Hollow." The residents were largely shut off from the outside world. Most of them spoke a corrupted dialect of Elizabethan English. They had only a vague understanding of time and distance and owned few clocks or calendars and virtually no automobiles. The Hoovers decided to create a school for the children. This included providing the initial funding; obtaining books, supplies, and furniture; heating the one-room school they constructed; hiring a teacher; and providing her with an apartment within the school building, an auto, and a horse. Lou spent more time and effort on the project than on any other charitable activity during the Depression. Once the backwardness of the mountaineers was learned, donations poured in, in money and in kind. The Hoovers and their staff personally contributed about $18,000 and selected the teacher, Miss Christine Vest, a 25-year-old graduate of Berea College and native of Appalachia who had also attended Columbia. The materials were purchased by the Hoovers, and local men, mostly unemployed, constructed the building, which furnished work relief. The institution, known as the Mountain School, opened on February 24, 1930, with an average of 6 to 16 attending daily, which rose to 32 students by May 1932. The pupils, eager to learn, caused no discipline problems and were earnest and hardworking. Vest taught practical skills, such as how to pay bills, write letters, and order from mail catalogues. The publisher Charles Scribner's Sons sent boxes of free books, and Lou purchased subscriptions to the *New York Times* and the *Washington Post*. The First Lady also donated a radio, a movie camera, and a projector and provided educational films. The Hoovers paid for the children to be vaccinated at the school, and they received a free hot lunch. Will Durant visited the school and signed donated copies of his classic, *The Story of Philosophy*. Vest started adult literacy classes at night and taught Sunday school. The school became the social center of the community where the people gathered evenings to sing and listen to music on the radio. Vest took some of the children to Washington, where they lunched at the White House. On April 17, 1930, former students gathered at the White House to present a bolt of cloth woven by mountaineer women sufficient to make a suit for the president and an ensemble for the First Lady. The Hoovers continued to underwrite the school and sustain its operation until they departed Washington in 1933. At about the same time, Vest married a Marine she had met from the nearby post and moved away. Attendance gradually dwindled. The school was incorporated into the state school system, but its graduates and other mountaineers, having been exposed to the outside world, gradually filtered away. By 1938, when Vest visited, most of the families had left. Yet many of the graduates of the Mountain School have gone on to college and succeeded in various professions. Hoover might have benefitted from publicizing his generosity, yet shunned publicity. When the press sought interviews with the Burraker family, Ray and his parents turned them away, stating that the president had asked them not to talk to reporters.[44]

When he left the presidency in 1933, Hoover deeded Rapidan and the Mountain School to the Shenandoah National Park. Virginia tried to preserve the school as long as it was needed, but the area was emerging from its cocoon into the modern world. Hoover left Camp Rapidan prepared for his successor. He had spent about $114,000 of personal funds on the camp and the school. The Hoovers said it was their intention that if Rapidan were not utilized by his successors, the rustic site, fully intact, be made available for camping by the Boy Scouts and the Girl Scouts. FDR visited the camp but once and found the terrain too rugged for his wheelchair. The facility gradually fell into disrepair. The Scouts rarely used it. President Eisenhower considered using Rapidan but preferred to fly fish in the Rocky Mountains. In 1954 ex-president Hoover made his final visit to the dilapidated camp after an absence of more than 20 years. The Boy Scouts used it sporadically until 1959, when the rotting buildings were torn down, and the usable lumber sold. Dr. Boone acted as the former president's consultant. Hoover, now living in New York, was too frail to travel to witness the demolition. Due to lack of use, the roads became useless, and the site could no longer be reached by auto. President Carter inspected Rapidan and fished there once, the first president since FDR to visit the camp personally. Vice President Mondale fished there frequently as did some of President Reagan's friends.[45]

The ghosts of Rapidan vanished like wisps of the Great Depression. The trout were there alone, and the murmuring of trees and the babbling of waters were the only voices left at the place Hoover once loved. Contrary to his image, the president had fun, yet, like everything he did, it was a personal, intimate type of fun, never raucous or boisterous. To those who saw the Hoovers in this relaxed, informal setting, it was impossible to believe the stereotype of the president as a hard-hearted man, indifferent and distant to ordinary people. On the contrary, this complex man enjoyed the simplest of pleasures. Visitors to Rapidan left with the conviction that the Hoovers were unusually pleasant.[46]

CHAPTER 17

The Fourth Estate

Until the Great Depression dimmed the luster of his reputation, Herbert Hoover led a charmed life with the press. During the Harding and Coolidge administrations, he chatted daily with journalists, some of them friends since his tenure as food administrator. He even leaked juicy tidbits, though he never undermined his superiors. Journalists considered him the most informative news source in Washington—honest, open, a man with nothing to hide. He was the only cabinet secretary familiar with all departments. Harding and Coolidge used Hoover as a conduit. The commerce secretary received a steady stream of requests to write articles. Lou Henry wrote an article about her experiences as a young girl for *American Girl*, the magazine of the Girl Scouts, in 1924. Hoover's closest journalistic friend was Mark Sullivan, who was invited to social gatherings. Hoover's circle included Edward Eyre Hunt, who had been on Hoover's staff during Belgian relief. He wrote positive accounts of Hoover for *Outlook*, *Survey*, and the *Nation*. Other journalist intimates included William Hard and Will Irwin, both of whom wrote early biographies. Still, he refused to divulge information about his private life. In 1925, the *Chicago Tribune* published a favorable story about Hoover and Lou Henry, including their courtship. The commerce secretary responded with an angry letter, protesting that he wanted stories to exclude personal information. He was sensitive not merely to criticism but to excessive praise. The Quaker preferred to let his accomplishments speak for themselves.[1]

As president it was impossible for Hoover to enjoy the camaraderie with journalists he had in the cabinet. His days were full, especially during the Depression. He could not focus on selected interests; he was spread thin.

Besides, he believed it was his job to make policy, not generate publicity. Now the president had to weigh his words carefully for their foreign and domestic impact. Reporters wrote for readers who craved juicy stories and editors driven by circulation. Both the presidency and the role of the press were changing in the 1930s, and it became a more adversarial relationship. Yet the charge that Hoover did not understand the press is as false as the charge that he lacked a sense of humor. He knew his job was different from theirs. If his policies succeeded, criticism would be muted. If his policies failed, no amount of political spin could make him popular. The president did not ignore the press, and he tried to be meticulously fair. Yet it ranked as a lower priority than other things he had to do. As president, he was held to greater accountability. The stakes were higher. His mistakes were magnified, and he had to shoulder the responsibility himself. The president alone—of any American public official—is responsible to all the people. The people are intensely curious about their president and when things go wrong, they quickly turn critical. Expectations had been lifted as high as Mount Everest. Even during normal times, it would have been impossible for him to sustain them, and he did not serve during normal times. The search for some explanation of the inexplicable economic decline—demanded from the man at the top, conspired to erode goodwill. Hoover believed personal attention distracted from focusing on goals he was striving to accomplish. He disdained hyperbole, even praise. Hoover fought criticism by working harder to achieve his goals. He was a problem solver, and in the seat of power he had a superb opportunity to resolve problems. The superficial blandness of Hoover's personality led some newsmen to depict him as a "do-nothing" president, though few, if any, presidents worked harder. Under the circumstances, he achieved a great deal. Still, what the public saw filtered through the press was the tip of the iceberg above the water. With the economy shipwrecked, glib news management alone could not have prevented the captain from going down with the ship.[2]

The president's initial relationship with most of the press began cordially yet gradually deteriorated. About 200 reporters attended his first press conference, a new record. The president told them that he would like to be as frank and open as possible. He planned to liberalize interaction. Hoover met reporters twice weekly, once in the morning and once in the afternoon, to accommodate the deadlines of morning and evening dailies. He appointed a committee of newsmen to devise ways in which he could make their jobs easier. The president intended to deal with the general outlines of policy to gatherings and cover details with small groups. He would not show favoritism. Hoover was the first president to permit reporters to quote him directly. Hoover seemed the opposite of dull. A poll of reporters in April 1929, considered him the most interesting personality in the world. He was a welcome contrast to Coolidge, who was grudging with news and parsimonious with words.[3]

White House correspondents concluded after Hoover's first month that he was off to a good start. In fact, if one compares Hoover's press clippings during the first six months of his presidency to those written in 1932, it is difficult to believe journalists were writing about the same man. Initially, he cultivated the press. Five weeks after his inauguration the new leader attended the Gridiron dinner, where he laughed about good-natured ribbing and delivered a brief, satirical speech. A week later, he was the featured speaker at the annual luncheon of the Associated Press in New York. Hoover continued by hosting Adolph Ochs, publisher of the *New York Times* and a Democrat, at the White House. Two weeks later, he granted an exclusive interview to Anne O'Hare McCormick for the *New York Times Magazine*. The article praised the president for his leadership and industriousness. In late May, the chief executive and Henry L. Stimson hosted a dozen foreign editors at the White House, and in July the president helped to dedicate a new printing plant for the *Chicago Daily News* in the Windy City. Hoover was fair and flexible. He gave each reporter an opportunity to question him. While the economy prospered, the president and the press got along. The nation's leader did not snub writers who criticized him. He invited *New York World* editor Walter Lippmann, who was often critical, to visit him at the White House.[4]

On May 24, 1929, an article appeared in the *Chicago Daily News* comparing Hoover to Theodore Roosevelt and stating that the Quaker had comparable traits of greatness. He was similar in "the prodigious number of his personal contacts outside the White House," the daily wrote. "He is also Rooseveltian in the quickness and firmness of his decisions." There were important differences in temperament, however. Hoover did not boast nor enjoy the limelight. "President Hoover is no back slapper like Roosevelt," it continued. Hoover was not boisterous like the Rough Rider, "nor does he expect his subordinates to ascribe to him infallibility or to credit him with everything good that happens." He did not aspire to glamour and cared more about accomplishments than about credit. "Hoover is as strong a character as Roosevelt," and received journalistic praise, "but is rather niggardly about using it, especially for personal aggrandizement." The thirty-first president knew much more about economics than his more uninhibited predecessor. "Mr. Roosevelt seemed, at times, to do his thinking out loud. He did it in such a way as to please the country," the journalist wrote. "Mr. Hoover, on the contrary, rarely announces himself except to make a final decision." Both were imaginative, but Hoover supplemented ideas with facts. "Every time the president gets a new idea he has it investigated." More people were engaged in working for Hoover, directly or indirectly, than for any president in history, and Hoover worked them hard. The mail was the heaviest in history and covered a greater variety of topics. The new occupant of the White House saw more visitors daily than any president since TR.[5]

Assessments after the first year were chiefly laudatory. Hoover was depicted as a gifted administrator, decisive and careful to determine facts, who had initiated significant reforms. He responded promptly to the stock market crash, reassuring business and labor. Some predicted he would be an extremely effective, perhaps even great, president, especially if he cured the economy. Newsmen wrote that the Hoovers enjoyed serious conversation in a city where the favorite participant sport was gossip. Quaker rectitude did not restrain the Hoovers from sparkling conversation, and, unlike the Rough Rider, the West Branch orphan did not insist on dominating the table talk. As to the stock market crash, the conservative press concluded that the president had handled a bad situation well, and they expected the prosperity of the Coolidge years to return. Nonetheless, acclaim was not universal. Some were less sanguine about economic conditions and were beginning to abandon the president by early 1930. He was hurt by the defection of the Western Progressives, and some complained that he had failed to exert strong leadership on the tariff. The *New York World* complained that Hoover had accomplished little during his first year. *Commonweal* weighed in that the president's reputation had been exaggerated. All such criticism appeared in liberal publications. The next to abandon the Quaker president would be the middle-of-the-road press. Some of the working press was becoming restive because Hoover failed to feed backstairs tidbits about the First Family. The reviews of Hoover's first year were mixed, but more of the press was in his corner than was consistently critical. Although many agreed that he had been oversold, this was tempered by the assessment that no one could have lived up to such expectations.[6]

Two press secretaries served for most of Hoover's term. Their trajectory followed that of their chief. It started rather high, arced, and then declined. His first, George Akerson, had worked under Hoover at the Department of Commerce since 1925, handling public relations. A hard-drinking, convivial ex-Harvard football star, Akerson broke in with the *Minneapolis Tribune*, became Washington correspondent, and joined Hoover's staff at Commerce in 1925. He worked on the engineer's campaign in 1928 then followed him to the White House. Akerson met reporters twice daily. At Hoover's instructions, he focused on hard news, not titillating trivia. Akerson also served as appointments secretary, and congressmen felt he denied them access to the president. A group of Republican congressmen demanded his dismissal. Eventually, Hoover was forced to let Akerson go in order to protect his standing on Capitol Hill. There was no acrimony between Akerson and Hoover. The president arranged a better-paying job for the ex-secretary at Paramount Pictures, working in public relations. Akerson resigned early in 1931. French Strother, the president's research assistant, departed in May 1931 to write fiction and was succeeded by George Aubrey Hastings, a professional press agent, though Strother later returned because he missed his relationship with Hoover.[7]

Akerson's successor, Theodore Joslin, became press secretary and appointments secretary in mid-March 1931. He said it was the only government position he would have considered and that Hoover was the only president he would have served. Immediately, he complained that his phone rang incessantly, and in 1932, nearing a breakdown from stress, he took time off for rest but returned shortly. Joslin served as Washington correspondent for the *Boston Transcript*, a conservative daily, and also wrote political articles for magazines. Only 41, he had covered every major party convention since 1916. A close friend of Coolidge, Joslin had been chief of the Washington bureau of the *Transcript* since 1924. The new secretary assumed his job at a point when the president's popularity was declining and his time to deal with public relations was dwindling due to intractable economic problems. Akerson's successor was discrete and tried to protect his boss, understanding as few did the burden Hoover carried. Joslin tried to use his boss's acts of kindness to children, as well as his love of fishing, to humanize him. Like most who worked closely with the president, Joslin remained intensely loyal. He was awed by Hoover's stamina.[8]

Hoover's relationship with the press frayed as the Midas touch that had made him famous failed to reverse the Depression. Moreover, the type of information the president was adept at providing—and that he considered important—was not what journalists craved. The media was undergoing a revolution. Radio and motion pictures helped generate an age of heroes and villains; sometimes headlines dramatized the trivial and ignored less important news. Celebrities such as Babe Ruth, Charles Lindbergh, and Charlie Chaplin generated public interest on a scale hitherto unknown, which fed circulation, generated intense competition for readers, and led journalists to seek stories with color rather than substance. Hoover was ill suited for this journalistic revolution. His press conferences were packed with facts but failed to reverberate with excitement. His answers to questions were short, crisp, and purely factual. Hoover worked best behind the scenes and was not a glad-hander. Readers wanted to be spoon-fed entertainment. Further, a new type of adversarial relationship between presidents and reporters was developing, which would have happened under any president but was aggravated by the Depression. Some later presidents created an elaborate media apparatus to promote themselves. John Kennedy, for example, used the media to manufacture an image almost diametrically the opposite of reality. Richard Nixon, Theodore Roosevelt, Ronald Reagan, and even occasionally Dwight D. Eisenhower manipulated the press, as did Hoover's successor. The Quaker's refusal to say anything insincere handicapped him. In self-promotion via the press, exaggeration, not honesty, was the best policy. Hoover complained the scrutiny of journalists made him feel like a microbe. Had the Depression ended on his watch, personality might not have mattered. Neither would shedding crocodile tears over unemployment have sufficed unless unemployed actually declined. Lady Nancy Astor, who praised Hoover, was surprised at his demeanor when she met him personally. She observed that he lacked a hearty glad-hand and a perpetual smile, the ability to pretend to be what he was not. To her, this was to his credit because it demonstrated his sincerity. The president believed hard work and sound solutions were more important than pizzazz. In reality, the orphan from West Branch actually *was* what the squire of Hyde Park *seemed* to be. FDR often acted differently in public than in private. Sometimes he was not sincere, while Hoover would not fake emotion nor demonize Wall St. to win votes. Behind the scenes, the New Yorker unsheathed the dagger; loyalty meant little. While Roosevelt wooed the masses but had no lifelong friends, Hoover lacked mass appeal but had scores of lifelong friends. FDR's priority was to win elections and remain in office as long as possible. Hoover was a problem solver whose main priority could not be judged in terms of political success. Hoover's motive was nobler, and given additional time his more focused approach might have been effective. If anything proved more intractable than the Depression itself, it was the bureaucracy created to deal with it.[9]

By the standards of his generation, Hoover held a moderately high number of press conferences. Compared with other twentieth-century presidents, Hoover's average per year (35) is lower than Coolidge and FDR but greater than Truman, Eisenhower, Kennedy, Johnson, Nixon, and Reagan. Hoover is charged with being overly formal in his press conferences, yet his early conferences were more informal than Coolidge's and other predecessors'. In later conferences, the president placed more emphasis on responding to written questions submitted 24 hours in advance because he believed this provided more time to ponder them. He responded to oral questions on breaking events but in less detail. At a few press conferences Hoover offered to answer unlimited oral inquiries. Some reporters believed they could elicit spicier stories if they could catch the president by surprise. Hoover's chief interest was accuracy.[10]

The chief executive preferred specific questions. He considered some of the vague questions fishing expeditions. Certain journalists hoped to evoke gaffes. Other reporters violated guidelines by attributing to the president material given on background. Hoover considered his fight against the Depression the equivalent of a war and wanted reporters to be discrete in what they printed. He felt that loss of confidence in the economic system was a major psychological factor that contributed to the sluggishness of business. He was discrete about information that might contribute to public anxiety, inspire a run on banks, or undermine delicate negotiations with foreign governments. The president patiently explained that to give the press everything it wanted to know would not be in the nation's interest. He pointed out that to print administration ideas that were just in the formative stage might arouse unnecessary alarm or provoke opposition. Some presidents, such as Nixon during the Vietnam War and the Watergate Scandal, deliberately lied to reporters. Hoover did not lie to journalists; he simply did not tell them the entire story. In fact, FDR, who seemed more open because of his outgoing personality, was actually quite secretive and liked to spring surprises. Sometimes he planted untrue stories or trial balloons. Because he appeared good-natured, reporters underestimated FDR's deceptiveness.[11]

Hoover's image suffered early because of the failure of the special session called in 1929 to enact a tariff. The battle was polarizing, and Congress adjourned without passing a bill. The skirmishing renewed the following fall, and the bill was not completed until after the stock market crash of October 29, 1929. The divisions over the tariff and Hoover's signing of it provoked more consternation in the press than any action in his first two years. It unveiled the divisions within the GOP and provided his opponents with ammunition for criticism. Whatever the economic effects of the tariff, it furnished a partisan scapegoat for hard times. The Democrats exploited the tariff in the 1930 congressional elections and in the 1932 presidential campaign. Adding to Hoover's troubles were attacks on him over Prohibition, farm policy, and appointments. The attacks focused on Hoover for signing the bill, not on Congress for passing the measure.[12]

Hoover hated wasting time on trivial matters, and as conditions worsened he wanted to concentrate on substance. The Hoover presidency reached a crossroads at which the job of journalists departed from that of the president. The journalists wanted a good story, preferably a scoop, at all costs even if it incited a bank panic. The president was sometimes testy, and each side questioned the other's motives. What had changed was less Hoover's attitude than his workload. Washington, in the best of times is a mill that grinds out rumors like sliced bread. Without lying, the president could not contain it. He refused to lie because the truth would come out eventually, embarrassing both reporters and the chief executive.[13]

The hard times upended Hoover's image from a man who commanded international respect to a pariah. As his presidency wore on, Hoover became the target of ad hominem attacks that not only criticized his policies but demonized him as a person. In comparison with Harding and Coolidge, Hoover was a dynamo, yet most people blamed him, rather than his predecessors, for the calamity. Almost any president would have been castigated, yet Hoover's reclusive nature; his belief that reporters lay in ambush to distort his ideas; his refusal to permit stories showing his caring, humane side; his prodigious work; and his behind-the-scenes style played into their hands. The president might have considered the press fairer if much of the criticism had not originated with correspondents employed by Democratic newspapers. The tragedy of Hoover's relationship with reporters was not merely personal; it damaged his credibility and his ability to soothe the nation's financial nerves. The opposition press, swelled by a chorus of Democratic politicians, helped shape the folklore that Hoover was a do-nothing president, a charge that was patently untrue but was plausible, given the amount of suffering in the nation.[14]

By the fall of 1930 Hoover was receiving more press criticism than any president since the final two years of Wilson's administration. The president came to feel that the less he said the better, because reporters turned it against him. Journalists attending press conferences dwindled from about 200 his first year to around 12. The conferences increasingly relied on printed handouts. On some days the president simply said that he had no news to announce. The chief executive felt dismayed. He felt the job of newsmen was to write accurate stories not to judge or pontificate. It is ironic that Harding, who was weak, and Coolidge, who was lackadaisical, received better treatment. Presidents can create news, but the media interpret it.[15]

By May 1931, Hoover drew criticism from many quarters. New York Governor Franklin D. Roosevelt called him a reactionary. The *New Republic* wrote, "He is a new and negative Janus, who turns, not his face, but his back in both directions at once."[16] The *Outlook* and *Independent* charged that he had consistently underestimated the dimensions of the Depression. The chief executive had refused to give sustenance to the poor while his Farm Board wasted $500 million (which overlooked the fact that farmers were among the poor). His speeches consisted of "platitudes but no plans."[17] Columnist Walter Lippmann was acerbic yet had little to offer as an alternative except that he would have slashed federal spending. In an article published on December 31, 1931, Lippmann blasted the incumbent for budget-busting. "The A B C of the deficit; balancing the Federal accounts is the central problem in combating the depression," Lippmann claimed. "All other projects revolve about this central question of how to balance the Federal accounts."[18] Joslin believed the "wets" and liberals had united to issue propaganda discrediting the president—"a sad commentary in such an emergency as this," he wrote.[19]

By mid-1931, some pundits attributed to Hoover a malign omnipotence to control events possessed by no human. He was a fake, a snake charmer. Some journalists once awed by Hoover became his greatest detractors. Newsmen complained he did not understand economics, a field in which he was once considered an expert. The legion of detractors helped create a new stereotype by persistent repetition. It became fashionable to hate Hoover, as if that would exorcise the demons of the Depression. Hoover suffered in stoic, dignified silence, refusing to complain publicly or to lash back. He refused to inflict gratuitous pain on others. They had enough pain already.[20]

Hoover's popularity with the press plunged to its lowest point between June 1930 and early June 1931. In addition to the tariff and Prohibition, he was criticized for opposing farm subsidies. Ironically, to modern readers, Hoover's most savage attacks stemmed from his handling of the tariff and Prohibition while he received his strongest support in the press for his handling of the Depression. However, his declaration of an international debt moratorium in late June reaped renewed praise in the nation's dailies. A summary of newspaper editorials shows 592 supporting the moratorium with only 45 opposed. The *Cleveland Plain Dealer* reported that the moratorium made common sense, while the *San Francisco Chronicle* considered it an event comparable to the armistice. From this point on, he became increasingly assertive on the domestic scene as well. It appeared that the nation craved action, and though he had been far from inactive earlier, he redoubled his efforts to fight the Depression, rein in excessive spending and retarget it toward creating jobs. In the summer and fall of 1931 the president stood firm against a dole and enormous veterans' pensions and waged political wars to obtain legislation that would fight the Depression without bankrupting the government. Although more of the nation's dailies supported these actions than opposed them and although he was praised for his vigor, journalists and editors did not back him on every issue. Aggressive action had the effect of polarizing the press and Congress, although his program moved through the Democrat-dominated Congress better than expected. Overall, the major papers, with varying degrees of enthusiasm, praised his show of determination. Some papers that had opposed him earlier now backed his attempts to restrain spending. Journalistic support, however, did not directly translate into public support. Hoover's third year, 1931, ended with some improvement in the president's image in the nation's press. Many journalists predicted that his chances for reelection depended on a business revival during the next four to five months. However, critics continued to complain that the Republican's recovery program was too narrow. Some in Congress and in the press demanded direct relief and more public works. Nonetheless, a poll of the nation's journalists indicates that Hoover had regained some of his tarnished reputation.[21]

In 1932, the fulcrum of political coverage pivoted over fiscal issues. The president wanted to bring the budget more nearly into balance. Republicans and Democrats alike favored retrenchment. If Hoover was later condemned for parsimonious fiscal policies, in 1932 he had an army of company. The Democrats flirted with a sales tax. To some, the administration's attempts to trim did not go far enough. "Can't Washington understand?" the *New York Evening Post* editorialized. "Can't Ogden Mills and the Administration understand that the great issue, the supreme issue is: Stop spending our money." The clamor to cut spending was bipartisan. The *New York Times*, a Democratic daily, advocated "the freeing of capital from the fear of confiscatory taxes." Most agreed that promoting a balanced budget was more important than increased spending to stimulate the economy. There was also general assent that preservation of the gold standard was essential to recovery.[22]

A few journalists had the opportunity to observe Hoover in informal settings and gained appreciation for his congeniality, warmth, and humor. Some writers accompanied the chief executive while he traveled to Puerto Rico and the Virgin Islands aboard the battleship *Arizona* in late March 1931. Within the relatively small confines of the ship, the reporters and the president mingled, chatted, and dined together. Up close, they saw Hoover in a new light, relaxed, convivial. The dispatches they wrote were quite favorable, though some of them had been among the president's harshest critics. In fact, few people who really knew Hoover disliked him. It was easy to hate him at a distance but virtually impossible in person. The journalists were impressed by his sincerity, generosity, and simplicity. They did not find him deadly serious or all business. Many who had known him only from press conferences were surprised. Reporters who knew the president found it difficult to understand the visceral anathema some journalists had developed toward him. Those close to Hoover found him inoffensive and in fact cooperative. He provided more hard news than his predecessors. "Now this feeling against him becomes all the more amazing when it is known that few if any presidents have ever been as cordial to the correspondents as Mr. Hoover has," the *Washington Herald* wrote.[23]

The Caribbean voyage reminded journalists what a sincere, genuine person Hoover was. When traveling, it was his practice to invite three or four accompanying reporters to dine with him at breakfast, lunch, and dinner, for informal chats. "The point is that no President has been more friendly or hospitable to the Washington correspondents," the *Washington Herald* stated. He was less aloof than most chief executives. Journalists often did not need an appointment to talk with him. "If he runs across you he will stop and talk," a journalist explained. "And when you talk with him there is an engaging warmth which leaves its impress," he added. Coolidge, who was actually less genuine and had less charm than Hoover, was depicted as more down-to-earth. Hoover enjoyed company while Coolidge was reclusive. Journalists complained that they did not know what Hoover was thinking, yet actually he was more transparent than Coolidge or, for that matter, FDR, whose banter sometimes shielded more than it revealed. Nonetheless, the letters and dispatches sent home from the Caribbean showed a new regard for the president. By the spring of 1931, Press Secretary Joslin had finally made some progress in diminishing Hoover's stereotype as an emotionless, wooden figure by leaking fragments of accounts that revealed his human element, usually without the president's consent. He also helped persuade the chief executive to get out of his office more. The First Couple greeted children who attended the annual Easter Egg Roll. Next, the president, who had discontinued the convention of handshaking, persuaded by Joslin, opened the south lawn of the White House to visitors between noon and 1:30 p.m.[24]

Hoover was always frank with the press, whether he was in a jovial mood or a serious one. He told a group of newsmen that he understood that being criticized came with his job. The important thing was that truth prevailed in the long run. "But above all this the president has for a few short years the opportunity to speed the orderly march of a glorious people."[25] The chief executive said he believed in a free press. Sometimes time provided perspective. In the short run, he pointed out, the president and those he governed might feel that events were taking them upon an emotional roller coaster. But time smoothed out the hills and valleys and dispelled emotions of the moment. The judgment of history was not necessarily identical to contemporary conclusions, which were subject to revision. Some "C" students in the first grade graduate valedictorian.

In early 1932 there were many journalists who believed Hoover was doing a remarkable job under difficult conditions and that he had changed over the course of his presidency. A reporter for the *Des Moines Register* who interviewed the president in January found he had accepted with equanimity three years of personal abuse. He was "almost Oriental in calm." He once winced under criticism but now took it in stride. Hoover believed his philosophy was correct, and criticism did not deter him. The president appeared more relaxed, more at ease with himself, than he had in 1928. Those who intimated that the president was insulated from criticism were wrong, he reported. His friends told him the truth, even when unpleasant. Hoover's old habit of avoiding the eyes of the person he talked to—looking at his shoes or his feet—had disappeared. The president now looked squarely at his conversation partner and did not doodle. He spoke quietly and directly, and words flowed easily. He did not attempt to mask his feelings behind a poker face. The nation's leader smiled and occasionally chuckled. Physically, he was somewhat thinner, his hair grayer, and there were lines around his eyes. This was not the round, smooth face of 1928, but his health was actually better. His mouth had a softer, more sympathetic line. Hoover's fingers no longer nervously tapped a pencil. Although he labored endlessly at a thankless job, the president had not grown cynical.[26]

In February 1932 Anne O'Hare McCormick wrote in the *New York Times*, "Mr. Hoover is important because he is a pivotal figure in a world completely out of balance." She continued, "'The only personalities that really matter today,' says a French observer, 'are Stalin, Mussolini and Hoover.' He means as symbols of ideas, of course, ideas of government and civilization," McCormick observed. "Of the three, the least dynamic as a personality but the most powerful as a force in the world readjustment is the President of the United States." McCormick reminded her readers that whatever happened in the next presidential election, Hoover would remain president for more than a year, and it might be the most eventful year of his presidency. Hoover was aware of it: "He is putting every ounce of energy he has into measures for economic reconstruction. Slow in recognizing the extent of the Depression, now, in his own way, he takes steps for the restoration of confidence and credit that lack neither magnitude nor audacity." Later that year, as the long session of the Seventy-Second Congress prepared to adjourn in the summer, the nation's press assessed its accomplishments, and most were pleasantly surprised by the degree of bipartisan cooperation and the new assertiveness of Hoover. The legislators had given the president much of what he requested, including the act establishing a greatly strengthened Reconstruction Finance Corporation (RFC) with additional appropriations for relief, the Glass-Steagall Act, a billion-dollar tax bill, and a Home Loan bill.[27]

Hoover's relationship with the press was symbiotic. He read newspapers omnivorously, habitually poring over them before dinner as well as in the morning. The president scanned some major dailies individually, including the three New York papers, the three Washington papers, a Philadelphia daily, and often the *Baltimore Sun*. Forty-five Eastern papers reached the White House on their day of publication—those in range of Washington. A second group from more distant cities arrived within three or four days and were clipped and pasted onto paper for the president's perusal. An additional 400 smaller dailies and weeklies were compiled, clipped, pasted, and placed upon the president's desk once a week. These represented a cross-section of the nation ideologically and geographically. In addition to serving the president well, the collection preserved at the Herbert Hoover Presidential Library is a gold mine for historians, because Hoover made news every day, and often more can be gleaned from a single article than from dozens of letters, especially Hoover's correspondence, which was terse and usually dictated. Hoover made more news during his presidency than during any other stage of his long career. News magazines were also clipped, and the president read three liberal magazines in their entirety: the *New Republic*, *Nation*, and the *American Mercury*. The chief executive never confined his reading to uncritical papers. However, he realized that reporters thrived on conflict because it made better news. The ordinary administration and legislation of government was considered routine. Hoover believed much of the political process was driven by emotion and wanted to minimize this. He wanted issues to be treated seriously not oversimplified.[28]

In addition to Washington correspondents, editors and publishers still exerted some control over stories published in their papers, although less than during previous administrations. The profession of journalism was evolving toward greater autonomy for reporters and toward the separation of news stories from editorial viewpoints. The president never lost the support of the majority of publishers. William Randolph Hearst, and Roy Howard, chairman of the Scripps-Howard chain, opposed Hoover and exerted their influence on content. Some Southern papers that had supported Hoover in 1928 returned to the Democratic fold, while the *Washington Post* reversed its support of candidate Hoover and the *New York Times*, though not completely alienated, cooled. Magazines were less important than newspapers in shaping public opinion, and their circulation declined during the 1930s. Hoover fared poorly among popular magazines during the second half of his presidency. Occasionally, the president telephoned publishers he had known before reaching the White House to ask for their help and occasionally met face-to-face, sometimes for lunch, even with critical publishers. On May 25, 1932, he conferred for 3 hours with 41 publishers representing news organs with a circulation of almost ten million. He told them that pessimistic psychology was an obstacle to recovery. Hoover did not ask them to support him personally, he did ask them to downplay stories that might frighten potential investors or create bank runs, to which they agreed.[29]

In January 1932, the National Press Club invited Hoover to the installation of its officers, which included entertainment and a ball. The industrious president was reluctant to take an evening off, but Joslin persuaded him to attend, promising they would remain only a few minutes. On that condition, the busy national leader agreed. The club welcomed him warmly, and the chief executive sat down and relaxed. Following the formalities comedians performed one of the best shows in years. As time wore on, Joslin glanced at his watch periodically, but the president was enjoying himself too much to disrupt his fun. Eventually, the Secret Service warned Joslin of the late hour, but the president continued to laugh at the jokes and skits. When Hoover finally asked how long they had been at the club, his press secretary fibbed and told him only a few minutes. The president replied that was fine, because he wanted to stay a while. The two did not leave until the janitors began removing chairs from the floor. As they departed, the nation's leader observed that he could not remember the last time he had enjoyed himself so much. Back at the White House, Hoover resumed work, though it was after midnight. He continued until 3 a.m. and then arose at 6 a.m. With only three hours of sleep, he was refreshed and ready for a full day. The president still retained the type of energy he had demonstrated in the dusty goldfields of Australia in his twenties.[30]

By Hoover's tenure, radio had begun to complement the print media in covering the White House, but the medium focused more on entertainment and advertising than news. However, networks did broadcast some presidential speeches, and the Hoover administration set new records. A radio enthusiast, as secretary of commerce, the president had helped bring order to national broadcasting. Hoover's son, Herbert Jr., was a pioneer in radio, working as an expert in linking air to ground communication for the Western Air Express of Los Angeles. During the 1928 campaign, most of Hoover's live speeches were also carried by radio. Hoover broadcast between 80 and 90 speeches during his term, only slightly less than FDR during the latter's first 4 years. The Iowan was a better speaker via radio than in person because his voice carried better and he lacked a regional accent. However, he did not enjoy broadcasting from his office or from a studio. Most of the speeches broadcast were delivered before a live audience with sound equipment. In the first three years of his presidency Hoover broadcast about one speech per month, increasing to about two per month during the election year of 1932. In 1930 alone he was on the air for 27 radio addresses. The entire cabinet used the new medium, especially Interior Secretary Wilbur. Like many of the world's leaders of that era, the president appeared uncomfortable in sound newsreels. He stiffened before cameras and appears a wooden, mechanical figure, his voice barely audible. Hoover thought newsreels made him look older. Nonetheless, he became the first president to have his inaugural address filmed with sound.[31]

During Hoover's presidency, especially after 1930, spurious books about the chief executive poured from small presses, written by obscure authors. The motives were political, ideological, and personal, full of antipathy, spite, and greed. Some books sold modestly well, but most were flops. However, several were reviewed in prominent journals and a few newspapers and were mined for quotes by the Democratic National Committee (DNC). The DNC encouraged some of the books. The biographies actually belonged on the fiction list. Most dealt with his early mining career and ended before he became secretary of commerce, although several continued up until the 1932 campaign. Political gossip columnist Robert S. Allen devoted the most attention to Hoover's presidency. The books were penned by inexperienced writers in a hurry. Most had written no previous books. None knew Hoover. The content overlapped because the writers pirated one another's material. Among their charges were that Hoover had been an incompetent engineer who made his fortune through fraud and stock manipulation; that he absconded with $900,000 of the wealth of his partnership (actually another partner did so, and Hoover helped repay it); that he worked his men to death in Australia and China; that he defrauded the Chinese government; and then used Chinese coolies as slave laborer in South Africa. Hoover's motive for feeding Belgium was to make himself rich. He stole food donated to feed Belgian children and sold it to the Germans, hoping to prolong the war even though he was actually a British citizen who lived and voted in London. His British citizenship made him ineligible to be president, but he had covered this up. He built his false reputation as a humanitarian on a mountain of lies.[32]

Among the quickly manufactured fabrications were *The Rise of Herbert Hoover* (1932) by Walter Liggett, *The Great Mistake* (1930) by John Knox, *The Strange Career of Mr. Hoover under Two Flags* (1931) by John Hamill, *Hoover's Millions and How He Made Them* (1932) by James J. O'Brien, and *Herbert Hoover: An American Tragedy* (1932) by Clement Wood.[33] Two books that appeared in 1932 were specifically intended to derail the president's reelection bid, Robert S. Allen's *Why Hoover Faces Defeat* and John L. Heaton's *Tough Luck—Hoover Again*. These authors demonized Hoover as an incompetent, amoral president. Allen wrote that the incumbent was destined for defeat because of "his abysmal incompetence, his pettiness and deviousness in personal relations, his shocking callousness to tragic suffering among millions of his countrymen, his timidity, his plain ignorance, and his blind reactionism."[34] Allen wrote that the president had foisted upon the nation the Smoot-Hawley Tariff, which led to "millions of unemployed, the thousands of closed banks, bankrupt businesses, and silent factories." He claimed Hoover lacked the courage or the intelligence to deal with the Depression. Allen charged the incumbent had subverted the democratic system "into a quasi dictatorship which functioned through secret midnight councils."[35]

Some of the authors quarreled among themselves, damaging their credibility. Hamill hired O'Brien as a researcher and then produced a manuscript that even O'Brien could not stomach. O'Brien sued for a share of the profits and then decided to write his own book. The two became embroiled in a lawsuit. The trial ultimately ended with the conclusion that both litigants were dishonest in 1933, after Hoover's defeat. "I am sorry I wrote it," Hamill said on the witness stand. The presiding judge was scathing. "The most superficial examination of *The Strange Career of Mr. Hoover under Two Flags* causes instant anger because of its patent unfairness and untruthfulness," he wrote. "The documents and records on which the spite with which the book reeks are patently excerpts garbled and selected, because standing alone, they permit inferences never intended," he added. He condemned both litigants for "searching over the dunghill of shameless insincerity."[36]

Liggett's motives were more envy and ideology than greed. A Communist, he had created an organization to feed the roiling Soviet Union during the Russian Civil War, which was upstaged by Hoover American Relief Administration (ARA). A supporter of Lenin's Reds, Ligget loathed Hoover as a reactionary. His nearly 400-page tome, including a verbose appendix and written in hyperbolic style, attributed the president's dark impulses to a blighted childhood. Liggett's study is more detailed and psychoanalytical than those of his money-grubbing competitors. He calls the GOP candidate's 1928 campaign for president "the most nauseous and utterly dishonest canvass ever conducted in the history of America." The author describes the president as "smug, unctuous, sanctimonious, surly, prying, [and] profane."[37]

Hoover never read any of the books, considering them a waste of time. He believed if he read all the criticism it would leave him time for nothing else.[38] The president knew that to reply would further divide the country and felt that he must set an example by being even-tempered. Some of Hoover's friends tried to defend him, especially those who had worked under him in the Commission for Relief in Belgium (CRB) and the ARA and who were personally offended. They considered legal action but concluded that it would detract the president from his work and lower the dignity of his office. Edgar Rickard obtained affidavits from the auditors of the CRB and the ARA. One of Hoover's friends traveled to Britain, where he dug up information about the president's mining career, which refuted some of the charges. In the February 1932, issue of *Collier's*, the writer Arthur Train, a friend of Hoover, systematically dissected some of the charges, focusing primarily on Hamill's *The Strange Career of Mr. Hoover under Two Flags*, which he found replete with falsehoods. At least one man was sufficiently outraged to write a 248-page book exonerating Hoover of the charge that he had abused his powers and enriched himself. Dr. Walter Frier Dexter, president of Whittier College, published *Herbert Hoover and American Individualism* on July 26, 1932, with a major publisher, the Macmillan Company, which traced his career through the presidency and concluded that the president never sought excessive power or personal glory and in all his pursuits had done his best to serve his country.[39]

The smear books did not play a significant role in Hoover's defeat in 1932, yet they did contribute to besmirching his reputation. Some of the canards are still repeated and half believed. Because most of the charges were vague and impossible to prove, it was equally impossible, or at least impractical, to refute them point by point. Given that Americans feed on conspiracy theories, there was an ample market for fables that make Aesop seem like an amateur. If the economy had bounced back like a pogo stick, the allegations might have faded. In part, the attacks on the president were signs of the times. Washington and Lincoln, after all, had been vilified by their contemporaries. FDR too would be seriously criticized, and one could compile a list of fables regarding his administration. Yet most of the egregious falsehoods about Roosevelt are forgotten or discredited because the Depression and World War II ended on his watch. Winners write history, although some of the authors of the smear books qualify as life's losers.

More devastating than the attacks by the smear book amateurs was a relentless barrage of Democratic propaganda that spewed from the typewriter of Charles Michelson. Michelson's demonization began in 1928, when he was hired by the Democratic National Committee and continued after Hoover's defeat in 1932. After 1932, Michelson worked for FDR and continued his withering criticism of Hoover because Roosevelt continued to fear Hoover as an adversary, first as a critic of the New Deal and second as a potential opponent in 1936. Roosevelt always considered Hoover the most formidable of his GOP critics. John J. Raskob, the Democratic National Chairman, possessed a fortune in the range of $500 million and was willing to use as much of it as necessary to rebuild the Democratic Party after three successive defeats in the 1920s. He also collected money from other Democratic millionaires including Pierre S. Du Pont, Vincent Astor, and Bernard M. Baruch. Not deterred by inconsistency, Michelson proceeded to use part of the cache to paint Hoover as a lackey of millionaires and a tool of Wall Street, who had, also inconsistently, plotted the Wall St. Crash. Raskob had the money and the will to propel the Democrats into power, abetted by the Depression, which must have appeared providential, but he was no political strategist. Initially, his motivation was to set up a rematch between Hoover and Al Smith in which Smith would win the second round. This time around they would concentrate on Hoover's vices rather than Smith's virtues. Raskob did not like Franklin Roosevelt, opposed his nomination in 1932, and became an even sharper critic of the New Deal than Hoover was, helping to found and finance the American Liberty League to protest against it. Thus Raskob achieved his first purpose of helping to destroy Hoover's reputation but not his second purpose of electing Smith.[40]

Raskob's concept was original, however. Rather than waiting until the election year to rev up his party, he would bombard the incumbent of the opposing party with salacious propaganda from the moment he took the oath of office. Raskob had no clue as to how to accomplish his goal and did not even know Michelson, who was hired by Jouett Shouse, the chairman of the Executive Committee of the Democratic National Committee, who barely knew Michelson himself. Michelson had outstanding credentials as a hired gun. A political journalist for 40 years, most of them for William Randolph Hearst, he excelled at wicked satire and catchy phrases. Under Hearst, Michelson had become a star reporter by covering murders and scandals in Chicago and New York. In 1923, he began writing short stories and movie scripts with the same prolificacy. However, he declined to move to Hollywood and instead became the Washington correspondent for the *New York World* until hired away for more money by Raskob. The ghostwriter was paid $25,000 annually, a large salary at that time. The attacks included ad hominem attacks against Hoover as a person and ridicule of all his policies, including some that were later borrowed by FDR. Michelson had a knack for vilifying opponents and never overestimated the gullibility of his readers. Any time Hoover took a moderate position, he accused him of waffling. If he took a strong position, the president was labeled reckless. Raskob excelled at hyperbole and relished his assignment as a character assassin. In fact, he was so proud of it that he later wrote a book, *The Ghost Talks*, in which he explained his tactics, a summary that could have served as a primer for Machiavelli.[41]

Michelson preyed on ignorance, employing guilt by association, repetition, exaggeration, and outright fabrication. He undermined the president's ability to unify the country, and he also helped polarize the Congress. Moreover, his work aggravated the shaky psychological state of the economy and its banking system. Some of Michelson's press releases were published by Democratic newspapers or disguised as speeches delivered by prominent Democrats and insurgent Republicans on the floor of Congress, where they were protected from slander suits by congressional immunity. Then they were inserted in the *Congressional Record*, which gave them the imprimatur of credibility, and historians later used them as fact, citing the *Congressional Record* as their source. He said little of a positive nature about the party that employed him. His mantra was that Hoover had no more notion of where he was leading the country than the headless horseman. As of 1930, the Depression had not yet become Michelson's primary line of attack. He hammered the tariff and cited the failure of the Farm Board to end rural poverty. It was largely due Michelson's ghosted speeches and stories of 1930, driven home with greater fury during the campaign of 1932, that the myth of Hoover as the do-nothing president ossified. Having devoted much of his life to alleviating human suffering, the president was hurt but resisted counterpunches. At any rate, it would have been difficult to punch a ghost veiled in anonymity. Michelson was gathering momentum for the maelstrom of murderous prose composed in 1932.[42]

By 1932 the Michelson Express had gathered full steam, and the Hoover legend rolled out of the station. The engineer of Hoover's alleged incompetency ground out invective on deadline. Some verged on conspiracy theories not to mention contradiction. The chief executive was a tool of Wall Street yet had instigated the Crash, certainly a masochistic act. He used the presidency, just as he had used his entire public career, to plunder the public treasury. He and his obsequious lieutenants gorged themselves in luxury while the people starved. The only question was whether they were more incompetent or more corrupt—maybe it was a dead heat. The president's engineer's mind understood only machines, not human beings. He was good at what he did, an engineer steering the country down the railroad of destitution. Secretive, he trusted no one and had no friends, which was understandable because he was feckless, selfish, and cold. A man who knew nothing about economics, he might be the most incompetent president in history. Evidently, he was lazy because he liked to fish. FDR, and others, read Michelson's speeches without checking facts. In one 1932 campaign address, the Democratic candidate read a Michelson speech that claimed Hoover had failed the children of America. Although no such document existed, he claimed to have a statement claiming that children in public schools were fainting in their desks due to lack of food. Roosevelt claimed the incumbent had slashed appropriations for the Children's Bureau when in fact the president had increased them every year. Another much-believed invention of Michelson was that, during the Bonus March in the summer of 1932, Hoover had ordered troops to fire on the jobless veterans. Michelson might have complained that the army was ill trained, too, since no one was hit.[43]

As Michelson manufactured malice on the assembly line, the stock of the GOP incumbent sunk to the level of Insull Utilities. Writing in a style punctuated by hyperbole, Michelson worked at the emotional level, orchestrating the Democratic demonization with the artistry of a maestro. Though some of the literature might have been implausible during ordinary times, it provided a human villain in times when people worldwide craved scapegoats. The withering abuse frustrated the president's attempt to adjourn politics for the duration of the Depression. The Democrats glimpsed an opportunity. If they could, by repetition, create the stereotype of a bungling, do-nothing president and a heartless bureaucrat, they might drive a stake through Hoover's reputation permanently enabling them to haul out the tin-man caricature relentlessly in subsequent campaigns, enabling them to win, not one, but numerous elections, indelibly stamping the imprimatur of the Democratic party as more caring, with superior expertise in the management of spending the taxpayer's money. Each piece of worthwhile legislation was labeled Democratic, although most legislation enacted during the productive stage of the Seventy-Second Congress was initiated by Hoover and hammered out as a bipartisan compromise. Some of Hoover's ideas, denounced as disastrous when Hoover proposed them, were later pronounced strokes of genius when the New Deal adopted similar measures.[44]

The mainstream press did not treat the president so shabbily, and even many of those who printed Michelson's poison pen work did more so more out of gullibility than malice and might not have done so if they had known its source. Doubtless, Hoover took a battering. If people had not considered him invincible at his inauguration, they might not have considered him solely culpable for the economic distress of March 1933. Not many who did not already hate Hoover took the smear book impresarios seriously. F. Scott Fitzgerald's epigram, "Find me a hero and I will write you a tragedy," nonetheless resonates. Yet there were still many journalists who admired the orphan from West Branch. Some who were no longer awed by the president nonetheless respected him. Those who knew him the best respected him the most, and the vast majority of those who knew him well genuinely liked him, even loved him. After emerging from the meat grinder of public opinion during the worst economic crisis in American history, he seemed diminished as a political figure but not as a man. Under the circumstances, perhaps even grudging respect was an honor. And if imitation is a form of flattery, the first hundred days of his successor brought redemption in that respect as well.

CHAPTER 18

Running for His Life

The Election of 1932

After three dismal years, the summer of 1932 seemed to offer a glimmer of hope. It appeared that most industrialized countries had turned the corner on recovery. The economy might not rebound in time to save Hoover at the polls, but economic revival seemed genuine. The recovery gathered momentum from July through September and held steady in October until mid-November. However, by February 1933, during one of the bitterest interregnums in American history, the economy came apart at the seams, and the Depression plunged to its lowest point. The collapse reflected fear and uncertainty, undermining the budding recovery.

From July through September, almost every vital sign showed gains. The stock market, often a precursor of better times, led the parade of improving statistics, with the greatest gains coming in July and August. In September, the *New York Herald Tribune* reported that since early July blue-chip stocks had more than doubled and railroad stocks had tripled. In July and August, values increased by 77.7 percent. August showed the greatest gains of any month since the Crash. Bonds advanced from a low index of 57.5 to 76.0 by September 7. Bonds offered by the Treasury were oversubscribed. A bull market raged. Confidence rose. The gold drain halted, and bullion returned to America. Domestic hoarding ceased, and bank failures dwindled. Bank suspensions, which had averaged 209 per month from September 1931 through July 1932, declined to 85 per month in August, September, and October

1932. Business failures declined from August through September. Hundreds of millions of dollars in new industrial orders were placed, and about 500,000 men returned to work during July, August, September, and October. This represented only gradual growth, but August was the first month in two years in which employment had grown rather than fallen. From midsummer to early October, manufacturing showed a 4 percent rise in employment. Mining improved, as did textiles. General Motors and U.S. Steel resumed paying dividends. Overall business production grew about 7 percent. The oil industry revived, as did coal. Retail trade showed a 7.2 percent increase in employment from July through September. Employment in rayon manufacturing rose by 41 percent, and the women's clothing industry added employees at the rate of 25.1 percent. Commodity prices advanced by 10 percent between June 14 and August 30. Farm and textile prices led the increases, especially wheat and cotton, which rose by more than 20 percent in August and September. Cotton mills, running at 51.5 percent in July, were running at 97 percent by October. Electric power use bottomed out in July 1932 and then grew progressively through October. Railroad freight car loadings increased from an average of 80,000 cars daily in early July to 96,000 during the first two weeks of October. The greatest improvements occurred in the stock market, and some employment sectors remained sluggish. The recovery was attributed to progress made in resolving international economic problems at Lausanne; the saving of the gold standard; the flow of loans to business, banks, and construction through the Reconstruction Finance Corporation (RFC) with more expected; and firmness in security markets. Job growth was gradual; it appeared to be the last sector of the economy destined to recover, as is usually the case in a deep recession or depression. Further, conditions abroad were volatile. The country remembered that hopes of recovery had been doused in the spring and fall of 1931 by turmoil in Europe.[1]

The upturn was not limited to America. By the midsummer of 1932, every major nation had gone through the wringer, and the power of the Depression appeared spent. No country could pronounce complete recovery, yet for most, the worst was over. The German bankers' forecast was optimistic. The 1932 business turnaround in England, France, Germany, Italy, and Belgium continued, but in the United States, the upward surge stalled after the presidential election. Following the election, merchants and manufacturers cancelled orders. This increased unemployment in manufacturing. Democratic condemnation of the tariff disturbed producers of some domestic products, while fears that FDR might tamper with the gold standard inspired fears of inflation, destabilizing the stock and bond markets. But the most damaging aspect of the period when the recovery sputtered to a halt, then reversed into a tailspin, was the sheer uncertainty of what lay ahead. Roosevelt's campaign focused on blaming Hoover, bankers, and big business, and his promises about what he would actually do were vague and inconsistent. The centerpiece of his ill-defined program, at that time, appeared to be to slash government spending to the bone. With a gulf of uncertainty looming, the march of recovery became a retreat. This did not happen in any other nation on the road to recovery. Although the argument that the coming of the New Deal initially retarded recovery can be disputed, it is certainly plausible. Adding to its plausibility is that no one has offered an equally plausible explanation of why the world economy continued to advance while the U.S. economy self-destructed. However, the caveat must be added that Hoover and for that matter Roosevelt were only actors in a much larger drama. While individuals make mistakes, they seldom manufacture or cure depressions single-handedly. More important is the national mood, which turned from relief at the end of the campaign to fear of what might come next. The implications remain, however, that the economy during the second half of 1932 was on an upward arc and that political, rather than purely economic factors, played a role in smothering the embers of recovery. The September Democratic victory in Maine stalled the recovery. Stocks remained reasonably steady in October, but the rise ceased. After Roosevelt's victory on November 8, markets and businesses, which had expected the outcome, cut back gradually then in a deluge, as it appeared the long interregnum would not be an interim of political truce. Edmund Platt, former vice governor of the Federal Reserve, remarked in 1933, "If 1932 had not happened to be a presidential year, the recovery begun that year might have continued without any serious interruption."[2]

At the time and during the immediate aftermath, a consensus of journalists and economists concluded that Hoover had been on the way to ending the Depression when the recovery was derailed by political developments. Walter Lippmann, often a critic of Hoover, wrote in 1936, "The historians will . . . see that President Hoover, Secretary Mills, and Governor Meyer had hold of the essence of the matter in the spring of 1932 when . . . they arrested the depression."[3] Shortly after the election, in November 1933, Lippmann had viewed the recovery in its worldwide context. "There is very good statistical evidence which goes to prove that as a purely economic phenomenon," he wrote, "that in all the leading countries a very slow but nevertheless real recovery began."[4] Other respected observers concurred that Hoover's contention that he had almost vanquished the Depression and could have completed the task during a second term, had a basis of fact. On July 16, 1934, 16 months into the New Deal, the *New York Times*, a Democratic daily, observed, "The change for the better in the last half of 1932 is beyond doubt. That this evident revival of confidence was suddenly reversed in February 1933 is equally true."[5] As Hoover left office, the *New York Herald Tribune* drove home the point. "By the end of last spring," the daily wrote on March 5, 1933, "the legislative program at Washington in connection with other stabilizing influences seemed to indicate that the bottom of the depression had been reached and the upgrade was ahead."[6] The *Saturday Evening Post* concurred not only with the general consensus but also with the causes for the end of the recovery. "History will record that the depression was overcome during the last year of Mr. Hoover's

Administration" the *Saturday Evening Post* explained in 1935, "that the march of recovery, which began in the late spring of 1932, was continuous in the rest of the world but was interrupted here by the presidential campaign and the results of the election of 1933," adding, "that the banking panic of 1933 was the result of fears concerning the monetary and other policies of the incoming Administration, which fears were subsequently justified."[7]

Certainly, numerous contemporary observers, many of whom had been among Hoover's critics, concluded that the New Deal claim to have resurrected the country from the wreckage left by Hoover was the opposite of reality. But the recovery, whatever one's interpretation of its origins and its demise, was too late and too little to save Hoover's political fate during the campaign of 1932, although it might help to modify his historical reputation. As the nominating season approached, Hoover remained perplexed. So many things that appeared obvious to him were not appreciated by the voters, who questioned his competence. He found the presidency a thankless job and sometimes claimed to be indifferent to his renomination. "I am not worried over the election because I don't give a damn," he told Joslin. "Hoover does want to succeed himself," his friend James H. MacLafferty wrote, "but there is one thing he wants more than that: He wants to serve the highest interests of the country whether he succeeds himself or not." Despite the frustration, Hoover accepted the challenge. His staff found it difficult to tear him away from his work to restore the economy and had to prod him to campaign. To the Quaker, promoting himself seemed selfish.[8]

There was ample reason for Hoover's angst. One of his friends wrote that businessmen were disenchanted and demanded change. Farmers, he added, "are simply bitter against anything and anybody that represents power and influence."[9] The Republican National Committee was rudderless. A faction led by New York committeeman Charles Hilles hoped the president would lose so his cronies could manipulate the party machinery in 1936. The committee voted to hold the nominating convention in Chicago, which was not Hoover's choice, but only one other city, Atlantic City, had applied to host the event. The party's fundraising had slackened. By April 1932 the National Committee lacked the money to pay staff salaries. The president brainstormed with MacLafferty about finding someone to head the RNC during the campaign. They considered War Secretary Hurley and Postmaster General Brown, both loyal and vigorous. But Hoover needed them in the cabinet. He planned to use Hurley as a stump speaker and Brown, a talented organizer, to orchestrate the campaign. In April, the president invited Colonel Frank Knox to lunch at the White House and asked him to chair the RNC, but the publisher felt he was needed to run his business, the *Chicago Daily News*, an important Republican newspaper. Shortly before the convention in mid-June, the president chose Everett Sanders, an ex-political secretary to President Coolidge, as national chairman and titular head of the campaign. Sanders, from Indiana, had served in Congress before joining Coolidge's staff. The president did not consider

Sanders an energetic, imaginative leader and picked him by default. Sanders' chief asset was his link to the Coolidge wing of the party, which would calm business. Sanders might also shore up swing states in the Midwest.[10]

One of the ironies of the 1932 election is that the chief criticism of historians, and of many of his contemporaries, is that Hoover was a "do-nothing" president. In fact, the phrase was employed so relentlessly by Democrats, especially by their gifted ventriloquist, Charles Michelson, that it stuck to Hoover like chewing gum. Ironically, some Republicans tried to resurrect the candidacy of the virtually inert Calvin Coolidge in the illusion that Silent Cal had a better chance to win. On May 1, 1932, the president's friend Henry M. Robinson telephoned the White House to inform the chief executive that 20 financial and business leaders had been summoned to New York by bankers Thomas Lamont and Otto Kahn a few days earlier. Hilles, the RNC fifth columnist, was a party to the scheme. Their purpose was to select a delegation to travel to Northampton, Massachusetts, to persuade Coolidge to abandon retirement and seek the Republican nomination. Two of the men considered this a lunatic idea, walked out, and phoned Robinson, who promptly told Hoover. The president did not think Coolidge would be interested. If he did obtain the nomination, it would be worthless to him, Hoover explained. Others believed the Coolidge magic might still work but also believed replacing Hoover would only divide and ruin the party. Their scheme was to find a popular stalking horse for vice president, such as Coolidge, put his name before the delegates, and incite a stampede to nominate him for president instead. Hilles became one of the principal architects of the plot. The GOP was playing Russian roulette with the nomination in the back rooms. On August 15, 1931, Hoover talked with Hilles and asked his help to kill the idea, but Hilles was noncommittal. Coolidge would not have been the canny politician he was if he had been duped into such a pratfall. The pro-Coolidge clique did not think beyond winning the election. They had no idea what policies the Vermonter might adopt to restore prosperity. Besides, Coolidge was in a state of serious physical decline. If he had won the election, he would have been dead before his inauguration, the victim of a weak heart. Coolidge was no Benedict Arnold, and he did not want the job. The ex-president spent much of his retirement writing pithy, lucrative newspaper and magazine articles. Near the end of September 1931, well before the nominating convention, he used the medium of the *Saturday Evening Post* to announce that he had no intention of returning to public life. In scathing language, Silent Cal condemned those who suggested "that a former president should use his prestige to attempt to secure a nomination against a president of his own party."[11]

The incumbent's prenomination campaign was perfunctory. On June 15, 1931, before a friendly audience of 5,000 Republican editors at Indianapolis, Hoover delivered an important speech in the critical Midwest. He defined his objective as achieving economic recovery without compromising individualism. Prosperity lay in the cumulative success of individual Americans, he continued. He said he was willing to temporarily expand the powers of the federal government but contended that outright doles might deter initiatives. He also knew the government lacked the revenues to pay every needy person in the nation a living wage. The chief executive advocated a tariff to benefit farmers and workers and the regulation of business but inveighed against unfair government competition with business. Times were hard, but temporary, the president vowed, remaining upbeat. Resilient Americans had triumphed over adversity before. Other speeches designed to sway the Midwest followed in Ohio and Illinois. As his train trekked through West Virginia, Kentucky, and Ohio, the president stepped out on the rear platform, where he was greeted warmly by crowds along the route.[12]

In January 1932, Postmaster General Brown, the president's campaign manager, officially announced Hoover's candidacy for reelection in order to qualify him for some of the early primaries. His friends entered slates of delegates pledged to the president, but Hoover did not campaign personally, and he did not officially enter all primary states. Most states selected delegates through conventions or by appointment, not in primaries. Hoover had only token opposition. Even a candidate who entered and won every primary could not have denied him the nomination. A *Literary Digest* poll in late April took the pulse of GOP voters. Of those who expressed an opinion, 487 predicted Hoover would capture the nomination with only 29 dissenters. Vice President Curtis, however, stood on shaky ground. Some 189 expressed a preference for him, but a large number of votes were scattered among other potential running mates for the president. Still, the lack of serious competition did not mean that Republicans were confident about their prospects. Hoover avoided primaries in some Western states where he was unpopular. Dissent also existed along the East Coast where there was sentiment to repeal Prohibition, which Hoover enforced. When polled about issues, voters believed the economy would be the major determining factor, followed by Prohibition, public electric power, the tariff, farm relief, and the World Court. Foreign policy was a low priority.[13]

Some of Hoover's closest friends believed he must organize at the grass roots, rather than from the top down. David Hinshaw, a New York writer who wrote a biography of Hoover, organized "Hoover '32" clubs to inspire mass participation and expand the base for fundraising. Each club consisted of 32 members who donated $1 each. The clubs started in California and expanded eastward. Hinshaw wanted clubs to operate in 2,000 counties but fell far short. James MacLafferty, Hoover's covert political confidant, told the president that contacts with local leaders was the most effective campaign tactic. Handouts were ephemeral and were often discarded. Voters needed a feeling that the president cared about them, which could be conveyed best by talking with them in their own communities. Recruitment of leaders at the local level was the key to MacLafferty's grassroots strategy. Hoover planned only a limited personal campaign. He had delivered six major speeches in 1928 and planned to deliver only three in 1932, one in New England, one in New York, and one in the Midwest. He would not begin until September 15. The president did not anticipate campaigning at all in the West. Most of the campaign would be conducted through surrogates, especially Hurley, Mills, and Hyde, who were charismatic. Though Postmaster Brown served as campaign manager, Hoover made the major decisions. The president wrote or edited many of the speeches delivered by his spokesmen. He insisted that the wording be precise and the meaning accurate, and he wanted the campaign to be based strictly on issues. The president asked his staff to compile notebooks on each issue summarizing his positions and the administration's accomplishments. These consisted of hard facts not platitudes. Hoover was a meticulous yet flexible strategist. He accepted support from former foes because he realized he drew strength from them. Borah's defection concerned the chief executive. He liked the senator personally, considered him an effective speaker, and had done his best to cultivate him.[14]

Hoover devoted the primary season almost wholly to combating the Depression. Virtually certain of renomination, he believed his fate in the general election would depend on the state of the economy. In most primary states, the president had no serious opposition. The Hoover campaign was methodical, rather than flashy. In many states, delegations officially were uninstructed but privately backed Hoover. The president was pleased by his victory in Wisconsin, where he defeated archrival George Norris, running as the Progressive Party candidate at the invitation of young Bob LaFollette. This denied Norris and LaFollette the status to deliver a nominating speech critical of Hoover on the convention floor. It was the first time in memory that Wisconsin had sent a delegation dominated by party regulars. Ohio led the parade of state central committees endorsing Hoover in January, giving the president virtually a free hand to select delegates. Brown entered Hoover in the Buckeye State primary in February, and the election was held in May. Like several states, the balloting was preferential, allowing voters to express their choice but not binding the delegates chosen. The president entered the slate, which won easily. By mid-February, Hoover's friends were predicting that he would quickly collect enough delegates to sew up the nomination. Already the state committees of Tennessee, Kentucky, Washington, Kansas, Oklahoma, and Ohio had adopted resolutions supporting the president. In March, he won the North Dakota primary, the first held west of the Mississippi, and in April, he won in Maryland. By early May, Hoover had amassed enough delegates to guarantee his nomination.[15]

Speculation focused on whether Vice President Curtis would remain on the ticket. A group of his friends advised Curtis to run for a Senate seat in Kansas instead, which he was more likely to win. Hoover played little role in vice presidential politics. On November 30, 1931, Curtis announced his intention to run with Hoover, which virtually ended the debate. There was scattered support for several alternatives but no single strong candidate.[16]

The president agonized more over Prohibition than about any other platform plank. Although the economy was more important, Prohibition was more polarizing, and, unlike the economy, there was a simple solution— repeal it. Repeal was popular nationally, and the Democrats seemed likely to advocate the action. At heart, Hoover was dry, and the GOP was drier than the Democrats. However, he had to employ finesse. The issue might divide the GOP, which even if united, faced an uphill struggle. Some Republicans, such as Borah, were resolutely dry. However, East Coast congressmen felt they could only win reelection on a wet platform. The president did not talk about the issue publicly during the primaries, but he discussed it almost daily with his staff and influential congressmen. Hoover wanted a compromise, or a "moist" plank that advocated resubmission of the amendment to the states, allowing state option. However, return of the saloon would be forbidden. This satisfied neither ardent wets nor dries. By conviction, the Quaker could not run on a wet platform, and his stringent enforcement of Prohibition would make repeal seem hypocritical. The Democrats scented victory and were aligned on the popular side of the issue. The South was both dry and Democratic, but party loyalty prevailed there. As the convention neared, Hoover took a hand in personally drafting the platform, especially the Prohibition plank. He hoped deft wording could bridge the party divide, though he considered it impossible to satisfy everyone. The president feared that even a moist platform might alienate zealous dries to the extent that they might not vote at all.[17]

While Hoover moved inexorably toward the Republican nomination, the Democrats battled for a nomination that was difficult to win but would be worth more in the general election. New York Governor Franklin D. Roosevelt, former Secretary of War Newton D. Baker, 1928 nominee Al Smith, and Maryland Governor Albert Ritchie led the field. Hoover wanted Roosevelt to win the nomination because he considered him the easiest to defeat. Like many Democrats at the time, he underestimated the New York governor, although it is likely any Democratic nominee would have won due to the Depression. Hoover did not believe Roosevelt could be an effective president because his paralysis would siphon his stamina and limit his ability to travel. The incumbent considered Baker the most formidable opponent. Many of Hoover's backers considered FDR glib and vague in his speeches, which they believed lacked substance, a feeling shared by some Democrats and journalists.[18]

The president did not want to appear heavy-handed about dictating to the convention and made few public statements prior to the Chicago conclave, yet behind the scenes he meticulously managed details. During late May, he wrote drafts of the platform. Hoover invited Borah to the White House and warned that a bone-dry platform would spell defeat. Angry, Borah refused to attend the convention or to campaign for his party. Still, Hoover said he would not run on a plank advocating outright repeal. Hoover stacked all the key committees with administration supporters. James A. Garfield of Ohio, son of a president and Hoover's choice to chair the Resolutions Committee, which shaped the platform, visited the White House. Garfield appointed a subcommittee packed with administration backers to draft the platform. The subcommittee included cabinet secretaries Mills and Hyde as well as Ambassador to France Walter E. Edge. The administration sought to avoid divisive floor fights, especially over Prohibition. The president also edited the keynote address of Senator L. J. Dickinson of Iowa, moderating the Prohibition paragraphs. Mills and Hyde, key surrogates of the president, conferred with Hoover prior to the gathering. Mills was the point man on the Resolutions Subcommittee and the leading administration spokesman in Chicago. Administration dominance was assured by a boycott of most of the Progressive bloc. Further, most congressmen remained in Washington to finish work on legislation.[19]

The president pared the number of callers to the White House for the duration of the conclave. George Akerson, a former press secretary, returned to help manage public relations and followed the proceedings with Hoover and Lou, who listened by radio from the Lincoln study, where the president set up telephone and telegraph lines to Chicago. Seven cabinet members were delegates, as was Hoover's political secretary, Walter Newton. His confidential secretary, Lawrence Richey, gathered intelligence and reported directly to the president. It was the most scrupulously stage-managed convention in decades. As delegates arrived, administration leaders fanned out in the lobbies, buttonholing them. The keynote address by Senator Dickinson on June 14 packed little drama. It was delivered poorly to a listless, nearly empty hall. Dickinson discussed the president's economic record and attacked the Democrats. The cornerstone of the GOP recovery effort, he said, was the RFC, which saved banks, businesses, and homes. The Credentials Committee decision to reject corrupt Southern delegations was upheld on the floor, vindicating the patronage policies of Postmaster Brown. The president's choices for delegations representing South Carolina, Mississippi, Georgia, Louisiana, and Tennessee were approved. Only in Mississippi did the administration compromise. Brown had attempted to remove black Republican Perry Howard, head of the Mississippi delegation, but gave up after several indictments resulted in acquittals. Aside from Mississippi, the Southern delegations were virtually handpicked by the administration.[20]

On June 16, the convention discharged its business of ratifying the platform hammered out in committee and nominated the ticket. The president stayed up until the early morning hours monitoring the debate over the Eighteenth Amendment. His resubmission plank was approved 681–472, a comfortable margin, yet the closest vote of any plank. Hoover had counted electoral votes and knew the GOP could not win without carrying wet states. His own cabinet was overwhelmingly wet. The president realized that support for Prohibition was declining among voters and in Congress. The rest of the platform followed Hoover's script, praising the president's accomplishments, including the debt moratorium, preservation of the gold standard, the tariff, naval reductions, public works, labor peace, the RFC, the Farm Board, and attempts to bring the budget closer into balance. Foreign policy was secondary, but planks backed membership in the World Court, better relations with Latin America, and adherence to the Stimson/Hoover Doctrine.[21]

Hoover's nomination was routine. He was nominated by Joseph L. Scott, a fellow Californian, in a speech barely 2,000 words long, which ignited a wild celebration. Scott emphasized patriotic and religious themes, not policy. He praised the president as a man who had not bartered his soul for ephemeral applause. Listening to the radio with his family and close friends, Hoover showed little emotion. Joslin remarked that he must be happy. "Yes, it came out as good as could be expected in the circumstances," was the president's only response. Lou ceased knitting and walked down the hall with her husband as he returned to his office. Hoover sent a telegram to Representative Bertrand H. Snell of New York, the convention's permanent chairman, accepting the nomination. He delivered his formal acceptance speech later, on his birthday, August 11, at Constitution Hall in Washington[22]

Later that night, the vice president was nominated. Without his permission or knowledge, a small group of delegates conspired to place Coolidge in nomination. Former Vice President Dawes wanted the nomination but was dissuaded by his brothers. The family bank in Chicago, with which Dawes was no longer affiliated, needed an RFC loan to survive, and they could not request one if Dawes became vice president. Ogden Mills, a brilliant, magnetic speaker, was mentioned, but he said that it would be disloyal for any cabinet member to challenge his own vice president. There were other minor contenders, but no consensus for any of them. The greater problem was unhappiness with Curtis. Many delegates felt he was too old to take over should something happen to Hoover, and he lacked the energy to wage an aggressive campaign. They wanted a president-in-waiting should the ticket win or someone who could rebuild the party after a loss. Hoover shared some misgivings yet appreciated Curtis's loyalty and had no desire to humiliate him. Furthermore, dumping him would divide the party. For lack of a better alternative, Curtis was duly nominated but without much enthusiasm, barely polling enough votes to win on the first ballot. The ticket would be identical in 1932, but the outcome would not.[23]

Unlike the Democratic nominee, Franklin D. Roosevelt, who flew to the convention to accept in person, the president made no attempt to dramatize his nomination. Hoover considered such melodrama cheap showboating, akin to gloating. The president's address at Washington's Constitution Hall before 5,000 friendly faces, including a few blacks, was carried nationwide by NBC and CBS to some 25 million to 40 million listeners. Fact-packed and sober, it dealt chiefly with the Depression. The president conceded the reality of hard times but denied GOP responsibility. A new president would not necessarily have a recipe for prosperity; indeed, he might even prolong the misery. Although largely positive, he pointed out that the Democrats offered few constructive alternatives. Hoover addressed Prohibition for one of the few times in his campaign. The president surprised some by stating honestly that repeal in some form was virtually inevitable and that he could accept any type of modification that did not include the return of the saloon. Essentially, FDR's position was identical, except that he promised immediate revision of the Volstead Act. Hoover emphasized that, unlike previous depression presidents, he had attacked the economic problems vigorously. He observed that he had created jobs without creating a bloated bureaucracy. Once individual freedoms had been sacrificed expediently they would never return, the Quaker warned. He noted that there had been fewer strikes and lockouts and less social disorder than in normal times. Infant mortality and overall mortality had declined, and there was less serious illness. He had saved the gold standard, and the nation's credit was sound. A moderate though imperfect tariff, with the flexibility for revision, was in place. He explained that he understood, as few did, human suffering. A *San Francisco Chronicle* editorial added, "He has brought a depth of human understanding and a profound sympathy with the common man to motivate his acknowledged mastery of economic questions."[24]

The campaign team Hoover assembled was not a strong one at the administrative level. Everett Sanders, the new chair of the RNC, by default, did not assume the position until the Democrats were already organized. An executive committee of 15 Hoover loyalists made the key decisions. Sanders merely implemented them. He ran the campaign headquarters from Chicago because Hoover did not want details to distract him from fighting the Depression, though the president made strategic decisions. Hoover established an Eastern headquarters in New York, where Franklin Roosevelt located his headquarters.[25]

Local campaigns were delegated to state committees. The president wanted the campaign to concentrate on the big electoral states in the East. Hoover felt that if he could win New York and New England and carry a few swing states in the Midwest, including Illinois, Ohio, and Indiana, he could patch together an electoral majority. He could not win without winning the East, but he could win without the West. The incumbent did not personally plan to travel west of Iowa. Hoover decided to delay his personal campaign until October 1. He believed voters forgot speeches delivered earlier. FDR campaigned vigorously, nationwide, beginning in mid-August and peaking in the week before the election. The president believed a comparable campaign by an incumbent was unprecedented and undignified. However, Joslin pointed out that Taft had waged a strenuous campaign for reelection in 1912 and Wilson had campaigned in 1916. Then Hoover reconsidered. GOP strategists decided to wait until after FDR spoke in the West and then rebut his speeches. The minimalist approach was also due to limited funds. The president believed fundraising wasted his time. The economic downturn pinched the coffers of both parties, and Raskob, disappointed that Smith had failed to win the nomination, shut his wallet. Ironically, the Democrats spent more in losing in 1928 than they did in winning in 1932. Helped by a $500,000 contribution from J. P. Morgan in October, the GOP slightly outspent the Democrats. The Republicans, who spent about $4 million in 1928, spent only $2.5 million in 1932. Many businessmen feared Roosevelt but considered Hoover a lost cause.[26]

In normal times, the Republicans held the upper hand. In 1932, about 48 percent of registered voters were Republican, compared to 42 percent Democrat and 10 percent Independent. The Democrats had placed only two different individuals in the White House in the 72 years since the Civil War. Yet the United States had experienced 15 panics or depressions, and each time, except in 1820, the incumbent had been defeated. Republicans did not need converts; they only had to hold Republican voters. Under ordinary circumstances, the GOP could expect a majority of from 6 to 11 million voters. The Democrats appealed to several blocs: machine politicians who expected jobs; veterans who wanted a generous bonus; and the largest group, destitute voters who believed any change would be a change for the better. The Democrats controlled some big city Northern machines, but their most certain vote lay in the South, glued to the Democratic standard since Reconstruction. Despite inroads by Hoover in 1928, they returned to the party of Jackson in 1932. Roosevelt largely took the Southern and urban vote for granted. As far as policy, the Democrats played it safe and kept promises vague. They realized that unless prosperity returned or they committed a colossal mistake, they were certain victors. The only real platform difference was over Prohibition, and FDR vacillated so much that any difference virtually disappeared by voting day. Roosevelt's speeches were written by his Brain Trust, and sometimes he did not even read them before he delivered them. Because the speeches were written by different persons who disagreed, FDR's orations were pockmarked with inconsistencies, contradictions, and airy generalities. His speechwriters were, quite literally, not on the same page. The campaign was a contrast in personalities. Roosevelt was a charmer, while Hoover was sober and direct. But this had been true in 1928 too, and the charming Al Smith had been slaughtered. Hoover wanted to debate the issues, while Roosevelt tried to gloss them over. The Democrat felt he did not need to persuade voters, he simply needed to avoid alienating them. FDR possessed a vibrant, ingratiating speaking voice, although sometimes he shouted unnecessarily into an amplifier. He could be extremely negative, cataloguing and exaggerating Hoover's deficiencies. Many however considered Roosevelt weak, eager to please everyone, and superficial. Still, all he had to do was to exploit the economic wreckage spawned by the Depression, especially unemployment, and ride to office on a wave of discontent. Hoover said the GOP had to overcome "10,000,000 unemployed, 10,000 bonus marchers, and 10 cent corn." It was simple but devastating.[27]

Hoover used his cabinet to reiterate the administration's accomplishments. However, voters found little comfort in the argument that things could be worse. Hoover allowed his cabinet to criticize Roosevelt's policy and to try to pin him down, at which they had little luck, but instructed them to refrain from ad hominem attacks. The cabinet began with a series of nationwide radio broadcasts, one per week, in the spring of 1932. In the early fall they hit the campaign trail hard. By September, administration spokesmen had fanned out across the country. Some 260 speakers were dispatched. The most important were cabinet members and the vice president. Treasury Secretary Ogden Mills, who like Hoover wrote his own speeches, carried the greatest load. The articulate ex-New York congressman was most effective before sophisticated Eastern audiences. Postmaster General Brown orchestrated the speakers and provided liaison with local leaders. Secretary of War Patrick Hurley cultivated veterans, while Labor Secretary William N. Doak courted workers. Hoover wanted Secretary of State Stimson to play an active role, especially in New York where he felt he might have credibility attacking his fellow New Yorker. Stimson made a few speeches, though he considered campaigning beneath him, and refused to condemn FDR. Nonetheless, Stimson believed Roosevelt deserved criticism because "he has done such bad things that it is necessary to handle them pretty severely." Although Vice President Curtis delivered numerous speeches, he was quoted sparsely by the press and failed to galvanize farmers as hoped. The GOP insurgents either sat out the campaign or worked for Roosevelt. George Norris, Robert LaFollette, Hiram Johnson, Bronson Cutting, and Harold Ickes campaigned for the Democrats. Borah remained aloof. The Democrats united behind Roosevelt, although Al Smith joined the campaign late and lackadaisically. Roosevelt had an army of foot soldiers hungry for the manna of patronage.[28]

Mills attacked FDR's record. He complained about the Democrat's reluctance to clean up New York City's corrupt Tammany machine. Mills said Roosevelt had pledged to reduce spending yet as governor had increased spending by one-third. The Democrats demonized the Smoot-Hawley Tariff, even though they had engaged in logrolling for their constituents. For example, they covertly slipped into the Revenue Act of 1932 high tariffs on their pet products such as coal, oil, copper, and timber. Their protests were loud, but their voting record was hypocritical. The party of Jackson still flourished on the spoils system, and they intended to make merit appointments an endangered species. Democrats added $4 billion to appropriation bills, many of a pork barrel nature, during the Seventy-Second Congress. When Roosevelt embarked on a western tour in early September, Mills, Hurley, Hyde, Wilbur, and Doak, shadowed him. Their rebuttals were broadcast throughout the West. Curtis and Ernest Lee Jahncke, assistant secretary of the navy, also pursued FDR. Jahncke accused the Democrat of waging class war, demagogically pitting the poor against the rich, scapegoating his adversary, and employing glib oversimplifications. The GOP hammered the theme that the president had a program while Roosevelt lacked one.[29]

Hurley accused FDR of distorting the president's position on electric power. In fact, the differences were minor and involved only distribution of power, not federal construction of dams or generation of power. Distribution of such power would compete with private companies and undersell them, discouraging these companies from developing other dam sites. The dogmatism of the Democrats would limit, not expand, the nationwide distribution of power. Some fanatics, such as Senator Norris, believed private companies gouged their customers, yet Hoover favored strong regulation of rates while Roosevelt did not. The enormous publicity devoted to a single site, Muscle Shoals, had detracted from other federal power projects, of which Hoover was one of the earliest and strongest supporters. The Democrats and insurgents with an axe to grind, such as Norris, had adopted a rule or ruin policy. Roosevelt had curried favor with them to gain their support, not because he had a genuine interest in electric power development. Hurley rebutted the Democrat on another front. Roosevelt had accused the president of encouraging wild speculation before 1929 by refusing to regulate stocks. Hurley revealed that the Supreme Court had ruled that stock transactions represented intrastate commerce and that Roosevelt, as governor, had done nothing to regulate them. The same applied to banking. Although governor of the state where the banking center and stock exchange of the nation were headquartered, Roosevelt had done nothing to reform or regulate either, nor had he warned about speculation. In fact, he had been a speculator himself. Hoover had proposed legislation to reorganize banking, denied by the Congress, since the beginning of his term. The GOP speakers denounced Roosevelt's speeches as naïve, vacuous platitudes. After FDR spoke in Topeka, Kansas, Senator Arthur Capper commented that a large audience of Kansas farmers had been disappointed by the candidate's "amiable nothings" and array of "glittering generalities." Mark Requa, a California member of the RNC, believed Roosevelt had reached a new low for triviality when he tried to ingratiate California voters by praising the weather of Los Angeles. Mills accused the Democratic candidate of intellectual dissonance. By contrast, he said, the incumbent had a focused, coherent program with an interlocking approach. At St. Louis, Mills described FDR's farm program as lacking content, in contrast to Hoover's, which he described as the most comprehensive of any administration to date. Roosevelt's pretensions to farming were hypocritical; he had dabbled at farming, never turning a profit while living off of inherited wealth. FDR had never worked with his hands. Hoover had grown up on farms and in farm towns and had done agricultural labor. Hoover had made himself an expert in scientific farming, marketing, and transportation. The president had a record of farm legislation dating to his Commerce days that dwarfed Roosevelt's legislative achievements in the farm sector. Roosevelt's program consisted merely of the statement that he would do everything he could to help farmers.

Republican speakers pointed out that FDR said different things in different states. National Chairman Everett Sanders noted that FDR continued to straddle the bonus issue by claiming he would postpone consideration until the budget was balanced. In fact, the tactic of straddling was applied to virtually every issue. The president considered Roosevelt a naïve, indecisive person who lacked imagination, a belief shared by some Democrats.[30]

Hoover tried to be president of all the people and usually scorned interest group politics. He felt, however, that blacks and American Indians had been held back by historical circumstances. However, he did not believe in patronizing them. He was tolerant and treated all classes, races, and religions equally. Any honest person was welcome in his home. One black whom Hoover had appointed to a minor position wrote to explain that this was precisely how he wanted to be treated and why he intended to vote for Hoover. He wanted an equal opportunity for a job and an education but no special favors or pork-barrel appropriations. Hoover had been evenhanded, had appointed blacks to jobs and important commissions, and had done more for blacks than any modern president. Many blacks wrote to thank the chief executive for appointing a black official in the Department of Agriculture whose specialty was to help black farmers and businessmen weather the Depression. The incumbent's effort to uplift black farmers was rewarded by the endorsement of the National Federation of Colored Farmers.[31]

Some blacks saw reasons to vote against FDR. The Democrat boasted of writing the Constitution of Haiti while assistant secretary of the navy when the United States seized control of that black nation. Roosevelt allied himself with the Southern Bourbon wing of his party and relied on them for his nomination. He was indebted to these the archconservatives. The Democrats still held "white primaries" that excluded blacks from voting in the one-party region. Democratic conventions were often segregated. New York blacks claimed that Roosevelt had done nothing for them as governor. Many blacks found no reason to switch from the party of Lincoln.[32]

Following the election of 1928, the National Negro Republican League, which served as a liaison with black voters, collaborated with state organizations. Black Young Republican Clubs were organized in every major Northern city. The League advocated universal suffrage, better educational facilities for blacks, the elimination of segregation, equal military training for all races, and equal pay for blacks. It called for reforms in the South that included fair judicial and penal systems, the outlawing of lynching, and the inclusion of blacks on juries. Under the Hoover administration, about 55,000 blacks were employed permanently by the federal government, not counting jobs created to counteract the Depression. The president met with black delegations to the White House. The largest group, about 150, met with Hoover on October 1. Their spokesman was Roscoe Conklin Simmons, a Chicago black Republican, who had been a delegate to the GOP convention and had been one of two blacks to second Hoover's nomination. The president told the gathering that the GOP had no intention of departing from its traditional commitment to black Americans. The group pledged its support. Hoover said he had learned of the abject poverty of Southern blacks for the first time when he supervised rescue and recovery operations during the Mississippi River flood of 1927 and that he wanted to help them. Hoover said that black progress since the Civil War had been remarkable and would accelerate given opportunity and education. He praised the contributions of black delegates to the White House Conference on Child Health and Development and the Conference on Building and Home Ownership. His brief speech was interrupted several times by applause. Still, the GOP had to struggle to hold black support in 1932 because of the ravages of the Depression, particularly endemic unemployment. Some, though not a majority, defected to the Democrats. For the first time, a majority of black newspapers did not endorse the Republican candidate. Like other Americans, blacks were less enthusiastic about Hoover in 1932 than in 1928.[33]

Although Hoover lost the support of many men who had supported him in 1928, he remained strong among women, who applauded his enforcement of Prohibition, and his support of suffrage, children, families, peace, wholesome recreation, spiritual uplift, and humanitarian causes. They praised his conferences on child health and his strengthening of the better homes movement. Some pointed to his strong marriage as a model and to Lou's educational attainments and her work for athletics, scouting, and charities. The women presidents of Mount Holyoke, Mills College, Wellesley, and Radcliff endorsed him. Several prominent Republican women and the wives of famous men campaigned for Hoover, including the widows of Theodore Roosevelt and Thomas Alva Edison; Alice Longworth Roosevelt, the daughter of Theodore Roosevelt; and suffrage leader Carrie Chapman Catt, who delivered a radio address for the president. Nonpolitical male celebrities also campaigned for the president. Henry Ford delivered his first political speech, broadcast nationwide, for his Quaker friend. Four ex-football stars teamed to stump for Hoover: "Albie" Booth, captain and quarterback at Yale; "Shipwreck" Kelley, star halfback at Kentucky; Eddie Mays, former Harvard halfback; and "Red" Cagle, captain and fullback at Army. Both candidates and their surrogates made extensive use of radio. Broadcasting consumed a major portion of the party budgets. Hoover used radio more than FDR. All his major speeches were broadcast nationally, as well as a speech in New York before a women's conference on current problems. The president delivered two speeches, directly from the White House, without a live audience.[34]

Although the surrogate campaign for Hoover had been long under way on a modest scale, the event that galvanized the GOP and motivated the president to wage a more aggressive personal campaign was the unexpected Democratic victory in Maine, a rock-ribbed Republican state, in mid-September. Maine, which voted before the national elections in November, cast ballots for three U.S. representatives and a governor, all seats held by Republicans. Maine had elected only three Democratic governors since the Civil War. Both parties expected GOP victories, though by smaller margins than in 1928. Prognosticators viewed the state as a barometer of the national elections in November. Both parties poured immense resources into the symbolic conflict. MacLafferty began speaking and organizing there in June. The outcome electrified both parties. The Democrats won two of three congressional contests, as well as the gubernatorial race. The Republican votes declined by 31,000 from 1928, while the Democratic votes increased by 53,000. Thousands of Republicans defected in a state where registered Republicans heavily outnumbered Democrats. The chief, indeed the only issue was discontent with the economy. "This impalpable but real political drift may be unreasonable, illogical, and perfectly unfair to President Hoover," the *New York Times* wrote. "But there it is." The *New York Herald Tribune* added, "No Maine election in modern times has appeared so ominous to Republican prospects." Bad news piled up. Republican workers reported that all the states from the Mississippi to the Rockies were lost. However, Hoover and much of the party was galvanized rather than demoralized. The president was motivated by desperation and a belief in his program. He finally realized that if he wanted another term, he would have to wade in personally. The last weeks of the campaign revealed a president more vocal than the public had ever seen. The emotion behind his speeches was greater; he was terribly earnest, and there was a sting to his words. The incumbent materialized as the fighting Quaker he had always been; he had, however, never applied his furious energy to campaigning. In the short time remaining, he launched an offensive and worked himself to exhaustion.[35]

The president's first foray into the battleground of the farm belt occurred on October 4, at Des Moines, in his native state. The GOP was pessimistic but rejuvenated. Fear of Roosevelt's potential policies stimulated donations to the RNC. Hoover labored ceaselessly until he perfected his draft, writing until 1 a.m. He would not let any member of his staff edit the speech; the message and the language had to be exclusively his. As his train rolled westward, traversing states that were almost certainly already lost, the reception was gratifying. The president was relaxed and genial. He appeared on the back of the train platform at each small town to receive souvenirs, shake hands, and sign autographs. At Rock Island, Illinois, his train was greeted by more than 12,000, and between 10,000 and 12,000 welcomed him to Iowa when he crossed the Mississippi at Davenport. Ten thousand awaited his arrival at Iowa City, and 5,000 attended at the small college town of Grinnell. The streets were lined by Iowans when he reached Des Moines, and 125,000 observed the parade from the train station to the Governor's Mansion, where the tired candidate lunched and rested. Then he continued to the packed Coliseum. The West Branch band played, and one of his former teachers, Mrs. Mollie Brown Carran, attended. The spontaneous welcome by Iowans was unrestrained. Journalists described it as the fondest reception ever for the president. The speech, delivered with passion, and its substance, which chiefly concerned agriculture, was applauded enthusiastically. For the first time, the president revealed that the United States had been only two weeks away from leaving the gold standard when it was saved by swift passage of the Glass-Steagall Act. Hoover reminded fellow Iowans of his rural roots and extolled the family farm as the glue of society. He outlined his efforts to help farmers. His administration had spent twice as much as any previous one to develop inland waterways and had signed a treaty to construct a St. Lawrence Seaway providing cheap transportation, which awaited ratification. He had tried to save farm homes and land from foreclosure and had propped up rural banks. He recited statistics indicating that the tariff had kept American agricultural prices, however low, well above world prices. In addition, he had blocked harmful legislation, such as the Democratic attempt to print unbacked currency, which would have inflicted ruinous inflation. Des Moines was doubtless the most rewarding speech of Hoover's campaign. He received more than 100 congratulatory telegrams before entraining for the return trip to Washington. After speaking, he regaled a small group of journalists with reminiscences of his Iowa boyhood—sledding in the snow, his swimming hole, and how fishing that was better than trout angling at Rapidan. Then Hoover traveled east, making 16 brief stops between Chicago and Johnstown, Pennsylvania. The friendly crowds varied from 1,000 to 15,000. "It will be said that it was a new Hoover who disclosed himself yesterday in Iowa," the *New York Times* wrote on October 5, "making an appeal to his countrymen with an emotion not hitherto supposed to be characteristic of him."[36]

During a short stopover at Fort Wayne, Indiana, another Midwestern swing state, Hoover forcefully defended his administration. He refuted the Democratic charge that he felt no sympathy for suffering Americans and did nothing to relieve it. The president asserted, "I say to you that such statements are deliberate, intolerable falsehoods."[37] The president dismissed as sheer fiction the Democratic mantra that his administration created the Depression then perpetuated it via the Smoot-Hawley Tariff. Such political hyperbole was historically inaccurate. The roots of the Depression antedated 1929 and required sophisticated cures not Democratic patent medicines. The worldwide decline in purchasing power, not the Smoot-Hawley Tariff, caused the decline of world trade. The Depression began abroad before it leaped the Atlantic to America. As for predicting the Crash, "I did not notice any Democratic Jeremiahs." Pinning total blame on Republicans was like pinning the tail on the donkey—far too simple. The Democrats wanted to wring political advantage from human suffering.[38] The president returned to Washington gratified yet exhausted. During the final weeks of the campaign, adrenaline sustained him. His speech to the American Bar Association in Washington reflected his exhaustion, and he failed to duplicate the energy of Des Moines. He shook too many hands and had to retire early after cutting his right hand on the stone of a woman's ring. Further, he found the GOP nearly bankrupt, and he had to divert himself away from campaigning to raise money at a critical juncture in the contest.[39]

After Des Moines, the president decided to make additional public appearances, placing FDR on the defensive. Focusing on the critical Midwest, he delivered his next major speech at Cleveland on October 15. He improvised short, back-platform speeches at about a dozen communities as he traversed West Virginia, Maryland, Pennsylvania, and Ohio. Some 75,000 supporters greeted him at train stations along the route. The president spoke at the Cleveland auditorium to a crowd of about 24,000 as well as to a national radio audience. He defended the Smoot-Hawley Tariff, for protecting American workers and keeping farm prices above the world level. The president challenged Roosevelt to take an unequivocal stand on the veterans' bonus. Hoover's tone was sober as he discussed unemployment and his efforts to create jobs. The speech was successful, but the audience lacked the enthusiasm in Des Moines, and the president's voice had lower voltage. The conclusion was spiritual and inspirational. To succeed economic reform must be accompanied by a spiritual commitment.[40]

Hoover attempted to save another battleground state at Detroit. On October 21, he left the Capital and made 13 short stops along the way, greeting voters at train stations. He made longer addresses at Charleston, West Virginia, and at Akron, Columbus, and Toledo in Ohio. The auto capital presented an imposing challenge. Detroit staggered under a 50 percent unemployment rate due to the decline of automobile sales. For the first time, the president was booed briefly, yet inside the Olympia Arena the crowd of 22,000 was friendly. Hoover renewed his attack on the Democrats, describing Roosevelt's campaign as relentlessly negative and unoriginal. The president termed FDR's promise to give every unemployed American a government job "cruel," a false hope that no government could fulfill. He warned that the Democratic nominee might experiment with inflated currency, which would retard business recovery and shrink savings. Peppering his speech with facts and figures, Hoover described his efforts to preserve sound money. Hoover vowed to complete recovery and reform in a second term, providing aid for mortgaged homes and farms. The economic indicators showed recovery was already under way.[41]

The president's last venture into the Midwestern cauldron came at Indianapolis on October 28. He whistle-stopped his way through the coal and industrial states of West Virginia, Ohio, and Indiana and spoke for ten minutes to a large crowd at Cincinnati. A day earlier, Hoover had conferred with United Mine Workers President John L. Lewis, a personal friend, about improving conditions in the coal fields. Hoover spoke at the Butler University field house, packed to its capacity of 22,000. He said that, while a banker, FDR had advised his clients to speculate in German marks, which became worthless. Further, after months of attacking the Smoot-Hawley Tariff, the governor had conceded he would not lower tariffs on agriculture, the centerpiece of the legislation. A *Los Angeles Times* editorial commented that the people "cannot fail to concede that President Hoover knows of what he speaks at every turn, while his rival has floundered hopelessly in the midst of problems too big for him." Hoover displayed Democratic tracts entitled *How President Hoover Has Failed Children* and *The Bunk of the Home Loan Bank*, deliberate fabrications that Roosevelt used in his speeches.[42]

Hoover's speech at New York's Madison Square Garden on October 31 climaxed the campaign he had begun four weeks earlier at Des Moines. Later speeches were delivered as he traveled west to vote at Palo Alto, including addresses at St. Louis and Minneapolis, complemented by brief whistle stops. Crowds lined the tracks to watch the president's train roll by and greeted him at stations. Some 75,000 watched in Newark, where the president stopped to deliver a brief talk. He emphasized improving business conditions since midsummer and the number of unemployed returning to work. In New York, the Garden was filled, and 25,000 were turned away. The speech provided an overview of the president's personal and political philosophy that wove together the themes of his earlier, more combative addresses. The Quaker contrasted his policies with Roosevelt's and defended his program and his character. He depicted the campaign as a battle not simply between two parties but between two philosophies of government. The president said he feared the election of Roosevelt would mean the creation of the greatest government bureaucracy in American history, even in wartime, a bureaucracy that would entrench itself, devouring dollars on patronage and pork-barrel spending. Such a government would undermine American liberties. Other nations had bartered their liberties in exchange for perceived economic security, and totalitarianism had followed. He warned that such a powerful government would become the master of its peoples' souls, emasculate liberty, and stifle innovation. Hoover advised Americans not to abandon institutions that had served them well in a moment of desperation. He specifically pointed out that he did not believe in business monopoly, or in any type of monopoly, nor did he advocate laissez faire. The resources belonging to all Americans must be protected from predatory exploitation. Hoover dissented from FDR's claim that our nation's industrial infrastructure was complete and that no new frontiers remained. Americans were capable of much greater achievements and virtually infinite progress and should not feel limited by temporary hard times. Such pessimism sowed self-destruction and defeatism. Stylistically, this was Hoover's most eloquent speech, yet his audience might have overlooked its subtleties. His staff wanted fury, not philosophy. But the president wanted to delineate what government should and should not do. Moreover, by that time, he knew the election was lost. Yet Hoover had no intention of quitting until the ballots were counted. Both candidates, throughout much of the campaign, had been preaching to the choir. Yet as a testament, Hoover's speech included accurate prophesies. Even on his way out, he remained a realist. His regrets were not personal regrets. The *New York Herald Tribune* wrote, "Mr. Hoover has stated his case with a frankness, with a force, that have gained him the decision generally among thinking men and women." There were no bells and whistles, for that was not Hoover's forte. Some considered it the epistle of a tragic hero, but Hoover never considered himself either tragic or heroic.[43]

The candidate enlisted the aid of Coolidge early, and the ex-president agreed to help, especially after the Democrats blamed him along with Hoover for causing the crash and the Depression. However, his health limited travel and prevented a strenuous campaign. In early September the *Saturday Evening Post* published an article by Coolidge that used strong language, for the reticent Vermonter, to back his former commerce secretary. The icon of prosperity also cited, as Hoover had, many origins for the Depression beyond the American stock market, dating to the dislocations, punitive treaties, and slicing and dicing of Europe after the Great War. Coolidge's major address was delivered at Madison Square Garden before 20,000 and a national radio audience, on October 11. Coolidge's speech, the longest he ever delivered, was the most important in the Eastern campaign except for Hoover's own speech at the Garden. Hoover's former boss was critical of Roosevelt, claiming that his "forgotten man" speech verged on demagoguery. In contrast to the president, the challenger had never worked for a living, and his entrée into politics was his family name. Coolidge asserted that his successor had taken the proper approach to resurrect the economy and that recovery was under way. The speech infused the party faithful with an incentive to vote for the president and to work as volunteers, but it probably made few converts. Its purpose was to cement the party base. The retired president's second speech, a 15-minute radio address on election eve designed to increase voter turnout, was delivered from his Northampton home immediately following the GOP candidate's last national broadcast.[44]

The finale to Hoover's campaign was a transcontinental railroad journey home to vote at Palo Alto, departing Washington on November 3 and arriving on election day, November 8. He planned speeches at Springfield, Illinois; St. Louis; St. Paul; and Salt Lake City, culminating in a final radio address from Elko, Nevada. Before departing, the GOP standard bearer painstakingly scripted his speeches, employing original language and content in each. The president had finally decided that every region was a battleground. While he was not optimistic, he wanted to satisfy himself that he had done his best. Hoover fired his opening volley on November 4 at Springfield, followed by an address at St. Louis later that day. By this time, harsh invective had infected both campaigns, and the candidates had become bitter personal foes, a relationship that persisted. By the time he reached St. Paul on November 5, the president was exhausted. Joslin, who listened by radio from Washington, believed the candidate's delivery betrayed his physical condition. Hoover spoke haltingly and lost his place in the manuscript. The president charged the Democrats with budget-busting pork-barrel projects for their constituents and massive appropriation for nonproductive public works. Then they rewarded their most notorious pork-barrel politician, Garner, with the vice presidential nomination. In St. Paul, the president made a special appeal to women, who nurtured children, stabilized politics, promoted world peace, and sometimes took a longer view than men.[45]

Near the end of his metaphorical and geographical journey, Hoover delivered his last major live speech before 10,000 Latter Day Saints at the Old Mormon Tabernacle. Hoover returned to the theme that, in the early flickers of his term, before the axe fell on Wall Street, he had hoped to make the cornerstone of his administration, world peace. In the campaign's dying embers, he was returning frequently to that dream, which had motivated him to enter public life. The candidate had not mentioned it much previously because there were few votes in it. Indeed, foreign policy played a miniscule role in the 1932 campaign even as Storm Troopers tromped in Europe. The Depression would end in time, he said at Salt Lake City, but the necessity for world peace was eternal, if elusive. His Mormon audience was responsive. At Elko, Hoover spoke earnestly in his final nationwide broadcast, again mentioning the quest for peace. That quest must be assertive, not passive, he believed. Peace was more than the absence of war. Leaving Nevada, where the governor had refused to greet him and where he was pelted with eggs at Elko, the train rolled toward home at Palo Alto. He had not been there since 1928. Polls poured in predicting that Roosevelt would win by anything from a comfortable margin to a landslide. None showed Hoover in the lead. Party leaders realized that their standard bearer stood no more chance than a mouse in a cat's mouth. Earlier during the trek, a man was spotted pulling up spikes in an effort to derail the presidential train. One morbid wit cabled Hoover that he should vote for Roosevelt and make it unanimous. The memory of his past successes, even of his thumping of Al Smith, was dim, and the one thing that remained indelibly attached to him was the demon of the Great Depression. A realist, Hoover was aware of the inevitability of his fate. He wanted to win essentially for two reasons. First, he wanted to leave the White House on his own terms. He believed he had ushered in recovery and wanted historical justice. Second, he believed Roosevelt might retard recovery and that the Democrat was naïve and unqualified. He would not have bet on his own victory, but the Quaker was no betting man. Hoover's hectic, last-minute campaign might have gained few votes, but it earned him a measure of grudging respect. The campaign, which covered 10,000 miles and included ten major speeches and dozens of smaller ones, had been the most strenuous by an incumbent since Taft's in 1912. It was heated and involved tough language on both sides. At the weary end, he wondered if even historical vindication was in the cards.[46]

On November 8, as voters went to the polls, Hoover returned home. Despite discouraging polls, smaller samples found him winning a substantial majority of college students and clergymen. Among Stanford students, 63.4 percent backed him, and back in Iowa he won three-fourths of the West Branch vote. Among those who knew him best, he fared well. The Hoovers voted at their Stanford precinct, where later returns showed him winning with 176 votes to 45 for Roosevelt and 17 for Socialist candidate Norman

Thomas. That evening, the Hoovers received returns with family and friends in the great living room of their Spanish Hopi-style home. The entire family was there, including their two sons, daughter in law, and three grandchildren. Outside, Stanford students gathered to show and voice their support, as they had in 1928. The president conceded early, at 9:30 p.m., and then went out to thank the students for their loyalty. He shook hands with friends, including Wilbur, who had been there throughout the evening. The mood was sober but not grim. After all, it was not unexpected. Outwardly, the Quaker remained stoic, as he had in victory. To those around him, the president did not seem bitter. He promptly went to bed and slept for 12 hours.[47]

Nationwide, the returns resonated like a thunderclap. It was the end of one man's political career and of an era of his party's dominance. Roosevelt received 22.8 million votes, or 59 percent, to Hoover's 15.8 million and 41 percent. Roosevelt won all but six states. Most of Hoover's electoral votes came from the Northeast: Delaware, Connecticut, Maine, New Hampshire, and Vermont. The only large industrial state he carried was Pennsylvania. His margin of defeat was slightly greater than his margin of victory in 1928. Socialist Norman Thomas won about 900,000 votes—the highest total for a third-party candidate to that time. Hoover won a clear majority of the black vote, even while losing the white vote overwhelmingly. The election was the last time the Republicans won the black vote until 1956, shortly after the *Brown* ruling by an Eisenhower-appointed chief justice. The voters sent Republicans hurtling like pariahs into political exile. The mood for change resembled a tsunami, regardless of ideology. Representative Fiorello H. La Guardia of New York—an insurgent Republican, harsh critic of Hoover, and one of the most liberal members of the House—was defeated. The top-heavy new Congress contained Democratic majorities of 60–35 in the Senate and 310–117 in the House. The backbone of the Republican Old Guard was broken. Among those defeated were Reed Smoot of Utah, James Watson of Indiana, Wesley L. Jones of Washington, and George H. Moses of New Hampshire, some of the longest-tenured, most influential GOP senators. The incoming Congress would include a sufficient majority of wets to alter the Volstead Act promptly and to repeal the Eighteenth Amendment.[48]

In reality the campaigns of Hoover and Roosevelt were only marginally relevant. The Republicans had already lost before the campaign began, indeed, before the nominating conventions met, defeated not by a human foe but by an economic scourge. Even a strong campaign by Hoover and a weak one by FDR would have affected only the margin of victory, not the outcome. In the simplest terms, it was a crude referendum of the ins against the outs, of the status quo against the unknown. In that sense, the hoopla was redundant. Roosevelt was a superb campaigner, and Hoover was not, but had Roosevelt been the incumbent, the superb campaigner would have lost. Neither did the campaign conclusively demonstrate that Roosevelt was the potentially strongest Democratic candidate. Al Smith or Newton D. Baker might have fared as well. Pericles himself could not have swayed voters with his oratory had he been in Hoover's place. As one archivist at the Hoover Library observed, "You could have run Jesus Christ on the Republican ticket in 1932 and He would have finished second." It is perhaps equally true that Satan, running against Hoover, would have won easily. In fact, some Republicans still think Satan actually did.[49]

The only thing that mattered was economic misery. Mark Sullivan observed that the Depression was not really an issue but a condition that molded the election. "It is an emotional association: 'Hoover-depression: depression-Hoover,'" he wrote. In the world of politics, Hoover did not have to be responsible for the Depression to suffer from it. "The people remember that they have had a desperately unhappy time, and the word 'Hoover' recalls the time of their unhappiness." Sullivan pointed out that it was not even that most people really disliked Hoover. They simply wanted to escape the unpleasant association. It was only an emotional, not a rational, relationship, but it was profoundly powerful. They did not even intend to "vote" against Hoover, they just wanted to vote against the unpleasant feeling. They only wanted better times, not a formula. Roosevelt was a famous name, but it could have been Brown or Jones. Roosevelt simply had to reap discontent. Yet it is quite possible, Sullivan wrote, that Hoover was actually the right person in the right place at the right time. "It was the first time that Washington took responsibility for this kind of leadership," he wrote. The response meant that "henceforth the resistance to panic is to be conducted from the political capital."[50] In March 1933, the *Boston Herald* added that "the worst that can be said of Mr. Hoover is that he failed where nobody could have succeeded." He had not been the master of his fate, but he remained the captain of his soul. As for the calamities of his term, "It was his misfortune, not his fault."[51]

CHAPTER 19

The Hard Interregnum

Hoover had hoped to enjoy a short vacation at Palo Alto before returning to Washington after the election, but events determined otherwise. On November 10, two days after the election, Stimson notified him that some European powers had requested a delay in the next installment of their war debt payment, due January 15. The Europeans had met at Lausanne, Switzerland, in July and cancelled most German reparations on the condition that the United States relieve the former allies of war debts. The president had no authority to cancel or reduce debts without the consent of Congress, which opposed concessions. The European powers presented a solid front against America, hoping to exploit the four-month transition period between Roosevelt's election and his inauguration. The president rushed back to deal with the imminent deadline. He hoped to exact concessions on trade and disarmament from the Europeans while the United States still retained the leverage of the debts. Once they defaulted, the United States would lose the entire $11 billion.[1]

While Hoover's train paused at Yuma, Arizona, he dispatched a long telegram to the president-elect outlining the gravity of the situation and requesting a meeting with him at the White House. The outgoing president knew that, alone, he stood little chance of dealing effectively with Congress or foreign powers as a lame duck. Because the problems would overlap the new president's administration, Hoover wanted him to share in their resolution. The chief executive planned a large bipartisan meeting, including congressional leaders and economic advisers. It offered the opportunity to leave behind the bitter campaign and unite for a common purpose. Never before had an incoming and departing president met to discuss major policies prior to inauguration. The incumbent hoped they could hammer out a response before the debts fell due. He believed the discussion should include related issues such as the World Economic Conference scheduled to convene in London in 1933 and the Geneva Disarmament Conference already under way. The incumbent's purpose was not to commit Roosevelt to his policies. Rather, it was just the opposite. It was to seek his advice about decisions that would have consequences for him. Moreover, Hoover wanted to dampen nationalistic fires raging on both sides of the Atlantic. The European public and their parliaments and the American public and its Congress were equally obstinate. The debtors argued that it was unfair to expect them to ante up when they had recently released Germany from its obligation to pay reparations. Americans countered that they had opposed reparations all along and had renounced them. Further, the money for loans had been obtained from bonds sold to Americans. Redeeming the loans by imposing tax burdens on Americans in order to relieve European taxpayers of their obligations did not appear just in America and was politically unpopular. An American senator pointed out that if the Europeans reneged, the United States might be less willing to intervene the next time a crisis occurred. Hoover avoided an all-or-nothing approach. He favored reconstitution of a debt commission such as the Dawes and Young commissions of the 1920s, which had reduced reparations. The president was willing to give FDR veto power over appointments to such a commission and asked him to recommend members. He did not believe such a commission could or should complete its work during his term, but it could begin. Its appointment might stave off default. The president believed that total cancellation was unachievable. But he warned his fellow Americans that unless some compromise were worked out, default would result. Further, he insisted on dealing with debtor nations individually, based on their ability to pay.[2]

Roosevelt delayed his reply. A political animal, he considered it inconceivable that Hoover had no political motive. The governor feared that the president was trying to entrap him. Further, the incoming president planned a nationalistic approach, including currency inflation and devaluation and perhaps abandonment of the gold standard. His policies had not solidified, but they excluded any major international commitment. Although the president-elect realized he could not reject the invitation outright, he and his advisers were annoyed. In fact, with the election over, politics was far from Hoover's mind. As Robert H. Ferrell writes, "Herbert Hoover was no person to set traps, especially if they involved the welfare of his country."[3]

Roosevelt's response reached Hoover's train during a brief stop at Hutchinson, Kansas. The president-elect, who took a more casual approach to governing than Hoover, was noncommittal. The New Yorker suggested a brief chat with Hoover alone. Roosevelt disavowed responsibility. Using an expedient evasion, the governor said he was not clothed in constitutional authority until March 4. He could not sign bills or treaties, of course, but he could certainly block them or facilitate their implementation. Nor did he share the president's sense of urgency, although Congress convened on December 5 and the loans fell due on December 15. Hoover was disappointed. It might have been a step toward reconciliation. Instead, it marked the opening volley of the most bitter twentieth-century transition. Nonetheless, the president intended to use the meeting to persuade Roosevelt of the need for a prompt, unified front in the face of a major diplomatic challenge.[4]

Before the meeting took place on November 22, Roosevelt had changed his mind about the arrangements. The incoming chief executive knew little about the issue of war debts and was insecure about facing Hoover alone. Therefore, he invited Raymond Moley, head of his Brain Trust, to accompany him. Moley was ignorant of the problem. He did perfunctory research and wrote out questions on note cards from which the governor could read at the meeting, a tactic later used by President Ronald Reagan. Hoover and Ogden Mills did most of the talking during the three-hour meeting at the Red Room. Roosevelt seemed pleasant but detached and only nodded, seemingly in agreement. Speaking without notes, Hoover opened the conversation and spoke for an hour. "Before he finished," Moley recalled later, "it was clear that we were in the presence of the best-informed individual in the country on the question of war debts. His story showed a mastery of detail and a clarity of arrangement that compelled admiration." FDR was uneasy in the presence of Mills. The New Yorkers were opposites: Mills brusque and organized, the governor, genial and vague. Roosevelt feared and respected Mills' incisive mind and had studiously avoided a direct debate with him during the campaign.[5]

Hoover suggested that Roosevelt help him select a delegation to the Economic Conference that could also deal with war debts. Congress, which must ratify any agreement, should be represented. The president suggested making some concessions on debts in exchange for arms reductions. This would save enough to retire the debts. The president-elect let Moley do the talking. Moley improvised. The professor opposed the appointment of a special commission and insisted that negotiations be conducted by the regular diplomatic corps. Hatched on the spur of the moment, without input from Roosevelt or a clear rationale, this idea became the cornerstone for policy of the new administration for the remainder of the interregnum. Hoover countered that such a decentralized approach, which would require negotiating in scattered capitals simultaneously would be totally disorganized. Our ambassadors were not economic experts. Moreover, most ambassadors were Hoover appointees, which would deprive the incoming administration of any input. Debtors might not take the proposals of a lame duck administration seriously. The governor suggested appointing a fact-finding commission to report to Congress. Hoover explained that this would allow the debtor nations to drag out negotiations beyond December 15. Hoover said the jointly appointed commission could begin work immediately. Its conclusions would not be reached until after March 4, which would give Roosevelt the final word. FDR remained silent. Hoover wanted the parties to issue a joint statement, but Roosevelt said he preferred to meet with Democratic leaders that evening first. He asked Hoover to issue his own statement. Meanwhile, the governor asked to confer with Mills and Moley at his hotel at 9 a.m. the next morning in order to help him write his statement. Although the principals did not concur on all details, Hoover believed Roosevelt agreed on general principles. After Mills and Moley departed, the leaders talked privately for 17 minutes.[6]

Hoover found Roosevelt affable, perhaps overly affable, yet uninformed and unfocused. He delegated substance to Moley. Hoover's disillusionment grew the following day, when the chief executive met with ranking members from both parties. The Democrats opposed any negotiations and rejected a commission. They dared Europeans to default. Prominent Republicans said nothing could be accomplished without the Democrats. Because support of congressional Democrats meant more to FDR than policy questions, he backed away from endorsing anything advocated by the president. Roosevelt said on radio that the responsibility for settling war debts lay with the present administration and he did not intend to intervene with Congress.[7]

When Mills called upon Roosevelt and Moley at their hotel, he was told that the governor was unavailable and would soon depart for his vacation at Warm Springs, Georgia. Moley told Mills that Hoover should release his statement and that Roosevelt's would follow later that day. However, before departing, the president-elect held a spontaneous press conference that undercut the previous day's work. He commented that the debt problem was Hoover's responsibility, not his, and quipped that the debts "were not his baby" and that he would "leave that baby on Mr. Hoover's lap." Later that day, en route to Warm Springs, Roosevelt released a noncommittal statement. He took no position on debt reduction and said he would play no role in the negations before inauguration. The White House conclave had been an exercise in futility. The hopes of businessmen that the old and new administrations might cooperate and move forward were dashed. The abruptness, flippancy, and tone of FDR's reply embarrassed Hoover and dismayed the former allies, who considered it callous. The evasive response implied little serious thought. The financial community on both sides of the Atlantic was left in limbo at a precarious point in the Depression. Roosevelt remained confident in his ability to breeze through international problems without preparation. The press condemned the governor's cavalier attitude. "It is highly unfortunate that Governor Roosevelt was unable to bring himself to meet the president half way," the *Detroit Free Press* observed, adding that FDR's "statement that the matter was 'not his baby' revealed pettiness and a disturbing lack of vision." It concluded, "Mr. Roosevelt had an opportunity unique in the history of the American presidency, and he failed to grasp it." The *Baltimore Sun* wrote that the debts "may not be legally his baby until the fourth of March, but it seems to us that Mr. Roosevelt might wisely have given thought to the possibility that this baby, which is not now his, may soon develop into an unruly stepchild, permanently lodged under his roof, and disposed to play with matches."[8]

Secretary Stimson replied to the British request courteously, insisting on payment of the December 15 installment but offering hope of future negotiated reductions. The administration believed the debtor nations needed some incentive to negotiate. Meanwhile, the British and French met. The British attempted to persuade the French to meet the next installment. Although French Premier Eduard Herriot personally favored payment of the December 15 installment with a stipulation demanding future concessions, payment threatened the collapse of his cabinet in the hostile Chamber of Deputies. The duel pitted not so much Herriot against Hoover, who wanted to compromise, as the Chamber of Deputies against Congress. The French argued that the United States expected them to pay even though France had excused Germany from reparations. The powers played Russian roulette with the world economy. Sooner or later, someone was going to pull the trigger. Congress failed to appreciate the passion the French attached to the issue. Opposition to paying further installments incited violent demonstrations in Paris. French proponents of default were encouraged by a press report from Warm Springs quoting Roosevelt as stating that he did not consider payment of the December 15 installment a precondition for negotiations. The Chamber of Deputies assumed it could skip payments and then resume negotiations with a new, more sympathetic administration. The deputies toppled Herriot and defaulted on December 15. Some small debtors such as Belgium, Hungary, Poland, and Yugoslavia also defaulted. The animosity between America and France remained bitter until they became allies in the Second World War. Great Britain, Czechoslovakia, and a few minor debtors paid, yet the British attached a reservation stipulating that this installment did not imply a resumption of future payments. The United States collected $98,685,000 out of the $125,000,000 owed. Some nations continued to make token payments of less than the full amount. This ended in 1934 when Congress passed the Johnson Act prohibiting further loans to nations that had not paid in full. Only Finland paid its entire debt.[9]

Six months before the 1932 presidential election, President Hoover had initiated the calling of a World Economic Conference to meet in London in early 1933, officially sponsored by British Prime Minister Ramsay MacDonald. The purpose was to standardize and stabilize international exchange rates. Chaos had reigned since Britain abandoned the gold standard in September 1931. Inconsistency among exchange rates jeopardized world trade, crucial to recovery. On December 17, the president dispatched a long telegram to the president-elect asking him to participate in the planning. The situation was urgent because the world economy was deteriorating daily. Moreover, the Economic Conference overlapped with the meeting of the Geneva Disarmament Conference, and the issues were related. Money saved on weapons could be used to create jobs. The president explained that if America failed to plan for the conference, other nations would have an advantage. Roosevelt's reply on December 19 disappointed the incumbent. The president-elect, for unclear reasons, insisted on separating economic from arms negotiations, stating that he saw "a relationship but not an identity." FDR rejected responsibility for a participating in selection, "which would be both improper for me and inadvisable for you." That evening, Secretary Stimson, who liked FDR personally and shared his aristocratic caste, confided to his diary his impression of the president-elect's December 19 response. "The telegram showed a laughable, if it were not so lamentable, ignorance of the situation in which Roosevelt is going to find himself when he gets in March 4," Stimson wrote. "He really doesn't know what his is up against."[10]

On December 19, the same day he received a reply from the president-elect to his letter of December 17, Hoover sent a message to Congress outlining his program for addressing international financial problems. He had not given up on war debts and hoped the next installment, due on June 5, might be collectable, given some flexibility. It seemed fair to give the debtors a hearing, and America would only lose by a total default, which would delay recovery. On December 20, he addressed yet another telegram to Hyde Park. "I am unwilling to admit," he wrote, "that cooperation cannot be established between the outgoing and incoming administrations which will give earlier solutions and recovery from these difficulties."[11]

Toning down his earlier recommendation for a jointly appointed commission, the president asked Roosevelt to select two eminent Democrats using as examples Colonel Edward H. House and Owen D. Young. They would not negotiate with foreign governments but would observe and report back to the president-elect. Roosevelt's reply was tart. He indicated that the appointment of eminent Democrats might imply a commitment to policies. The exchange between December 17 and 21 had been frustrating to Hoover, who had repeatedly revised and tweaked his proposal to satisfy the president-elect. On December 21, Stimson learned from a Democratic informant the real reason for FDR's evasions. Roosevelt, working secretly and employing Colonel House as his intermediary, planned to stage a summit extravaganza after March 4 at which he would meet face-to-face with the foreign heads of state, including Britain and possibly France, to settle the war debts issue himself. That way he would not have to share credit with Hoover. He thought it would be a simple matter that required little study. The governor had been negotiating in bad faith all along. No individual could command the knowledge and judgment to settle such problems, and by March 4, the window of opportunity would have closed, with most nations in default. During the flurry of confidential telegrams and telephone calls during the week before Christmas, garbled versions had been published in the press, apparently leaked by Roosevelt. For the record, Hoover published both sides of the correspondence on December 22 without mentioning Roosevelt's plan for a summit. Roosevelt was embarrassed. The governor was condemned for duplicity and wasting valuable time. An editorial in the *New York Herald Tribune* declared, "The example set by the president-elect is about as bad as it could be."

FDR claimed he had cooperated—by observing a wholly passive form of cooperation.[12]

Hoover conceded there was little he could do and left Washington on December 23 for a Christmas vacation that took him deep-sea fishing in Georgia and Florida.[13] Politics did not rest. Roosevelt wanted to embellish his image. Some in both camps wanted to thaw relations, which were arctic. Hoover began to transcribe telephone conversations. Roosevelt worked indirectly through emissaries such as Felix Frankfurter, Lewis Douglas, and Norman Davis. They approached Stimson, in order to arrange a rapprochement. Douglas, about to become Roosevelt's budget director, was a conservative who privately agreed with Republican fiscal policy. Davis, a Democrat serving as a diplomat in the Hoover administration, was on good terms with the president and the governor. Stimson and Frankfurter were friends, and Stimson had not attacked Roosevelt during the campaign, although he had private qualms about his ability. At Roosevelt's request, Frankfurter invited Stimson to visit Hyde Park. Stimson was amenable, but Hoover and Mills vetoed the idea. After the president returned from Florida, the Roosevelt team renewed its entreaties, and Hoover conceded. Stimson traveled with Hoover, Mills, and Lou to Coolidge's funeral at Northampton, where the ex-president had died suddenly of a heart attack. The secretary of state rode with the party on their return and then disembarked at New York, where he spent the night. The next morning, January 9, he headed for Hyde Park, arriving at about 11 a.m. Stimson and Roosevelt chatted informally about foreign policy and lunched, spending five hours together before Stimson departed for New York. The meeting ranged over nearly every foreign policy topic, and there was little disagreement except for the touchy issue of war debts, which Stimson did not press. They spent most of their time on the crisis in Manchuria, and Roosevelt agreed to endorse the Stimson Doctrine. Moley, who was not consulted, was furious. The conference was simply a briefing by Stimson at which the president-elect said little. FDR seemed to agree with the secretary of state, though he was noncommittal on Philippine independence and Soviet recognition. Stimson noticed large gaps in the incoming president's knowledge. Afterward, the secretary left without comment and let Roosevelt describe the meeting to reporters.[14]

Stimson's personal diplomacy helped bring Hoover and Roosevelt together for a second meeting at the White House on January 20. In preparation, the secretary talked with the president and with the president-elect in Washington. Both sides now openly aired Roosevelt's plans to bring the British prime minister to Washington for personal negotiations. The administration decided that because FDR was set on his course, they would try to help facilitate it. Stimson told the president-elect that it would be useful to begin developing a policy he could present to the British leader. Apparently, this had not occurred to Roosevelt, who did not appear to have a specific policy in mind. Roosevelt was a man of alternating moods who resembled Ronald Reagan in some respects. He could remain passive much of the time and did not bother with details, yet on certain occasions he became intransigently stubborn, like Reagan, on subjects about which he knew little. Again, like Reagan, he relied more on personal finesse than on intellect and deflected serious issues with humor. When Stimson mentioned war debts, FDR summoned Moley and Davis. Thereafter Moley did most of the talking. It was difficult to discern whether Moley was Roosevelt's alter ego or Roosevelt was Moley's.[15]

The president-elect, accompanied by Moley and Davis, arrived at the White House at 11 a.m., where they met Hoover, Stimson, and Mills. Seated in a circle, they talked until about 12:15. The discussion focused on war debts, and again there was little agreement. The president realized that he could not budge Roosevelt from his plan to deal individually with foreign leaders. Hoover suggested that the Americans seek to persuade Britain to return to the gold standard in return for concessions on war debts, but the Democrats refused. The incoming president also declined a suggestion by Hoover that he inform the French that they must pay the December installment, still in arrears, before negotiating future reductions. FDR seemed eager to dispel the idea that he had been uncooperative. He did, as he had in his private meetings with Stimson, agree to support the Stimson Doctrine and also announced his backing of the Kellogg-Briand Pact. Substantial time was devoted to the mechanics of the discussions with foreign governments. Mills, Stimson, and Hoover saw no tactical advantage in separating debts, disarmament, and trade, yet the Democrats insisted. Roosevelt equated the questions to human twins who were related yet not identical. Then he suggested a strange approach. The problems should be discussed by different individuals in separate rooms within the same building. Then, when the discussions were terminated, the negotiators would gather in one room. The rationale for this arrangement was never specified. Hoover was tactful and drafted a statement that seemed to satisfy FDR, who later summoned Moley to determine the details. The group agreed that preliminary work involving the gathering of facts would begin at once. The State Department placed itself at the disposal of Roosevelt. The amount of work accomplished depended partly on the speed with which FDR selected his key experts and diplomats. Hoover emphasized that time was expiring.[16]

After January 20, Roosevelt worked with the British ambassador directly, through a personal intermediary. Stimson and the State Department acted as buffers between the president and the president-elect. Roosevelt's aides joined with Stimson's assistants in drafting notes to foreign governments. The wording had to be precise to avoid offending anyone. The process was tedious, nerve-wracking, and unprecedented. On February, 25, Stimson met his successor, Cordell Hull, a tall, courtly Southerner. Stimson found Hull slow and ponderous and believed that his lack of physical vitality would prevent him from keeping abreast of his work. Hull told Stimson that Roosevelt had informed him that he intended to handle foreign affairs himself. Stimson felt that he would not have accepted the job under such terms. It was a bad omen, Stimson believed, because Roosevelt underestimated the complexities of the State Department. Shortly before the inauguration, Hull confidentially told Stimson that the British had responded to Roosevelt's invitation for a summit by stating they wanted no meeting unless war debts were settled on their terms as the first issue. Hull was much more sympathetic to the position of the departing administration than Roosevelt had been. Stimson considered Hull too much in Roosevelt's shadow, although he had a better command of the situation than his boss and understood its urgency. Roosevelt's vaunted summit was never held. Most nations defaulted on June 15. Stimson remained on friendly terms with Roosevelt and occasionally visited the White House. Yet his last visit on October 30, 1934, ended in a disagreement over Far Eastern policy, and the relationship cooled. Stimson remained on friendly terms with Hull but was denied access to the president.[17]

FDR evolved into a great president but got off to a tortoise-like start. America paid a price for Roosevelt's narrowly nationalistic approach to the Depression, which alienated foreign leaders and damaged the world economy. Roosevelt overlooked the potential of both the Economic Conference at London and the Disarmament Conference at Geneva, and both disintegrated on his watch. FDR made clear in his inaugural address that he did not take the London Conference seriously. He dispatched a delegation divided in its economic views with vague instructions and later sent Raymond Moley to untangle affairs, but the American position became so muddled it ultimately undermined the entire conference, which adjourned without accomplishing anything on June 27, 1933. Moley confessed in 1948 that he never learned FDR's motive for sabotaging the conference.[18]

As president, Hoover had not asked Roosevelt to do anything unconstitutional or unethical but simply to cooperate during the transition lest vital time be squandered. The president-elect stated that it would be improper for him to play a role, yet he used his clout to influence the Democratic Congress to defeat Hoover's policies during the short session of the Seventy-Second Congress. FDR's tendency to procrastinate, which resembled Coolidge's, dismayed even his friends. Lacking Hoover's focus, the New Yorker delegated important details to subordinates. Like Reagan, he often waited for them to bring things to him. While he called for vigorous action rhetorically, he was not proactive in a policy sense and tended to let things slide until someone brought him ideas, which he adopted almost randomly. This is the aspect of Roosevelt's character that made some who knew him dubious of his ability in 1932. He relied on luck and charm to pull himself through. The most ominous response to the lost interregnum came from the American business community. By the last week in November commercial stagnation had set in. *Bradstreet's Weekly* trade review wrote, "Reports to *Bradstreet's Weekly* from 55 key cities throughout the country indicate that business is at a standstill and shows little definite promise of early improvement." It added, "Orders are small, buying extremely cautious."[19]

From the available evidence relating to the interregnum, it appears why many insiders considered FDR shallow and an intellectual lightweight in 1932. Yet in a political sense, he was enormously calculating and intuitively sophisticated, as apt at politics as he was inept at economics. Nonetheless, his apathy in the midst of a crisis is the indication of confusion, perhaps underlying insecurity that exacerbated inexperience. He overcompensated for this insecurity at the personal level by never divulging his private thoughts, by trusting no one, and by being aggressively ambitious at the political level. Unloved by intimates, he wanted love from the masses or at least approval; thus he tried to do the popular thing. It is doubtful he ever understood this about himself. In fact, he does not seem to have had much personal insight, at least none that he ever vocalized. Perhaps his mind was more troubled than is commonly believed. Deep within, he knew what it meant to profoundly fear, fear itself—fear of revealing himself, of making a political miscalculation. He was unusually sensitive about his handicap, much more so than most handicapped individuals, although he had made a courageous fight against paralysis. It was a form of denial that refused to permit him to admit that he could have weaknesses like other people. In a practical sense, it prevented him from moving on. Acceptance, not denial, is the sign of a healthy personality. During the interregnum and later, he demonstrated a strong vindictive streak. In political matters, FDR was quite flexible, but in personal matters it was extremely difficult for him to admit ever making a mistake. Roosevelt was genuinely unprepared to take the reins of government in 1932. Some, even of Roosevelt's own party, understood this. Roosevelt possessed great inner strength, but like other people one of the origins of his strengths might have arisen from weaknesses in other areas. Further, FDR was unduly alarmed that Hoover's efforts at cooperation were a subterfuge designed to undermine the New Deal. He had known Hoover long enough to know that the Quaker did not operate that way. Sabotage the New Deal? At the time, neither Hoover nor Roosevelt knew what the New Deal was going to be. His confidence existed in a vacuum. Roosevelt could proceed with a blithe confidence unjustified by reality. FDR did not know how much he did not know.

Roosevelt's inspirational qualities consisted largely of the ability to persuade people to vote for him and contributed little of a tangible nature to ending the Depression. It is true that the masses worshipped FDR, as less fortunate nations sometimes worshipped their leaders. It is true as well that Huey P. Long and Father Charles E. Coughlin, who contributed little of a constructive nature to recovery, could also mesmerize. In American politics, the ability to inspire is often the ability to promise. Inspiration in the political vernacular often consists of oversimplifying complex problems. Roosevelt did not have to inspire a Congress that was overwhelmingly Democratic. If Washington politicians believe voting for a political measure will aid their reelection, they rarely need much inspiration to vote for it.

It has sometimes been overlooked that Congress sat in session during the turbulent interregnum, though it was hardly a beehive of constructive activity. Frustrated by his inability to find common ground with the president-elect, Hoover approached the short session of the Seventy-Second Congress determined to extract from it integral parts of his program for recovery and reform. It was essentially the same body that had given the president much of what he requested during its long session. Yet in the face of a declining economy and a backlog of legislation, the motor of Congress idled during the interregnum. The president's program included balancing the budget, banking regulation, bankruptcy reform, and government reorganization in the interest of economy and efficiency; ratification of the St. Lawrence Seaway treaty; increased appropriations for the Reconstruction Finance Corporation and repeal of the provision permitting publication of RFC loans, which had ignited a run on banks; and expansion of the Home Loan Discount Banks. Some of these ideas, or similar ones, had been proposed in the Democratic platform, yet behind the scenes Roosevelt manipulated the wires to prevent their enactment on Hoover's watch, lest the outgoing president receive credit. The president-elect also instructed congressional Democrats to block the confirmation of all pending Hoover appointments, including some 100,000 patronage jobs and about 2,000 civil service positions. This left so many vacancies that some departments languished in limbo. Hoover leftovers remained on the job, cooperating during the transition and until the New Deal geared up with the full knowledge that they would soon lose their jobs. As in foreign policy, domestic policy remained gridlocked while the economy disintegrated. The beleaguered president's standoff with Congress and with his successor was the equivalent of Custer's Last Stand, and Hoover fared about as well as General Custer. When the dust settled the legislative cupboard was virtually barren of achievement. It was the most frustrating period of Hoover's entire presidency and the apogee of the Great Depression. While hunger stalked the streets and banks collapsed, Congress sat on its hands. The most appropriate song for the session might have been "Silent Night." While Hoover still held the baton, he no longer conducted the band. For all his hopes and the country's need for urgent action, the session ended on the tempo of a dirge.[20]

In 1932, the American public, most economists, the majority of Congress, and especially Wall Street concurred that the Ship of State was listing, destined to sink into a sea of red ink. Balancing the budget, which in a literal sense was impossible, was a priority in both party platforms and the cornerstone of the Democratic critique of Hoover, who was labeled a spendthrift. Ironically, Roosevelt also accused him of doing nothing. FDR promised that, if elected, he would slash the federal budget by 25 percent. During the interregnum, Hoover attempted to implement fiscal austerity, and Roosevelt blocked it, even though he had earlier disavowed intervention in affairs of state on the grounds that he lacked attendant authority. Yet FDR controlled congressional Democrats and insisted that they defeat every important measure the president submitted. Hoover's economic plan was less draconian than Roosevelt's rhetoric. He believed lower deficits would reassure business. The budget-making process as it existed until implementation of the Twentieth Amendment was an anachronism. A president and much of a Congress, soon to be missing in action, were required by constitutional mandate to shape the budget for the fiscal year lasting from July 1, 1933, to June 30, 1934. Unless they did so, the government would have no operating funds. Hoover proposed a sales tax that would raise $500 million and budget reductions of about $800 million. The president also submitted a government reorganization plan that would save money and provide better service. Congress had authorized him to do so, and the plan would go into effect automatically unless vetoed by one House. There was a consensus in both parties that a more nearly balanced budget was prudent.[21]

Speaker Garner supported Hoover's revenue program including a sales tax, as did a majority of Democrats. Combined with Republicans, it seemed likely to pass. On December 29, however, Roosevelt ordered Democrats to defeat the sales tax. He next directed Democrats to defeat Hoover's plan for government reorganization, which also died. On January 5, 1933, the president-elect convened a conference of Democratic congressional leaders at New York. He told the delegation to defeat all efforts to balance the budget. However, on March 10, six days after Hoover left office, President Roosevelt called upon Congress to implement drastic economies, terming it vital to recovery. But he went further: He claimed that the bank debacle during the interregnum was due largely to the failure of the Hoover administration to rein in spending. "For three long years the Federal Government has been on the road toward bankruptcy," he said. "It has contributed to the recent collapse of our banking system." This was virtually an echo of what Hoover had told Roosevelt during the interregnum, during which FDR blocked retrenchment and banking reform as banks shut down. The new president piously added, "Upon the unimpaired credit of the United States Government rest the safety of deposits." Now the business of budget control would be "his baby."[22]

During the interregnum, the president labored for banking reform. He had submitted legislation to strengthen banks every year since 1929 and now pressed for legislation as banks toppled throughout the country. Most of the bill's provisions were long overdue. After delaying for years, Senator Glass, the procreator of the Federal Reserve, agreed to lend his prestige by attaching his name as the chief sponsor. The president pointed out that bank failures, even during depressions, were not inevitable. Neither Britain nor Canada, for example, had suffered significant failures. To prevent the excesses that had contributed to the Crash, the bill separated deposits from investment banking to prevent bankers from speculating with their depositors' money. The president considered state banks, which operated under 48 different sets of laws, a weak link in the system. All banks engaging in interstate commerce would be regulated by the federal government and required to join the Federal Reserve System. Consolidation of weak banks would be facilitated by permitting branch banking on a statewide basis. The Federal Reserve would be empowered to implement the prompt, orderly liquidation of closed banks and the distribution of their assets to depositors. Such strong federal regulation would protect depositors. However, the proposal was opposed by most bankers, who wanted no regulation. Senator Huey P. Long delayed consideration in the Upper House by a lengthy filibuster, but on January 26 it passed the Senate. Then it was killed in the House in the midst of the banking crisis because Democratic leaders, on the instructions of the president-elect, refused to permit it from coming to a vote. Hoover pleaded with FDR for his help, but the incoming administration refused. The Glass bill was finally enacted, including many of the original provisions, but not until Roosevelt took office, and it is usually chalked up as one of the accomplishments of the New Deal. Roosevelt initially opposed federal insurance of deposits, but the provision was included in the final measure. If Nero fiddled while Rome burned, the last session of the Seventy-Second Congress lay paralyzed in the wake of the most devastating banking crisis in the nation's history, moving at the pace of a snail rushing to put out a fire. In the end, it proved as penurious with beneficial legislation as Scrooge was with Christmas turkeys.[23]

The president considered bankruptcy reorganization another crucial reform. Property values dropped during the downturn, yet debtors were expected to pay the full amount of installments and interest based on the purchase price. Hoover believed bankruptcy regulation by the federal government would make the system more humane to debtors while remaining fair to creditors. He submitted legislation that provided for swift reorganization of corporate and private debts under the protection of the courts. Further, insolvent estates could be liquidated and distributed promptly. Finally, fraud and waste should be purged from the system. After the Democratic Congress rejected the legislation on January 11, 1933, Hoover made a further plea. The House passed a bill, but it was held up in the Senate. The president argued that, amid the chaos of vast liquidations with more imminent, the purpose of the measure was simply to provide cooperation between debtors and creditors in settling debts to mutual advantage. Had the bill been passed promptly, it might have alleviated suffering of many foreclosed homeowners. The measure was finally enacted during the waning days of the short session, stripped of some of its provisions, after the damage had been done and too late for Hoover to receive credit.[24]

Congress did enact legislation, some of it important but unrelated to the collapsing economy. It repealed Prohibition, which was inevitable, but the expeditious passage was a surprise. Congress also passed the Hawes-Cutting Act phasing in Philippine independence over the president's veto. Stimson, who had been governor-general of the islands, and Hurley felt the measure was premature, would expose the islands to Japanese aggression, and damage their economy. Many Filipinos opposed the bill on the grounds that it subjected their exports, especially sugar, to American tariffs. It also curtailed Filipino immigration, which many of the islanders opposed. They attributed the law to selfishness and to the lobbying of U.S. sugar interests. Emilio Aguinaldo, who had led the war for Cuban independence after the Spanish-American War, and Filipino Senate leader Manuel Quezon denounced the override of Hoover's veto. Ultimately the Filipino legislature, because of the tariff provisions, refused to ratify the law, nullifying it. In 1934, after Hoover's term ended, it ratified an amended measure that provided for a "commonwealth" government until 1946 when the islands would become independent. Diplomatic historian Robert H. Ferrell argues that the measure sent the wrong message to the Japanese by encouraging them to believe that the American government would not defend the Philippines.[25]

With Hoover's term expiring, prospects for ratification of the St. Lawrence Seaway treaty dimmed. Eastern shippers, railroads, and the ports of New York and Buffalo opposed it. Washington in transition was Washington in chaos. Nothing had been done on the most pressing problems of these months: the Glass banking bill, farm relief, aid to the unemployed, taxation, and economy in government. The Seventy-Second Congress was expiring with a whimper, not a bang. In February, Senator Robinson, the Democratic floor leader, agreed with his Republican counterpart, Senator Watson, that Congress was tied in knots. Congress, however, was a tool of the president-elect, a quite dull tool. "But there is no use blinking the fact that the thirty-second President of the United States, Franklin D. Roosevelt, is off to a bad start," the *New York Evening Post* complained.[26]

On January 2, 1933, the President's Research Committee on Social Trends, chaired by Wesley C. Mitchell, finally issued the report Hoover had commissioned in 1929. It took the committee of 500 scholars and social scientists over three years to sift through mountains of statistics, compile data, digest it, and condense it into two hefty volumes, which Hoover hoped would serve as a blueprint for reform for him and his successors. This summary was followed by 13 monographs addressing specific problems. Costing $1 million, financed entirely by foundations and private donations, it was the most ambitious, comprehensive study of its time, a treasure trove for researchers. Hoover thrived on facts, and he realized his time was too short to make use of the study, but it has proved invaluable to historians and social scientists in the long run. The work was divided into academic specialties but written in layman's language. It indicated the scope and approach Hoover might have pursued in areas such as race, unemployment, income disparities, education, health care, and urban decay. The clue to stability, the committee concluded, lies in the pace of social change, which occurs unevenly. In the economic crisis, for example, production outpaced consumption. All facets of society are intertwined, and the key to orderly progress is proper balance. Technology leads the parade but also costs jobs and changes the nature of employment. Education holds the key to progress, and government involvement in business and economic planning should increase. Religion remains the nation's moral compass, and families are its anchor, while individual citizens cumulatively produce national vitality. The study shows that Hoover envisioned a progressive, dynamic society. He pondered the findings, and although he felt some writers tilted too heavily in the direction of a leviathan state, Hoover appreciated the magnitude, quality, and craftsmanship of the study. He had aspired to implement some of its findings during a second term. Hoover did not believe society could or should be engineered in a literal sense, but he believed that research is the raw material for humane reform.[27]

By January 1933 Hoover faced a crisis in banking that eclipsed the peril over war debts. The financial community, with good reason, feared that Roosevelt intended to devalue the dollar, inflate currency, and abandon the gold standard, although he had promised sound money during the campaign. The issue concerned the business community, and devaluation would erode the value of the money saved by every American and reduce salaries, in real money, for all earning a steady income. It would help debtors, part of Roosevelt's constituency, but hurt creditors. Panics thrive on uncertainty. After improving from July to late September, the economy soured from November 8 to late December. Uncertainty manufactured the panic of the interregnum, and FDR contributed by refusing to clarify his plans. Businesses cancelled orders and dismissed workers. Unemployment increased from about 10 million to approximately 13 million during the period. The fate of the gold standard lay in limbo. People began to demand gold in exchange for currency, draining the treasury and creating instability among banks. Insiders, privy to Roosevelt's intentions, exported bullion or invested in foreign bonds. Depositors in rural banks moved their money to stronger Eastern banks. Some, distrusting all banks, hoarded money, drying up credit and contracting the economy. Consumption fell. Domestic manufacturers, fearing the loss of tariff protection, drew down inventories. In late January, Senator Carter Glass, a Virginia Democrat, the financial oracle of Congress, rejected Roosevelt's offer to become secretary of the treasury because Roosevelt refused to promise that he would not tamper with the currency. Because of Glass's prestige, the financial community was shaken. Any one of these omens would have been destabilizing, but cumulatively they spread a contagion of fear. The fragile economy, volcanic underground, rumbled ominously, ready to erupt in an economic calamity of biblical proportions. The president strove to soothe the financial community and smother the volcano of fear. But would-be allies, including Congress, the Federal Reserve, and the president-elect, denied responsibility. Many believed Wilson's creation of the Federal Reserve System would douse an incipient panic. They were about to be proven wrong.[28]

The decision of the Democratic House to publish RFC loans to banks retroactively fueled the fiasco. The Emergency Relief and Construction Act of July 1932, over the objections of Hoover and the RFC board, permitted piecemeal revelations, but Speaker Garner pledged not to use the authority. Publication was superfluous because the loan data was already available to members of Congress. Garner reneged on his promise and published the loans in newspapers. Many depositors misinterpreted loans as signs of the weakness of their banks and impulsively withdrew their money, inspiring a cascade of failures. On January 5, 1933, the House approved a resolution authorizing retroactive publication of past loans as of January 26. The timing could not have been worse. By late January, banks were failing at the rate of ten per day. On February 2, Senator Joseph T. Robinson, an Arkansas Democrat, denounced this gratuitous publicity on the Senate floor but ceased objecting when he learned that Roosevelt supported the policy. Release of not only current but cumulative loans defied common sense. Not even political capital could be gained; the elections had ended in November. Vindictively, it plunged a dagger into the heart of the fragile banking system, creating spasms of hemorrhaging withdrawals. The publication of some 400 loans simultaneously terrified jittery depositors. The multiplying failures less resembled falling dominoes than an avalanche. It helped provoke the implosion of large yet struggling banks in Detroit. In addition to inspiring a wave of withdrawals, many banks famished for loans became reluctant to apply for them. The policy sucked the economy dry of credit. Publication contributed to the fleeing of gold and currency to safer havens abroad. Fear drove the panic. Ironically, most banks that received RFC loans gained strength from the influx of capital and were actually sound. However, no bank retains sufficient reserves to pay everyone if their entire clientele demands their money simultaneously. Roosevelt's backing of the publication policy shows his dark side. On March 14, 1933, a few days after his resignation, former RFC chairman Atlee Pomerene, a Democrat, said of the deliberate release of the loan data, "It was the most damnable and vicious thing that was ever done." He added, "It almost counteracted all the good work we had been able to do," which evidently was exactly what it was intended to accomplish. Confirming the partisan motives behind the publication of loans is the fact that in May 1933, shortly after Roosevelt assumed office, the authorization of any publication of RFC loans, whether in part or retroactively, was repealed by the massive Democratic majorities in both houses. But it had worked its deadly deed.[29]

Regional instability surfaced in Iowa. During the first week of January, the American Trust Company of Davenport fell. To contain the failures, the governor declared a moratorium on January 20, 1933. Like a deadly disease spread by human hysteria, the infection leaped to Tennessee, Kansas, and Missouri. By the end of January, bank failures had reached 245, the highest monthly total since the creation of the RFC. More was to come. The RFC deterred a panic in New Orleans with a loan to the venerable Hibernia Bank and Trust Company, but it only patched a crevice before the earthquake.

Everyone watched nervously, awaiting the next blow. It came in Detroit, whose major banks relied upon the stagnant auto industry. Two important banking groups, the Guardian Union and the Detroit Bankers' Company, had acquired weaker, smaller banks. Yet their size was no barometer of strength. Both had speculated with depositors' money during the mania that preceded the Crash and reaped the whirlwind of greed. Hoover knew a failure of the banks would cost some one million innocent depositors their savings. The crisis was fractured by politics and bitter personal enmity between two wealthy men, millionaire Senator James Couzens of Michigan and Henry Ford. Ford had invested in the Guardian Trust Company, an affiliate of the Guardian-Detroit-Union Group, and had deposited $7.1 million in the bank, partly to prop it up. The Union Group applied for a $50 million RFC loan. Couzens blocked the loan, based partly on his grudge against Ford. Seeking to exploit the crisis for political gain, Couzens charged that the Hoover administration should help the poor, not rich bankers, ignoring the looming loss of savings by his own constituents. The RFC feared that if it made the loan, Couzens might flex his political muscle to undermine the RFC. The RFC knew, as it reported to the president, that the failure of the banking syndicate would lead to the closure of every bank in Detroit, possibly every bank in Michigan. Yet Couzens refused to compromise, preferring to see the bank fail. Liberals, Progressives, and Father Coughlin joined Couzens in waging class war against the prostrate banks. Henry Ford offered to personally bail out the Detroit banks if he could name their boards of directors, yet Couzens denounced Ford as a selfish rich man. On February 13, the Detroit banks closed, and the following day Governor William A. Comstock declared a ten-day statewide closure. The Michigan failures vaulted across state lines and ignited a firestorm of bank holidays. When the Michigan holiday expired, Governor Comstock found it was easier to close banks than to reopen them.[30]

Meanwhile, the sounds heard from the president-elect were the sounds of silence. At the height of the banking crisis he took a two-week fishing vacation aboard Vincent Astor's yacht, though he continued to demonize the rich. The Hoover administration learned the reason for Roosevelt's lassitude amid a tidal wave of bank failures. While the governor was mum, his advisers had embarrassingly loose tongues. On February 25, 1933, Joslin received a telephone call from industrialist James H. Rand, who had just lunched with Rexford G. Tugwell, one of FDR's key advisers. "He said they were fully aware of the bank situation and that it would collapse in a few days which would place the responsibility in the lap of President Hoover," Rand reported. "We should not worry about anything except the rehabilitation of the country after March 4," Tugwell added. Speaking to Herbert Feis, who expressed concern after 27 states had closed their banks, Tugwell responded curtly, "Let 'em bust; then we'll get things on a sound basis." Raymond Moley, the intellectual leader of Roosevelt's Brain Trust, later wrote that the president-elect "preferred to have conditions deteriorate and gain for himself the entire credit for the operation" of recovery. On February 26, William Woodin, the incoming treasury secretary, confirmed Rand's statement in a conversation with Mills. According to Mills, Woodin told him that the new administration wanted to take over at the lowest point possible and did not intend to stem the tide until the Democrats took over. David Lawrence, the distinguished Washington commentator, also blamed Roosevelt for the panic. "The bank holiday should never have occurred," Lawrence later wrote, "and it would not have been necessary if there had been real leadership on the part of Mr. Roosevelt in the period between the election in November and his inauguration in March."[31]

Hoover felt stymied in his efforts to halt the downwardly spiraling economy. Congress, the public, and even the Federal Reserve Board were not prepared to follow the president's recommendations without the approval of the incoming administration. Any decisions made on financial policy would have to be confirmed by Congress, which would listen only to Roosevelt, and any decisions made by Hoover by late February would be ineffective without FDR's support because implementation would occur during the new administration. In desperation, the president wrote a ten-page handwritten letter to the president-elect explaining that some type of statement from him, or some indication of cooperation, was the only possible way to galvanize Congress and restore the confidence of business, bankers, and the public. The economy lay bound in a hangman's noose, dangling by a rope of uncertainty. The longer action was delayed, Hoover stated, the greater the financial wreckage, and the more effort it would take to revive the banks, leaving millions of depositors bankrupt. Roosevelt was now the fulcrum on which the economy pivoted. Hoover offered numerous proposals for solutions. The government could ensure deposits, at least in part, a relatively novel idea then, which was later folded into the Glass-Steagall Act of the New Deal. Hoover asked for the termination of publication of RFC loans and for clarification of the plans of the incoming administration that would relieve the Damocles Sword of uncertainty. He said any reasonable compromise that would arrest the decline was amenable to him. The need for action was urgent. Roosevelt, who would piously proclaim in his inaugural address that "this nation asks for action, and action now," was in no mood for action on Hoover's watch. In fact, he was annoyed by the letter and laid it aside without responding.[32]

Ten days later, having received no reply, the president dispatched a second letter, hand carried to the governor by the Secret Service. The situation, bad on February 18, was now spinning out of orbit. Since his last letter, banks had fallen in Cleveland and Washington, DC, with failures imminent in New York City, the nation's financial nerve center. Hoover offered to be helpful in any way he could, at the convenience of the president-elect. The economy was withering, without credit and with bank vaults empty and gold fleeing the country. A statement by the president-elect providing some indication of his administration's plans might arrest some of the fear that propelled the panic. By the time the president received Roosevelt's reply it was March 1, three days before inauguration. The president-elect prevaricated that he had written Hoover on March 21, yet the missive had been mishandled by his secretary and he had discovered it only after the second letter arrived. The governor enclosed a copy of the March 21 letter to prove his good faith. Unfortunately, the letter demonstrated anything but good faith. In it were facts that had not become known until after March 21. It was an artless cover up worthy of the Nixon White House. More importantly, it failed to address the situation at hand. While Hoover was determined to fight to the end, Roosevelt told him it was time to quit. "I am equally concerned with you in regard to the gravity of the banking situation," he wrote, "but my thought is that it is so very deep-seated that the fire is bound to spread in spite of anything that is done by way of mere statement."[33]

On March 2, Hoover invited influential Democratic Senators Robinson and Glass to lunch in order to discuss the financial crisis. He asked Glass for help in enacting his banking bill during the little time remaining before Congress adjourned. Glass agreed to consult Roosevelt and seek his aid in passing the bill. The president believed there was still time to salvage something if they agreed on a common plan. He offered several options: the Treasury could place deposits in selected banks to shore them up; bank deposits might be guaranteed up to a certain limit by the federal government; or the comptroller of the currency might reorganize weak banks in collaboration with state governors. If bank closures were necessary, Hoover wanted to close them selectively, leaving strong banks open in order to permit trade. The president said that FDR and his advisers had not suggested any plan and had rejected every idea he had proposed. Hoover implored the Democratic senators to explain to the president-elect that he had a moral, if not legal, obligation, to help lead the country. Despite past failures, Hoover said he wanted to exhaust every possibility. Robinson and Glass were also frustrated with Roosevelt's indifference. The governor had dismissed them abruptly when they tried to talk with him about the bank panic. Robinson said he had been limited to a ten-minute conversation while Roosevelt was in the bathroom. Glass said that he had been given only ten minutes as well to discuss the entire economic situation. They also expressed disillusionment with the caliber of men Roosevelt had selected for the cabinet. The governor had rejected their recommendations and picked mediocrities. They detected weakness, as if the president-elect feared competent men might overshadow him. The Democrats told the president that FDR had decided, as a political tactic, to postpone all action until after March 4. They agreed to transmit Hoover's options to Roosevelt and to solicit the incoming president's own ideas. Hoover never received a response.[34]

At 6:30 p.m. that evening, Adolph Miller of the Federal Reserve Board called the president from New York. He said the banking situation in the metropolis had deteriorated and asked the president to close banks nationwide under authority of the Trading with the Enemy Act of 1917. Hoover asked Miller to obtain a written recommendation from the entire board, which met later that day. The president said he believed that a proclamation prohibiting withdrawals unnecessary for commerce, a move designed to prevent hoarding and coupled with a ban on speculation in foreign currencies and the export of gold abroad, could contain the situation without a total nationwide closure. A total closure would paralyze the economy. It was overkill. Miller agreed. Then he called Mills, conveyed the options, and asked him to contact incoming Treasury Secretary William Woodin to seek Roosevelt's consent. Any measure would require congressional approval, and Congress would not act on Hoover's word alone. Shortly afterward, Attorney General Mitchell informed the president that a total shutdown based on the Trading with the Enemy Act, which was meant to apply to different circumstances, would be constitutional only if confirmed by Congress. Meanwhile, the Fed, after meeting all night in New York, finally agreed upon a document recommending the closing all banks. Roosevelt refused to lend his weight to either a closure or a mitigation to limit withdrawals to essential needs. The governor also instructed Congress to refuse to enact the Glass bill during its waning hours. Conferences in which Mills and Woodin were the major figures worked continuously until the early morning of inauguration day.[35]

On Friday morning, March 3, the day before the inauguration, Mills met Hoover at 9:30 a.m. at the White House. Mills had learned that the new administration intended to abandon the gold standard, which would disrupt international trade, already in disarray. The president discussed the remaining options as time ran out on the administration. In the morning, Mills had agreed with Hoover that the New York banks could survive without government intervention, but by midafternoon he had changed his mind and believed a nationwide banking shutdown was necessary. By that time, every state except New York and Illinois had declared whole or partial holidays. The president arranged for Mills and Meyer to join him at the White House when the president-elect paid a courtesy call for tea at 4 p.m. After the formalities, Hoover brought up the banking collapse. Roosevelt called Moley to join them, and Hoover invited Mills and Meyer to participate. Meyer presented a rambling argument for a national holiday. Hoover responded that it would be a pity to close the strong banks along with the weak ones. He pointed out that conditions were different in each state and could be handled more effectively by state governors in tandem with federal auditors. Mills, who remained after the meeting, wanted a national holiday. Mills and Hoover clashed that evening while financial discussions continued all night at the White House, the Treasury, Roosevelt's hotel suite, and the Federal Reserve in New York. Groups of influential private bankers met at New York and Chicago. The bankers, especially the New York group, opposed a total shutdown. Hoover was in almost constant contact with Roosevelt by telephone. Despite the urgency of the banking crisis, the president-elect spent time tinkering with revisions in his inaugural address that evening, having postponed the work until the last minute. His political image remained his priority. Hoover continued to resist a blanket closure, believing more limited measures would suffice. Glass, who was with Roosevelt, advised him against a shutdown. Roosevelt refused to collaborate in any joint announcement, whether for a national holiday or for Hoover's more limited plan to prevent hoarding and the export of bullion. By this time Roosevelt's intention to abandon gold had leaked to the financial community, and gold fled the United States. At 11:15 p.m., Hoover talked with Roosevelt. FDR said, and repeated for the benefit of those in the room with Hoover, that he did not consider either a holiday or even a limited proclamation halting hoarding and capital flight necessary. The principals talked for the last time at midnight and retired at about 1 a.m. Nothing had been resolved.[36]

On March 4, inauguration day, the president arose at 6 a.m. after four hours of sleep. He had not slept for more than five hours any night for the past ten days. Near sunrise, the last remaining states, New York and Illinois, shut their banks. The nation's economy lay prostrate. Banks were completely closed in 32 states and operated on a part-time basis in 16 others. There had not been a darker time in American history since the firing on Fort Sumter. Throughout the day and night, with the exception of the inauguration itself, Mills and other Hoover financial advisers worked alongside Woodin and the new Treasury team to put the finishing touches on the Emergency Banking Act of 1933, which was almost complete by the time Hoover left office. The first bill enacted under the New Deal followed closely the measure drafted during the Hoover administration. Many of the suggestions Roosevelt had rejected during the interregnum were included in the bill, and Congress, which had balked at passing it, rubber-stamped it without reading the measure. Enacted earlier, it could have saved thousands of banks and millions of depositors. Hoover's belief that there was no necessity for a total closure appears vindicated by the fact that after FDR's emergency holiday, 92 percent of the banks were deemed solvent and reopened within a few days. Washington awaited the future uncertainly. People had voted for change but not for any specific type of change, and the interregnum had been a nightmare. All hotels posted notice that because of the banking collapse, no out-of-town checks would be accepted, even from senators, representatives, and ambassadors. Thousands were stranded, and many simply remained home. With virtually a total shutdown of banking declared by state governors, Roosevelt's proclamation of a national bank holiday after taking office was largely superfluous, in a practical sense, important chiefly for its symbolism.[37]

Hoover's final day as president was frenzied. The tempo was fast because work and good-byes remained. The cabinet meeting in the morning was a farewell to the chief. The cabinet, led by Wilbur, presented Hoover with a going-away gift, a complicated desk set that included a calendar, a clock, a barometer, a thermometer, and two pens, set within a carved cabinet into which the names of the members had been engraved. A stream of visitors peeked into the president's office to bid good-bye. Representative Snell dropped by to say he expected no new business to come before the House. At the White House, the personal possessions of the Hoover family were loaded into vans for their journey to California. The president held his last press conference, said he had no important news, thanked the correspondents, told them that he had enjoyed his tenure despite disagreements, and invited them to visit him in California. The Washington correspondent for the *Baltimore Sun* spoke for the journalists and said they wished him well and a long life. One of Hoover's final official acts was to sign into law the bankruptcy bill for which he had long lobbied, intended to provide relief for individuals, farmers, and railroads groaning beneath debts. Hoover rode to the inauguration with Roosevelt. The president, who considered the event solemn, said little, not because he was angry or depressed but because he remained, as he had always been, a stoic Quaker of few words, not inclined to idle chatter. Instead of calming bankers, FDR attacked them as "money changers" in his inaugural address, which poured oil on the flames.[38]

After the ceremonies, the former First Couple drove to the railroad station. The atmosphere there was upbeat and sentimental. Although Washington was no longer the Hoovers' home, 5,000 friends cheered their departure. "You've done your duty," someone in the crowd shouted, which summed up the ex-president's life. He smiled shyly. A contingent of Girl Scouts gave roses and candy to their former First Lady and First Scout. The Chief appeared stoic until just before he turned from the rear platform to enter his car. Then he rushed in before the tears burst. Before the end of the day he received a death threat. Churlishly, Roosevelt summarily terminated Secret Service protection usually assigned to ex-presidents. Lou continued to California, but Hoover moved into a suite at New York's Waldorf-Astoria to make his help available during the remainder of the economic emergency. The White House never called. Hoover patched up relations with Ogden Mills, and on the day following Roosevelt's inauguration, he borrowed Mills' car to drive to Connecticut to visit his old friend Edgar Rickard, who had handled Hoover's personal financial affairs during the presidency. He was accompanied by his son Allan and his former secretary, Richey. Hoover loyally announced public support for the new president's bank holiday. The exhausted former chief executive refreshed himself with 2 consecutive nights of 12 hours of uninterrupted sleep. He regretted losing the election but felt released from the burden. Shunning press interviews, he spent most of his time for the next week in his hotel room, chatting with friends and advising officers for charities he supported. Hoover promised to observe a moratorium on political comments while his successor established his administration. Hoover continued his long, productive life outliving his successor by nearly 20 years. He wrote about his experiences; devoted substantial time to charitable fundraising, especially for the Boys' Clubs of America; and chaired presidential commissions under Truman and Eisenhower. Lou, who loved California, finally resigned herself to the fact that her husband wanted to remain close to the center of action. Leaving her dream house at Palo Alto behind, she returned to New York to live with him.[39]

Franklin D. Roosevelt and Herbert Hoover never really understood each other. Their policy differences were probably less profound than their personality differences. Each arose from the Progressive tradition, served together in the Wilson administration, and at one time were mutual admirers and friends. Until Roosevelt reached the White House, Hoover was the senior partner in the relationship. Hoover was brighter than FDR, but Roosevelt was a superior politician. Outside of politics, Hoover's accomplishments are more impressive, yet Roosevelt had unparalleled political skills. FDR was kinder on the outside, yet Hoover was kinder on the inside. Roosevelt was externally articulate and optimistic—so much so that before he became president many considered him glib and superficial. Yet inside there was a part of him that was calculating and cold, even selfish, as one raised as a pampered only child might be. He liked to get his way and held grudges when he could not. There was a part of him even his closest friends—or his wife or his lovers—could never penetrate. Roosevelt also displayed a stain of arrogance, yet at the time of the interregnum he had no accomplishments to be arrogant about. The humble Quaker, Hoover, was also stubborn and liked to get his way. He was frustrated by unparalleled economic distress, human suffering, a divided Congress, his own divided party, and an image that became stamped in history that was more a caricature than a reality.

For the sake of the country and of Roosevelt's reputation, it is fortunate that the shakiest portion of his entire presidential experience came at the very beginning. The interregnum was a tragically inauspicious start. The New Deal became a machine lubricated by patronage and the myth that it ended the Depression is just that, a myth. The Depression continued for nearly a decade and expired with the winds of war and the burst of postwar spending based on pent-up consumer demand, a factor more important than the war itself, because the jobs created by the war were no more permanent than the jobs created by the New Deal. Roosevelt grew on the job, mastered the art of government, and gained confidence. He always tended to let other men do his thinking, though he made the final decisions. But at no time after the desultory interregnum, though there were periods of vacillation, was he shown in such adverse light as during the transition. If he had continued along that line be would be ranked near the bottom of presidents, not near the top. In retrospect, it is clear why many observers tended to underestimate Roosevelt in 1932 and 1933 and also why they were not entirely wrong. Much of his personal life was quite unhappy, a certain hollowness beneath the public persona. But power proved an elixir, and he thrived on it. FDR flourished, at least for a time, though he also floundered at times, and the internal tribulations that he never discussed persisted. But no one could have anticipated in the vague, indecisive figure of the interregnum, the degree to which he loved power, perhaps too much, and enjoyed manipulating people, which were tactical political advantages but human vices. For Herbert Hoover, the interregnum was the most frustrating experience of his life. For Roosevelt, it showed his worst side as a crass, even cruel, purely political animal. Fortunately for both men, it was the exception rather than the rule in the stories of their lives.

CHAPTER 20

Fighting Quaker

Polls of historians ranking presidents, from the 1930s to the present, even those confined to conservative historians, place Hoover near the bottom of chief executives, and polls of the general public rank him yet lower. In the twenty-first century, the only thing most Americans remember about Hoover is that he failed to end the Great Depression. However, many historians who have studied Hoover carefully, especially since the opening of the Herbert Hoover Presidential Library to researchers in 1966, are more positive. There are reliable studies of Hoover in print, yet few major scholarly syntheses of Hoover's life exist. The best are David Burner's balanced yet dated biography published in 1979 and Richard Norton Smith's more popular life study, *An Uncommon Man: The Triumph of Herbert Hoover*, published five years later. Martin L. Fausold's *The Presidency of Herbert C. Hoover* (1985) is the most valuable study confined to Hoover's presidency. There are perceptive monographs, dissertations, and articles about Hoover, but these have not received comparable attention to some of the prominent books denigrating the Quaker president as a total failure, some penned by distinguished historians. Even the best of the major published works do not fully illuminate Hoover's personality, his private life, or his relationship with his family and friends, although Smith goes further than the others. Burner's title, *Hebert Hoover: A Public Life*, for example, is indicative of the fact that he eschews dissecting the private man. Attempting to resurrect Hoover's reputation from the graveyard of presidents is a task comparable to that of Samson or even Atlas. Images of the Depression are etched in black-and-white photographs and bleak newsreels of breadlines, hobos, and bonus marchers, and Hoover's visage is indelibly imprinted in that stark collage depicting the hardest of hard times. He seems irredeemable unless God is extremely forgiving. Fortunately, there exists a trove of documents and a supporting cast of monographs to dispel some of the mist of misunderstanding and the greater sin of neglect.[1]

There is a subjective element in evaluating presidents. History is a mixture of storytelling and analysis. It is necessary to provide accurate information and to make sense of it, which is partly intellectual, partly intuitive. Historians are umpires, and sometimes umpires, however scrupulous, miss calls. This is especially important in understanding the "Why?" behind past events. Historical context is essential to understanding a president. Too often, Hoover is judged solely in terms of his successors, especially his immediate one, rather than including his predecessors and other presidents who have grappled with economic crises. In the latter perspective, he appears among the most activist peacetime presidents up to his time. The extent of Hoover's efforts to deal with the Depression is not widely appreciated. The Quaker, for example, erected more public works than any previous president, with most of the buildings still in use today. He believed that relief should begin with private charity and ascend, in turn, to the cities, states, and the federal government. His achievements include the massive Hoover Dam, negotiations of agreements with business and labor to maintain wages and refrain from striking (which lasted almost two years), arranging farm and home mortgage credit, creating the Reconstruction Finance Corporation to loan money to banks and businesses, disseminating information about scientific farming, encouraging agricultural cooperatives, discouraging hoarding, expanding the currency, and advocacy of insuring bank deposits and social security. For someone often dismissed as an inept politician, he extracted a plethora of useful legislation from a divided Congress in which even his own party was factionalized. Hoover's legislative record on domestic policy was better than those of Harding, Coolidge, Truman, Eisenhower, Kennedy, Ford, Carter, George H. W. Bush, and George W. Bush. The Norris-La Guardia Act, passed by the Seventy-Second Congress, limited the use of injunctions to end strikes, a practice Hoover had opposed since the Harding administration. Hoover consistently supported a constitutional amendment to restrict child labor. Hoover's signing of the Smoot-Hawley Tariff was imprudent. It was not the kind of bill he wanted, yet he had failed to exert strong executive leadership to temper the logrolling of the high protectionists. Passed after the Crash of 1929, it did not precipitate the debacle and was only a minor factor in retarding recovery because foreign trade was not then a major element in the American economy.

After the prolonged tariff conflict in Congress, Hoover grasped the reins of congressional leadership more firmly. The president was realistic about the Depression, treading the line between despair and false hope. Recognizing the Depression's psychological dimensions, he utilized radio more than any predecessor and almost as much as his successor. Hoover was never a mindless cheerleader, yet several false recoveries deceived him, due to declining economic conditions and rising political instability in Europe. Under his leadership, America fared better economically than much of the Western World. Moreover, Hoover did not panic at the helm, and America did not topple into the abyss of totalitarianism on his watch. It was not Franklin Roosevelt alone who saved capitalism.

Hoover's actions during an economic downturn may be compared with those of the man he considered his political mentor, Theodore Roosevelt, whose extravagant oratory was not always matched by his actions. When the Panic of 1907 struck, the Rough Rider was relatively passive compared to Hoover. His legislative achievements and their originality, while appreciable, are not comparable to Hoover's. Too often, Hoover's subdued personality has concealed the significance of his activist record. The Quaker president was a quintessential problem solver. However, he considered the belief that the federal government has solutions to all problems hopelessly utopian. Hoover felt that government spending could only mitigate, not end, depressions. The idea that the government can "jump start" the economy is only a metaphor, not a literal fact. A stagnant economy is not, in fact, a dead battery. Neither is the economy literally a "pump" that can be primed. These metaphors are only colorful clichés, misleading because they imply a quick solution for complex problems. There was no quick fix for the Great Depression.

Hoover learned on the job, under circumstances that offered no precedents. The best idea man in his own administration, he established lasting precedents. As the Depression deepened, his policies grew increasingly aggressive, culminating in the Emergency Relief and Construction Act of 1932. He understood that a wholly balanced budget was impossible under the circumstances, yet he also resisted fiscal policy that would irretrievably mire the nation in a quicksand of debt. The president feared, justifiably, that expedient actions to mitigate the Depression might produce temporary relief at the cost of permanently undermining democracy and self-reliance. Bartering one's inheritance for a bowl of pottage was no better a bargain in the 1930s than it was in Jacob's time. Hoover preferred voluntarism to compulsory government programs because he believed that giving ennobled the giver, as well as aided the recipient. He wanted to serve Americans without reducing them to servitude. He took pride in "American individualism" and capitalism with the sharp edges smoothed because Hoover wanted America to be a meritocracy with a heart.

Hoover was prophetic in some of his Cassandra-like warnings. He foresaw that the welfare state would evolve into a massive, cumbrous bureaucracy, more impersonal than humane, inciting a scramble for spoils that once ignited could not be doused. He foresaw that deficit spending on a consistent basis was the easy way out. The president was not penurious, yet he realized that money did not solve all problems. He also knew that somebody, sometime, would have to pay the Piper for a spree of spending or he would pipe the children of Hamlin into a cave and seal it. Hoover predicted Communism would implode and was wrong only in the timing. Like Woodrow Wilson, he was sometimes right in principle but wrong in degree. Some of his jeremiads were unpopular, yet we live in a land much shaped by his vision, not a better place for ignoring his warnings. If many who lived from 1914 into the twenty-first century were still around to reflect, they might conclude that Hoover was more often ahead of his times than behind them. Of all the national leaders of his time—Roosevelt, Churchill, Hitler, Stalin, and Hoover himself—only Hoover avoided some degree of recklessness. Churchill's bipolar disorder gave him the advantage in imagination, but Hoover probably exceeded them all in intelligence. Each exhibited relative degrees of stubbornness, which might more charitably be termed tenacity or in some cases courage—Roosevelt in fighting a hopeless disease, Churchill in fighting a hopeless war. Stalin and Hitler had to deal with the demons of their own dark sides.

The idea that the more activist a president is, the better, does not apply to all circumstances. Activism must be prudent, tempered, and coupled with sound judgment. There is a time to make things happen and a time to let things happen. An activist president who imprudently leads the nation into war might be justly chastised. If Hoover had involved America in a land war with Japan over Manchuria in 1931 or 1933, it is a war America probably would have lost. At best, it might have produced a bloody, prolonged stalemate followed by an occupation of indefinite duration. He approved of the Stimson Doctrine of nonrecognition of conquests by aggression, yet warned that imposing economic sanctions on Japan might lead to war. Later, they did. The foundation of Hoover's foreign policy was to erect lasting peace on the basis of the Kellogg-Briand Pact, employing the leverage of public opinion to deter aggression, coupled with a more tangible deterrent, disarmament. His leadership produced the largely successful London Naval Disarmament Conference of 1930. The president's 1932 disarmament proposal at the Geneva Conference, in the unlikely event of its acceptance, would have made offensive war nearly impossible. An internationalist before and during his presidency, although he later warned against involvement in the Second World War, Hoover endorsed the Versailles treaty and the World Court, defying the position of many in his own party. He favored the League of Nations yet was more realistic about it than Wilson, who considered it the cornerstone of the treaty. Hoover was willing to accept Republican reservations to win ratification while Wilson refused to compromise and lost. Hoover initiated the Good Neighbor Policy toward Latin America and cemented better hemispheric relations with systematic military disengagement from nations in Central America and the Caribbean. He resolutely opposed colonialism, although he felt the Philippines were unprepared for independence, economically and militarily, and might be seized by Japan, which they were during World War II.

Hoover's leadership style caused many to underestimate him. He led by example and by moral conviction rather than boasting or self-promotion, unlike Theodore Roosevelt. This type of flamboyance can exaggerate actual accomplishments, misleading the public and historians. Further, some who attempt to establish Hoover's place in history find the task befuddling because he is complex; it is difficult to plumb his depths though in reality, no more difficult than plumbing the depths of FDR's personal philosophy. Was Hoover forward looking or backward looking, ahead of his times or behind them? Although he was consistent in his religious and moral philosophy, he evolved and sometimes changed his mind. Hoover was hardly reactionary. A product of Progressivism, he was an assertive if subdued personality, who sometimes led by indirection and relied on surrogates. The Quaker did not like to browbeat people. He preferred to reason with them and to persuade them do things that were in their own self-interest. More of a classical liberal than a modern conservative, at least during his presidency, he was above all an original thinker and an unconventional politician whose aspirations did not include winning at all costs. However, he did want a second term to complete his work. He declined to barter patronage and disliked fundraising and campaigning. He resisted fraternizing with congressmen, unless it served a tangible purpose. Hoover shunned personal publicity, the manna upon which most politicians gorge. He believed work that produced results was more important than showcasing his persona. Among our presidents, only Hoover had never previously sought electoral office, except for successful military men. Uninterested in money or fame, he had quit a lucrative mining career to feed Belgium during the Great War. At times he could be stubborn. This followed from the fact that he was principled and trusted his judgment because it had usually proved sound. However, most of the time, he was quite flexible. Those who consider politics the art of the possible sometimes fail to appreciate that everything desirable was not possible in the political, economic, institutional, and international context in which Hoover operated and with the knowledge and options available to him at the time. He was a principled pragmatist. Consistently intellectually honest, perhaps to a fault in a political sense, he was a rare political specimen. Although his accomplishments are substantial, part of his reputation rests upon his character. On Judgment Day, no one will ever say: "Herbert Hoover did not try."

Like the last battle in a war, the last election of a politician's career often defines his place in history, especially if it ends in a defeat. Most one-term presidents, unless they die by assassination, are labeled failures. As comforting as it might be to believe in instant gratification, "Happy Days" did not immediately follow the election of 1932 and ridding the nation of Hoover did not rid the nation of the Depression. Historical revisionism often awaits a contemporary event, such as the Great Recession that began in 2007, to focus on events in the past that appear to have parallels, at least in a metaphorical sense. Perhaps, in this respect, justice delayed is better than justice denied.

Senator Mark Hatfield of Oregon wrote that "He has been . . . completely oversimplified because of his association with the Great Depression."[2] For example, Hoover possessed a logical mind, yet he was no prisoner of logic and never allowed it to inhibit his humanitarianism. Many modern Americans do not appreciate how people-oriented he was. Although not a politician, he was gifted at inspiring those who knew him well. The view of Hoover as a technocrat is at least half false. He understood technology superbly, possibly better than any modern president. He knew the composition of materials used for dams, roads, and buildings that were used in his public works program. He had worked on farms, lived in farm communities, and began his mining career as an ordinary laborer. What most interested him, however, was the fate of people not technology or efficiency as an end itself. If he had felt otherwise he would have directed his philanthropies into scientific causes rather than humanitarian ones, such as the welfare of children. He probably melded these two aspects of his personality better than any American since Benjamin Franklin. In his later life, Hoover wrote prodigiously and became a spokesman for the Republican opposition. His criticism of the New Deal sometimes makes him appear more conservative than he actually had been as president. Still, his criticism was directed at policies, and he avoided hyperbole. While he espoused political policies and tried to cobble together a GOP in disarray, he also made time to answer personal letters from children; to write humorously about fishing; to raise money for charities, especially the Boys' Clubs of America; and to write and visit old friends. He wrote more books as a postpresident than any other chief executive. Many were histories, such as his mammoth four-volume *American Epic*, about the relief efforts he had directed. Hoover never ceased believing that he had something to contribute and something new to say to the American people. As a politician, he had obvious flaws. He was a poor speaker, lacked charisma before the masses, had no zeal for political combat, and demonstrated little patience with politics as an end in itself. That would have taken a different person, with a different set of life experiences. The American people knew the man they were voting for when they elected him president in 1928, and they voted for him because of his personal qualities, not in spite of them.

Hoover was not a great president because there must be some singular, extraordinary accomplishment to place an individual in that category. Yet neither was the Quaker an incompetent or inert president, and he is undeserving of the bottom rung in presidential polls. James Olson points out that "He rarely received credit for the Reconstruction Finance Corporation Act, the Emergency Relief and Construction Act, and the Emergency Banking Act." Significantly, "For the first time in American history, the federal government had accepted direct responsibility for controlling the business cycle." Olson further observes, "Under the authority of the Emergency Relief and Construction Act of 1932, the RFC accepted direct responsibility for maintaining the quality of life in the United States until the economy revived." He sums up, "The federal government would never be able to abandon these commitments. Later presidents would only expand on that foundation."[3] Clair Everett Nelson writes that "far from being indifferent, he used the power of his office to a greater extent than had Wilson even in war-time." Nelson explains that the president's relations with Congress are often misunderstood. The Democratic Congress elected in 1930 actually gave him most of what he requested. While some goaded him to do more, greater numbers urged him to slash the budget. Hoover, she concludes, was ahead of his times and especially ahead of his party.[4] Joseph S. Davis argues that there is no basis for the belief that Hoover was a laissez-faire president. "Indeed, for better or worse, he was the first president to assume government responsibility (contrary to Secretary Mellon's strong views) for coping with incipient depression," Davis explains, arguing that the New Deal really began during Hoover's presidency. Neither did the president surround himself with men who parroted his own thinking. "He differed sharply with Secretary Mellon on at least three crucial issues and with Secretary Stimson on others," Davis continues. "Secretaries Charles Francis Adams, Ray Lyman Wilbur and Ogden Mills were by no means docile yes men." Hoover himself observed that he and his advisers did not always agree, but they refused to air their differences publicly. "In brains, knowledge, experience, and dedication, he towered above most men of his time, including his predecessors in the White House," Davis concludes.[5]

Hoover was one of the few public figures who combined the abilities to think big, as well as to practice meticulous administration—adept at details, aided by a prodigious memory and by imagination, connecting dots that others did not even see. Yet history has tried to encase him within a procrustean model perhaps because he did not conform to the image of a conventional politician. His thoughts and actions were consistent to an uncanny degree for a politician. He was direct and to the point. The president always considered educating the public an important task, and, though he communicated effectively in small groups, he was ineffective at doing so on a mass basis. He did not dominate his assistants; rather, he let them do their jobs. Like all leaders, his inspirational qualities were situational. When one asks what FDR's vaunted inspirational qualities contributed, of a tangible nature, to ending the Depression, the answer is, very little. He did not have to inspire the jobless to accept government jobs when no other jobs were available. Nor did he have to persuade Congress, top-heavy with Democrats, to pass his bills. When the Democratic majorities diminished, so did Roosevelt's ability to steamroll bills through. Neither did he inspire businessmen; rather, he frightened them into hoarding their cash. The New Yorker's inspirational qualities and personal charisma were far more effective in getting himself reelected than in pulling the nation out of the Depression, and in 1940 and 1944, voters made the safe choice because of the roiling waters of a European war.

There was nothing fickle about Hoover's friendships. He craved good friends and good conversation. He was intensely loyal to his large cohort of personal friends, which included people from almost every conceivable occupation. He could disagree with friends, but he never betrayed them nor expediently sacrificed them, and they did not desert him. After he left the

White House, Hoover continued to correspond with many of his journalistic friends, such as Mark Sullivan and William Allen White. He had frequent exchanges with Ogden Mills and Supreme Court Justice Harlan Stone. Walter Lippmann, although sometimes critical, nonetheless continued to respect Hoover. When these friends disagreed with him, it was often only to a matter of degree. Many of his friends were Stanford alumni, and a multitude had been comrades in his undertakings during the Great War. They stuck to each other like glue.

Hoover's mind, which was both quick and deep, probably ranked in the top ten among all our presidents. In honesty, public and private, his reputation was spotless. No twentieth-century president achieved more before becoming president. Only Carter achieved as much afterward. "As a person who has been a historian of presidents," writes FDR biographer Frank Freidel, "the more I think about Hoover the more I am convinced that the only reason he did not become one of our greatest presidents was simply because he could not cope with the depression." Yet "Mr. Roosevelt largely did not cope with it either. But Hoover did bring about a good bit of the modern presidency." Moreover, "Hoover was a man of transcendental world importance."[6]

If the criterion for judging Hoover's administration is dealing successfully with the Great Depression, it was not a failure but an incomplete success. By that standard, the New Deal was also an incomplete success. The Quaker had limitations and economic inhibitions, but they were smaller than those of most men of his time. In 1932 his most severe and most numerous critics complained that he was moving too fast and spending too much. Among them was Franklin D. Roosevelt. Hoover moved deliberately, and the New Deal sped supersonically. But the New Deal was not planned that way. The New Deal got Americans through the Depression and made life more bearable without restoring prosperity. In 1938, after five years of the New Deal, 11 million remained unemployed, and farm prices in constant dollars were at their lowest level in history. Throughout the course of the New Deal, unemployment never dipped below eight million. Perhaps it never would have completely ended the Depression. Hoover was not averse to change; he was a trial-and-error, pragmatic president, much like FDR, but the risks he took were calculated, not random experiments, and he never used jobs or public works as a form of political patronage. His chief criticism of the New Deal was that it had politicized relief programs in order to reelect incumbents. That largely explains FDR's electoral successes. The New Dealers employed patronage ruthlessly.[7]

Perhaps the image of a prophet fits Hoover better than that of a politician, a prophet who never reached the Promised Land. Prophets are meant to lead but not to govern. They provide more questions than answers. They are often ignored and sometimes labeled insane. They might become scapegoats, especially if they are correct. Sometimes an angry general slays the messenger. Hoover had little faith in massive bureaucratic government, but he never lost faith in the American people. He thought long term. "He was conscious of the choices he made, and guilty of nothing more than farsightedness," Olson writes. "His fears of the long-range consequences of governmental activism and insensitive bureaucracies wedded by mutual interest to the powerful economic elites have been fulfilled in American life." Olson believes that Hoover would have become a great president during normal times, "for his sophisticated understanding of corporate, industrial, and bureaucratic realities would have permitted him to simultaneously regulate the economy and restrain the federal government."[8] Hoover has been portrayed as a failure because of his belief in limited government. Yet big government has not proven a total success either and has created problems and dogmas of its own. The new dogmas are as intransigent as the old ones. Criticisms that other policies would have worked better or that the federal government, with some tinkering, can solve every problem have not survived the test of time. Hoover understood human nature. He comprehended the intricate and subtle relationship between the individual, the community, and the state, and how it might become corrupted. He knew individuals needed to establish their places in the transcendent order, as well as in the political and economic order. He did not believe that economic problems transcended all other problems. The Quaker believed that government must be humane yet practical. At the very least, he posed questions that endure. Hoover, if not a major political philosopher, was a synthesizer of many of the ideas and issues of his generation. The questions he asked and the solutions he proposed remain worthy of consideration.[9]

Hoover's tangible accomplishments, even if they had ended in 1920, would remain substantial. Yet, in the final analysis, his reputation rests more on his character than on his achievements, less on what he did than on who he was. He knew what many men in public life never realize: that the only kind of morality that really counts is when no one is looking. Certainly his reputation and his legacy were forged in adversity. The test of a person or a nation occurs not when everything is going well. The test of a football team comes not when it wins the big game but when it loses the big game. "The fact that he was to become the victim of one of history's cruel ironies does not negate what Hoover represented," Wilton Eckley writes. "Indeed, it underscores what he represented." According to Eckley, "Hoover is preeminently a man of ideals." It is easy to ridicule idealists. Yet Hoover was no Don Quixote; he was tough, mentally and physically, as well as kind and pragmatic. On a personal basis, there have been few kinder presidents. Moreover, ideals often outlive ephemeral problems. Hoover was a public servant during an age of glitz—the 1920s—and in an age of suffering—the 1930s. He remained steady through both, never yielding to the false hopes in good times or yielding to loss of faith in hard times. He rejected the smug cynicism of Sinclair Lewis. "I have resented the sneers at Main Street," he said, "for I have known that in the cottages that lay behind the street rested the strength of our national character."

Eckley concludes, "Hoover was not willing to give up his optimistic faith in America. And also in that sense, his ideas are worth revisiting."[10]

Whiplashed between the extremes of his own party, soundly rejected by the voters in 1932, he might have been tempted, as Richard Nixon did in 1962, to indulge in self-pity, yet he never did. Hoover, like William Howard Taft, was undermined by the feud within his own party between the Old Guard and the Progressive factions. The Old Guard feared that, unlike Harding, Hoover would refuse to be their puppet, which was accurate. Hoover deliberately avoided factional politics and appealed instead on the basis of the merits of his ideas. In better times, this might have succeeded. In fact, this was the only practical means of achieving compromise and bringing Democrats into a bipartisan coalition necessary to govern.[11] Hoover's tireless efforts won respect as well as enthusiastic praise, sometimes from former foes, especially as time passed and his presidency was viewed in a less inflammatory atmosphere. "The sustaining virtues of history are always measured by the accomplishment of an individual in his serving for bettering the life of his fellow men," George E. Sokolsky wrote in 1947. "In that realm, Herbert Hoover stands a colossus in our age."[12] Raymond Moley, perhaps Roosevelt's most key adviser during the interregnum and throughout the early phases of the New Deal, later developed a profound appreciation for Hoover's character and for his ability and felt that the Quaker had been shortchanged by history. Writing in 1964, shortly after the ex-president's death, Moley praised the "great integrity and personal characteristics of the man for whom a nation offers a belated tribute of affection and respect." During the New Deal, Moley had been a Democratic partisan. Later, after leaving the administration of FDR, he became disillusioned with Roosevelt's policies. Moley wrote that he still considered some of Hoover's policies wrong, yet "I learned to respect not only the vast knowledge of the man, but the sincerity with which he held his views. He had no reason to love me," Moley wrote of Hoover, "since I had actively participated in his defeat in 1932. But he was a singularly generous man of great honor."[13] In another context, the former mastermind of FDR's Brain Trust wrote, "Hoover, in the abundant resources of his own conscience, can know that he will live as the greatest Republican of his generation."[14]

The Depression changed America's perception of Hoover. In fact, it almost turned it on end. From a man who could do no wrong, virtually overnight, he became a man who could do nothing right. By the time he left office in 1933, he had become a symbol of the Depression. There was a new Hoover legend, much less accurate, in its own way, than the old legend. Today, most historians who have studied Hoover in detail, admittedly a limited number, do not consider him a failure. Most agree that he did not do as badly as the entrenched stereotype suggests. The fact that Hoover has been demonized does not, on the other hand, mean that he should be elevated to the status of a demigod as an antidote. It simply means that the history of his presidency be leavened by accuracy and fairness, and that standards be applied to presidents equally, rather than segregating the Quaker president as a pariah. History is full of might-have-beens.

Hoover enlarged the role of government prudently, without creating a leviathan state. Some wanted him to move further and faster, though at least as many accused him of extravagance and bloating the bureaucracy. He paid a price for moderation. It is also true that many of the evils Hoover predicted would occur under a vast, centralized, bureaucratic federal government have materialized and become virtually impossible to root out. As Hoover realized, huge expenditures and the bureaucracy needed to implement them feeds on itself and becomes self-sustaining. Programs designed for a temporary emergency do not disappear once the emergency ends. There is an iron law that bureaucracies are self-perpetuating. Even Franklin Roosevelt intended the bureaucracy he created to be situational, not the closest thing on earth to eternal life. Hoover was no politician, but he realized that politicians, thinking in the short-term interest of self-preservation, tend to give their constituents what they want, even if some people want more than they should have and even if there is never enough to go around. The idea that government benefits are free can be refuted by perusing one's tax bill or tabulating the national debt. Hoover understood that government is neither good nor bad in the abstract. It is a tool, an imperfect tool, and only one of many. It cannot compensate for bad luck or lack of talent or drive. Hoover, who probably had excessive drive, did not believe there was anything he could do about these realities because the problems were beyond the magnitude of any individual to solve, had existed since the beginning of time and probably would remain until the end of time.

If dreams really do come true, then, perhaps, so do nightmares. Hoover dreamed of becoming president, but he feared that the people expected too much and that if some great catastrophe occurred on his watch, it would be blamed on him. The greater the anticipation of success, the greater the disappointment when it is crushed. Ironically, the chief complaint of his contemporaries was a conservative one: that he did not preserve the *status quo* of Coolidge prosperity. However, Coolidge prosperity was running on empty. It is ahistorical to blame Hoover alone for either the Crash or the economic wreckage worldwide. Still, neither can Hoover be completely exonerated. Some of his personal virtues were political flaws. Nonetheless, the temptation to flinch before difficult decisions never deterred Hoover. If one examines his reputation at the time he took office, his fate in history cannot help but produce some empathy, even if all of us are, to some degree, responsible for our fates, a belief Hoover shared. Even sadder is that so many years later, Hoover still lingers near the bottom of the presidential heap. Scapegoating is ugly. Hoover outlived most of his enemies and his friends. To the end, he strove to rehabilitate his reputation, and to some extent he did, though the bitter taste of the presidency during those harsh years never really left. Among the general public, he has been more forgotten than forgiven and when remembered is remembered for a single reason. It is said that a nation that has heroes is lucky, but a nation that needs them is weak. Perhaps a nation that manufactures villains, to a certain extent, deserves them.

The man from West Branch revered democracy, even when it frustrated him. He knew how to give people space. Unlike FDR, he could be comfortable in silence and did not need to be the center of attention or to dominate every conversation. He was confident in his judgment. Unlike many politicians, he was not a compulsive talker, though he genuinely liked people. He also possessed a sense of presence that impressed those he met. He was wealthy yet neither pretentious nor stuffy. He was intuitive. At a relatively early age and with primitive equipment, he demonstrated a rare ability to determine the profitability of mines and what lay beneath the surface that cannot be attributed to intellectual analysis alone. The president was also a gifted organizer who seldom used diagrams, flowcharts, or notes but relied on memory. Hoover hoped to build on the prosperity of the Coolidge years and implement overdue reforms. He would have been an activist president even without the Great Depression. Hoover's life was anything but that of a cautious coward. He perceived some of the dangers of the welfare state and of entitlements long before Ronald Reagan made it fashionable, long before the Great Recession of 2007 made it urgent. As Ellis Hawley perceptively points out, there has been an international trend since the New Deal away from state regulation and relying more on corporate structures. American society itself might be pushed in that direction. In that case, the New Deal will be viewed as an intermediate stage between Hoover's type of state organization and the next one, which will resemble Hoover's more closely than Roosevelt's.[15]

Although the stereotype of Hoover as a laissez-faire president persists in the public imagination, it is by no means fully representative of informed opinion. "If President Hoover had acted during the first three years of the depression in the way previous depression Presidents had acted, nothing would have been tried and nothing world have been learned," Albert U. Romasco writes. "But instead of imitating the example of patient forbearance, President Hoover had established a precedent of action."[16] James Olson writes of Hoover: "The United States has never really understood him nor, for that matter, ever really appreciated him."[17] On March 3, 1933, at the culmination of the hard interregnum, as Franklin D. Roosevelt prepared to step into the limelight and Hoover slid into the shadows of the postpresidency, a host of newspapers, Democratic and Republican alike, rendered grateful assessments of his tenure in office. Some came from newspapers that had opposed him in 1932, such as the *New York Times*, a Democratic paper. "With unsparing application he gave himself night and day to the discharge of the duties of his office," the *Times*, explained. "What bore him up was apparently a high resolve to omit nothing which might contribute to better the morale of the people and help to bring in brighter days." It pointed out that the administration had functioned without scandal: "If the country had continued to be prosperous he would have been heralded as a great President." To sum up, "With extraordinary ability, an almost unequaled grasp of facts and tendencies and developments, and with an iron industry that amazed all observers, he gave his utmost to his country with indomitable purpose through four anxious and battling years."[18]

The trend of newspaper editorials and feature stories was unmistakable. For all the battering he had taken, they would miss him. "In character, in high mentality, in tenacious courage, in the face of crumbling circumstances, Herbert Hoover has been a great President," the *State Journal* of Lansing, Michigan, wrote. "If national crisis demanded our best in sacrifice, then it has been given." Even his enemies respected him. Some feared him, but they feared his ability, not his inclination to extract retribution. He was no Machiavellian.[19] In the Far West, the *Tacoma Journal* joined the accolades. "The true measure of any man can only be had when he is tested in the fire of adversity," it claimed. "When one can stand up and take it on the chin, under criticism which was as unjust and unfair as it was vitriolic, the way Hoover has done, all in the genuine (not false) interests of the country, then indeed should we pay him homage." The editorial continued, "Had it not been for the sheer courage of President Hoover, economic chaos would long since have been the order." The president had notable tangible accomplishments. However, "Mr. Hoover's greatest victory has been moral and social rather than political." American democracy under his helm had weathered the storm. "Lincoln preserved a nation; Hoover preserved a world." There were more trials to come, but Hoover had got the country over the hump.[20]

On the day before FDR's inaugural, the *Kansas City Star* joined the chorus of editorials extolling Hoover for his strenuous efforts against insurmountable odds. It acknowledged that he had entered office with no political experience, but said that he had mastered the art. "The legislation that he wrested from a hostile Congress in his last year was amazing." He was able to exert his uncanny command of facts and persuasive powers among small groups. Initially, the president believed too strongly in the separation of power. But later, he had seized the reins and furnished brilliant, almost unexampled, leadership during a financial crisis. The overpowering influence of the Depression overshadowed his achievements in other fields, though they were significant. In foreign policy, he had befriended Latin America; offered respect to small countries; engineered disarmament at the London Naval Conference; and had attempted, albeit unsuccessfully, to forge the Kellogg Pact into a more practical instrument of peace. Hoover had endured setbacks but had played with skill the hand dealt him by fate. "In a time that tried men's souls he proved himself a great leader, a great American."[21]

"No man has ever shown more moral courage," the *Columbus Dispatch* of Ohio wrote of Hoover. "Assailed cruelly, unreasonably, dishonestly," it continued, "handicapped at every move by enemies within and without his party; balked in his highest aims to help us, he has labored and sacrificed and has not uttered a complaint." Over time, the politicians attempted to carve him into

political mincemeat, but he never became cynical, never fought with their
tools. He managed, nonetheless, to accomplish a great deal without doing
things the old way. He took his lumps, but he remained a formidable figure.
Few dared challenge him one-on-one. The president never lost his head, even
when many in Washington and on Wall Street were losing theirs.[22] The *Boston Herald*, writing at the end of the interregnum, believed Hoover deserved
the accolades of his countrymen and their gratitude. Certainly, he had earned
their respect. Among our presidents, it editorialized, "None has had a greater
regard for his fellow countrymen or made more earnest efforts to improve the
lot of common humanity." In a philosophical sense, the man "who has failed
because it was not possible for anybody to prevail often deserves more praise
than the man whose lot is cast in happier times and who wins the glory."[23]
According to the *New York Evening Post*, Hoover could retire with a clear
conscience. His mettle was tested. "That he did as much and possibly more
than any man in his position could have done to combat the effects of the
depression cannot be successfully disputed," it stated. A greater achievement
than the mitigation of suffering was Hoover's preservation of the strands of
democracy that bound America. He had carried a burden greater than virtually any president and could be proud of the job he had done.[24]

Nonetheless, the Quaker president's leadership style was not a perfect fit
for the era during which he led the nation. He never recovered from the shell
shock of his shellacking in 1932, more because of the nature of the sins attributed to him and the dimensions of his rejection than from the loss itself. This
preyed on his mind for the remainder of his life and deprived him of a degree
of peace of mind, though he complained less about his own fate than about the
direction of the nation. Harsh, unjust criticism always hurts, but Hoover's was
far more intense and enduring than that of any twentieth-century president.
Further, he was highly sensitive, disliked attention, and yet could not escape it
as his name was echoed in subsequent elections, with the same refrain. He had
rarely experienced criticism of such decibel level before entering the White
House; in fact, neither had anyone else. Because of his inhibitions, he found
it difficult to find emotional release from the drumbeat of criticism. His
speeches against the New Deal as a former president dealt with legitimate
issues. Never puritanical, he had minor personal vices, inveterately smoking
a cigar or later a pipe. Lou was a teetotaler, but Hoover drank lightly before
and after Prohibition. Except during his presidency, he did not attend church
regularly, though he was a spiritual person.

After leaving the White House, he ended his regimen of exercise, except
for walks and fishing. Though he mellowed as he aged, there remained a certain loneliness inculcated by the trauma of being orphaned. He craved human
company and sorely missed Lou after her death in 1944. Most men who have
sat in the White House reflect on the loneliness of the job and the vacuum
that follows. The elder statesman poured himself into worthy projects but
lacked the degree of purpose men find in the presidency and find missing

afterward. He continued to work prodigiously, largely as a writer and speaker, crafts he improved yet never fully enjoyed. He still found it difficult to completely relax. Industriousness is not a flaw, merely a character trait that under most circumstances is a virtue, and Hoover's energies were chiefly directed at reform and humanitarian endeavors. In short, he changed somewhat but remained in character, and he never became an anachronism. Hoover loved people and he loved work, in that order, and that never changed.

Hoover appeared outwardly stoic in later years, yet he softened somewhat, and more people came to appreciate his undercurrent of humor. He revealed a vulnerability that had always been present but had been submerged beneath his competitive drive. His personality is difficult to pigeonhole because, although he was often characterized as the most conventional of men, he was in his own way an example of the kind of individualism he extolled. He had wrung the most out of his years in the White House, and those years had wrung the most out of him. Over his lifetime, the Quaker combined philosophical insight with the will to act decisively. He was more than a Quaker, an orphan, or a president. He had insecurities, yet within him lay rock-hard self-assurance, quiet assertiveness, pride in doing a hard job well, and the inner resources to persevere against the odds. Like all people, he experienced sadness. The presidency has seen many varieties of occupants. Yet, in a relative sense, Hoover's route to the White House, his tribulations there, and his road back to partial redemption might be the most unlikely, the most tragic, and the most wonderful, intertwined.

Most one-term presidents are labeled failures, and few presidents, even relatively successful ones, leave office as popular as they entered it. What Hoover should have done about the Depression, even if one believes his policies were wrong—or wrong in degree—is still not clear. Many books, unlike this one, are "Yes, but," accounts of Hoover's presidency. "Yes, he did this, but he should have done more of it or he should have done that instead." Some studies concentrate on lecturing the president about what he should have done. Even from the hindsight of the twenty-first century, it remains unclear how much control any national leader has over the national economy. Events we confidently state cannot happen again because of earlier reforms do in fact happen again, in substance if not in degree. In a cosmic sense, one question humans beings must ponder, whether they are ordinary people, philosophers, theologians, poets, or politicians, is whether we determine our fates or float along with them, meet them half way, have unlimited free will, or none at all. Anyone tempted to believe that people completely control their destiny must be jolted when a brick falls on their head. Are some doors open to us but not others? These questions bear on the origins and destination of humanity itself, but they are relevant to the story of Herbert Hoover. He was not powerless: He had a variety of choices, yet he could not pull prosperity out of a hat. Timing is as important in politics, as it is vital to hitting a baseball, telling a joke, or meeting a soul mate. Sometimes individuals and nations do the right things for the wrong reasons or the wrong things for the right reasons. Sometimes it is better to be lucky than good. Over the course of his lifetime, Hoover had a mixture of fortune, both good and bad, and although he had mostly good fortune, it is the bad that is memorable. He was blessed with wisdom but was not infallible. It is easy to play the game of "could've, would've, should've." What pitcher has never regretted hanging a curve ball? Comedy is usually based on someone else's minor tragedy. But Hoover's tragedy was not minor; it was set against a tragedy of worldwide dimensions. Sophocles could not have written it better.

Hoover was a great man and, more importantly, a good man, although his presidency was only a partial success. Still, even great presidents make mistakes and have flaws. As a president during a time of emergency, Americans could have done much worse. Few presidents have faced crises of such staggering proportions and Hoover dealt with them competently and, on the whole, wisely. At least publicly, he refrained from blaming others. Even though vilified, he reflected that serving as president had been an honor, one he had sought. It was doubtless a burden, yet he endured stress much better than most people. He somewhat contained the Depression, at least until the rudderless interregnum, and he kept the country from turning on itself and destructing—an outcome that, in retrospect, was not inevitable. Hoover made a valiant fight against the economic Furies and, more important in a personal sense, emerged with his idealism intact though sobered. There are many who believe he should have acted differently. But in those paths not taken, there is no guarantee of success either. Hoover ran for president chiefly because it gave him the opportunity to serve at the pinnacle, where he could do the most good. Perhaps, even if he could have foreseen the future and perhaps especially then, he still would have sought the office.

Hoover's administration was an incubator of ideas—some that hatched later, some that he simply could not navigate through Congress. Even so, both the quality and the quantity of legislation actually passed, requiring bipartisan leadership, is formidable. Some included ideas that had never been tried before or were ahead of their time or for which his opponents coveted political credit. An important member of Franklin D. Roosevelt's Brain Trust, Rexford G. Tugwell, reflected in 1974: "We didn't admit it at the time, but practically the whole New Deal was extrapolated from programs that Hoover started."[25] Hoover might have partly disagreed, because he believed parts of the New Deal were excessive and set bad precedents, yet there is no question that he sowed vast fields of seeds. In retrospect, Hoover was correct in his argument that nations cannot simply spend themselves out of depressions any more than a pitcher can thrive on a steady diet of fastballs. Infinite spending, even if feasible, would not ensure infinite prosperity. That is a transparently reductionist argument, the equivalent of an economic perpetual motion machine. The government must take money away before it can spend it. The permanent bureaucracy Hoover feared has exceeded his expectations, and, as he predicted, cemented itself in place. There is still debate over what causes depressions and what ends them. If national leaders knew the precise answers they would never occur, or, if they did occur, they would not last long. Considering ourselves superior to our predecessors who dealt with serious problems in a serious manner is too smug. The much celebrated lessons of history are not literal. They indicate only human tendencies, not inevitable outcomes. History does not consist of recycled Xeroxed copies of past events. Historians, like generals, sometimes fall into the fallacy of assuming that the present is like the past and base their battles on skirmishes fought long ago, with different men and different weapons. Hannibal's tactic of employing elephants in the Alps is no longer logistically brilliant. Were life's lessons so literal, life itself would be simple; we could lounge back and watch reruns of history. It is also true that all trials but life itself are ephemeral. A nation, like an individual, can find redemption in suffering. But for America it was delayed beyond Herbert Hoover's term. It is more important, in the end, to conquer oneself than to conquer a city, and in this, Hoover succeeded.

A good case can be made that Hoover was a near-great president because he managed insurmountable problems with a dedication and deftness that no one else electable in 1928 could have achieved. If one leaps to the conclusion that Franklin Roosevelt could have done better, it is only realistic to concede that in 1928 Roosevelt was no more electable than Al Smith. In fact, he could not even have won the Democratic nomination. Like all presidents, Hoover had weaknesses, but perhaps after all he was the right man in the right place for his times. Certainly the country could hardly have leaped the gorge from Coolidge to the New Deal without Hoover in between, and Roosevelt's bag of tricks fared hardly better than Hoover's over a longer period, despite enormous congressional majorities and vast appropriations. Also, unlike the Hoover years, the New Deal was flawed by waste, corruption, and the return of the spoils system. Hoover's great achievement was that he held the nation together, preserving the essence of its system of government while expanding its scope, and handed it over to his successor intact. What might have happened during a second term, or during his first term without a depression, is less important than what actually did happen, which is enough to justify his place in history. Further, Hoover's public service did not begin or end at the White House door. He continued to be a productive public servant to his country—and to the world—for the remainder of his life. He was one of the most unselfish public servants in American history and, in his own unique way, one of the great lovers of his time. A person, or a people, who is tested and endure, is stronger than those who are never tested at all. Hoover led unpretentiously, by example, while the decibel level rose around him, with restrained dignity, in the eye of the storm. He accepted criticism, though he did not enjoy it, and never paid back insults, however invidious. He was a man of principle, yet willing to change, within limits, as conditions changed. The president once offered up as the high prophet of material plenty, never considered material plenty the greatest prerequisite for happiness. There had been, he knew, indigent Saints and miserable kings. He stretched government further than he wanted to, but he wanted the changes he produced to be temporary, not permanent. He was willing to do what had to be done, but gratuitous change, any more than gratuitous language, was not in his lexicon. Hoover bonded with people, but his greatest bond was with his country, which gave a poor orphan boy from an obscure Iowa village the opportunity to become president, a debt he repaid in full. The stress or violence of the presidency in times of discord brought early deaths to Lincoln, Wilson, Roosevelt, and Lyndon Johnson. Hoover, however, lived long with the memories, ever trying to understand them.

Notes

Prologue

1. *Chicago Daily News*, Feb. 21, 1929, Clipping File (hereafter CF), Herbert Hoover Presidential Library (hereafter HHPL), West Branch, IA; Maude Stratton, *Herbert Hoover's Home Town: The Story of West Branch* (1948; Wichita, KS: Macy Genealogy Project, 2000), 154; Mitchell V. Charnley, *The Boy's Life of Herbert Hoover* (New York, 1931), 264.
2. David Burner, *Herbert Hoover: A Public Life* (New York, 1979), 6; Martin Fausold, *The Presidency of Herbert C. Hoover* (Lawrence, KS, 1985), 1–3; Stratton, *Herbert Hoover's Home Town*, 62.
3. Fausold, *The Presidency of Herbert C. Hoover*, 3–4.
4. Herbert Hoover, *Hoover after Dinner* (New York, 1933), 125–32; Eugene Lyons, *Herbert Hoover: A Biography* (Garden City, NY, 1964), 6–7; Herbert Hoover to Lewis L. Strauss, Presidential Papers (hereafter PP), Subject File (hereafter SF), Box 1, Christmas, 1933, HHPL. In this letter Hoover describes his Quaker beliefs in impressive detail.
5. Hoover to Strauss, Christmas, 1933; Fausold, *The Presidency of Herbert C. Hoover*, 4; Marian M. McGregor, "The Early Environment of Herbert Hoover," 3–6, in PCP, SF, Box 25, Articles about or by Herbert Hoover, HHPL.
6. Burner, *A Public Life*, 6–7, 11–12; Hoover, *Hoover after Dinner*, 126–33; Kendrick A. Clements, *Hoover, Conservation, and Consumerism: Engineering the Good Life* (Lawrence, KS: 2000), 11.
7. Burner, *A Public Life*, 10–11; George H. Nash, *The Life of Herbert Hoover: The Engineer, 1874–1914* (New York, 1983), 8–12; Clements, *Hoover, Conservation, and Consumerism*, 13; Harold Wolfe, *Herbert Hoover: Public Servant and Leader of the Loyal Opposition* (New York, 1956), 15; Richard Norton Smith, *An Uncommon Man: The Triumph of Herbert Hoover* (New York, 1984), 65–66.
8. Nash, *The Life of Herbert Hoover: The Engineer*, 13–17; Burner, *A Public Life*, 13–16; Charnley, *The Boys' Life of Herbert Hoover*, 52–53.
9. Joan Hoff, *Herbert Hoover: Forgotten Progressive* (Boston, 1975), 10–11; Hal Elliott Wert, *Hoover, the Fishing President: Portrait of the Private Man and His Life Outdoors* (Mechanicsburg, PA, 2005), 46; Wolfe, *Public Servant*, 17.
10. Burner, *A Public Life*, 18–19; George H. Nash, *Herbert Hoover and Stanford University* (Stanford, CA, 1988), xi–xii, 15–19; Charnley, *The Boys' Life of Herbert Hoover*, 67–70; Hoff, *Forgotten Progressive*, 11; Ray Lyman Wilbur, "Herbert Hoover: A Personal Sketch," 6–7, Pre-Commerce Papers (PCP), SF, Box 26, Articles about or by Herbert Hoover, HHPL.

11. Nancy Beck Young, *Lou Henry Hoover: Activist First Lady* (Lawrence, KS, 2004), 7–12.

12. Young, *Activist First Lady*, 12.

13. Hoff, *Forgotten Progressive*, 12–13; Wolfe, *Public Servant*, 19–20; Wert, *The Fishing President*, 69; "American Romances—II, Herbert Clark Hoover," *The Delineator*, March 1920, p. 8, PCP, SF, Box 32, HHPL.

14. Burner, *A Public Life*, 28–32; Nash, *Hoover and Stanford University*, 2; J. W. Kirwan, "Hoover in Western Australia, Some Goldfield Memories," abbreviated from an article in the *Western Australian*, p. 1, PCP, SF, Box 25, Articles about Hoover in Western Australia, HHPL.

15. Wolfe, *Public Servant*, 21–22; Young, *Activist First Lady*, 13.

16. Young, *Activist First Lady*, 13–15; Burner, *A Public Life*, 36–37.

17. Wert, *The Fishing President*, 71–73; Wolfe, *Public Servant*, 23–24; Herbert Hoover, "History, June 17th to 23rd, 1900 [an account of the Boxer Rebellion siege]," 1–11, PCP, SF, Box 30, China—Boxer Rebellion, HHPL; Dale Mayer, *Lou Henry Hoover: A Prototype for First Ladies* (Hauppauge, NY, 2004), 106.

18. Burner, *A Public Life*, 49; Nash, *Hoover and Stanford University*, 23; Hoff, *Forgotten Progressive*, 14–15.

19. Wilbur, "Hoover: A Personal Sketch," 19; Hoff, *Forgotten Progressive*, 14–17; Wolfe, *Public Servant*, 30; Burner, *A Public Life*, 52; "Hoover's Seven American Business Pilgrimages," *The Magazine of Business* (April 1928), 1–6, CP, SF, Box 268, Hoover, Herbert, Biography, 1928, HHPL; Burma Corporation, *Limited Report*, reprinted from *The Mining World*, Nov. 13, 1915, PCP, SF, Box 50, Mining—Burma Corporation, Ltd, 1914–1920, HHPL.

20. Clements, *Hoover, Conservation, and Consumerism*, 28; Wolfe, *Public Servant*, 36–37; Wert, *The Fishing President*, 91.

21. Nash, *The Life of Herbert Hoover: The Humanitarian, 1914–1917* (New York, 1988), 29–33, 86–96, 124; Burner, *A Public Life*, 72–83, 94; Speech by Lou Henry Hoover on the CRB, Oct. 1915, PCP, SF, Box 32, HHPL.

22. Nash, *The Life of Herbert Hoover: The Humanitarian*, 96.

23. Johnson Brigham, "Herbert C. Hoover, Mining Engineer—World Promoter—Philanthropist—Chief Conserver of the Nation's Food Resources," May 15, 1918, pp. 7–8, PCP, SF, Box 26, Articles About or by Herbert Hoover, HHPL; Wilbur, "Hoover: A Personal Sketch," 19; George H. Nash, *The Life of Herbert Hoover: Master of Emergencies, 1917–1918* (New York, 1996), 34–40; Ray Lyman Wilbur, *The Memoirs of Ray Lyman Wilbur*, eds. Edgar Eugene Robinson and Paul Carroll Edwards (Stanford, CA, 1960), 260–61.

24. Nash, *The Life of Herbert Hoover: Master of Emergencies*, 465–504; Wolfe, *Public Servant*, 52–53, 73–79; Burner, *A Public Life*, 114–30; David Hinshaw, *Herbert Hoover: American Quaker* (New York, 1950), 108–17; Vance McCormick Diary, Paris Peace Conference, 1919, pp. 47, 83–117, PCP, SF, Box 48, HHPL.

25. Herbert Hoover, *The Memoirs of Herbert Hoover*, vol. 2, *The Cabinet and the Presidency, 1920–1933* (New York, 1952), 10–12; Memorandum presented by Hoover to Democratic leaders on Nov. 19, 1919; Hoover interview with *Washington Star*, March 18, 1920; and Extract from Hoover address at Johns Hopkins University, Feb. 23, 1920, all in *Some Notes on the League of Nations* [n. d.], CP, SF, Box 365, League of Nations, 1920, HHPL; Royal J. Schmidt, "Hoover's Reflections on the Versailles Treaty," in *Herbert Hoover: The Great War and the Aftermath, 1914–1923*, ed. Lawrence E. Gelfand (Iowa City, IA, 1979), 61–83; Burner, *A Public Life*, 149; Herbert Hoover, *The Ordeal of Woodrow Wilson* (New York, 1958). Hoover, as a former president, is on the whole sympathetic to Wilson.

26. Gary Dean Best, "The Hoover-for President Boom of 1920," *Mid-America* 35, no. 4 (Oct. 1971), 227–22, PP, SF, Box 74, 1920 Press & Public Opinion, Hoover Institution Archives, Stanford University; [no author], "New Man for a New Era," *Saturday Evening Post* (April 24, 1920), 29; Wilbur, *Memoirs*, 374–76; Louis W. Liebovich, *Bylines in Despair: Herbert Hoover, the Great Depression, and the U.S. News Media* (Westport, CT: 1994), 14–17.

27. Hoff, *Forgotten Progressive*, 78–80; Wolfe, *Public Servant*, 89–91.

28. Hoff, *Forgotten Progressive*, 80; Liebovich, *Bylines in Despair*, 30; Wolfe, *Public Servant*, 92. Hoover commented to his press secretary that after attending one poker party he would not go again. See *Theodore G. Joslin Diaries*, Box 10, File 7, HHPL. On May 11, 1921, Hoover

wrote Harding that one of the first priorities of the new administration should be to plan a naval disarmament conference in Washington. Harding responded that he would take the initiative. See Hoover to Harding, May 11, 1921, and Harding to Hoover, May 14, 1921, in CP, SF, Box 480, President Harding, 1921, May–June, HHPL. Harding asked Hoover to draft memos he could send out as replies to policy questions. See George B. Christian Jr. to Hoover, April 14, 1921, Commerce Papers (CP), SF, Box 480. Harding accepted Hoover's recommendation for appointment of director of the census. See Hoover to Harding, April 26, 1921; George B. Christian Jr. to Hoover, April 29, 1921, both in CP, SF, Box 480, President Harding, 1921, April, HHPL. Hoover's suggestions for appointments as Commissioner of Internal Revenue and Director of the War Finance Corporation were also approved by the president. See Hoover to Harding, March 17, 1921; Hoover to Harding, March 23, 1921; and George B. Christian to Hoover, March 24, 1921, all in CP, SF, Box 480, President Harding, 1921, March, HHPL.

29. Hoff, *Forgotten Progressive*, 122–23. Hoover and Coolidge became friends while Coolidge was vice president. In Nov. 1921, Coolidge invited Hoover to use the vice president's room any time he was on the Senate side of the Capitol, and Hoover accepted. See Coolidge to Hoover, Nov. 10, 1921, and Hoover to Coolidge, Nov. 15, 1921. CP, SF, Vice President Coolidge, Nov. 1921, HHPL. Coolidge asked Hoover to handle the coal crisis in 1923, and Hoover drafted a memorandum for the president entitled "The Anthracite Coal Situation." See Memo, Aug. 11, 1923, CP, SF, Box 476, President Coolidge, Aug.–Sep., 1923, HHPL. In response to a man who complained about the price of coal to Coolidge, Coolidge's Secretary, C. B. Slemp, referred the letter to Hoover, who wrote a letter for Coolidge to sign. See Hoover to C. B. Slemp, Oct. 22, 1923 in CP, SF, Box 476, President Coolidge, Oct. 1923, HHPL.

30. Hoover was instrumental in drafting the Republican platform in 1924, especially as it affected the Western states and the issue of water power. See Hoover to Charles B. Warren, June 10, 1924, CP, SF, Box 515, Republican National News Services, 1921–1923, and Undated, HHPL. Hoover ghostwrote passages to be inserted in Coolidge's speeches pertaining to Muscle Shoals and development of the Colorado River and the St. Lawrence Seaway. See CP, SF, Box 476, President Coolidge, 1923–Nov., HHPL.

31. Burner, *A Public Life*, 163–64.

32. Ibid., 166–67; Fausold, *The Presidency of Herbert C. Hoover*, 120; Hoff, *Forgotten Progressive*, 94. Burner considers the Conference on Unemployment a constructive and an incremental move in countercyclical measures.

33. Hoff, *Forgotten Progressive*, 85–86, 103–5, 110–14; Fausold, *The Presidency of Herbert C. Hoover*, 16–17; Wolfe, *Public Servant*, 96–100; Burner, *A Public Life*, 146, 159–61, 168–71; Ray Lyman Wilbur and Arthur Mastick Hyde, *The Hoover Policies* (New York, 1937), 102–15.

34. Hoover, *Memoirs*, vol. 2, 28–29; Wolfe, *Public Servant*, 101–2; Burner, *A Public Life*, 174; Fausold, *The Presidency of Herbert C. Hoover*, 120–21.

35. Hoover, *Memoirs*, vol. 2, 334–35; Edward Eyre Hunt to Lawrence Richey, May 1, 1935, Hoover Presidential Papers, Box 335, Hoover Archives, Stanford University; Maury Klein, *Rainbow's End: The Crash of 1929* (New York, 2001), 142; Burner, *A Public Life*, 245–46.

36. Bruce Alan Lohof, "Herbert Hoover and the Mississippi Valley Flood of 1927: A Case Study of the Political Thought of Herbert Hoover" (PhD diss., Syracuse University, 1968), 55, 95–96, 131–32, 165; Hoff, *Forgotten Progressive*, 115–16; John M. Barry, *Rising Tide: The Great Mississippi Flood of 1927 and How It Changed America* (New York, 1997), 262–66. Lohof is the best single source, because he focuses specifically on Hoover's role in flood rescue and relief. Barry is a more general, popular account of the flood as a whole.

37. Lohof, "Herbert Hoover and the Mississippi Valley Flood of 1927," 125–27; Barry, *Rising Tide*, 275–79; Hoover, *Memoirs*, vol. 2, 126.

38. Mrs. J. Gardner to Hoover, May 18, 1927; George Akerson to Garner, May 31, 1927; Hoover to Mrs. Paul L. Dennis, May 29, 1927, all in CP, SF, Box 396, Mississippi Valley Flood Relief Work, Misc., May 16–20, HHPL; New Orleans *Item-Tribune*, May 22, 1927,

in CP, SF, Box 396; Hoover Speech on Flood, June 11, 1927, in CP, SF, Box 397; Hoover to
Frederick J. Haskin, Dec. 13, 1927, in CP, SF, Box 397, Sep.–Dec., HHPL.

39. Lohof, "Herbert Hoover and the Mississippi Valley Flood of 1927," 186–91; Statement
of Hoover to the Press, June 14, 1927, CP, SF, Box 397, June 11–30, HHPL; Hoover to
Frederick J. Haskin, Dec. 13, 1927, CP, SF, Box 397, Sep.–Dec., HHPL; Clements, *Hoover,
Conservation, and Consumerism*, 117.

Chapter 1

1. Quotes are in William Allen White, *A Puritan in Babylon: The Story of Calvin Coolidge* (New
York, 1965), 359–61. See also Louis W. Liebovich, *Bylines in Despair: Herbert Hoover, the
Great Depression, and the U.S. News Media* (Westport, CT, 1994), 57–58; Martin L. Fausold,
The Presidency of Herbert C. Hoover (Lawrence, KS, 1985), 30.

2. David Burner, *Herbert Hoover: A Public Life* (New York, 1979), 190; Glen Jeansonne, *A Time
of Paradox: America from Awakening to Hiroshima, 1890–1945* (Lanham, MD, 2007), 138;
John M. Barry, *Rising Tide: The Great Mississippi Flood of 1927 and How It Changed America*
(New York, 1997), 262; Maury Klein, *Rainbow's End: The Crash of 1929* (New York, 2001),
241.

3. James H. MacLafferty Diary, March 4, 1929, Box 1, Herbert Hoover Presidential Library,
West Branch, Iowa (hereafter HHPL). Copyright Stanford University. MacLafferty wrote
his impressions after the fact, not necessarily at the time they occurred.

4. Craig Lloyd, *Aggressive Introvert: Herbert Hoover and Public Relations Management, 1912–
1932* (Columbus, OH, 1972), 84–85.

5. Joan Hoff, *Herbert Hoover: Forgotten Progressive* (Boston, 1975), 125–26; Harold Wolfe,
Herbert Hoover: Public Servant and Leader of the Loyal Opposition (New York, 1956), 114–15;
Liebovich, *Bylines in Despair*, 59.

6. Dale Carnegie to Hoover, Dec. 15, 1927, Commerce File (hereafter CP), Subject File (SF),
Box 78, Carnegie, Dale, 1927, HHPL.

7. Liebovich, *Bylines in Despair*, 60.

8. Lloyd, *Aggressive Introvert*, 79–80.

9. Roy V. Peel and Thomas C. Donnelly, *The 1928 Campaign: An Analysis* (New York, 1931),
7–9, 14.

10. Fausold, *The Presidency of Herbert C. Hoover*, 33; *New York Times*, Dec. 12, 1927, Clipping
File (hereafter CF), HHPL.

11. MacLafferty Diary, Box 1, March 4, 1929, HHPL.

12. Lloyd, *Aggressive Introvert*, 85.

13. Lloyd, *Aggressive Introvert*, 95–96.

14. Fausold, *The Presidency of Herbert C. Hoover*, 34.

15. Donald R. McCoy, "To the White House, Herbert Hoover, Aug. 1927–March 1929," in *The
Hoover Presidency: A Reappraisal*, eds. Martin L. Fausold and George T. Mazuzan (Albany,
NY, 1974), 30.

16. Hoover Biographical Draft, 1928, p. 8, CP, SF, Box 8, HHPL.

17. Harris Gaylord Warren, *Herbert Hoover and the Great Depression* (New York, 1967), 32;
Liebovich, *Bylines in Despair*, 49–50.

18. Ray Lyman Wilbur, *The Memoirs of Ray Lyman Wilbur*, eds. Edgar Eugene Robinson and
Paul Carroll Edwards (Stanford, CA, 1960), 387–89; Herbert Hoover, *The Memoirs of Herbert Hoover*, vol. 2, *The Cabinet and the Presidency, 1920–1933* (New York, 1952), 191–94.

19. Lloyd, *Aggressive Introvert*, 96.

20. Wilbur, *Memoirs*, 388.

21. Telegram, D. W. Griffith to Mark L. Requa, April 20, 1928, CP, SF, Box 273, Hoover,
Herbert, Presidency, 1923–1928 and undated, HHPL.

22. *Chicago Daily News*, Jan. 5, 1928, CF, HHPL; Jackson, Michigan, *Citizen Patriot*, Sep. 7,
1927, CP, SF, Box 273, Hoover, Herbert, Presidency, 1923–1928, HHPL.

23. Statement by James R. Howard, undated prenomination endorsement, 1928, CP, SF, Box 273, Hoover, Herbert, Presidency, 1923–1928, and undated, HHPL.

24. Katherine Langley, Congresswoman from Kentucky, undated prenomination endorsement, CP, SF, Box 273, Hoover, Herbert, Presidency, 1923–1928, and undated, HHPL.

25. Statement by C. D. Street, Republican National Committeeman of Alabama, Feb. 7, 1928, CP, SF, Box 273, Hoover, Herbert, Presidency, 1923–1928, and undated, HHPL.

26. Donald J. Lisio, *Hoover, Blacks, and Lily-Whites: A Study of Southern Strategies* (Chapel Hill, NC, 1985), 38–39; *Houston Informer*, Feb. 25, 1928, CP, SF, Box 2, Press Statements, Hoover's Nomination, HHPL; *Chicago Tribune*, Feb. 13, 1928, CF, HHPL.

27. Lisio, *Hoover, Blacks, and Lily-Whites*, 55.

28. Burner, *A Public Life*, 197–98.

29. CP, SF, Box 273, Hoover, Herbert, Presidency, 1923–1928, and undated, HHPL.

30. Statement by Professor Michael I. Pupin, CP, SF, Box 273, Hoover, Herbert, Presidency, 1923–1928, and undated, HHPL.

31. Statement by E. G. Pranter, CP, SF, Box 273, Hoover, Herbert, Presidency, 1923–1928, and undated, HHPL.

32. Silas Bent, "Herbert Hoover: A Political Portrait," *Outlook* 148, no. 8 (Feb. 22, 1928), 283–84.

33. Hoover to Borah, Feb. 23, 1928, CP, SF, Box 56, Borah, Senator William E., 1921–1928, and undated, HHPL.

34. "Hoover on Prohibition," *Outlook* 148, no. 10 (March 7, 1928), 374; *Portland Morning Oregonian*, Feb. 24, 1928, CP, SF, Box 484, Press Summaries, Hoover's Nomination, #1; *Chicago Daily News*, Feb. 24, 1928, CF, HHPL.

35. Dale Mayer, *Lou Henry Hoover: A Prototype for First Ladies* (Hauppauge, NY, 2004), 231–32.

36. *New York Herald-Examiner*, March 14, 1928, CF, HHPL

37. *Chicago Tribune*, May 22, 1928, CF, HHPL; Liebovich, *Bylines in Despair*, 59; *Chicago Daily News*, April 20, 1928, CF, HHPL.

38. "Mr. Hoover's Obstacles," *Outlook* 148, no. 16 (April 18, 1928), 609–10.

39. Eugene Lyons, *Herbert Hoover: A Biography* (Garden City, NY, 1964), 174.

40. Thomas H. Gammack, "A Wall Street View of Hoover," *Outlook* 149, no. 9 (June 27, 1928), 350.

41. "Mr. Hoover's Qualifications," *Outlook* 149, no. 9 (June 27, 1928), 350.

42. Legal Opinion, Irvine L. Lenroot, Dec. 5, 1927, CP, SF, Box 548, Lenroot, Irvine L., 1923–1927, HHPL.

43. *Chicago Daily News*, April 20, 1928, CF, HHPL.

44. Charles H. Betts to unmarked newspaper, June 6, 1928, CF, HHPL.

45. *New York Times*, Feb. 6, 1928, CF, HHPL; Hoover, *Memoirs*, vol. 2, 191; James W. Davis, *Presidential Primaries: Road to the White House* (Westport, CT, 1980), 295; Hal Elliott Wert, *Hoover, the Fishing President: Portrait of the Private Man and His Life Outdoors* (Mechanicsburg, PA, 2005), 148–50; McCoy, "To the White House," 33–34.

46. Coolidge to Mr. Prescott of Massachusetts, April 20, 1928, CP, SF, Box 479, President Coolidge, 1928, March–June, HHPL.

47. Warren, *Hoover and the Great Depression*, 31.

48. Wolfe, *Public Servant*, 117.

49. Peel and Donnelly, *The 1928 Campaign*, 7–9, 14; Robert H. Ferrell, *The Presidency of Calvin Coolidge* (Lawrence, KS, 1998), 88–94.

50. Davis, *Presidential Primaries*, 45, 161–62, 295–98.

51. *Chicago Tribune*, May 11, 1928, CF, HHPL.

52. Burner, *A Public Life*, 200; Davis, *Presidential Primaries*, 295–98.

53. *Utica Observer-Dispatch*, n.d. [Feb. 1928]; *Binghamton Sun*, n.d. [Feb. 1928]; *Utica Press*, n.d. [Feb. 1928]; [Olean, NY] *Herald*, Feb. 22, 1928; *Endicott Bulletin*, Feb. 24, 1928; *Franklin Dairyman*, Feb. 3, 1928; CP, SF, Box 484, Press Summaries, Hoover's Nomination, #2.

54. *Chicago Tribune*, May 23, 1928; *Chicago Daily News*, Jan. 25, March 25, 1928, CF, HHPL.

55. *Chicago Tribune*, June 8, 1928; *Chicago Daily News*, June 9, 1928, CF HHPL; Edgar Rickard Diary, June 11, 1928, Box 1, "1928," HHPL.

56. *Chicago Daily News*, June 7, 1928; *Chicago Tribune*, June 8, 1928; *Kansas City Star*, June 12, 1928; and *Kansas City Post*, June 13, 1928, all in CF, HHPL; Rickard Diary, June 12, 1928, Box 1, "1928." HHPL.

57. Unmarked clipping, Associated Press, Aug. 8, 1929, CF, HHPL.

58. *Chicago Daily News*, June 11, 1928, CF, HHPL; Helen B. Pryor, *Lou Henry Hoover: Gallant First Lady* (New York, 1969), 151; Liebovich, *Bylines in Despair*, 72–73.

59. *Chicago Daily News*, June 13, 1928, CF, HHPL; Lisio, *Hoover, Blacks, and Lily-Whites*, 58–61.

60. *Chicago Daily News*, June 15, 1928; *Chicago Tribune*, June 15, 1928, CF, HHPL; E. S. Rochester, *Coolidge-Hoover-Work: An Intimate Review of an Epochal National Campaign for the Presidency of the United States* (Washington, DC, 1929), 48; *World Almanac and Book of Facts for 1929* (New York, 1929), 847.

61. *Chicago Tribune*, June 15, 16, 1928; *Kansas City Star*, June 17, 1928; and *New York Herald Tribune*, June 17, 1929, all in CF, HHPL; Rochester, *Coolidge-Hoover-Work*, 51–52.

62. *Chicago Daily News*, June 15, 1928, and *Chicago Tribune*, June 15, 16, 1928, both in CF, HHPL.

63. *Chicago Daily News*, June 15, 1928, and *Chicago Tribune*, June 16, 1928, both in CF, HHPL; Hoover, *Memoirs*, vol. 2, 195.

64. *Toledo Times*, June 29, 1928, CP, HHPL; *Washington Post*, July 1, 1928, Box 1, HHPF; Rochester, *Coolidge-Hoover-Work*, 51–52.

65. Rochester, *Coolidge-Hoover-Work*, 51–52; Nathan William MacChesney to Hoover, Nov. 7, 1928, Campaign and Transition Papers (hereafter C&TP), SF, Box 163, Hoover-Curtis Organization Bureau, Republican National Committee, HHPL; *Philadelphia Inquirer*, Aug. 26, 1928; *Chicago Tribune*, July 3, 5, 1928, CF, HHPL; Box 1, Work Scrapbook, HHPF.

66. *Chicago Daily News*, July 9, 10, 16, 17, 1928; *Chicago Tribune*, July 11, 13, 19, 1928, CF, HHPL.

67. *Chicago Daily News*, July 18, 20, 1928; *Chicago Tribune*, July 18, 19, 20, 1928, CF, HHPL; Pryor, *Gallant First Lady*, 151–52.

68. *Chicago Daily News*, July 23, 24, 1928; *Chicago Tribune*, July 26, 28, 1928, CF, HHPL.

69. Wert, *The Fishing President*, 161, 169–70; Wilbur, *Memoirs*, 306, 397–98; *Chicago Daily News*, July 31, Aug. 1, 1928; *Chicago Tribune*, Aug. 2, 1928; *New York Times*, Aug. 22, 1928, CF, HHPL.

70. Herbert Hoover, *The New Day: Campaign Speeches of Herbert Hoover, 1928* (Stanford, CA, 1928), 11–42; Wilton Eckley, *Herbert Hoover* (Boston, 1980), 62–64; *Chicago Daily News*, Aug. 13, 1928, CF, HHPL.

71. For Smith's portrait, I have drawn upon the excellent study by Robert A. Slayton, *Empire Statesman: The Rise and Redemption of Al Smith* (New York, 2001), though I differ with some conclusions. See also Burner, *A Public Life*, 200–201; Fausold, *The Presidency of Herbert C. Hoover*, 25; Wolfe, *Public Servant*, 120–23; and Lyons, *Herbert Hoover: A Biography*, 177–78.

72. Warren, *Hoover and the Great Depression*, 39–42; Burner, *A Public Life*, 204.

73. Unmarked clipping analyzing the campaign, probably *Chicago Daily News*; *Chicago Tribune*, Feb. 13, 1928, CF, HHPL; McCoy, "To the White House," 37–38.

74. Ed., *Christian Science Monitor*, Aug. 14, 1928, and *Chicago Daily News*, July 3, 1928, both in CF, HHPL.

75. *Chicago Daily News*, June 22, July 24, Oct. 13, 24, 1928; Ed., *Chicago Daily News*, Aug. 14, 1928, CF, HHPL; Burner, *A Public Life*, 207.

76. *Chicago Daily News*, Oct. 26, 1928, CF, HHPL; Robert Sobel, *Herbert Hoover at the Onset of the Great Depression, 1929–1930* (Philadelphia, 1975), 33; Burner, *A Public Life*, 204.

77. Press Release, "The National Negro Republican League—What it is and What it Stands for," Nov. 25, 1931, PP, SF, Box 106, Colored Quest., Corres., 1931, Sep.–Dec., HHPL; Lisio, *Hoover, Blacks, and Lily-Whites*, 61–71, 82–89, 108; Burner, *A Public Life*, 196.

78. *Chicago Daily News*, Feb. 21, 22, 1928; Ed., *New York Herald Tribune*, Aug. 19, 1928; and Ed., *Washington Post*, Aug. 19, 1928, all in CF, HHPL.

79. *New York World*, Aug. 22, 1928; *New York Herald Tribune*, Aug. 24, 1928; *Chicago Daily News*, Aug. 23, 24, 1928; *Chicago Tribune*, Aug. 22, 23, 24, 1928; and *Washington Times*, Aug. 23, 1928, all in CF, HHPL; Hoover, *The New Day*, 46–50.

80. *Chicago Daily News*, Sep. 18, 1929, CF, HHPL.
81. *Chicago Daily News*, Sep. 18, 1928; Ed., *Chicago Daily News*, Sep. 18, 1928; and *Chicago Tribune*, Sep. 19, 1928, all in CF, HHPL; Hoover, *The New Day*, 62–85; Eckley, *Hoover*, 64–65.
82. *Chicago Daily News*, Oct. 6, 16, 1928; Ed., *Chicago Daily News*, undated [Oct. 1928]; *Chicago Tribune*, Oct. 6, 1928; and *Washington Star*, Oct. 3, 1928, all in CF, HHPL; Hoover, *The New Day*, 88–110.
83. *Chicago Daily News*, Oct. 15, 16, 1928; Ed., *Chicago Daily News*, Oct. 16, 1928; and *Chicago Tribune*, Oct. 16, 1928, all in CF, HHPL; Hoover, *The New Day*, 115–45; Eckley, *Hoover*, 66.
84. *Chicago Daily News*, Oct. 22, 23, 1928; Ed., *Chicago Daily News*, Oct. 23, 1928; *Chicago Tribune*, Oct. 21, 1928; and *Washington Post*, Oct. 23, 1928, all in CF, HHPL; Hoover, *The New Day*, 148–76; Eckley, *Hoover*, 66–68.
85. *Chicago Daily News*, Nov. 2, 3, 1928; and *Chicago Tribune*, Nov. 2, 3, 1928, all in CF, HHPL; Eckley, *Hoover*, 68–69; *The New Day*, 178–208. Quotation from *The New Day*, 207.
86. Liebovich, *Bylines in Despair*, 65–68; Clair Everet Nelsen, "The Image of Hoover as Reflected in the American Press" (PhD diss., Stanford University, 1956), 56, and *Chicago Daily News*, Aug. 16, 1928, and *Chicago Tribune*, June 13, 1928, both in CF, HHPL.
87. Liebovich, *Bylines in Despair*, 72–74; Wilbur, *Memoirs*, 399.
88. *Philadelphia Public Ledger*, July 31, 1928; *New York Herald Tribune*, Oct. 12, 1928; *Chicago Tribune*, Sep. 13, Oct. 24, 1928; *Chicago Daily News*, Nov. 3, 1928; Ed., *Chicago Daily News*, undated clipping, CF, HHPL; Hubert Work Scrapbook, Box 1, HHPF; McCoy, "To the White House," 39–40; Claude M. Fuess, *Calvin Coolidge: The Man from Vermont* (Boston, 1940), 430.
89. Pryor, *Gallant First Lady*, 149–55; Nancy Beck Young, *Lou Henry Hoover: Activist First Lady* (Lawrence, KS, 2004), 43–48; Mayer, *A Prototype for First Ladies*, 240; *Chicago Daily News*, Aug. 22, Oct. 29, 1928; *Chicago Tribune*, Aug. 1, Oct. 22, Nov. 9, 1929, CF, HHPL.
90. Hoover, *The New Day*, 210–14; Liebovich, *Bylines in Despair*, 72; *Chicago Daily News*, Nov. 6, 1928, CF, HHPL.
91. George H. Nash, *Herbert Hoover and Stanford University* (Stanford, CA, 1988), 91–92; *Chicago Daily News*, Nov. 6, 7, 1928; Ed., *Chicago Daily News*, Nov. 7, 1928, CF, HHPL.
92. Fausold, *The Presidency of Herbert C. Hoover*, 30; Mayer, *A Prototype for First Ladies*, 241; David M. Kennedy, *Freedom from Fear: The American People in Depression and War, 1929–1945* (New York, 1999), 32; Lisio, *Hoover, Blacks, and Lily-Whites*, 90–92; Ed., *Chicago Daily News*, undated, CF, HHPL; Ed., *Washington Post*, Nov. 8, 1928, CF, HHPL.
93. *Congress, Senate, Presidential Campaign Expenditures, Senate Report 204*, 70th Cong., 2d. sess. (Washington, DC, 1929), 26–31; MacLafferty Diary, Box 1, April 2, 1932, HHPL,
94. Quote from *Washington Post*, Nov. 8, 1928, CF, HHPL; Mark Sullivan, "Personal Quality Wins for Hoover," *New York Herald Tribune*, undated, CF, HHPL; Liebovich, *Bylines in Despair*, 75–76.
95. Quote from *Chicago Daily News*, Nov. 8, 1928. See also *Chicago Daily News*, Nov. 7, 1928, CF, HHPL. Hoover's remarks are also carried in Hoover, *The New Day*, 217.

Chapter 2

1. *Chicago Daily News*, July 19, 1929; *Chicago Tribune*, Nov. 10, 1928; and Unmarked clipping, all in Clipping File (hereafter CF), Herbert Hoover Presidential Library (hereafter HHPL), West Branch, IA; Alexander DeConde, *Herbert Hoover's Latin American Policy* (Stanford, CA, 1951), 15–17; Robert H. Ferrell, *American Diplomacy in the Great Depression: Hoover-Stimson Foreign Policy, 1929–1933* (New Haven, CT, 1957), 217; Martin L. Fausold, *The Presidency of Herbert C. Hoover* (Lawrence, KS, 1985), 183–85.
2. Fausold, *The Presidency of Herbert C. Hoover*, 183–85; William Starr Myers, *The Foreign Policies of Herbert Hoover, 1929–1933* (New York, 1940), 43–49.
3. DeConde, *Hoover's Latin American Policy*, 20–27; David Burner, *Herbert Hoover: A Public Life* (New York, 1979), 286.

4. *Chicago Daily News*, Dec. 12, 14, 17, 1928; and *Chicago Tribune*, Dec. 14, 15, 1928, all in CF, HHPL: Burner, *A Public Life*, 286.

5. *Chicago Tribune*, Dec. 17, 18, 1928; *Chicago Daily News*, Dec. 18, 1928, CF, HHPL.

6. *Chicago Daily News*, Dec. 21, 1928; Ed., *Chicago Daily News*, Dec. 4, 1928; and *Chicago Tribune*, Dec. 22, 24, 1928, all in CF, HHPL; DeConde, *Hoover's Latin American Policy*, 24.

7. Ferrell, *American Diplomacy in the Great Depression*, 215–17; Republican National Committee, *The Hoover Administration: Its Policies and Its Achievements in the First Sixteen Months*, Presidential Papers (hereafter PP), Subject File (hereafter SF), Box 55, Accomp. of the Admin., 1931, HHPL; *Chicago Daily News*, Dec. 22, 26, 31, 1928; Jan. 9, 1929; and *Chicago Tribune*, Dec. 28, 29, 1928, all in CF, HHPL.

8. Fausold, *The Presidency of Herbert C. Hoover*, 33–34; *Chicago Tribune*, Dec. 16, 1928; Jan. 7, 1929; *Chicago Daily News*, Dec. 26, 1928; Jan. 9, 1929, CF, HHPL.

9. Hal Elliott Wert, *Hoover, the Fishing President: Portrait of the Private Man and His Life Outdoors* (Mechanicsburg, PA, 2005), 177–80; *Chicago Tribune*, Jan. 21, 22, 28, 29, 30, 1929; *Chicago Daily News*, Jan. 24, 28, 29; Feb. 14, 1929, CF, HHPL.

10. *Chicago Daily News*, Feb. 20, 21, 1929; *Chicago Tribune*, Feb. 21, 1929, CF, HHPL.

11. David Hinshaw, *Herbert Hoover: American Quaker* (New York, 1950), 182; *Chicago Daily News*, Jan. 21, 1929, CF, HHPL.

12. John O. Hart to Hoover, Feb. 5, 1929, PP, SF, Box 92, Cabinet, The, Corres., 1929.

13. W. E. Cummings to Hoover, Feb. 9, 1929, PP, SF, Box 92, Cabinet, The, Corres., 1929.

14. *Chicago Daily News*, Jan. 11, 12, Feb. 13, 14, 15, 19, 20, 22, 1929, and *Chicago Tribune*, Jan. 8, Feb. 11, 1929, all in CF, HHPL; Burner, *A Public Life*, 209–10.

15. *Chicago Daily News*, Feb. 20, 1929, CF, HHPL.

16. The portraits of Hoover's friends are gleaned from Frederic William Wile, "The Hoover Era," *World's Work* 8, no. 3 (April 1929), 42–45, 156–58, 162–63, Reprint File (hereafter RF), HHPL.

17. *Chicago Daily News*, Feb. 7, 20, 28, 1929, CF, HHPL; J. Joseph Huthmacher and Warren I. Susman, eds., *Herbert Hoover and the Crisis of American Capitalism* (Cambridge, MA, 1973), 38; Burner, *A Public Life*, 166; Fausold, *The Presidency of Herbert Hoover*, 33.

18. *New York Jewish Tribune*, Nov. 16, 1929, Campaign and Transition Papers (hereafter C&TP), SF, Box 160, Jews, HHPL.

19. Harris Gaylord Warren, *Herbert Hoover and the Great Depression* (New York, 1967), 4.

20. *New York Times*, May 12, 1929, CF, HHPL.

21. "Hoover Halfway," *Time* 17, no. 9 (March 2, 1931), 12.

22. *The Memoirs of Herbert Hoover*, vol. 2, *The Cabinet and the Presidency, 1920–1933* (New York, 1952), 233.

23. Maury Klein, *Rainbow's End: The Crash of 1929* (New York, 2001), 5.

24. Ed., "The Trend of Events," *Outlook and Independent* 151, no. 12 (March 20, 1929), 450–51.

25. *San Bernardino Telegram*, Sep. 4, 1929, CF, HHPL.

26. *Herbert Hoover, Hoover after Dinner* (New York, 1933), 10.

27. Dale Mayer, *Lou Henry Hoover: A Prototype for First Ladies* (Hauppauge, NY, 2004), 242. The quote is also included in Burner, *A Public Life*, 211, and Richard Norton Smith, *An Uncommon Man: The Triumph of Herbert Hoover* (New York, 1984), 103. Willis recollected the conversation in the *Christian Science Monitor*, Nov. 27, 1932.

28. *Chicago Daily News*, March 2, 1929, CF, HHPL; Fausold, *The Presidency of Herbert C. Hoover*, 40–41.

29. Hoover, *Memoirs*, vol. 2, 222; Theodore G. Joslin, *Hoover off the Record* (Garden City, NY, 1934), 28–29; Fausold, *The Presidency of Herbert C. Hoover*, 39–40; Harold Wolfe, *Herbert Hoover: Public Servant and Leader of the Loyal Opposition* (New York, 1956), 129–30; Louis W. Liebovich, *Bylines in Despair: Herbert Hoover, the Great Depression, and the U.S. News Media* (Westport, CT, 1994), 89; Helen B. Pryor, *Lou Henry Hoover: Gallant First Lady* (New York, 1969), 163–66; Nancy Beck Young, *Lou Henry Hoover: Activist First Lady* (Lawrence, KS, 2004), 5.

30. Hoover, *Memoirs*, vol. 2, 219; Fausold, *The Presidency of Herbert C. Hoover*, 34–37; *Illinois State Journal*, March 3, 1929, PP, SF, Box 92, Cabinet, The, Corres., 1929, HHPL; Joan

Hoff, *Herbert Hoover: Forgotten Progressive* (Boston, 1975), 134; Fausold, *The Presidency of Herbert C. Hoover*, 37.

31. Theodore G. Joslin Diary, Box 10, File 7, Aug. 27, 1931; Jan. 20, 1932, HHPL.
32. Klein, *Rainbow's End*, 68–71; Joslin Diary, Feb. 4, 1932, HHPL; *New York Times*, Feb. 4, 1932, CF, HHPL.
33. *New York Herald Tribune*, Sep. 15, 1929, CF, HHPL; Ed., "Back in Washington," *Outlook and Independent* 151, no. 10 (March 6, 1929), 30; James H. MacLafferty Diary, Box 1, March 1, 1929, HHPL; Burner, *A Public Life*, 209.
34. Fausold, *The Presidency of Herbert C. Hoover*, 37; Robert Sobel, *Herbert Hoover at the Onset of the Great Depression, 1929–1930* (Philadelphia, 1975), 28; MacLafferty Diary, March 1, 1929, HHPL; *New York Times*, Nov. 14, 1929, Dec. 7, 1929; *New York World*, Nov. 19, 1929; *New York Herald Tribune*, Nov. 21, 1929; Unmarked clipping, Associated Press, July 7, 1929; Unmarked clipping, Aug. 8, 1929, all in CF, HHPL.
35. Fausold, *The Presidency of Herbert C. Hoover*, 35–36; Ray Lyman Wilbur, *The Memoirs of Ray Lyman Wilbur*, eds. Edgar Eugene Robinson and Paul Carroll Edwards (Stanford, CA, 1960), 403–8; *New York Post*, Aug. 13, 1929, CF, HHPL; PP, SF, Box 93, Cabinet, The, Corres., 1930–1933, HHPL; Wolfe, *Public Servant*, 128.
36. *New York Times*, Aug. 4, 1932; *New York Evening Post*, July 30, 1929; and *New York Herald Tribune*, Sep. 15, 1929, all in CF, HHPL; *Illinois State Journal*, March 3, 1929, PP, SF, Box 92, Cabinet, The, Corres., 1929; Hoover to Robert P. Lamont, Aug. 9, 1932, PP, SF, Box 93, Cabinet, The, Corres., 1930–1933, HHPL; Fausold, *The Presidency of Herbert C. Hoover*, 36, 45; Warren, *Hoover and the Great Depression*, 55; Joslin Diary, Box 10, File 7, April 23, 1932, HHPL; Ray Lyman Wilbur and Arthur Mastick Hyde, *The Hoover Policies* (New York, 1937), 537.
37. Wilbur, *Memoirs*, 542–43; Fausold, *The Presidency of Herbert C. Hoover*, 44–45; Memo on Cabinet Meetings, April 15, 1932, PP, SF, Box 93, Cabinet, The, Corres., 1930–1933; Lawrence Richey to Professor Kenneth Colegrove, Aug. 25, 1932, PP, SF, Box 93, Cabinet, The, Corres., 1930–1933, HHPL.
38. *New York Evening Post*, Sep. 26, 1931; *New York Times*, May 12, 1929; *Chicago Daily News*, April 14, 1929, CF, HHPL; Theodore G. Joslin, "Hoover's First Year," *World's Work* 59 (March 1930), 118; Joslin, *Hoover off the Record*, 79–80; Liebovich, *Bylines in Despair*, 84–85.
39. *New York Herald Tribune*, March 31, Aug. 25, 1932; and *New York Times*, Feb. 11, 1932, all in CF, HHPL.
40. Fausold, *The Presidency of Herbert C. Hoover*, 66; Warren, *Hoover and the Great Depression*, 12–13.
41. David E. Hamilton, *From New Day to New Deal: American Farm Policy from Hoover to Roosevelt, 1928–1933* (Chapel Hill, NC, 1991), 27–50.
42. *New York Times*, April 15, 16, 1929, CF, HHPL.
43. *New York Times*, April 15, 21, 1929; *New York World*, April 2, 1929; *Chicago Daily News*, June 15, 1929; and *Chicago Tribune*, June 16, 1929, all in CF, HHPL; Edward Eyre Hunt, "Fight on the Depression: Phase I," book II, part 4 (1935), Box 335, Herbert Hoover Presidential File (Hoover Institution, Stanford University [hereafter HHPF]), 82–85; Albert U. Romasco, *The Poverty of Abundance: Hoover, the Nation, the Depression* (New York, 1968), 106–9; William J. Schaefle, "How President Hoover Serves His Country," *American Globe* (Oct. 1929), PP, SF, Box 55, Accomp. of the Admin., 1929, 5–13.
44. Hunt, "Fight on the Depression: Phase I," HHPF; *Chicago Daily News*, April 27, 1929, CF, HHPL; Clair Everet Nelsen, "The Image of Herbert Hoover as Reflected in the American Press" (PhD diss., Stanford University, 1956), 74–75; Victor L. Albjerg, "Hoover: The Presidency in Transition," *Current History* 39, no. 230 (May 1960), 215.
45. MacLafferty Diary, Address at Charleston, WV, Feb., 12, 1932, Box 1, HHPL.
46. *Chicago Daily News*, Sep. 24, 25, 29, 1929, all in CF, HHPL; Hoover, *Memoirs*, vol. 2, 293–94.
47. Jordan A. Schwarz, *The Interregnum of Despair: Hoover, Congress, and the Depression* (Urbana, IL, 1970), 6–11; Myers, *The Foreign Policies of Herbert Hoover*, 124–27; Romasco, *The Poverty of Abundance*, 215.

48. Warren, *Hoover and the Great Depression*, 85–87; Joslin, *Hoover off the Record*, 30–31; David M. Kennedy, *Freedom from Fear: The American People in Depression and War, 1929–1945* (New York, 1999), 49.

Chapter 3

1. George H. Nash, *The Life of Herbert Hoover: The Humanitarian, 1914–1917* (New York, 1988), 374–76; William Hard, "Hoover, the President," *World's Work* 58 (Sep. 1, 1929), 88; Donald Wilhelm, "Working with Hoover," *World's Work* (Aug. 16, 1928), 410–15, Reprint File (hereafter RF), Herbert Hoover Presidential Library (hereafter HHPL).
2. Theodore G. Joslin, *Hoover off the Record* (Garden City, NY, 1934), 192–95.
3. Craig Lloyd, *Aggressive Introvert: Herbert Hoover and Public Relations Management, 1912–1932* (Columbus, OH, 1972), 19, 75–77.
4. Joslin, *Hoover off the Record*, 77–78.
5. Eugene Lyons, "The Little-Known Side of Herbert Hoover," *Family Weekly* (Aug. 9, 1964), unpaginated, RF, HHPL.
6. Wilhelm, "Working With Hoover," 415.
7. Lyons, "The Little-Known Side of Herbert Hoover," unpaginated.
8. *New York Herald Tribune*, Oct. 5, 1931; *New York Times*, Nov. 3, 1931, Clipping File (hereafter CF), HHPL.
9. *New York Times*, Nov. 12, 1931; *Washington Herald*, Dec. 13, 1931, CF, HHPL.
10. Harris Gaylord Warren, *Herbert Hoover and the Great Depression* (New York, 1967), 56.
11. *Chicago Daily News*, Sep. 3, 1929, CF, HHPL; Carl N. Degler, "The Ordeal of Herbert Hoover," *Yale Review* 52 (June 1963), 578, RF, HHPL.
12. Theodore G. Joslin Diary, Box 10, File 7, Jan. 3, 1932, HHPL; Joslin, *Hoover off the Record*, 4; *New York Times*, April 19, 1932; *New York World*, Jan. 29, 1930, CF, HHPL.
13. *New York Herald Tribune*, Sep. 22, 1932, CF, HHPL.
14. Anne O'Hare McCormick, [untitled clipping], *New York Times Magazine* (Feb. 5, 1933), 1, RF, HHPL.
15. Joslin, *Hoover off the Record*, 16.
16. Henry F. Pringle, "The President," *New Yorker* (Dec. 27, 1930), 23; Edward G. Lowry, "Mr. Hoover at Work and Play," *Saturday Evening Post* 202, no. 9 (Aug. 31, 1929), 39–40; Edwin Balmer and William B. Crawford, "When You Meet the President," *Redbook* 58 (March 1932), 115, RF, HHPL.
17. Lowry, "Mr. Hoover at Work and Play," 40.
18. Ibid., 42.
19. Ibid., 40; Hard, "Hoover, the President," 104.
20. Nash, *The Life of Herbert Hoover: The Humanitarian*, 369.
21. Herbert Hoover, *Hoover after Dinner* (New York, 1933), 65–66.
22. Eugene Lyons, *Herbert Hoover: A Biography* (Garden City, NY, 1964), 206–10.
23. Hoover, *Hoover after Dinner*, 56–58.
24. Anecdotes, 1928, Campaign and Transition Papers (hereafter C&TP), Subject File (hereafter SF), Box 75, HHPL.
25. Degler, "The Ordeal of Hoover," 577.
26. Lyons, *Hoover: A Biography*, 328.
27. Darwin Lambert, *Herbert Hoover's Hideaway* (Luray, VA: Shenandoah National History Association, Inc., 1971), 118–19.
28. Frank Kent to Bernard Baruch, May 13, 1929, cited in Jordan A. Schwarz, *The Interregnum of Despair: Hoover, Congress, and the Depression* (Urbana, IL, 1970), 6.
29. Joslin, *Hoover off the Record*, 14–18.
30. James H. MacLafferty Diary, Box 1, Feb. 7, 1932, HHPL, Copyright Stanford University.
31. Joslin, *Hoover off the Record*, 14.
32. Davis W. Houck, "Rhetoric as Currency: Herbert Hoover and the 1929 Stock Market Crash," *Rhetoric and Public Affairs* 3, no. 2 (Summer 2000), 160.

33. *New York Times*, Feb. 19, 1930, CF, HHPL.

34. "Memo on Hoover's Remarkable Memory," Anecdotes, 1928, C&TP, SF, Box 75, HHPL.

35. Joslin, *Hoover off the Record*, 14–15.

36. Anecdotes, 1928, C&TP, SF, Box 75, HHPL.

37. George H. Nash, "Herbert Hoover: Political Orphan," in *Uncommon Americans: The Lives and Legacies of Herbert and Lou Henry Hoover*, ed. Timothy Walch (Westport, CT, 2003), 14; James R. Bowers, "Herbert Hoover: Ambivalent Quaker" (MA thesis, University of Illinois Legal Studies Center, Springfield, IL, 1981), 118–19.

38. Nash, *The Life of Herbert Hoover: The Humanitarian*, 96.

39. Martin L. Fausold, *The Presidency of Herbert C. Hoover* (Lawrence, KS, 1985), 45–46.

40. Football, 1931–1932, Presidential Papers (hereafter PP), SF, Box 163, PP, SF, Box 55, Accomp. of Admin., 1930, Jan.–June, HHPL; Lyons, *Hoover: A Biography*, 188–90.

41. Nancy Beck Young, *Lou Henry Hoover: Activist First Lady* (Lawrence, KS, 2004), 25.

42. Lyons, *Hoover: A Biography*, 188.

43. Jordan A. Schwarz, "Hoover and Congress: Politics, Personality and Perspective in the Presidency," in *The Hoover Presidency: A Reappraisal*, eds. Martin L. Fausold and George T. Mazuzan (Albany, NY, 1974), 93.

44. Albert U. Romasco, "Hoover's Policies for Dealing with the Great Depression: The End of the Old Order or the Beginning of the New?" in *The Hoover Presidency: A Reappraisal*, eds. Fausold and Mazuzan, 71–72.

45. Fausold, *The Presidency of Herbert C. Hoover*, 40–45; Joslin, *Hoover off the Record*, 20–23.

46. Joan Hoff, *Herbert Hoover: Forgotten Progressive* (Boston, 1975), 28; Joslin, *Hoover off the Record*, 7.

47. Houck, "Rhetoric as Currency," 172–73.

48. Joslin, *Hoover off the Record*, 44; *New York World*, Oct. 23, 1929, CF, HHPL.

49. Hoff, *Forgotten Progressive*, 26–27; Joslin, *Hoover off the Record*, 45; Joslin Diary, June 11, 1931, HHPL.

50. Joslin, *Hoover off the Record*, 45; Lyons, *Hoover: A Biography*, 193–94; *New York World*, Aug. 24 and Oct. 3, 1929, CF, HHPL.

51. Both quoted in Lloyd, *Aggressive Introvert*, 92.

52. Nash, *The Life of Herbert Hoover: The Humanitarian*, 370–71.

53. David Hinshaw, *Herbert Hoover: American Quaker* (New York, 1950), 35–51; Thomas D. Hamm, "The Divergent Paths of Iowa Quakers in the Nineteenth Century," *Annals of Iowa*, Third Series 61, no. 2 (Spring 2002), 125–26.

54. Bowers, "Herbert Hoover: Ambivalent Quaker," 25–27; Kendrick A. Clements, *Hoover, Conservation, and Consumerism: Engineering the Good Life* (Lawrence, KS, 2000), 16–17.

55. Ray Lyman Wilbur and Arthur Mastick Hyde, *The Hoover Policies* (New York, 1937), 297.

56. Hamm, "The Divergent Paths of Iowa Quakers," 125; Mitchell V. Charnley, *The Boy's Life of Herbert Hoover* (New York, 1931), 15–16; Gerald D. Nash, [n.t.], in *Herbert Hoover and the Crisis of American Capitalis*, eds. J. Joseph Huthmacher and Warren I. Susman (Cambridge, MA, 1973), 94; unmarked clipping titled "Quakers," CP, SF, Box 488, Quakers, 1921–1928 and undated, HHPL.

57. *Chicago Tribune*, July 31, 1928, CF, HHPL.

58. Wilbur and Hyde, *The Hoover Policies*, 23.

59. Robert Bolt, "Herbert Clark Hoover of West Branch, Iowa: U.S. President of Quaker Stock," *Quaker Life* (Sep. 1984), 22; Hoff, *Forgotten Progressive*, 4; Hinshaw, *American Quaker*, 40; *Chicago Tribune*, Feb. 24, 1929; *Washington Times*, May 10, 1929; unmarked clipping, May 18, 1931, CF, HHPL; George H. Nash, *Herbert Hoover and Stanford University* (Stanford, CA, 1988), 98.

60. Checked out for Hoover by his secretary, B. D. Nash, in Oct. 1927, CP, SF, Box 488, Quakers, 1922–1928, and Undated, May 22, 1928, and Undated, HHPL.

61. George Akerson to Elizabeth Gannon, May 22, 1928, Religious Denominations, 1921, 1928, CP, SF, Box 513, HHPL; PCP, SF, Box 26, Articles about or by Herbert Hoover, "Herbert Hoover: A Personal Sketch," by Ray Lyman Wilbur (1919), HHPL.

62. *Chicago Daily News*, May 20, 1929, CF, HHPL.

63. Wilbur and Hyde, *The Hoover Policies*, 23.
64. William Starr Myers and Walter H. Newton, *The Hoover Administration: A Documented Narrative* (New York, 1936), 504.
65. Hinshaw, *American Quaker*, 161–62; Wilbur and Hyde, *The Hoover Policies*, 8–12.
66. Herbert Hoover, *American Individualism* (New York, 1922), 8–11, 13–16, 21–22, 26–28, 31; Herbert Hoover, *The New Day: Campaign Speeches of Herbert Hoover, 1928* (Stanford, CA, 1928) 162–64; Charnley, *The Boy's Life of Herbert Hoover*, 16.
67. Herbert Hoover, *The Memoirs of Herbert Hoover*, vol. 3, *The Great Depression, 1919–1941* (New York, 1952), 25; Carol Green Wilson and Neil H. Petree, eds., "Herbert Hoover: Master Engineer," *Stanford Illustrated Review* 21, no. 2 (Nov., 1919), 77; Hoover Dinner, Sep. 16, 1919, PCP, SF, Box 43, HHPL; Clements, *Hoover, Conservation, and Consumerism*, 56–57.
68. Hoover, *American Individualism*, 17–19.
69. David Burner, *Herbert Hoover: A Public Life* (New York, 1979), 143–45; Hoff, *Forgotten Progressive*, 7; Carl Parrini, "Hoover and International Economics," in *Herbert Hoover: The Great War and Its Aftermath, 1914–1923*, ed. Lawrence E. Gelfand (Iowa City, IA, 1979), 183–86.
70. Ellis W. Hawley, "Herbert Hoover and American Corporatism, 1929–1933," in *The Hoover Presidency: A Reappraisal*, ed. Fausold and Mazuzan, 114.
71. Hoover radio address to the convention of the National Electric Light Association at Atlantic City, May 21, 1924, CP, SF, Box 120, Comm. Dept. Achievements, 1924, May–June, HHPL.

Chapter 4

1. Herbert Hoover, *The Memoirs of Herbert Hoover*, vol. 2, *The Cabinet and the Presidency, 1920–1933* (New York, 1952), 223.
2. Ray Lyman Wilbur and Arthur Mastic K. Hyde, *The Hoover Policies* (New York, 1937), 575; Hoover, *Memoirs*, vol. 2, 217; Martin L. Fausold and George T. Mazuzan, eds., *The Hoover Presidency: A Reappraisal* (Albany, NY, 1974), 7.
3. Joan Hoff, *Herbert Hoover: Forgotten Progressive* (Boston, 1975), 136; Summary of Accomp. of the Admin., 1929, Presidential Papers (hereafter PP), Subject File (hereafter SF), Box 55, Herbert Hoover Presidential Library (hereafter HHPL), West Branch, IA; Frederic William Wile, "The Hoover Era," *World's Work* 58, no. 3 (April 1929), 43; David M. Kennedy, *Freedom from Fear: The American People in Depression and War, 1929–1945* (New York, 1999), 11–12; William Starr Myers and Walter H. Newton, *The Hoover Administration: A Documented Narrative* (New York, 1936), 373.
4. William J. Schaefle, "How President Hoover Serves His Country," *American Globe* (Oct. 1929), 11–12, PP, SF, Box 55, Summary of Accomp. of the Admin., 1929, HHPL.
5. *Literary Digest*, Sep. 21, 1929, 12, Accomp. of the Admin., 1929, SF, Box 55, HHPL.
6. *New York World*, March 2, 1930, Clipping File (hereafter CF), HHPL.
7. Non-Governmental Activities, PP, Taylor/Gates Coll., Box 3, A-IV-7, HHPL.
8. Memo from Hoover to Secretary of the Navy, March 22, 1929, PP, SF, Box 120, Economy-Corres., 1929–1931; J. Kelly Smith to Hoover, May 23, 1932, PP, SF, Box 120, Economy-Corres., 1929–1931; David B. Burner, "Before the Crash: Hoover's First Eight Months in the Presidency," in *The Hoover Presidency: A Reappraisal*, eds. Fausold and Mazuzan, 51–52.
9. "Mr. Hoover and the People," *Outlook* (April 1, 1929), 535–536, Reprint File (hereafter RF), HHPL; *Chicago Daily News*, Feb. 20, 1929, and *New York Times*, July 5, 1929, both in CF, HHPL; Wilbur and Hyde, *The Hoover Policies*, 575.
10. "Playing Politics for the Country," *World's Work* (Sep. 1930), 22, RF, HHPL; *Chicago Daily News*, April 12, 1929, CF, HHPL.
11. Vaughn Davis Bornet, "Herbert Hoover's Planning for Unemployment and Old Age Insurance Coverage, 1921 to 1933," in *The Quest for Security: Papers on the Origins and the Future of*

the American Social Insurance System, ed. John N. Schacht (Iowa City, IA: 1982), RF, HHPL; Kennedy, *Freedom from Fear*, 90.

12. Hoover, *Memoirs*, vol. 2, 316; Bornet, "Hoover's Planning for Unemployment," 35–48, RF, HHPL.

13. Herbert Hoover, *Hoover after Dinner* (New York, 1933), 16–19; *Philadelphia Inquirer*, Feb. 22, 1930, PP, SF, Box 55, Accomp. of the Admin., 1930, Jan.–June, HHPL.

14. Myers and Newton, *A Documented Narrative*, 419.

15. *Washington Herald*, March 2, 1930; *New York Evening Post*, July 9, 1931; and Ed., *Washington Post*, July 22, 1929, all in CF, HHPL.

16. Report of the Committee on Economic Changes submitted by Arch W. Shaw to Hoover, Dec. 10, 1930; Theodore Joslin to George L. Cain, April 15, 1931, PP, SF, Box 120, Econ.-Corres., 1931.

17. Harold Wolfe, *Herbert Hoover: Public Servant and Leader of the Loyal Opposition* (New York, 1956), 159; Martin L. Fausold, *The Presidency of Herbert C. Hoover* (Lawrence, KS, 1985), 59–61; Wilbur and Hyde, *The Hoover Policies*, 52–53; French Strother, "Four Years of Hoover: An Interpretation," *New York Times*, Feb. 26, 1933, Section 8, 114–17, RF, HHPL; Bornet, "Hoover's Planning for Unemployment," 57.

18. Wolfe, *Public Servant*, 154; *Chicago Tribune*, July 20, 1929; Ed., *Washington Post*, July 22, 1929; and Ed. *New York Evening Post*, Aug. 20, 1930, all in CF, HHPL; Theodore G. Joslin, "Hoover's First Year," *World's Work* 59 (March 1930), 61–65, RF, HHPL; Hoover, *Memoirs*, vol. 2, 281.

19. Quoted in *Chicago Daily News*, March 1, 1929, CF, HHPL; *New York Herald Tribune*, Dec. 17, 1929, CF, HHPL; Hoover, *Memoirs*, vol. 2, 540.

20. Hoover, *Memoirs*, vol. 2, 243–45; Wilbur and Hyde, *The Hoover Policies*, 219–22; Myers and Newton, *A Documented Narrative*, 430–31.

21. Hoover, *Memoirs*, vol. 2, 248; U.S. Shipping Board and Merchant Fleet Corp., Taylor/Gates Coll., Box 2, AII-25, HHPL; Wolfe, *Public Servant*, 139.

22. *New York World*, June 11, 1930; Unmarked clipping, June 25, 1930, CF, HHPL; Myers and Newton, *A Documented Narrative*, 445.

23. *New York Times*, Dec. 24, 1930; Dec. 6, 1931, CF, HHPL.

24. David Burner, *Herbert Hoover: A Public Life* (New York, 1979) 233–34; Fausold, *The Presidency of Herbert C. Hoover*, 116–17; Wolfe, *Public Servant*, 139.

25. Memo, Fed. Board for Vocational Education, Taylor/Gates Coll., Box 2, A-II-13, HHPL; Memo, "Hoover on Latin," [1928], Campaign and Transition Papers (hereafter C&TP), Box 75, SF, Anecdotes, HHPL.

26. Burner, *A Public Life*, 224; Kendrick A. Clements, *Hoover, Conservation, and Consumerism: Engineering the Good Life* (Lawrence, KS, 2000), 145.

27. Ray Lyman Wilbur, *The Memoirs of Ray Lyman Wilbur*, eds. Edgar Eugene Robinson and Paul Carroll Edwards (Stanford, CA, 1960), 511–15; Wolfe, *Public Servant*, 162.

28. Quote from Wilbur and Hyde, *The Hoover Policies*, 80. See also, *Chicago Daily News*, Feb. 20, 1932; *New York Evening Post*, Jan. 5, 1933; and *New York Times*, Jan. 5, 1933, all in CF, HHPL; Myers and Newton, *A Documented Narrative*, 178.

29. Raymond H. Muessig, "Herbert Hoover and Education," *School and Society* 95, no. 2293 (Summer 1967), 309–13. The best monograph dealing with Hoover's relation with Stanford is George H. Nash, *Herbert Hoover and Stanford University* (Stanford, CA, 1988).

30. Harris Gaylord Warren, *Herbert Hoover and the Great Depression* (New York, 1967), 67; Burner, *A Public Life*, 223; Burner, "Before the Crash," 59.

31. Burner, *A Public Life*, 219; Hoff, *Forgotten Progressive*, 8; Hoover, *Memoirs*, vol. 2, 276–77; *Christian Science Monitor*, March 11, 1925, Commerce Papers (hereafter CP), SF, Box 89, *Christian Science Monitor*, 1922–1925, HHPL.

32. Theodore G. Joslin, *Hoover off the Record* (Garden City NY, 1934), 210–14; *Buffalo Evening News*, Aug. 8, 1928, C&TP, Box 75, SF, Anecdotes; *Chicago Daily News*, Sep. 21, 1928; June 21, 27, 1929; and *Chicago Tribune*, Aug. 4, Sep. 12, 1930, all in CF, HHPL.

33. *Chicago Tribune*, June 19, 1929; Jan. 24, 1931; Ed., *Chicago Tribune*, Jan. 24, 1931; *Chicago Daily News*, Jan. 23, 1931; Feb. 29, 1932; and *New York World*, Nov. 9, 1930, all in CF,

HHPL; James H. MacLafferty Diary, Box 1, Feb. 16, 1932, HHPL; James D. Calder, "Herbert Hoover's Contributions to the Administrative History of Crime Control Policy," prepared for the Southwest Political Science Association Convention, Dallas, TX, 1981, 18–21, RF, HHPL; Hoover, *Memoirs*, vol. 2, 276–77; David Hinshaw, *Herbert Hoover: American Quaker* (New York, 1950), 209; Dale Mayer, *Lou Henry Hoover: A Prototype for First Ladies* (Hauppauge, NY, 2004), 297–98.

34. *Chicago Tribune*, May 29, Sep. 29, 1929; *Chicago Daily News*, Jan. 19, 1931, CF, HHPL; Strother, "Four Years of Hoover," CF, HHPL.

35. *New York Herald Tribune*, Jan. 14, 1930; Jan. 21, 1931; CF, HHPL; Myers and Newton, *A Documented Narrative*, 467–68; Joslin, *Hoover off the Record*, 74; Burner, *A Public Life*, 220–21.

36. *Chicago Daily News*, Jan. 20, 21, Feb. 11, 1931; and *Chicago Tribune*, Dec. 26, Jan. 26, 1929; Jan. 21, 1932, all in CF, HHPL; Wolfe, *Public Servant*, 152–53; Myers and Newton, *A Documented Narrative*, 444.

37. Bills sponsored by the Dept. of Justice since March 4, 1929, which have been enacted into law, Feb. 20, 1933, Taylor/Gates Coll., Box 1, Justice Dept.; "Recommendations for Legislation in the First Wickersham Committee Report," Feb. 22, 1933, Taylor/Gates Coll., Box 1, A II-4, Justice Dept., HHPL.

38. MacLafferty Diary, Nov. 22, 29, Dec. 3, 11, 30, 1930, Box 1, HHPL; Clair Everet Nelsen, "The Image of Herbert Hoover as Reflected in the American Press" (PhD diss., Stanford University, 1956), 105–6; *Chicago Tribune*, Sep. 23, 1930; *Chicago Daily News*, Oct. 4, 1929; *Washington Post*, Nov. 17, 1930; *New York Times*, Dec. 17, 1931, all in CF, HHPL.

39. Schaefle, "How President Hoover Serves His Country," 5; Strother, "Four Years of Hoover," RF, HHPL; *New York Herald Tribune*, April 13, 1929; *Washington News*, July 31, 1929; *Chicago Daily News*, Jan. 13, 1929; *Chicago Tribune*, Jan. 15, 21, 23, 24, 1931; and *Christian Science Monitor*, May 1, 1929, all in CF, HHPL.

40. Hoover, *Memoirs*, vol. 2, 273–74; Theodore G. Joslin Diary, 1931–1933, Box 10, File 10, March 2, 1932, HHPL; Burner, *A Public Life*, 213–15; Burner, "Before the Crash," 55–56; Myers and Newton, *A Documented Narrative*, 537; Calder, "Herbert Hoover's Contributions," RF, HHPL.

41. Calder, "Herbert Hoover's Contributions," 25, RF, HHPL; Dept. of Justice, "List of Accomp.," Taylor/Gates Coll., Box 1, Justice Dept., HHPL; Myers and Newton, *A Documented Narrative*, 489–96, 535, 536.

42. *New York World*, Aug. 3, 1929; *Chicago Daily News*, Aug. 6, 1929, CF, HHPL.

43. *Washington Herald*, May 15, 1930; [Washington, DC] *U.S. Daily News*; and *New York World*, Aug. 16, 1930, all in CF, HHPL; Wolfe, *Public Servant*, 150–51; Warren, *Hoover and the Great Depression*, 69; Myers and Newton, *A Documented Narrative*, 433.

44. Clements, *Hoover, Conservation, and Consumerism*, x, 1–8, 20, 29, 78; Mark O. Hatfield in *Understanding Herbert Hoover: Ten Perspectives*, ed. Lee Nash (Stanford, CA, 1987), 45–48.

45. Wilbur, *Memoirs*, 410–14; Clements, *Hoover, Conservation, and Consumerism*, 130.

46. Burner, *A Public Life*, 232.

47. Murray N. Rothbard, in *Herbert Hoover and the Crisis of American Capitalism*, eds. J. Joseph Huthmacher and Warren I. Susman (Cambridge, MA, 1973), 50; "Mr. Hoover and the People," *Outlook* 51, no. 14 (April 3, 1929), 536; Strother, "Four Years of Hoover," RF, HHPL.

48. Wolfe, *Public Servant*, 138; *New York Herald Tribune*, April 9, 1931, CF, HHPL.

49. *New York Times*, Oct. 3, Oct. 26, Oct. 29, 1930; *New York Herald Tribune*, Feb. 12, 1931; and [Washington, DC] *U.S. Daily News*, Feb. 27, 1931, all in CF, HHPL; Wilbur, *Memoirs*, 415–19.

50. [Washington, DC] *U.S. Daily News*, Aug. 27, 1929, Oct. 30, 1929; Ed., *New York Times*, July 21, 1929; *New York Times*, March 8, 1931; April 10, 1932; and *Chicago Tribune*, Aug. 28, 1929, all in CF, HHPL; Burner, *A Public Life*, 229; Wilbur and Hyde, *The Hoover Policies*, 229–33; Clements, *Hoover, Conservation, and Consumerism*, 148–68.

51. Clements, *Hoover, Conservation, and Consumerism*, 91.

52. *Chicago Daily News*, Oct. 16, 1929, CF, HHPL; Wilbur, *Memoirs*, 439.

53. Rothbard, [n.t.], 50; Clements, *Hoover, Conservation, and Consumerism*, 139.

54. Wilbur, *Memoirs*, 431–33; Myers and Newton, *A Documented Narrative*, 477, 537–39; Burner, *A Public Life*, 228–30; Wilbur and Hyde, *The Hoover Policies*, 233–34.
55. Wilbur, *Memoirs*, 436–38.

Chapter 5

1. David Burner, *Herbert Hoover: A Public Life* (New York, 1979), 247; Harold Wolfe, *Herbert Hoover: Public Servant and Leader of the Loyal Opposition* (New York, 1956), 215–16.
2. Senator Irvine L. Lenroot to Daniel R. Crissinger, Nov. 25, 1925; Lenroot to Lawrence Richey, May 3, 1933 [copy]; Crissinger to Lenroot, Dec. 10, 1925; Lenroot to Crissinger, Dec. 23, 1925, Commerce Papers (hereafter CP), Subject File (hereafter SF), Box 548, Senate, Lenroot, Irvine L., 1923–1927, Herbert Hoover Presidential Library (hereafter HHPL), West Branch, IA; Susan L. DuBrock Wendel, "Herbert Hoover and Banking Reform" (MA thesis, Northeastern Illinois University, 1985), 10–14; Edward Eyre Hunt, "Fight on the Depression: Phase I," book II, part 4 (1935), Box 335, Herbert Hoover Presidential File (Hoover Institution, Stanford University [hereafter HHPF]), unpaginated.
3. David M. Kennedy, *Freedom from Fear: The American People in Depression and War, 1929–1945* (New York, 1999), 54–57.
4. Eugene Lyons, *Herbert Hoover: A Biography* (Garden City, NY, 1964), 218; Hunt, "Fight on the Depression: Phase I," 4–8, 12, 16–20; Herbert Hoover, *The Memoirs of Herbert Hoover*, vol. 3, *The Great Depression, 1929–1941* (New York, 1952), 8–11, 334–35; James Stuart Olson, *Herbert Hoover and the Reconstruction Finance Corporation, 1931–1933* (Ames, IA, 1977), 8–10.
5. William Starr Myers, *The Foreign Policies of Herbert Hoover* (New York, 1940), 189–98; Joan Hoff, *Herbert Hoover: Forgotten Progressive* (Boston, 1975), 179–81; Wolfe, *Public Servant*, 257; Harris Gaylord Warren, *Herbert Hoover and the Great Depression* (New York, 1967), 10–11; Joan Hoff, "A Reevaluation of Herbert Hoover's Foreign Policy," in *The Hoover Presidency: A Reappraisal*, eds. Martin L. Fausold and George T. Muzuzan (Albany, NY, 1974), 176–77.
6. Wolfe, *Public Servant*, 216; Burner, *A Public Life*, 247.
7. Robert Sobel, *Herbert Hoover at the Onset of the Great Depression, 1929–1930* (Philadelphia, 1975), 56.
8. Kennedy, *Freedom from Fear*, 38–40; Maury Klein, *Rainbow's End: The Crash of 1929* (New York, 2001), 207–42; Sobel, *Hoover at the Onset*, 54–55; Richard Norton Smith, *An Uncommon Man: The Triumph of Herbert Hoover* (New York, 1984), 118; *New York Herald Tribune*, Oct. 26, 1929; *New York Evening Post*, Oct. 29, 1929; *New York World*, Oct. 29, 1929, all in Clipping File (hereafter CF), HHPL.
9. Kennedy, *Freedom from Fear*, 40–41; Louis W. Liebovich, *Bylines in Despair: Herbert Hoover, the Great Depression, and the U.S. News Media* (Westport, CT, 1994), 106–7, 122–23.
10. Liebovich, *Bylines in Despair*, 102; David Hinshaw, *Herbert Hoover: American Quaker* (New York, 1950), 231–33.
11. Kennedy, *Freedom from Fear*, 9.
12. Walter Starr Myers and Walter H. Newton, *The Hoover Administration: A Documented Narrative* (New York, 1936), 21; *New York Times*, Oct. 31, 1929, CF, HHPL; Dale Mayer, *Lou Henry Hoover: A Prototype for First Ladies* (Hauppauge, NY, 2004), 245.
13. Lyons, *Hoover: A Biography*, 212.
14. Martin L. Fausold, *The Presidency of Herbert C. Hoover* (Lawrence, KS, 1985), 77.
15. E. C. Stokes to Hoover, Oct. 18, 1930, Presidential Papers (hereafter PP), SF, Box 159, Financial Matters, New York Stock Exchange, Corres., 1930, July–Dec., HHPL.
16. See Amity Shlaes, *The Forgotten Man: A New History of the Great Depression* (New York, 2007). Shlaes turns the traditional liberal historiography on end. Her argument is plausible, but it would require additional research to substantiate it. It remains an interesting "what if" question that should be taken seriously.
17. Lyons, *Hoover: A Biography*, 246.

18. Hunt, "Fight on the Depression: Phase I," unpaginated; Sobel, *Hoover at the Onset*, x; Davis W. Houck, "Rhetoric as Currency: Herbert Hoover and the 1929 Stock Market Crash," *Rhetoric and Public Affairs* 3, no. 2 (Summer 2000), 167–69.

19. David Hamilton, "War on a Thousand Fronts," in *Uncommon Americans*, ed. Timothy Walch (Westport, CT: Praeger, 2003), 147–49; Kennedy, *Freedom from Fear*, 54–57; Klein, *Rainbow's End*, 246; Hoff, *Forgotten Progressive*, 137–38; *New York Evening Post*, Nov. 21, 1929, CF, HHPL.

20. Hunt, "Fight on the Depression, Phase I," unpaginated; Albert U. Romasco, *The Poverty of Abundance: Hoover, the Nation, the Depression* (New York, 1968), 31–32; *New York Evening Post*, Nov. 15, 1929; *New York Herald Tribune*, Nov. 16, 1929, CF, HHPL.

21. *Chicago Daily News*, Oct. 29, 1929, and *Chicago Tribune*, Oct. 29, 1929, both in CF, HHPL.

22. Kennedy, *Freedom from Fear*, 52–54; Minutes of Meeting Held with Railroad Presidents, Nov. 19, 1929, PP, SF, Box 91, Business, Pres. Bus. Conf., 1929, HHPL; *New York Herald Tribune*, Nov. 19, 1929, and *New York Evening Post*, Nov. 19, 1929, both in CF, HHPL.

23. *New York World*, Nov. 21, 1929, and *New York Herald Tribune*, Nov. 22, 1929, both in CF, HHPL; Kennedy, *Freedom from Fear*, 52–55; Myers and Newton, *The Hoover Administration*, 26–27; Hoover, *Memoirs: The Great Depression*, 43–46.

24. *New York Times*, Nov. 22, 1929, CF, HHPL; Burner, *A Public Life*, 252; Ellis W. Hawley, in *Herbert Hoover and the Crisis of American Capitalism*, eds. J. Joseph Huthmacher and Warren I. Susman (Cambridge, MA: 1973), 21.

25. *New York Herald Tribune*, Nov. 19, 27, 1929; *New York Evening Post*, Nov. 25, 1929, CF, HHPL; Klein, *Rainbow's End*, 243; John Spargo, *The Legend of Hoover Who "Did Nothing,"* [pamphlet], Box 226, March 21, 1936, HHPF; Myers and Newton, *The Hoover Administration*, 30.

26. *Chicago Daily News*, Nov. 23, 1929, and *New York Evening Post*, Nov. 23, 1929, both in CF, HHPL.

27. Hunt, "Fight on the Depression: Phase I," unpaginated; Lyons, *Hoover: A Biography*, 252–53.

28. Ed., *New York Times*, Nov. 29, 1929, CF, HHPL.

29. Ed., *New York Evening Post*, Dec. 4, 1929, CF, HHPL.

30. *Chicago Tribune*, Nov. 29, 1929, CF, HHPL.

31. Carlton A. Shively, "Stimulating Business," *Outlook* 153 (Dec. 11, 1929), 585, RF, HHPL.

32. Lippman is quoted in Hunt, "Fight on the Depression: Phase I," 59.

33. Ibid., 60.

34. Kennedy, *Freedom from Fear*, 58–59; Burner, *A Public Life*, 248–49; Lyons, *Hoover: A Biography*, 253; Ed., *New York Evening Post*, Nov. 26, 1929, CF, HHPL; Hunt, "Fight on the Depression: Phase I," 98–102; Mayer, *A Prototype for First Ladies*, 279.

35. *New York Herald Tribune*, May 4, 1930; *New York World*, Oct. 11, 21, 25, 1930; and *New York Times*, Oct. 16, Dec. 31, 1930, all in CF, HHPL; Edward Eyre Hunt, "Fight on the Depression: Phase II," Book II, Part 5, 1935, Box 336, HHPF.

36. [Washington, DC] *U.S. Daily News*, Sep. 21, 1931, CF, HHPL.

Chapter 6

1. Robert Sobel, *Herbert Hoover at the Onset of the Great Depression, 1929–1930* (Philadelphia, 1975), 59; Harris Gaylord Warren, *Herbert Hoover and the Great Depression* (New York, 1967), 88–97; William Starr Myers and Walter H. Newton, *The Hoover Administration: A Documented Narrative* (New York, 1936), 424.

2. Harold Wolfe, *Herbert Hoover: Public Servant and Leader of the Loyal Opposition* (New York, 1956), 235–36; Herbert Hoover, *The Memoirs of Herbert Hoover*, vol. 2, *The Cabinet and the Presidency, 1920–1933* (New York, 1952), 294–98; *New York Herald Tribune*, March 27, 1930, Clipping File (hereafter CF), Herbert Hoover Presidential Library (hereafter HHPL), West Branch, IA.

3. *New York Times*, March 26, May 5, 1930; and *New York Herald Tribune*, March 26, May 5, 1930, all in CF, HHPL; Theodore G. Joslin, "Hoover's First Year," *World's Work* 59 (March 1930), 63–64.

4. Ed., *New York Evening Post*, March 25, 1930; Ed., *New York Times*, March 25, 1930; *New York Times*, June 16, 1930; *New York World*, June 17, 1930; and *New York Evening Post*, June 17, 1930, all in CF, HHPL.

5. Edwin Balmer and William Crawford, "When You Meet the President," *Redbook* 58 (March 1932), 112; U.S. Dept. of Commerce, *National Income and Product Accounts of the United States*, vol. 1, *1929–1958* (Washington, DC, 1993).

6. Hoover, *Memoirs*, vol. 2, *The Cabinet and the Presidency, 1920–1933*, 291–93, 299; Julius Klein, "The Tariff and the Depression," *Current Events* 34, no. 4 (July 1931), 497–99, Accomp. of the Admin., 1931, Presidential Papers (hereafter PP), Subject File (SF), Box 55, HHPL.

7. David M. Kennedy, *Freedom from Fear: The American People in Depression and War, 1929–1945* (New York, 1999), 49.

8. Warren, *Hoover and the Great Depression*, 90.

9. Charles F. Scott, [n.t.], *The Republican*, March 10, 1932, 1–3, PP, SF, Box 55, Accomp. of the Admin., 1932, Jan.–March; [no author], "Profiles, The President," *New Yorker* (Dec. 27, 1930), 21; Christina D. Romer, "The Nation in Depression," *Journal of Economic Perspectives* 7, no. 2 (Spring 1993), 19–39; Barry Eichengreen, "The Political Economy of the Smoot-Hawley Tariff," *Research in Economic History* 12 (Aug., 1986), 1–43; Myers and Newton, *A Documented Narrative*, 440–41.

10. Unmarked clipping, June 1, 1931; *New York Herald Tribune*, Dec. 18, 1931; and *New York Times*, Feb. 29, 1932, all in CF, HHPL; John Conybeare, "Trade Wars: A Comparative Study of Anglo-Hanse, Franco-Italian, and Hawley-Smoot Conflicts," *World Politics* 38, no. 1 (Oct. 1985), 165–66, Reprint File (hereafter RF), HHPL; Richard N. Cooper, "Trade Policy in Foreign Policy," in *U.S. Trade Policies in a Changing World Economy*, ed. Robert M. Stern (Cambridge, MA, 1987), 291–92.

11. Joslin, "Hoover's First Year," 61–65.

12. *Chicago Daily News*, Feb. 25, 1930, CF, HHPL.

13. Ray Lyman Wilbur and Arthur Mastick Hyde, *The Hoover Policies* (New York, 1937), 332–37; Memo to Attorney General [summary], Aug. 26, 1931, PP, SF, Box 155, Finan. Matters, Banking and Bankruptcy, Corres., July, Jan.–Aug., HHPL; Carl N. Degler, "The Ordeal of Herbert Hoover," *Yale Review* 52 (June 1963), 567, RF, HHPL.

14. *Washington Star*, Oct. 20, 1929, and *New York Times*, June 28, 1931, both in CF, HHPL; Ray Lyman Wilbur, *The Memoirs of Ray Lyman Wilbur*, eds. Edgar Eugene Robinson and Paul Carroll Edwards (Stanford, CA, 1960), 466–67; Ray Harris, "The President's Record," *Woman Republican* 9, no. 12 (Dec. 1931), 3–7, RF, HHPL; Republican National Committee, *The Hoover Administration: Its Policies and Its Achievements in the First Sixteen Months*, PP, SF, Box 55, Accomp. of the Admin., 1931, HHPL.

15. Wilbur and Hyde, *The Hoover Policies*, 194–200; Myers and Newton, *A Documented Narrative*, 198, 441–45; *Washington Star*, June 2, 1930, CF, HHPL.

16. Kennedy, *Freedom from Fear*, 63; Wolfe, *Public Servant*, 134–35; [Washington, DC] *U.S. Daily News*, Dec. 28, 1929; *New York Times*, April 2, 1930; and *New York Herald Tribune*, April 17, 1930, all in CF, HHPL.

17. Theodore Joslin, *Hoover off the Record* (Garden City, NY, 1934), 71–73; Kendrick A. Clements, *Hoover, Conservation, and Consumerism: Engineering the Good Life* (Lawrence, KS, 2000), 89; Warren, *Hoover and the Great Depression*, 72–77; Wolfe, *Public Servant*, 57; *New York World*, May 27, July 26, 1930, CF, HHPL.

18. Clements, *Hoover, Conservation, and Consumerism*, 180; David E. Hamilton, "Herbert Hoover and the Great Drought of 1930," *Journal of American History* 68, no. 4 (March 1982), 850–54; Report of Arthur M. Hyde to Hoover, Sep. 2, 1930, PP, SF, Box 118, Drought-Corres.-1930, Sep. 1–15, HHPL.

19. *New York World*, Aug. 5, 7, 12, 19, 1930; *New York Herald Tribune*, Aug. 5, 7, 9, 10, 1930; *New York Times*, Aug. 10, 12, 15, 19, 1930; *New York Evening Post*, Aug. 9, 12, 1930; [Washington,

DC] *U.S. Daily News,* Aug. 9, 1930; and *Chicago Daily News,* Aug. 12, 1930, all in CF, HHPL; George P. Street to Hoover, Aug. 12, 1930, PP, SF, Box 118, Drought, Corres., 1930, Aug. 12, HHPL.

20. *New York Herald Tribune,* Sep. 3, 1930, CF, HHPL; DeWitt Smith to Mr. Fieser, Weekly Drought Relief Report, Red Cross, Sep. 26, 1930, PP, SF, Box 118, Drought, Corres., 1930, Sep. 16–30, HHPL.

21. Radio talk delivered by G. E. Farrell, Asst. Secy., National Drought Relief Committee, Nov. 17, 1930, NBC, PP, SF, Box 119, Drought-Press Releases, 1930, Oct.–Dec., HHPL; C. W. Warburton to George Akerson, Oct. 15, 1930; PP, SF, Box 118, Drought, Corres., 1930, Oct.–Dec., HHPL; *New York Herald Tribune,* Nov. 17, 1930, CF, HHPL; Press Release, Dept. of Agriculture, Nov. 3, 1930, PP, SF, Box 119, Drought, Press Releases, Oct.–Dec., HHPL.

22. *New York Times,* Dec. 4, 1930, CF, HHPL; Special Report on the Feed Situation, U.S. Dept. of Agriculture, Dec. 4, 1930, PP, SF, Box 119, Drought, Press Releases, 1930, Oct.–Dec., HHPL; "Wheat Surplus Reduced by Heavy Feeding, Press Release by U.S. Dept. of Agriculture," Dec. 8, 1930, PP, SF, Box 119, Drought, Press Releases, 1930, Oct.–Dec., HHPL.

23. Hoover to Arthur M. Hyde, Aug. 18, 1930, PP, SF, Box 118, Drought, Corres., Aug. 16–20, HHPL.

24. Macon Chamber of Commerce to Hoover, Aug. 7, 1930, PP, SF, Box 118, Drought, Corres., Aug. 8, 1930; Memos of Aug. 8, 1930 by Hoover, PP, SF, Box 118, Drought, Corres., 1930, Aug 8, 1930; Statement of the Commissioner of Intermediate Credit Banks, PP, SF, Box 118, Drought, Corres., 1930; *The Official Record,* U.S. Dept of Agriculture, Sep. 4, 1930, PP, SF, Box 118, Drought, Corres., 1930-Aug. 14, HHPL; Myers and Newton, *A Documented Narrative,* 42–44; *New York Herald Tribune,* Aug. 16, 1930, CF, HHPL.

25. Recommendations of the National Drought Committee on Drought Finance [Aug., 1930], PP, Box 118, Drought, Corres., 1930, Aug. 26–30; Problem of Farm Credit, Memorandum, National Drought Relief Comm., Oct. 10, 1930, PP, SF, Box 118, Drought, Corres., 1930, Oct.–Dec.; Memo on Banking Committees, Drought of 1930, PP, SF, Box 118, Drought, Corres., 1930, Aug. 26–30; Report of Banker Members of State Committees, Oct. 15, 1930, PP, SF, Box 118, Drought, Corres., 1930, Oct.–Dec., HHPL.

26. C. W. Warburton to Dr. Louise Stanley, Chief, Bureau of Home Economics, Oct. 20, PP, SF, Box 119, Drought, Press Releases, 1930, Oct.–Dec.; Talk by C. W. Warburton, Oct. 27, 1930, PP, SF, Box 119, Drought, Press Releases, 1930, Oct.–Dec.; Henry M. Robinson to Hoover, Aug. 27, 1930, PP, SF, Box 118, Drought, Corres., Aug. 26, 1930, HHPL; Hamilton, "Hoover and the Great Drought of 1930," 854–58, RF, HHPL.

27. Clements, *Hoover, Conservation, and Consumerism,* 180; Hamilton, "Hoover and the Great Drought of 1930," 850–54, RF, HHPL; David E. Hamilton, *From New Day to New Deal: American Farm Policy from Hoover to Roosevelt* (Chapel Hill, 1991), 91–93; Address by Dr. C. W. Warburton, NBC, Dec. 29, 1930, PP, SF, Box 119, Drought, Press Releases, 1930, Oct.–Dec. 1; Walter F. McGinnis, Jr. to Hoover, April 19, 1932, enclosed unmarked clipping, PP, SF, Box 55, Accomp. of the Admin., 1932, April-June; *New York World,* Feb. 11, 1931; and *New York Times,* Feb. 11, 1931, both CF, HHPL.

28. *Time,* Aug. 4, 1930, unpaginated clipping, RF, HHPL; *New York Times,* Sep. 22, 1929; July 26, 1930; *New York Herald Tribune,* July 20, 1930; *New York World,* Oct. 15, 1930; and *New York Evening Post,* Oct. 10, 1930, all in CF, HHPL.

29. Clair Everet Nelson, "The Image of Herbert Hoover as Reflected in the American Press" (PhD diss., Stanford University, 1956), 94–99, HHPL; *New York Times,* Sep. 16, 1930; *New York Herald Tribune,* Oct. 14, 1930; and *New York World,* July 14, 1930, all in CF, HHPL. Michelson describes his role in Charles Michelson, *The Ghost Talks* (New York, 1944).

30. *New York Herald Tribune,* Oct. 14, 1930, CF, HHPL.

31. *New York Times,* Oct. 21, 1930, CF, HHPL.

32. "National Affairs: Election Footer," *Time* 16, no. 20 (Nov. 17, 1930), 15, RF, HHPL; Warren, *Hoover and the Great Depression,* 190.

33. Myers and Newton, *A Documented Narrative*, 54–56; Jordan A. Schwarz, *The Interregnum of Despair: Hoover, Congress, and the Depression* (Urbana, IL, 1970), 18–21; Kennedy, *Freedom from Fear*, 59–61; *New York Times*, Nov. 11, 1930, CF, HHPL.
34. *New York Herald Tribune*, Oct. 1, 4, 1930, CF, HHPL.
35. Martin L. Fausold, *The Presidency of Herbert C. Hoover* (Lawrence, KS, 1985), 135–36; *New York Herald Tribune*, Nov. 17, 1930; March 4, July 14, 1931; *New York World*, Jan. 8, Feb. 18, 1931; *New York Times*, Feb. 23, 1931; and *U.S. Daily News*, March 4, 1932, all in CF, HHPL; James H. MacLafferty Diary, Jan. 8, 1931, Box 1, HHPL.
36. *New York World*, Feb. 14, 17, 20, 21, 27, 1931; Ed., *New York Evening Post*, Feb. 17, 1931; Ed., *New York Times*, Feb. 17, 1931; and *New York Herald Tribune*, Feb. 17, 1931, all in CF, HHPL; James H. MacLafferty Diary, Dec. 20, 1930, Box 1, HHPL; Fausold, *The Presidency of Herbert C. Hoover*, 134.
37. Ed., *New York World*, Jan. 16, 1931, CF, HHPL.
38. *New York Times*, Dec. 6, Dec. 20, 1930; *New York Herald Tribune*, Dec. 19, 20, 1930; Jan 16, 17, 1931; *New York World*, Dec. 17, 1930; [Washington, DC] *U.S. Daily News*, Dec. 20, 1930; and Ed., *Washington Post*, Dec. 10, 1930, all in CF, HHPL; John Barton Payne, Chairman, Central Committee on Resolutions, Jan. 29, 1931, PP, SF, Box 118, Drought, Corres., 1931, Jan.–March, HHPL.
39. *New York Evening Post*, Feb. 3, 1931; *New York Herald Tribune*, Jan. 11, 17, 9, 15, 1931; and *New York Times*, Dec. 20, 1930; Jan. 20, Feb. 15, 1931, all in CF, HHPL.
40. Glen Jeansonne, *Messiah of the Masses: Huey P. Long and the Great Depression* (New York, 1993), 117–18, 123–25; Richard D. White, Jr., *Kingfish: The Reign of Huey P. Long* (New York, 2006), 195–200.
41. [Washington, DC] *U.S. Daily News*, Dec. 4, 1930; *New York Times*, Dec. 14, 1930; Ed., *New York Times*, Jan. 6, 1931; *New York World*, Jan. 5, 1931; *New York Herald Tribune*, undated clipping, CF, HHPL.
42. *New York World*, Feb. 14, 1931, CF, HHPL.
43. *Chicago Daily News*, Feb. 10, March 9, 1931; *New York Herald Tribune*, Feb. 13, 1931, March 10, 1931; and *New York World*, Feb. 20, 1931, all in CF, HHPL; Hoover to William Green [summary], March 9, 1931, PP, SF, Box 193, Labor, Corres., 1931–1932, HHPL.

Chapter 7

1. For this summary, I have relied chiefly on the books in this series which precede the presidency, although my interpretation differs from theirs in some respects. See the excellent studies by George H. Nash, *The Life of Herbert Hoover: The Engineer, 1874–1914* (New York, 1983); *The Life of Herbert Hoover: The Humanitarian, 1914–1917* (New York, 1988); and *The Life of Herbert Hoover: Master of Emergencies, 1917–1918* (New York, 1996); and the more recent study by Kendrick H. Clements, *The Life of Herbert Hoover: Imperfect Visionary, 1918–1928* (New York, 2010). Two older life studies remain quite useful: David Burner, *Herbert Hoover: A Public Life* (New York, 1979), and the succinct work by Joan Hoff, *Herbert Hoover: Forgotten Progressive* (Boston, 1975), both of which include valuable insights.
2. Ray Lyman Wilbur and Arthur Mastick Hyde, *The Hoover Policies* (New York, 1937), 577–84; Burner, *A Public Life*, 284–85; David Hinshaw, *Herbert Hoover: American Quaker* (New York, 1950), 184; Robert Bolt, "Herbert Clark Hoover of West Branch, Iowa: U.S. President of Quaker Stock," *Quaker Life* (Sep. 1984), 23; David A. Quigley, "Assessing the Hoover Presidency," in *Uncommon Americans: The Lives and Legacies of Herbert and Lou Henry Hoover*, ed. Timothy Walch (Westport, CT, 2003), 185.
3. Hoff, *Forgotten Progressive*, 8–9, 173–74, 189–91; Harold Wolfe, *Herbert Hoover: Public Servant and Leader of the Loyal Opposition* (New York, 1956), 171–73.
4. James R. Bowers, "Herbert Hoover: Ambivalent Quaker" (MA thesis, University of Illinois Legal Studies Center, Springfield, IL, 1981), 87–102; Bolt, "Herbert Clark Hoover of West Branch, Iowa: U.S. President of Quaker Stock," 23; French Strother, "Four Years of

Hoover: An Interpretation," *New York Times*, Feb. 26, 1933, Section 8, 114–17, Reprint File (hereafter RF), Herbert Hoover Presidential Library (hereafter HHPL), West Branch, IA.

5. Henry L. Stimson and McGeorge Bundy, *On Active Service in Peace and War* (New York, 1948), 188.

6. William Starr Myers and Walter H. Newton, *The Hoover Administration: A Documented Narrative* (New York, 1936), 531; Herbert Hoover, *The Memoirs of Herbert Hoover*, vol. 2, *The Cabinet and the Presidency, 1920–1933* (New York, 1952), 331–32; Quigley, "Assessing the Hoover Presidency," 185; Mark Sullivan, "President Hoover in International Relations," *Yale Review* 19 (Dec. 1929), 217–31.

7. Robert H. Ferrell, *American Diplomacy in the Great Depression: Hoover-Stimson Foreign Policy, 1929–1933* (New Haven, CT, 1957), 35–37; Stimson and Bundy, *On Active Service*, 155–61; Richard N. Current, *Secretary Stimson: A Study in Statecraft* (New Brunswick, NJ, 1954), 43.

8. Stimson and Bundy, *On Active Service*, 197.

9. Ibid., 195.

10. Current, *Secretary Stimson*, 6.

11. Theodore G. Joslin Diary, Box 10, File 7, July 23, 1931; Jan. 6, Feb. 1, 1932, HHPL.

12. Ferrell, *American Diplomacy in the Great Depression*, 29; Stimson and Bundy, *On Active Service*, 200; Hoover, *Memoirs*, vol. 2, 336–37.

13. Stimson and Bundy, *On Active Service*, 161; Ferrell, *American Diplomacy in the Great Depression*, 19–26, 38–40.

14. Alexander DeConde, *Herbert Hoover's Latin American Policy* (Stanford, CA, 1951), 124.

15. DeConde, *Hoover's Latin American Policy*, ix, xii, 66–78, 111–21; *New York Times*, June 11, 1931, Clipping File (hereafter CF), HHPL; Theodore G. Joslin, "Hoover's First Year," *World's Work* 59 (March 1930), 62; Hoover, *Memoirs*, vol. 2, 333–34; Burner, *A Public Life*, 285–86.

16. *New York Herald Tribune*, Sep. 18, 1930, CF, HHPL; DeConde, *Hoover's Latin-American Policy*, 52–56, 90–96; Current, *Secretary Stimson*, 52, 58–59; Stimson and Bundy, *On Active Service*, 175–79; Burner, *A Public Life*, 286–87.

17. The quotation is from Herbert Hoover, *Hoover after Dinner* (New York, 1933), 9. The account of Hoover's Latin American policies is gleaned from the introduction to Martin L. Fausold and George T. Mazuzan, eds., *The Hoover Presidency: A Reappraisal* (Albany, NY, 1974), 23; Sullivan, "President Hoover in International Relations," 225–28; Current, *Secretary Stimson*, 56–57; Burner, *A Public Life*, 288; Ferrell, *American Diplomacy in the Great Depression*, 218–21.

18. *New York Times*, Dec. 7, 9, 1929; March 21, April 18, 1930; *U.S. Daily News*, Dec. 7, 1929; *New York Herald Tribune*, March 15, Oct. 15, 1930; and *New York Evening Post*, April 21, 1930, all in CF, HHPL.

19. Burner, *A Public Life*, 287; Unmarked newspaper, Portland, ME, March 18, 1930; Ed., *New York Herald Tribune*, March 19, 1930; *New York World*, March 22, 1930; and *New York Times*, March 29, July 15, 1930, all in CF, HHPL.

20. *New York Times*, Dec. 7, 1929, CF, HHPL.

21. Burner, *A Public Life*, 287; *New York Times*, Dec. 29, 1929; and Ed., *New York Herald Tribune*, March 19, 1930, all in CF, HHPL.

22. Republican National Committee, *The Hoover Administration: Its Policies and Its Achievements in the First Sixteen Months*, Accomp. of the Admin., 1931, Presidential Papers (hereafter PP), SF, Box 55, HHPL.

23. *New York Times*, May 18, 1929, and *U.S. Daily News*, May 19, 1929, both in CF, HHPL; DeConde, *Hoover's Latin American Policy*, 27–30; Ferrell, *American Diplomacy in the Great Depression*, 223–25.

24. Ferrell, *American Diplomacy in the Great Depression*, 52–60; Alexander DeConde, "Herbert Hoover and Foreign Policy: A Retrospective Assessment," in *Herbert Hoover and the Historians*, ed. Mark M. Dodge (West Branch, IA, 1989), 105–7; Current, *Secretary Stimson*, 46–47.

25. *New York Times*, July 19, 23, Nov. 27, 28, 29, 30, Dec. 5, 1929; Ed., *New York Times*, Nov. 26, 1929; and *New York Herald Tribune*, July 24, Aug. 25, 1929, all in CF, HHPL; Ferrell, *American Diplomacy in the Great Depression*, 49–60.

26. William Starr Myers, *The Foreign Policies of Herbert Hoover* (New York, 1940), 55–63; Theodore G. Joslin, *Hoover off the Record* (Garden City, NY, 1933), 41–43, 85; Thomas Herbert Bernard Dressler, "The Foreign Policies of American Individualism: Herbert Hoover, Reluctant Internationalist" (PhD diss., Brown University, 1973); *Chicago Daily News,* April 6, 25, May 30, June 2, Aug. 29, 1929; *New York Times,* April 22, 23, 1929; and *New York Evening Post,* April 22, 1929, all in CF, HHPL.

27. Sullivan, "President Hoover in International Relations"; *Chicago Daily News,* April 4, 1929; *U.S. Daily News,* April 24, 1929; *New York Times,* April 25, 27, 1929; and *New York Evening Post,* July 24, 1929, all in CF, HHPL.

28. *New York Times,* June 27, July 26, 1929; and Ed., *New York Times,* July 26, 1929, all in CF, HHPL.

29. *New York Times,* May 6, July 25, Sep. 14, 1929; [Washington, DC] *U.S. Daily News,* July 26, 1929; *New York Herald Tribune,* Aug. 1, 1929; and *New York World,* Sep. 3, 1929, all in CF, HHPL.

30. *New York Times,* Sep. 13, Oct. 5, 6, 1929; *Chicago Daily News,* Oct. 5, 1929; *New York Evening Post,* Oct. 5, 7, 1929; and *New York Herald Tribune,* Oct. 6, 7, 1929, all in CF, HHPL; Ferrell, *American Diplomacy in the Great Depression,* 80–86; Fausold, *The Presidency of Herbert C. Hoover,* 172–73; Darwin Lambert, *Herbert Hoover's Hideaway* (Luray, VA: Shenandoah National History Association, Inc., 1971), 71–81.

31. Ferrell, *American Diplomacy in the Great Depression,* 87–103; Fausold, *The Presidency of Herbert C. Hoover,* 174–75; Burner, *A Public Life,* 291–93; Stimson and Bundy, *On Active Service,* 162–67; *Chicago Daily News,* Jan. 21, 1930, and *Chicago Tribune,* March 15, 1930, both in CF, HHPL.

32. Stimson and Bundy, *On Active Service,* 167–73; Ed., *New York Herald Tribune,* Dec. 28, 1929, and *New York World,* March 25, 1930, both in CF, HHPL.

33. Current, *Secretary Stimson,* 49–52; *Chicago Daily News,* April 11, 1930, and *New York Herald Tribune,* April 15, 1930, both in CF, HHPL; Republican National Committee, *The Hoover Administration: Its Policies and Its Achievements in the First Sixteen Months,* Accomp. of the Admin., 1931, PP, SF, Box 55, HHPL.

34. *New York Times,* April 11, 1930, CF, HHPL; Fausold, *The Presidency of Herbert C. Hoover,* 176.

35. Raymond G. O'Connor, *Perilous Equilibrium: The United States and the London Conference of 1930* (Westport, CT, 1969), 114–15; *Chicago Daily News,* June 7, 1930, and *New York Evening Post,* July 7, 1930, both in CF, HHPL; Hoff, *Forgotten Progressive,* 193; Ferrell, *American Diplomacy in the Great Depression,* 104.

36. *Chicago Daily News,* July 7, 1930, CF, HHPL.

37. Wilbur and Hyde, *The Hoover Policies,* 593.

38. *Denver Post,* July 22, 1930, and *Chicago Tribune,* Oct. 28, 1930, both in CF, HHPL.

39. *New York Herald Tribune,* July 22, 1930, CF, HHPL.

40. Ed., unmarked clipping; Ed., *New York Herald Tribune,* July 22, 1930; *New York Evening Post,* March 2, 1931, CF, HHPL; Republican National Committee, *The Hoover Administration: Its Policies and Its Achievements in the First Sixteen Months,* 1931, PP, SF, Box 55, HHPL.

41. *Chicago Tribune,* Jan. 17, 1929; *Chicago Daily News,* July 26, 1929; and *New York Times,* Oct. 5, 1930, all in CF, HHPL.

42. *Chicago Tribune,* Feb. 11, 1928; *Chicago Daily News,* July 23, Aug. 28, Sep. 19, 1929; *New York Herald Tribune,* July 27, 1929; Ed., *New York Herald Tribune,* July 25, 1929; Ed., *New York Evening Post,* July 24, Aug. 5, 1929; *New York Times,* July 27, 1929; and *U.S. Daily News,* July 31, 1929, all in CF, HHPL; Hoover, *Memoirs,* vol. 2, 338–39.

43. Benjamin D. Rhodes, "Herbert Hoover and War Debts, 1919–1933," *Prologue* 6, no. 2 (Summer, 1974), 130–44, RF, HHPL; Hoff, *Forgotten Progressive,* 183–85; Joan Hoff, "A Reevaluation of Herbert Hoover's Foreign Policy," in *The Hoover Presidency: A Reappraisal,* eds. Martin L. Fausold and George T. Mazuzan (Albany, NY, 1974), 178; Ferrell, *American Diplomacy in the Great Depression,* 32–33; Ray Harris, "The President's Record," *Woman Republican* 9, no. 12 (Dec., 1931), 3, RF, HHPL; *New York Herald Tribune,* July 7, 1929, and *Chicago Daily News,* Dec. 18, 1929, both in CF, HHPL; William J. Schaefle, "How President

Hoover Serves His Country," *American Globe* (Oct. 1929), PP, SF, Box 55, in Accomp. of the Admin., 1929, HHPL.

44. Hoff, "A Reevaluation of Herbert Hoover's Foreign Policy," in *The Hoover Presidency: A Reappraisal,* 185–86; *New York Times,* Dec. 7, 1930, CF, HHPL.

Chapter 8

1. The best overview of Congress and its factions during the Hoover administration is Jordan A. Schwarz, *The Interregnum of Despair: Hoover, Congress, and the Depression* (Urbana, IL, 1970). See also David Hinshaw, *Herbert Hoover: American Quaker* (New York, 1950), 46–59, 173–80; Clair Everet Nelsen, "The Image of Herbert Hoover as Reflected in the American Press" (PhD diss., Stanford University, 1956), 85–86; Theodore G. Joslin, *Hoover off the Record* (Garden City, NY, 1934), 22.
2. James H. MacLafferty Diary, Box 1, Jan. 4, 1931, Herbert Hoover Presidential Library (hereafter HHPL), West Branch, IA. [All MacLafferty Diary citations are from Box 1]. David Burner, *Herbert Hoover: A Public Life* (New York, 1979), 199; *New York Evening Post,* July 31, 1929, Clipping File (hereafter CF), HHPL.
3. MacLafferty Diary, Dec. 24, 1930; *New York Herald Tribune,* Dec. 25, 1930, CF, HHPL.
4. MacLafferty Diary, June 7, 1932; *Washington Star,* June 28, 1929, and Ed., *New York Herald Tribune,* June 9, 1932, both in CF, HHPL.
5. Charles Walcott and Karen M. Hult, "Management Science and the Great Engineer: Governing the White House during the Hoover Administration," *Presidential Studies Quarterly* 20, no. 3 (Summer 1990), 557–79; MacLafferty Diary, Dec. 13, 1930.
6. Joslin, *Hoover off the Record,* 21–22.
7. J. Joseph Huthmacher and Warren I. Susman, eds., *Herbert Hoover and the Crisis of American Capitalism* (Cambridge, MA, 1973), xi; French Strother, "Four Years of Hoover: An Interpretation," *New York Times,* Feb. 26, 1933, Section 8, 114–17, transcript, Reprint File (hereafter RF), HHPL.
8. Edward Eyre Hunt, "Evaluation of the Hoover Presidency," Jan. 26, 1932, unpaginated, Herbert Hoover Presidential File (hereafter HHPF), Box 73, Herbert Hoover Administration, E. E. Hunt, Hoover Institution Archives, Stanford University.
9. MacLafferty Diary, Sep. 1, 1930; Edward Eyre Hunt, "Fight on the Depression: Phase I," 1935, HHPF, Box 335; *New York Evening Post,* Aug. 31, Nov. 1, 1929; and *Chicago Daily News,* Sep. 3, 1929, all in CF, HHPL.
10. *New York Times,* March 4, 1930, CF, HHPL.
11. *New York World,* March 5, 1930, CF, HHPL.
12. *New York Times,* March 4, 1930, CF, HHPL.
13. *New York Times,* March 5, 1930, and *New York Herald Tribune,* March 31, 1930, both in CF, HHPL.
14. *New York Evening Post,* May 9, 1930, CF, HHPL.
15. *New York Times,* July 15, 1930, CF, HHPL.
16. *New York World,* March 5, 1930, and unidentified Boston newspaper, March 11, 1930, both in CF, HHPL.
17. MacLafferty Diary, Jan. 4, 1931.
18. MacLafferty Diary, Dec. 11, Dec. 19, 1930; Jan. 4, 1931; *New York Evening Post,* March 18, 1932, CF, HHPL; Burner, *A Public Life,* 258.
19. MacLafferty Diary, April 14, Dec. 11, Dec. 16, 1931; June 2, 1932; Theodore G. Joslin List of Comments, Observations, Joslin Papers, 1932, p. 1, HHPL; *Chicago Daily News,* Feb. 17, 1930; *New York Herald Tribune,* April 9, 1931, CF, HHPL; Taylor/Gates Coll., Box 2, A-IV, President's Relations with Congress, July 25, 1933, PP, HHPL.
20. Viola Jennings Cameron to Hubert Work, Aug. 28, 1929, Hubert Work Scrapbook, Box 2, Hoover Institution Archive, Stanford University; *Washington Post,* Sep. 9, 1929; *New York Times,* March 22, June 30, 1930; *New York World,* April 2, 1930; and Ed., *New York World,* June 13, 1930, all in CF, HHPL.

21. MacLafferty Diary, July 8, Aug. 7, 1930; Paul Y. Anderson, "Huston Stays On," *Nation* (July 30, 1930), 119; *New York Herald Tribune*, July 11, July 25, Aug. 8, 1930; *New York Evening Post*, July 25, 1930; *New York World*, July 10, 1930; and *New York Times*, July 26, 1930, all in CF, HHPL.

22. MacLafferty discusses Raskob's role in financing the Democrats in his diary entry of Dec. 24, 1931, and in an undated entry in 1932.

23. MacLafferty Diary, Aug. 7, 1930; Jan. 28, 1932; *New York Times*, Nov. 30, 1931, and *New York Evening Post*, Dec. 15, 1931, both in CF, HHPL.

24. *Chicago Daily News*, March 16, 1929, CF, HHPL.

25. MacLafferty Diary, March 4, 1929; Nov. 22, Dec. 8, 1930; Jan. 14, 1932. Quote from MacLafferty Diary, Dec. 13, 1930.

26. MacLafferty Diary, Nov. 14, Nov. 29, Nov. 30, 1930; March 15, April 16, 1931. Copyright Stanford University.

27. MacLafferty Diary, Summary, June 1931-Nov., 1931. See especially, June 7, 9, 20, July 29, Sep. 6, Oct. 14, 1931. Copyright Stanford University.

28. Ellis W. Hawley, in *Hoover and the Crisis of American Capitalism*, eds. J. Joseph Huthmacher and Warren I. Susman (Cambridge, MA, 1973), 119.

29. Burner, *A Public Life*, 235; Harris Gaylord Warren, *Herbert Hoover and the Great Depression* (New York, 1967), 68.

30. Harold Wolfe, *Herbert Hoover: Public Servant and Leader of the Loyal Opposition* (New York, 1956), 147–48; Unmarked clipping, "Chief Justice Hughes," SF, PP, Box 193, Judiciary-Sup. Court, Appointment of Hughes as Chief Justice, HHPL; *Los Angeles Times*, Feb. 8, 1930, SF, PP, Box 193, Judiciary-Sup. Court, Appointment of Hughes as Chief Justice, HHPL; Editorial Summary, Feb. 24, 1930, SF, PP, Box 193, Judiciary-Sup. Court, Appointment of Hughes as Chief Justice, HHPL; Hughes to Hoover, April 12, 1931, SF, PP, Box 193, Judiciary-Sup. Court, Appointment of Hughes as Chief Justice, HHPL; Judiciary-Sup. Court of the U.S., Biographies of Men Considered, SF, PP, Box 193, Judiciary-Sup. Court, Appointment of Hughes as Chief Justice, HHPL; *New York Herald Tribune*, Feb. 4, 1930; *New York Times*, April 27, 1930, CF, HHPL.

31. *New York Herald Tribune*, March 9, 1930, and *New York Times*, March 22, 1930, both in CF, HHPL; Donald J. Lisio, *Hoover, Blacks, and Lily-Whites: A Study of Southern Strategies* (Chapel Hill, NC, 1985), 205–7; Biography of John J. Parker, PP, SF, Box 193, Judiciary-Sup. Court of the U.S., Biographies of Men Considered, HHPL; William Starr Myers and Walter H. Newton, *The Hoover Administration: A Documented Narrative* (New York, 1936), 427–28.

32. *New York Times*, April 12, 1930; Ed., *New York Times*, May 5, 1930; and *New York Evening Post*, April 21, 1930, all in CF, HHPL; Gerald D. Nash, in *Hoover and the Crisis of American Capitalism*, eds. J. Joseph Huthmacher and Warren I. Susman (Cambridge, MA, 1973), 105; Lisio, *Hoover, Blacks, and Lily-Whites*, 208–9, 228–30.

33. *New York Times*, April 6, 25, 28, 1930, and *New York Herald Tribune*, March 29, April 14, 1930, all in CF, HHPL.

34. *New York Herald Tribune*, April 30, 1930; *New York Evening Post*, April 25, 29, 1930; Ed., *New York World*, April 18, 1930; *New York World*, April 19, 1930; Ed., *New York Times*, April 14, 1930; and *New York Times*, April 18, 19, 1930, all in CF, HHPL; Wolfe, *Public Servant*, 148.

35. *New York Evening Post*, April 25, May 10, 1930; *New York Times*, May 3, 1930; and *New York Herald Tribune*, May 21, 1930, all in CF, HHPL; Burner, *A Public Life*, 236; Lisio, *Hoover, Blacks, and Lily-Whites*, 246; Biography of Owen J. Roberts, PP, SF, Box 193, Judiciary-Sup, Court of the U.S., Biographies of Men Considered, HHPL.

36. Lisio, *Hoover, Blacks, and Lily-Whites*, 246; Herbert Hoover, *The Memoirs of Herbert Hoover*, vol. 2., *The Cabinet and the Presidency, 1920–1933* (New York, 1952), 268–69; Burner, *A Public Life*, 236; Theodore G. Joslin Diary, Feb. 15, 1932, HHPL; MacLafferty Diary, Feb. 16, 1932; Ed., *New York Evening Post*, Feb. 16, 1932; and *New York Herald Tribune*, Jan. 24, 1932, all in CF, HHPL.

Chapter 9

1. Jordan A. Schwarz, *The Interregnum of Despair: Hoover, Congress, and the Depression* (Urbana, IL, 1970), 14.

2. *Christian Science Monitor,* Jan. 2, 1931, Clipping File (hereafter CF), Herbert Hoover Presidential Library (hereafter HHPL), West Branch, IA.

3. Susan L. DuBrock Wendel, "President Hoover and Banking Reform" (MA thesis, Northeastern Illinois University, 1985), 31.

4. Robert Sobel, *Herbert Hoover at the Onset of the Great Depression, 1929–1930* (Philadelphia, 1975), 35.

5. Eugene Lyons, *Herbert Hoover: A Biography* (Garden City, NY, 1964), 263.

6. Wendel, "President Hoover and Banking Reform," 32.

7. David M. Kennedy, *Freedom from Fear: The American People in Depression and War, 1929–1945* (New York, 1999), 57; Joan Hoff, *Herbert Hoover: Forgotten Progressive* (Boston, 1975), 93; Murray N. Rothbard, in *Herbert Hoover and the Crisis of American Capitalism,* eds. J. Joseph Huthmacher and Warren I. Susman (Cambridge, MA, 1973), 36–37.

8. French Strother, "Four Years of Hoover: An Interpretation," *New York Times,* Feb. 26, 1933, Section 8, 114–17, transcript, Reprint File (hereafter RF), HHPL; Ray Lyman Wilbur and Arthur Mastick Hyde, *The Hoover Policies* (New York, 1937), 360–65; Joslin, *Hoover off the Record,* 47–50, 81–84; Edward Eyre Hunt, "Fight on the Depression, Phase II," 1935, Box 336, Herbert Hoover Presidential File (hereafter HHPF), Hoover Archives, Stanford University.

9. The quotations and the statistics on relief overhead are from Lyons, *Hoover: A Biography,* 288. Also see Robert Bolt, "Herbert Clark Hoover of West Branch, Iowa, U.S. President of Quaker Stock," *Quaker Life* (Sep. 1984), 22–23; Strother, "Four Years of Hoover," transcript, RF, HHPL; Kennedy, *Freedom from Fear,* 47–48; David Burner, in *Understanding Herbert Hoover: Ten Perspectives,* ed. Lee Nash (Stanford University, 1987), 62.

10. Quotes from Harris Gaylord Warren, *Herbert Hoover and the Great Depression* (New York, 1967), 193–94; *New York Evening Post,* Oct. 17, 1930, CF, HHPL; Edward Eyre Hunt, "Fight on the Depression, Phase I," 1935, Box 335, HHPF, Hoover Archives, Stanford University, 102; David Burner, *Herbert Hoover: A Public Life* (New York, 1979), 259–60.

11. Sobel, *Hoover at the Onset,* 68.

12. Martin L. Fausold, *The Presidency of Herbert C. Hoover* (Lawrence, KS, 1985), 97–99; Burner, *A Public Life,* 249.

13. [Washington, DC] *U.S. Daily News,* Aug. 21, 1933, CF, HHPL.

14. Burner, *A Public Life,* 259–60; Strother, "Four Years of Hoover," 14, RF, HHPL; James H. MacLafferty Diary, Box 1, Dec. 12, 1930, HHPL, Copyright Stanford University. For unemployment rates, see U.S. Bureau of the Census, *Historical Statistics of the United States: Colonial Times to 1970,* Bicentennial Edition (Washington, DC, 1975). On the whole, the overall average of unemployment was lower for the four Hoover years than for the pre-war Roosevelt years. The year 1933 fell under Hoover until March; afterwards, under FDR.

15. *Chicago Daily News,* Aug. 8, Aug. 15, 1931, CF, HHPL.

16. *New York Herald Tribune,* Dec. 16, 1929, CF, HHPL; Presidential Papers (hereafter PP), Subject File (hereafter SF), Box 55, Accomp. of the Admin., 1930-Jan.–June.

17. *New York Evening Post,* Oct. 21, 22, 23, 1930; *New York Times,* Jan. 5, 1932, CF, HHPL; *Time* (Nov. 3, 1930), unpaginated clipping, RF, HHPL; Hunt, "Fight on the Depression, Phase I"; Burner, *A Public Life,* 266–67; Walter Starr Myers and Walter H. Newton, *The Hoover Administration: A Documented Narrative* (New York, 1936), 53; Lyons, *Hoover: A Biography,* 287–88; Wilbur and Hyde, *The Hoover Policies,* 374–75.

18. [Washington, DC] *U.S. Daily News,* April 28, 1931, and *New York Herald Tribune,* April 28, 1931, both in CF, HHPL; Burner, *A Public Life,* 265–67.

19. *New York Times,* Nov. 30, 1929; March 10, Oct. 19, 1930; *New York World,* Oct. 21, 1930, CF, HHPL.

20. Wilbur and Hyde, *The Hoover Policies*, 141; Albert U. Romasco, *The Poverty of Abundance: Hoover, the Nation, the Depression* (New York, 1968), 71.

21. Hoover, *Memoirs*, vol. 3, 21–27; Harold Wolfe, *Herbert Hoover: Public Servant and Leader of the Loyal Opposition* (New York, 1956), 236–38; Burner, *A Public Life*, 269–70; Wendel, "President Hoover and Banking Reform," 32–35.

22. Wendel, "President Hoover and Banking Reform," 37–38; Kennedy, *Freedom from Fear*, 64–69; Myers and Newton, *A Documented Narrative*, 50.

23. Fausold, *The Presidency of Herbert C. Hoover*, 151–52; Romasco, *The Poverty of Abundance*, 72–74.

24. Robert F. Himmelberg in *Herbert Hoover and the Crisis of American Capitalism*, eds. J. Joseph Huthmacher and Warren I. Susman (Cambridge, MA, 1973), 68–74.

25. Burner, *A Public Life*, 252–53; Richard Norton Smith, *An Uncommon Man: The Triumph of Herbert Hoover* (New York, 1984), 39; Taylor/Gates Coll., Box 2, A-II-9, Accomp. of the Admin., Pub. Works; Taylor/Gates Coll., Box 2, II-8, Agriculture Dept. List, HHPL; Unmarked clipping, July 1, 1930, CF, HHPL; Myers and Newton, *A Documented Narrative*, 211.

26. Schwarz, *The Interregnum of Despair*, 143–44; Myers and Newton, *A Documented Narrative*, 59, 532; Hoover, *Memoirs*, vol. 3, 145–46; *New York Times*, June 25, Dec. 24, 1930, CF, HHPL.

27. Kennedy, *Freedom from Fear*, 57–58.

28. Herbert Hoover, *The Memoirs of Herbert Hoover*, vol. 2, *The Cabinet and the Presidency, 1920–1933* (New York, 1952), 249–151; Ferry K. Heath, "Washington's Vast New Public Buildings," Master Memo and General Description, Taylor/Gates Coll., Box 1, A-1, PP, SF; Myers and Newton, *A Documented Narrative*, 385; Accomp. of the Admin., 1929, Public Buildings and Parks, HHPL; *New York Times*, July 5, 1929; [Washington, DC] *U.S. Daily News*, Sep. 3, 1930; *Chicago Daily News*, June 10, 1929; *New York Herald Tribune*, May 5, 1929; March 15, 1931, CF, HHPL.

29. Hoover, *Memoirs*, vol. 2, 251; Lyons, *Hoover: A Biography*, 225; Taylor/Gates Coll., "Stabilization of Relief of Business and Employment," Box 2, A IV-4, 1933, HHPL.

30. Taylor/Gates Coll., "Stabilization of Relief of Business and Employment," 1933, HHPL.

31. Hoover, *Memoirs*, vol. 2, 226–33; Wilbur and Hyde, *The Hoover Policies*, 266–69; Wolfe, *Public Servant*, 156.

32. "Outstanding Accomplishments in River and Harbor Work, 1929–1933," Taylor/Gates Coll., Box 1, A II-3; War Dept., Box 1, A II-3, Box 2, A II-26; Inland Waterway Corp., Memo to Mr. John W. Martyrn, Aug. 23, 1932, Taylor/Gates Coll., Box 1, A II-3, HHPL; *New York Herald Tribune*, Aug. 24, 1930, CF, HHPL.

33. Warren, *Hoover and the Great Depression*, 63–64; Myers and Newton, *A Documented Narrative*, 522–23; "The March of Events," *World's Work* 58 (Sep. 1929), 38–39; *New York Times*, July 8, 1930; [Washington, DC] *U.S. Daily News*, June 22, 1929, CF, HHPL; Ray Lyman Wilbur, *Memoirs*, 442–61.

34. Ray Lyman Wilbur, *The Memoirs of Ray Lyman Wilbur*, eds. Edgar Eugene Robinson and Paul Carroll Edwards (Stanford, CA, 1960), 442–48; [Washington, DC] *U.S. Daily News* Nov. 15, 1930, CF, HHPL; Wolfe, *Public Servant*, 131–32.

35. *New York Herald Tribune*, Jan. 10, Sep. 19, 1930; *New York Evening Post*, Sep. 17, 1930, CF, HHPL; Wilbur, *Memoirs*, 451.

36. George E. Sokolsky, "Long Delayed Tribute Paid Herbert Hoover," unmarked clipping, April 1947, Box 227, HHPF, Hoover Archives, Stanford University; Eugene Lyons, "The Ordeal—and Triumph—of Herbert Hoover," *Reader's Digest* 85, no. 512 (Dec. 1964), 165; Wilbur, *Memoirs*, 462–65; David Hinshaw, *Herbert Hoover: American Quaker* (New York, 1950), 198.

37. Burner, *A Public Life*, 181–82, 229–30, 289; Kendrick A. Clements, *Hoover, Conservation, and Consumerism: Engineering the Good Life* (Lawrence, KS, 2000), 86–87, 194–95; Wolfe, *Public Servant*, 132; Hoover, *Memoirs*, vol. 2, 230–31; Warren, *Hoover and the Great Depression*, 64.

38. *New York Times*, Dec. 31, 1930; Ed., *New York Herald Tribune*, Dec. 30, 1931; *New York Herald Tribune*, Dec. 30, 1930; Jan. 2, 1931, CF, HHPL; James Stuart Olson, *Herbert Hoover and*

the Reconstruction Finance Corporation, 1931–1933 (Ames, IA, 1977), 98; Hinshaw, *American Quaker*, 195; Burner, *A Public Life*, 278; Wilbur and Hyde, *The Hoover Policies*, 322–31.

39. *New York Times*, July 3, 1931, CF, HHPL; Wilbur and Hyde, *The Hoover Policies*, 288; Clements, *Hoover, Conservation, and Consumerism*, 173–74.

40. Myers and Newton, *A Documented Narrative*, 499–50; Hoover, *Memoirs*, vol. 2, 251–52.

41. Wilbur, *Memoirs*, 518–19; Hoover Conference with Roy A. Young, Governor of the Federal Reserve Board, March 24, 1930, PP, SF, Box 154, Financial Matters Corres., 1929–1930, HHPL; H. S. Sackett to Hoover, Telegram, Nov. 16, 1929, PP, SF, Box 91, Business, Presidential Business Conference, Nov. 16, HHPL.

42. Wilbur, *Memoirs*, 518–21; Ed., *Los Angeles Times*, Aug. 7, 1930, CF, HHPL; Sigmund Wurf to French Strother, Sep. 25, 1930, PP, SF, Box 193, Labor, Alien Labor, HHPL.

43. Myers and Newton, *A Documented Narrative*, 44.

Chapter 10

1. Jordan A. Schwarz, *The Interregnum of Despair: Hoover, Congress, and the Depression* (Urbana, IL, 1970), 76–77; *New York Times*, Dec. 2, 9, 1931, Clipping File (hereafter CF), Herbert Hoover Presidential Library (hereafter HHPL), West Branch, IA; James H. MacLafferty Diary, Box 1 [All MacLafferty citations are from Box 1], Dec. 2, 1931, HHPL.

2. E. Francis Brown, "Mr. Hoover Faces Nation's Problems," *Current History* (Jan. 1932), 578; John Spargo, *The Legend of Herbert Hoover Who "Did Nothing"* (Old Bennington, VT, 1936), 30–32, Herbert Hoover Presidential File (hereafter HHPF), Box 226, March 21, 1936, Hoover Archives, Stanford University.

3. *New York Times*, Dec. 9, 1931; [Washington, DC] *U.S. Daily News*, Dec. 9, 1931, CF, HHPL; Edward Eyre Hunt, "Fight on the Depression, Phase II," 1935, Box 336, HHPF, Hoover Archives, Stanford University, 40–44; James Stuart Olson, *Herbert Hoover and the Reconstruction Finance Corporation, 1931–1933* (Ames, IA, 1977), 33; Martin L. Fausold, *The Presidency of Herbert C. Hoover* (Lawrence, KS, 1985), 156.

4. Quotation from James S. Olson, "The End of Voluntarism: Herbert Hoover and the National Credit Corporation," *Annals of Iowa* 41 (Fall 1972), 1104; Ed., *New York Times*, Jan. 22, 1932; *New York Times*, Jan. 15, 23, 1932; *New York Evening Post*, Jan. 22, 1932, CF, HHPL; Olson, *Hoover and the Reconstruction Finance Corporation*, 12, 34–38, 58; Fausold, *The Presidency of Hoover*, 153–54; Herbert Hoover, *The Memoirs of Herbert Hoover*, vol. 3, *The Great Depression, 1919–1941* (New York, 1952), 107–8; David Quigley, "Assessing the Hoover Presidency," in *Uncommon Americans: The Lives and Legacies of Herbert and Lou Henry Hoover*, ed. Timothy Walch (Westport, CT, 2003), 189; Schwarz, *The Interregnum of Despair*, 88–92; MacLafferty Diary, Jan. 2, 1932; David Burner, *Herbert Hoover: A Public Life* (New York, 1979), 272–75.

5. *New York Times*, Jan. 26, 1932, CF, HHPL; Albert U. Romasco, *The Poverty of Abundance: Hoover, the Nation, the Depression* (New York, 1968), 191; William Starr Myers and Walter H. Newton, *The Hoover Administration: A Documented Narrative* (New York, 1936), 164; Ray Lyman Wilbur and Arthur Mastick Hyde, *The Hoover Policies* (New York, 1937), 424–25.

6. David M. Kennedy, *Freedom from Fear: The American People in Depression and War, 1929–1945* (New York, 1999), 76–77; Burner, *A Public Life*, 270.

7. Kennedy, *Freedom from Fear*, 77; Theodore G. Joslin, *Hoover off the Record* (Garden City, NY, 1934), 170–73; Olson, "The End of Voluntarism," 1104; Mastick and Hyde, *The Hoover Policies*, 470.

8. [Washington, DC] *U.S. Daily News*, Dec. 18, 1931; *New York Herald Tribune*, Nov. 27, 1931; *New York Herald Tribune*, Jan. [undated], 1932, CF, HHPL.

9. Hunt, "Fight on the Depression, Phase II," 48.

10. Schwarz, *The Interregnum of Despair*, 96–98; MacLafferty Diary, Feb. 11, 16, 17, 29, 1932, HHPL; *New York Times*, Jan. 29, 1932; Ed., *New York Herald Tribune*, Feb. 17, 1932; *New York Herald Tribune*, Feb. 24, 25, 1932, CF, HHPL; Theodore G. Joslin Diaries, Feb. 14, 28, 1932, HHPL.

11. *New York Herald Tribune*, Feb. 11, 1932; *New York Times*, Feb. 12, 27, 1932; *New York Evening Post*, Feb. 27, 1932, CF, HHPL; Romasco, *The Poverty of Abundance*, 191–93; Joslin Diary, Feb. 11, 1932, HHPL.
12. Schwarz, *The Interregnum of Despair*, 100–101; Kennedy, *Freedom from Fear*, 62–63.
13. Hoover, *Memoirs*, vol. 3, 101–2.
14. Schwarz, *The Interregnum of Despair*, 62–63, 65–67, 69–71, 102–4, 117; Kennedy, *Freedom from Fear*, 61–62.
15. Kennedy, *Freedom from Fear*, 62.
16. Kennedy, *Freedom from Fear*, 62. For insights into Michelson's work see his own book, Charles Michelson, *The Ghost Talks* (New York, 1944).
17. Hoover, *Memoirs*, vol. 3, 104.
18. Joslin Diary, Box 10, File 7, March 30, 1932, HHPL.
19. *New York Times*, Feb. 21, 1932, CF, HHPL.
20. *New York Evening Post*, Feb. 20, 1932; *Chicago Daily News*, Feb. 24, 1932; *New York Times*, Feb. 19, 1932; *U.S. Daily News*, Dec. 30, 1931, CF, HHPL; MacLafferty Diary, Feb. 17, 19, 23, 1932; HHPL; Harold Wolfe, *Herbert Hoover: Public Servant and Leader of the Loyal Opposition* (New York, 1956), 154; Harris Gaylord Warren, *Herbert Hoover and the Great Depression* (New York, 1967), 70–71; Joslin, *Hoover off the Record*, 205–6; Herbert Hoover, *The Memoirs of Herbert Hoover*, vol. 2, *The Cabinet and the Presidency, 1920–1933* (New York, 1952), 282–84.
21. Susan L. DuBrock Wendel, "President Hoover and Banking Reform" (MA thesis, Northeastern Illinois University, 1985), deserves reading in its entirety. For specific details see Hoover, *Memoirs*, vol. 3, 124; Warren, *Hoover and the Great Depression*, 164; Eugene Lyons, *Herbert Hoover: A Biography* (Garden City, NY, 1964), 279; Myers and Newton, *A Documented Narrative*, 166–67.
22. *New York Herald Tribune*, April 25, 1932; *New York Times*, April 25, 1932; *New York Evening Post*, April 25, 1932, CF, HHPL; Lyons, *Hoover: A Biography*, 216–17; Warren, *Hoover and the Great Depression*, 112–13.
23. *Time*, "Business and Finance: Bear Hunt" (April 25, 1932), 49, Reprint File (hereafter RF), HHPL.
24. *New York Times*, June 25, 1932, CF, HHPL.
25. Kennedy, *Freedom from Fear*, 81; David E. Finley, "The Admin.'s Reconstruction Program," in *New York Times*, Feb. 28, 1932, Presidential Papers (hereafter PP), Subject File (hereafter SF), Box 55, Accomp. of the Admin., 1932-Jan.–March, HHPL; Ed., *New York Evening Post*, Aug. 1, 1932, CF, HHPL; David Hinshaw, *Herbert Hoover: American Quaker* (New York, 1950), 70; Text of Speech by Will R. Wood, Chairman of the Congressional National Committee, Rebutting Shouse Attack on Hoover, March 28, 1932, NBC Broadcast, in MacLafferty Diary, undated entry, HHPL.
26. *New York Times*, June 1, July 1, Dec. 31, 1931; Jan. 3, Feb. 10, 1932; *New York Sun*, June 3, 1931, CF, HHPL.
27. *New York Times*, May 1, 2, July 25, 1931; *New York Herald Tribune*, May 12, 1931; Myers and Newton, *A Documented Narrative*, 197; Taylor/Gates Coll., Box 2, A-IV-2, Budget, HHPL.
28. *New York Herald Tribune*, April 16, 1932; *Chicago Daily News*, April 11, July 16, 1932; *New York Evening Post*, April 26, 30, 1932, HHPL; Joslin Diary, April 4, 5, 8, 11, 1932, HHPL; MacLafferty Diary, April 17, 29, 1932, HHPL.
29. Joslin Diary, May 5, 1932, HHPL.
30. *New York Times*, June 9, 15, 30, 1932; [Washington, DC] *U.S. Daily News*, June 30, 1932; *Chicago Daily News*, June 17, 30, 1932, CF, HHPL; Joslin Diary, June 11, 1932, HHPL; Myers and Newton, *A Documented Narrative*, 219–23; Wilbur and Hyde, *The Hoover Policies*, 462.
31. Myers and Newton, *A Documented Narrative*, 174.
32. *New York Herald Tribune*, March 24, 25, 1932; *New York Times*, March 27, 1932, CF, HHPL; Burner, *A Public Life*, 281; Fausold, *The Presidency of Herbert C. Hoover*, 161; MacLafferty Diary, March 8, 10, 11, 16, 18, 21, 23, 24, 26, 31, 1932, HHPL; Schwarz, *The Interregnum of Despair*, 120–30; Joslin Diary, Box 10, File 7, March 21, 1932, HHPL.

33. *New York Times*, May 6, 22, 5, 27, 28, June 3, 7, July 17, 1931; *New York Herald Tribune*, May 22, 31, June 4, 7, 1931, CF, HHPL; Joslin Diary, May 31, 1931, HHPL; Kennedy, *Freedom from Fear*, 81.

34. Fausold, *The Presidency of Herbert C. Hoover*, 164–65; Schwarz, *The Interregnum of Despair*, 151–56; *New York Times*, Feb. 13, 17, 1932; *New York Herald Tribune*, Jan. 30, 1932, CF, HHPL; MacLafferty Diary, May 28, 1932, HHPL. Copyright Stanford University.

35. *New York Times*, May 22, 28, 1932; *New York Herald Tribune*, June 25, 1932, CF, HHPL.

36. Schwarz, *The Interregnum of Despair*, 165.

37. *New York Times*, May 22, 28, 1932; *New York Herald Tribune*, June 25, July 7, 1932; *New York Evening Post*, May 19, 1932; Ed., *New York Evening Post*, July 7, 1932, CF, HHPL; MacLafferty Diary, June 2, 7, 24, 1932, HHPL.

38. Schwarz, *The Interregnum of Despair*, 165–71; Clair Everet Nelsen, "The Image of Herbert Hoover as Reflected in the American Press" (PhD diss., Stanford University, 1956), 137; Joslin Diary, July 9, 1932, HHPL: MacLafferty Diary, July 7, 8, 1932, HHPL; Statement of John Nance Garner, Speaker of the House, From Hearings Before the House Committee on Ways and Means, May 31, June 1, 2, in PP, SF, Box 248, Reconstruction Finance Corporation, History of, HHPL; Statement of Ogden L. Mills Before the House Ways and Means Committee, June 2, 1932, Reconstruction Finance Corporation, History of, PP, SF, Box 248, HHPL.

39. Olson, *Hoover and the Reconstruction Finance Corporation*, 67–69.

40. Myers and Newton, *A Documented Narrative*, 205–6; Schwarz, *The Interregnum of Despair*, 160–64; Olson, *Hoover and the Reconstruction Finance Corporation*, 69–71.

41. *New York Herald Tribune*, July 12, 1932; *Chicago Daily News*, July 21, 1932; *New York Times*, July 17, 1932, CF, HHPL; Olson, *Hoover and the Reconstruction Finance Corporation*, 87.

42. Olson, *Hoover and the Reconstruction Finance Corporation*, 71–72; Wendel, "President Hoover and Banking Reform," 63–66; MacLafferty Diary, July 14, 1932, HHPL.

43. Olson, *Hoover and the Reconstruction Finance Corporation*, 73, 89; Joslin, *Hoover off the Record*, 257–59; Fausold, *The Presidency of Herbert C. Hoover*, 166.

44. Unmarked clipping, Nov. 13, 1932; *New York Times*, Feb. 8, June 12, 16, 26, 1932; *New York Herald Tribune*, Dec. 1, 1931; July 23, 1932, CF, HHPL; Wendel, "President Hoover and Banking Reform," 51–52; Home Loan Bank Board, Taylor/Gates Coll., Box 2, A-II-27; Wilbur and Hyde, *The Hoover Policies*, 439–41; Myers and Newton, *A Documented Narrative*, 506–7; Joslin Diary, July 16, 1932, HHPL; Joslin, *Hoover off the Record*, 149–51, 260.

45. Wendel, "President Hoover and Banking Reform," 63, 80–97.

46. Warren, *Hoover and the Great Depression*, 69; Wolfe, *Public Servant*, 149–50.

47. William Allen White, ed., *Emporia Gazette*, July 13, 1932, CF, HHPL.

48. Romasco, *The Poverty of Abundance*, 221–23.

Chapter 11

1. Louis W. Liebovich, *Bylines in Despair: Herbert Hoover, the Great Depression, and the U.S. News Media* (Westport, CT, 1994), 148–49; Edward Eyre Hunt, "Fight on the Depression, Phase II," 1935, Box 336, Herbert Hoover Presidential File (hereafter HHPF), Hoover Archives, Stanford University, 79; Herbert Hoover, *The Memoirs of Herbert Hoover*, vol. 3, *The Great Depression, 1919–1941* (New York, 1952), 152.

2. Theodore G. Joslin, *Hoover off the Record* (Garden City, NY, 1934); *New York Herald Tribune*, March 4, 1932, Clipping File (hereafter CF), Herbert Hoover Presidential Library (hereafter HHPL), West Branch, IA.

3. Edwin Balmer and William Crawford, "When You Meet the President," *Redbook* (March 1932), 112, Reprint File (hereafter RF), HHPL.

4. Theodore G. Joslin Diary, Box 10, File 7, March 28, 1932, HHPL. [All citations from Joslin are from the same box and file].

5. *Chicago Daily News*, April 1, 1932, CF, HHPL.

6. James S. Olson, "Herbert Hoover and the Analogue of War," *Palimpsest* 54 (July/Aug. 1973), 28, RF, HHPL.
7. Albert U. Romasco, *The Poverty of Abundance: Hoover, the Nation, the Depression* (New York, 1968), 178–79.
8. *Chicago Daily News*, May 25, 26, 1932, CF, HHPL.
9. [Washington, DC] *U.S. Daily News*, June 9, 1931; *Chicago Daily News*, July 29, 1931, CF, HHPL; Business Stabilization of Industry Plans, Presidential Papers (hereafter PP), Subject File (hereafter SF), Box 92, 1931, June-July and undated, HHPL.
10. *Chicago Daily News*, Aug. 13, 17, 20, 21, 25, 1931; [Washington, DC] *U.S. Daily News*, Aug. 20, Sep. 26, 1931; *New York Evening Post*, Aug. 20, 1931; *New York Evening Post*, Aug. 20, 1931; *New York Herald Tribune*, Aug. 23, 1931, CF, HHPL; David M. Kennedy, *Freedom from Fear: The American People in Depression and War, 1929–1945* (New York, 1999), 88; Hunt, "Fight on the Depression, Phase II."
11. *New York Times*, Sep. 18, Oct. 29, 1931; *New York Herald Tribune*, Sep. 19, 1931; [Washington, DC] *U.S. Daily News*, Sep. 26, 1931, CF, HHPL.
12. [Washington, DC] *U.S. Daily News*, July 22, Nov. 28, 1931; *New York Times*, Aug. 7, 13, 1931; *New York Herald Tribune*, Aug. 30, 1931; *Chicago Daily News*, Oct. 31, CF, HHPL.
13. Joslin Diary, Feb. 18, 1932, HHPL; William Starr Myers and Walter H. Newton, *The Hoover Administration: A Documented Narrative* (New York, 1936), 225; David Burner, *Herbert Hoover: A Public Life* (New York, 1979), 276; Hunt, "Fight on the Depression, Phase II," unpaginated.
14. *New York Herald Tribune*, Feb. 6, 1932; *New York Times*, May 2, 1932, CF, HHPL.
15. Hunt "Fight on the Depression, Phase II," unpaginated.
16. [Washington, DC] *U.S. Daily News*, Aug. 24, 1932; *New York Herald Tribune*, Aug. 27, 1932; Hunt, "Fight on the Depression, Phase II," unpaginated.
17. *New York Herald Tribune*, Aug. 30, Sep. 16, Oct. 17, 1932, CF, HHPL; Hunt, "Fight on the Depression, Phase II," unpaginated.
18. *New York Times*, Feb. 4, 1932; *New York Herald Tribune*, Sep. 30, 1931; *New York Evening Post*, Feb. 8, 9, 1932; *Chicago Daily News*, Feb. 4, 1932; *Chicago Tribune*, Feb. 4, 1932, CF, HHPL; James H. MacLafferty Diary, Box 1, Feb. 19, 1932, HHPL, Copyright Stanford University; Joslin Diary, Oct. 12, 1931, HHPL; Hunt, "Fight on the Depression, Phase II," unpaginated; James Stuart Olson, *Herbert Hoover and the Reconstruction Finance Corporation, 1931–1933* (Ames, IA, 1977), 49.
19. *New York Evening Post*, Feb. 29, March 7, 1932; *Chicago Daily News*, March 7, 11, 1932; *New York Times*, March 18, 1932; Ogden L. Mills, "The Reconstruction Program," *New York Herald Tribune Magazine*, March 20, 1932, 1–3, 20, CF, HHPL.
20. *New York Times*, Nov. 22, 1931, CF, HHPL.
21. *New York Times*, Jan. 26, 1932; *New York Herald Tribune*, Jan. 26, 1932, CF, HHPL.
22. *New York Herald Tribune*, April 4, Aug. 8, 1932, CF, HHPL.
23. [Washington, DC] *U.S. Daily News*, Nov. 7, 1932, CF, HHPL.
24. Martin L. Fausold, *The Presidency of Herbert C. Hoover* (Lawrence, KS, 1985), 99–100.
25. Joan Hoff, *Herbert Hoover: Forgotten Progressive* (Boston, 1975), 132, 152; Fausold, *The Presidency of Herbert C. Hoover*, 117–18; Hunt, "Fight on the Depression, Phase II," unpaginated; *New York Herald Tribune*, Sep. 16, 1931, CF, HHPL; Stabilization of Industry Plans, 1931-Swope Plan, Statement of U.S. Senator Felix Hebert on the Subject of Stabilization of Industry, PP, SF, Box 92, Business, Stabilization of Industrial Plans, 1931, p. 4, HHPL; William Donovan, Analysis of Swope Plan, Sep. 4, 1931, PP, SF, Box 92, Business, Stabilization of Industry Plans, 1931, Sep. 1-15, p. 6, HHPL; Opinion of Acting Attorney General Howard Thatcher on Constitutionality of the Swope Plan, Oct. 1, 1932, p. 2, PP, SF, Box 92, Business, Stabilization of Industry Plans, Oct., 1931, HHPL.
26. Charles A. Beard, "A Five-Year Plan for America," *Forum* 86 (July 1931), 1–11, PP, SF, Box 92, Business, Stabilization of Industry Plans, Sep. 1-15, HHPL.
27. Fausold, *The Presidency of Herbert C. Hoover*, 142.
28. *New York Times*, Dec. 6, 19, 1931; July 24, Nov. 22, Dec. 13, 1932; *New York Herald Tribune*, Dec. 20, 1931; July 26, 1932, CF, HHPL.

29. *New York Herald Tribune,* June 9, 1931, CF, HHPL.
30. *Chicago Daily News,* Aug. 9, 1931; *New York Times,* Dec. 18, 1931, CF, HHPL.
31. *New York Times,* Dec. 14, 1931; Jan. 2, 1932; *Chicago Daily News,* Sep. 6, 10, 1932, CF, HHPL; Burner, *A Public Life,* 267; Myers and Newton, *A Documented Narrative,* 165.
32. *Chicago Daily News,* Sep. 9, 1932; *New York Herald Tribune,* Sep. 10, 1932; *New York Times,* Sep. 13, 1932, CF, HHPL; Hoover, *Memoirs,* vol. 3, 450.
33. Murray N. Rothbard, in *Herbert Hoover and the Crisis of American Capitalism,* eds. J. Joseph Huthmacher and Warren I. Susman (Cambridge, MA, 1973), 46; Hoover, *Memoirs,* vol. 3, 145; Harris Gaylord Warren, *Herbert Hoover and the Great Depression* (New York, 1967), 66; John Spargo, *The Legend of Herbert Hoover Who "Did Nothing"* (Old Bennington, VT, 1936), HHPF, Box 226, March 21, 1936, Hoover Archives, Stanford University.
34. Hoover to Herbert S. Crocker, May 22, 1932, pp. 1–10, PP, SF, Box 248, RFC, History of, HHPL; Text of Hoover letter on Public Works Plan, May 23, 1932, Associated Press, in James H. MacLafferty Diary, Box 1, HHPL, Copyright Stanford University.
35. *New York Evening Post,* Oct. 6, 7, 1931; *New York Times,* Oct. 6, 7, 1931; *New York Herald Tribune,* Oct. 7, 1931; Olson, *Hoover and the Reconstruction Finance Corporation,* 24–27; Myers and Newton, *A Documented Narrative,* 118, 127–28; Romasco, *The Poverty of Abundance,* 89–90; Fausold, *The Presidency of Herbert C. Hoover,* 153; Hunt, "Fight on the Depression, Phase II," unpaginated.
36. *New York Herald Tribune,* Oct. 8, 1931; *New York Times,* Oct. 9, 30, 1931; *U.S. Daily News,* Oct. 10, 1932; *Chicago Daily News,* Oct. 31, 1931, CF, HHPL; Olson, *Hoover and the Reconstruction Finance Corporation,* 27–28.
37. *New York Times,* Nov. 7, 9, 1931; Romasco, *The Poverty of Abundance,* 92–95; James S. Olson, "The End of Voluntarism: Herbert Hoover and the National Credit Corporation," *Annals of Iowa* 41 (Fall 1972), 1110–12; Olson, *Hoover and the Reconstruction Finance Corporation,* 27–29; Myers and Newton, *A Documented Narrative,* 144; Hoover, *Memoirs,* vol. 3, 97.
38. Olson, *Hoover and the Reconstruction Finance Corporation,* 3–32.
39. Ibid., 40–48; *New York Times,* Jan. 26, Feb. 3, 1932, CF, HHPL; James S. Olson, "Herbert Hoover and the Analogue of War," 30–31.
40. Olson, *Hoover and the Reconstruction Finance Corporation,* 39–49; *New York Evening Post,* Feb. 6, 1932; *New York Times,* Feb. 9, 12, 1932, CF, HHPL.
41. Olson, *Hoover and the Reconstruction Finance Corporation,* 50; Liebovich, *Bylines in Despair,* 150; Victor L. Albjerg, "Hoover: The Presidency in Transition," *Current History* 39, no. 230 (May 1960), 218; Statement by Charles G. Dawes Before House Ways and Means Committee, April 21, 1932, PP, SF, Box 248, RFC, History of; [Washington, DC] *U.S. Daily News,* April 22, 1932, CF, HHPL.
42. Joslin Diary, Box 10, File 7, Feb. 12, March 16, 22, 1932, HHPL.
43. *New York Times,* June 6, 1932; *New York Herald Tribune,* Oct. 5, 1932; *Washington Herald,* June 6, 1932, PP, SF, Reconstruction Finance Corporation, History of, 3–6; Burner, *A Public Life,* 274–75.
44. Joslin Diary, June 5, 1932, HHPL; Olson, *Hoover and the Reconstruction Finance Corporation,* 57–58.
45. Joslin Diary, May 23, 1932, HHPL; Dawes to Hoover [letter of resignation], June 6, 1932, PP, SF, Box 248, RFC, History of, 1–2, HHPL; MacLafferty Diary, June 7, 1932, HHPL, Copyright Stanford University.
46. Olson, *Hoover and the Reconstruction Finance Corporation,* 59; Harold Wolfe, *Herbert Hoover: Public Servant and Leader of the Loyal Opposition* (New York, 1956), 239; Joslin Diary, June 27, 1932, HHPL; Myers and Newton, *A Documented History,* 219.
47. Olson, *Hoover and the Reconstruction Finance Corporation,* 51–61, 117. Quotation on 117.
48. Joslin Diary, July 6, 24, Sep. 16, 1932, HHPL; Joslin, *Hoover off the Record,* 286–89; *New York Evening Post,* July 29, 1932, CF, HHPL; Olson, *Hoover and the Reconstruction Finance Corporation,* 75–77.
49. Olson, *Hoover and the Reconstruction Finance Corporation,* 77–79, 84–86.
50. Ibid., 93–97.

51. *New York Evening Post*, Aug. 17, 24, 1932, CF, HHPL; Susan L. DuBrock Wendel, "President Hoover and Banking Reform" (MA thesis, Northeastern Illinois University, 1985), 66; Joslin Diary, Aug. 18, 1932, HHPL.
52. *New York Times*, Aug. 10, 27, Oct. 14, 16, 1932; [Washington, DC] *U.S. Daily News*, Feb. 9, Aug. 8, 1932, CF, HHPL; J. E. McDonough, "The Federal Home Loan Bank System," *American Economic Review* 24 (Dec. 1934), 671–75.

Chapter 12

1. Albert U. Romasco, *The Poverty of Abundance: Hoover, the Nation, the Depression* (New York, 1963), 102–3.
2. Romasco, *The Poverty of Abundance*, 98–99; David Burner, *Herbert Hoover: A Public Life* (New York, 1979), 167; Harold Wolfe, *Herbert Hoover: Public Servant and Leader of the Loyal Opposition* (New York, 1956), 232; David E. Hamilton, *From New Day to New Deal: American Farm Policy from Hoover to Roosevelt, 1928–1933* (Chapel Hill, NC, 1991), 59.
3. Glen Jeansonne, *A Time of Paradox: America from Awakening to Hiroshima, 1890–1945* (Lanham, MD, 2007), 145; Hamilton, *From New Day to New Deal*, 67.
4. Romasco, *The Poverty of Abundance*, 113; Burner, *A Public Life*, 238.
5. "The March of Events," *World's Work* 58 (Sep. 1929), 35–36, Reprint File (hereafter RF), Herbert Hoover Presidential Library (hereafter HHPL), West Branch, IA; *New York Herald Tribune*, June 30, 1929; *New York Times*, July 30, 1929, Clipping File (hereafter CF), HHPL.
6. C. C. Teague to Laurence Richey, Jan. 9, 1930; C. R. Hare to A. R. Rule, Jan. 7, 1930; Carl Williams to Herbert Hoover, July 10, 1930, Presidential Papers (hereafter PP), Subject File (hereafter SF), Box 127, Farm Matters—Cooperative Marketing, 1930–1933, HHPL.
7. *New York World*, Feb. 4, 7, Nov. 26, 1930; Ed., *New York World*, June 27, July 16, 1930; *New York Times*, Feb. 11, 26, 27, 28, July 15, Nov. 17, 21, Dec. 6, 1930; *New York Herald Tribune*, Nov. 18, 1930; *Chicago Daily News*, March 8, 1930, CF, HHPL.
8. C. Roger Lambert, "Herbert Hoover and the Federal Farm Board Wheat," *Heritage of Kansas* no. 10 (Spring 1977), 28, RF, HHPL.
9. Lambert, "Herbert Hoover and the Federal Farm Board Wheat," 25–27; *New York World*, July 12, 1930, CF, HHPL; Martin L. Fausold, *The Presidency of Herbert C. Hoover* (Lawrence, KS, 1985), 108–10.
10. Burner, *A Public Life*, 240; Hoover Objectives for Congress, 1932, PP, SF, Box 81, Bills-Relief-Drafts, 1932, HHPL.
11. *New York Times*, Feb. 19, July 10, Aug. 1, Nov. 6, 7, 9, 1931; Ed., *New York Times*, Nov. 3, 1931; *New York Herald Tribune*, June 10, 1931, CF, HHPL; Hamilton, *From New Day to New Deal*, 105–8.
12. Theodore G. Joslin Diary, Box 1, Aug. 12, 1931, HHPL; *New York Times*, Aug. 11, 13, Sep. 9, 11, 1931; *New York Herald Tribune*, Sep. 10, 1931, CF, HHPL.
13. *New York Times*, Feb. 15, March 23, 24, Sep. 10, 1931; Ed., *New York Evening Post*, Feb. 17, 1931; *New York Herald Tribune*, April 5, 1931; unmarked clipping, March 29, 1931; CF, HHPL; "National Affairs," *Time* (March 16, 1931), 14.
14. *New York Times*, April 22, June 27, 19, Aug. 22, Sep. 12, 1931; Ed., *New York Times*, Aug. 21, 1931; *New York Times*, July 31, Sep. 26, Dec. 9, 1932; *New York Evening Post*, Aug. 20, June 29, 1931; *New York Herald Tribune*, July 2, 1931; [Washington, DC] *U.S. Daily News*, Aug. 31, 1931; July 5, 7, 1932, CF, HHPL; Burner, *A Public Life*, 241–43; Fausold, *The Presidency of Herbert C. Hoover*, 110; Wolfe, *Public Servant*, 233–34.
15. James C. Stone, "A Fair Deal for the Farmer," *New York Herald Tribune Magazine*, May 8, 1932, CF, HHPL; James H. MacLafferty Diary, March 4, 1932, Box 1, HHPL, Accomp. of the Federal Farm Board, Taylor/Gates Coll., Box 2, A II-13, Federal Farm Board, 1933, HHPL.
16. List of Accomp. of the Dept. of Agriculture, 1933, Taylor/Gates Coll., Box 2, A II-8, HHPL.
17. List of Accomp, Dept. of Agriculture, Taylor/Gates Coll., Box 2, A II-8, 1933, HHPL.

18. Ray Lyman Wilbur and Arthur Mastick Hyde, *The Hoover Policies* (New York, 1937), 442–46; Hamilton, *From New Day to New Deal*, 150–54, 168, 195; Federal Farm Loan Board [Memo on], May 26, 1933, Taylor/Gates Coll., Box 1, A II-6, Federal Farm Loan Board, HHPL; Herbert Hoover, *The Memoirs of Herbert Hoover*, vol. 3, *The Great Depression, 1929–1941* (New York, 1952), 156–57; *New York Times*, Feb. 1, 1933; *New York Herald Tribune*, Oct. 8, 1931; *Chicago Tribune*, Oct. 20, 1931, CF, HHPL.

19. Romasco, *The Poverty of Abundance*, 120.

20. *New York Times*, Dec. 10, 1931, Ed., Dec. 10, 1931; *New York Herald Tribune*, March 5, 1933, CF, HHPL; Wilbur and Hyde, *The Hoover Policies*, 158–62; Romasco, *The Poverty of Abundance*, 118–23; Martin L. Fausold and George T. Mazuzan, Eds., *The Hoover Presidency: A Reappraisal* (Albany, NY, 1974), 12.

21. Hamilton, *From New Day to New Deal*, 132, 140, 147, 247; Wilbur and Hyde, *The Hoover Policies*, 169–72.

22. Burner, *A Public Life*, 279.

23. Ed., *New York Herald Tribune*, March 7, 1932; Ed., *New York Times*, March 6, 1932, CF, HHPL.

24. *New York Herald Tribune*, March 5, 1932, CF, HHPL.

25. Donald J. Lisio, *The President and Protest: Hoover, Conspiracy, and the Bonus Riot* (Columbia, MO, 1974), 6–8; Louis W. Liebovich, *Bylines in Despair: Herbert Hoover, the Great Depression, and the U.S. News Media* (Westport, CT, 1994), 155–56; Herbert Hoover, *The Memoirs of Herbert Hoover*, vol. 2, *The Cabinet and the Presidency, 1920–1933* (New York, 1952), 286–90; Harris Gaylord Warren, *Herbert Hoover and the Great Depression* (New York, 1967), 225–27; Eugene Lyons, *Herbert Hoover: A Biography* (Garden City, NY, 1964), 266–67.

26. Lisio, *The President and Protest*, 22–23, 27–29, 34–37, quote on 27; David Hinshaw, *Herbert Hoover: American Quaker* (New York, 1950), 213–14; Burner, *A Public Life*, 309.

27. Burner, *A Public Life*, 309; MacLafferty Diary, Jan. 21, 1932, HHPL, Copyright Stanford University; *New York Times*, May 31, 1932, CF, HHPL.

28. William Starr Myers and Walter H. Newton, *The Hoover Administration: A Documented Narrative* (New York, 1936), 66–69; Warren, *Hoover and the Great Depression*, 225–27; Liebovich, *Bylines in Despair*, 156; Theodore G. Joslin, *Hoover off the Record* (Garden City, NY, 1934), 64–67; Wilbur and Hyde, *The Hoover Policies*, 1937), 201–3; *New York Times*, Sep. 4, 22, 1931; *New York Herald Tribune*, Sep. 20, 1931, CF, HHPL.

29. Lisio, *The President and Protest*, 49; MacLafferty Diary, June 2, 1932, HHPL; *New York Times*, June 15, 1932, CF, HHPL.

30. Lisio, *The President and Protest*, 71; Liebovich, *Bylines in Despair*, 157–59.

31. Lisio, *The President and Protest*, 54, 71–77, 80–87, 96–99, 104–5; Liebovich, *Bylines in Despair*, 159; Lyons, *Hoover: A Biography*, 241; Burner, *A Public Life*, 309.

32. Lisio, *The President and Protest*, 107–8, 110–11, 113–15, 118–25, 133–38, 140–48; Hoover, *Memoirs*, vol. 3, 225–27; *New York Evening Post*, July 9, 1932; *New York Herald Tribune*, July 13, 1932, CF, HHPL.

33. *New York Times*, Sep. 12, 1932, CF, HHPL.

34. Lisio, *The President and Protest*, 157; *New York Herald Tribune*, July 27, 28, 1932; *New York Times*, July 28, 1932; *Chicago Daily News*, July 27, 1932, CF, HHPL.

35. *Washington Evening Star*, Aug. 4, 1932; *New York Times*, Sep. 12, 1932, CF, HHPL.

36. Burner, *A Public Life*, 310–11; *Washington Evening Star*, Aug. 4, 1932, CF, HHPL; Lisio, *The President and Protest*, 186–213; Joslin, *Hoover off the Record*, 267–80.

37. *New York Times*, Sep. 12, 1932, CF, HHPL.

38. Lisio, *The President and Protest*, 214–23, 276, 285–90; Burner, *A Public Life*, 311–12; Interview with General MacArthur by the Press at 11 p.m., July 28, 1932, PPP, SF, Box 214, MacArthur, General Douglas, Corres., 1942–1964, HHPL; *New York Herald Tribune*, July 30, Sep. 13, 1932; *New York Times*, Sep. 13, 1932, CF, HHPL.

39. Liebovich, *Bylines in Despair*, 160–61; Hinshaw, *American Quaker*, 215–16; Hoover, *Memoirs*, vol. 3, 232; Warren, *Hoover and the Great Depression*, 229–31; *New York Times*, Sep. 12, Sep. 13, 1932, CF, HHPL.

40. *New York Times*, Sep. 13, 1932, CF, HHPL.

41. Lisio, *The President and Protest*, fn. 275.
42. Glen Jeansonne, *Transformation and Reaction: America, 1921–1945* (Long Grove, IL, 2004), 119.
43. Lisio, *The President and Protest*, 285.
44. Ibid., 281.
45. Ibid., 295.
46. Ibid., 298.
47. Patrick J. Hurley, "The Facts About the Bonus March," *McCall's* 77, no. 143 (Nov. 1949), unpaginated copy, Box 227, Herbert Hoover Presidential File (HHPF), Hoover Institution, Stanford University.

Chapter 13

1. Robert Sobel, *Herbert Hoover at the Onset of the Great Depression, 1929–1930* (Philadelphia, 1975), 27.
2. Donald J. Lisio, *Hoover, Blacks, and Lily-Whites: A Study of Southern Strategies* (Chapel Hill, NC, 1985), 187–89.
3. Lisio, *Hoover, Blacks, and Lily-Whites*, 187–89, 311; David Burner, *Herbert Hoover: A Public Life* (New York, 1979), 215; Joan Hoff, *Herbert Hoover: Forgotten Progressive* (Boston, 1975), 135–36; *New York Herald Tribune*, Aug. 8, 1929, Clipping File (hereafter CF), Herbert Hoover Presidential Library (hereafter HHPL), West Branch, IA.
4. Kelly Miller, "The Negro's Place under Hoover Assayed by a Negro Educator," *New York Times*, CF, HHPL; Lisio, *Hoover, Blacks, and Lily-Whites*, 11–12.
5. Herbert Hoover, "Herbert Hoover's Mississippi Valley Land Reform Memorandum: A Document," ed., Bruce A. Lohof, *Arkansas Historical Quarterly* 29, no. 2 (Summer 1970), Reprint File (hereafter RF), HHPL; Lisio, *Hoover, Blacks, and Lily-Whites*, 15–19; David E. Hamilton, *from New Day to New Deal: American Farm Policy from Hoover to Roosevelt, 1928–1933* (Chapel Hill, NC, 1991), 40.
6. Burner, *A Public Life*, 196, 216.
7. Martin L. Fausold, *The Presidency of Herbert C. Hoover* (Lawrence, KS, 1985), 58; Nancy Beck Young, *Lou Henry Hoover: Activist First Lady* (Lawrence, KS, 2004), 66; Burner, *A Public Life*, 214–15.
8. Quote from Lisio, *Hoover, Blacks, and Lily-Whites*, 21. See also, George F. Garcia, "Herbert Hoover and the Issue of Race," *Annals of Iowa* 44, no. 7 (Winter 1979), 507–15. For Hoover's desegregation of the Commerce Dept. see William Pickett Helm, "Political Winds Against Hoover," *Outlook and Independent* 157 (April 15, 1931), 530–32; Lisio, *Hoover, Blacks, and Lily-Whites*, 31; B. D. Nash to Hoover, March 13, 1926, CP, Subject File (hereafter SF), Box 427, National Association for the Advancement of Colored People, 1921–1928, HHPL.
9. David S. Day, "A New Perspective on the 'DePriest Tea' Historiographic Controversy," *Journal of Negro History* 75, no. 314 (Summer–Autumn 1990), 121–23; Young, *Lou Henry Hoover: Activist First Lady* (Lawrence, KS, 2004), 67–71; Dale Mayer, *Lou Henry Hoover: A Prototype for First Ladies* (Hauppauge, NY, 2004), 246–47; Lisio, *Hoover, Blacks, and Lily-Whites*, 135; *Houston Chronicle*, June 14, 1929; *New York World*, June 15, 1929, CF, HHPL; Statement by Mrs. Hoover [1929], Presidential Papers (hereafter PP), SF, Box 106, Colored Quest., DePriest Incident, Corres., 1929, June 14, HHPL.
10. Mayer, *A Prototype for First Ladies*, 246–47; Young, *Activist First Lady*, 67–71; *New York Times*, July 7, 1929; *New York World*, June 16, 17, 1929, CF, HHPL; *Tallahassee Daily Democrat*, June 16, 1929, PP, SF, Box 106, Colored Quest., DePriest Incident, Corres., 1929, June 16–20, HHPL.
11. Helen B. Pryor, *Lou Henry Hoover: Gallant First Lady* (New York, 1969), 179–81.
12. [Jackson, MS] *Daily News*, excerpt carried in *New York World*, June 21, 1929, CF, HHPL.
13. *New York Times*, July 4, 1929; *New York World*, June 17, 1929, CF, HHPL; Harold Wolfe, *Herbert Hoover: Public Servant and Leader of the Loyal Opposition* (New York, 1956), 164; Lisio, *Hoover, Blacks, and Lily-Whites*, 137.

14. David S. Day, "Herbert Hoover and Racial Politics: The DePriest Incident," *Journal of Negro History* 65, no. 1 (Winter 1980), 11–12; Ed., *New York World*, July 23, 1929, CF, HHPL.

15. Telegram, Walter H. Newton to Colonel Henry W. Anderson, June 16, 1929, PP, SF, Box 106, Colored Quest., DePriest Incident, Corres., 1929, June 16–20, HHPL.

16. Excerpts carried in *New York World*, June 21, 1929, CF, HHPL.

17. *New York Times*, June 30, 1929, CF, HHPL.

18. *Chicago Tribune*, June 27, 1929, CF, HHPL; *Chicago Daily News*, June 24, 1929, CF, HHPL.

19. Young, *Activist First Lady*, 65–66, 71.

20. Ray Lyman Wilbur, *The Memoirs of Ray Lyman Wilbur*, eds. Edgar Eugene Robinson and Paul Carroll Edwards (Stanford, CA, 1960), 78, 478; Garcia, "Herbert Hoover and the Issue of Race," 514–15; Lisio, *Hoover, Blacks, and Lily-Whites*, 191–92; Hoover to Dr. John Hope, July 16, 1931, PP, SF, Box 106, Colored Quest., Corres., 1931, Jan.–Aug., HHPL; *New York Times*, June 11, 1932, CF, HHPL.

21. Lisio, *Hoover, Blacks, and Lily-Whites*, 191.

22. Wilbur, *Memoirs*, 476–77.

23. Lisio, *Hoover, Blacks, and Lily-Whites*, 191–92.

24. Garcia, "Herbert Hoover and the Issue of Race," 514–15; *New York Times*, April 23, 1931, CF, HHPL; Ray Lyman Wilbur to Mordecai W. Johnson, Dec. 10, 1931, PP, SF, Box 106, Colored Quest., Corres., 1931, Sep.–Dec., HHPL; Lawrence Richey to Mrs. J. E. Clinton, Nov. 1, 1932, PP, SF, Box 106, Colored Quest., Corres., 1932, Oct.–Dec., HHPL.

25. T. J. Woofter, Jr., *Industrial Background of the Economic Status of the Negro*, 3–9, 19–30, 32–38, PP, SF, Box 106, Colored Quest., Corres., 1930, June-Oct., HHPL; Harry E. Newcomer to Hoover, Dec. 4, 1931; Robert Jordan to Hoover, Nov. 10, 1931, PP, SF, Box 106, Colored Quest., Corres., 1931, Sep.–Dec., HHPL.

26. Burner, *A Public Life*, 216; Statement Concerning Negroes Appointed by Hoover and Employed by the Federal government, Aug. 2, 1932, PP, SF, Box 106, Colored Quest., Corres., 1932, Aug., HHPL; Memo on Federal government [1932], PP, SF, Box 106, Colored Quest., Corres., 1932, Sep., HHPL.

27. Transcript [1931] marked "General Resolution," PP, SF, Box 106, Colored Quest., Corres., 1931, Sep.–Dec., HHPL; Edgar Rickard, Confidential Memoranda of the Twenty-Second Conference of the National Association for the Advancement of Colored People, Pittsburgh, PA, June 30 to July 6, 1931, PP, SF, Box 106, Colored Quest., Corres., 1931, Jan.–Aug., HHPL.

28. Simon P. Drew and J. N. Bearman to Theodore G. Joslin, Secretary to the President, May 14, 1931; Joslin to Drew, May 31, 1931, PP, SF, Box 106, Colored Quest., Corres., 1931, Jan.–Aug., HHPL.

29. Walter White to Patrick J. Hurley, Secretary of War, Oct. 2, 1931, PP, SF, Box 106, Colored Quest., Corres., 1931, Sep.–Dec., HHPL; Press Release, Press Service of the National Association for the Advancement of Colored People, Sep. 25, 1932, PP, SF, Box 106, Colored Quest., Corres., 1931, Sep.–Dec., HHPL; *New York Herald Tribune*, Sep. 4, 1931, CF, HHPL.

30. James A. Jackson to Walter Newton, Sep. 13, 1932, PP, SF, Box 106, Colored Quest.-Corres., 1932, Sep., HHPL; [Greenville, MS] *Leader*, Sep. 10, 1932, PP, SF, Box 106, Colored Quest., Corres., 1932, Sep., HHPL; Memo, Hoover to Kerry Heath, Sep. 12, 1932, PP, SF, Box 193, Labor, Corres., 1931–1932, HHPL; Ray Lyman Wilbur to Mark L. Requa, May 5, 1932, PP, SF, Box 106, Colored Quest., Corres., 1932, May-July, HHPL; Memo on government Contracts, Hoover to Ferry K. Heath, Assistant Secretary of the Treasury, Sep. 12, 1932, PP, SF, Box 106, Colored Quest., Corres., 1932, Sep., HHPL; Memorandum on Flood Control, Oct. 26, 1932, Directive from Hoover Appointing Commission, PP, SF, Box 106, Colored Quest., Corres., 1932, Oct.–Dec., HHPL; Statement issued by the White House, Oct. 19, 1932, PP, SF, Box 193, Labor, Corres., 1931–1932, HHPL; Secretary of War to Secretary Newton, Feb. 24, 1933, PP, SF, Box 106, Colored Quest., Corres., 1933, HHPL.

31. Garcia, "Herbert Hoover and the Issue of Race," 507.

32. Quoted in Charles H. Martin, "Negro Leaders, the Republican Party, and the Election of 1932," *Phylon* 32, no. 1 (1st Quarter 1971), 86.

33. Martin, "Negro Leaders, the Republican Party, and the Election of 1932," 86–87.

34. Lisio, *Hoover, Blacks, and Lily-Whites*, 253; Burner, *A Public Life*, 217.

35. Lisio, *Hoover, Blacks, and Lily-Whites*, xv, 72–77.

36. Herbert Hoover, *The Memoirs of Herbert Hoover*, vol. 2, *The Cabinet and the Presidency, 1920–1933* (New York, 1952), 279–80; William Starr Myers and Walter H. Newton, *The Hoover Administration: A Documented Narrative* (New York, 1936), 377–78; Wolfe, *Public Servant*, 153; Presidential Statement, undated, PP, SF, Box 254, Republican National Committee, Colored Voters, HHPL; *New York Herald Tribune*, Aug. 6, 1930; *Chicago Tribune*, Oct. 22, 1929, CF, HHPL.

37. *New York World*, Oct. 16, 1929; May 2, 3, 27, Aug. 4, 1930; *Washington Post*, Aug. 8, 1930; *New York Evening Post*, Aug. 14, 1930, CF, HHPL; James H. MacLafferty Diary, Box 1, Dec. 11, 1931, HHPL, Copyright Stanford University.

38. *New York Times*, April 19, 1931, CF, HHPL; Lisio, *Hoover, Blacks, and Lily-Whites*, 173–79, 182–85.

39. Lisio, *Hoover, Blacks, and Lily-Whites*, 135.

40. Raymond Henle, Oral History interview with General Leslie R. Groves, U.S. Army, Retired, Aug. 9, 1968, Washington, DC, for the Hoover Presidential Library and the Hoover Institution on War, Revolution, and Peace, 50–51. I am grateful to Craig Wright for calling this interview to my attention.

41. James R. Bowers, "Herbert Hoover: Ambivalent Quaker" (MA thesis, University of Illinois Legal Studies Center, Springfield, IL, 1981), 94–96; Wolfe, *Public Servant*, 162; Burner, *A Public Life*, 222–25; David Burner, "Before the Crash: Hoover's First Eight Months in the Presidency," in *The Hoover Presidency: A Reappraisal*, eds. Martin L. Fausold and George T. Mazuzan (Albany, NY, 1974), 60.

42. Burner, *A Public Life*, 226–27; Burner, "Before the Crash," 62.

43. Kendrick A. Clements, *Hoover, Conservation, and Consumerism: Engineering the Good Life* (Lawrence, KS, 2000), 142–44; Wilbur, *Memoirs*, 481–83. Quotation in Wilbur, *Memoirs*, 489.

44. Wilbur, *Memoirs*, 484–85; Burner, *A Public Life*, 227; *U.S. Daily News*, Sep. 20, 1931, CF, HHPL.

45. Burner, *A Public Life*, 224–27; Wilbur, *Memoirs*, 401, 481–83; Fausold, *The Presidency of Herbert C. Hoover*, 85; *New York Times*, April 17, 1929, CF, HHPL.

46. *New York Times*, Aug. 11, 1930, CF, HHPL.

47. *New York Times*, Aug. 11, 1930, CF, HHPL; Ray Lyman Wilbur and Arthur Mastick Hyde, *The Hoover Policies* (New York, 1937), 88–89.

48. On Lou Henry Hoover see Mayer, *A Prototype for First Ladies*; Dale Mayer, ed., *Lou Henry Hoover: Essays on a Busy Life* (Worland, WY, 1994); Young, *Activist First Lady*; and Pryor, *Gallant First Lady*.

49. [Columbus, OH] *Dispatch*, Dec. 8, 1929, PP, SF, Box 370, Women, Corres., 1929–1930, HHPL; "Hoover's Administration Takes Kindly View toward Trend of Modern Feminism," *New York World* (Dec. 4, 1929), CF, HHPL.

50. Reprint from *The Women's Journal*, unpaginated, undated, RF, HHPL; Women Appointed to Important Positions Since March 4, 1929, PP, SF, Box 70, Appointments, Women, 1929, HHPL; Taylor/Gates Coll., Box 3, A-IV-6, Women's Interests; PP, SF, Box 370, Women, Equal Rights For, 1929–1931, HHPL; *New York Herald Tribune*, Dec. 25, 1932, CF, HHPL.

51. Hoover, *Memoirs*, vol. 2, 101, 221–22; Robert K. Murray, "Herbert Hoover and the Harding Cabinet," in *Herbert Hoover as Secretary of Commerce: Studies in New Era Thought and Practice*, ed. Ellis W. Hawley (Iowa City, IA, 1981), 83–87; Burner, *A Public Life*, 145–46, 173–74; Wilbur and Hyde, *The Hoover Policies*, 117–19, 128; Industrial Waste Committee, PCP, SF, Box 38, Labor Unions, Nov. 1920-Feb. 1921; *New York Times*, Oct. 5, 1930, CF, HHPL.

52. Murray, "Herbert Hoover and the Harding Cabinet," 28–29; Wilbur and Hyde, *The Hoover Policies*, 125–27; Hoover, *Memoirs*, vol. 2, 104–8; Hoff, *Forgotten Progressive*, 94–95.

53. *New York Times*, July 10, 14, 23, 1931; Jan. 5, 1932; Ed., *New York Times*, July 23, 1931; Ed., *New York Evening Post*, July 21, 1931; *New York Herald Tribune*, March 2, July 1, 1932; *U.S. Daily News* Sep. 1, 1931, CF, HHPL; Herbert Hoover, *Hoover after Dinner* (New York, 1933), 6.
54. Wilbur and Hyde, *The Hoover Policies*, 130–32, 142–43; *New York Times*, Aug. 6, Nov. 10, 1930; Sep. 24, 1931; *New York Herald Tribune*, May 16, July 28, Aug. 22, Sep. 24, 1931, CF, HHPL.
55. President Hoover's Labor Record, PP, SF, Box 55, Accomp. of the Administration, HHPL; Taylor/Gates Coll., Box 2, A-II-9, Commerce Dept., HHPL.
56. *New York Times*, March 24, 1932, CF, HHPL; Fausold, *The Presidency of Herbert C. Hoover*, 122; Harris Gaylord Warren, *Herbert Hoover and the Great Depression* (New York, 1967), 191–92; Burner, *A Public Life*, 279; President Hoover's Labor Record, PP, SF, Box 55, Accomp. of the Administration, HHPL.
57. Wilbur and Hyde, *The Hoover Policies*, 143; Burner, *A Public Life*, 197; Hoover, *Memoirs* vol. 3, 47–48.
58. Myers and Newton, *A Documented Narrative*, 541; Wilbur and Hyde, *The Hoover Policies*, 140; *New York Times*, Sep. 11, 1930; *New York Herald Tribune*, July 10, 1930; [Washington, DC] *U.S. Daily News*, June 25, Oct. 17, 1932, CF, HHPL.

Chapter 14

1. Eugene Lyons, *Herbert Hoover: A Biography* (Garden City, NY, 1964), 256.
2. David M. Kennedy, *Freedom from Fear: The American People in Depression and War, 1929–1945* (New York, 1999), 72–74; Herbert Hoover, *The Memoirs of Herbert Hoover*, vol. 3, *The Great Depression, 1919–1941* (New York, 1952), 75; Lyons, *Hoover: A Biography*, 269.
3. Kennedy, *Freedom from Fear*, 71–72; David Burner, *Herbert Hoover: A Public Life* (New York, 1979), 300; Robert H. Ferrell, *American Diplomacy in the Great Depression: Hoover-Stimson Foreign Policy, 1929–1933* (New Haven, CT, 1957), 111–12.
4. Kennedy, *Freedom from Fear*, 72–74; William Starr Myers and Walter H. Newton, *The Hoover Administration: A Documented Narrative* (New York, 1936), 74–75; *New York Times*, July 8, 1931; [Washington, DC] *U.S. Daily News*, June 10, 23, 1931, Clipping File (hereafter CF), Herbert Hoover Presidential Library (hereafter HHPL), West Branch, IA.
5. Myers and Newton, *A Documented Narrative*, 88–96; Theodore G. Joslin, *Hoover off the Record* (Garden City, NY, 1934), 96–105; *New York Times*, July 8, 1931, CF, HHPL.
6. *New York Times*, June 20, June 21, 22, 23, July 2, 4, 1931; *New York Herald Tribune*, June 22, 24, 25, 1931; *New York Evening Post*, June 22, July 30, 1931; *Washington Star*, July 24, 1931, CF, HHPL.
7. Jordan A. Schwarz, *The Interregnum of Despair: Hoover, Congress, and the Depression* (Urbana, IL, 1970), 80–87; *New York Herald Tribune*, Dec. 20, 1932; *New York Evening Post*, Dec. 15, 22, 1931; *New York Times*, Dec. 15, 1931, CF, HHPL.
8. Myers and Newton, *A Documented Narrative*, 103–5; *New York Times*, Jan. 24, July 24, 1931, CF, HHPL.
9. *New York Times*, June 26, July 9, 24, 1931; *New York Herald Tribune*, June 21, 1931, CF, HHPL.
10. *New York Times*, Aug. 2, 11, 17, 23, 1931; *New York Herald Tribune*, Aug. 20, 21, 1931; Unmarked clipping, Dec. 24, 1931, CF, HHPL.
11. *New York Times*, July 13, 14, 21, Aug. 2, Sep. 4, Oct. 8, 1931; Ed., *New York Times*, July 21, Aug. 1, 1932; *New York Herald Tribune*, July 12, 16, 29, Oct. 10, 1931; CF, HHPL.
12. Hoover, *Memoirs*, vol. 3, 81–83; *New York Times*, July 23, 24, Aug. 2, 6, Sep. 19, 20, 1931; *New York Herald Tribune*, July 16, Sep. 21, 1931; *New York Evening Post*, Sep. 21, 1931, CF, HHPL; Theodore G. Joslin Diary, Box 10, File 7, Sep. 21, 1931, HHPL.
13. Kennedy, *Freedom from Fear*, 75–79; Harris Gaylord Warren, *Herbert Hoover and the Great Depression* (New York, 1967), 141; *New York Times*, Sep. 22, 24, 25, Oct. 1, 26, 1931; *New York Herald Tribune*, Sep. 21, 1931, CF, HHPL.

14. William Starr Myers, *The Foreign Policies of Herbert Hoover* (New York, 1940), 178–82; Joslin, *Hoover off the Record*, 146–48; Richard Current, *Secretary Stimson: A Study in Statecraft* (New Brunswick, NJ, 1954), 64; Warren, *Hoover and the Great Depression*, 137; *New York Times*, Sep. 20, 1931, CF, HHPL.

15. *New York Times*, Oct. 25, 26, 1931; *New York Evening Post*, Oct. 26, 1931; Ed., *New York Evening Post*, Oct. 26, 27, 1931; *New York Herald Tribune*, Oct. 27, 1931, CF, HHPL; Joslin Diary, Box 10, File 7, Oct. 21, 25, 1931, CF, HHPL.

16. *New York Evening Post*, Nov. 7, 19, 1931; *New York Times*, Nov. 18, 1931; Ed., *New York Herald Tribune*, Nov. 18, 1931, HHPL.

17. Ed., *New York Evening Post*, July 21, 1932, CF, HHPL.

18. Ray Lyman Wilbur and Arthur Mastick Hyde, *The Hoover Policies* (New York, 1937), 513–18; Joan Hoff, "A Reevaluation of Herbert Hoover's Foreign Policy," in *The Hoover Presidency: A Reappraisal*, eds. Martin L. Fausold and George T. Mazuzan (Albany, NY, 1974), 179–80; *New York Times*, Dec. 20, 1931; *New York Herald Tribune*, Dec. 20, 1931, CF, HHPL.

19. *U.S. Daily News*, May 15, 1931; Ed., *Chicago Daily News*, June 23, 1932, CF, HHPL; Ferrell, *American Diplomacy in the Great Depression*, 194–98; Harold Wolfe, *Herbert Hoover: Public Servant and Leader of the Loyal Opposition* (New York, 1956), 180–82; Joslin, *Hoover off the Record*, 86.

20. Wilbur and Hyde, *The Hoover Policies*, 605–7; Ferrell, *American Diplomacy in the Great Depression*, 194–98; Wolfe, *Public Servant*, 180–82; *Chicago Daily News*, June 23, 1932, CF, HHPL.

21. Henry L. Stimson and McGeorge Bundy, *On Active Service in Peace and War* (New York, 1948), 272–77; *New York Times*, July 22, 1931; Ed., *New York Evening Post*, July 22, 1931, CF, HHPL.

22. Stimson and Bundy, *On Active Service*, 270–72.

23. Myers, *The Foreign Policies of Herbert Hoover*, 151–52; Wilbur and Hyde, *The Hoover Policies*, 608–10; Herbert Hoover, *The Memoirs of Herbert Hoover*, vol. 2, *The Cabinet and the Presidency, 1920–1933* (New York, 1952), 353–56; Joslin Diary, Box 10, File 7, June 22, 1932, HHPL; *New York Herald Tribune*, June 23, 1932; *Chicago Tribune*, Feb. 10, 1932, CF, HHPL.

24. *New York Herald Tribune*, June 23, 26, 1932; *New York Evening Post*, June 24, 1932; *Chicago Daily News*, June 23, 1932; *Chicago Tribune*, Sep. 15, 1932, CF, HHPL.

25. *New York Herald Tribune*, May 10, 1931; *New York Times*, June 28, 1931; CF, HHPL; Wolfe, *Public Servant*, 169–71.

26. *New York Herald Tribune*, March 23, 25, 26, 1931; *New York Times*, March 23, 1931; *Washington Evening Star*, March 28, 1931, CF, HHPL.

27. Alexander DeConde, *Herbert Hoover's Latin American Policy* (Stanford, CA, 1951), 103–7; Myers, *The Foreign Policies of Herbert Hoover*, 49–53.

28. DeConde, *Hoover's Latin American Policy*, 31–33, 79–83; *New York Times*, Feb. 14, 1931; *New York Evening Post*, April 16, 1931, CF, HHPL.

29. DeConde, *Hoover's Latin American Policy*, 89; *New York Times*, Sep. 9, 1932, CF, HHPL.

30. DeConde, *Hoover's Latin American Policy*, 35–38; Ed., *New York Times*, Aug. 5, 1932; *New York Times*, Sep. 11, 1932, CF, HHPL.

31. DeConde, *Hoover's Latin American Policy*, 39–44.

32. Myers, *The Foreign Policies of Herbert Hoover*, 153–58; Burner, *A Public Life*, 293–95; Current, *Secretary Stimson*, 66–70.

33. Ferrell, *American Diplomacy in the Great Depression*, 123–37, 139–48; Hoover, *Memoirs*, vol. 2, 363–66; Wolfe, *Public Servant*, 191–94.

34. Stimson and Bundy, *On Active Service*, 226–33; Wolfe, *Public Servant*, 195–97; Hoover, *Memoirs*, vol. 2, 369–70.

35. Current, *Secretary Stimson*, 75–79, 84–86, 89–91; Fausold, *The Presidency of Herbert C. Hoover*, 178–81; Stimson and Bundy, *On Active Service*, 234–39; Ferrell, *American Diplomacy in the Great Depression*, 149–63; Wolfe, *Public Service*, 198–201; Alexander DeConde, "A Retrospective Assessment," in *Herbert Hoover and the Historians*, ed. Mark M. Dodge (West Branch, IA, 1989), 107–9; Hoover, *Memoirs*, vol. 2, 373.

36. Stimson and Bundy, *On Active Service*, 239–44; Ferrell, *American Diplomacy in the Great Depression*, 170–78; Joslin Diary, Box 10, File 7, Jan. 29, 1932, HHPL; Joslin, *Hoover off the Record*, 176–77.

37. Current, *Secretary Stimson*, 92–102, 104–7; Stimson and Bundy, *On Active Service*, 257–63; Ferrell, *American Diplomacy in the Great Depression*, 169, 185–87; Fausold, *The Presidency of Herbert C. Hoover*, 181–82; Joan Hoff, *Herbert Hoover: Forgotten Progressive* (Boston, 1975), 206–7; *New York Times*, May 15, 1932; *New York Herald Tribune*, May 15, 1932, CF, HHPL.

38. Fausold, *The Presidency of Herbert C. Hoover*, 182, 374–77; Ferrell, *American Diplomacy in the Great Depression*, 149–68, 248 [quote on 168]; Wolfe, *Public Servant*, 203, 294; Burner, *A Public Life*, 295–97.

Chapter 15

1. George H. Nash, *Herbert Hoover and Stanford University* (Stanford, CA, 1988), 16; Dale Mayer, *Lou Henry Hoover: A Prototype for First Ladies* (Hauppauge, NY, 2004), 4, 26–29; Helen B. Pryor, *Lou Henry Hoover: Gallant First Lady* (New York, 1969), 3, 16–19.

2. Pryor, *Gallant First Lady*, 10–12.

3. Articles and Addresses, 1886–1898, Earlier Writings Preserved by Father in Articles, Addresses and Statements by Mrs. Hoover, Subject File (hereafter SF), Box 3, Lou Henry Hoover Papers (LHHP), Herbert Hoover Presidential Library (hereafter HHPL), West Branch, IA.

4. Lou Henry Hoover, historical essay, undated, untitled, SF, Articles, Addresses, and Statements by Mrs. Hoover, Box 3, LHHP, HHPL; Mayer, *A Prototype for First Ladies*, 134; David Burner, *Herbert Hoover: A Public Life* (New York, 1979), 70; Lou Henry Hoover, undated, 1898 and 1919, SF, PCP, Box 43, HHPL; Joan Hoff, *Herbert Hoover: Forgotten Progressive* (Boston, 1975), 22; Nancy A. Colbert, *Lou Henry Hoover: The Duty to Serve* (Greensboro, NC, 1998), 44–45; *New York Evening Post*, June 10, 1929, Clipping File (hereafter CF), HHPL.

5. For the information on Lou's geology degree see Colbert, *The Duty to Serve*, 26. The Odell citation is from Harriette Miles Odell to Lou Henry Hoover, Jan. 4, 1912, Odell, Harriette, Personal Corres., HHPL; Quoted in Mayer, *A Prototype for First Ladies*, 43.

6. Quoted in Mayer, *A Prototype for First Ladies*, 52.

7. Mitchell V. Charnley, *The Boy's Life of Herbert Hoover* (New York, 1931), 117–18; Mayer, *A Prototype for First Ladies*, 32–33, 36–38.

8. Mayer, *A Prototype for First Ladies*, 33–40; Pryor, *Gallant First Lady*, 23–29.

9. Susan Estabrook Kennedy, "Pioneer Girl: Lou Henry Hoover and the Girl Scouts," in *Uncommon Americans: The Lives and Legacies of Herbert and Lou Henry Hoover*, ed. Timothy Walch (Westport, CT, 2003), 79; Hoff, *Forgotten Progressive*, 18.

10. Nancy Beck Young, *Lou Henry Hoover: Activist First Lady* (Lawrence, KS, 2004), 18–19; Hoff, *Forgotten Progressive*, 17–18.

11. For the above paragraphs providing insights into the Hoover family, see Young, *Activist First Lady*, 18–19, 23–24, 29–32; Mayer, *A Prototype for First Ladies*, 149; Colbert, *The Duty to Serve*, 66; *Chicago Tribune*, April 29, 1985; *Chicago Daily News*, June 15, 1928; *Chicago Daily News*, Material prepared for the obituary of Lou Henry Hoover, undated, CF, HHPL; Walch, ed., *Uncommon Americans*, 4; James H. MacLafferty Diary, Box 1, Feb. 1, 1932, HHPL, Copyright Stanford University. The interpretation is the author's.

12. Mayer, *A Prototype for First Ladies*, 151; Nancy Beck Young, "Searching for Lou Henry Hoover," in *Uncommon Americans*, ed. Timothy Walch, 21–22.

13. Quotes from Articles, Addresses and Statements by Mrs. Hoover, 1922, Jan., Comments on Fun of Scout Camping, Savannah, GA, Box 3, LHHP, HHPL; Mayer, *A Prototype for First Ladies*, 208–19; Young, *Activist First Lady*, 30–37; Young, "Searching for Lou Henry Hoover," 22; Kennedy, "Pioneer Girl," 82–89; Hoff, *Forgotten Progressive*, 19.

14. Young, *Activist First Lady*, 40–41; Mayer, *A Prototype for First Ladies*, 225–28.

15. *New York Times*, April 29, 1929; *New York Herald Tribune*, June 24, 1929; *Chicago Daily News*, March 6, 11, 20, 24, 30, April 5, May 19, Nov. 26, 1929; March 11, Nov. 7, 1931; *Chicago Tribune* April 5, 1929; Nov. 7, 1931, CF, HHPL; Young, *Activist First Lady*, 23, 157, 94, 100–101, 105–9, 128–35, 145–48, Mayer, *A Prototype for First Ladies*, 284.

16. Kendrick A. Clements, "The New Era and the New Woman: Lou Henry Hoover and 'Feminism's Awkward Age'," *Pacific Historical Review* 73, no. 3 (Aug. 2004), 425–61; Herbert Hoover, *The Memoirs of Herbert Hoover*, vol. 2, *The Cabinet and the Presidency, 1920–1933* (New York, 1952), 323–25; Young, "Searching for Lou Henry Hoover," 22; *Chicago Daily News*, Sep. 1, 1931, CF, HHPL.

17. *Chicago Daily News*, July 18, 1928; June 3, 1929; June 10, 1930; Oct. 17, 1931; May 14, June 13, 1932; *Chicago Daily News*, undated, "Sketch of Lou Henry Hoover prepared in Case of Death"; *New York Herald Tribune*, May 1, 15, June 14, 1932; CF, HHPL; Young, *Activist First Lady*, 51–57, 61–65, 76–77; Pryor, *Gallant First Lady*, 150, 225; Colbert, *The Duty to Serve*, 78.

18. Pryor, *Gallant First Lady*, 225.

19. Young, *Activist First Lady*, 190.

20. *New York World*, Feb. 3, 1931; *New York Times*, Feb. 15, 1931, CF, HHPL.

21. Unmarked clipping, New York newspaper, Sep. 28, 1930; *New York World*, May 11, 1929; *U.S. Daily News*, July 9, 1929, CF, HHPL; Edward G. Lowry, "Mr. Hoover at Work and Play," *Saturday Evening Post* 202, no. 9 (Aug. 31, 1929), 10–11, 39–40, RF, HHPL.

22. *New York Times*, Sep. 1, 1929; *New York Herald Tribune*, June 28, 1929; Jan. 2, 20, 1930; *Washington Star*, Aug. 21, 1929, CF, HHPL; William J. Schaefle, "How President Hoover Serves His Country," *American Globe* (Oct. 1929), 5–13, Presidential Papers (hereafter PP), SF, Box 55, Accomp. of the Admin., 1929, HHPL.

23. *New York Evening Post*, Sep. 22, Oct. 30, 1930; *New York World*, Sep. 17, Oct. 18, 1930; *New York Herald Tribune*, Nov. 18, 1930; March 7, 1931; *New York Times*, April 29, 1931, CF, HHPL; MacLafferty Diary, Box 1, Nov. 9, 1930, HHPL, Copyright Stanford University; Young, *Activist First Lady*, 149–52; Pryor, *Gallant First Lady*, 188, 209.

24. *New York Evening Post*, June 23, 1930; *Washington Herald*, July 27, 1930; *New York Herald Tribune*, Sep. 22, Dec. 31, 1930; *Indianapolis Star*, June 16, 1931; *Chicago Daily News*, Jan. 20, 1932, CF, HHPL; Pryor, *Gallant First Lady*, 193.

25. *Chicago Tribune*, March 7, 11, 12, June 22, July 4, Aug. 10, 1929; Jan. 2, 1930; Feb. 2, 1932; *Chicago Daily News*, April 12, May 22, June 7, 22, 1929; Oct. 14, 1932; *New York Herald Tribune*, Jan. 2, 1931; *New York Times*, Oct. 14, 1932; *New York Evening Post*, Feb. 10, 1932, CF, HHPL; "The March of Events," *World's Work* 58 (Sep. 1929), 35–40; Lowry, "Mr. Hoover at Work and Play," 40, RF, HHPL; John P. Schumacher to Walter H. Newton, Sep. 29, 1932, PP, SF, Box 225, President, The, Power and Duties, April–Dec.; Joslin Diary, Box 10, File 7, Jan. 1, 1932, HHPL.

26. Hoover, *Memoirs*, vol. 2, 327.

27. *New York World*, Dec. 25, 1929; *Philadelphia Inquirer*, Dec. 26, 1929; [Washington, DC] *U.S. Daily News*, Dec. 28, 1929; *Chicago Daily News*, Dec. 20, Dec. 23, Dec. 24, Dec. 26, 1929; *Chicago Tribune*, Dec. 25, 1929, CF, HHPL; Pryor, *Gallant First Lady*, 174–75; Young, *Activist First Lady*, 77.

28. Mary Roberts Rinehart, "A New First Lady Becomes Hostess for the Nation," *World's Work* 58, Part I (March 1929), 34–39, 170, RF, HHPL; *Chicago Daily News*, March 9, 1929; *New York Evening Post*, Oct. 31, CF, HHPL.

29. *Chicago Tribune*, March 12, 1929; *New York Evening Post*, May 11, 1929, CF, HHPL; Pryor, *Gallant First Lady*, 166–70; Mayer, *A Prototype for First Ladies*, 253; Burner, *A Public Life*, 59; Young, *Activist First Lady*, 75–77.

30. *Chicago Daily News*, Nov. 6, 1929, CF, HHPL; Young, *Activist First Lady*, 74, 79; Ray Lyman Wilbur, *The Memoirs of Ray Lyman Wilbur*, eds. Edgar Eugene Robinson and Paul Carroll Edwards (Stanford, CA, 1960), 529.

31. Young, *Activist First Lady*, 77–82; Colbert, *The Duty to Serve*, 86–87; Wilbur, *Memoirs*, 541; *New York World*, June 2, 1930, CF, HHPL.

Chapter 16

1. William Starr Myers and Walter H. Newton, *The Hoover Administration: A Documented Narrative* (New York, 1936), 425.
2. Boys Week, 1924–1926, CP, Subject File (hereafter SF), Box 58, Herbert Hoover Presidential Library (hereafter HHPL), West Branch, IA.
3. *New York Evening Post*, Nov. 20, 1930, Clipping File (hereafter CF), HHPL.
4. Herbert Hoover, *Hoover after Dinner* (New York, 1933), 139–40.
5. Ray Lyman Wilbur and Arthur Mastick Hyde, *The Hoover Policies* (New York, 1937), 31.
6. Myers and Newton, *A Documented Narrative*, 457.
7. Herbert Hoover, *On Growing Up*, ed. William Nichols (New York, 1962), 10.
8. James P. Johnson, "Herbert Hoover: The Orphan as Children's Friend," *Prologue* 12, no. 4 (Winter 1980), 202–3.
9. Herbert Hoover, "Our Goal-Oriented Normal Child," President's Address to the American Child Health Association, Atlantic City, May 18, 1926, CP, SF, Box 87, Child Health, 1922–1926, HHPL.
10. Hoover, *On Growing Up*, 68.
11. Richard Norton Smith and Timothy Walch, "Orphan Boy: Herbert Hoover and Children," in *Uncommon Americans: The Lives and Legacies of Herbert and Lou Henry Hoover*, ed. Timothy Walch (Westport, CT, 2003), 76–77.
12. Hoover, *On Growing Up*, 16, 29, 35–36.
13. Memo, Jan. 23, 1931, Presidential Papers (hereafter PP), SF, Box 93, Cabinet, The, Corres., 1930–1933, HHPL.
14. Summary of Address by Secretary Hoover Before First Annual Session of the ACHA, Detroit, Oct. 15, 1923, CP, SF, Box 87, Child Health, 1922–1926, HHPL; James N. Giglio, "Voluntarism and Public Policy between World War I and the New Deal: Herbert Hoover and the American Child Health Association," *Presidential Studies Quarterly* 13, no. 3 (Summer 1983), 431–43; Philip Van Ingen, "The Story of the American Child Health Association," reprinted from the Sep.–Nov. 1935 Issue of the *Child Health Bulletin* 11, no. 5 and 6, 149–88 published by the American Child Health Association, 14–20, Reprint File (hereafter RF), HHPL; Harold Wolfe, *Herbert Hoover: Public Servant and Leader of the Loyal Opposition* (New York, 1956), 100–101; Herbert Hoover, *The Memoirs of Herbert Hoover*, vol. 2, *The Cabinet and the Presidency, 1920–1933* (New York, 1952), 100.
15. Smith and Walch, "Orphan Boy," 75–76.
16. Johnson, "The Orphan as Children's Friend," 205–6.
17. Local Color and Anecdotes on Herbert Hoover, PPP, SF, Box 75, Boys' Clubs of America, Corres.-Undated, HHPL.
18. Hoover, *On Growing Up*, 64–66; Hoover to James E. West, Dec. 14, 1922, CP, SF, Box 57, Boy Scouts of America, 1921–1922; James E. West to Hoover, June 7, 1924, CP, SF, Box 57, Boy Scouts of America, 1923–24, HHPL.
19. Myers and Newton, *A Documented Narrative*, 541–52; Kendrick A. Clements, *Hoover, Conservation, and Consumerism: Engineering the Good Life* (Lawrence, KS, 2000), 145; Summary of the Address of Secretary Hoover to the National Conference of Social Work, Providence, RI, June 27, 1922, CP, SF, Box 87, Child Labor, 1923–1926; Hoover Press Releases, June 3, 1924, March 5, 1925, CP, SF, Box 87, Child Labor, 1923–1926, HHPL.
20. Johnson, "The Orphan as Children's Friend," 203.
21. Johnson, "The Orphan as Children's Friend," 203; Smith and Walch, "Orphan Boy," 66; Theodore G. Joslin Diary, Box 10, File 7, May 28, 1932, HHPL; Theodore G. Joslin, *Hoover off the Record* (Garden City, NY, 1934), 9–11.
22. Johnson, "The Orphan as Children's Friend," 203; Joslin, *Hoover off the Record*, 81; *New York Times*, April 30, 1931; *New York Evening Post*, April 30, 1931, CF, HHPL.
23. Joslin, *Hoover off the Record*, 198–99.
24. *Chicago Daily News*, Nov. 15, 1929, CF, HHPL.
25. *Chicago Tribune*, May 26, 1929, CF, HHPL.

26. *New York Times*, Feb. 25, 1932, CF, HHPL.
27. Smith and Walch, "Orphan Boy," 74.
28. *Washington Star*, Nov. 24, 1929; *Boston Post*, Aug. 30, 1929; *Philadelphia Public Ledger*, April 28, 1929; *New York Times*, Feb. 7, 1933, CF, HHPL; Joslin, *Hoover off the Record*, 55–57; Theodore G. Joslin, "Hoover's First Year," *World's Work* 59 (March 1930), 118–19, RF, HHPL; Hoover, *Memoirs*, vol. 2, 327.
29. Edward G. Lowry, "Mr. Hoover at Work and Play," *Saturday Evening Post* 202, no. 9 (Aug. 31, 1929), 42, RF, HHPL; Unmarked Editorial, CF, HHPL; Hoover, *Memoirs*, vol. 2, 166; Hoover, *On Growing Up*, 77; Richard Norton Smith, *An Uncommon Man: The Triumph of Herbert Hoover* (New York, 1984), 174.
30. Hal Elliott Wert, *Hoover, the Fishing President: Portrait of the Private Man and His Life Outdoors* (Mechanicsburg, PA, 2005), xiv.
31. *New York Herald Tribune*, Sep. 6, 1930, CF, HHPL.
32. Hoover, *Hoover after Dinner*, 98.
33. Ibid., 94.
34. Wert, *The Fishing President*, xiii.
35. Wilbur and Hyde, *The Hoover Policies*, 246.
36. Kendrick A. Clements, "Herbert Hoover and the Fish," *Journal of Psychohistory* 10, no. 3 (Winter 1983), 334–35.
37. *Washington Evening Star*, Oct. 22, 1932; *Chicago Daily News*, Oct. 27, 1932, CF, HHPL.
38. Ray Lyman Wilbur, *The Memoirs of Ray Lyman Wilbur*, eds. Edgar Eugene Robinson and Paul Carroll Edwards (Stanford, CA, 1960), 546–48; Wert, *The Fishing President*, 182–85.
39. Darwin Lambert, *Herbert Hoover's Hideaway* (Luray, VA: Shenandoah National History Association, Inc., 1971), vii–viii, 11–13, 25–29, 37–40; *New York Herald Tribune*, Aug. 2, 1932, CF, HHPL; Helen B. Pryor, *Lou Henry Hoover: Gallant First Lady* (New York, 1969), 170–71; Hoover, *Memoirs*, vol. 2, 322–23; Wilbur, *Memoirs*, 546–48; Wert, *The Fishing President*, 182–85; Dale Mayer, *Lou Henry Hoover: A Prototype for First Ladies* (Hauppauge, NY, 2004), 265–69.
40. Nancy Beck Young, *Lou Henry Hoover: Activist First Lady* (Lawrence, KS, 2004), 58–59; Lambert, *Herbert Hoover's Hideaway*, ix, 58–59, 101–5, 11–117; Wilbur, *Memoirs*, 548–49; *New York World*, Aug. 3, 1929; *Chicago Daily News*, Aug. 20, 1932, CF, HHPL.
41. Lambert, *Herbert Hoover's Hideaway*, vii–x, 41–43, 104–5; Lowry, "Mr. Hoover at Work and Play," 1–11, 39–40, 42; Mary Hornaday, "Where the President Puts Care Aside: Informality Rules at Rapidan Camp, Isolated in Wild Mountains and Enveloped by the Peace of The Woods, where the President Rests," *New York Times Magazine*, June 12, 1932, 6, 16; Pryor, *Gallant First Lady*, 184; Wilbur, *Memoirs*, 548.
42. Lambert, *Herbert Hoover's Hideaway*, 65, 53–62; *Chicago Daily News*, Aug. 17, 1929, CF, HHPL.
43. Lambert, *Herbert Hoover's Hideaway*, x, 82–86; *Chicago Daily News*, Sep. 2, 1929, CF, HHPL.
44. Mayer, *A Prototype for First Ladies*, 272–77; Hornaday, "Where the President Puts Care Aside," 16; Lambert, *Herbert Hoover's Hideaway*, 87–100; Young, *Activist First Lady*, 84–90; *New York Herald Tribune*, Feb. 18, 1930; *U.S. Daily News*, Aug. 22, 1929; *Chicago Daily News*, April 17, 1930, CF, HHPL.
45. Lambert, *Herbert Hoover's Hideaway*, 122–42.
46. Ibid., 105.

Chapter 17

1. Louis W. Liebovich, *Bylines in Despair: Herbert Hoover, the Great Depression, and the U. S. News Media* (Westport, CT, 1994), 32–38; Fauneil J. Rinn, "President Hoover's Bad Press," *San Jose Studies* 1, no. 1 (Feb. 1975), 33–35.
2. Theodore G. Joslin, *Hoover off the Record* (Garden City, NY, 1934), 70; Harris Gaylord Warren, *Herbert Hoover and the Great Depression* (New York, 1967), 57–59.

3. *Chicago Daily News*, March 18, 1929; Feb. 7, 1930; unmarked clipping, byline from New York, United Press, April 15, 1929, Clipping File (hereafter CF), Herbert Hoover Presidential Library (hereafter HHPL), West Branch, IA.; Harold Brayman, "Hooverizing the Press," *Outlook and Independent* 156, no. 4 (Sep. 24, 1930), 123–25; Republican National Committee, *The Hoover Administration: Its Policies and Its Achievements in the First Sixteen Months*, Presidential Papers (hereafter PP), Subject File (hereafter SF), Box 55, Accomp. of the Admin., 1931, pp. 18–19, HHPL; William J. Schaefle, "How President Hoover Serves His Country," *American Globe* (Oct. 1929), 5–6, PP, SF, Box 55, Accomp. of the Admin., 1929, HHPL.

4. Liebovich, *Bylines in Despair*, 90–92, 112–15.

5. *Chicago Daily News*, May 24, 1929, CF, HHPL.

6. Liebovich, *Bylines in Despair*, 108–10; Martin L. Fausold, *The Presidency of Herbert C. Hoover* (Lawrence, KS, 1985), 87.

7. Liebovich, *Bylines in Despair*, 46, 119–20; David Burner, *Herbert Hoover: A Public Life* (New York, 1979), 256; James H. MacLafferty Diary, Box 1, Nov. 18, Dec. 16, 1930, HHPL; *New York World*, Jan. 3, 1931, CF, HHPL.

8. Theodore G. Joslin Diary, Box 10, File 7, April 6, 1930, Aug. 28, 1931, HHPL; Liebovich, *Bylines in Despair*, 47, 120; *New York Herald Tribune*, March 17, 1931, CF, HHPL.

9. Liebovich, *Bylines in Despair*, 86–88, 140–46; Eugene Lyons, *Herbert Hoover: A Biography* (Garden City, NY, 1964), 187–90; Kendrick A. Clements, *Hoover, Conservation, and Consumerism: Engineering the Good Life* (Lawrence, KS, 2000), 37–38; Burner, *A Public Life*, 255–56.

10. Rinn, "President Hoover's Bad Press," 35–37.

11. Ibid., 40–44.

12. *New York Times*, Nov. 24, 1929, CF, HHPL; Clair Everet Nelsen, "The Image of Herbert Hoover as Reflected in the American Press" (PhD diss., Stanford University, 1956), 90–93.

13. Joslin, *Hoover off the Record*, 70–71.

14. Liebovich, *Bylines in Despair*, 143–48; Craig Lloyd, *Aggressive Introvert: Herbert Hoover and Public Relations Management, 1912–1932* (Columbus, OH, 1972), 165–69.

15. Liebovich, *Bylines in Despair*, 109–15; Lloyd, *Aggressive Introvert*, 166; Brayman, "Hooverizing the Press," 123.

16. Nelsen, "The Image of Herbert Hoover," 109–10.

17. Ed., "Mr. Hoover's Apologia," *Outlook* 158, no. 8 (June 24, 1931), 233–34, Reprint File (hereafter RF), HHPL.

18. Walter Lippmann, *Interpretations, 1931–1932* (New York, 1932), 57–60.

19. Joslin Diary, Box 10, File 7, Aug. 25, 1931, HHPL.

20. Albert U. Romasco, *The Poverty of Abundance: Hoover, the Nation, the Depression* (New York, 1968), 205–11; Lloyd, *Aggressive Introvert*, 165; David Hinshaw, *Herbert Hoover: American Quaker* (New York, 1950), 21; Robert Bolt, "Herbert Clark Hoover of West Branch, Iowa: U.S. President of Quaker Stock," *Quaker Life* (Sep. 1984), 22–23, RF, HHPL.

21. Nelsen, "The Image of Herbert Hoover," 100–104, 111–18, 125, 129.

22. Ibid., 130–31.

23. *Washington Herald*, March 29, 1931, CF, HHPL.

24. Ibid.; Unmarked clipping, April 5, 1931; *New York Evening Post*, April 13, 1931, CF, HHPL.

25. *Chicago Daily News*, Jan. 12, 1930, CF, HHPL.

26. *Des Moines Register*, Jan. 17, 1932, PP, SF, Box 225, President, The, Powers and Duties 1932, Jan.–March, HHPL.

27. Anne O'Hare McCormick article in *New York Times* quoted in MacLafferty Diary, Box 1, File 7, HHPL; Nelsen, "The Image of Herbert Hoover," 139–40.

28. Edward G. Lowry, "Mr. Hoover at Work and Play," *Saturday Evening Post* 202, no. 9 (Aug. 31, 1929), 40, 41; *New York Herald Tribune*, Sep. 15, 1929; April 16, 1930, CF, HHPL.

29. Liebovich, *Bylines in Despair*, 141–43; Joslin Diary, Box 10, File 7, May 25, 1932, HHPL.

30. Joslin, *Hoover off the Record*, 168–70.

31. Liebovich, *Bylines in Despair*, 132–38; Joan Hoff, *Herbert Hoover: Forgotten Progressive* (Boston, 1975), 140–41; *New York Herald Tribune*, July 14, 1929; Dec. 28, 1930; *Chicago Daily News*, Oct. 18, 1929; and *New York Times*, June 24, 1930, all in CF, HHPL.

32. Lloyd, *Aggressive Introvert*, 155; Joslin, *Hoover off the Record*, 37–38; Rosanne Sizer, "Herbert Hoover and the Smear Books, 1930–1932," *Annals of Iowa* 47, no. 2 (Spring 1984), 350–55; John Hamill, *The Strange Career of Mr. Hoover: Under Two Flags* (New York, 1931), 53–88, 150–61, 306–24; Clement Wood, *Herbert Clark Hoover: An American Tragedy* (New York, 1932), 139–52, 243–75; Walter W. Liggett, *The Rise of Herbert Hoover* (New York, 1932), 125–30, 340–60.

33. Burner, *A Public Life*, 317.

34. Sizer, "Herbert Hoover and the Smear Books," 343–45.

35. *New York Times*, July 14, 1932, CF, HHPL.

36. *New York Herald Tribune*, Jan. 13, 1933, and *New York Evening Post*, Jan. 13, 1933, both in CF, HHPL.

37. Sizer, "Herbert Hoover and the Smear Books," 351–52. For Liggett's interpretation of Hoover's childhood, see *The Rise of Herbert Hoover*, 3–31.

38. Joslin, *Hoover off the Record*, 37.

39. Sizer, "Herbert Hoover and the Smear Books," 353–61; Joslin, *Hoover off the Record*, 37, 53; MacLafferty Diary, Box 1, File 7, Jan. 8, 1932, HHPL; *New York Herald Tribune*, Feb. 11, 1932; *Chicago Daily News*, Feb. 12, 1932; *New York Times*, July 26, 1932, CF, HHPL.

40. Charles Michelson, *The Ghost Talks* (New York, 1944), 14–16, 20–25, 29–33; Warren, *Hoover and the Great Depression*, 122.

41. Michelson, *The Ghost Talks*, 16–33; William Starr Myers and Walter H. Newton, *The Hoover Administration: A Documented Narrative* (New York, 1936), 46; Alva Johnston, "The Great Silent Orator," *Saturday Evening Post* 208, no. 48 (May 30, 1936), PPP, SF, Box 219, Michelson, Charles, 1935–1939, HHPL.

42. Fausold, *The Presidency of Herbert C. Hoover*, 101–2; Joslin, *Hoover off the Record*, 34; Harold Wolfe, *Herbert Hoover: Public Servant and Leader of the Loyal Opposition* (New York, 1956), 279; Ed., *New York Times*, Feb. 23, 1933, CF, HHPL.

43. Robert Sobel, *Herbert Hoover at the Onset of the Great Depression, 1929–1930* (Philadelphia, 1975), 44–48; Hinshaw, *American Quaker*, 226–27; Roy V. Peel and Thomas C. Donnelly, *The 1932 Campaign: An Analysis* (New York, 1935), 54; "The Ordeal—and Triumph—of Herbert Hoover," *Reader's Digest* 85, no. 512 (Dec. 1964), 161–62, 164–65, 167–68.

44. Joslin, *Hoover off the Record*, 34–37, 67; Myers and Newton, *A Documented Narrative*, 181; Lyons, *Hoover: A Biography*, 231–37; Fausold, *The Presidency of Herbert C. Hoover*, 204–5; "The Ordeal—and Triumph—of Herbert Hoover," 162–64.

Chapter 18

1. Lawrence Sullivan, *Prelude to Panic: The Story of the Bank Holiday* (Washington, DC, 1936), 8–11; Ray Lyman Wilbur and Arthur Mastick Hyde, *The Hoover Policies* (New York, 1937), 525–27; Pamphlet composed of four articles published in the *Saturday Evening Post*, June 8, 15, 22, 29, 1935, 4–5, Postpresidential Papers (hereafter PPP), Subject File (hereafter SF), Box 30; Banking Crisis, "Origins of the Banking Crisis," Herbert Hoover Presidential Library (hereafter HHPL), West Branch, IA; William Starr Myers and Walter H. Newton, *The Hoover Administration: A Documented Narrative* (New York, 1936), 271–73; David Hinshaw, *Herbert Hoover: American Quaker* (New York, 1950), 272–73; Herbert Hoover, Chapter 1, "The Economic Situation at November 7," *Origins of the Banking Panic*, 7–11, PPP, SF, Box 30, 1935, HHPL; *New York Times*, Aug. 1, 24, Sep. 11, Oct. 27, 1932; *New York Evening Post*, Aug. 9, 1932, Clipping File (hereafter CF), HHPL.

2. Sullivan, *Prelude to Panic*, 3–6, 35; Myers and Newton, *A Documented Narrative*, 275–76; Hinshaw, *American Quaker*, 157, 258–59; R. Gordon Hoxie, "Hoover and the Banking Crisis," Commentary on Hoover Presidential Seminar, Aug. 7, 1974, Reprint File (hereafter RF), HHPL; *New York Evening Post*, Dec. 22, 1932, CF, HHPL; Platt quoted in Eugene Lyons, *Herbert Hoover: A Biography* (Garden City, NY, 1964), 310.

3. Herbert Hoover, *The Memoirs of Herbert Hoover*, vol. 3, *The Great Depression, 1929–1941* (New York, 1952), 165.

4. *New York Herald Tribune*, Nov. 14, 1933, quoted in Sullivan, *Prelude to Panic*, 11.

5. Quoted in Lyons, *Hoover: A Biography*, 258.

6. *New York Herald Tribune*, March 5, 1933, CF, HHPL.

7. Pamphlet composed of four articles in the *Saturday Evening Post*, 6, PPP, SF, Box 30, Banking Crisis, *Origins of the Banking Crisis*, HHPL.

8. Theodore G. Joslin, List of Comments and Observations, Jan., 1931–1933, HHPL; Theodore G. Joslin Diary, Box 10, File 7, Nov. 30, 1931, HHPL; James H. MacLafferty Diary, Box 1, Jan. 2, 1932; also, undated entry, 1932, Box 1, HHPL, Copyright Stanford University.

9. R. L. Underhill to M. L. Requa, Nov. 23, 1932, PP, SF, Box 55, Accomp. of the Admin., HHPL.

10. MacLafferty Diary, Box 1, Dec. 16, 1931; Jan. 8, Feb. 16, March 6, April 19, June 18, 1932, HHPL; Joslin Diary, Box 10, File 7, April 10, June 12, 1932, HHPL.

11. Theodore G. Joslin, *Hoover off the Record* (Garden City, NY, 1934), 226–27; Joslin Diary, Box 10, File 7, Sep. 22, 29, 1931; May 1, 1932, HHPL; MacLafferty Diary, Box 1, June 9, 1932, HHPL; *Washington Herald*, Aug. 16, 1931; *New York Evening Post*, Sep. 29, 1931, CF, HHPL; Roy V. Peel and Thomas C. Donnelly, *The 1932 Campaign: An Analysis* (New York, 1935), 23.

12. *New York Times*, March 14, June 15, 1931; *U.S. Daily News*, July 16, 1931; *New York Evening Post*, June 16, 1931, CF, HHPL.

13. Joslin, *Hoover off the Record*, 168; Joslin Diary, Box 10, File 7, Jan. 14, 1932, HHPL; MacLafferty Diary, Box 1, Jan. 14, 15, 16, 1932, HHPL; *Chicago Daily News*, Jan. 14, 1932; *New York Herald Tribune*, April 26, 1932; *Chicago Tribune*, Feb. 23, 1932, CF, HHPL.

14. Joslin, *Hoover off the Record*, 168; Joslin Diary, Box 10, File 7, Jan. 14, Feb. 24, July 21, 1932, HHPL; MacLafferty Diary, Box 1, Jan. 9, 12, 14, 15, 16, 19, March 11, April 13, June 18, 1932, HHPL; *Chicago Daily News*, Jan. 14, 1932; *New York Times* March 13, April 29, 1932, CF, HHPL.

15. Joslin Diary, Box 10, File 7, Feb. 19, May 11, 1932, HHPL; MacLafferty Diary, Box 1, April 6, 8, 1932, HHPL; *Chicago Daily News*, Jan. 22, Feb. 27, April 27, May 3, 1932; *Chicago Tribune*, Feb. 18, April 17, 1932; *New York Herald Tribune*, Jan. 17, Feb. 13, Feb. 14, March 10, 1932; *New York Times*, Jan. 22, March 18, 1932, HHPL.

16. *New York Herald Tribune*, March 27, 1931; *New York Evening Post*, Nov. 30, 1931, CF, HHPL; MacLafferty Diary, Box 1, Dec. 2, 5, 1931, HHPL.

17. MacLafferty Diary, Box 1, Dec. 19, 1931; Jan. 4, 6, Feb. 17, March 6, 8, 11, 16, 1932, HHPL; Joslin Diary, April 1, May 20, June 8, 1932; *Chicago Daily News*, Feb. 11, 1932; *Chicago Tribune*, May 25, 26, June 2, 1932, CF, HHPL.

18. MacLafferty Diary, Box 1, Dec. 29, 1931; March 16, 18, April 12, 18, 21, 28, 29, June 9, 1932, HHPL; Joslin Diary, Box 10, File 7, April 26, 27, June 24, 1932, HHPL.

19. *New York Herald Tribune*, April 12, June 10, 12, 1932; *Chicago Tribune*, May 31, June 10, 1932; *New York Times*, June 10, 15, 17, 1932, CF, HHPL.

20. *New York Times*, June 15, 1932; *New York Herald Tribune*, June 16, 1932; *Chicago Daily News*, June 9, 1932, CF, HHPL; Republican Keynote Speech by Senator L. J. Dickinson of Iowa, Temporary Chairman of the Republican National Convention at Chicago, IL, June 14, 1932, PP, SF, Box 248, Reconstruction Finance Corporation, History of, HHPL.

21. Harold Wolfe, *Herbert Hoover: Public Servant and Leader of the Loyal Opposition* (New York, 1956), 273–76; Peel and Donnelly, *The 1932 Campaign*, 86; Joslin Diary, Box 10, File 7, June 13, 14, 1932, HHPL; *Chicago Sun*, June 16, 1932; *Chicago Daily News*, June 16, 1932, CF, HHPL.

22. Joslin Diary, Box 10, File 7, June 16, 1932, HHPL; Joslin, *Hoover off the Record*, 245–46; *Chicago Sun*, June 16, 1932; *Chicago Tribune*, June 17, 1932; *Chicago Daily News*, June 16, 1932, CF, HHPL.

23. Joslin Diary, Box 10, File 7, June 15, 1932, HHPL; MacLafferty Diary, Box 1, June 18, 1932, HHPL; *New York Herald Tribune*, June 10, 1932; *New York Times*, June 17, 18, 1932, CF, HHPL.

24. Wolfe, *Public Servant*, 284–86; Myers and Newton, *A Documented Narrative*, 250; *Chicago Daily News*, Aug. 11, 12, 1932; *New York Times*, Aug. 14, 1932; Ed., *San Francisco Chronicle*, Aug. 13, 1932, CF, HHPL.

25. *New York Herald Tribune*, June 16, 17, July 19, 1932; *New York Times*, June 18, Sep. 7, 1932, CF, HHPL; Joslin Diary, Box 10, File 7, Sep. 27, 1932, HHPL.

26. *New York Times*, Sep. 10, 13, 1932; *New York Evening Post*, Sep. 6, 1932; *New York Herald Tribune*, Aug. 31, Sep. 24, 1932, CF, HHPL; Joslin Diary, Box 10, File 7, Sep. 11, Oct. 16, 18, 19, 1932, HHPL; David Burner, *Herbert Hoover: A Public Life* (New York, 1979), 307–9.

27. MacLafferty Diary, Box 1, Feb. 12, HHPL; Peel and Donnelly, *The 1932 Campaign*, 107, 163–67, 179; Harris Gaylord Warren, *Herbert Hoover and the Great Depression* (New York, 1967), 257–58; George R. Nutter to Hoover, Oct. 4, 1932, PP, SF, Box 252, Republican National Committee, Corres.-Speech Suggestions, 1932, Oct., HHPL. For the final quotation see Joslin, List of Comments, Observations, Jan. 1932–1933, HHPL.

28. Ray Lyman Wilbur, *The Memoirs of Ray Lyman Wilbur*, eds. Edgar Eugene Robinson and Paul Carroll Edwards (Stanford, CA, 1960), 566; Martin L. Fausold, *The Presidency of Herbert C. Hoover* (Lawrence, KS, 1985), 211–12; *New York Evening Post*, Oct. 19, 1932, CF, HHPL. For Stimson quote see Henry Lewis Stimson Diaries, XXIV, Microfilm Ed., Reel 5, Manuscripts and Archives, Yale University Library, New Haven, CT.

29. *New York Herald Tribune*, July 12, Sep. 25, 1932; Ed., *New York Herald Tribune*, July 12, 1932, CF, HHPL.

30. *New York Herald Tribune*, Sep. 29, Oct. 1, 14, 19, 21, 1932; *New York Times*, Sep. 30, Oct. 23, 1932, CF, HHPL; MacLafferty Diary, Box 1, Aug. 9, 1932, HHPL.

31. "Political Paragraphs," Capital News Service Feature, Sep. 5, 1932, Colored Quest.-Corres., 1932, Sep., HHPL; Walter H. Newton to Judge James A. Cobb, Aug. 14, 1932, PP, SF, Box 106, Colored Quest.-Corres., 1932, Aug.; D. M. Baxter to Hoover, Sep. 19, 1932, PP, SF, Box 106, Colored Quest.-Corres, 1932, Sep.; B. F. Abbott to Hoover, Sep. 26, 1932, PP, SF, Box 106, Colored Quest.-Corres, 1932, Sep.; Bishop W. J. Walls to Hoover, Sep. 17, 1932, PP, SF, Box 106, Colored Quest.-Corres., 1932, Sep.; Telegram, National Federation of Colored Farmers of Chicago to Hoover, Oct. 29, 1932, PP, SF, Box 106, Colored Quest.-Corres., 1932, Oct-Dec., HHPL; Rev. L. P. Herring to Hoover, Oct. 28, 1932, PP, SF, Oct. 28, 1932, Colored Quest.-Corres., 1932, Oct.–Dec., HHPL.

32. J. M. Marques, Exalted Ruler of the Black Elks to U.S. Representative James M. Beck, May 26, 1932, PP, SF, Box 106, Colored Quest.-Corres., 1932, Jan.–June, HHPL; Unmarked clipping, Oct. 1, 1932, PP, SF, Box 106, Colored Quest.-Corres., 1932, Oct.–Dec., HHPL.

33. John R. Hawkins, "The National Negro Republican League—What It Is and What It Stands For," Press Release, Nov. 25, 1931, PP, SF, Box 106, Colored Quest.-Corres., 1931, Sep.–Dec.; Press Release [untitled], PP, SF, Box 106, Colored Quest.-Corres., 1932, July; *The Afro-American*, week of July 23, 1932, PP, SF, Box 106, Colored Quest.-Corres., 1932, July; John R. Hawkins to Everett Sanders, Chairman, Republican National Committee, Aug. 4, 1932, PP, SF, Box 106, Colored Quest.-Corres., 1932, Aug., HHPL; *New York Times*, Oct. 1, 1932; *Chicago Daily News*, Oct. 1, 1932, CF, HHPL. The Moton quotation is from John M. Barry, *Rising Tide: The Great Mississippi Flood of 1927 and How It Changed America* (New York, 1997), 415.

34. *New York Times*, Oct. 11, 15, Nov. 3, 1932; *Chicago Daily News*, Aug. 26, 1932; *New York Herald Tribune*, Sep. 29, Oct. 11, 20, 1932; unmarked clipping, Oct. 23, 1932, CF, HHPL; MacLafferty Diary, Box 1, Feb. 16, Oct. 28, 1932, HHPL; Louis W. Liebovich, *Bylines in Despair: Herbert Hoover, the Great Depression, and the U.S. News Media* (Westport, CT, 1994), 193–194; Peel and Donnelly, *The 1932 Campaign*, 116–21.

35. For quotes see Ed., *New York Times*, Sep. 14, 1932; and *New York Herald Tribune*, Sep. 14, 1932, CF, HHPL. The remainder is gleaned from MacLafferty Diary, Box 1, June 18, 1932, HHPL; Joslin Diary, Box 10, File 7, Sep. 13, 1932, HHPL; Joslin, *Hoover off the Record*, 300–304; *New York Times*, Aug. 13, Sep. 15, 16, 1932; *New York Evening Post*, Sep. 3, 1932; *Chicago Tribune*, Sep. 14, 1932, CF, HHPL.

36. For the quotation see Ed., *New York Times*, Oct. 5, 1931, CF, HHPL. The remainder of the account is found in Joslin Diary, Box 10, File 7, Sep. 3, 18, 19, 30, Oct. 5, 6, 7, 1932, HHPL;

Joslin, *Hoover off the Record*, 299–313; Wolfe, *Public Servant*, 288–92; Myers and Newton, *A Documented Narrative*, 255–259; unmarked clipping, Iowa newspaper, undated, 1932, CF, HHPL.

37. John Spargo, "The Legend of Hoover Who 'Did Nothing'," Hoover Papers, Box 226 (March 21, 1936), Herbert Hoover Presidential File (hereafter HHPF), Hoover Institution Archives, Stanford University.

38. Wolfe, *Public Servant*, 293–294.

39. Joslin Diary, Box 10, File 7, Oct. 9, 12, 1932, HHPL; Joslin, *Hoover off the Record*, 316–317.

40. *New York Herald Tribune*, Oct. 16, 17, 1932; *New York Times*, Oct. 12, 15, 1932, CF, HHPL; Joslin Diary, Box 10, File 7, Oct. 15, 1932, HHPL; Wilton Eckley, *Herbert Hoover* (Boston, 1980), 72.

41. *New York Times*, Oct. 21, 23, 1932; *New York Herald Tribune*, Oct. 18, 20, 1932, CF, HHPL; Eckley, *Hoover*, 73; Liebovich, *Bylines in Despair*, 194–195; Wolfe, *Public Servant*, 297–99.

42. *New York Herald Tribune*, Oct. 27, 1932; Ed., *Los Angeles Times*, Oct. 31, 1932, CF, HHPL; Timothy Walch and Dwight M. Miller, eds., *Herbert Hoover and Franklin D. Roosevelt: A Documentary History* (Westport, CT, 1998), 56–61.

43. Wolfe, *Public Servant*, 299–308; *New York Times*, Nov. 1, 1932; *New York Herald Tribune*, Nov. 1, 1932, CF, HHPL; Joslin Diary, Box 10, File 7, Oct. 31, 1932, HHPL.

44. *Boston Transcript*, Aug. 2, 1932; *New York Times*, Sep. 6, Oct. 16, Nov. 5, 1932; *New York Evening Post*, Oct. 10, 1932; *New York Herald Tribune*, Oct. 12, 1932, CF, HHPL; Wolfe, *Public Servant*, 315.

45. Wolfe, *Public Servant*, 310–14; Joslin, *Hoover off the Record*, 323–24; Joslin Diary, Box 10, File 7, Nov. 4, 5, 1932, HHPL; Walch and Miller, *Hoover and Roosevelt*, 64; Eckley, *Hoover*, 73; *New York Herald Tribune*, Nov. 3, 1932, CF, HHPL.

46. *New York Herald Tribune*, Nov. 8, 1932; *New York Times*, Nov. 8, 1932; CF, HHPL; Eckley, *Hoover*, 73–74; Joslin Diary, Box 10, File 7, Nov. 1, 7, 1932, HHPL; Burner, *A Public Life*, 316–17.

47. *New York Times*, Nov. 9, 1932; *Washington Post*, Nov. 9, 1932, CF, HHPL; George H. Nash, *Herbert Hoover and Stanford University* (Stanford, CA, 1988), 101–2; James Quinten Cahill, "Herbert Hoover's Early Schooling in Iowa and Its Place in Presidential Politics, Community Memory, and Personal Identity," *Annals of Iowa*, Third Series, 61, no. 2 (Spring 2002), 181; Joslin, List of Comments, Observations, 1931–1933, HHPL.

48. Burner, *A Public Life*, 316–18; Liebovich, *Bylines in Despair*, 197; *New York Times*, Nov. 13, 1932; *New York Evening Post*, Nov. 10, 1932, CF, HHPL.

49. The Hoover Library archivist quoted is Lynn Smith.

50. Mark Sullivan, "Hoover First President to War on Slump," *New York Herald Tribune*, Oct. 23, 1932, CF, HHPL.

51. Ed., *Boston Herald*, March 1933 [date not legible], CF, HHPL.

Chapter 19

1. Lawrence Sullivan, *Prelude to Panic: The Story of the Bank Holiday* (Washington, DC, 1936), 25–27; Harold Wolfe, *Herbert Hoover: Public Servant and Leader of the Loyal Opposition* (New York, 1956), 320–21.

2. David M. Kennedy, *Freedom from Fear: The American People in Depression and War, 1929–1945* (New York, 1999), 105; *New York Herald Tribune*, Nov. 12, 16, 1932; and *New York Times*, Nov. 14, 1932, all in Clipping File (hereafter CF), Herbert Hoover Presidential Library (hereafter HHPL), West Branch, IA.

3. Robert H. Ferrell, *American Diplomacy in the Great Depression: Hoover-Stimson Foreign Policy, 1929–1933* (New Haven, CT, 1957), 235.

4. *New York Herald Tribune*, Nov. 15, 1932, CF, HHPL.

5. Moley is quoted in William Starr Myers, *The Foreign Policies of Herbert Hoover, 1929–1933* (New York, 1940), 210.

6. Hoover Memorandum, Nov. 22, 1932, in Timothy Walch and Dwight M. Miller, eds., *Herbert Hoover and Franklin D. Roosevelt: A Documentary History* (Westport, CT, 1998), 73–76; Frank Friedel, "The Internal Struggle Between Hoover and Roosevelt," in *The Hoover Presidency: A Reappraisal*, eds. Martin L. Fausold and George T. Mazuzan (Albany, NY, 1974), 140–42; Herbert Hoover, Chapter 7, "The Disastrous Delay in Settling War Debts and Currency Stabilization," *Origins of the Banking Panic*, 11–13, PPP, Subject File (hereafter SF), Box 36, HHPL.
7. Theodore G. Joslin Diary, Box 10, File 7, Nov. 22, 23, 1932, HHPL; *U.S. Daily News*, Nov. 25, 1932, CF, HHPL; Hoover, Chapter 7, *Origins of the Banking Panic*, 14–16, PPP, SF, Box 30, HHPL; Stimson Diary, XXIV, Mic. Ed., Reel 5, Nov. 23, 1932, p. 120, Manuscripts and Archives, Yale University Library, New Haven, CT.
8. Wolfe, *Public Servant*, 325–26; Sullivan, *Prelude to Panic*, 30–33; Roosevelt Statement, Nov. 23, 1932, in *Hoover and Roosevelt*, eds. Walch and Miller, 77–78; Herbert Hoover, *The Memoirs of Herbert Hoover*, vol. 3, *The Great Depression, 1929–1941* (New York, 1952), 181–83; *New York Times*, Nov. 21, 22, 1932; *New York Evening Post*, Nov. 21, 1932; and *New York Herald Tribune*, Nov. 21, 1932, all in CF, HHPL. The *Detroit Free Press* is quoted in Dale Mayer, *Lou Henry Hoover: A Prototype for First Ladies* (Hauppauge, NY, 2004), 306. The *Baltimore Sun* is quoted in Hoover, *Memoirs*, vol. 3, 184.
9. William Starr Myers and Walter H. Newton, *The Hoover Administration: A Documented Narrative* (New York, 1936), 290–93; Harris Gaylord Warren, *Herbert Hoover and the Great Depression* (New York, 1967), 139; Stimson Diary, XXIV, Mic. Ed., Reel 5, Dec. 11, 1932, pp. 203–5, Dec. 13, 1932, p. 216, Dec. 1, 1932, p. 3; XXV, Dec. 15, 1932, pp. 1–3, Yale University; Benjamin D. Rhodes, "Herbert Hoover and the War Debts, 1919–1933," *Prologue* 6, no. 2 (Summer 1974), 141–43; Hoover, Chapter 7, *Origins of the Banking Panic*, 18, PPP, SF, Box 30, HHPL; Theodore G. Joslin, *Hoover off the Record* (Garden City, NY, 1934), 333–36; Henry L. Stimson and McGeorge Bundy, *On Active Service in Peace and War* (New York, 1948), 217–18; *New York Times*, Dec. 4, 14, 15, 16, 1932; *New York Herald Tribune*, Dec. 4, 15, 1932; and *New York Evening Post*, Dec. 15, 1932, all in CF, HHPL.
10. Telegram, Hoover to Roosevelt, Dec. 17, 1932, and Telegram, Roosevelt to Hoover, Dec. 19, 1932, in *Hoover and Roosevelt*, eds. Walch and Miller; Stimson Diary, Dec. 20, 1932, in *Hoover and Roosevelt*, eds. Walch and Miller, 83–85; Wolfe, *Public Servant*, 329.
11. Wolfe, *Public Servant*, 329–30; *New York World Telegram*, Dec. 20, 1932, and *New York Times*, Dec. 20, 1932, both in CF, HHPL; Joslin Diary, January, 1933, quoted in *Hoover and Roosevelt*, eds. Walch and Miller,123.
12. Stimson Diary, XXV, Mic. Ed., Reel 5, Dec. 21, 1932, pp. 31–32, Yale University; Telegram, Roosevelt to Hoover, Dec. 12; Telegram, Hoover to Roosevelt, Dec. 20; Telegram, Roosevelt to Hoover, Dec. 21; Telegram, Hoover to Roosevelt, Dec. 22; Roosevelt Press Release, Dec. 22, 1932, in *Hoover and Roosevelt*, eds. Walch and Miller, 89–94; *New York Times*, Dec. 25, 1932; *New York Herald Tribune*, Dec. 20, 22, 23, 1932; Ed., *New York Herald Tribune*, Dec. 23, 1932, CF, HHPL.
13. Hal Elliott Wert, *Hoover, the Fishing President: Portrait of the Private Man and His Life Outdoors* (Mechanicsburg, PA, 2005), 206–17; *New York Times*, Dec. 24, 31, 1932; *New York Herald Tribune*, Dec. 17, 24, 1932; and unmarked clipping, Dec. 23, 1932, all in CF, HHPL.
14. Stimson Diary, XXV, Mic. Ed., Reel 5, Jan. 7, 9, 1933, pp. 86–103, Yale University; Stimson Memorandum of Conversation with Franklin D. Roosevelt, Monday, Jan. 9, 1933, at Hyde Park, NY; Hoover to Stimson, Jan. 15, 1933, in *Hoover and Roosevelt*, eds. Walch and Miller, 101–3; Stimson and Bundy, *On Active Service*, 289–93; Martin L. Fausold, *The Presidency of Herbert C. Hoover* (Lawrence, KS, 1985), 220–21; Richard Current, *Secretary Stimson: A Study in Statecraft* (New Brunswick, NJ, 1954), 119–22; Ferrell, *American Diplomacy in the Great Depression*, 238, 245.
15. Stimson Diary, XXV, Mic. Ed., Reel 5, Jan. 16–20, 1933, pp. 3–4, 129–30, 142–46, Yale University; Stimson Diary, Jan. 15, 19, 1993, in *Hoover and Roosevelt*, eds. Walch and Miller, pp. 105–10; *New York Herald Tribune*, Jan. 21, 1933, CF, HHPL.
16. Stimson Diary, XXV, Mic. Ed., Reel 5, Jan. 20, 1933, pp. 149–51, Yale University; David Burner, *Herbert Hoover: A Public Life* (New York, 1979), 321; *New York Herald Tribune*,

Jan. 21, 1933; *New York Times,* Jan. 20, 1933, CF, HHPL; Hoover, Chapter 7, *Origins of the Banking Panic,* 29–36, PPP, SF, Box 30, HHPL.

17. *New York Times,* Jan. 24, 1933, CF, HHPL; Stimson Diary, Mic. Ed., Reel 5, XXVI, Feb. 25, 26, March 1, 1933, pp. 96–97, 105–6, 117–20, Yale University; Current, *Secretary Stimson,* 128–31.

18. Ferrell, *American Diplomacy in the Great Depression,* 260–73.

19. Sullivan, *Prelude to Panic,* 34.

20. Warren, *Hoover and the Great Depression,* 274–80.

21. Sullivan, *Prelude to Panic,* 55; Pamphlet composed of articles from the *Saturday Evening Post,* June 8, 15, 22, and 29, 1935, pp. 31–33, Box 30, SF, PPP, HHPL; Wolfe, *Public Servant,* 337–40; Hoover, Chapter 4, *Origins of the Banking Panic,* 1–10, PPP, SF, Box 30, HHPL; Hoover, *Memoirs,* vol. 3, 192–93; *New York Herald Tribune,* Dec. 7, 8, 1932; *U.S. Daily News,* Nov. 21, Dec. 7, 1932, CF, HHPL.

22. Quotes are from Myers and Newton, *A Documented Narrative,* 313–14. For the remainder of the account see pamphlet composed of articles from *Saturday Evening Post,* 33–35, Box 30, SF, PPP, HHPL; Sullivan, *Prelude to Panic,* 57–65; *New York Herald Tribune,* Dec. 28, 1932; *New York Times,* Dec. 28, 1932; and *New York Evening Post,* Dec. 28, 1932, all in CF, HHPL.

23. James Stuart Olson, *Herbert Hoover and the Reconstruction Finance Corporation, 1931–1933* (Ames, IA, 1977), 108–9; Susan L. DuBrock Wendel, "Herbert Hoover and Banking Reform" (MA thesis, Northeastern Illinois University, 1985), 68–71; R. Gordon Hoxie, "Hoover and the Banking Crisis," *Presidential Studies Quarterly* 4, no. 3 14–5, no. 1 (Summer/ Fall 1974–Winter 1975), 25–28; Hoover, Chapter 6, *Origins of the Banking Panic,* 1–7, PPP, SF, Box 30, HHPL; Pamphlet composed of articles from the *Saturday Evening Post,* 36–41, Box 30, SF, PPP, HHPL; Myers and Newton, *A Documented Narrative,* 315–24.

24. *New York Herald Tribune,* Jan. 31, 1933, CF, HHPL; Pamphlet composed of articles from the *Saturday Evening Post,* 41–43, Box 30, SF, PPP, HHPL; Hoover, Chapter 6, *Origins of the Banking Panic,* 8–10, PPP, SF, Box 30, HHPL; Joslin, *Hoover off the Record,* 345–46.

25. *New York Times,* Dec. 19, 23, 30, 1932; Jan. 14, 17, 18, Feb. 6, 21, 1933; *New York Herald Tribune,* Jan. 18, 1933; *New York Evening Post,* Jan. 6, 1933, CF, HHPL; Ferrell, *American Diplomacy in the Great Depression,* 252–53.

26. Kennedy, *Freedom from Fear,* 130; *New York Times,* Feb. 6, 1933, and *New York Herald Tribune,* Nov. 17, Dec. 8, 1932, all in CF, HHPL. The final quotation is from the *New York Evening Post,* Jan. 12, 1933, CF, HHPL.

27. Burner, *A Public Life,* 326; Joan Hoff, *Herbert Hoover: Forgotten Progressive* (Boston, 1975), 138; Myers and Newton, *A Documented Narrative,* 527; *New York Herald Tribune,* Jan. 1, Jan. 3, Jan. 4, 1933; *New York Times,* Jan. 1, 1933; and *New York Evening Post,* Jan. 3, 1933, all in CF, HHPL.

28. Pamphlet composed of articles from the *Saturday Evening Post,* 8–13; Sullivan, *Prelude to Panic,* 23, 67, 71–78; *New York Times,* Feb. 20, 1933, CF, HHPL.

29. Mark Sullivan, "Recent Runs on Banks Traced to Publicity of R. F. C. Loans," *New York Herald Tribune,* Feb. 7, 1933, CF, HHPL; Sullivan, *Prelude to Panic,* 45–53. The Pomerene quote is on p. 53. Olson, *Hoover and the Reconstruction Finance Corporation,* 99–101; Pamphlet composed of articles from the *Saturday Evening Post,* 22; David Hinshaw, *Herbert Hoover: American Quaker* (New York, 1950), provides the same quote from Pomerene on p. 278.

30. Olson, *Hoover and the Reconstruction Finance Corporation,* 101–4; Fausold, *The Presidency of Herbert C. Hoover,* 231; Sullivan, *Prelude to Panic,* 83–87; *New York Evening Post,* Feb. 15, 1933, CF, HHPL.

31. Theodore Joslin to Hoover, Feb. 25, 1933, Banking Crisis, President's Log and Documents, 1933, Box 30, SF, PPP, HHPL. The conversation between Woodin and Mills is recorded in the President's Log, Feb. 26, 1933, Banking Crisis, Box 30, PPP, SF, HHPL. The Tugwell-Rand conversation is documented in Kennedy, *Freedom from Fear,* 110, and Mayer, *A Prototype for First Ladies,* 308; Lawrence Sullivan to Bernice Miller, Miller Papers, Hoover Institution Archives, Stanford University. Enclosed is a clipping by Sullivan in the *Washington Star,* March 4, 1958.

32. Kennedy, *Freedom from Fear*, 109; Burner, *A Public Life*, 322–23; Hoover to Roosevelt, Feb. 18, 1933, in *Hoover and Roosevelt*, eds. Walch and Miller, 130–32; Pamphlet composed of articles from the *Saturday Evening Post*, 13–17, Box 30, SF, PPP, HHPL; President's Log and Documents, 1933, Banking Crisis, pp. 13–20, Box 30, SF, PPP, HHPL.
33. Hoover to Roosevelt, Feb. 28, 1933, in *Hoover and Roosevelt*, eds. Walch and Miller, 134; Wolfe, *Public Servant*, 352–56; Roosevelt to Hoover, March 1, 1933, in *Hoover and Roosevelt*, eds. Walch and Miller, 135; Fausold, *The Presidency of Herbert C. Hoover*, 229–32.
34. President's Log, March 2, 1933, Banking Crisis, President's Log and Documents, 1933, pp. 1–3, Box 30, SF, PPP, HHPL.
35. Ibid.; Olson, *Hoover and the Reconstruction Finance Corporation*, 109–11.
36. President's Log, March 3, 1933, Banking Crisis, President's Log and Documents, 1933, pp. 1–2, 30–34, B30, SF, PPP, HHPL; *New York Times*, March 4, 1933, CF, HHPL; Hoover Memorandum, March 3, 1933, in *Hoover and Roosevelt*, eds. Walch and Miller, 137–45; Joslin Diary, March 3, 1933, in *Hoover and Roosevelt*, eds. Walch and Miller, 145.
37. Myers and Newton, *A Documented Narrative*, 365–67; Wert, *The Fishing President*, 218; Burner, *A Public Life*, 323; *New York Evening Post*, March 4, 1933, and *New York Times*, March 4, 1933, both in CF, HHPL.
38. *New York Times*, March 4, 1933, CF, HHPL; Hoover account [notes not used in *Memoirs*], 1–3, Box 30, SF, PPP, Bank Failure, undated, HHPL.
39. Nancy A. Colbert, *Lou Henry Hoover, The Duty to Serve* (Greensboro, NC, 1998), 95; Joslin, *Hoover off the Record*, 366–67.

Chapter 20

1. For Hoover standing in presidential polls see George H. Nash, "Herbert Hoover: Political Orphan," in *Uncommon Americans: The Lives and Legacies of Herbert and Lou Henry Hoover*, ed. Timothy Walch (Westport, CT, 2003), 10. The major academic studies include David Burner, *Herbert Hoover: A Public Life* (New York, 1979), and Martin L. Fausold, *The Presidency of Herbert C. Hoover* (Lawrence, KS, 1985).
2. Hatfield is quoted in James R. Bowers, "Herbert Hoover: Ambivalent Quaker" (MA thesis, University of Illinois Legal Studies Center, Springfield, IL, 1981), iii.
3. James Stuart Olson, *Herbert Hoover and the Reconstruction Finance Corporation, 1931–1933* (Ames, IA, 1977), 118.
4. Clair Everet Nelsen, "The Image of Herbert Hoover as Reflected in the American Press" (PhD diss., Stanford University, 1956), 205–6.
5. Joseph S. Davis, "Herbert Hoover, 1874–1964: Another Appraisal," *South Atlantic Quarterly* 68, no. 3 (Summer 1969), 307–18.
6. Fausold, *The Presidency of Herbert C. Hoover* (Lawrence, KS, 1985), 242–47; Joan Hoff, *Herbert Hoover: Forgotten Progressive* (Boston, 1975), 273–74; Frank Freidel in *Understanding Herbert Hoover: Ten Perspectives*, ed. Lee Nash (Stanford, CA, 1987), 128.
7. Herbert Hoover, *Further Addresses upon the American Road, 1938–1940* (New York, 1940), 3, 5, 22.
8. James S. Olson, "The Philosophy of Herbert Hoover: A Contemporary Perspective," *Annals of Iowa* 43, no. 3 (Winter 1976), 190–91.
9. Ellis W. Hawley, ed., *Herbert Hoover as Secretary of Commerce: Studies in New Era Thought and Practice* (Iowa City, IA, 1981), 248, 254.
10. Wilton Eckley, *Herbert Hoover* (Boston, 1980), 154, 156, 159.
11. Harris Gaylord Warren, *Herbert Hoover and the Great Depression* (New York, 1967), 300–301.
12. George E. Sokolsky, "Long Delayed Tribute Paid Herbert Hoover," unmarked clipping, April 1947, Box 227, Herbert Hoover Presidential File (hereafter HHPF), Hoover Institution Archives, Stanford University.
13. *New York Herald Tribune*, Oct. 25, 1964, Clipping File (hereafter CF), Herbert Hoover Presidential Library (hereafter HHPL), West Branch, IA.

14. Moley is quoted in Memorandum by Edgar Rickard, Oct. 1949, p. 2, Box 227, HHPF, Hoover Institution Archives.
15. Ellis W. Hawley, "Neo-Institutional History and the Understanding of Herbert Hoover," in *Understanding Hoover*, ed. Lee Nash, 73.
16. Albert U. Romasco, *The Poverty of Abundance: Hoover, the Nation, the Depression* (New York, 1968), 200.
17. Olson, *Hoover and the Reconstruction Finance Corporation*, 119.
18. Ed., *New York Times*, March 3, 1933, CF, HHPL.
19. Ed., *Lansing* (MI) *State Journal*, March 3, 1933, CF, HHPL.
20. Ed., *Tacoma Journal*, March 3, 1933, CF, HHPL.
21. Ed., *Kansas City Star*, March 3, 1933, CF, HHPL.
22. Ed., *Columbus* (OH) *Dispatch*, March 3, 1933, CF, HHPL.
23. Ed., *Boston Herald*, March 3, 1933, CF, HHPL.
24. Ed., *New York Evening Post*, March 4, 1933, CF, HHPL.
25. Burner, *A Public Life*, 61.

A Note on the Sources

I initially planned to write a full-scale biography of Herbert Hoover, and during the 15 consecutive months of my sabbatical in 2006–2007 as well as parts of 2 earlier summers, I researched his entire life at the Herbert Hoover Presidential Library at West Branch, Iowa. I dipped into the subject files of every period of his career and selectively into personal files of Hoover and his friends. In researching the presidency I found the president's newspaper clipping file far richer than his letters, which were often sparse and impersonal, usually dictated. I used the Reprint File (RF) of the Presidential Library extensively for articles on his presidency. My assistants and I were able to flesh out many incomplete citations. Some we simply cited as RF. The rare incomplete citations in the president's newspaper clipping file (CF) are cited as CF. The Clipping File represents a vast sampling of clippings nationwide, without regard to ideological persuasion. My selection was based on the significance of the events covered. We photocopied more than three hundred oral history interviews, but I used them sparsely because they contain little original material on the presidency. They are more useful for the postpresidential period. My research included reading and taking notes on every published book about Hoover, old and new, as well as every PhD dissertation and Master's thesis relevant to the presidency, although not all were included in the book or the bibliography. Some of the early biographies are virtually primary sources because the authors talked to Hoover personally, and many of them knew him well in the prime of his life.

In addition to 15 consecutive months and parts of 2 summers at West Branch, I spent several weeks at the Hoover Institution Archives on the campus of Stanford University at Palo Alto working primarily in the Herbert Hoover papers. Unlike my initial research at West Branch, by the time I traveled to California I was already directing my attention solely to Hoover's presidency. The Stanford collection focuses largely on Hoover's early career rather than his presidency, and there is some overlap with the West Branch collection. I obtained substantial information on the 1928 election from the scrapbook of Hubert Work and from a study written by Edward Eyre Hunt. By the time I reached Stanford, much of the research was done, and it was a matter of filling gaps.

I have attempted to define my research strategy as a prerequisite for understanding the bibliography that follows and to indicate why I relied on certain types of sources. The problem, when the research ran against a hard deadline, was not a paucity of information but an overabundance that needed to be boiled down. This long book could have been much longer.

Bibliography

Manuscripts and Collections
Herbert Hoover Presidential Library, West Branch, Iowa

Papers

Herbert Hoover Papers, Precommerce Period
Herbert Hoover Papers, Commerce Period
Herbert Hoover Papers, Campaign and Transition Period
Herbert Hoover Papers, Presidential Period
Herbert Hoover Papers, Postpresidential File
"The Bible" (typed copies of Hoover's articles, addresses, and public statements, 1892–1964)
George Edwards Akerson Papers
American Child Health Association Papers
American Relief Administration Bulletins
Theodore G. Joslin Papers
Allan Hoover Papers
Lou Henry Hoover Papers
Lawrence Richey Papers
Edgar Rickard Diaries

Unpublished Diaries

Boone, Joel T., Diary
Joslin, Theodore G., Diary
MacLafferty, James H., Diary, Copyright, Stanford University
Rickard, Edgar, Diary
Stimson, Henry L. Diary, Microfilm Edition, Manuscripts Collection, Yale University Library

Unpublished Manuscripts

Hoover, Herbert. "Origins of the Banking Panic" (1935), Postpresidential Papers (PPP), Box 30, Herbert Hoover Presidential Library (HHPL), West Branch, IA.
Hunt, Edward Eyre. "Fight on the Depression: Phase I and Phase II" (1935), Herbert Hoover Presidential Files, Box 335, Stanford University, irregularly paginated typescript.

Oral Histories

Raymond Henle
Allan and Margaret Hoover

Hoover Institution Archives, Stanford, California

George Barr Baker Papers
Herbert Hoover Subject Collection
Edward Eyre Hunt Papers
Mark Sullivan Papers
Ray Lyman Wilbur Papers

Books

Abels, Jules. *In the Time of Silent Cal.* New York: G. P. Putnam's Sons, 1969.

Allen, Anne Beiser. *An Independent Woman: The Life of Lou Henry Hoover.* Westport, CT: Praeger, 2000.

Barber, William J. *From New Era to New Deal: Herbert Hoover, the Economists, and American Economic Policy, 1921–1933.* New York: Cambridge University Press, 1985.

Barry, John M. *Rising Tide: The Great Mississippi Flood of 1927 and How It Changed America.* New York: Simon & Schuster, 1997.

Best, Gary Dean. *Herbert Hoover: The Postpresidential Years 1933–1964.* Vol. 1, 1933–1945. Stanford, CA: Hoover Institution Press, Stanford University, 1983.

———. *Herbert Hoover: The Postpresidential Years 1933–1964.* Vol. 2, 1946–1964. Stanford, CA: Hoover Institution Press, Stanford University, 1983.

Brandes, Joseph. *Herbert Hoover and Economic Diplomacy: Department of Commerce Policy, 1921–1928.* Pittsburgh, PA: University of Pittsburgh Press, 1962.

Burner, David. *Herbert Hoover: A Public Life.* New York: Alfred A. Knopf, 1979.

Charnley, Mitchell V. *The Boy's Life of Herbert Hoover.* New York: Harper and Brothers, 1931.

Clements, Kendrick A. *Hoover, Conservation, and Consumerism: Engineering the Good Life.* Lawrence, KS: University Press of Kansas, 2000.

———. *The Life of Herbert Hoover: Imperfect Visionary 1918–1928.* New York: Palgrave Macmillan, 2010.

Colbert, Nancy A. *Lou Henry Hoover: The Duty to Serve.* Greensboro, NC: Morgan Reynolds, 1998.

Corey, Herbert. *The Truth about Hoover.* Boston: Houghton Mifflin Company, 1932.

Crowther, Samuel. *The Presidency vs. Hoover.* Garden City, NY: Doubleday, Doran & Company, Inc., 1928.

Current, Richard. *Secretary Stimson: A Study in Statecraft.* New Brunswick, NJ: Rutgers University Press, 1954.

Daniel, Pete. *Deep'n as It Come: The 1927 Mississippi River Flood.* New York: Oxford University Press, 1977.

Davis, James W. *Presidential Primaries: Road to the White House.* Westport, CT: Greenwood, 1980.

DeConde, Alexander. *Herbert Hoover's Latin American Policy.* Stanford, CA: Stanford University Press, 1951.

Dennis, Ruth. *The Wit and Wisdom of Herbert Hoover: A Compilation of Many of His Quotations.* New York: Vantage Press, 1995.

Dodge, Mark M., ed. *Herbert Hoover and the Historians.* West Branch, IA: Herbert Hoover Presidential Library Association, 1989.

Eckley, Wilton. *Herbert Hoover.* Boston: Twayne, 1980.

Ellis, Edward Robb. *A Nation in Torment: The Great American Depression 1929–1939.* New York: Capricorn Books, 1970.

Ellis, L. Ethan. *Republican Foreign Policy, 1921–1933*. New Brunswick, NJ: Rutgers University Press, 1968.

Emerson, Edwin. *Hoover and His Times*. Garden City, NY: Garden City Publishing Company, 1932.

Emery, Anne. *American Friend: Herbert Hoover*. n.p.: Rand McNally, 1967.

Ewy, Marvin. *Charles Curtis of Kansas: Vice President of the United States, 1929–1933*. Emporia, KS: Kansas State Teachers College, 1961.

Fausold, Martin L. *The Presidency of Herbert C. Hoover*. Lawrence, KS: University Press of Kansas, 1985.

Fausold, Martin L., and George T. Mazuzan, eds. *The Hoover Presidency: A Reappraisal*. Albany, NY: State University of New York Press, 1974.

Ferrell, Robert H. *American Diplomacy in the Great Depression: Hoover-Stimson Foreign Policy, 1929–1933*. New Haven, CT: Yale University Press, 1957.

———. *The Presidency of Calvin Coolidge*. Lawrence, KS: University Press of Kansas, 1998.

Finan, Christopher M. *Alfred E. Smith: The Happy Warrior*. New York: Hill and Wang, 2002.

Free, A. M. *Herbert Hoover*. Published by the Author, 1928.

Garraty, John A. *The Great Depression*. San Diego, CA: Harcourt Brace Jovanovich, 1986.

Gelfand, Lawrence E., ed. *Herbert Hoover: The Great War and Its Aftermath, 1914–1923*. Iowa City, IA: University of Iowa Press, 1979.

Gilbert, Robert F. *The Tormented President: Calvin Coolidge, Death, and Clinical Depression*. Westport, CT: Praeger, 2003.

Greenberg, David. *Calvin Coolidge*. New York: Times Books/Henry Holt, 2006.

Hamill, John. *The Strange Career of Mr. Hoover: Under Two Flags*. New York: William Faro, Inc., 1931.

Hamilton, David E. *From New Day to New Deal: American Farm Policy from Hoover to Roosevelt, 1928–1933*. Chapel Hill, NC: University of North Carolina Press, 1991.

Handlin, Oscar. *Al Smith and His America*. Boston: Little, Brown, 1958.

Hard, William. *Who's Hoover?* New York: Dodd, Mead and Company, Inc., 1928.

Hatfield, Mark O., compiler. *Herbert Hoover Reassessed: Essays Commemorating the Fiftieth Anniversary of the Inauguration of Our Thirty-First President*. Washington, DC: Government Printing Office, 1981.

Hawley, Ellis W., ed. *Herbert Hoover as Secretary of Commerce: Studies in New Era Thought and Practice*. Iowa City, IA: University of Iowa Press, 1981.

Hinshaw, David. *Herbert Hoover: American Quaker*. New York: Farrar, Straus and Company, 1950.

Hodgson, Godfrey. *The Colonel: The Life and Wars of Henry Stimson 1867–1950*. New York: Alfred A. Knopf, 1990.

Hoff, Joan. *Herbert Hoover: Forgotten Progressive*. Boston: Little, Brown, and Company, 1975.

Hoover, Herbert. *Addresses upon the American Road, 1933–1938*. New York: Charles Scribner's Sons, 1938.

———. *America's First Crusade*. New York: Charles Scribner's Sons, 1942.

———. *An American Epic*. Vol. 1, *The Relief of Belgium and Northern France, 1914–1930*. Chicago: Henry Regnery, 1959.

———. *An American Epic*. Vol. 2, *Famine in Forty-Five Nations: Organization behind the Front, 1914–1923*. Chicago: Henry Regnery, 1960.

———. *An American Epic*. Vol. 3, *Famine in Forty-Five Nations: The Battle on the Front Line, 1914–1923*. Chicago: Henry Regnery, 1961.

———. *An American Epic*. Vol. 4, *The Guns Cease Killing and the Saving of Life from Famine Begins, 1939–1963*. Chicago: Henry Regnery, 1964.

———. *American Individualism*. New York: Doubleday, Doran & Company, Inc., 1922.

———. *A Boyhood in Iowa*. New York: Aventine Press, 1931.

———. *Campaign Speeches of Herbert Hoover, 1928*. Stanford, CA: Stanford University Press, 1928.

———. *The Challenge to Liberty*. Rockford, IL: Herbert Hoover Presidential Library Association, 1971.

———. *Fishing for Fun—And to Wash Your Soul*. Edited by William Nichols. West Branch, IA: Herbert Hoover Presidential Library, 1963.

———. *Further Addresses upon the American Road, 1938–1940*. New York: Charles Scribner's Sons, 1940.

———. *Herbert Hoover, Hoover after Dinner*. New York: Charles Scribner's Sons, 1933.

———. *Herbert Hoover, The New Day: Campaign Speeches of Herbert Hoover*. Stanford, CA: Stanford University Press, 1928.

———. *The Memoirs of Herbert Hoover*. Vol. 1, *Years of Adventure, 1874–1920*. New York: Macmillan Company, 1951.

———. *The Memoirs of Herbert Hoover*. Vol. 2, *The Cabinet and the Presidency, 1920–1933*. New York: Macmillan Company, 1952.

———. *The Memoirs of Herbert Hoover*. Vol. 3, *The Great Depression, 1929–1941*. New York: Macmillan Company, 1952.

———. *On Growing Up*. Edited by William Nichols. New York: William Morrow & Company, 1962.

———. *The Ordeal of Woodrow Wilson*. New York: McGraw-Hill, 1958.

———. *Public Papers of the Presidents*. Vol. 1, *1929*. Washington, DC: United States Government Printing Office, 1974.

———. *Public Papers of the Presidents*. Vol. 2, *1930*. Washington, DC: United States Government Printing Office, 1976.

———. *Public Papers of the Presidents*. Vol. 3, *1931*. Washington, DC: United States Government Printing Office, 1976.

———. *Public Papers of the Presidents*. Vol. 4, *1932–1933*. Washington, DC: United States Government Printing Office, 1977.

Hoover, Herbert, and Hugh Gibson. *The Basis of Lasting Peace*. New York: D. Van Nostrand Company, 1945.

———. *The Problems of Lasting Peace*. Garden City, NY: Doubleday, Doran & Company, Inc., 1942.

Hughes, William, and Frederick Patterson, eds. *Robert Russa Moton*. Chapel Hill, NC: University of North Carolina Press, 1956.

Huthmacher, J. Joseph, and Warren I. Susman, eds. *Herbert Hoover and the Crisis of American Capitalism*. Cambridge, MA: Schenkman Publishing Company, 1973.

Irwin, Will. *Herbert Hoover: A Reminiscent Biography*. New York: Grosset & Dunlap, 1928.

Jeansonne, Glen. *Messiah of the Masses: Huey P. Long and the Great Depression*. New York: HarperCollins, 1993.

———. *A Time of Paradox: America from Awakening to Hiroshima, 1890–1945*. Lanham, MD: Rowan and Littlefield, 2007.

———. *Transformation and Reaction: America, 1921–1945*. Long Grove, IL: Waveland Press, 2004.

Johnson, Claudius O. *Borah of Idaho*. Seattle: University of Washington Press, 1936.

Joslin, Theodore G. *Hoover off the Record*. Garden City, NY: Doubleday, Doran & Company, Inc., 1934. Reprint, Freeport, NY: Books for Libraries Press, 1971.

Kellogg, Vernon. *Herbert Hoover: The Man and His Work*. New York: D. Appleton and Company, 1920.

Kennedy, David M. *Freedom from Fear: The American People in Depression and War, 1929–1945*. New York: Oxford University Press, 1999.

———. *Over Here: The First World War and American Society*. New York: Oxford University Press, 1980.

Kennedy, Hugh A. Studdert. *Hoover in 1932*. San Francisco: Farallon Press, 1931.

Kennedy, Susan Estabrook. *The Banking Crisis of 1933*. Lexington, KY: University Press of Kentucky, 1973.

Keynes, John Maynard. *The Economic Consequences of the Peace*. London: Macmillan Company, 1920.

Kindleberger, Charles P. *The World in Depression, 1929–1939: Revised and Enlarged Edition*. Berkeley, CA: University of California Press, 1986.

Klein, Maury. *Rainbow's End: The Crash of 1929*. New York: Oxford University Press, 2001.

Krog, Carl E., and William R. Tanner, eds. *Herbert Hoover and the Republican Era: A Reconsideration*. Lanham, MD: University Press of America, 1984.

Lambert, Darwin. *Herbert Hoover's Hideaway.* Luray, VA: Shenandoah Natural History Association, Inc., 1971.

Lane, Rose Wilder. *The Making of Herbert Hoover.* New York: Century, 1920.

Lerski, George J. *Herbert Hoover and Poland: A Documentary History of a Friendship.* Stanford, CA: Hoover Institution, 1977.

Leuchtenburg, William E. *Herbert Hoover.* New York: Henry Holt, 2009.

——. *The Perils of Prosperity, 1914–1932.* Chicago: University of Chicago Press, 1958.

Liebovich, Louis W. *Bylines in Despair: Herbert Hoover, the Great Depression, and the U.S. News Media.* Westport, CT: Praeger, 1994.

Liggett, Walter W. *The Rise of Herbert Hoover.* New York: H. K. Fly Company, 1932.

Lippmann, Walter. *Interpretations, 1931–1932.* New York: MacMillan, 1932.

Lisio, Donald J. *Hoover, Blacks, and Lily-Whites: A Study of Southern Strategies.* Chapel Hill, NC: University of North Carolina Press, 1985.

——. *The President and Protest: Hoover, Conspiracy, and the Bonus Riot.* Columbia, MO: University of Missouri Press, 1974.

Lloyd, Craig. *Aggressive Introvert: Herbert Hoover and Public Relations Management, 1912–1932.* Columbus, OH: Ohio State University Press, 1972.

Lochner, Louis P. *Herbert Hoover and Germany.* New York: Macmillan Company, 1960.

Lower, Richard Coke. *A Bloc of One: The Political Career of Hiram W. Johnson.* Stanford, CA: Stanford University Press, 1993.

Lyman, Robert Hunt, ed. *World Almanac and Book of Facts for 1929.* New York: New York World, 1929.

Lyons, Eugene. *Herbert Hoover: A Biography.* Garden City, NY: Doubleday, 1964.

Marsh, William J., Jr. *Our President Herbert Hoover.* New Milford, CT: William J. & Chas. Marsh, 1930.

Mayer, Dale. *Lou Henry Hoover: A Prototype for First Ladies.* Hauppauge, NY: Nova History Publications, 2004.

——, ed. *Lou Henry Hoover: Essays on a Busy Life.* Worland, WY: High Plains Publishing Company, 1994.

McCoy, Donald R. *Calvin Coolidge: The Quiet President.* New York: Macmillan Company, 1967.

McGee, Dorothy Horton. *Herbert Hoover: Engineer, Humanitarian, Statesman.* New York: Dodd, Mead and Company, Inc., 1967.

McKenna, Marian C. *Borah.* Ann Arbor, MI: University of Michigan Press, 1961.

McLean, Hulda Hoover. *Genealogy of the Herbert Hoover Family.* Stanford, CA: Hoover Institution on War, Revolution and Peace, 1967.

——. *Uncle Bert: A Biographical Portrait of Herbert Hoover.* Published by the author, 1974.

McLean, Hulda Hoover, compiler. *Hulda's World: A Chronicle of Hulda Minthorn Hoover, 1848–1884.* West Branch, IA: Hoover Presidential Library Association, 1989.

Michelson, Charles. *The Ghost Talks.* New York: G. P. Putnam's Sons, 1944.

Moley, Raymond. *After Seven Years: A Political Analysis of the New Deal.* Lincoln, NE: University of Nebraska Press, 1939.

——. *Master of Politics: In a Personal Perspective.* New York: Funk & Wagnalls Company, 1949.

Murray, Robert K. *The Harding Era: Warren G. Harding and His Administration.* Minneapolis: University of Minnesota Press, 1969.

Myers, William Starr. *The Foreign Policies of Herbert Hoover, 1929–1933.* New York: Charles Scribner's Sons, 1940.

Myers, William Starr, and Walter H. Newton. *The Hoover Administration: A Documented Narrative.* New York: Charles Scribner's Sons, 1936.

Nash, George H. *Herbert Hoover and Stanford University.* Stanford, CA: Hoover Institution Press, Stanford University, 1988.

——. *The Life of Herbert Hoover: The Engineer, 1874–1914.* New York: Norton, 1983.

——. *The Life of Herbert Hoover: The Humanitarian, 1914–1917.* New York: Norton, 1988.

——. *The Life of Herbert Hoover: Master of Emergencies, 1917–1918.* New York: Norton, 1996.

Nash, Lee, ed. *Understanding Herbert Hoover: Ten Perspectives.* Stanford, CA: Hoover Institution, 1987.

Neal, Donn C. *The World beyond the Hudson: Alfred E. Smith and National Politics, 1918–1928.* New York: Garland, 1983.

Norris, George. *Fighting Liberal: The Autobiography of George W. Norris.* New York: Macmillan Company, 1945. Reprint, Lincoln, NE: University of Nebraska Press, 1972.

Nye, Frank T., Jr. *Doors of Opportunity: The Life and Legacy of Herbert Hoover.* West Branch, IA: Herbert Hoover Presidential Library Association, Inc., 1988.

O'Connor, Raymond G. *Perilous Equilibrium: The United States and the London Conference of 1930.* Westport, CT: Greenwood Press, 1969.

Olson, James Stuart. *Herbert Hoover and the Reconstruction Finance Corporation, 1931–1933.* Ames, IA: Iowa State University Press, 1977.

Peare, Catherine Owens. *The Herbert Hoover Story.* New York: Thomas Y. Crowell Company, 1965.

Peel, Roy V., and Thomas C. Donnelly. *The 1928 Campaign: An Analysis.* New York: Richard R. Smith, 1931. Reprint, New York: Arno Press, 1974.

———. *The 1932 Campaign: An Analysis.* New York: Farrar and Rinehart, 1935.

Pryor, Helen B. *Lou Henry Hoover: Gallant First Lady.* New York: Dodd, Mead and Company, Inc., 1969.

Reeves, Earl. *This Man Hoover.* New York: A. L. Burt Company, 1928.

Robinson, Edgar Eugene, and Vaughn Davis Bornet. *Herbert Hoover: President of the United States.* Stanford, CA: Hoover Institution Press, Stanford University, 1975.

Rochester, E. S. *Coolidge-Hoover-Work: An Intimate Review of an Epochal National Campaign for the Presidency of the United States.* Washington, DC: Terminal Press, 1929.

Romasco, Albert U. *The Poverty of Abundance: Hoover, the Nation, the Depression.* New York: Oxford University Press, 1968.

Rosen, Elliot A. *Hoover, Roosevelt, and the Brains Trust: From Depression to New Deal.* New York: Columbia University Press, 1977.

Rothbard, Murray N. *America's Great Depression.* Los Angeles: Nash Publishing, 1972.

Russell, Francis. *The Shadow of Blooming Grove: Warren G. Harding and His Times.* New York: McGraw-Hill, 1968.

Saul, Norman E. *Friends or Foes? The United States and Soviet Russia, 1921–1941.* Lawrence, KS: University Press of Kansas, 2006.

Schlesinger, Arthur M., Jr. *The Age of Roosevelt: The Crisis of the Old Order, 1919–1933.* Boston: Houghton Mifflin Company, 1957.

Schwarz, Jordan A. *The Interregnum of Despair: Hoover, Congress, and the Depression.* Urbana, IL: University of Illinois Press, 1970.

Scroop, Daniel. *Mr. Democrat: Jim Farley, the New Deal, and the Making of Modern American Politics.* Ann Arbor, MI: University of Michigan Press, 2006.

Self, Robert C. *Britain, America, and the War Debt Controversy: The Economic Diplomacy of an Unspecial Relationship, 1917–1941.* London: Routledge, 2006.

Shannon, David A., ed. *The Great Depression.* Englewood Cliffs, NJ: Prentice-Hall, 1960.

Shlaes, Amity. *The Forgotten Man: A New History of the Great Depression.* New York: Harper, 2008.

Slayton, Robert A. *Empire Statesman: The Rise and Redemption of Al Smith.* New York: Free Press, 2001.

Smith, Gene. *The Shattered Dream: Herbert Hoover and the Great Depression.* New York: William Morrow, 1970.

Smith, Richard Norton. *An Uncommon Man: The Triumph of Herbert Hoover.* New York: Simon and Schuster, 1984.

Sobel, Robert. *Herbert Hoover at the Onset of the Great Depression, 1929–1930.* Philadelphia: J. B. Lippincott Company, 1975.

Stimson, Henry L., and McGeorge Bundy. *On Active Service in Peace and War.* New York: Harper & Brothers, 1948.

Stratton, Maud. *Herbert Hoover's Home Town: The Story of West Branch.* Published by the author, 1948. Reprint, Wichita, KS: Macy Genealogy Project, 2000.

Sullivan, Lawrence. *Prelude to Panic: The Story of the Bank Holiday.* Washington, DC: Statesman Press, 1936.

Surface, Frank M., and Raymond L. Bland. *American Food in the World War and Reconstruction Period: Operations of the Organization under the Direction of Herbert Hoover, 1914 to 1924.* Stanford, CA: Stanford University Press, 1931.

Train, Arthur. *The Strange Attacks on Herbert Hoover: A Current Example of What We Do to Our Presidents.* New York: John Day Company, 1932.

Trani, Eugene P., and David L. Wilson. *The Presidency of Warren G. Harding.* Lawrence, KS: University Press of Kansas, 1977.

Tucker, Ray, and Frederick R. Barkley. *Sons of the Wild Jackass.* Seattle: University of Washington Press, 1932.

Turner, Paul V. *Mrs. Hoover's Pueblo Walls: The Primitive and the Modern in the Lou Henry Hoover House.* Stanford, CA: Stanford University Press, 2004.

U.S. Bureau of the Census. *Historical Statistics of the United States: Colonial Times to 1970.* Bicentennial Edition. Washington, DC: U.S. Department of Commerce, 1975.

United States Congress. Senate. Special Committee Investigating Presidential Campaign Expenditures. Senate Report. 70th Cong., 2nd sess. Washington, DC: Government Printing Office, 1929, 1–31.

U.S. Department of Commerce. *National Income and Product Accounts of the United States.* Vol. 1, *1929–1958.* Washington, DC: Government Printing Office, 1993.

Walch, Timothy, ed. *Uncommon Americans: The Lives and Legacies of Herbert and Lou Henry Hoover.* Westport, CT: Praeger, 2003.

Walch, Timothy, and Dwight M. Miller, eds. *Herbert Hoover and Franklin D. Roosevelt: A Documentary History.* Westport, CT: Greenwood Press, 1998.

———. *Herbert Hoover and Harry S. Truman: A Documentary History.* Worland, WY: High Plains Publishing Company, 1992.

Warren, Harris Gaylord. *Herbert Hoover and the Great Depression.* New York: W. W. Norton & Company, 1967.

Watkins, T. H. *The Hungry Years: A Narrative History of the Great Depression in America.* New York: Henry Holt and Company, 1999.

Wert, Hal Elliott. *Hoover, the Fishing President: Portrait of the Private Man and His Life Outdoors.* Mechanicsburg, PA: Stackpole Books, 2005.

White, Richard D., Jr. *Kingfish: The Reign of Huey P. Long.* New York: Random House, 2006.

White, William Allen. *A Puritan in Babylon: The Story of Calvin Coolidge.* New York: Macmillan Company, 1938. Reprint, New York: Capricorn Books, 1965.

Wilbur, Ray Lyman. *The Memoirs of Ray Lyman Wilbur.* Edited by Edgar Eugene Robinson and Paul Carroll Edwards. Stanford, CA: Stanford University Press, 1960.

Wilbur, Ray Lyman, and Arthur Mastick Hyde. *The Hoover Policies.* New York: Charles Scribner's Sons, 1937.

Wilson, Carol Green. *Herbert Hoover: A Challenge for Today.* New York: Evans Publishing Company, 1968.

Wolfe, Harold. *Herbert Hoover: Public Servant and Leader of the Loyal Opposition.* New York: Exposition Press, 1956.

Wood, Clement. *Herbert Clark Hoover: An American Tragedy.* New York: Michael Swain, 1932.

Young, Nancy Beck. *Lou Henry Hoover: Activist First Lady.* Lawrence, KS: University Press of Kansas, 2004.

Articles

Albjerg, Victor L. "Hoover: The Presidency in Transition." *Current History* 39, no. 230 (May 1960), 213–19.

Anderson, Paul Y. "Huston Stays On." *Nation* (July 30, 1930), 119.

Ed., "Back in Washington." *Outlook and Independent* 151, no. 10 (March 6, 1929), 30.

Balmer, Edwin, and William Crawford. "When You Meet the President." *Redbook* 58 (March 1932), 112–15.

Beard, Charles A. "A Five-Year Plan for America." *Forum* 86 (July 1931), 1–11.

Bent, Silas. "Herbert Hoover: A Political Portrait." *Outlook* 148, no. 8 (February 22, 1928), 283–84.

Bolt, Robert. "Herbert Clark Hoover of West Branch, Iowa: U.S. President of Quaker Stock." *Quaker Life* (September 1984), 22–23.

Bornet, Vaughn Davis. "Herbert Hoover's Planning for Unemployment and Old Age Insurance Coverage, 1921 to 1933." In *The Quest for Security: Papers on the Origins and the Future of the American Social Insurance System*, edited by John E. Schacht. Iowa City, IA: Center for the Study of the Recent History of the United States, 1982.

Brayman, Harold. "Hooverizing the Press." *Outlook and Independent* 156, no. 4 (September 24, 1930), 123–25, 155.

Brown, E. Francis. "Mr. Hoover Faces Nation's Problems." *Current History* (January 1932), 578.

Cahill, James Quinten. "Herbert Hoover's Early Schooling in Iowa and Its Place in Presidential Politics, Community Memory, and Personal Identity." *Annals of Iowa*, Third Series, 61, no. 2 (Spring 2002), 151–91.

Carter, Paul. "The Campaign of 1928 Re-Examined: A Study in Political Folklore." *Wisconsin Magazine of History* 46 (Summer 1963), 263–72.

Clements, Kendrick A. "Herbert Hoover and the Fish." *Journal of Psychohistory* 10, no. 3 (Winter 1983), 333–48.

———. "The New Era and the New Woman: Lou Henry Hoover and 'Feminism's Awkward Age.'" *Pacific Historical Review* 73, no. 3 (August 2004), 425–61.

Conybeare, John. "Trade Wars: A Comparative Study of Anglo-Hanse, Franco-Italian, and Hawley-Smoot Conflicts." *World Politics* 38, no. 1 (October 1985), 147–72.

Cooper, Richard N. "Trade Policy in Foreign Policy." In *U.S. Trade Policies in a Changing World Economy*, edited by Robert M. Stern, 291–92. Cambridge, MA: MIT Press, 1987.

Cowley, Robert. "Drought and the Dole: Herbert Hoover's Dismal Dilemma." *American Heritage* (February 1972), RF, HHPL.

Croly, Herbert. "How Is Hoover?" *New Republic* (June 27, 1928), 138–40.

Davis, Joseph S. "Herbert Hoover, 1874–1964: Another Appraisal." *South Atlantic Quarterly* 68, no. 3 (Summer 1969), 295–18.

Day, David S. "Herbert Hoover and Racial Politics: The DePriest Incident" *Journal of Negro History* 65, no. 1 (Winter 1980), 6–17.

———. "A New Perspective on the 'DePriest Tea' Historiographic Controversy." *Journal of Negro History* 75, no. 3 14 (Summer–Autumn 1990), 120–24.

Degler, Carl N. "The Ordeal of Herbert Hoover." *Yale Review* 52 (June 1963), 563–83.

Eichengreen, Barry. "The Political Economy of the Smoot-Hawley Tariff." *Research in Economic History* 12 (August 1986), 1–43.

Gammack, Thomas H. "A Wall Street View of Hoover." *Outlook* 149 (June 27, 1928), 350.

Garcia, George F. "Herbert Hoover and the Issue of Race." *Annals of Iowa* 44, no. 7 (Winter 1979), 507–15.

Giglio, James N. "Voluntarism and Public Policy between World War I and the New Deal: Herbert Hoover and the American Child Health Association." *Presidential Studies Quarterly* 13, no. 3 (Summer 1983), 430–52.

Ginzl, David. "Lily Whites versus Black and Tans: Mississippi Republicans during the Hoover Administration." *Journal of Mississippi History* 42 (August 1980), RF, HHPL.

Hamilton, David E. "Herbert Hoover and the Great Drought of 1930." *Journal of American History* 68, no. 4 (March 1982), 850–75.

Hamm, Thomas D. "The Divergent Paths of Iowa Quakers in the Nineteenth Century." *Annals of Iowa*, Third Series, 61, no. 2 (Spring 2002), 125–50.

Hard, William. "Hoover the President." *World's Work* 58 (September 1, 1929), 88.

Harris, Ray. "The President's Record." *Woman Republican* 9, no. 12 (December 1931), 3–7.

Hatfield, Mark. "President Hoover's Early Days in Oregon." *Congressional Record* (August 13, 1974), RF, HHPL.

Hawley, Ellis W. "Herbert Hoover, the Commerce Secretariat, and the Vision of an 'Associative State,' 1921–1928." *Journal of American History* 41 (June 1974), 116–40.

———. "Secretary Hoover and the Bituminous Coal Problem, 1921–1928." *Business History Review* 42 (Autumn 1968), 247–70.

Hoover, Herbert. "Herbert Hoover's Mississippi Valley Land Reform Memorandum: A Document." Edited by Bruce A. Lohof. *Arkansas Historical Quarterly* 29, no. 2 (Summer 1970), 112–18.

"Herbert Hoover: The Man without a Party." *Literary Digest* (March 13, 1920), 47–52.

"Hoover Halfway." *Time* 17, no. 9 (March 2, 1931), 12.

"Hoover on Prohibition." *Outlook* 148 (March 7, 1928), 374.

Hornaday, Mary. "Where the President Puts Care Aside: Informality Rules at Rapidan Camp, Isolated in Wild Mountains and Enveloped by the Peace of The Woods, where the President Rests." *New York Times Magazine* (June 12, 1932), 6, 16.

Houck, Davis W. "Rhetoric as Currency: Herbert Hoover and the 1929 Stock Market Crash." *Rhetoric and Public Affairs* 3, no. 2 (Summer 2000), 155–81.

Hurley, Patrick J. "The Facts About the Bonus March." *McCall's* 77, no. 143 (November 1949), 2, 142–43.

Johnson, James P. "Herbert Hoover: The Orphan as Children's Friend." *Prologue* 12, no. 4 (Winter 1980), 193–206.

Johnston, Alva. "The Great Silent Orator." *Saturday Evening Post* 208, no. 48 (May 30, 1936).

Joslin, Theodore G. "Hoover's First Year." *World's Work* 59 (March 1930), 61–65 and 118–19, RF, HHPL.

Kellogg, Vernon. "Herbert Hoover as I Know Him." *Outlook* (October 19, 1927), 203–6, and (October 26, 1927), 239–41, 244.

Klein, Julius. "The Tariff and the Depression." *Current Events* 34, no. 4 (July 1931), 497–99.

Kottman, Richard N. "Herbert Hoover and the Smoot-Hawley Tariff: Canada, A Case Study." *The Journal of American History* (December 1974), RF, HHPL.

Lambert, C. Roger. "Herbert Hoover and the Federal Farm Board Wheat." *Heritage of Kansas* 10 (Spring 1977), 28.

Lohof, Bruce A. "Herbert Hoover, Spokesman of Humane Efficiency: The Mississippi Flood of 1927." *American Quarterly* 22 (Fall 1970), 690–700.

Lowry, Edward G. "Mr. Hoover at Work and Play." *Saturday Evening Post* 202, no. 9 (August 31, 1929), 39–41.

Lyons, Eugene. "The Little-Known Side of Herbert Hoover." *Family Weekly* (August 9, 1964), RF, HHPL.

"The March of Events." *World's Work* 58 (September 1929), 35–40.

Martin, Charles H. "Negro Leaders, the Republican Party, and the Election of 1932." *Phylon* 32, no. 1 (1st Quarter 1971), 85–93.

McCormick, Anne O'Hare. [untitled clipping], *New York Times Magazine* (February 5, 1933), 1.

McDonough, J. E. "The Federal Home Loan Bank System." *American Economic Review* 24 (December 1934), 668–85.

McMillen, Neil. "Perry Howard, Boss of Black-and-Tan Republicanism in Mississippi, 1924–1960." *Journal of Southern History* 48 (May 1981), RF, HHPL.

"Mr. Hoover and the People." *Outlook* 151, no. 14 (April 3, 1929), 536.

"Mr. Hoover's Apologia." *Outlook* 158, no. 8 (June 24, 1931), 233–34.

"Mr. Hoover's Obstacles." *Outlook* 148 (April 18, 1928), 609–10.

"Mr. Hoover's Qualifications." *Outlook* 149 (June 27, 1928), 350.

Muessig, Raymond H. "Herbert Hoover and Education." *School and Society* 95, no. 2293 (Summer 1967), 309–13.

Murray, Robert K. "President Harding and His Cabinet." *Ohio History* 75 (1966), 125–68.

Nash, George H. "The Social Philosophy of Herbert Hoover." *Annals of Iowa* (Fall 1980), RF, HHLP.

Nash, Gerald D. "Herbert Hoover and the Origins of the Reconstruction Finance Corporation." *Mississippi Valley Historical Review* 46, no. 3 (December 1959), 455–68.

"National Affairs: Election Footer." *Time* 16, no. 20 (November, 17, 1930), 15.

O'Brien, Patrick G., and Philip T. Rosen. "Hoover and the Historians: The Resurrection of a President." *Annals of Iowa* 46, no. 2 (Fall 1981), RF, HHPL.

Olson, James S. "The End of Voluntarism: Herbert Hoover and the National Credit Corporation." *Annals of Iowa* 41 (Fall 1972), 1104–13.

———. "Herbert Hoover and the Analogue of War." *Plimpsest* 54 (July/August, 1973), 26–31.

———. "The Philosophy of Herbert Hoover: A Contemporary Perspective." *Annals of Iowa* 43,
no. 3 (Winter 1976), 181–91.

"The Ordeal—and Triumph—of Herbert Hoover." *Reader's Digest* 85, no. 512 (December 1964),
161–62, 164–65, 167–68.

Pickett Helm, William. "Political Winds against Hoover." *Outlook and Independent* 157 (April 15,
1931), 530–32

Pringle, Henry F. "Hoover: An Enigma Easily Misunderstood" *World's Work* 56 (June 1928),
131–32, 134.

———. "The President" *New Yorker* (December 27, 1930), 23.

Rhodes, Benjamin D. "Herbert Hoover and War Debts, 1919–1933." *Prologue* 6, no. 2 (Summer
1974), 130–44.

Rickard, T. A. "Herbert Hoover: A Sketch." *Mining and Scientific Press* (April 3, 1920), 494–96.

Rinehart, Mary Roberts. "A New First Lady Becomes Hostess for the Nation." *World's Work* 58,
no. 1 (March 1929), 34–39.

Rinn, Fauneil J. "President Hoover's Bad Press." *San Jose Studies* 1, no. 1 (February 1975), 32–44.

Romer, Christina D. "The Nation in Depression." *Journal of Economic Perspectives* 7, no. 2 (Spring
1993), 19–39.

Schaefle, William J. "How President Hoover Serves His Country." *American Globe* (October
1929).

Schofield, Kent. "The Public Image of Herbert Hoover in the 1928 Campaign." *Mid-America* 51
(October 1969), RF, HHPL.

Shively, Carlton A. "Stimulating Business." *Outlook* 153 (December 11, 1929), 585, RF, HHPL.

Sizer, Rosanne. "Herbert Hoover and the Smear Books, 1930–1932." *Annals of Iowa* 47, no. 2
(Spring 1984), 343–61.

Snyder, J. Richard. "Hoover and the Hawley-Smoot Tariff: A New of Executive Leadership."
Annals of Iowa (Winter 1973), RF, HHPL.

Soule, George. "Herbert Hoover: Practical Man." *New Republic* 53 (December 28, 1927), 161.

Strauss, Lewis, Jr. "Herbert C. Hoover and the Jews." *American Hebrew* (April 23, 1920), 747,
759.

Strother, French. "Herbert Hoover." *World's Work* 39 (April 1920), 578–85.

Ed., "The Trend of Events." *Outlook and Independent* 151, no. 12 (March 20, 1929), 450–51.

Van Ingen, Philip. "The Story of the American Child Health Association." reprinted from the
Child Health Bulletin 11, no. 5–6 (September–November 1935), 149–88.

Walcott, Charles and Karen M. Hult. "Management Science and the Great Engineer: Governing
the White House during the Hoover Administration." *Presidential Studies Quarterly* 20, no.
3 (Summer 1990), 557–79.

Wile, Frederic William. "The Hoover Era." *World's Work* 58, no. 3 (April 1929), 42–45, 156–58,
162–63.

Wilson, Carol Green and Neil H. Petree, eds., "Herbert Hoover: Master Engineer." *Stanford
Illustrated Review* 21, no. 2 (November 1919), 75–77, 111–16.

"The Woman's Party and Mr. Hoover." *Nation* (October 3, 1928), 312.

Dissertations

Dressler, Thomas Herbert Bernard. "The Foreign Policies of American Individualism: Herbert
Hoover, Reluctant Internationalist." PhD diss., Brown University, 1973.

Lohof, Bruce Alan. "Herbert Hoover and the Mississippi Valley Flood of 1927: A Case Study of
the Political Thought of Herbert Hoover." PhD diss., Syracuse University, 1968.

Nelsen, Clair Everet. "The Image of Herbert Hoover as Reflected in the American Press." PhD
diss., Stanford University, 1956.

Theses

Bowers, James R. "Herbert Hoover: Ambivalent Quaker." MA thesis, University of Illinois Legal Studies Center, 1981.

Kuglitsch, Ryan. "A Study of the Contributions Made by Herbert Hoover on American Policy during World War Two." MA thesis, University of Wisconsin-Milwaukee, 2006.

Smith, Marisa A. "A Reconsideration of Herbert Hoover." MA thesis, University of Wisconsin-Milwaukee, 2010.

Wendel, Susan L. DuBrock. "Herbert Hoover and Banking Reform." MA thesis, North Eastern Illinois University, 1985.

Newspapers

Binghamton Sun (1928–1933)
Boston Herald (1928–1933)
Boston Star (1928–1933)
Boston Transcript (1928–1933)
Buffalo Evening News (1928–1933)
Chicago Daily News (1928–1933)
Chicago Sun (1928–1933)
Chicago Tribune (1928–1933)
Christian Science Monitor (1928–1933)
Columbus [OH] *Dispatch* (1928–1933)
Endicott Bulletin (1928–1933)
Franklin Dairyman (1928–1933)
Houston Informer (1928–1933)
Illinois State Journal (1928–1933)
Indianapolis Star (1928–1933)
Kansas City Post (1928–1933)
Kansas City Star (1928–1933)
Lansing [MI] *State Journal* (1928–1933)
New York Evening Post (1928–1933)
New York Herald-Examiner (1928–1933)
New York Herald Tribune (1928–1933)
New York Jewish Tribune (1928–1933)
New York Post (1928–1933)
New York Times (1928–1933)
New York World (1928–1933)
Olean, NY *Herald* (1928–1933)
Philadelphia Inquirer (1928–1933)
Philadelphia Public Ledger (1928–1933)
Portland Morning Oregonian (1928–1933)
San Bernardino Telegram (1928–1933)
Saturday Evening Post (1928–1933)
Tallahassee Daily Democrat (1928–1933)
Toledo Times (1928–1933)
Utica Observer-Dispatch (1928–1933)
Utica Press (1928–1933)
U.S. Daily News [Washington, DC] (1928–1933)
Washington Herald (1928–1933)
Washington Post (1928–1933)
Washington Star (1928–1933)
Washington Times (1928–1933)

Films and Documentaries

Blumer, Ronald H. *The Crash of 1929*. Produced by Ellen Hovde and Muffie Meyer. Directed by Alicia Weber. WGBH, PBS, 1990. DVD.

Landslide: A Portrait of President Herbert Hoover. Produced by Chip Duncan and Tracy Dorsey with Bob Hack and Patricia Ostermick. Directed by Chip Duncan. Stamats Communications, Iowa Public Television, 2009. DVD.

Index

Abbot, Willis J., 52
Adams, Charles Francis, 47, 55, 56, 160, 169, 457
Adams, John Quincy, 155
Addams, Jane, 21
Aguinaldo, Emilio, 440
Akerson, George, 18, 28, 42, 44, 56, 57, 187, 285, 386, 411
Albright, Horace, 111
Allen, Henry J., 38
Allen, Robert S., 396
Anderson, Marian, 307
Angell, James G., 20
Arnold, Benedict, 407
Asquith, Herbert, 81
Astor, Vincent, 398, 443
Autry, Gene, 372

Baker, George Barr, 50
Baker, Newton D., 260, 274, 410, 425
Barbour, William Warren, 236–37
Barnes, Julius, 49, 125
Baruch, Bernard M., 18, 195, 228, 398
Bates, Sanford, 107
Bauer, George, 349
Beard, Charles A., 264
Bent, Silas, 22
Bestor, Paul, 271
Bismarck, Otto von, 131
Bissing, Moritz von, 81
Blease, Cole, 23
Bonus Army, 293–301, 377, 400, 451
Boone, Joel, 360, 375

Booth, "Albie," 418
Borah, William, 22, 26, 48, 60, 97, 101, 129, 134, 136, 160, 179, 190, 193, 224, 239, 344, 364, 410
Borno, Louis, 163
Bouimistrow, W. W., 21
Brand, Charles, 22
Brandeis, Louis D., 18, 193
Branner, John Casper, 3
Brewster, Ralph Owen, 50
Briand, Aristide, 331
Brookhart, W. Smith, 35, 60, 61, 97, 129, 134, 179–80, 182, 190, 212, 227
Brown, Walter, 28, 186, 314, 406, 408, 409, 411, 415
Brown, Warren, 54, 56, 181, 186
Bruening, Heinrich, 333, 334
Bryan, William Jennings, 34, 178, 281
Burke, Francis, 185
Burke, James, 314
Burner, David, 193, 310, 451
Burraker, Ray, 380, 382
Bush, George H. W., 452
Bush, George W., xx, 452
Butler, Pierce, 193
Byoir, Carl, 259
Byrd, Harry F., 380

Cagle, "Red," 418
Calhoun, John C., 79
Camp Rapidan, 374, 378–82
Capone, Al, 102
Capper, Arthur, 67, 90, 416

Caraway, Thaddeus, 306
Cardozo, Benjamin, 193, 194
Carnegie, Andrew, xvi, 280
Carnegie, Dale, 17
Carran, Mollie Brown, 419
Carter, Jimmy, 1, 382, 456, 458
Castle, William R., Jr., 53, 161, 344, 345
Cates, Louis S., 196
Catt, Carrie Chapman, 418
Cellar, Emmanuel, 295
Chapin, Roy Dickman, 55
Chaplin, Charlie, 387
Chiang Kai-Shek, xvi, 165
Church, Robert, 315
Churchill, Winston, xvi, 454
Clark, Edward T., 57
Clark, Reuben J., 162
Cleveland, Grover, 121, 190, 293, 306, 313
Comstock, William A., 443
Coolidge, Calvin, xix, 9–10, 12, 13, 15–16, 18,
    24, 25, 27, 29, 31, 33, 36, 37, 38, 39, 42, 43,
    46, 47, 48, 50, 52, 54, 57, 60, 66, 67, 80, 89,
    90, 91, 95, 102, 108, 115, 116, 117, 137,
    156, 159, 164, 180, 186, 190, 206, 211, 228,
    261, 279, 291, 306, 310, 324, 341, 354, 361,
    363, 364, 383, 384, 388, 389, 390, 392, 362,
    377, 406, 407, 423, 433, 435, 452, 461, 462
Coolidge, Calvin, Jr., 15
Coolidge, Grace, 16
Costigan, Edward E., 224, 233
Cotton, Joseph P., 161
Coughlin, Charles, 293, 436, 443
Couzens, James J., 212, 239, 443
Cox, James M., 46, 146
Crissinger, D. R., 116
Croxton, Fred. C, 256–57, 259–60
Curley, James, 299
Curtis, Charles, 1, 17, 25, 27, 28, 34, 42, 53,
    56, 146, 192, 193, 229, 364, 408, 409, 412,
    415
Custer, George A., 437
Cutting, Bronson, 224, 415

Daugherty, Harry, 324
Davis, James J., 55, 124
Davis, Joseph S., 457
Davis, Norman, 433, 434
Dawes, Charles G., 17, 25, 28, 29, 37, 42,
    167, 169, 220, 222, 271, 273, 412
DeConde, Alexander, 161
DeMille, Cecil B, 20
DePriest, Jessie, 306, 307
DePriest, Oscar, 305–7
Dexter, Walter Frier, 397

Dickinson, L. J., 411
Dilling, Elizabeth, xv
Doak, William N., 47, 55, 266, 415
Donovan, William J., 48
Doughton, Robert L., 231
Douglas, Lewis, 433
DuBois, W. E. B., 312
Du Pont, Pierre S., 398
Durant, Will, 381

Earhart, Amelia, xvi
Ecker, Frederick, 93
Eckley, Wilton, 459
Edge, Walter E., 411
Edison, Thomas, xvi, xviii, 20, 46, 47, 75
Eisenhower, Dwight D., 80, 173, 297, 316,
    387, 388, 452

Faushold, Martin L., 120, 451
Feagan, Charles, 373
Feis, Herbert, 443
Ferrell, Robert H., 440
Fess, Simeon D., 183, 185, 188
Firestone, Harvey, 46–47
Fitzgerald, F. Scott, 400
Forbes, W. Cameron, 163
Ford, Gerald, 452
Ford, Henry, xvi, 20, 46, 75, 124, 137, 443
Ford, James W., 299
Fort, Franklin W., 276
Fox, George, 81
Frankfurter, Felix, 300, 433
Franklin, Benjamin, 86
Free, Arthur, 183
Freidel, Frank, 458

Galbraith, John Kenneth, xvii
Gandhi, Mahatma, xvi
Gann, Dolly, 364, 365
Garfield, James A., 411
Garfield, James R., 110, 202
Garner, John Nance, 217, 218, 220, 223, 224,
    225, 229, 231, 234–35, 237, 276, 331, 423,
    438, 442
Gaylord, Harris, 133
Gibson, Hugh, 167, 169–70, 333, 338, 339
Gifford, Walter S., 202, 257, 258–59, 260
Glass, Carter, 136, 220, 222–23, 227, 239,
    438, 439, 441, 445, 447
Glassford, Pelham, 294, 296, 298, 299
Glass-Steagall Act, 219, 222–23, 227, 439
Glen, Otis, 27
Goff, Guy, 17, 25

Gompers, Samuel, 324
Good, James W., 27, 28, 54, 173, 365
Gorbachev, Mikhail, 340
Grandi, Dino, 336–37, 340
Grant, Ulysses S., 121, 306
Great Depression, xix, xx, 11, 19, 66, 70, 71,
   78, 79, 80, 85, 89, 92, 95, 97, 98, 99, 110,
   113–28, 130, 134, 156, 158
Green, William, 50, 191, 230, 264–65, 324, 327
Gregory, Thomas, 28, 49
Griffith, D. W., 20
Groves, Leslie, R., 316

Haggerston, Fred H., 184
Hague, Frank, 35
Hamill, John, 396, 397
Hannibal, 467
Hard, William, 38, 375, 383
Harding, Warren G., 9, 17, 28, 33, 60, 80, 89,
   90, 107, 108, 109, 123, 134, 164, 189, 202,
   206, 310, 324, 325, 354, 357, 361, 377, 383,
   389, 390, 452
Harris, James M., 350
Harrison, Benjamin, 184
Hastings, George A., 57, 386
Hatfield, Mark, 455
Hawley, Ellis W., 190, 462
Hayes, Rutherford B., 306
Hays, William H., 261
Hearst, William Randolph, 118, 299, 394
Heaton, John L., 396
Hebert, Felix, 266
Henle, Raymond, 316
Henry, Charles D., 29, 348
Herter, Christian, 20, 55
Hilles, Charles, 406, 407
Hindenburg, Paul von, 331, 334
Hines, Frank T., 136, 292
Hinshaw, David, 408
Hitler, Adolf, xvi, 119, 330, 333, 334, 338, 454
Hoaf, Joan, 83
Holmes, Oliver Wendell, 193
Holt, Hamilton, 81
Hoover, Allan, 18, 44, 52, 352, 353, 354, 355,
   358, 359, 360, 362, 365, 380, 448
Hoover, Herbert
   agricultural policy, 11, 24–25, 32, 35, 36,
      38, 50, 57–58, 59–61, 125, 139–44,
      150–51, 154, 279–91, 420
   Australia, 4–5, 70, 395, 396
   banking crisis and reform, 136, 203–5,
      219, 220–26, 227–28, 237, 239–40,
      269–77, 335, 420, 437, 438–39, 441–47,
      452

Belgium, 6–7, 13, 38, 69, 73, 74, 77, 81,
   121, 123, 141, 182, 198, 322, 350, 352,
   396, 397
Bonus Army, 293–301, 377, 400, 451
   books about, 396, 451
Burma, 6, 70
cabinet, 46–49, 52, 53–57, 72, 447–48
childhood, xviii, 1–3, 66
children's issues, 368–73
China, 5–6, 23, 32, 70, 312, 351, 396
Commerce Secretary, 9–13, 16–17, 21,
   22, 23, 24, 31, 38, 49, 51, 92, 94, 100,
   114, 189, 197, 198, 204, 205, 206, 305,
   323–24, 416
Congress, relations with, 60–63, 78–79,
   129–54, 159, 177–79, 181, 183, 188–89,
   199, 217–14, 269–77, 389, 391, 427,
   439–49
Cuba, 341
disarmament, 154, 157–59, 166–73,
   338–40, 420, 454, 463
economic policy, 11, 17, 115–19, 120–25,
   175, 267–68
education policy, 98–99
engineer, as, 4, 5, 6, 38, 74–75
environmentalism, 107–8, 109, 110,
   111–12, 213, 377
foreign policy, 30, 43–46, 50, 53, 155–75,
   301, 329–45, 427, 428, 454
government, philosophy of, 22, 53, 76, 85,
   86–87, 89–90, 91–92, 96, 97–98, 110,
   123, 180–81, 189–90, 226, 408, 422–23,
   453–54, 459, 462, 466
Great Depression, xix, xx, 11, 19, 66, 70,
   71, 78, 79, 80, 85, 89, 92, 95, 97, 98, 99,
   110, 113–28, 130, 134, 156, 158,
   189–90, 195–215, 219–24, 253–77,
   279–301, 450–51
Haiti, 163–64, 341–42, 417
humor, sense of, 73–74, 465
immigration policy, 326–27
inauguration (1929), 52–53
inauguration (1933), 447–48
labor policy and relations, 29, 33, 125, 154,
   191–92, 201, 214, 230, 323–27, 452
Latin America, 43–46, 161–63, 164–65,
   332, 337, 340–42, 359, 412, 454, 463
Mississippi River Flood, 11–13, 33, 121,
   123, 141, 182, 198, 304, 418
Nicaragua, 164, 341
outdoorsman, as, 375–77, 378, 379–80
personality and personal life, xvi–xvii, xxi,
   19, 65–87, 347–65, 367–68, 457–58,
   464–65

Hoover, Herbert (*continued*)
    Philippines, 439–40, 454
    Poland, 8
    president, as, xx, 43–63, 71–73, 77, 85,
        89–128, 456
    presidential election (1928), 15–42, 52
    presidential election (1932), 236, 403–26
    press, relations with, 383–401
    prison reform, 106–7
    Prohibition, 22, 30, 32, 34, 48, 54,
        100–105, 106, 144, 146–47, 153, 188,
        321, 357, 389, 390, 410, 411, 413, 414,
        464
    public speaker, 34, 79–80, 456, 465
    public works, 11, 32, 35, 36, 137–38,
        152–53, 154, 182, 200–203, 206–14,
        219, 233–34, 266–67, 274–75, 420
    Quaker, xvii, xviii, 1–2, 21, 30, 33, 36,
        37–38, 42, 65, 69, 71, 76, 78, 81–87,
        106, 108, 156, 159, 172, 187, 198, 317,
        452, 464
    race relations, 20, 21, 23, 30, 32, 33–34,
        191, 303–21, 348, 364, 417–18
    Republican Party, relations with, 177–94
    retirement insurance, 92–94
    Roosevelt administration, transition to,
        428–30
    Russia, 6, 8, 21, 69, 70, 121, 282
    social policy, 53, 95
    Stanford University, xvi, 1, 3–4, 19, 29, 40,
        49, 68–69, 83, 99–100, 317, 348, 349,
        350–51, 358, 359, 364, 369, 424, 458
    Supreme Court nominations, 190–94
    tariff debate, 61–63, 129–35, 389, 390, 452
    thinker, as, xviii, 3, 155–56
    transportation policy, 96–97
    Versailles Peace Conference, 8, 18, 38, 49,
        74, 81, 156, 157
    veterans policy, 136–37, 149–50, 153,
        291–301
    war debt, World War I, 174–75, 431–34
    women's issues, 321–23
    World War I, 7–8, 23, 32, 38, 49, 69, 81,
        121, 123, 156, 157, 158, 198, 282, 322,
        352
    writer, as, xxi, 80–81, 350, 371, 376, 456,
        465
Hoover, Herbert, Jr., 18, 96, 352, 353, 354,
    355, 358, 359, 360, 362, 365, 378, 395
Hoover, Herbert, III, 360
Hoover, Huldah, 1, 3, 82
Hoover, Ike, 70
Hoover, J. Edgar, 106
Hoover, Jesse, 1, 3

Hoover, Joan, 360
Hoover, Lou Henry, 4, 5, 18, 22, 28, 29, 39,
    44, 53, 71, 83, 155, 169, 262, 305, 306, 322,
    347–65, 378, 381, 383, 411, 412, 433, 448,
    449, 464
Hoover, Mary, 3
Hoover, Peggy, 360
Hoover, Peggy Ann, 360, 374
Hoover, Theodore, 3, 358
Hoover Dam, 154, 210–12, 311–12, 452
Hopkins, Harry, 201, 269, 291
Houdini, Harry, 80
House, Edward, 48, 187, 432
Howard, James R., 20
Howard, Perry, 411
Howard, Roy, 394
Hughes, Charles Evan, 48, 53, 103, 117, 160,
    190, 192, 193, 199, 341
Hull, Cordell, 434–35
Hunt, Edward Eyre, 181, 265, 383
Hurley, Patrick J., 54, 193, 296, 298, 300–301,
    344, 406, 409, 415, 416, 439
Huston, Claudius H., 184, 185, 188, 314
Hyde, Arthur M., 55, 56, 125, 140, 142, 151,
    203, 262, 283, 285, 290, 409, 411, 415

Ickes, Harold, 201, 211, 415
Irwin, Will, 18, 19, 38, 50, 67, 68, 383

Jackson, Andrew, 318, 414
Jahnecke, Ernest Lee, 53, 415
Janin, Louis, 4
Jardine, William M., 10, 47
Jefferson, Thomas, 86, 90
Joan of Arc, xvii
Johnson, Hiram, 9, 59, 129, 134, 192, 332,
    364, 415
Johnson, Lyndon B., 52, 70, 158, 180, 190,
    388, 468
Johnson, Mordecai, 308
Jones, Wesley L., 425
Jordan, David Starr, xvi, 3
Joslin, Theodore, 54, 57, 74, 81, 160, 181,
    187, 225, 254, 273, 362, 373, 386, 390, 392,
    395, 406, 412, 413, 423

Kahn, Otto, 407
Kelley, Ralph S., 109
Kellogg, Frank B., 46, 47, 160, 162, 164
Kellogg, Vernon, 49, 370
Kennedy, David, 133, 207
Kennedy, John F., xvi, 32, 79, 80, 82, 83, 387,
    388, 452

Kennedy, Joseph P., 118
Kent, Frank, 17
Keynes, John Maynard, xvi, 18, 74, 228, 233
Klein, Julius, 49, 53
Knox, Frank, 261, 406
Knox, John, 396

LaFollette, Robert, 59, 94, 95, 129, 134, 182, 224, 233, 295, 409, 415
La Guardia, Fiorello H., 151, 224, 231, 295, 326, 425
Lamb, Charles, 73
Lamont, Robert P., 55, 124, 126, 203, 214
Lamont, Thomas, 407
Landon, Alfred, 80
Lane, Rose Wilder, 19
Langley, Katherine, 20
Laval, Pierre, 158, 333, 335, 336, 337
Lawrence, David, 67, 444
Legge, Alexander H., 125, 140, 151, 283, 284, 285, 286, 289
Lehman, Monte, 104
Lenin, Vladimir, xvi, 397
Lenroot, Irvine L., 23, 28, 116
Leuchtenburg, William E., 196
Levine, Emmanuel, 299
Lewis, John L., 48, 324, 325, 421
Lewis, Sinclair, 459
Liggett, Walter, 396, 397
Lincoln, Abraham, xix, 70, 90, 128, 306, 398, 417, 468
Lindbergh, Ann, 379
Lindbergh, Charles, xvi, 106, 379, 380, 387
Lippman, Walter, 126, 385, 390, 405, 458
Lisio, Donald J., 193, 292, 300
Lloyd, Craig, 17
Lloyd George, David, 81
Long, Huey P., xv, 151–52, 436, 439
Longworth, Nicholas, 184
Lowden, Frank O., 17, 25, 26, 27
Lucas, Robert, 185, 188
Luis, Washington, 45
Lyman, Ray, 19
Lyons, Eugene, 68, 120

MacArthur, Douglas, xvi, 18, 173, 297–98, 300
MacDonald, Isabel, 168–69
MacDonald, Ramsay, 158, 167, 168–69, 337, 379, 431
Machado, Gerardo, 341
Machiavelli, 399

MacLafferty, James H., 16, 18, 57, 74, 181, 187, 188, 406, 408, 419
MacReynolds, James Clark, 193
Mann, Horace, 21, 28, 46, 314
Marconi, Guglielmo, 75
Mayer, Louis B., 20
McCormick, Anne O'Hare, 385, 393
McGrath, Myra, 57
McKelvie, Samuel R., 283
McNab, John L., 27
McNary, Charles L., 55, 193
McReynolds, James C., 192
Mellon, Andrew, 9, 11, 18, 26, 47, 53, 54, 55, 90, 115–16, 118, 121, 124, 149, 206, 228, 230, 269, 333
Merriam, Charles E., 95
Meyer, Eugene, 205, 220, 222, 269, 271, 272, 273, 405, 446
Michelson, Charles S., 145, 148, 225, 398, 399, 400, 407
Miles, Laban, 316
Miller, Adolph C., 49, 445–46
Miller, Charles A., 274
Mills, Ogden, 28, 53, 54, 124, 222, 230, 236, 271, 295, 336, 391, 405, 409, 411, 412, 415, 416, 429, 430, 433, 444, 446, 448, 457, 458
Milne, John, 349
Minthorn, John Henry, 3, 82, 316
Mitchell, Wesley C., 95, 440
Mitchell, William D., 48, 54, 56, 91, 102, 105, 182, 193, 263, 446
Moley, Raymond, 429, 430, 434, 443, 460
Mondale, Walter, 382
Monroe, James, 162
Mooney, Thomas J., 304
Morgan, J. P., 414
Morley, Christopher, 71
Morrow, Dwight L., 160, 169, 171, 183
Moses, George H., 27, 28, 145, 186, 217, 425
Mosley, George Van Horn, 297
Moton, Robert R., 305, 306, 307, 309, 312, 315
Murray, Augustus T., 83
Mussolini, Benito, 340, 393

Nelson, Clair Everett, 456–57
Nero, 439
Newton, Isaac, xx
Newton, Walter, 56, 91, 185, 186, 411
Nixon, Richard, 387, 388, 445, 460
Norris, George F., 25, 26, 27, 59, 97, 129, 130, 134, 137, 138, 148, 179, 190, 193, 232, 241, 295, 409, 415, 416

Nutt, Joseph R., 185
Nye, Gerald P., 35, 109

O'Brien, James J., 396
Ochs, Adolph, 385
Odell, Harriette Miles, 350
Odum, Howard W., 95
O'Hare, Anne, 71
Olson, James S., 220, 273, 274, 462, 456

Pace, John T., 299
Paderewski, Ignacy Jan, xvi, 262
Page, Walter Hines, 6, 7, 77
Parker, John J., 191, 192, 194, 199
Patman, Wright, 293
Patton, George, 297
Payne, John Barton, 142, 150, 262
Peek, George M., 23
Penn, William, 81, 316
Penny, J. C., 46
Perez, Leander, xv
Pershing, John J., 362
Picasso, Pablo, 75
Pickford, Mary, xvi
Pinchot, Gifford, 200, 275
Pittman, Key, 217
Platt, Edmund, 405
Poe, Edgar Allan, 73
Pomerene, Atlee, 274, 275
Pont, Pierre du, 124
Pratt, W. V., 173

Quezon, Manuel, 440

Rainey, Henry T., 235
Rand, James H., 443–44
Rankin, John, 293
Raskob, John J., 41, 145, 186, 398, 399, 414
Reagan, Ronald, 79, 80, 340, 382, 387, 388,
   429, 433–34, 462
Reed, David A., 170, 172
Requa, Mark L., 49, 68, 416
Rhine, George W., 296
Rhoads, James C., 319, 320
Richey, Lawrence, 56, 188, 378, 411
Rickard, Edgar, 28, 48, 68, 397, 448
Ritchey, Albert, 410
Roberts, Owen J., 103, 193, 199
Robinson, Henry M., 48, 260, 407
Robinson, Joseph T., 120, 151, 170, 172, 182,
   183, 193, 218, 234, 236, 331, 440, 442
Rockefeller, John D., 99, 112

Rockne, Knute, 77
Rogers, Will, 90
Romasco, James U., 462
Roosevelt, Eleanor, xvi, 300–301, 306, 347
Roosevelt, Franklin D., xvi, 8, 16, 44, 52, 66,
   70, 80, 95, 123, 190, 196, 199, 201, 206,
   212, 228, 255, 291, 298, 300, 313, 316, 342,
   347, 354, 361, 382, 388, 389, 392, 400, 422,
   442, 454, 460, 462, 463, 466, 467, 468
   agricultural policy, 290
   economic policy, 122, 126, 135, 263
   foreign policy, 159, 431–32, 433–35
   government, philosophy of, 94, 455, 461
   governor of New York, 93, 115, 146, 258,
      227, 389
   inauguration (1933), 444, 448
   presidency, transition from election to,
      428–30, 431–41, 443–44, 445–47,
      449–50
   president, as, 164, 226, 277, 395, 398,
      449, 457
   presidential election (1932), 149, 173, 236,
      375, 403–26
Roosevelt, Theodore, xvi, xx, 37, 51, 54, 76,
   95, 108, 110, 121, 159, 178, 180, 224, 305,
   306, 364, 375, 385, 387, 418, 453, 454
Roosevelt, Theodore, Jr., 341
Root, Elihu, 18
Rosenwald, Julius, 48, 99, 124, 305
Rowe, John S., 6
Roy, Eugene, 163
Russell, John H., 163
Ruth, Babe, 74, 387

Sanders, Everett, 188, 413
Sandino, Augustine, 341
Sanford, Edward T., 191
Scattergood, J. Henry, 319
Schwarz, Jordan A., 235
Scott, Joseph L., 412
Scottsboro Boys, 311
Shankey, Ann, 57
Shaw, Arch W., 38, 68
Shlaes, Amity, 121
Shouse, Jouett, 218, 398
Simmons, Roscoe Conklin, 417
Slemp, Bascom, 315
Sloan, Alfred P., 124
Smith, Adam, 121
Smith, Alfred E., 30–31, 32, 35, 38, 39,
   40–42, 80, 146, 152, 218, 304, 398, 414,
   425, 467
Smith, Gerald L. K., xv
Smith, Richard Norton, 371, 451

Smoot, Reed, 151, 425
Snell, Bertrand H., 217, 225, 291, 412, 448
Sobel, Robert, 118, 303
Sokolsky, George E., 211, 460
Sousa, John Philip, 40
Spargo, John, 73
Stalin, Josef, 393, 454
Steagall, Henry, 222
Stimson, Henry L., 55, 56, 103, 159, 160, 161, 164, 165, 166, 169, 170–71, 175, 333, 335, 337, 338, 343, 344, 345, 385, 415, 431, 432, 433, 434, 435, 439
Stone, Harlan D., 48, 103, 193, 458
Stone, James C., 283, 286
Strauss, Lewis, 18, 49, 68
Street, C. D., 20
Strong, Benjamin, 205
Strother, French, 57, 95, 386
Stude, Henry, 262
Sullivan, Mark, 20, 38, 50, 67, 375, 426, 458
Sutherland, George, 193
Swope, Gerard, 263, 264

Taft, William Howard, 18, 52, 80, 103, 190, 192, 365, 413, 424
Tang Shao-yi, 23
Tarbell, Ida, 67
Tarkington, Booth, 20
Teague, C. C., 283
Thomas, Elmer, 293
Thomas, Norman, 41
Thoreau, Henry David, 349
Tilson, John Q., 47, 182, 184, 217, 291
Train, Arthur, 397
Truman, Harry, 80, 211, 388
Tugwell, Rexford G., 443, 466
Turner, Frederick Jackson, 57, 281

Untied, Bryan, 373–74

Van Buren, Martin, 121
Vandevanter, Willis, 190
Vare, William S., 26

Vest, Christine, 381
Vinson, Fred, 316

Wagner, Robert, 152, 182, 224, 233–34, 235, 236, 265, 295
Walch, Timothy, 371
Walker, James J., 168
Wallace, Henry, 10, 11
Warren, Earl, 316
Washington, Booker T., 305–6
Washington, George, 1, 111, 398
Washington, Martha, 357
Waters, Walter W., 294–96, 299
Watson, James E., 25, 26, 27, 35, 47, 184, 185, 225, 239, 425, 440
Watson, Margaret, 353
Webster, Daniel, 79
Wendel, Susan L. DuBrock, 195
Westinghouse, George W., 75
White, Walter, 191, 312
White, William Allen, 38, 67, 81, 241, 458
Whitney, Richard, 227–28
Wickersham, George W., 103–5
Wiggins, Albert W., 333–34
Wilbur, Ray Lyman, 48, 89, 55, 56, 84, 95, 99, 108, 109, 110, 111, 112, 211, 213, 214, 308, 311, 318, 319, 321, 375, 377, 395, 415, 457
Willebrandt, Mabel Walker, 106, 304
Williams, Carl, 283
Willis, Frank B., 17, 23–24, 25
Wilson, Woodrow, xvi, xx, 7, 8, 9, 17, 22, 44, 48, 70, 76, 89, 95, 100, 116, 131, 146, 153, 156, 158, 178, 180, 187, 190, 192, 232, 333, 389, 413, 441, 449, 454, 457, 468
Wolman, Leo, 264–65
Wood, Clement, 396
Woodin, William, 444, 446, 447
Woods, Arthur, 10, 202, 256, 257
Wordsworth, William, 349
Work, Hubert, 27, 28, 184, 188

Young, Owen D., 124, 202, 257, 259, 261, 274, 432
Young, Roy A., 213

CPSIA information can be obtained at www.ICGtesting.com
Printed in the USA
LVOW10*1425090615

441769LV00001B/1/P